Affecting Performance

Smithsonian Series in Ethnographic Inquiry

William L. Merrill and Ivan Karp, series editors

Ethnography as fieldwork, analysis, and literary form is the distinguishing feature of modern anthropology. Guided by the assumptions that anthropological theory and ethnography are inextricably linked, this series is devoted to exploring the ethnographic enterprise.

Affecting Performance

MEANING, MOVEMENT, AND EXPERIENCE
IN OKIEK WOMEN'S INITIATION

Corinne A. Kratz

SMITHSONIAN INSTITUTION PRESS

Washington and London

Portions of this book first appeared, in different form, as "Persuasive Suggestions and Reassuring Promises: Emergent Parallelism and Dialogic Encouragement in Song." *Journal of American Folklore* 103 (1990); "Sexual Solidarity and the Secrets of Sight and Sound: Shifting Gender Relations and Their Ceremonial Constitution," *American Ethnologist* 17, no. 3 (1990); "Amusement and Absolution: Transforming Narratives during Confession of Social Debts," *American Anthropologist* 93, no. 4 (1991); and "'We've Always Done It Like This . . . Except for a Few Details': 'Tradition' and 'Innovation' in Okiek Ceremonies," *Comparative Studies in Society and History* 35, no. 1 (1993), and are reproduced with permission.

Edited by Susan Warga.
Production editing by Rebecca Browning.
Designed by Alan Carter.
Indexed by Andrew Christenson.

Library of Congress Cataloging-in-Publication Data

Kratz, Corinne Ann, 1953–
    Affecting performance : meaning, movement, and experience in Okiek
women's initiation / by Corinne A. Kratz.
     p. cm. — (Smithsonian series in ethnographic inquiry)
    Includes bibliographical references and index.
    ISBN 1-56098-234-9 (cloth).—ISBN 1-56098-273-X (paper)
    1. Women, Dorobo—Rites and ceremonies. 2. Initiation rites—
Kenya—Mau Escarpment. 3. Puberty rites—Kenya—Mau Escarpment.
4. Language and culture—Kenya—Mau Escarpment. 5. Mau Escarpment
(Kenya)—Social life and customs. I. Title. II. Series.
DT433.545.D67K73   1993
306'.089927624—dc20 92-35663

British Library Cataloguing-in-Publication Data is available.

Manufactured in the United States of America.
5 4 3 2 1
97 96 95 94 93

∞ The paper used in this publication meets the minimum requirements of the American National Standard for Permanence of Paper for Printed Library Materials Z39.48-1984.

Contents

Appendixes   339

List of Illustrations

List of Tables

Preface: Linguistic Setting and Orthography

Okiek is a Southern Nilotic language, one of the related languages of the Kalenjin branch. Maa, the language spoken by Maasai neighbors to Okiek, is an Eastern Nilotic language. Other Kalenjin languages are Kipsigis (the most similar to Kipchornwonek Okiek), Nandi, Tuken, Keiyo, Sebei, Pokot, and Marakwet. Kalenjin languages have been described by Tucker and Bryan (1966), Toweett (1979a), and Creider (1981). I have discussed Okiek linguistic repertoires, lexical borrowing, and language use elsewhere (Kratz 1986). I remark here on some of the most prominent aspects of Okiek language structure that come up in the course of talking about Okiek initiation.

First, unmarked word order in Okiek is verb initial. Orders that front other constituents are used for clarification, emphasis, or other rhetorical purposes in various discourse conditions. The change is marked by the particle *ko* after the fronted word or phrase (cf. Creider 1976).

Nouns occur in two forms, primary and secondary. These terms are used by Tucker and Bryan (1964–65), who base the distinction on formal criteria rather than frequency of use; secondary forms are primary forms with suffixes. Secondary noun forms are by far the most common in conversational use; primary forms are used more frequently in song than in speech. The semantic distinctions between the two forms have yet to be precisely characterized.

According to Toweet 1979, referents of nouns in primary form are in implicit comparison with other members of the set denoted by the noun, while referents of nouns in secondary form are in implicit comparison with members of sets denoted by other nouns. Thus *tany'* "cow" (primary form) refers to some cow (but not another), and *teeta* "cow" (secondary form) refers to a cow (and not to a goat or a human). (Creider 1982:27–28).

Toweet calls the two noun forms inclusive and exclusive instead of primary and secondary.

Okiek use a number of affective particles that indicate a range of attitudes. The particles relate to the speaker's relation to the addressee (for example, -*wei*, a friendly marker, used between age-mates among others), attitude to what is said (for example, *ara,* indicating doubt, uncertainty, tentativeness), and/or the ongoing interaction (for example, -*a,* -*ai,* which have some senses similar to "then" or "now" in English examples such as "take it, then"). These are difficult to translate, and a number of them appear in text translations here inadequately rendered as "then," "now," or "friend."

One of the most ubiquitous and difficult to translate is -*toi,* used in Maa as well as Okiek. -*toi* has the sense of "friend" in some interchanges and is commonly used between age-mates. Yet in other contexts it indicates exasperation, something like "buddy" in an English example such as "listen, buddy," though still retaining a friendly sense that is not entirely ironic. In the texts included here, -*toi* is common in accounts of *pesenweek* (social debts), where I usually translate it simply as "friend."

I have maintained one feature of Okiek in the English translations, the use of -*ii* at the end of phrases. -*ii* is said with a jump of pitch, higher than the rest of the utterance, sometimes with rising pitch. This raised pitch is incorporated into the final syllable if it is a vowel. It occurs in several contexts. First, it is question intonation, added to the end of the sentence. Second, it is listing intonation, which can be used at the end of each item when going through a list; the pitch of listing intonation rises but does not jump as much as that of questions. Occurring by itself, *ii?* is a request for clarification, repetition, or an indication that the listener has heard or agreed. With repeated use, *ii* can take on a tone of insistence or anger, as in arguments.

When Okiek hesitate in speaking, they usually say *in* or *en.* This is the equivalent of English speakers' hesitations such as "uh" or "um."

The rendering of Okiek here is simplified in one important way: I do not indicate tonal distinctions, which carry both semantic meaning and grammatical information. This impoverishes the detail and accuracy of the transcription, but tonal distinctions are not central to the analyses presented here.

Okiek has a series of four unvoiced stop phonemes that become voiced after nasals, and after /l/: /p/, /t/, /c/, and /k/. Between vowels, /p/ and /k/ also become voiced. The stop /c/ sounds much like "ch." Nasal phonemes also number four, corresponding to the stops in place of articulation: /m/, /n/, /ny'/, and /ng'/. The other consonant phonemes in Okiek are /s/, /l/, /r/, /w/, and /y/.

The distinction of vowel quality within a five-vowel system produces ten vowel phonemes in Okiek, each further differentiated by length. Vowel quality distinguishes between vowels pronounced with advanced tongue root and those with retracted tongue root. The latter are shown here with underlining (cf. Creider and Creider 1980). Aurally, these correspond to some extent to distinctions heard between tense and lax vowels, though the distinction is not one of height. The difference between /a/ and /o/ is the most difficult to hear.

The following list of sound correspondances will guide pronunciation of Okiek words.

Phoneme	Example
/i/	English "beat"; Kiswahili "*nini*"
/i̱/	English "bit"
/e/	English "bake"; Kiswahili "*cheza*"
/e̱/	English "bet"
/u/	English "boot"; Kiswahili "*uma*"
/u̱/	English "but"
/ō/	English "boat"; Kiswahili "*ona*"
/o/	English "bought"
/a/	English "bought," but with a fuller, more open sound
/a̱/	English "father"; Kiswahili "*ama*"

The Maa language uses a similar vowel system; scholars of that language distinguish the difference in quality as open and close vowels (Tucker and Ole Mpaayei 1952; Mol 1980). Open vowels in Maa correspond to the vowels pronounced with retracted tongue root in Okiek (and other Kalenjin languages such as Kipsigis and Nandi). When Maa words appear in this book, the open vowels are underlined. Unlike Okiek nouns, Maasai nouns are usually preceded by gender prefixes (masculine: *ol-* in singular, *il-* in plural; feminine: *en-* in singular, *in-* in plural).

Acknowledgments

This book is the product of almost twenty years of work. Over that time, many people and institutions have helped me, far more than I can mention here by name. My research in Kenya would have been impossible without affiliation with the Sociology Department, University of Nairobi, and the permission of the Office of the President, Government of Kenya. Thanks to all who helped make it possible in both 1974–75 and the period from 1982 to 1991.

Many of the people with whom I lived and worked most closely were the same in 1974–75 and from 1982 through 91. Once again I acknowledge Mentegai Leboo, my co-wife Laato, her sister Kaina, Kirutari Meitukut, Simion and Lutia Sina, and their families with gratitude for friendship, hospitality, and patience over the years. The families in whose ceremonies I participated in 1983 were also generous with their time, hospitality, and reflections, especially those of Arapkiplet, Kap Leboo, and Kap Changoroi. Margaret Wanjiku Ngugi and Daniel Ngugi became good friends and neighbors as well as giving me a place to store supplies and vehicles. John Sena provided a room at Nkaroni during the start of my 1983 research. I cannot name everyone in my research area, but my appreciation extends much further than those I list here, to all those with whom I lived, worked, and talked.

Several assistants helped with tape transcription: David Cheriro, Fredrick Kilagui Salimu, and Simon Ole Nchoe. Joseph Mapelu was my research assistant in 1974–75. He helped out again when I first returned in 1982; David Cheriro was my general guide and interpreter in early 1983.

Thanks for hospitality, equipment loans, storage space, and much more to: Jane and Michael Barbour, Dismas and Christine Masolo, Harry Merrick, Donna Klumpp Pido, Denyse and Pete Robertshaw, Inez and John Sutton, the British Institute in Eastern Africa, the Institute of African Studies, and the National Museums of Kenya.

One version of this book was a dissertation for the University of Texas at Austin. My committee there gave advice and acute readings at many points: Dick Bauman, Amy Burce, Chet Creider, Jim Denbow, Steve Feld, Joel

Sherzer, and Greg Urban. Long before I began the dissertation, Johannes Fabian was a critically influential teacher and has remained a friend and colleague.

Other wonderful colleagues and friends commented on portions of earlier drafts: Jeanne Bergman, Bill Bravman, Chet Creider, Micaela di Leonardo, Paulla Ebron, Carolyn Harford, Donna Klumpp Pido, and Franz Rottland. Ed Wilmsen's careful reading and suggestions guided me through the final revisions. Many thanks to the congenial and talented people with whom I worked at Smithsonian Institution Press, especially Daniel Goodwin, Rebecca Browning, and Alan Carter. Susan Warga was a marvelous editor and a sympathetic, knowledgeable, and meticulous critic. I especially appreciate her steady attention to my manuscript when on the verge of leaving for her own research in Côte d'Ivoire (indeed, even later in Abidjan).

Ivan Karp has lived with the ups and downs of this book, ever supportive, ever willing to read, ever critical. Several other friends were also especially supportive while I was writing and revising: Carolyn Harford, Urs Herren, Mona Moore, Donna Klumpp Pido, Odoch Pido, Susan Russell, all the Slow Moving Fun Seekers, Paul Smoke, Ed Steinhart, Pam Swing, Frank Trechsel, Luise White, Justin Willis, and James Woodburn. My mother has sustained me in all my decisions and efforts with faith, support, and many candles.

Dr. Elizabeth Meyerhoff-Roberts gave permission to cite and quote from her doctoral dissertation on Pokot. Rod Blackburn collegially shared material from Okiek ceremonies he attended in 1968–69. Laura Tindimubona drew all maps, except for figures 1 and 6, which were done by Marcia Bakry.

Research between 1982 and 1986 was supported by the National Science Foundation, the Fulbright-Hays program, the Wenner Gren Foundation for Anthropological Research, the Institute for Intercultural Studies, the University of Texas at Austin, and the Joint Committee on African Studies of the Social Science Research Council and the American Council of Learned Societies. Sigma Xi provided a small transcription grant in 1987. A fellowship in the Anthropology Department at the Smithsonian Institution in 1990–91 supported me while I began final revisions on the manuscript. I completed revisions at the Institute for Advanced Study and Research in the African Humanities at Northwestern University.

Part 1

The Challenge of
Ritual Efficacy

1

Introduction

If you usually go about laughing and thinking, "Initiation is a game," well, it's no longer a game today. It's tomorrow that you will put your body down. That woman [comes] and cuts. If you yell, you'll see what happens. All these people in the house will laugh and leave. We'll leave this liquor [without drinking it]. . . . Do you hear? If you shame people? It's not a game.

Daniel Arap Sityene, 9 December 1983

Initiation is something that everyone has done. *ii?* But initiation—initiation—we must be completely brave for initiation. . . . It's something you do bravely. And sit still like a person. . . . The only thing to say is just do that job that you have chosen for yourselves early in the morning. We'll stand [and watch]. But don't jump, don't do what [squirm or twitch]. Just be still. So the woman comes and you lean against her. She just holds your arms and you just do this and are still. Even if she doesn't come to hold you, you just be still and lean against something in your own way, [like] a person. Until you are finished. Somebody's child who has become a person.

Tiongik Kiamar, 9 December 1983

This book explores how Okiek children in Kenya are made into adults through initiation and the diverse experiences involved in that process. The central problem concerns ritual efficacy: how does ceremonial performance and participation effectively transform the children? The book's secondary aim is to consider Okiek conceptions of gender and cultural identity as they relate to initiation. I set each of these themes historically so as to bring into focus their interconnections with each other and the broader settings and processes of their cultural production.

The problem of ritual efficacy presents a double challenge. Complexly orchestrated ceremonial performances introduce the analytical challenge of unraveling the intricacies, interweavings, and effects of multiple media, multiple events, and multiple participants and perspectives. As the encouraging speeches excerpted above make clear, physical trials are an important part of Okiek initiation. But girls' excision or boys' circumcision is just one moment—a dramatic, climactic, and painful one—in a long and elaborate process.[1]

At the same time, ritual efficacy presents challenges grounded in culture and history: how can diverse participants with different interests and experiences be joined, affected, and persuaded of the transformation through ceremonial performance? How are such complex, affecting performances reproduced and reinterpreted in changing circumstances over time? Okiek initiation ceremonies re-create ideal representations that are familiar to all participants—representations of gender, adulthood, and other social relations. Simultaneously, ceremonial performances incorporate questions about and challenges to those representations, arising from the different locations, perspectives, and contradictions of daily life. Children become adults through initiation, but never ideal men, women, or adults. Contradictions are not resolved, but life goes on.

One Okiek question about gender representations is carried in the language of the quotes at the start of this chapter and by the situation in which they were spoken, an event in which men deliver encouraging speeches to initiates. Two men are speaking to girls on the first night of initiation, giving speeches made only when girls are initiated. If they were to encourage boys, they would tell them to be brave like men. They cannot tell the girls to be like men, but neither can they tell them to be brave like women. Women are considered intrinsically weak-willed and uncontrolled, yet the girls are about to undergo a test of stoic forbearance equivalent to boys' initiation. Thus the men tell the girls to be "like a person," that is, like an adult; in many circumstances, "person" is understood to mean a man (for example, "the person of the house" [ciit aap kaa] is the man of the house).

I address problems of ritual efficacy in Okiek initiation through analyses of the ceremonies that I attended and my discussions with Okiek. Both the ceremonies and the discussions were products of their histories and of my own history with Okiek. Before explaining my particular approach to ritual efficacy and the ceremonial transformations of initiation, then, I describe the history I share with Okiek, the research experience and theoretical positions I bring to this study, and how I plan to proceed.

Research Circumstances

Kaplelach and Kipchornwonek are the southernmost Okiek groups on the forested slopes of the western Mau Escarpment in west-central Kenya. As the crow flies, these Okiek live about one hundred miles northwest of Nairobi, Kenya's capital city (see figure 1). The highland forest continues to their north, with other Okiek groups living on other parts of the escarpment. Their southern neighbors, pastoral Maasai, reside on savannah plains at the foot of the escarpment. In the past, Maasai came into the lower reaches of Okiek forest for dry season grazing. Maasai also live east of Kaplelach; other Okiek groups live farther northeast, on the eastern Mau Escarpment.

To the west live Kipsigis, Kalenjin-speaking linguistic cousins to Okiek. Increasingly over the past thirty years, agropastoral Kipsigis have moved into western Kipchornwonek areas from the rolling hills and plains they occupy in Kericho District. Since the mid-1980s, they have been purchasing land and moving into Kaplelach areas in significant numbers as well.[2]

Most Kaplelach and Kipchornwonek Okiek are multilingual, with linguistic repertoires and abilities varying by age, gender, and Okiek group (Kratz 1986). Apart from their own Okiek language, many people also speak Maa (the Maasai language) and adapt their Okiek lexically and tonally to communicate with Kipsigis. A fair number know rudimentary Kiswahili, one of Kenya's national languages; some speak it well. Younger Okiek now in school and a handful educated in the past also know some English, the other national language.

I first stayed with Okiek for a year in 1974–75, working from two research bases. The Kipchornwonek base was near Sogoo at Olkerei, a twenty-minute walk from a slightly larger Okiek settlement at Nkaroni. My other base was with Kaplelach at Sukumeriet, about ten miles to the east (see figure 2).

I returned to Kenya in September 1982 to do further research with similar arrangements. I first stayed with Kaplelach friends at Mbokishi. In February 1983, we all moved to new houses at Ng'apng'eenta, two or three miles away. At the Kipchornwonek side, I found most people from Olkerei had moved nearer to Nkaroni, closer to their gardens, a shift that was already starting when I left in 1975. From January 1983 to May 1984, my Kipchornwonek home was at Nkaroni; I then moved to a friend's house at nearby Cumpek for another year.

During both research periods, I moved back and forth, alternating bases every four to six weeks, always hearing about my other home from visitors. When the pace of preparation for a ceremony quickened at one place, I stayed there two months or more, with only short visits to the other.

I moved to Nairobi in June 1985, after more than two and a half years in the forest. Based there until April 1990, I made return visits several times a year;

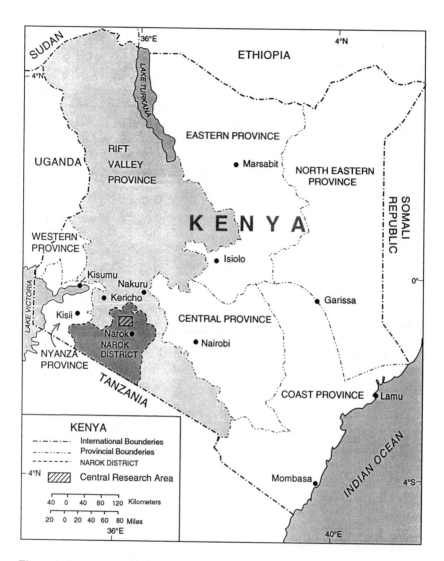

Figure 1. Research area within Kenya

occasional Okiek visitors also brought me news in Nairobi. During that time, I also visited other Okiek groups in Kenya and Tanzania.

Since my analyses and interpretations rely heavily on language, it is important to give more than the usual nod to the question of my own competence in the languages of Okiek life. When I first began research, I spoke only European languages. I worked mainly through an interpreter-

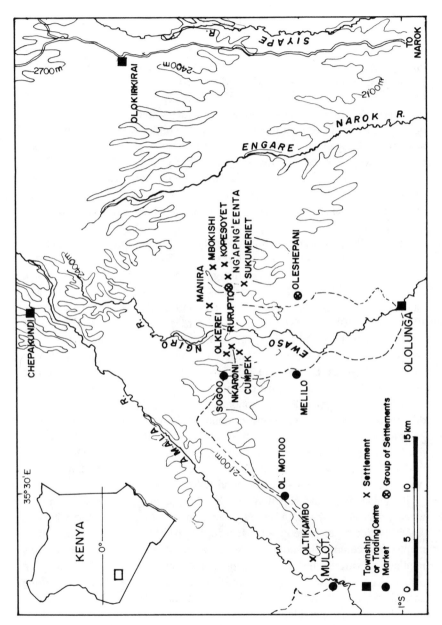

Figure 2. Central research area and Okiek settlements mentioned

assistant, although after a time I had enough grammatical proficiency and vocabulary in Okiek to follow discussions and participate in a basic way.

When I returned in 1982, I was fluent in Kiswahili and armed with further linguistic training and with recently published Kalenjin grammars (Toweett 1979a; Creider 1981). After intensive training in Nandi, a Kalenjin language closely related to Okiek, I moved to the forest to concentrate my language learning on Okiek. For the first five months of 1983, I employed a Maresionik Okiot from near Njoro as field assistant, interpreter, and often linguistic informant. When he returned home, I could communicate in Okiek adequately, if haltingly. Miscommunication and frustration were common on both sides when I began my communicative self-reliance. Still, with laughter and patience, we managed. As my language ability increased, so too did my sensitivity to differences between Kaplelach and Kipchornwonek Okiek and between Okiek and Kipsigis. I, too, adapted my vocabulary for Kipsigis, but I never fully mastered the intonational changes that Okiek make to sound more like Kipsigis.

I am not fluent in Maa, the final component of an ideal linguistic repertoire for Okiek research. While in the forest, my efforts at Maa suffered at the expense of Okiek. Nonetheless, I did gain a basic grasp of its grammar, a moderate vocabulary, and some conversational comprehension in that language from published grammars and dictionaries (Tucker and Ole Mpaayei 1952; Mol 1980), field experience, and, later, Maa language training.

Both friendships and understanding of another culture gain in depth and complexity over time as personal knowledge, respect, and affection grow with shared experiences. Extended research with continuing relations and repeated visits to the same area can give depth and history to cultural analysis, which work based on a first field trip cannot achieve (cf. Colson 1984). Yet cultural differences remain, evident even in mundane daily activities. I cultivated no garden, kept no livestock, had no beehives and no children of my own to care for. I roamed and visited people according to my own plans, accountable to no husband or father, as Okiek women were, even though my fictive kin network was based on a joking status as second wife.

Both Kaplelach and Kipchornwonek were planning initiation ceremonies when I arrived in 1982. A month after I moved to the forest, a series of shaving ceremonies (celebrated before initiation) began. I attended and documented all ceremonies possible. When allowed, I visited female initiates regularly during seclusion; we spent many hours talking and transcribing songs. Uninitiated myself, I was not allowed to attend the secret parts of the ceremonies. I stayed nearby with others who could not attend—the uninitiated and adults of the opposite sex.

The final coming-out ceremonies of initiation are public, however, so I was there. Girls' initiation is followed almost immediately by marriage; during the initiates' seclusion, each girl's family was engaged in discussions about her marriage. I documented those occasions also, along with the weddings held soon after.[3] In my analyses of Okiek initiation, I have worked intensively with tape recordings; I was able to record every scheduled event at a number of ceremonies, producing some forty-five hours of recordings. Their transcription became a major research task as well as an opportunity to raise questions and clarify issues with Okiek. Selections from these transcriptions are included in the appendixes.

Some Basic Concepts and Balances

Communicative conventions, patterns, and language use condition and are conditioned in multiple ways by social interaction and experience (including research). Research attentive to such patterns and interconnections is critical to learning about and interpreting cultural patterns and processes, and equally critical to understanding the epistemological bases of cultural knowledge and of our own research. It can elucidate the production of cultural understandings whether or not a tradition of explicit exegetical interpretation exists (or is created in the interaction of the anthropologist and her interlocutors). Further, such attention can be a beginning toward collaborative research that tries not only to preserve the different perspectives involved, but also to recognize and consider the communicative and intersubjective basis of anthropological research (Fabian 1979, 1990a, 1990b).

Specific circumstances and associations influence and contribute to the meanings of all signs, so it is methodologically fundamental to record and discuss the many kinds of information necessary for contextual analysis. Each kind of information relates to contextual analyses of different, interpenetrating scopes. How widely the contextual net is thrown raises important questions: How to integrate microanalyses full of significant detail with analyses of broader social and historical processes? How to show the influences of the latter in social relations represented in the microanalyses, and vice versa (Gluckman 1964; Clifford and Marcus 1986; Marcus and Fisher 1986)?

The scholarly traditions whose insights and concepts are so useful to detailed analysis of ceremonies in a communicative framework have a common weakness here. They are almost invariably weighted toward local considerations, with little regard for processes and interactions of wider scope. Some recent works have tried to strike a different balance. Fernandez 1982 sets detailed symbolic analysis of Bwiti religion within broader historical and political processes, and Sahlins 1981 integrates interpretive structural analysis with historical concerns.

My own far-from-ideal solution brackets detailed analyses of Okiek initiation (part 3) with chapters that set the ceremonies into wider context historically, geographically, and socially. Part 2 outlines general historical and political processes referred to later in the detailed analyses, and reviews some forms they take in daily life at the household level. It includes discussions of Okiek gender relations and regional ethnic relations over time, all experiential forms that are incorporated into Okiek ceremonies. The fourth and final part considers historical shifts in ceremonial form and their relations to changing circumstances of Okiek life.

To discuss ceremonial structure, I draw on concepts that identify components of different scales and communicative resources that crosscut and/or define them, for example, ritual events, communicative channels, and framing. "Initiation" refers to the entire process by which Okiek children become young adults through a series of ceremonies. Each ceremony is an occasion that includes formally defined and scheduled ritual events as well as periods of informal discussion, interaction, and celebratory consumption. Ritual events include a number of ritual acts that combine communicative resources from a variety of channels, both verbal and nonverbal.

When concentrating on communicative resources of various scales and kinds, their differentiation into channels, and different modes of signification, I lean more heavily on a semiotic vocabulary. The Peircian distinction among icon, index, and symbol is fundamental here, and is reviewed in chapter 2. The semiotic perspective emphasizes interrelations among components so as to reunite in another sense what is distinguished structurally. Ceremonies, ritual acts, ritual objects, and ritual events are all signs, and the communicative channels combined there not only constitute structural distinctions but also simultaneously crosscut them and weave them together. I balance the dry formality of semiotic analysis with detailed description, expanded contextual analysis, and varied perspectives from personalized accounts of particular occasions.

Cultural analysis involves not only picking things apart to consider significant details but also putting them back together again for a broad view of cultural processes informed by particularities. In ceremonial analysis, this involves returning time and again to ceremonial sequence and orchestration, relating what emerges from looking at each ritual event or each channel to ceremonial structure and process as a whole.

Orchestration is an apt metaphor for speaking of ceremonial structure and performance, of the ways diverse communicative resources are combined through time to accomplish cultural transformations. In performance, people re-create and experience familiar and meaningful ceremonial patterns. The patterns fulfill general expectations of what initiation is, but at the same time create affecting, dramatic tensions. Those dramatic tensions build and recede during the performance; they are sometimes inherent in the ceremonial structure. At times, emotional tension concentrates at moments when cultural expectations can be violated (cf. Meyer 1956). It is also especially felt when the general structure of ritual events is particularized or personalized in performance.

While ceremonial orchestration is bound up with dramatic tension and emotional engagement, the scheduled sequence and combination of communicative resources are the concurrent means through which ceremonial transformation is worked. As people are drawn into ceremonial experience it is the emotional involvement that both makes the cultural background of the transformation (including the cultural understanding and forms of emotion involved) seem natural and focuses attention and involvement on the central change created and its personal implications.

I consider within this communicative framework the processes by which cultural transformation is accomplished through the structure and performance of ceremonies. The other chapter in this first part outlines my theoretical priorities and stance in more detail.

Organization

The book is divided into four parts. The parts and chapters differ in style and perspective in ways related to their different foci and purposes. Some are highly analytic, others are closer to a first-person journalistic account. Some concentrate on details and particularities of personal experience; others look at broader patterns and processes. Different kinds of scholarly practice and intentions shape the nature and construction of discourse and writing.

I did not fully realize I had written with such shifts until someone reading an earlier draft pointed it out. Rather than smooth them over, I decided to accentuate the differences a bit. My intent in varying the style and focus was twofold. The first was to benefit from the different kinds of insights possible with these varied perspectives. The understanding that emerges by drawing them together is not the kind of holistic system that social scientists once constructed in their writing, but a more fragmented view of multiple networks of influences, interconnections, and relations of authority that stretch in many far-flung directions. Yet it is a more holistic view than that possible from concentrating on any single analytical level because it is more encompassing and more broadly informed.

At the same time, the view is more precisely located because the style shifts help keep the authorial presence in sight. The second reason for presenting different perspectives on Okiek initiation in various chapters is to give a sense of my relations with Okiek, of the different understandings of initiation I could glimpse through different people and different sources, and of the other kinds of relations that affect Okiek life (relations where other dimensions of power and authority come into play).

My concentration on the themes of cultural identity and gender also varies over the course of the book. Cultural identity is especially prominent in the broad, historical chapters, though it figures in the fine-grained analyses as well. Gender issues are more important in chapters concentrating on ceremonial performance, though they also appear in general and historical considerations.

The second part of the book provides the background necessary for detailed analyses of Okiek initiation. Chapter 3 introduces Kipchornwonek and Kaplelach Okiek with a historical sketch of the social and economic contexts of their lives. I discuss the local contexts of daily life as well as the regional and national standpoints that are central to understanding Okiek ethnic identity and contemporary life.

Chapter 4 provides a preliminary description of the process of initiation. Most of it describes the initiation of a particular group of girls, emphasizing the more personalized, experiential side of the process. The personalities and politics of that initiation are not the focus of analysis here, but a particular description brings structure to life and gives a better sense of the complexity and experience of the ceremonial occasions. Material analyzed later always comes in part from the initiation described in chapter 4; a photographic essay illustrating the initiation process follows chapter 4.

Part 3 consists of three analytical chapters. Chapter 5 considers ritual roles, costume, spatial locations, and ritual materials. Verbal aspects of initiation are the focus of chapters 6 and 7, the first concentrating on the speech of initiation and the second on song. One of my central premises is that the organization of communicative resources over time in ceremonial structure is essential to the production of ritual efficacy in performance. The analyses in part 3 are presented in terms of communicative channels in order to concentrate on that organization and its effects.

This mode of presentation initially makes clear the interconnections and sequential relations between signs using the same media and mode, and then facilitates consideration of the interrelations among them. Significant relations that extend beyond the ritual event or the ceremony become salient with this perspective as well. Communicative channels are an analytically useful choice for organization, and might be picked for cross-cultural and comparative reasons as well. The channels discussed here are the material bases of human communication in all societies. How they are used, divided, combined, and interpreted is historically and culturally specific, and relations between channels may also change historically.

Organization by channel introduces the common academic difficulty of dissecting intrinsically multimedia ceremonies into separate strands. Further, the analytically motivated separations do not always coincide with the way Okiek categorize and divide experience. I try to compensate for this analytical violence in several ways. First, I describe initiation in its entirety prior to focusing on selected parts. In later chapters, when I focus on particular aspects of initiation, that earlier description can serve as background. Similarly, I balance formal considerations along the way by filling out the cultural context, including Okiek categorizations and views.

Finally, I move back and forth between channel and ritual event as the unit of description and analysis within chapters (ultimately both are essential) and return frequently to the perspective of the ceremonial sequence as a whole. This entails some repetition, but ceremonial progression and movement through time are essential to understanding performative efficacy. Each part of the analysis must be related back to that perspective.

The analyses in chapters 5 through 7 have three foci. First, I consider performance contexts through detailed descriptive interpretation of various significant aspects. The second involves formal and thematic analysis. With nonverbal signs, this includes patterns of participation and ritual roles during initiation as well as the sources and associations of ritual materials. With verbal aspects, the analysis includes narrative structure and development, thematic patterns and concentrations, and poetic structures and devices.

The final focus is on the pragmatic and rhetorical aspects of initiation. Pragmatic analysis proceeds in conjunction with the formal and contextual analyses, inasmuch as pragmatics is the study of "how speech forms are used as effective action in specifiable cultural contexts" (Silverstein 1977:1). With these three analytical foci, I show how Okiek work efficacious transformations through the creation of meaning, movement, drama, and engagement in ceremonies.

Part 4, the final part of the book, returns Okiek initiation to its wider historical context and reviews the analyses presented and their implications. Chapter 8 traces the history of Okiek initiation in relation to changing social and economic circumstances. It also discusses the image of tradition Okiek endow on their ceremonial practice, how it is created, and how it relates to Okiek cultural identity. Chapter 9 reviews the key processes of ritual efficacy and the linked contradictions in cultural identity, gender, and age that emerge in Okiek initiation. I also consider the general significance of my analyses of Okiek initiation for studies of ritual, performance studies, linguistic anthropology, and work on gender and cultural identity. In conclusion, I discuss the overall structure of Okiek initiation as a metaphoric progression that relates Okiek initiation and social organization.

Five appendixes and a glossary follow the main text. The first appendix discusses issues related to excision and circumcision. The other four appendixes contain selections from material analyzed for chapter 6. Examples discussed in the main text are included in tables there for convenient reference. Those interested in more detail, a better sense of performance context, aspects of discourse over longer sequences, or other questions can turn to the appendixes.[4]

2

Meaning, Movement, and Experience: Efficacy and Performance

Both rituals and storytelling constitute rich means by which Kaguru themselves try to imagine what their way of life signifies. In part these explain how some things have come about; more important, they present and play with the profound contradictions and ambiguities within Kaguru social life.

T. O. Beidelman, *Moral Imagination in Kaguru Modes of Thought*

Calves become cows simply by growing and maturing, just as children become adults. But while biological maturity develops simply with nurturance and the passage of time, social maturity is created. What it means to be an adult in a particular place and time varies widely, in terms of cultural definitions and in terms of social rights, relations, and responsibilities. Similarly, how biological maturation and social maturation are entwined varies in different cultures.[1] In many societies, the change from child to adult is ceremonially marked, and the transformation of social identity is effected through ceremonial performance. Even cows have culturally defined stages of growth: calf, heifer, cow. Okiek living in Kenya make children into adults with initiation ceremonies after about fifteen years. When they are girls becoming women, they are first turned metaphorically into wild creatures, and then into heifers.

The aim of this work is to understand how Okiek produce that transformation through ceremonies, how the structure and performance of initiation ceremonies are implicated in the cultural transformation from child to adult, and specifically from girl to woman. The book also contributes to theoretical discussions about ceremony, ritual, language, communication, and cultural

14

experience by looking at their coordination, combinations, and interrelations in detailed, specific analyses of both verbal and nonverbal aspects of Okiek initiation.

Ceremonies are complex cultural performances, often dramatic and compelling. Understandably, scholars have found them fertile fields of study for diverse questions. Yet oddly enough, a critical question—perhaps the most obvious one raised by ceremonies—has not been adequately addressed: the question of ritual efficacy. Just how do people accomplish what they say they do through ceremonies? That question is the focus of this study.

To address the issue of symbolic and performative efficacy is to explore the relations among ceremonial structure, performance, and effects. This requires attention to what actors see themselves as doing through ceremonial performance, by the actual enactment. I focus on the goal Okiek acknowledge for their ceremonies on the assumption that what people believe a ceremony does will be a factor (though not the only one) that motivates its structure and content, shapes people's understandings and interpretations of it, and shapes their experiences of ceremonial performances. The initiation ceremonies I discuss here are intended to make girls into women—a transformation of personhood.

This emphasis takes up Malinowski's observation, now familiar wisdom, that ceremonies are pragmatic, purposive action. An equally standard observation provides the analytical key to demonstrating how ceremonial purposes are accomplished: ceremonies are multimedia events. In essence, my approach here puts together the implications of these two observations and explores them in terms of the question of ritual efficacy.

All social interaction involves simultaneous communication in multiple channels and modes. However, the multimedia nature of ceremonies is particularly important for analyses of their structure and performance. While one can see patterns within communicative channels, varied channels might be scheduled in relation to one another as well. The coherence, dramatic pacing, and affective meter of ceremonies are created in part by the combined patterns, each of which is based on several different types of sign relations (Kratz 1986). Analyzing the multimedia nature of ceremonies requires a fundamentally communicative approach that is capable of considering language and other media of communication in context and use as well as interrelations among media.

This approach differs somewhat from previous work and entails other kinds of analysis in addition to those normally used. The extensive work available on ritual and ceremonies is enormously helpful in looking at ritual efficacy, but each major approach to the field also has some limitations. In the following sections, I elaborate my approach to ceremonies and ritual efficacy by critically considering five major figures who represent different approaches. This is not an exhaustive survey. I discuss these scholars because they have important strengths that I want to combine and/or because they raise issues and emphases that I consider central.

An initial consideration of the communicative and metacommunicative nature of ceremonies will preview ceremonial processes discussed later in the chapter and lead into discussion of Victor Turner and the Manchester school. I begin with Turner because he defined the terms and methodology of much later work on ritual. Many of his insights can be retained and refined with semiotic adaptation, but Turner's view of social process seems to lack a broad historical setting. Maurice Bloch's recent effort to consider ceremonies in Madagascar historically is discussed next. Bloch identifies important problems, but his assumptions about ritual and ideology prevent him from solving them. The third figure is Pierre Bourdieu, whose theory of how cultural meaning is embodied and reproduced has been useful and influential. However, Bourdieu gives priority to questions of logic, seeking to define modes of knowledge in terms of types of logic (theoretical and practical). This results in a severely restricted picture of the experience and emotion of social life. Consideration of Bourdieu leads to a final discussion of the phenomenological approach to ritual practiced by a number of Oxford-trained anthropologists, focused on the work of Godfrey Lienhardt and T. O. Beidelman.

After considering these five figures, I return to outline ceremonial processes more fully. I concentrate on three key processes in order to understand the ritual efficacy of Okiek initiation and how the power of ceremonial experience arises from its structure and performance.

Communicative and Metacommunicative Processes: A Preview

Each performance of a ceremony transforms (or tries to transform) some aspect of a shared cultural definition of the world—this child is now an adult, that person is now the king, it is now the season to plant. The transformation works through the communicative forms with which that definition is created, in a forum agreed to have the authority and ability to effect that change. It is not only the multimedia nature of communication that is central in ceremonies, then. Ceremonies are also fundamentally metacommunicative enactments through which cultural understandings of the world are redefined by changing the significance or application of some of its aspects (cf. T. Turner 1977). It is this metacommunicative character, in part, that makes ceremonies appropriate occasions for and means of cultural transformation.

However, ceremonies are metacommunicative in two senses. The classic Batesonian sense is that ceremonial occasions define and are defined by a metacommunicative frame in which intended changes in cultural categorization can take place (Bateson 1936, 1972). They establish the frame "This is ceremony" in performance, marking and defining spatial and temporal contexts for transformation. The frame establishes the way to interpret the unfolding enactment, that is, as the occasion when transformation can and does occur. At the same time, it enables ceremonial transformation by creating an appropriate, authoritative occasion for it. The opening processional song of initiation, for example, is not taken as part of a ceremony when children sing and wave sticks that they pretend are ceremonial saplings. The event is different, the context is different, and no one becomes a young adult. That interpretive frame is "This is play." The metacommunication is about how to frame and interpret the ongoing communicative interaction.

The second sense of ceremonial metacommunication applies within the frame that is established. Within that frame, the uses of communicative forms are redefined through ceremonial performance. The metacommunication is about understandings and applications of specific communicative forms; for example, X means "girl" but no longer applies to the particular girl undergoing initiation. As cultural understandings of experience are re-created, some bit of experience is transformed by the way they are redefined. This is part of the key process that I call semiotic movement, described more specifically later in this chapter.

Transformations accomplished through ceremonies are not changes in cultural categories or social orders per se, but changes within them. Ceremonies transform particular cases and by doing so perpetuate the general practice on which they are based; they produce historical and cultural continuity as well as changes within that continuity. Many signs in ceremonies come into the transformation largely as context; they maintain the same sense, associations, and applications throughout. Ceremonies are metacommunicative, but their enactments also simply communicate, portray, and bring to mind aspects of daily life, social relations, and cultural assumptions and values. Communicative forms essential to metacommunicative transformation are embedded in and surrounded by others that frame them and place them in a larger cultural context, incorporate them into the evaluations people make of the ideas and values associated with them, and connect them into the unfolding ceremonial enactment. This is part of another key process I discuss below, contextual re-creation.

Ceremonies are not just efficient metacommunicative cultural tinkering, but also potentially affecting performances. Cultural transformation is worked in an atmosphere that becomes charged with emotion at times during the performance. This emotional power is central to ceremonial experiences, to performative efficacy, and to re-creating and confirming cultural tradition. It is also part of another ceremonial transformation that is rarely recognized as such by participants: the continuity of cultural tradition in individual form.

[T]he socialization of primary experience on the one hand and the rendering of social experience primordially relevant on the other . . . Ritual dramas in which these symbols are manipulated create an exchange between physiological and social experiences ennobling the former and investing the latter with emotional significance. (Fernandez 1977:127)

The affective senses of signs, like their representational aspects, are also culturally created and also refract into multiple experiences and expressions. However, the emotional power of ceremonies does not arise only from the presence of emotionally evocative signs. Dramatic orchestration, staging, and timing are also essential components of ceremonial structure, also instrumental in the effectiveness, affective force, and authority of its transformative power. This is part of the third and final key process I discuss below, experiential and emotional engagement.

Refining Turner Semiotically

Victor Turner's work on ritual and symbolism combines two important dimensions: exegesis of cultural meaning and analysis of the social jockeying carried on during ceremonies. His concept of key symbols is integral to the first, while his discussions of conflict and social action in ceremonial context are central to the second, which I consider later. The two dimensions of Turner's work are paralleled by different analytical foci.[2]

Turner's work develops a typology and general methodology for the study of symbols. He often explicates through example, outlining the multiple meanings of specific symbols. Turner discusses a symbol's uses in different ceremonial contexts in terms of canonical, general ceremonial form; specificities of ceremonial performance are not central to his symbolic interpretations. However, when Turner focuses on the political maneuverings of social interaction, he uses the details of specific ceremonial performances as his primary mode of analysis—a version of Gluckman's case study method. His attention centers on the ways personal relations are played out in the performance, however, not on ceremonial form.

Turner's symbolic typology makes a central distinction between dominant (key) symbols and instrumental symbols. Dominant symbols are emotionally evocative and central to ceremonial events. They are multivocal, with multiple layers of meanings and associations. The metacommunicative aspects of ceremonial structure and process outlined above lend another significance to Turner's emphasis on the multiple condensed, multivocal signs found in ceremonies. Metacommunicative adjustments are most productive when some sign vehicles carry associations from many contexts; they ramify into interactions and relations in dispersed contexts.

When Turner considers the Durkheimian question of the effectiveness of symbols—that is, how people become committed to representations—he proposes a further morphology of dominant symbols. He suggests that such symbols have two poles, ideological and sensory, each a cluster of different associations, either social or physical-psychological. Emotional power arises from the interaction of the two poles (V. Turner 1967:28).

> At one pole cluster a set of referents of a grossly physiological character, relating to general human experience of an emotional kind. At the other pole cluster a set of referents to moral norms and principles governing the social structure. . . An exchange of qualities may take place in the psyches of the participants under the stimulating circumstances of the ritual performance, between orectic [sensory] and normative [ideological] poles. (V. Turner 1967:55)

Turner makes two problematic assumptions here: first, that the sensory pole's associations represent primordial, universal experiences; and second, that there is a relatively clear-cut division between the two poles. Mauss's concept of habitus (later used by Bourdieu) undermines both, showing that understandings of the body and bodily experiences are cultural categories that are literally embodied and taken on in social interaction (Mauss 1979).

Turner underplays the cultural definition of emotional potential. Further, his somewhat Freudian solution stresses only the emotional power associated with particular key symbols. While he shows that different associations prevail in different contexts, he does not consider how emotional potential is mobilized in particular settings. His image of isolated, powerful, dominant symbols popping up at the center of ritual episodes is a most unsatisfactory depiction of ceremonies and ritual efficacy. An adequate explanation must consider the efficacy of symbols and the efficacy of ceremonies together. It must also consider the way a ceremony's performative nature, its structure over time, both draws on that potential and contributes to its force.

Turner's instrumental symbols are mainly connectors, filling out ritual acts that center on key symbols and leading from act to act and/or from symbol to symbol. Their associations are considered less rich and less layered, and they "could be regarded as mere signs or referential symbols," though they, too, have powerful associations. Turner suspects that they may "approximate to the condition of condensation symbols," but gives them little sustained attention because he considers them beyond the "limits of competence of anthropological explanation" (V. Turner 1967:32).[3] What Turner calls "dominant" and "instrumental" are not distinct types of symbols, but rather involve different emphases and combinations of sign modes. Both are critical to understanding ceremonial efficacy and both can be subject to elaboration, as Karp shows in his study of beer as an instrumental symbol (Karp 1980).

Turner's methodology discovers and traces symbolic layers, looking specifically at associations based on material properties, ceremonial uses (operational meaning), and the foregrounding of the relevant symbolic sense (positional meaning). The final layer comes from indigenous commentary on the symbol (exegetical meaning), which is in fact the source of knowledge about many of the other meanings. The method is very fruitful. Many wonderful studies have unpacked important cultural themes from key symbols or looked at processes of social transformation by treating ceremonial form and sequence as a progression of cultural categories, sketching their content through key symbol analysis.

But the method also has shortcomings. It stresses the cognitive, representational aspects of signs at the expense of their performative aspects. Further, it seems to direct study especially to material signs, such as objects, though Turner explicitly includes acts and events as possibilities. The dichotomy of dominant/instrumental symbols, which implicitly devalues instrumental symbols as objects of interpretation, hinders appreciation of their relations. This emphasis, due in part to a Saussurean approach to signs and symbols, has serious consequences.

Central ceremonial processes remain unexamined: for example, exactly how ceremonial structure and sequence are involved in ceremonial transformation, the nature of multimedia coordination and interaction, and different modes of ceremonial participation and experience. When "instrumental symbols" are consigned to a merely connective role,[4] the importance of that role in constituting significant links to other contexts, and in creating the orchestrated sequence of experience, emotional power, and efficacy in performance, falls by the wayside. Overall ceremonial structure—the orchestration of communicative means over time—is thus lost to view. The insights key-symbol analysis provides into the representational aspects of ceremonies should be better integrated with their performative aspects (cf. Tambiah 1979; Bloch 1986:181) in a more comprehensive analysis of ceremonial performances, their dramatic and emotional tensions, and the processes and interactions through which their layers of significance are created.

The semiotic notion of signs, based on the work of C. S. Peirce, can facilitate this necessarily intricate analysis. Semiotic distinctions retain and refine Turner's important insights and at the same time overcome some difficulties in his approach. For instance, the Peircian distinction among iconic, indexical, and symbolic sign modes captures and elucidates relations among a sign's many associations. It can also clarify continuities and differences between communicative media.

The iconic sign mode is based on formal resemblance, whether a similarity of relations (as in a map or photographic image) or of physical properties (as in the whiteness of both mother's milk and the sap of a *mudyi* tree, to use a famous Turnerian example). Indexical signification is based on spatial or temporal contiguity (as smoke is a sign of fire, or *mudyi* is the "flag of Ndembu women" because they dance around it during *nkang'a* rites [V. Turner 1967:23]). The symbolic mode relies on cultural convention for the significance of its relations. Thus, white can be taken as a sign of purity when there is no relation of similarity or contiguity between the color and the property. Such conventions are established through language and social interaction.

For Peirce, icon, index, and symbol are not disparate types of signs, but kinds of signification with different foundations, necessarily combined in some cases. He posits an implicational hierarchy among the three sign modes. The implicational hierarchy means that a sign can be simply iconic, but every indexical sign necessarily implies the simultaneous existence of an iconic mode, and every symbolic sign necessarily includes both indexical and iconic modes. This framework shows that Turner's suspicion was right: dominant and instrumental symbols differ not in kind, but in their combinations of sign modes. Obviously, then, both must be part of a full understanding of ceremonies. Peirce's hierarchy also highlights the intrinsic potential of signs for multifunctionality, an important corrective to the priority often given to reference and representation in anthropological description. In the study of ritual and symbolism, that priority has been peculiarly combined with a latent bias against the verbal. Linguistic materials have typically been handled in an undifferentiated, almost offhand way, with little detailed consideration of language use in ceremonies.

Turner's sense of multivocality highlights the essential role of associations that cross and unite contexts in constituting cultural meaning. With semiotic notions, however, it seems better to keep in mind the idea that objects, acts, events, occasions, words, phrases, texts, and languages can all be considered both as sign vehicles themselves and as constituting part of other sign vehicles. Shifting perspective and scale among these various signs can illuminate webs of varied significance and connections to many communicative contexts and interactions. It points to the complex embedding and crosscutting of sign vehicles and sign relations, the meaningful affective texture created, and "the complicated system by which signs carry and constitute sociocultural meaning" (Mertz 1985:1).

Associations are formed on various bases across time, space, context, and communicative channel; again, signs of various scales are included.[5] Some associations are salient, overtly significant, and readily accessible in discussions. The significance of others may be less explicit, based chiefly on tacit knowledge and pragmatic features, which are not topics of referential discourse. Still others might be part of the constitution and definition of the structure of an event or interaction, an enabling aspect not explicitly recognized.

The symbolic associations of signs are fundamental in cultural analysis. In fact, discussion about signs from other contexts, the formal similarities between signs, and other such topics is already a symbolic overlay. A semiotic perspective elucidates the way that language constitutes much of the symbolic mode of signs through establishing shared cultural conventions. Methodologically and epistemologically, this is important.

Iconic and indexical sign relations are based on physical properties: formal resemblance or spatiotemporal co-presence. The bases exist whether or not they are taken as meaningful and interpreted as signs. An infinity of possible indexical connections and iconic resemblances could be meaningful in a situation, but only a limited number are actually taken as cultural signs. Language use in various contexts picks these out and helps create the ways in which they are significant.

Explicit exegesis or teaching is one kind of language use that obviously does this, but it may be uncommon in some cultures or with respect to some domains of signs. Nonetheless, significant associations and cultural meaning are constituted in many contexts and in diverse interactions through other kinds of language use. Comments or discussions may be dispersed and fragmentary, may involve oblique reference or metaphoric extension, and may be playful, peremptory, or solemn.

Olerienit can serve as a brief example. When growing up, Okiek children learn about the properties and uses of different trees and plants. The wood of the *olerienit* tree, they learn, is excellent firewood—hard, slow-burning, and fragrant. Boys see their father or brother using a bundle of *olerienit* brands to smoke out fierce bees; girls are told by their mother not to bring bad, smoky firewood, and may be told to bring *olerienit*. Other conversational comments, daily interactions, and observations also contribute to their understanding of the tree, its wood, and its uses. In addition, people are told in blessings to "become *olerienit* trees," metaphorically transferring key properties of the wood to people. *Olerienit* wood is also used in ceremonies, but these examples suffice to show how fragments of daily life, conversation, and interaction help constitute the cultural significance of signs and the important role of language use in different contexts in doing so.

The example also demonstrates the importance for cultural analysis of sustained research, participation in many contexts and circumstances, and knowing the languages in which people converse regularly. Interpretive interviews can, of course, be translated and may convey important cultural information. However, an assistant might count statements such as a mother's admonition about firewood as too trivial to translate, even though they might be fundamental in creating the patterns and associations of cultural knowledge.

Finally, it underlines an important epistemological point. Varied communicative contexts and interactions can have different implications for the understanding that is created and can illuminate in various ways the cultural processes that are involved. Studies of symbols and ceremonies rarely highlight the distinctions among general conversations held by members of the culture, a researcher's discussions with specialists and others (which take place both in contexts conducive to thoughtful reflection, such as interviews, and in the middle of ceremonies), and the language of songs, prayers, speeches, or instruction that are themselves part of a ceremony (cf. Briggs 1986:41).[6] All are synthesized in description and analysis, but the product is a generalized common culture, with conflicting, "unofficial" versions homogenized out.

The multifunctionality of language and other communicative media is central to ceremonial analysis. The semiotic perspective establishes that signs are potentially multifunctional in terms of their mode of signification; Roman Jakobson and other scholars associated with the Prague Circle have explored other critical kinds of communicative multifunctionality, stressing the diversity and simultanity of modes of language use. In anthropology, their insights have been incorporated and developed particularly in the ethnography of communication and performance analysis.

Beginning with a model of communicative context, Jakobson defines communicative functions in terms of differential emphasis on contextual components (Jakobson 1960). The semiotic sign modes can figure in any of the communicative functions. For instance, iconic repetitions can contribute to poetic form (Jakobson 1968), clarify comprehension, or establish a communicative channel by attracting an interlocutor's attention (Jakobson's poetic, referential, and conative functions).

In the course of communicative interchanges, aesthetic tensions arise from different functional foregroundings and shifts between them. Shifts and tensions of this sort are the very stuff of ceremonial poetics and performance. Jakobson also considered tensions between cultural form and performance, but Bakhtin developed this concern most fully, highlighting social and ideological aspects of language use (e.g., Volosinov 1987). His notion of heteroglossia is a valuable conceptual tool, which I will use to discuss the multiple and contradictory perspectives of ceremonial performance.

The homogenization of cultural meaning in ceremonial analyses raises other questions of a Bakhtinian sort about Turner's sense of multivocality. Whose voices are multiply represented and combined? From what perspectives do various aspects of multivocality emerge? What other, "unofficial" perspectives are there, and where are they voiced? These questions project the formal strengths of semiotics into social theory.

Turner's alternative term, "polyvalent," actually seems more suited to the sense in which he uses it. Different values and meanings can be assigned to the same form, and can overlap and influence one another. His central message concerns the elaboration of these symbolic values, all apparently shared and agreed upon. When Turner considers contradiction in ceremonies, he locates conflicting messages in different media but does not find conflicting messages contained within a single voice or within a single medium. For example, during the *nkang'a* ceremony opposition and conflict between the novice's mother and other women is mimed in a competition to grab the "porridge of *chipwanpwilu*" while songs praise the solidarity of women and jeer at men (V. Turner 1967:55–56). Opposing principles of social organization are given expression, Turner notes, but expressed contradictions can be overlooked through media separation (and other versions of complementary distribution). Turner's multivocality shows one cultural voice saying different things in different media—not multiple voices saying different things simultaneously, at times in the same medium.

Bakhtin's sense of multiple voices (heteroglossia) is radically different. His voices have speakers who are communicating in particular contexts and who have particular interests. Bakhtin's implicit social theory is akin to that of Giddens, a theory with knowledgeable human agents, contested interpretations, and a sense that "power is integral to the constitution of social practices" (Giddens 1979:54).[7] Bakhtin's special concern is with multiple voices and purposes carried simultaneously by the same communicative forms and exchanges, not simply multiple associative meanings. He is concerned with contradictions and tensions that arise when different perspectives and different interests meet (sometimes within a single person) and with tensions between "official" and "unofficial" understandings of culture carried simultaneously in the same cultural forms.

These sources of ambiguity escape attention in most work on ritual, perhaps because they often emerge as nuances of ceremonial performance. Their recognition entails not only an emphasis on the kind of Jakobsonian multifunctionality mentioned above, but also a keen appreciation of the melding of rhetoric and poetics in ceremonial form, of the ideological uses of language, and of the ironies possible in ceremonial performance.[8]

Turner's closest attention to social politics and conflict was reserved not for ceremonial form but for negotiations about social relations through ceremonial performance. This is the second dimension of his work, complementing work on symbolic types and interpretation. Here Turner looks at the same competing principles of social organization that he saw expressed in different media during ceremonies, and focuses on the ways those contradictions are played out in daily life. He considers cases where people have different involvements in social relations that are defined according to certain principles of social organization. They thus have different vantage points and interests that conflict. Turner's classic analyses follow social dynamics in detail as contradictory interests emerge, are exacerbated, and erupt into open conflict of some sort, and then as compromises are reached, appeasement made, or other interventions separate opponents or defuse the situation. These are the dynamics described in Turner's social dramas, his development of the Manchester school's interest in situational analysis and conflict.

Turner's image of social process in these analyses privileges repetitive cycles. It is not an unchanging picture; his sketches of the particularities and personalities of social dynamics make plain the novelty of each situation. But the novelty is variation rather than innovation. It is not clear whether or how contradictions of social organization might lead to structural changes, or how people might successfully contest or resist some contradictory aspects. One fundamental reason for these lacunae in Turner's representation of social process is that he has not linked the Ndembu to any larger world. What their disputes and ceremonies might have to do with larger historical and political circumstances was not a question that entered Turner's framework. His sense of history and politics remained local and specific to Ndembu interpersonal relations, set in the context of social processes such as village and household formation and fission.

This discussion of Turner's work has led to issues that Maurice Bloch puts at the center of his recent work—issues concerning relations between ceremonial forms and their historical and political circumstances. Though Bloch raises issues important for any analysis of ceremonies, his answers are unsatisfactory.

Essentialist and Structuralist Pitfalls: Bloch's Ceremonial History

A historical perspective on ceremonial structure and form is needed to understand ritual efficacy because the transformative work of a ceremony is specifically defined by and through the circumstances in which it is performed. Those circumstances, the ways in which they are understood, and the ways in which they become incorporated into ceremonies are all social products shaped over time. People eventually abandon ceremonies that are unresponsive or unrelated to their lives, though the relations of ceremonies to broader sociopolitical circumstances can be redefined. *From Blessing to Violence,* Bloch's book on the history of male circumcision ceremonies in Madagascar, traces such changing relations, showing how ceremonies can be put to uses other than those intended by the people who perform them. However, he fails to explore how the ceremonies work for those performers, or whether their recognized reasons for conducting ceremonies have changed as well. These are serious difficulties when his intention is to bring together formal and functionalist approaches and "show that the meaning and nature of a ritual can be understood in the process of its historical formation" (Bloch 1986:11).

Bloch's book is important because there has been so little scholarly attention to the history of ceremonial form.[9] The commonly overdrawn Durkheimian distinction between ceremonies and daily life may have contributed to this deficiency, but other factors are clearly involved as well, since this strong contrast is not made by scholars such as Bateson, Simmel, and Bourdieu. The exaggerated contrast is defined and justified by concepts about the nature of ritual, concepts bound up with ideas about tradition, social change, and animal behavior (Kratz 1993).

Ceremonies do have special (though not necessarily unique) characteristics, such as their metacommunicative aspects, but the ways in which ceremonial contexts interpenetrate with nonceremonial ones are critical to both. Ceremonial experiences are constituted by and help constitute a "daily life" set in specific circumstances at a particular historical time. A detailed sense of that connectivity is essential to understand the question of ritual efficacy and the particular voices and contradictions that may emerge in ceremonial performance. It is equally important for ceremonial history.

Bloch flounders into the traps of the overdrawn distinction, beginning with the false assumptions that typically accompany it. He first describes the Merina ceremonies as he observed them in 1971. His adept structuralist analysis finds their central oppositions and explicates their meanings both as ceremonial logic and as cultural context for later discussion. In addition, the analysis isolates ritual elements that become Bloch's historical markers. He then embarks on a history of Merina circumcision ceremonies, tracing the fate of those elements over the last two hundred years.

The ceremonies were appropriated by various political camps and adapted to different political purposes in different circumstances. They went from locally based ritual to royal state ritual, to a self-conscious alternative to Christianity, to ceremonies that incorporated Christian elements relatively harmoniously, to opposition to the urban bourgeois associations of Christianity. Throughout these changes, Bloch finds formal stability in "the most important ritual acts, symbols and songs" and their central cultural oppositions, relations, and mediations. The changes he describes are a matter of minor tinkering and symbolic flourishes that leave the basic structure unchanged (Bloch 1986:165). Puzzling over such formal stability in a ceremony whose functions, as he sees them, have changed so radically over the past two centuries, he explains this stability by invoking the nature of ritual.

Bloch is right when he says that ceremony and ritual "combine the properties of statements and actions" (Bloch 1986:181; cf. Finnegan 1969; Tambiah 1979; Silverstein 1981; Fernandez 1982). But he develops from that assertion conclusions about the nature of ritual that are fundamentally wrong; he sees it as essentially uncreative, nonpropositional, and timeless. I consider each of Bloch's proposals in turn, using Okiek initiation to provide counterexamples or counterinterpretations.

"Ritual is revealed as an area of human activity very low indeed in creativity," Bloch asserts, because of the relative stability in ritual acts, songs, and symbols (Bloch 1986:186). Bloch has been criticized before for correlating formal definition with lack of creativity and coercive authority, an argument he also applies to political language (Bloch 1975).[10] Okiek initiation demonstrates that the overstatement is no more true of ritual in general than it is of political language. Okiek ceremonies show a relative continuity of ceremonial form within which creativity and implicit recognition of historical change can be and are accommodated in a number of ways (see chapter 8). As

Irvine 1979 shows, there are continua of formal definition of different kinds and continua of creativity that combine in different ways in different cultures, in different ceremonies, and in different ritual events.

Bloch's argument for the nonpropositional nature of ritual leads to another overstatement that sweeps away an essential part of the efficacy and performative nature of ceremonies.

[T]hey are not governed by rules of syntax that make recombination meaningful. Ritual language and material symbols can never express propositions similar to the propositions expressed in other language uses. (Bloch 1986:182)

Bloch must be challenged here for tossing out the syntactic baby with the propositional bathwater. Since reordering and meaningful recombination are not possible, Bloch concludes that syntax, that is, ceremonial sequence, is meaningless repeated formula, frozen into irrelevance. However, Okiek initiation shows that sequential ordering is crucially meaningful in the experience and efficacy of ceremonial transformation. As Fernandez observes, "[R]itual sequences are . . . arguments of images and not fully syntactical in the linguistic sense." Nonetheless, the "transformative interaction of syntax and paradigm" is fundamental to the metamorphosis of ceremonial experience (Fernandez 1986:174; cf. also Fernandez 1982). Silverstein 1981 also suggests that sequence in the form and figures of ritual language effects cultural transformations. Other semiotic means are carefully ordered and orchestrated in ceremonies as well.

In fact, Bloch's otherwise sensitive symbolic analysis of Merina ceremonies pays little attention to their progression and its effect, with only passing references to transformation through language and song (for example, pages 98–99). He concentrates on structural oppositions and categories, their associations and eventual mediation, all to the end of creating an image of transcendent authority to which people acquiesce in its legitimated earthly form.

Bloch mentions the emotional power of the ceremonies but concludes rather weakly and vaguely that it results from the joint ideological collusion of all the people involved in ritual. "For a society such as the Merina, ritual has the main burden of carrying ideology" (Bloch 1986:176). Without considering the sequential and dramatic structure of the ceremonies, he cannot be more specific about the ways that power is created and reaches different participants or about its specific cultural definitions. By overlooking the realm of implicit ideology created through practice, a realm whose importance Bourdieu demonstrates, Bloch also misses an important source of emotional resonance and relations to other contexts of daily life.

Finally, I come to Bloch's case for the timeless nature of ritual. He makes an important point about continuity, but once again argues through hyperbole, ending in misrepresentation and overgeneralization.

Rituals represent events as though they were general occurrences. The circumcision of each particular boy becomes that of any and every boy. . . . Rituals reduce the unique occurrence so that they become a part of a greater fixed and ordered unchanging whole. . . . Ritual makes the passage of time, the change in personnel, and the change in situation, inexpressible and therefore irrelevant. (Bloch 1986:184)

A universalizing capacity is indeed central to ceremonial experience and efficacy, but the individuality and uniqueness of a particular ceremony is not thereby abolished. On the contrary, general ceremonial form and sequence is always personalized and particularized in Okiek initiation; that, too, is an essential aspect of the process (cf. Wagner 1981:50).

Bloch's ritual timelessness is derived from the same exaggerated premise of formal fixity. Okiek initiation does not present a timeless order, but one with considerable temporal continuity that nonetheless accommodates creative responses within shifting social and material circumstances. The simple example of schoolchildren's initiation shows this: people schedule ceremonies and shorten seclusion periods to coincide with school holidays. An *image* of timelessness is asserted, but not without the simultaneous recognition of adaptations and shifts within the overall process. In chapter 8, I consider how that image is created and show that changes in Okiek initiation practice are not simply symbolic flourishes but are related to their changing historical circumstances.

Despite his false conclusions, Bloch's discussion of Merina circumcision contains material that supports a different interpretation. Another view of formal stability and of relations between specific formal shifts and changing historical circumstances can be salvaged from his discussion. Bloch was so blinded by his conclusions about syntax, timelessness, and unanimity that he did not recognize alternative explanations within his own discussion. First, he wants to explain the continuity of symbolic forms without considering how they are tied to the structured transformative sequence central to the ceremony. Second, he does not look at how symbols become a "natural" idiom, felt as well as said and done during ceremonies.

Bloch's puzzle is the continuity of form in a ceremony whose specific political contexts and functions have varied greatly over two hundred years. There are other continuities, however, that Bloch fails to recognize. First, there may be more continuity in the ceremony's political function than he admits. As he describes it, the circumcision ritual represents and legitimates an authority structure that is similar in all the historical situations. Its scale, representatives, and opposing alternatives differed, but in each period Bloch notes institutional continuity: existing institutions were strengthened, not replaced; traditional institutions were used, renovated, and reorganized; under the British treaty, the Merina state expanded and was consolidated; later, when opposition to Merina state administration grew, ancestral customs were strengthened to reinforce legitimacy. Similarly, those involved have always had a Merina background and Merina experience (and sometimes other kinds of experience as well) and understood and felt the "natural" idiom of descent on which both circumcision and political hierarchy draw.[11]

Second, the basic transformative sequence of Merina ceremonies has persisted through time, as have the symbolic forms. The stability Bloch notes is a basic structural continuity that must take forms and sequence together. Though the specific historical situation has changed considerably, the legitimating transformative capacity of the ceremonies has remained effective and responsive in part by means of formal changes and reevaluations within the structure.

Bloch reviews these changes in his historical account, noting changes in scale, costume, ritual events, and ritual materials used, and sometimes crucial changes in those who perform the rite (for example, rulers appropriate the descent idiom, as the king takes the role of elder and the royal administrators those of kinsmen). However, he sees them as unimportant variations that do not affect the stability of symbolic content, which is defined by basic symbolic oppositions and acts. Bloch created the elements of history by isolating them through structuralist analysis; his emphasis on the continuity of these symbolic oppositions then leads him to dismiss these other shifts as unimportant.

Bloch's paradox of formal stability and functional diversity ignores these other formal changes and makes no mention of the continuity in the transformative function of the ceremonies. The structural continuity and formal changes must be taken together. Merina circumcision has such stability through time both because the kind of transformation achieved by its affectively powerful structure and idiom is of continued relevance and because the transformative structure and felt idiom have remained creatively responsive to particular situations through formal shifts and changes. With this perspective, ritual is hardly Bloch's essentially uncreative and ideologically frozen phenomena.

Bloch's sense of social process is bound up with and crippled by his notions about the nature of ritual. He staunchly asserts his materialist orientation and insists that ideology is created by human agency (Bloch 1986:6). Yet he looks to history to escape the unending search for what ritual means for participants. He wants to get at the nature of ritual not "through seeing what it means for the participants, [but through] . . . a much more easily graspable phenomena [sic]: the way rituals are affected by events" (Bloch 1986:11).

What kind of human agency is this? What kind of actors does it assume? What are his "events" but a way to keep human actors and agency at one remove, a result of Bloch's frustration at the ongoing and creative nature of social process? Or is Bloch suggesting that such meanings can be disregarded because actors' understandings do not affect events? Surely that is not the case in, for instance, many colonial encounters, where "policy developed inadvertently in the course of a long, slow, clumsy [cross-cultural] dialogue, replete with systematic misunderstanding" (Feeley-Harnik 1984:7). If actions and events are produced by knowledgeable actors, then the meanings they attach to the world *must* be part of the actors' effects; the attribution of meaning is necessarily an open-ended process.

Bloch's frustration may come from his inability to explain the processes through which rituals become meaningful for participants. This difficulty is the product of his radical dichotomy between ritual and daily life, his insistence that ritual knowledge is opposed to practical knowledge and that the "construction of ideology takes place in very specific and limited kinds of activities, in this example . . . almost entirely in ritual" (Bloch 1986:178).

Bloch resorts to "real history," he says, to avoid reductionism in either the complexity of ritual or the intricate process of "determination." But by removing the actors whose agency should be manifest and denying that their participation in ritual is somehow informed by the rest of their lives (and vice versa), the reality of the social process portrayed becomes somewhat questionable. Despite his stress on the intricacies of determination, Bloch looks for one-way causalities without recognizing the interactive complexities of mutual determination. Ceremonies can be at once a means through which actors understand their lives and interactions, a product of those interactions, and also a force that affects their lives.

The Limits of Logic: Bourdieu's Social World

Pierre Bourdieu argues quite persuasively the opposite of Bloch's view of ideology: that ideology is constructed in a vast array of seemingly inconsequential daily activities as well as in ritual. For Bourdieu, ritual knowledge is a kind of practical knowledge, based on the same schemes of habitus as daily life. The patterns of ritual and daily activities interpenetrate and interact to create the cultural significance of the lived-in world. Despite a view of ideology different from that of Bloch, however, Bourdieu sketches a social world in which the roles of ritual, language, actors, and agency are remarkably similar to those Bloch outlines.

Bourdieu combines a Weberian concern with modes of rationality, legitimation, power, and social action with Maussian notions of body techniques and habitus in his approach to ritual and daily life, first developed at length in *Outline of a Theory of Practice* (1977a). He has since reworked that provisional presentation in *The Logic of Practice,* made "fundamental transformations" in it (1990:284 n. 1), and elaborated his view of language (1977b, 1982).

Bourdieu frames his work as an epistemological exploration of the organization and production of two modes of knowledge, theoretical logic and practical logic. He elaborates practical logic with detailed examples from

Algerian Kabyle. Bourdieu sets a goal for theoretical knowledge: a scientific process that is aware of the effects its own means of knowing, systematizing, and synchronizing have on what it seeks to know. He uses the Kabyle examples to show these effects. It is within this framework that Bourdieu asks what kind of sense ritual makes and how it relates to other domains of practice and to other kinds of knowledge.

The key notion in Bourdieu's practical logic, habitus, leads to his emphasis on cross-contextual links. A set of generative schemes of perception, action, and appreciation that are learned and reinforced by actions and discourses produced according to the same schemes (Bourdieu 1990:14), habitus is applied equally in agricultural labor and calendrical rites, in daily interaction and ceremonial action. This wide-ranging application of a small set of schemes gives practical logic its approximate cohesion, its "fuzzy" regularity.

Bourdieu's habitus gives Turner's notion of multivocality a twist. Stress is placed less on symbols themselves as multivocal than on their incorporation into multiple schemes of action; they are apprehended through different aspects and in different contexts. Bourdieu's argument for cross-contextual considerations is stronger than Turner's, and is accompanied by a more faithfully Saussurean system of relational meaning (Bourdieu 1990:4). His exquisitely detailed Kabyle material leaves no doubt that daily acts, just as much as ritual acts, are part of a continuous creation of significant cultural divisions and values.

Yet Bourdieu still gives greater weight to ritual practice because, he says, it leads more directly to deep-rooted schemes of the habitus. Proverbs, sayings, and riddles are his corresponding linguistic keys, offering similar objectified and codified paths. The condensed allusions and symbolic representations of proverbs and ritual are certainly a boon for theoretical research projects, but Bourdieu claims that schemes of practical knowledge remain outside the universe of thought for those living that practical knowledge, except in "intermittent and partial ways." It thus remains unclear whether or how such objectified forms are similarly primary for practical knowledge; the priority Bourdieu accords them seems to be an artifact of his theoretical enterprise.[12]

While Bourdieu's attention to schemes of habitus illuminates the interpenetration of cultural contexts, his relational understanding of them tends to displace other associations that rely less extensively on interreferencing, positive meanings that do not rely on oppositions to other schemes or objects. The significance of ritual elements and schemes can be understood neither by reducing it to intercontextual relations nor by ignoring those relations.

There is a corresponding displacement of attention from the actors involved, that is, those who live and know the habitus, to the habitus itself and its approximate systematicity. This means that Bourdieu's analyses become more and more a kind of expanded structuralism, his portrayal of Kabyle an increasingly Lévi-Straussian exercise. By the final chapter of The Logic of

Practice, Bourdieu boils the complexity of Kabyle ritual down to two basic abstract schemes: reuniting separated contraries and separating reunited contraries. Like Lévi-Strauss's myths, which think themselves in the minds of men, a certain "autonomy to produce actions or symbols" is also attributed to these schemes (Bourdieu 1990:238).

Such reduction precludes appreciation of the dramatic and persuasive effects of ceremonial sequence and performance. Bourdieu notes the importance of time and tempo to some kinds of practice, like gift giving, where timing is a matter of strategy. Despite his discussion of the calendar of agrarian rites, he does not see the related importance of ceremonial sequence and tempo, nor their role in dramatic effect. He recognizes ritual syntax only as a way to isolate contradictions in meaning, or a way to specify the singularity of a symbol within its Saussurean set of differences. When Bourdieu speaks of efficacy, he refers to the adaptability of practical logic (Bourdieu 1990:261). He does not address the question of why those symbols or those rites are effectively felt by Kabyle during particular ceremonies.

That question would lead into the sphere of emotion, a realm quite foreign to Bourdieu's interest but nonetheless central to the material he discusses. Cross-contextual associations created by multiple sign uses are not affectively neutral. Bourdieu does not stress the point, but these associations can be emotionally evocative as well as cognitively significant, creating and synthesizing particular cultural understandings of emotion and emotionalizing other cultural categories and experiences. Repeated use of signs in similar contexts on similar ceremonial occasions can also create a sense of cultural continuity (or change) that both contributes to and draws on evocative and cognitive resonances.

Bourdieu concentrates on practical knowledge as an alternative to theoretical thinking, but logic is still paramount. His emphasis on the system and structure of practical logic presents a life without feeling, where affect has no effect. He views emotion as "a hallucinatory 'presenting' of the impending future, which . . . leads a person to live a still suspended future as already present, or even already past" (Bourdieu 1990:292). This disregard for emotion and ceremonial sequence means that Bourdieu overlooks the dramatic and rhetorical power of ritual. They are missing from his understanding of language as well.

The limits of Bourdieu's theory are particularly clear when he turns to language. Rhetorical and performative effects are not the only dimensions of communication he overlooks. As others have noted, Bourdieu also gives insufficient attention to the content people communicate through language, thus overlooking the logical power of persuasion as well (Thompson 1984:64).[13] These dimensions are critical to ritual efficacy.

Bourdieu's critique of Saussure and Chomsky (1977b) centers on familiar issues, leading him to the same position from which Gumperz and Hymes

(1964, 1972), Ardener (1971), and others began an important turn toward language in anthropology: the notion that the cultural understandings and social organization of language use are highly variable, an important means through which to understand social interaction, and an indispensable part of understanding verbal communication. Bourdieu proposes a marketplace analogy to deal with the social dimensions of language, but this is an unclear and oversimplifying metaphor (cf. Irvine 1989).

One problem is that Bourdieu assumes a single linguistic marketplace and a single set of values that are recognized and shared by all concerned (Bourdieu 1977b:654, 658). Different attitudes and values toward the same practice can and often do coexist, as Bakhtin has emphasized. Thompson (1984:59) also demonstrates the imprecise and ambiguous sense of Bourdieu's "recognition." Furthermore, Bourdieu's concepts of discourse and communication include little interaction between speakers and are void of the normal negotiations over definitions of context or formality. The only negotiation he acknowledges is "between the expressive interest and the censorship inherent in particular linguistic production relations" (Bourdieu 1977b:651). In fact, there is no real negotiation, for censorship always wins, according to Bourdieu; "material conditions of existence determine discourse" (Bourdieu 1977b:653).

Multidimensional social relations, multifaceted notions of identity, and crosscutting ties disappear in Bourdieu's social world, as do interpersonal relations on anything resembling an equal footing. Verbal communication is similarly limited in function; Bourdieu stresses indexical roles with a single association (often class in European examples). His examples show a simplistic understanding of language use that even a preliminary perusal of the available literature could have dispelled. A few illustrations will suffice.

Discussing language choice and bilingual switching, Bourdieu notes only one of the two kinds of code-switching that Blom and Gumperz (1972) distinguish as situational and metaphorical. By citing only situational switching, he leaves aside multidimensional and playful language uses emphasized in metaphorical switching.[14]

Bourdieu's examples of *tu/vous* usage in French and of matters of phrasing, questions, and politeness are also inadequate, ignoring available work on precisely those topics (for example, Brown and Gilman 1960; Friedrich 1967; Goody 1978). Again, the work disregarded would give a richer comparative basis for the issues involved and show the importance of creative and negotiated aspects of language use. Bourdieu uses common-sense examples, but a general theory of language in social interaction cannot afford to ignore evidence of direct relevance, especially when Bourdieu himself has shown that the social construction of common sense can run counter to understandings constructed through theoretical logic.

The studies just cited on the uses of language in social context are a small sample of the work on language and culture that has been flourishing since the mid-1960s. Diverse studies have been done on the political dimensions of language use (Bloch 1975; Brenneis and Myers 1984; Parkin 1980, 1984), the social aspects of poetics (Jakobson 1960, 1968; Fabian 1982), narrative structure and experience (Labov and Waletsky 1967; R. Rosaldo 1980; Sherzer 1987a; Bauman 1986), figurative speech (Sapir and Crocker 1977; Fernandez 1974; Friedrich 1979), the pragmatics of ritual language (Silverstein 1981; Kratz 1990a), verbal performance (Bauman 1977; Hymes 1975; Fernandez 1977), and the relations among speech, song, and sentiment (Feld 1982; Abu-Lughod 1986), to cite only a few topics and authors. Ceremonies commonly include diverse ways and genres of speaking, which are variously related to cultural understandings of communication in other contexts. This body of work provides a battery of methods and concepts with which to consider language use in ceremonies. The challenge is to relate diverse ways of speaking to one another and to other dimensions of ceremonial structure in order to understand the ritual efficacy of their combinations in performance.

This work on language also conveys a more complicated sense of social actors as people with multiple interests, abilities, and identities, which are communicated and negotiated in interaction. As knowledgeable actors, people's actions are effective, though not always in anticipated ways. Bourdieu limits too severely the extent to which actors are knowledgeable, denying them any real possibility of making a difference in their own situations. He does not allow for degrees of recognition and knowledge of the schemes of practical knowledge or of wider situations, or for various moments and contexts of self-reflection. As a result, Bourdieu's theory cannot accommodate historical contingencies and conjunctions. How do the rituals he describes incorporate changing aspects of daily life? The habitus is generative, but how it changes is unclear. Bourdieu's actors, like Bloch's, are in the end censored and coerced by habitus and language, part of a rather humorless life with little irony or creativity. As Karp and Maynard note, "there is little room for agency here" (Karp and Maynard 1983:501).

Bourdieu's general picture of social life, social actors, communication, and interaction is oversimplified, overemphasizing constraints and underemphasizing not only how contingency, multiple perspectives, and interests are accommodated but also how felt experience is culturally defined in emotional concepts that figure in social life. Social theory that acknowledges actors as knowledgeable and effective recognizes better the complexities of individuals and social life. Bourdieu cites Bakhtin on carnival reversals (Bourdieu 1977b:663), but leaves aside his discussions of heteroglossia and the simultaneous holding of multiple, sometimes contradictory perspectives. Despite the difficulties with Bourdieu's larger social theory, however, his intricate understanding of how diverse contexts and activities interpenetrate and the general concept of practical knowledge are important contributions to the study of cultural knowledge and ritual processes.

Ceremonial Experience and Emotion: Leads from Lienhardt and Beidelman

Experience is a central focus for a number of Oxford-trained anthropologists, as the title of Godfrey Lienhardt's study of Dinka religion suggests: *Divinity and Experience*. Their notion of experience is complex, encompassing both an apprehension of social and physical environments and a cognitive, affective, and moral interpretation of them. Scholars such as Lienhardt and T. O. Beidelman combine a phenomenological approach with Durkheim's and Mauss's concern with topics such as the relation of individual and society, cultural categories and understandings of the world, and the philosophical dimensions of symbolic imagery. The combination produces hermeneutical elaborations that trace the interconnections among landscape, economic cycles, body attitudes, aesthetics, social relations, metaphor, song, and ceremonies, weaving and circling back and forth among aspects of life that are analytically distinguishable but experientially united.

Their exegeses describe the contours and shadings of various "configurations of experience," a formulation through which these scholars recognize and address the meaningful interconnections that Turner discusses in terms of associations and Bourdieu with the schemes of habitus. Several important distinctions in the renderings of social actors and ceremony are bound up with these related but dissimilar notions.

Human experience overflows the categories through which we think and live it, so the categories' associations cannot exhaust their meaning (Lienhardt 1961:162–70; Beidelman 1970:507). Such categories image lived experience but neither contain it nor fully limit it. Variation and change are intrinsic to human experience (for example, individual, regional, and historical variations), and so cultural associations and understandings necessarily retain a certain elusiveness. That inherent openness provides an important way for historical contingency and change to be incorporated in representations of experience.

"Configurations of experience" seems both broader and more vague than either Turner's associative methodology or Bourdieu's habitus, but the vagueness arises not from imprecision but from Lienhardt's conception of actors, their agency, and their creative engagement with the world. In both Lienhardt's and Beidelman's social worlds, actors are not only knowledgeable but reflective (Beidelman 1986:1–10; Lienhardt 1961:15–27). Analogies of thought and idioms of reasoned argument are as powerful in shaping their understandings and intentions as analogies based on schemes of action. Configurations of experience are fuzzy sets of interconnections that figure in such analogies and reasoning, serving as resources for what in a more general sense is called moral imagination. Moral imagination brings together the imaging of lived experience, the practice and conventions of social interaction, and the material constraints of historical and physical circumstances.

The reflective dimension of moral imagination connotes neither passivity nor reclusivity, as Western notions of reflection would often have it (Beidelman 1986). Reflection and action are mutually infusing features of human experience, synthesized in social life. Poetic performances, ceremonies, and legal deliberations are themselves among the means through which actors can control the world (in part), act upon it, and sometimes change it. Individuals can rarely, if ever, accomplish this on their own, however; the strength to shape the world arises out of joint action and the collective power of social groups.

For instance, Beidelman's cogent reanalysis of Swazi royal ritual discusses "some of the ways, through ritual acts, by which Swazi believe that they themselves can manipulate symbols to achieve certain states and effects in themselves and the world about them" (Beildelman 1966:376). Lienhardt speaks of people modeling hopes and desires, controlling mental and moral dispositions, confirming intentions, and "modulating" experience through ceremonies and symbolic acts (Lienhardt 1961:282–91). He cites legal councils as one example:

[T]he whole of the situation [was presented] to the disputants and to the community, so that its rights and wrongs, the true . . . and the false, were apparent in such a way as to transcend the individual views of truth held by those in conflict. . . . Those who were in disagreement will, ideally, adjust their separate views to each other in the light of that representation. (Lienhardt 1961:248)

Lienhardt may implicitly recognize contradictions within the politics of public compromise, between such public adjustments and more individual demands of self-respect, justification, and personal control, or among cultural understandings from radically different contexts that might be drawn together in the experience of some individuals. However, he does not clearly factor such dimensions into his image of social process, whether in the form of open contestation, implicit resistance, or cultural disenchantments (Holmes 1989). D'Azevedo (1962) reports that Gola disputants return from counsels, where they have reworked public representations of a case through debate and consensus, only to reaffirm their own versions as the "real truth" in variants temporarily confined to family contexts. In other words, their versions persist as representations of personal autonomy and identity, or as a means of future challenge should political circumstances or relations of power and authority shift.

Lienhardt's attention to internal social divisions and power imbalances is very selective. He notes structural parallels among Dinka representations of divinity and powers, relations between fathers and sons, and relations between elder and younger brothers. He concentrates, however, on the collective sense of clan, lineage, and tribe (by which he means section or ethnic subgroup) represented in ontological categories and sacrificial rites. One result is a very unelaborated picture of Dinka women's positions and perspectives, though

Lienhardt does not discount their importance. He notes women's critical role in Dinka myth and also concludes that the sacrificial cattle that deflect human death represent women. Yet he does not consider the possible alternatives of women's experiences, their representations of activity and passivity in sacrifice (Lienhardt 1961:152), or their takes on the idiom of cattle and wealth, which seems to limit their participation in important ways. The specific nature of women's ritual roles, for example, the dance and song they perform at key points, is similarly unelaborated.

An underdeveloped cognizance of contestation, authority, and power in ceremonial performance also limits Lienhardt's discussion of disputatious, ironic, and paradoxical possibilities in Dinka imaging of experience. Such considerations may not be possible, however, until there are analyses that begin from participants' viewpoints and understandings of what they are doing in ceremonies. Oddly enough, these are relatively rare. Beidelman shows how critical this is to the question of ritual efficacy, taking Swazi understandings of ritual categories, intention, and effect as his analytical starting point. He underscores the importance of psychological aspects in ritual effect, meaning attention to actors' beliefs, intentions, and agency. Karp combines the Oxford anthropologists' concern with symbolic classification and definitions of the person with Bakhtin's focus on heteroglossia to show that performance can ironically contradict the official definition encoded in classificatory schemes (Karp 1987).

The other component necessary to study ritual efficacy is a detailed consideration of ceremonial structure, sequence, and performance. In effect, this is a corollary and elaboration of the actor-centered starting point. Both Lienhardt and Beidelman pay attention to this, but they look at ceremonial components and form in a gross sense rather than at detailed interweavings of communicative resources and orchestrations of dramatic and affective sequence.[15] For instance, Lienhardt describes the main parts of sacrificial ceremonies, but doesn't clarify their sequential relations, their repetitions, or the significance of certain actors (Lienhardt 1961:270). He realizes that verbal repetitions can be significant and effective, but omits them in favor of more general thematic exposition (Lienhardt 1961:233).

Both Lienhardt and Beidelman rely on linguistic material to examine cultural philosophy and ritual thematics. The important word *ring* (flesh) is traced through the course of a Dinka ceremony (Lienhardt 1961:136). Prayer texts illustrate concepts; metaphors link different realms of experience. Dinka and Swazi actors speak, in a sense, thereby providing a feel for cultural idiom (in translation), something that is essential to understanding the ceremonies.

When Lienhardt looks at a series of ceremonies in the latter part of his book, he separates their verbal and "manual" aspects for clarity of exposition, a practice I adopt in this study as well. He uses Dinka texts as "actually said," but by that he means a running thematic translation. He notes his omission of repetitions and punctuating sounds, but that omission means many poetic and rhetorical structures of the performances are lost. With them is lost a way to specify the effective means of ceremonial performance.

Beidelman notes a general relation between song sequence, the development of Swazi ritual, and the supernatural development in the rites (Beidelman 1966:396). Similarly but more generally, Lienhardt notes that genres of song and speech are interspersed and that people "lose themselves" more and more as the ceremony progresses (Lienhardt 1961:244). He does not, however, look at the significance of verbal patterning over the course of the ceremony for clues to this effect. Lienhardt's division of verbal and manual aspects does not result in a clearer sense of their interrelations; his concern is with the way Dinka cosmology is enacted in sacrificial rites rather than with understanding how Dinka create effective ceremonial performances.

The limited thematic treatment of verbal aspects of Dinka ceremonies has another casualty as well. "No aspect of language is immune from appropriation by the semiotic of emotion" (Lutz and White 1986:423). By confining his attention to broad referential dimensions of language, Lienhardt loses the opportunity to explore *how* affective movement defines existential truth and moral reality, though he recognizes that it does (Lienhardt 1961:250). He describes Dinka trembling and trance chiefly in physiological terms (Lienhardt 1961:234), with reference to concepts of divinity but without placing them within a Dinka economy of emotion, sentiment, and personhood.

Neglect of these matters is a real shortcoming and constraint for a study that seeks to understand cultural experience in ceremonies from participants' perspectives. Emotional categories figure importantly in cultural understandings of personhood, that is, who participants are. "The fact that emotions are, in many societies, a critical link in cultural interpretations of action implies that emotion concepts are likely to be actively used in the negotiation of social reality" (Lutz and White 1986:420). Furthermore, the different means and contexts for the expression of emotions, all culturally shaped, might well reveal different sets of values—official and unofficial views of the world and of social relations (Abu-Lughod 1986:256). Lienhardt's underemphasis of alternative perspectives has already been noted.

The social and cultural construction of emotion became a prominent topic of anthropological research only in the past twenty years (Lutz and White 1986), but that work has begun to specify the ways language, culture, emotion, and social action are entwined (Abu-Lughod 1986; Lutz and Abu-Lughod 1990). Many of these interests and perspectives resonate with Lienhardt's phenomenological studies. Surely he would concur that "discourses [of sentiment] are not templates, but rather languages that people can use to express themselves. In enabling people to express experiences, these discourses may enable them to feel those experiences. But the fact remains that it is people who make the statements" (Abu-Lughod 1986:258).

Ceremonial Processes and Paradoxes

The preceding critiques define issues and topics on which I focus in examining Okiek initiation. I also propose a combination of approaches in order to consider ritual efficacy most productively. "[W]e need it all: a formal poetics of performance, an ethnographic understanding of events and social interactions in terms of the constitutive role of discourse, and a sense of form-function interrelationships" (Bauman 1986:114). The mix must also include express attention to the interplay of structure and history through the diversity of cultural experience. The final synthesis presents a processual and historical view of continuities between marked performances (such as ceremonies) and other contexts and illuminates the constitutive relations between communicative channels and the "heightened intensity of communicative interaction" and "power inherent in performance" (Bauman 1977:43–45). The synthesis aims for a balanced blend of formal analysis, pragmatic analysis, and a semiotics of social situations—one that can consider questions of authority and social power and accommodate the whimsy, contradictions, and creative tensions of cultural processes (Wagner 1981; Giddens 1979; Karp 1986a:32–35).

This section formulates more specifically the way this synthetic approach can help explore the ritual efficacy of Okiek initiation. I will focus on three key processes involved in producing ceremonial transformation: contextual re-creation, semiotic movement, and experiential and emotional engagement. These processes emerge in different ways in different ritual events over the course of initiation, combined in different modalities. Such shifts and variation make it essential to consider the varied uses and combinations of communicative resources in ceremonies.

The process of contextual re-creation represents important cultural assumptions that are the background and context for the specific transformation. Re-created in ceremonial structure and performance, these assumptions establish the frame of cultural understandings and social relations within which transformation takes place. At the same time, this process re-creates, continues, and often legitimates a sociopolitical organization based on those understandings.

For instance, Okiek conceptions of gender roles and relations are an important context for initiation. The organization of ceremonial participation, ways of speaking, and other communicative modes all carry and re-create assumptions about gender that are the framework for the change from girl to woman. The ceremonial transformation is understood in terms of those assumptions and can also perpetuate them.

The second process, semiotic movement, concentrates on the transformation itself. It creates significant movement over the course of initiation ceremonies through coordinated changes in several series of related signs. Girls move toward cultural definition as women through sequential changes in a series of indexical signs over the course of initiation: costume, location, action, mode of verbal participation, song, and so forth.

The third process, experiential and emotional engagement, concerns the potentially strong emotional experiences of ceremonies. The ways sentiments are understood, experienced, and expressed in ceremonies are not the same for all participants, but each is part of a culturally specific emotional economy. This process focuses on the cultural creation of affective potential through the dramatic structure of ceremonies, the coordination of communicative means, combinations of significant, affectively resonant signs, patterns of participation, and, finally, the personalization of general ceremonial structure in particular performances. Without this third process, the first two seem so much mechanical manipulation. Of course, the three are inseparable in experience, and are distinguished analytically only to clarify the cultural processes through which people shape, understand, and experience their lives.

I should make clear what I mean to accentuate when I talk of the emotional power of ceremonies, for "power" has become a buzzword in recent years. The currency of "power" reflects a heightened interest in questions of influence and authority, ideology, and cultural hegemony, but buzzwords often accumulate interpretative mutations until the resultant ambiguity obscures what they are intended to elucidate. Arens and Karp (1989:xii) emphasize the multicentered nature of power and argue that "power must be viewed in part as an artifact of the imagination and a facet of human creativity." They make a useful distinction between the notion of power as force or control and that of power as energy or capacity. In collective events, the two often intertwine.

Okiek initiation, for instance, is partly about access to and control of cultural resources, an adult power that men enjoy to a greater degree than women. Initiation is a culturally created danger point, with both personal, physical danger from the operation and the wider danger of public shame and cowardice. In braving those dangers, initiates move away from parental control, display their personal control, and emerge with the power of adult capacities. Self-control in the service of both self and others leads to the capacity to control and influence others.[16] How does this relate to the emotional experience of initiation? What kind of power is that?

A collective sense of emotional engagement and the corresponding sense of powerful, strong emotion is almost palpable at some moments during initiation. This sense of emotional power is produced through interactive intensification over the course of the ceremony. *-nereec* is the term Okiek apply to the emotional state of most participants in the ceremony, and means in a general sense "to be worked up." It refers to different sorts of emotional engagement, however, which are expressed in a number of ways during the ceremony. The power of the emotion glossed as *-nereec* also varies.[17]

When relatives and friends attending the ceremony get worked up, they might be anxious or worried as they remember the pain of their own initiation, proud of their daughter dancing so beautifully, and/or ambivalent at the changes the ceremony will bring to their personal relations. Whatever the particulars, they are *nereece* in their heightened emotional state and show it in specific, culturally defined ways. Young men might have a kind of fit; women might harangue the initiates, have a fit, or cry; older men introduce emotional exclamations and pauses when they address the girls. In each case, the display is a personal expression of emotion and engagement and simultaneously an encouragement (*ceerset*) to initiates. These emotional displays have the power to induce an effect in initiates, to make them worked up in turn and more determined to succeed at initiation.

Initiates also describe their emotional state during the ceremonies with the verb *-nereec,* but theirs remains a more internal state, a mounting energy. They show their strong emotion through an increasing stoicism and an ever more intense physical control rather than through being overcome and unable to contain their emotion, as other people are. The initiates' growing engagement—a hardening resolve and determination, in their case—is none-theless visible to those who can interpret its stylization in the girls' decreasing animation and interaction, their unchanging facial expressions. These obser-vations can set off more emotional displays by others, especially at turning points of the ceremony. These in turn show the girls their relatives' anxiety, make the girls more determined, and so on. This kind of mutual effect and heightening is what I mean by interactive intensification.

The initiates' controlled emotional engagement, however, does not just have power to induce an effect in others. It also has another power, critical to their success: the power to make them actualize their capacity for self-control and so ratify their claim to adult capacities and powers.[18] In summary, this is the logic (and one of the outcomes) of the process of experiential and emotional engagement in Okiek initiation.

Okiek effect the ceremonial transformation that occurs during initiation through these three central processes. Much of the background established through contextual re-creation and much of the semiotic movement work with cultural ideals and norms, are representations of the way things "should" be. Yet another face appears in ceremonial performance as well. Personal experi-ence always creates individual, "unofficial" understandings that counter re-ceived, "official" ones in some ways (cf. Bakhtin 1976).

Immense social effort goes into attaching orderly "official" meanings to action and communication. But as played out in events those official meanings can often be seen to have ambiguous and contradictory counterparts attached to them. (S. F. Moore 1987:735)

While these counterparts are related to familiar analytical oppositions, such as individual and group interests or "ideal images" and "real experiences," there is more to them than such totalizing oppositions would suggest. Official meanings and ideal norms represent a certain perspective on social life, a perspective that favors and empowers certain people rather than others. Ambiguous and contradictory counterparts of official viewpoints may reflect a difference of perspective that is collective as well as individual. Those who subscribe to and benefit from official views are not immune to ambiguity and contradiction either, for unofficial and official meanings and perspectives can be understood and felt simultaneously. Further, both conflict and contestation are socially experienced, expressed, and even constructed in events such as ceremonies. Any sociopolitical organization engenders tensions between people with different interests and motivations (sometimes within the same individual simultaneously), and incorporates particular structural contradictions as well. Although they are often bound up together, the two need to be considered separately.

Following Lockwood's distinction, the interpersonal tensions are related primarily to social integration while the structural contradictions are related more to system integration. "Whereas the problem of social integration focuses attention upon the orderly or conflictful relationships between the actors, the problem of system integration focuses on the orderly or conflictful relationships between the parts of a social system" (Lockwood 1964:245). Structural contradictions may be highlighted when two official views meet (as, for example, in Okiek notions of gender and initiation) or in the space between official and unofficial (such as when norms of adult-child interaction are questioned from the collective perspective of Okiek children). Interpersonal tensions related to social integration emerge in particular relationships, for example, in arguments between a woman and her husband or between a man and one of his sons.

I use the term "contradiction" in a way that is fairly standard in social theory (cf. Giddens 1979), deriving from Marx but focusing on one of several senses in his work, the sense that Lockwood identifies with questions of system integration. Contradictions arise when structural principles central to the reproduction of a sociopolitical formation work in opposition to each other. Such contradictions are typically seen as central in historical transformations of sociopolitical formations, but the existence of structural contradictions does not automatically result in transformation. Nor do contradiction and conflict always coincide—one point of Lockwood's distinction and a theme in Bakhtin's work as well.

I identify contradictions in the structure of Okiek life that have been fundamental to its transformation (Kratz 1990b) and will also consider historical shifts in Okiek socioeconomic organization. They are not the focus of this study, however, but essential historical background for my analysis of contemporary ceremonial performance. My concentration on performance highlights the way central contradictions are embodied in cultural forms and emerge in cultural performance. Particular contradictions emerge in ceremonies in varied ways, with various degrees of conscious recognition by actors involved. So, too, does the mode of recognition vary.

Contradictions are sometimes recognized most clearly in crisis situations, but at times they also emerge as part of the very structure and definition of ritual events, and even more often in asides, in the ways events unfold, in jokes and irony, and in the sometimes chaotic uncertainties of performance.[19] Cultural forms and events carry contradictory purposes and interpretations simultaneously. They too add another facet to the emotional tenor and experience of the occasions.

The early Manchester school often studied conflicts in ceremonies arising from contradictory social principles, such as the combination of matrilineality and patrilocality, but these system conflicts were considered in terms of specific social conflicts—how they created contradictory personal interests and impulses at a moment in time. The need for choice and action in social situations necessitates a temporary reconciliation of personal ambiguities. Social conflict is resolved, but contradictory principles remain. As historical circumstances change, those structural contradictions can become exacerbated and may eventually be transformed; local understandings of social relationships are modified concurrently. Thus in studying ceremonial forms, attention must be given to their complex semiotic history within changing historical circumstances as well as to the contemporary politics and accommodations they can illustrate.

Later students of the Manchester school maintain a focus on ritual as resolving particular situations and contradictory viewpoints, but also pay greater attention to the performative and aesthetic nature of ceremonies, "their aesthetic structure in practice" (Kapferer 1983:8, 1979a, 1979c). Kapferer's detailed study of exorcism rituals is a sophisticated frame analysis that takes account of the multiple media involved in performance and sets modes of Sri Lankan healing in sociological perspective. Nonetheless, the historical dimension is still missing.

Contradictions may produce tensions between different social groups, but not necessarily open conflict. People can often accommodate contradictions through contextual separation or through imaginative cultural forms (Beidelman 1986). The ways that contradictions emerge in ceremonial performance sometimes merge with distinctions such as ideal/real and official/unofficial; they also play on ambiguous meanings and the possibility of multiple interpretations. All are part of cultural politics and ideology in culturally and historically particular ways (Giddens 1979:190–97).

Three key contradictions emerge in Okiek initiation, emphasized differentially during the process. They concern cultural identity, gender, and age; the three intersect in concepts of personhood, concepts fundamental to initiation. Later chapters will discuss the ways Okiek experience these contradictions and how they figure in situations and interpersonal judgments Okiek make about themselves and others as persons. At present, I outline the bases of the three contradictions in the organization of Okiek social life, looking at gender and cultural identity in more detail. The axis of contradiction in each case is defined by different principles of equality versus hierarchy.

Okiek cultural identity combines two elements: first, forest-dwelling hunters and honey-gatherers who diversified with farming and herding, and second, a regional minority long in interaction with pastoral and agricultural neighbors who look down on them. In this sphere, hierarchy and equality appear not as contradictory structural principles, but rather in contradictory views held by Okiek and their neighbors of the same regional interactions.

Okiek emphasize their distinctive habitat, history, and subsistence activities. They cast themselves as accommodators of cultural difference rather than as simply the disparaged, impoverished minority their neighbors portray. Both views figure in Okiek cultural identity, however, and are linked through categories, metaphors, and interactions that are shared by Okiek and their neighbors but which they evaluate in different ways (Kratz 1981a; Galaty 1979, 1986; Klumpp and Kratz 1992).

Cultural identity is both contextually and historically mutable; the contemporary Kenyan mosaic of ethnicity developed largely after 1880 (Lonsdale 1977; Ambler 1988; Spear and Waller 1992). The current categories of "Okiek" (what Okiek call themselves) and "Torrobo" (the more common name for Okiek, derived from a derogatory Maasai term) and the emphases that define them now must be seen in this context. The same is true of gender categories, but historical transformations in concepts of gender can be more difficult to reconstruct.

Initiation establishes an equality among all adult men and, separately, among all adult women. At the same time, it creates a contradictory set of hierarchical intragender relations based on age; that is, within each community of initiated equals there are differences of authority, influence, and ritual knowledge relative to age. Initiation could also imply equality between adult men and women, but that equality is not recognized or borne out in social life. Okiek gender relations are defined by a contradiction between complementarity in household production (with men and women contributing services and products that are equally essential but distinct) and a gender-defined hierarchy of access to and control of productive resources and sociopoliticial influence.

This contradiction in gender relations arises through certain conjunctions of Okiek understandings about and organization of gender, economy, power, and authority. Various configurations of these four domains emerge repeatedly in studies of gender in diverse cultures, in history, and in the academic practice of science, literary studies, and history (Reiter 1975; Rogers 1975; Cott 1977; Young, Wolkowitz, and McCullagh 1981; Harding 1986; Kauffman 1986; Scott 1988; Haraway 1989). The Okiek slant on this convergence and the ways Okiek gender relations are played out and played with through ceremonial performance brings out other dimensions of cultural processes through which such conjunctions are re-created, naturalized, legitimated, and questioned.

Gender, Ethnicity, Identity, and Difference

At different points in the development of gender studies, scholars would have asked different questions about Okiek gender relations and their social, economic, and political circumstances, questions shaped by changing theoretical perspectives. In the 1970s, debate over the reasons for women's universally low status dominated women's studies, with various scholars arguing for the priority of either natural or cultural reasons (Quinn 1977). The general conclusion of this debate, that nature and culture entwine and interact in all gender relations, raised questions about the terms in which it had been phrased. "Domination," "discrimination," and "low status" are categories that must be disentangled into specific, culturally relevant dimensions and then often qualified and differentiated relative to historical moment, social relations, the life cycle, women's subsistence roles, and various other aspects of social life (cf. Rosaldo and Lamphere 1974:13; MacCormack and Strathern 1980). For instance, Okiek women's current mixed agricultural production provides them with different possibilities compared to earlier decades, when Okiek relied more on hunting and gathering. Similarly, older women often have greater influence on family decisions than younger women.

The most important conceptual distinction to emerge from this literature was clearly developed by the mid-1970s: gender versus sex (for example Rubin 1975; Davis 1976). The gender concept underlines the social and historical constitution of identities and relations related to sexual differences. It emphasizes that these identities and relations are not innate products of biological sex. The gender/sex distinction directed research to interpretive issues, especially cultural and historical representations of gender. This produced a growing archive of case studies that examine gender-related particulars, seeking to define modes of domination, types of status and gender relations, and their distributions. However, a catalogue of details proved an insufficient research goal, particularly in light of the feminist political program implicitly coupled with the work.

As case studies that were focused on gender accumulated, scholars began to ask a fundamental question: how are gender relations and representations produced, legitimated, changed, and perpetuated? This question has been asked increasingly often since the early 1980s, and signals a reorientation that was part of a general increase in emphasis on process-oriented theories (Bourdieu 1977a; Giddens 1979; Ortner 1984). The question pointed to the need for comparative analyses of cultural and historical processes related to gender hierarchies and inequalities, and at the same time could sustain a critical and political turn within academic fields (Kauffman 1986:21, 314; Scott 1988:29). Recent work that focuses on these processes also emphasizes non-gender-based commonalities and connections among the situations of ethnic minorities, women, and third world scholars (Bhabha 1986:150; Scott 1988:3; Prakash 1990:403).[20] Cases that replace gender with ethnicity in the gender-economy-power-authority conjunction can easily be found; both conjunctions are at play in the Okiek situation.

The developments I have outlined in this cursory overview of women's studies seem to convey a progressive, unified image that can be misleading. Previous scholarly work has indeed been built on, and sometimes corrected, but such development is only one tale. Many feminist positions coexist inside and outside academe, often at odds with one another. Some positions represent alternative developments stemming from the concerns and periods mentioned. "Behind the facade of progress is a complex history of roads traveled and then abandoned, new starts, and alliances and fissures across disciplines and among anthropological subfields" (di Leonardo 1991c:1).

For instance, in one line of work (including most of the scholars cited above) the notion of gender is used to emphasize relationality, understanding "women" as always part of a set of culture-specific gender categories and identities. However, the concept of gender is also incorporated into work that loses sight of this central relationality, espousing separatist and/or nationalist agendas, as well as into work that conflates biology and culture. Both of the latter build on extremely problematic notions of "women's culture" (di Leonardo 1991a).[21] All these strands can be seen in the growing literature on "seeing like a woman," "speaking like a woman," or generally "doing X like a woman." To illustrate the very different approaches and assumptions that cluster under this gender umbrella, I take two books published in 1986 as examples. The first considers gender and writing, the second gender and reading.

Linda Kauffman's *Discourses of Desire* gives a very clear sense of the multiple layers of cultural artifice involved in representations of gender. Her study of fiction cast in the form of love letters distinguishes portrayals of gender that relate to text characters and to authors, that is, gender representations in writing about women and in "writing like a woman." In elucidating these intricacies, Kauffman pushes her discussion beyond the cultural construction and conventions of gender to "reevaluate the very concepts of author, of genre, of mimesis and challenge the traditional models of academic criticism" (Kauffman 1986:20–21) by showing how tacit assumptions about gender affect interpretation.

Gender and Reading, a contemporaneous edited volume on "reading like a woman," is a sad contrast. Its authors worry about creating a false universal by glossing over distinctions of race, class, and sexual orientation among women. But their unacknowledged universe of reference—contemporary Euro-American society—becomes as clear as their inadequate sense of the cultural and historical specificity of gender and the politics of gender. This is evident, for instance, in their consistent failure to interrogate the category "third world women" and even in such apparently innocent generalizations as "gender identity is acquired with literacy" (Flynn and Schweickart 1986:xxi). The volume shows how specific cultural and historical definitions and perceptions become universalized and naturalized, how reading or writing like a middle-class, educated, white, American woman in the 1980s is redefined as reading or writing like a woman.[22] There are many examples of feminist rifts along race lines or among women of color that issue from such exclusive and essentialist claims (Sargent 1981; E. F. White 1990; Mohanty, Russo, and Torres 1991). This process of synecdoche is one way the myths of "women's culture" are created.

When specific cultural and historical contexts are elevated to natural universals and a relational perspective is lost (a combination of problems not unique to feminism), separatist politics often result, in some cases as a reaction. Important relationalities glossed over include not only those within the same system of inequality (such as in gender), but also the articulation of different systems of inequality in the same setting and across settings (race, class, ethnicity, gender, and so on). The separatism espoused may merely invert the terms of the system that is being contested, a counterhegemony that reproduces the same power relations with different valences rather than rethinking them. Edward Said notes this danger in subaltern studies:

For if subaltern history is construed to be only a separatist enterprise—much as early feminist writing was based on the notion that women had a voice or a room of their own, entirely separate from the masculine domain—then it runs the risk of just being a mirror opposite of the writing whose tyranny it disputes. It is also likely to be as exclusivist, as limited, provincial, and discriminatory in its suppressions and repressions as the master discourses of colonialism and elitism. (Said 1988:viii)

In such politics of identity and/or difference, which contest identities and roles and challenge power and authority, the politics of representation are critical to disputes over specific issues and over the terms of debate. Whether the inequities at stake involve androcentricity, Eurocentricity, Afrocentricity, bourgeois-centricity and/or postcoloniality, the further question of whose androcentricity, whose Afrocentricity, must be specifically addressed. Questioning and specifying perspectives is a corollary of relationality, though it is rarely applied consistently. "Perspective conditions comprehension and interpretation. Perspective here signifies the capacity for certain insights as well as the limitation of vision" (Flynn and Schweickart 1986:xxi). Perspective also involves political positioning; the limitations of one's own perspective are often denied.

Feminist and postmodern critiques of essentialist identities share an emphasis with Bakhtin's heteroglossic literary analyses, all insisting on multiple, simultaneous perspectives. These critiques bring into focus twin problems and pitfalls in identity politics. First, precipitate generalization disguises important distinctions and divergent interests within groups that share some identity. Conversely, such heightened attention to ever more particularized divisions can be so balkanizing that little sense of shared identity remains, common interests seem elusive, and any generalization becomes a sign of insensitivity. Critical reformulations suggest not that a balance be struck between these poles but that identity be reconceptualized in multiple terms, emphasizing the simultaneity and interplay of intersecting identities and perspectives.

A comparative approach would help illuminate the many ways that multiple identities can intersect, overlap, and influence one another in different times and places, as it helped broaden and clarify questions in women's studies. Specific case studies can explore relevant cultural categories and modes of representation, and then look critically at how such categories and representations are created, how they intersect and interact, how they are inscribed and naturalized as identities, what social, political, and economic locations they encode in particular periods and circumstances, and how they change over time. Comparative analyses of these processes can be based only on case studies. It is those cultural and historical processes that are the relevant and interesting locus for comparison and generalization, rather than the specific categories and examples of representational strategy.

Marilyn Strathern's telling critique of misplaced universalism in the anthropology of women (Strathern 1981) turns on a related point: the fallacy of generalizing about all women and the meaning of womanhood from the way women are represented and understood in any particular culture. This is the same problem discussed above, but Strathern examines a case that elevates the categories of a non-Western culture to universal. Her careful comparison of Hagen and Wiru gender representations and relations illustrates the absurdity of misplaced universalism. It also underlines the importance of relational analyses of gender that are "informed by concepts of the person, individuality, will and so forth to be read from the data and not into them" (Strathern 1981:683). These more general concepts are essential for understanding concepts and relations of gender, but the ways they are "read from the data" into anthropological analyses deserve the critical attention that analytical concepts in other fields have been receiving (Haraway 1988; Scott 1989; Prakash 1990; di Leonardo 1991a, 1991c).

Strathern also notes that "there are differences both in the qualities attributed to womanhood and in the manner in which symbols are generated out of a male-female dichotomy. . . . As soon as the concept [i.e., "woman"] is given cultural value . . . the proper focus for comparative analysis becomes not women but the values so assigned" (Strathern 1981:682). Particular representations of women must be considered in conjunction with related representations and through time (cf. Riley 1988). Those representational configurations, their processes of representation, and their placements and institutional interconnections in multiple spheres of power and influence are the appropriate material for comparison. Each point in the configuration also defines a location in and perspective on the processes and institutional interconnections.

Within this enterprise, work on gender and language is particularly significant. Ways of speaking associated with gender in various cultures—from details of pronunciation to gender-linked styles, topics, contexts, and vocabulary—are important avenues for considering many important issues: how relations of authority are constituted and legitimated, how different expectations and modes of social interaction are re-created, and how gender becomes one "natural" dimension of personal identity articulated with others (Labov 1973; Brenneis and Myers 1984; Silverstein 1985; Sherzer 1987b; Tannen 1990; Gal 1991). Even studies of gender and language that do not trace these interconnections explicitly can provide careful descriptive material with which to examine them.

Considerations of gender and language are never about gender alone, but about how representations of gender, relations of authority, and processes of cultural politics are linked. Gender-inflected vocabularies are used to signify other relations of power, creating interconnected systems of inequality rather than parallel ones (Riley 1988; Scott 1988:42). The vocabulary of gender is one tip of this iceberg. As I consider Okiek initiation in this book I discuss gender-related distinctions of language use and participation and the ways they are implicated in Okiek notions of gender and relations of authority. Initiation ceremonies simultaneously inculcate and perpetuate those notions and relations. They also provide a forum in which they are exposed and questioned.

Parallels among systems of inequality have been highlighted in recent years at the same time that notions of identity fundamental in those systems have come into question. Gender, class, race, and ethnicity become linked with other minority positions through a "politics of difference" (West 1990:94), though issues may be shared only superficially at times. This politics of difference denies exclusive and essentialist definitions of identity, deconstructing them as part of a critique of dualistic categories, which are taken to be hegemonic Western constructs. Hegemonic devices they may well be, but essentialist categories are not confined to Euro-American thinking (Bayly 1990:1314). Holquist argues convincingly that dualistic thinking and stereotypes are part of the nature of linguistic processes, though their specifics vary widely. "The universality of stereotypes is imposed by language; their particularity derives from history" (Holquist 1988:468). He finds parallels "between Bakhtin's attempts to theorize his way out of . . . binarism, teleology, and closure and the attempts . . . to rethink the categories of alterity" (Holquist 1988:454).

Alternative, relational ways to think of identity that have been developed along with the politics of difference stress the co-presence of intersecting facets of identity and the articulation of forms of difference (Bhabha 1986:150; Mouffe 1988; Prakash 1990:399). Identity is conceived "as a nexus of relations and transactions actively engaging a subject," with "exchange rather than [separate] identity" as fundamental (Clifford 1988:344). This complicates but does not eliminate the need to look critically for systematic conjunctions and interconnections among modes of economic organization, relations of power and authority, and cultural representations. Nor is critique of essence a critique of history. In fact, historical specificity is important for any antidote to essentialism.

Before returning to specific articulations of Okiek identities, there are two realms in which to take up issues of systematic interconnections and intersecting differences: ethnicity and personhood. When the term "tribe" became an issue in the 1960s, its offensive assumptions were criticized. "Ethnic group," a notion previously used for urban native groups and associations or European minorities became the safe substitute. In addition to the assumed sense of continuity, history, and emotional identification that "tribe" carried, the notion of ethnicity came to convey a mutable, negotiable, and situationally variable understanding of identity as well (Leach 1954; Barthes 1969; Southall 1970; Mafeje 1971).[23]

Despite changes in understanding the workings of ethnicity, however, the substitution of "ethnic group" for "tribe" rarely involved rethinking either notion. Ethnicity has become another subject for critiques of essentialist notions of bounded, unitary, and ahistorical entities, notions that have been downplayed and denigrated but nonetheless carried over from "tribe" (Kratz 1981a; Galaty 1982:1; O'Brien 1986:899; Bentley 1987; Wilmsen 1989; Klumpp and Kratz 1992). The best critiques combine two tactics, at once historicizing particular cases and specifying their dynamics.

The concept of ethnicity itself is historically variable, the claim to an ethnic identity figuring in social relationships in different ways at different times (if at all). In eastern Africa, for instance, there seems to have been a shift, beginning in the late nineteenth century, from loosely defined social amalgams to more exclusively defined ethnic categories, a shift encouraged and at times partially created by missionary and colonial expectations, interactions, and administrative organizations (Lonsdale 1977; Ranger 1979; Ambler 1988; Ojwang and Ocholla-Ayayo 1989:181; Bravman 1990; Spear and Waller 1992). Further research is needed to trace connections among the formation of ethnicities, precolonial regional politics, the caravan trade, and early colonial contacts within the broader political economy of the area; an excellent example is Wilmsen's (1989) incisive account of the Kalahari region in southern Africa.[24]

Wilmsen outlines the dynamics of labor, trade, and the creation of ethnicity in the Kalahari region over several centuries. His is perhaps the most broadranging and significant study of these processes yet to appear. His work shows the historical development of different kinds of sociopolitical interactions and relations (each of which might have been glossed in something like ethnic terms, but with very different senses of "ethnic") and the convergence of those processes with colonial interests and administration to solidify the contemporary ethnicities of people of the Kalahari region. Maasai regional dominance in eastern Africa in the late nineteenth century differed substantially from the Tswana polities he describes, and labor dynamics in the Maasai area did not involve the two-tiered system of extraction later associated with migrant mine workers. There are some similarities in the way Kipsigis were encouraged to become tea workers and to take up cash cropping, but how these different ethnic policies worked their way into regional interactions has yet to be studied.

Historical and regional studies of ethnicity explode images of the isolated ethnic group as a font of primordial identity and continuity. They show the changing senses and social settings of ethnicity as a concept, the interconnections between ethnic categories and larger economic and political systems, and that ethnic categories are the product of long patterns of social relations (O'Brien 1986). Studies focused on specific negotiations of ethnicity in interaction blast the images from another direction, deconstructing ethnicity into the various signs and social networks relevant at a given time. Work on ethnicity as process and practice looks at what it means to claim an ethnic identity, how such claims are made and mediated in social interaction, and how interconnections of ethnicity and political and economic hierarchy play out in individuals' lives.

Galaty's work on Maasai ethnic categories, evaluations, and hierarchy explicates one such regional system, taking the perspective of those at the top (Galaty 1979, 1982, 1992). Elsewhere he considers shifts in Maasai identity, politics, and economy related to the national Kenyan context, shifts tied to landholding, education, and development (Galaty 1980, 1981). He has yet to bring these two strands of work together, to discuss corresponding shifts in the regional system of ethnicity within national and international contexts, but he does provide some elements with which it is possible to do so.

The Okiek perspective on this same ethnic system gives the view from the bottom of the hierarchy, suggests ways in which common signs of ethnicity are differently used and valued, and may also give a different sense of these larger shifts. Okiek both are incorporated into and, by their manner of incorporation, contest Maasai cultural hegemony. Both Maasai and Okiek use ethnic labels in ways that seem to refer to "nonproblematical, unitary, and given social entit[ies]" as "natural categor[ies] . . . as concrete as geographical features, as biologically distinct as cattle, and as unique in practice as species of wild animals" (Galaty 1982:1, 3). The categories of people included and excluded by the labels, however, can shift in different circumstances; essentialist ethnic categories are used in ways that emphasize different essential facets at different times. For instance, ethnic categories are used to identify styles of beadwork, ceremonial performance, song, and various other activities and products. My own use of ethnic categories as adjectives in this book follows this practice, so I may write of Maasai color sequences in beadwork, Kipsigis initiation songs, Okiek baskets, and so forth.

Okiek take this a step further, deconstructing, as it were, signs of Maasai ethnic identity and reshaping, recombining, and reinterpreting them as their own, though the descriptive ethnic term may remain. Elsewhere I have discussed the ways they do this with a number of critical indicators of Maasainess, including language and personal ornament (Kratz 1981a, 1986, 1988b; Klumpp and Kratz 1992). Okiek initiation ceremonies also exemplify these processes: they include blessings in the Maa language, costumes and songs incorporated from Kipsigis, and modes of entertainment and decoration that are part of a general contemporary rural Kenyan style. In addition to slight changes that Okiek introduce to such signs of ethnicity, the very mixture, uses, and combinations are part of what make them "Okiek" to people. Ethnicity is marked by style and combination as much as by unique signs. But the regional system of ethnicity is not just a matter of style; it is also a matter of hierarchy, power, influence, and inequality. In the next chapter I discuss shifts in the regional rhetoric of ethnicity and in Okiek social orientations and ethnic coidentification over the past twenty years that are best understood in that light (see also Kratz 1990b).

Ethnicity and gender are entwined in Okiek experience and understandings of personhood, and are two important aspects among the intersecting differences of Okiek identities. They are also interconnected systems of inequality. A number of ideas and stereotypes about men and women are shared by Okiek, Maasai, Kipsigis, and other Kenyans. Okiek women, then, have a gender liability as well as an ethnic handicap to contend with in public contexts (Kratz 1990b). Gender ideology includes stereotypes of men and women, but their ambiguities differ from those of ethnic stereotypes. Ethnicity is considered a matter of history, heritage, upbringing, and style, something that can be assimilated and perhaps shared in part, with signs that can be appropriated and combined. Gender representations evoke immutable, "natural" differences between men and women. Gender stereotypes emphasize appropriate modes of relationship across a primordial division, while those of ethnicity play up continuity and tradition as the basis of social divisions and relations.

Ethnicity and gender are linked systems of inequality in which Okiek participate; both ethnic and gender differences involve an interplay of equality and hierarchy, of complementarity and control. Yet that interplay unfolds differently in the two domains, and embodies ambivalences and contradictions with different implications and locations in each. The gender interplay defines each encounter and event involving both women and men, and even close, daily domestic relations. It is a constant construction of difference, inequality, and authority that is countered by experiences that belie the distinctions on which it is based. Initiation is one such experience. The ceremonial creation of adult men and women demonstrates the strength and bravery of both but simultaneously insists that women are weak-willed and childlike. Okiek ethnicity is a backdrop for initiation, but gender roles are foregrounded, along with their ambivalences. Contradictions of gender cannot admit double meanings and double identities, as ethnic identities do; there is no realm of nongendered life to which to retreat like the seemingly nonethnic realm of Okiek life apart from their neighbors. There the stereotypes of ethnicity can be presented as perspectives, as alternative truths; the ambivalence and ambiguity of ethnic inequality can be playfully distanced and disarmed, temporarily bracketed. This is not possible with gender.

Chapter 3 continues this discussion by looking in more detail at the dynamics and history of Okiek relations with their neighbors and discussing the contemporary Okiek situation in Narok District. It also discusses Okiek gender roles, tracing the interplay and contradictions of complementarity and control in Okiek gender relations and the gendered contexts and experiences of daily life that are represented and re-created through initiation. That chapter begins part 2, which provides background for the focused analyses of Okiek initiation that follow in part 3.

Part 2

Ethnographic and
Historical Background

Poor Forest Demons/ Gracious Hunters of Game and Honey

We were told by the elders that when God came to prepare the world he found three things in the land, a Dorobo, an elephant, and a serpent, all of whom lived together.

> Maasai myth told by Justin Ol-omeni, quoted in A. C. Hollis, *The Masai: Their Language and Folklore*

"Dorobo, are you the one who cut God's thong? May you remain as poor as you have always been. You and your offspring will for ever remain my servants. Let it be that you will live off animals in the wild. May the milk of my cattle be poison if ever you taste it." This is why up to this day the Dorobo still live in the forest and they are never given milk.

> Same myth, quoted by Naomi Kipury, *Oral Literature of the Maasai*

Our origin is Dorobo. We used to live on wild game and honey. Then the hunting of animals was forbidden by the Government and we were told that we could not put our honey barrels in the forest, and were told to go out of the forest . . . because we were Masai . . . a proof that we are not Masai is that the Masai will not marry with us or let us drink their milk or mix with us in any way. . . . We take an oath we are not Masai.

> Evidence of Leratia Ole Turumet, given to the Kenya Land Commission in 1932

This chapter sketches the recent histories of Kaplelach and Kipchornwonek Okiek and their social and economic adaptations.[1] Like other Okiek groups, they interact regularly with pastoral or agropastoral neighbors, in this case

57

chiefly Maasai and Kipsigis. They are a minority group in the area, long regarded by their neighbors as low-status, poor, and not quite civilized.

Okiek life is part of a network of interethnic relations that are actively incorporated into Okiek economy, culture, history, and identity, as well as into those of their neighbors. A regional perspective is essential to understand the historical trajectory and contemporary lives of any of these peoples.[2] For Okiek, that includes not only neighboring ethnic groups but relations among different Okiek groups as well.

Most Kipchornwonek and Kaplelach presently live in family settlements in the Mau Escarpment's midaltitude forest, a residential pattern that has developed in conjunction with shifts in economic pursuits and land tenure. They till gardens of maize and millet, have a few head of cattle and some goats and sheep, and continue to various extents to hunt forest game and climb their hives to collect honey. During the 1980s, a small number of Okiek, mainly Kipchornwonek, opened shops at the growing center of Sogoo or bought *matatu* trucks (public transport vehicles) to serve the new Narok-Sogoo-Mulot route. That decade also saw community primary schools mushroom in the immediate area (going from zero to three with a fourth in the works) with a corresponding surge in school attendance. Contemporary Okiek life is in some ways typical of rural Kenya, but complex differences of local history and understanding pervade the situations in different parts of the country. Okiek initiation ceremonies cannot be considered without the background of these understandings.

This description is complicated by the need to include several versions of Okiek life. A double image pervades Okiek discourse about themselves—a Then and a Now represented in different lights at different times. The time called Then is when Okiek were living a forest life, following honey seasons, without regular gardens or livestock at home—a memory from childhood for most Kaplelach and Kipchornwonek over forty or forty-five. In contrast, Now is basically the time since Okiek began settling, gardening regularly, and keeping domestic animals.

The period considered to be Now is lengthy and encompasses considerable changes in the extent to which Okiek continue to hunt, have come to cultivate, go to school, and participate in the money economy, as well as significant changes in land tenure and use. The two periods when I was a daily part of Okiek life both fall within that time. My later research began when far-reaching changes in land tenure were starting to take effect; Okiek life at the beginning and end of that period were quite different. The first part of that research is my own narrative Now, my descriptive baseline. My earlier research is a different baseline for comparison when I talk about economic differentiation, incorporation into national development, and changes in ceremonial style and performance.[3]

What is called Then also covers a long time and undoubtedly includes significant changes. In fact, Then takes account only of recent history, from just before 1900. The economic and social processes Okiek portray as critical breaks with tradition are probably more common within a longer historical perspective. Represented as unchanging and continuous, what is considered tradition varies in different historical periods and between generations.

Nonetheless, Then is represented as the start in contemporary narration of local history. Fights and famines punctuate it, as do a few important colonial events,[4] but Okiek represent the period of game and honey as largely undifferentiated in daily practice. They knew things were happening elsewhere and visited new and growing trade centers, and some Okiek men spent several years working in security services in late colonial times, but Okiek talk of themselves as staying in the forest, doing what they had always done.

There is a certain truth to this version of history, for Kaplelach and Kipchornwonek came under little direct administration and for many years experienced colonial changes at some remove. This monolithic image of tradition and continuity, however, comes into play in other ways. Okiek have two versions of their forest life, a negative one that justifies subsequent economic diversification, and another that emphasizes the bounty of meat and honey enjoyed deep in the forest. I began to think of the latter as Golden Age narratives, "when we ate nothing but honey and meat, the flowerings were good, and no one was sick." Okiek commonly tell visitors these mythlike narratives, often spontaneously.

No mere nostalgic reminiscence, these narratives zero in on what their tellers see as especially Okiek, essential aspects that help define their particular identity. While these aspects are no longer as prevalent in daily life as they once were, Okiek history and tradition as forest-dwelling honey gatherers and hunters is still central in their sense of who they are. Some aspects of the daily practice, as well as the nostalgic image of forest life, are incorporated into Okiek ceremonies—in materials used, ritual locations, prayers, and songs—thereby recreating its role in constituting Okiek cultural identity. Historical representation of forest life as a continuing, virtually unchanging tradition that existed at the start of times remembered must be seen in conjunction with this.

If, when I was faced with an idyllic image, I asked Okiek why they began to diversify their economy, another side came out, also overdramatized—food uncertainties, hunger and cold in the rainy season, and the troubles of moving. However they represent the shift, Okiek do not mention people who disagreed with or resented the changes. Still, different evaluations of the changes can be discerned in stories Kaplelach and Kipchornwonek tell about each other. Few people envisaged the implications such apparently simple changes would have, since they unfolded gradually as diversification continued.

This universalizing of distinctions in and disagreements about economic diversification is part of a general characteristic of Okiek representation of the past. Dualistic representation as Then and Now masks historical process. It flattens changes that took place over time, often incrementally and differentially. Age-sets are an alternative, crosscutting Okiek periodization that helps counter this. Exploring the personal experiences of people of different age-sets can help restore processual distinctions otherwise camouflaged. While the Okiek dual periodization of Then and Now organizes the following description, I also discuss historical processes and differentiation within it. Table 1 lists Okiek age-sets with calendar equivalents as a guide to the discussion that follows.

Okiek and Torrobo

Discussions about Okiek are often muddled by misunderstandings of the term "Torrobo" (also encountered as Dorobo, Wandorobo, and Nderobo). *Il Torrobo* is what Maasai call Okiek, other hunters, and poor Maasai who have no cattle; the adoption of the term into other fields of discourse led to unfortunate confusions. The main problem has been the combination of two distinct clusters of hunting groups under the name Torrobo.[5]

The first includes Kalenjin-speaking Okiek throughout the central and western Kenyan highlands; the second consists of hunters in northern Kenya, who speak only Maa and call themselves Torrobo. To add to the difficulty, linguistically and historically distinct hunting groups have also been thrown into the Torrobo category; even Yaaku and El Molo have been listed as Torrobo or Okiek. There are some striking similarities in Okiek and Torrobo ecological adaptations and intergroup patterns of interaction, but there is no clear genealogical relation between them.[6] Within each diverse cluster, however, there are historical and genealogical relations, as well as linguistic, economic, and cultural commonalities.

Confusions resulting from the term "Torrobo" and its variations, which are also used in the Kenya national census, and from the dispersed locations of Okiek groups make an estimate of the total Okiek population difficult. If other Okiek groups are roughly the size of Kaplelach and Kipchornwonek, about five to six hundred each, then there might be roughly fourteen or fifteen thousand Okiek in Kenya, though that figure could be far too high or too low.

Kaplelach and Kipchorwonek are the southernmost of some ten Okiek groups on the western Mau Escarpment (figure 3). About eight other groups live on the eastern escarpment, and at least four more in forests north of Nakuru (figure 4).[7] Many on the eastern Mau now speak Maa as their home language instead of Kalenjin. Formerly, Kalenjin-speaking hunters also lived in highland forests around Mount Kenya and the Aberdares, but they were pushed back and eventually absorbed by Kikuyu in the nineteenth century through "land sales," intermarriage, and adoption (Kenya Land Commission 1933, 1934; Muriuki 1975). Akie in Tanzania around the Maasai Steppe are

Table 1: Okiek Age-Sets

Joint Age-Set Name	Dates of Young Manhood (*murenik*)	Right/Left Subsets	Circumcision Dates
il peles	1866–1886	*i sampinonito*	started 1866
		il mangusha	started 1874
il talala	1881–1905	*il terito*	started 1881
		il chungen	started 1889
il tuati	1896–1917	*il merisho*	1896–1897
		i lemek	1898–1906
il tareto	1911–1929	*il meiruturut/il tareto*[1]	
		il kitoip	1911–1918
il terito	1926–1948	*il tiyeki*	1925–1927
		il kirmere[2]	
		il ny'echere	1930–1932
il ny'angusi	1942–1959	*il kalikal*	1939–1941
		il kamaniki	1946–1948
eseuri	1955–1974	*il terekeyani*	1954–1957
		il tiyogoni	1959–1961
i rambau	1967–1984?	*i rambau*	1967–1975
		i rantai	1970–1975
	1983–	*il kipalit*	1976–1981
		il kirupi	1985–

Dates based on Bernsten (1979:89–93). Closing date of the joint age-set of *i rambau* and dates for *il kipalit* and *il kirupi* are tentative. Subset information for *il peles* and *il talala* courtesy of R. Waller.

1. These two names refer to the same subset. Circumcision dates cannot be stated with precision.

2. This age-set had three subsets. It is not clear what the circumcision dates are for the second subset (*il kirmere*).

the southernmost groups who can be included with Okiek on linguistic grounds (Distefano 1985; Ehret 1971).

Two other Okiek groups live today on savannah plains and speak Maa. The first, Digiri, live in several places, but nonetheless maintain contact with one another. Some now north of Nanyuki near Doldol were once among the Kalenjin-speaking hunters near Mount Kenya (Herren 1987).[8] Others migrated from the Laikipia plateau with Purko during the Maasai moves and now stay on the Loita Plains (Blackburn 1976; Herren 1987). Kaplelach and Kipchornwonek consistently name Digiri of Loita as Okiek; Blackburn also records Digiri on the eastern Mau.

The other group is Omotik. Formerly living west of Kipchornwonek,[9] Omotik now live among Maasai in four related, intermarrying groups: near

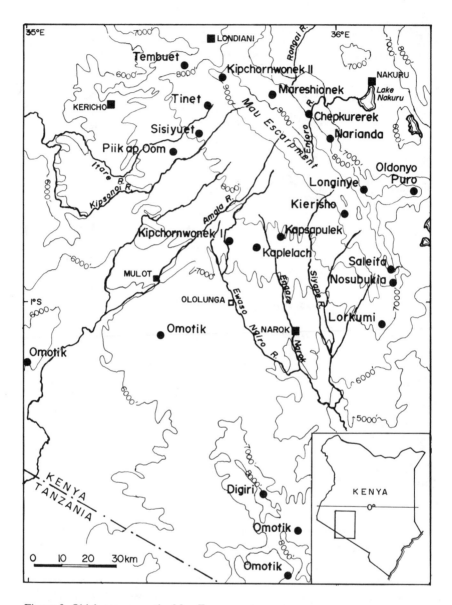

Figure 3. Okiek groups on the Mau Escarpment

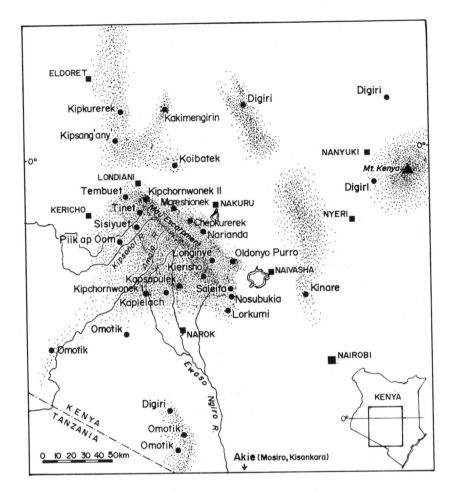

Figure 4. Okiek groups in Kenya

Lemek, northeast of Lolgorien, near Morijo, and near Entasekera (Heine 1973; Franz Rottland, personal communication). Other Okiek identify them as Okiek, and note that they used to speak a language somewhat like theirs.[10] Today the Omotik language is remembered only by very old people; Maa has become their daily language.

Known by particular names (Kaplelach, Maresionik, and others), Okiek local groups are socially constituted and territorially defined. Each consists of a core of exogamous patrilineages with adjacent forest territories who live together in settlements and often work together. Okiek recognize speech distinctions among local groups; Kaplelach and Kipchornwonek, for instance, differ lexically, morphologically, in intonation, and in loan word patterns.[11]

Most daily interaction takes place within a local group, but people also visit nearby groups regularly. Overlapping networks of interaction involving inter-marriage, visiting, temporary residence, and trade linked different Okiek local groups together, though each group had different networks of interaction with neighbors of various ethnic groups.[12] Western Mau Okiek were all in contact with one another, from Kaplelach and Kipchornwonek in the south to Mare-sionik in the north. Some Okiek groups in the north and west of this region, it seems, had Okiek to the north as their main contacts. Those of the southern part included southeastern Mau groups, such as Saleyta, in their visiting rounds as well.

Variations of social organization, costume, and language repertoire among Okiek groups stem in part from different histories and interactions with other neighbors.[13] However, there are also similarities—economic, linguistic, cul-tural, ecological, and social—that have been maintained through interaction among Okiek groups. Overlapping interaction networks created several col-lections of groups having stronger links and similarities with one another than with other Okiek farther away.[14] In the next section, I look at Kaplelach and Kipchornwonek interrelations with their neighbors before discussing their forest lives Then and Now.

Neighborly Relations, Stereotypes, and Cultural Identity

While Kaplelach and Kipchornwonek have been neighbors for as long as they can remember, their other neighbors have changed over the years; Kaplelach and Kipchornwonek interactions with these neighbors have differed slightly but significantly (Kratz 1986).

In the late nineteenth century, Maa-speakers were the dominant presence in the central Rift Valley. Others in the vicinity, who eventually formed present-day Kikuyu, Okiek, and other ethnic groups, interacted with them in various ways. Maasai of the il Damat section neighbored both Kipchornwonek and Kaplelach then. As a Maasai ethnic identity was formed in the course of political conflicts, population movements, and interactions with neighbors, forest-dwelling hunters and honey-gatherers became incorporated into the emerging Maasai ethnic system as Torrobo (see this chapter's epigraphs).

The inclusion of both hunters and poor Maasai without cattle in the Torrobo category indicates the standing of these groups in the regional system. From a Maasai viewpoint, they shared not only poverty but a peripheral position and were potentially exploitable in various ways. Poor Maasai Tor-robo could become clients and a source of pastoral labor for wealthy house-holds, while hunters could provide ritual services, honey, and other forest products. Unlike poor Maasai, however, some hunters called Torrobo entered such exchanges only on occasion and had another historical heritage, which was (or eventually became) summarized in their own ethnic identity as Okiek. Their understanding of themselves within that heritage recognized criteria of wealth and worth other than those held by cattle keepers and did not place them at the bottom of the ladder. What is unclear is how the sense of Okiek ethnic identity changed in conjunction with that of Maasai and Torrobo and was part of a formative stage of ethnicity arising out of a homogeneous treatment of diverse peoples (Wilmsen and Vossen 1990:12).[15]

Encounters between Okiek and il Damat Maasai were most common in low, open forest where Okiek spent four or more months a year for honey seasons and il Damat grazed cattle in dry seasons. Okiek and Maasai used different resources in the area—forest and fields—with no inherent conflict of interests. Kaplelach apparently had more contact with il Damat than did Kipchornwonek; il Damat did not regularly graze in fields near them.

Though individual Okiek may have lived for weeks, months, or years with little direct interaction with Maasai neighbors, they *were* part of the regional economy. What may have seemed a relatively peripheral involvement helped to develop and sustain an autonomous self-image while providing the personal contacts that allowed Okiek to participate at the bottom of the hierarchy on what could seem to them like their terms. Given the situation of Maasai influence and dominance, it was important and virtually inevitable to be linked into that regional economy in some way, "at the bottom of the heap, but in it" (Wilmsen and Vossen 1990:18).

Maasai regional preeminence and prestige have continued into this century; colonial agreements with Maasai leaders were at least as critical as those made with other local leaders. The British colonial government orchestrated Maasai moves in 1904 and in the period from 1911 to 1913, bringing Purko Maasai south to where il Damat had been. Okiek then interacted with Purko in more or less the same way as they had with il Damat.

Personal contacts were the basis of trade, gift exchanges, and invitations to ceremonies. Both Kipchornwonek and Kaplelach formed friendships and trading relations with Purko. Okiek invariably describe these relations as friendships; Maasai might consider them client relations. Considering both groups' respective reliance on goods exchanged, however, it is not at all clear that Okiek would be the clients.[16] Several Kaplelach and Kipchornwonek men of the *il tareto* and *il tuati* age-sets traveled widely to circumcise Maasai, a service that was appropriate, according to Maasai, because of the association between Okiek and "unclean" blood-spilling in the hunt.

Some encounters with Purko Maasai were less than friendly. Young Maasai men (*Il murran,* usually translated as "warriors") sometimes intimidated and threatened Okiek, arrogantly ordered them to prepare hide sword sheaths, or appropriated their honey. The attitude might have been a matter of convention at times, as Ole Kulet's description of Maasai boys going to get their "Torrobo" circumcisor suggests:

He was to be found in the black forest where his people dwelt. . . . They were to pretend to be annoyed and provoked and should tell him that if he did not accompany them they would kill him. (Ole Kulet 1972:90)

The boys' encounter with the circumcisor, Ole Sulunye, is an excellent stereotype of Maasai arrogance, emphasizing Okiek terror and abject submission to young boys as only a Maasai author could.[17] They find him collecting honey:

The man nearly fainted. He opened his eyes wide and they rolled from side to side. A brown stream of sweat rolled from his forehead down to his chin. . . . The boys stood over him with their spears pointing at him. Then he began to cry like one stabbed. He groaned. The groan slowly gave way to pleas for mercy.
"Please—please—I beseech you. Spare me."
"You are going to die," Mbulung told him firmly.
"Please—oi—please, don't kill me. I will give you whatever you want." . . .
"Let him give us honey then," Mbulung said roughly.
[Then on reaching the Okiot's home:]
Ole Sulunye spoke to the women in a language the boys could not understand. . . . They were filled with fear. Each went to her hut and came out holding a bag full of honey which they handed to the boys. Leshao did not want to take the honey. To him it was a kind of robbery which he resented, but to Mbulung it was the beginning of a show of his bravery and strength. The yielding of Ole Sulunye and the fear shown by the women on seeing them made him happy. (Ole Kulet 1972:93–94, 96)

A small number of Uas Nkishu, another Maasai section, began to move into the Kaplelach and Kipchornwonek area later, in the 1940s (*il ny' angusi* age-set), from around Nakuru and Baringo.[18] They settled year round in the savannah-forest boundary at Melilo, Oleshepani, and Oldomuyu, rather than coming for seasonal grazing. Okiek relations with Uas Nkishu are not as good as those with Purko. Many Uas Nkishu know Kalenjin, but they nevertheless speak Maa with Okiek.

Purko stopped grazing regularly in low Okiek areas in the early 1960s (*il tiyogo* age-set); the arrival of Uas Nkishu and increasing wheat cultivation were both factors in the shift. At roughly the same time that the Purko presence there began waning, Kipsigis were gradually moving closer to Kipchornwonek from the west.

Maasai sections share stereotypes about the people they call Torrobo. Maasai consider Torrobo not only poor, since cattleless, but despicable.[19] Torrobo are considered selfish, cowardly, incestuous, unrestrained in meat consumption, and unclean from the bloodshed of hunting, and are seen as living in an environment unfit for human dwelling (that is, for Maasai with cattle). Maasai cultural categories present

an ideal Maasai image in contraposition to images of the Torrobo, along fundamental scales of value and honor. This ideology is oriented to those dimensions of most significance to the Maasai, not to the Torrobo, and evaluations of the Torrobo are based on general stereotypic impressions of what they are, what they do, and what they are like. (Galaty 1977a:181)

Such stereotypes support the Maasai sense of superiority to Torrobo (including Okiek) and justify domineering treatment, though Maasai are not always rude or aggressive with Okiek. There are indeed strong interethnic friendships. Maasai assume Okiek would accept such treatment, though, further confirming their stereotypes. Domination often emerges in more subtle ways, such as in the use of the Maa language in all interactions. Maasai are also dominant in contemporary regional politics and decisions about the use of development resources. Maasai regional power is now part of a larger sociopolitical configuration, different from that at the turn of the century. Okiek have also retained and shifted their position within regional and national dynamics.

Okiek themselves redefine this implicit Maasai domination and devaluation of their language and life, reinterpreting it positively as gracious accommodation on their part and a special ability to learn the languages and ways of others. Yet there is also ambivalence about Maasai. In one breath Okiek speak of great Maasai friends and in the next call Maasai *puunik* (enemies). In recent years, Okiek have begun to stress their kinship with Kipsigis as much as their long history of interaction with Maasai (Kratz 1986, 1990b). As I discuss below, this is both an artifact of shifting regional patterns and a response to larger political forces.

Kipsigis ideas about Okiek have some things in common with Maasai stereotypes, but Okiek relations with Kipsigis have not been as oppressive or ambivalent. Many Kipsigis keep a few hives and occasionally hunt, so Okiek practice cannot be represented as so radically different. Still, Kipsigis also stress the differences between themselves and Okiek. They consider Okiek poor because they don't farm and accumulate livestock, and assume this shows shiftlessness. Kipsigis are also fearful and suspicious of Okiek, thinking they can kill strangers in the forest (Michael Donovan personal communication) or bewitch cows out of jealousy. Kipsigis portray Okiek as shy, but, like Maasai, also see them as wily, selfish, and inhospitable tricksters. Widespread Kipsigis accounts describe Okiek ruses to avoid sharing meat or other food (Kratz 1988c:63).

What Kipsigis perceive as selfishness, rudeness, and a lack of restraint lead them to see Okiek as antisocial. This arises in part from different conventions—of drunkenness, for using sexual expletives in anger, and of ceremonial organization. Kipsigis think Okiek are slightly wild and backward and lack basic social propriety.

While Kipsigis portray themselves as more civilized than Okiek, they also recognize and sometimes stress their connections through language and history. Their interactions have generally also been more evenhanded in trade and intermarriage. Kipsigis might well stress affinities in my research area today, as they rely on Okiek for land and initial aid as newcomers. Kipsigis come as temporary dependents and clients, but they see their arrival as an opportunity for Okiek to learn "modern" ways. Yet a comparative lack of savvy on the part of Okiek enables Kipsigis and others to buy their land cheaply. With their domination, more subtle than that of Maasai, Kipsigis portray their partially exploitative settlement as something that helps Okiek. Once again, Okiek accommodate Kipsigis linguistically.

How did this increase in Kipsigis neighbors develop? During the late nineteenth century, the nearest Kipsigis lived west of the Amala River. Kipsigis traded with Okiek, most frequently with Kipchornwonek, who lived nearer to them. When Purko Maasai replaced il Damat Maasai, Kipsigis were still in the same area. In 1910, about the same time as the Maasai moves, the colonial government declared the Amala River as the eastern boundary of the Kipsigis Reserve. Their allotted area soon proved insufficient.

Kipsigis continued grazing livestock south of the reserve, as in the past, and began to expand gradually eastward into Okiek land. There Kipsigis settled permanently and cleared forest for cultivation, which proved more devastating to Okiek forest subsistence than had Maasai complementary resource use. By the time Kipsigis reached Okiek areas, Okiek had already begun the economic diversification described below and were staying in midaltitude base camps for longer periods. Kipsigis and westernmost Kipchornwonek, then, became regular neighbors with more frequent and diverse interactions than before.

Kipsigis and Okiek date this crossing of the Amala at various times between the age-sets of il tareto (1910–1930) and il terekeyani (1950s), possibly referring to different times in the process. By 1975, Kipsigis were well established east of the Amala to Olmotiook; Kipchornwonek Okiek remained as pockets in their midst. By 1982, they had reached Nentolo (some five miles farther east) and were beginning to settle at Nkaroni (see figures 2 and 5). By 1985, Kipsigis had land agreements with many Kaplelach and some were arriving to live. By 1990, there were at least as many Kipsigis as Okiek in the western Kaplelach area. With the new possibility of land sales in this area (see below) and land scarcity elsewhere in Kenya, immigrant Kipsigis are no longer old neighbors encroaching gradually, but often leapfrog in from more distant places. News spreads; a few Kisii have also come to obtain land through purchase, loan, or, more rarely, marriage.

The history of interethnic relations between Kaplelach and Kipchornwonek and their neighbors shows the creation of the current regional network of social and economic interaction. At present, Kipsigis have become close neighbors for Kaplelach as well as for Kipchornwonek, living in their midst and quickly outnumbering them. Uas Nkishu Maasai remain where they

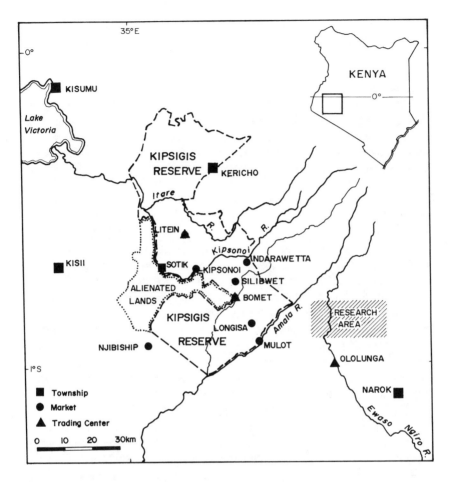

Figure 5. Markets and towns mentioned and former Kipsigis Reserve

settled, and are now legally joint owners of group-ranch land with Okiek. Purko remain the Maasai majority in Narok District, holding most of the influential political positions. Okiek encounter Purko in this capacity, informally in towns, and in reciprocal visits that help maintain already-established relations between families. (I discuss Okiek encounters with government administration and development in the next section.)

Perhaps as important for the present purpose, that history of interethnic relationships also reveals how stereotypes have become part of Okiek identity. Both Maasai and Kipsigis images of Okiek are ambivalent—devaluing their way of life, yet revealing discomfort with and fear of their apparently unrestrained behavior and their habitat. Okiek often reinterpret these relationships and stereotypes to their own advantage, emphasizing positive qualities such as adaptability. While the same ambivalence is present in Okiek cultural identity, only they have the perspective (from within forest life) to cast it favorably. This cultural strategy may help explain a relative lack of power, but does not negate it.

Two things are central to these derogatory images of Okiek: their forest domicile and their reliance on game and honey. The combined implications create and justify the low status attributed to Okiek by their neighbors. Yet these same things are central to Okiek identity and history, in which they are experienced and evaluated quite differently.

From Then to Now: The Lives of the Forest

This section discusses Okiek forest life more particularly, as people say it was in the past and as it is lived today. Between Then and Now, a split began to develop between Okiek daily practice and the traditional patterns of subsistence that are represented as central to Okiek identity. For Kipchornwonek, the split is wider and older than for Kaplelach. Okiek economic diversification began simply, but "seemingly small changes . . . can have vast reverberations in the lives of people" (R. Rosaldo 1980:28). Yet today's radically transformed Okiek life is still organized and lived through the same basic social structure, though now in different circumstances and with important differences and additions.

Temporal categories and representation are especially problematic in describing Then. First, as mentioned, the historical processes that created the structure and texture of Okiek life up to about 1940 are cloaked in an image of uniform continuity. A second problem mirrors that processual contraction: the risk of projecting back onto Then a homogeneous model of circumstances and processes that in reality have continued, shifted, and changed differentially up to now.

In describing forest life, for example, Okiek categorizations of forest zones and honey seasons are relevant both Now and Then. Yet Okiek patterns of settlement and honey gathering have shifted gradually, and land tenure has changed in complicated ways. The forest was divided into lineage-held tracts of land when economic diversification began; national legislation in the late 1960s changed the legal tenure system and set the stage for a change. Though another landholding system now prevails, lineage divisions are still critical for hive placement, use of unsettled high forest, and land claims in lower and middle forests. With these caveats in mind, I sketch how Okiek forest life Then became that of Now.

The forested western Mau Escarpment where Kaplelach and Kipchornwonek live rises in altitude from about 1,800 to 2,800 meters over roughly forty miles, creating several ecological zones. Okiek recognize five kinds of forest, distinguished by their most common flora and fauna.[20] Differences in altitude, rainfall, and species create different honey seasons in each. Okiek moved accordingly a few times a year. The first three zones were most important for Kaplelach and Kipchornwonek honey. From lowest to highest they are: (1) *soyua*—open, bushy forest from about 1,800 to about 2,100 meters, with acacia trees, buffalo, and elephant; (2) *sasaontet*—forest with glades and fields from about 2,100 to about 2,400 meters; *perekeyuet* trees,[21] tree hyrax, and bushbuck; (3) *tirap*—thick forest from about 2,400 to about 2,600 meters; much distinctive flora (for example, *celumpuut, seketeetik, tikeltit*),[22] giant forest hog, and bongo; (4) *sisiyuet*—roughly the same altitude as *tirap,* increasingly thick bamboo stands; and (5) *mau*—forest becomes open moorland, about 2,600 meters.

Until recent land reforms, Okiek divided land into lineage-owned, patrilineally transmitted parcels that climbed through the forest zones; such a tract (*konoito*) was usually a ridge bounded by streams (see figure 6). Each *konoito* was subdivided into named areas (*kooreet,* pl. *kooroosyek*). Some lineages gave *kooreet* use rights for honey to particular families; others used the entire *konoito* cooperatively. Everyone could hunt throughout the forest.[23]

This tenure system gave each lineage access to each forest zone during each honey season throughout the year. Honey availability determined Okiek moves; they hunted animals that were available where the honey was. They moved to high-altitude *tirap* during the dry season in December and January to eat honey until the rains several months later. Low-altitude *soyua* had honey from May through September. From August through November, honey ripened in *sasaontet.*[24] Honey was eaten, stored for future consumption, brewed into beer, traded, and/or sold. The rains were the worst time for Okiek, with slippery trees, little honey, and uncomfortable hunting. Cold, wet conditions brought by rain ended their stay in high, dense *tirap* early in the year.

Residence groups were small extended families, for example, a father and his adult sons or a group of brothers. The patrilineal core was often joined by affines for a while, though Okiek frown on long coresidence with affines. Other families lived on neighboring ridges, often within shouting distance. Traveling across ridges, through different lineage territories, one could visit different families and relatives.

Six to ten adjacent lineages constituted a local group, which is a significant unit in distinctions of cultural identity and history, though it is accompanied by no unique rights. Lineage was (and is) more salient and important in matters of property, marriage, residence, and legal responsibilities. Land was held patrilineally and rights in it inherited by sons; sons also inherited other property, such as hives. Men of the family also decided on marriages for their children, though mothers and other women who had married into the lineage participated as well.

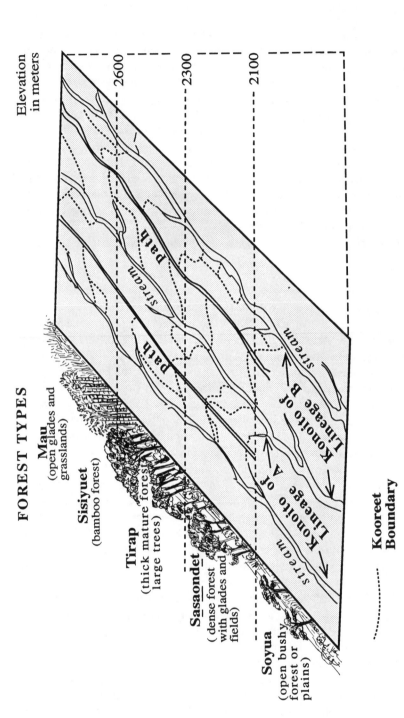

Figure 6. Okiek forest types and lineage territories

Legal cases and general problems are discussed in meetings of men who live together in an area. Attendance is drawn from a number of lineages, neighborhoods,[25] and perhaps ethnic groups. The residential group brought together in meetings is loose, unnamed, and was more fluid when people moved more often.

Age-set relations crosscut those of lineage, uniting men of different lineages into a cohort of equals enjoined to observe norms of friendship. Okiek women have no distinct, parallel age-set system; they are integrated into the male one through key male relations, first fathers and then husbands. Named age-sets group men initiated over defined periods of some fourteen to twenty years.[26] Male age-set identity was forged not only by shared initiation experiences but afterwards as *murenik* (young men), when they went visiting, hunting, raiding, and looking for girls. Age-sets also create a hierarchy of gerontocratic authority. Men of an age-set should respect and honor senior age-sets, particularly the next age-set but one and beyond, who are like their fathers and grandfathers. As they mature they will initiate younger age-sets and expect the same respect in turn.

The major social groups just outlined defined and still define the organization of social relations in Okiek life. Okiek diversified their life of honey and meat Then through a number of choices. Adding grain and milk production were perhaps most important, but these additions were part of several interconnected processes, which I trace now. The following section will discuss in more detail changes in the organization of daily work as Then became Now.

Okiek place their adoption of their neighbors' subsistence practices between the 1930s and 1950s (*il terito* and *il ny'angusi* age-sets). Kipchornwonek and Kaplelach began diversifying in parallel ways beginning ten to fifteen years apart. Why Okiek began to farm and keep animals at precisely that time is difficult to know, but a number of factors and influences were involved.

The process began gradually; Okiek cite no particular reason or decisive difficulty. Adding a small garden simply meant another food supply, fairly reliable if small and temporary. After the fact, Okiek complain that honey yields have decreased. I have found no ecological or climatic differences beginning then, but the period followed major changes in land distribution and use, including the colonial creation of native reserves and the appropriation of fertile highlands for white settlers. Continued development of settler lands and increasing pressure on the insufficient reserves led to migration and/or increased forest clearing for settlement by both whites and indigenous peoples. These changes might well have affected the Okiek forests south of the White Highlands.[27]

Kipsigis were moving closer to Okiek, taking over some western Kipchornwonek land; land appropriation and other pressures prevented their expansion in other directions. Nonetheless, they were still some distance from most Kipchornwonek and farther yet from Kaplelach. Okiek had a few livestock at that time, before they began planting gardens, but kept them elsewhere, where they interfered little with forest pursuits. Similarly, they did not alter their usual movements and activities for some time after first sowing crops.

Okiek initially regarded domestic animals mainly as another source of meat. They wouldn't drink milk and slaughtered animals received through gifts or trade. Thus, they preferred male animals for meat, not females to build a herd.[28] If any Okiot kept a few animals, they were left with Maasai friends—not always a satisfying solution, since the animals' offspring might be hidden. Nonetheless, it was not until the mid-1950s (*il teregeyani* age-set) that Kipchornwonek began keeping animals at home and building small herds. Kaplelach started later, around *i rambau* (1960s). This change was accompanied by increasing involvement in agriculture as well as changes in some aspects of forest life.

Kipchornwonek were first with gardens, too, sowing very small plots with millet from Kipsigis in the late 1930s and early 1940s. These early gardens did not curtail seasonal forest movements; Okiek planted seed and left it until harvest. It took forest animals some time, so they say, to learn about the tasty new plants. Kipchornwonek began planting maize later, in the 1950s and early 1960s, again with Kipsigis seed. The maize gardens were somewhat larger, and agriculture began taking more time and effort. A tendency toward increasingly settled life in the midaltitude *sasaontet* forest developed concurrently, though Okiek emphasize that their early gardens did not disrupt hunting and honey gathering. This tendency also coincided with decisions to keep livestock at home. Shortly after Kipchornwonek began planting maize, Kaplelach started farming, beginning with small maize gardens that they left until harvest.

Millet was ground for porridge; maize was boiled or roasted. Okiek learned only later of *akimiet* (stiff porridge; Kiswahili *ugali*), the current staple made from maize flour. Kipchornwonek at Nkaroni got their first hand-operated maize mill in the 1950s, though doubtless they had been using other mills before that. The approximate coincidence of the mill's arrival with garden expansion, however, seems significant.

Though they still moved to *tirap* for honey, by the 1940s Kipchornwonek were beginning to maintain more permanent *sasaontet* homes. Learning from Kipsigis, they built sturdier, mud-walled, thatched houses instead of ones made with leaves and bark. Kipchornwonek date increased settlement to *il ny'angusi* age-set, the same significant period in the 1950s when they began planting larger maize gardens and keeping herds.[29] Kaplelach built these houses later, in the 1960s, when they, too, began settling.

As mentioned earlier, Kipchornwonek and Kaplelach began to diversify their economic practices similarly, although ten to fifteen years apart.

Kipchornwonek cite a slight decrease in mobility as the first change in forest practice, more or less concurrent with their early millet gardens (maize for Kaplelach later). They may have gradually increased garden size and become more sedentary over the next ten to twenty years, but Okiek recognize the 1950s as a watershed for Kipchornwonek: greater settlement, larger gardens, maize, home-based herds, the first hand-operated mill, and houses suited to longer residence in one place. Okiek do not discuss these shifts causally, but the coincidence was certainly mutually reinforcing. Soon after this watershed, Kaplelach began a similar economic diversification.

I call the process diversification because Okiek continued to hunt, make beehives, and collect honey. They simply added other practices to them, though there were eventually shifts of organization. Men could still gather honey from the full forest range from more permanent homes, visiting hives on short trips; when honey was ripe in *tirap,* families still moved there for several months. Eventually entire families stopped moving to the forest. Instead, the men and older boys went for a week or more, while the women stayed home to care for things, coming later to carry honey home.

This was the case with Kipchornwonek in the mid-1970s. Ten years later, few men still went to the forest regularly and fewer still stayed there any length of time. Kaplelach, on the other hand, were still going for months at a time, moving with the family, though someone stayed home to watch things.

Incorporating new subsistence practices presented no contradiction initially to continuing a forest livelihood because of both scale and division of labor. Early cultivation was on too small a scale to interfere much with other activities, including seasonal movements. Men and women both could divert work occasionally to a tiny plot. When people began to work more on gardens and enlarge them, an aspect of Okiek forest production that contrasts with other African gatherer-hunters became especially important. Vegetable foods gathered by women played an extremely minor role in Okiek subsistence. This meant Okiek women were comparatively freer to expend additional labor on cultivation when it became more time-consuming.

Changes in settlement patterns and house type and eventual increases in the amount of purchased goods also influenced shifts in women's work. Men could and did continue their main forest work, though they helped with new kinds of work; women's work changed and included most of the cultivation after the initial clearing. Children became herders and helped in the gardens. These shifts in labor organization and Okiek household economy will be discussed in greater detail in the next section. The important point here is that initially, economic diversification involved more people in directly productive work.

This initial balance of labor has continued shifting, however, particularly for Kipchornwonek. They have been organizing their time, work, interests, and goals increasingly toward agropastoralism. Many other factors, some quite recent, have influenced the direction and extent of their reorientation, producing repercussions that increasingly will encompass both Kaplelach and Kipchornwonek.

Each of the described changes in Okiek life took shape in the setting of their relations with neighbors. Maasai and Kipsigis were both possible sources of animals for Okiek and models for livestock keeping. Kipsigis also facilitated the adoption of agriculture by serving as the initial sources of seed, mills, and, more recently, ox-drawn plows. Their mixed farming and herding was one model Okiek could observe and discuss with them as they diversified economically. These neighbors may have influenced Okiek diversification, but Okiek had long been living with them without trying other economic pursuits. The question remains: why then? Other factors and influences must have coincided with these and reinforced, perhaps indirectly, the idea that some aspects of their neighbors' lives were worth trying.

First, events and changing circumstances among their neighbors, who often felt more direct colonial administration and influence, were important. The Maasai moves opened ranching land in Laikipia and near Nakuru by confining Maasai to a southern reserve, bringing other Maasai sections to the area near Okiek where formerly only il Damat had been. The moves were completed shortly after 1913. Afterward, the administration in the Maasai area was concerned largely with cattle trade and movement, market development, and other ways to control, develop, and exploit the Maasai pastoral economy; it had little direct relevance for Okiek in the forest. The trading center at Ololunga began early in the century, during il tareto age-set, with two Somali shops and one Asian one; until about 1980 it remained the nearest place for many Kaplelach to buy blankets, clothing, sugar, salt, and other items.

In Kipsigis areas, however, administration and European settlement was another matter. Reviewing Kipsigis economy and land tenure between 1900 and 1960, Manners (1967) emphasizes the northern area as the center of significant changes, oriented toward the market and communications that were developed early around Kericho and the tea estates established nearby.

The Kipsigis near Kipchornwonek Okiek are at the far south of the area he discusses.[30] Similarly linked processes involving shifts in land use and tenure, the adoption of maize, and increasing incorporation into the money economy also occurred in southerly Kipsigis areas, though slightly later. Donovan (1987) describes similar land tenure shifts in the 1940s in the southeastern part of the reserve, near Ndaraweta, begun by immigrant Kipsigis who also brought maize with them. During that decade, Okiek and Kipsigis there began to buy maize and sell honey for cash, and roads and markets also began to reach the area.

There are three key differences between Manners's northern Kipsigis area and Donovan's southeastern part (and the area farther southeast, near the Amala River). First, communications were developed initially in the north; the network of roads, markets, and what came with them reached farther south only gradually. Second, the south had no close, regular, and growing market for the new maize like there was in the north where demand was fueled by tea plantation labor. When maize reached the south, then, it could not be a cash crop on the scale it was in the north until transport and marketing were improved.

The third difference, related to land, eventually had the most important implications for Kipchornwonek and Kaplelach. Kipsigis land was first alienated for European settlement near Kericho, beginning in 1906–7. That area became the center of tea production and the initial market of orientation for Kipsigis in the northern part of the reserve. Soon after these land grants, another area was opened to Europeans around Sotik, west of the Kipsonoi River near the southern part of the reserve, reaching to Bomet (see figure 5).

Alienating the more densely settled Sotik area entailed forcibly moving Kipsigis to the eastern side of the Kipsonoi. As settler farms developed, some people returned as squatter-laborers, bringing relatives' and friends' herds to use grazing rights granted African workers. In the 1940s, however, new controls and limits were put on squatters' herds, eventually eliminating their right to keep them.

Those dispossessed Kipsigis who tried to take their cattle back into the Reserve encountered difficulties because by now—the late forties and the fifties—pasture and even house space was in increasingly short supply. Many of them were forced to find living space outside the Reserve. Thus, this late crop of migrants has been motivated not nearly so much by the desire to escape the interminable efforts of the agricultural officers to get them to plant more maize or to cull out their herds and flocks, but by an acute and growing land hunger. (Manners 1967:286)

Kipsigis expansion east over the Amala River, which some Kipsigis and Okiek date to this time, might reasonably be related to these land pressures. Maize planting was catching on in the southeastern part of the Kipsigis Reserve about this same time, as the market system also expanded to the area.[31]

Okiek remember maize as recent (after the arrival of Europeans) and clearly identify Kipsigis as their source of seed (millet and maize) and farming techniques. They are less explicit about Kipsigis influences in Kipchornwonek decisions to settle and plant larger maize gardens in the 1950s, yet the coincidence with these developments in Kipsigis life is striking.

When the European settlers came to the country of the Kipsigis and moved to the lands on which many of the tribe had pastured their flocks and herds and had grown their few vegetables and their modest crops of finger millet, a series of changes was precipitated which came to affect not only those Kipsigis who were embraced by the leasehold, or those who were forced to leave for other parts, but the entire tribe. (Manners 1967:285)

Though the influences were more removed and mediated, Okiek living east of the Kipsigis Reserve must surely be added to those eventually touched by these colonial policies and decisions.

Similar, concurrent processes in other areas might have influenced Okiek decisions to garden, with similar mediation. Maresionik Okiek near Elburgon, west of Nakuru, lived adjoining land appropriated for the White Highlands and came into earlier, more direct contact with the colonial administration and with other Kenyans who came to European farms as squatters and laborers. Kikuyu who came from central Kenya showed Maresionik how to farm and helped with seed. Maresionik began maize gardens slightly before the early Kipchornwonek millet gardens, perhaps in the 1930s. Kipchornwonek and Kaplelach visited Maresionik and could have talked about the gardens. Visiting Okiek might have identified more closely with the Maresionik example than with other neighbors long known as farmers.

Undoubtedly, many interacting factors influenced Okiek economic diversification, some more immediately than others. Once started, however, it continued and spread, with related shifts in settlement and labor patterns. As it did, still other factors, such as ecological shifts, interactions with Kipsigis, the colonial administration's emphases, schooling, and wage labor, contributed and reinforced the processes, fundamentally transforming Kipchornwonek life.

Kaplelach began diversifying later but have yet to plant much besides maize or to enlarge their gardens substantially. Most have continued hunting and gathering honey to a greater extent. These differences relate to more concentrated development efforts among Kipchornwonek and to increasing Kipchornwonek intermixture with Kipsigis. Kipsigis present a picture of market- and cash-oriented farming as well as subsistence cultivation. They value education, aspire to houses with *mabati* (iron-sheet) roofs and certain breeds of cow,[32] and at the same time want, ask for, and present good reasons for increasing development services there.

Roads, schools, health services, and shops are planned for or beginning to be available in Kaplelach areas as well; until now, Ololunga had been the closest place for these. This infrastructure first developed in the Kipchornwonek area, however, partially reorienting Kaplelach visits. In 1979, a road was cut from Ololunga through Sogoo, west of Nkaroni, to join one between Olmotiook and Mulot. Since then, Sogoo has mushroomed and become a small weekly market.[33] Kipchornwonek with means used the road to get to a private mission hospital in Tenwek, north of Mulot. Kaplelach continued to go to the Ololunga dispensary, opened in the early 1960s. A new government health center opened at Sogoo in 1987. Both Kaplelach and Kipchornwonek now visit that center, by far the closest, despite its periodic drug shortages and the communication difficulties it presents for Okiek women with limited Kiswahili.

The provision of other services also followed. The post of assistant chief for Sogoo began about 1978 or 1979, and has been held since then by an Okiot from Nkaroni. Agricultural and veterinary officers came in 1984. The assistant chief is one of the few Okiek, most of them Kipchornwonek, to attend Ololunga school briefly in the late 1950s or early 1960s.[34] One or two, including him, finished primary school.

In the 1970s, some Okiek children were in school at Ololunga or elsewhere. Distance was a problem, but things began to change dramatically for Kipchornwonek in 1978, when a primary school opened at Sogoo. Though it was still far for small children, older children could now live at home and go to school. In the early 1980s, most families at Nkaroni had some older children in school for at least some time, joining children of Kipsigis and other immigrants.

In January 1984, Nkaroni Primary opened with Standard One, adding a class each year after that. Soon after, in 1985, Mekenyo nursery class was started in the Kaplelach area and is now a growing primary school. Attendance was sporadic among Kaplelach due to distance, school fees, and the loss of children's labor.[35]

All these developments have opened up the Kipchornwonek area east of Nentolo, integrating it more into district and national economy and culture. The adjoining Kaplelach area is quickly following. Coupled with that area's development, recent changes in land tenure have brought about radical changes in settlement patterns and a flood of immigrants.

General land demarcation was legislated in Kenya in 1969, but before that a group-ranch division policy was being developed for districts with predominantly Maasai population (Kajiado, then Narok). Kipchornwonek and Kaplelach forests were included in Narok District even though they were high- or medium-potential land rather than the semiarid savannah the group-ranch plan was devised for.[36] Division began in the mid-1970s. Most Kaplelach and Kipchornwonek became members of group-ranches, tracts combining land from several lineage territories (and superseding those territories). Neighbors who had settled in Okiek territories were also registered. Other tracts of former Okiek land were demarcated to non-Okiek individuals. The farthest reaches of Okiek forest were to become forest reserve, under county council jurisdiction. The group-ranch system involved Okiek with government administration in direct and critical ways, and introduced not only different ideas about land but also embryonic groups in which new land politics could develop. Actual land use changed little initially, but the groundwork had been laid for later developments.

Currently Okiek are subdividing group-ranches into individual plots, with most titles given to male heads of households. When this began, in the early 1980s, Okiek started to disperse. Households settled alone or with one or two close relatives, claiming an area or going to the area determined by a local committee in anticipation of official adjudication. By 1986, most Kipchorn-wonek had gone to live individually on locally allocated plots, leaving their joint settlement of some fifteen years at Nkaroni, now the assistant chief's land.[37] Kaplelach started homesteading in 1983. By 1986, they still had not begun local subdivision, but people were acting as if their claims were official, which was by no means always the case. Official adjudication was yet to be done in 1991.

There is fundamental disagreement over subdivision in some group-ranches held jointly by Kaplelach and Maasai. A major conflict, not entirely an ethnic split, pits joint use of pasture and water, beneficial to those with herds, against subdivision and individual development, which allows people to sell land. Maasai accuse Okiek of having sold the land even before the Maasai have agreed to subdivide.

Unfortunately, they are right. With subdivision, individuals can sell, lease, or otherwise use or dispose of their land, a consequence with far-reaching repercussions. Poor, cattleless "Torrobo" are suddenly land-rich, with large, fertile, well-watered forest tracts and any number of clients ready to convert that wealth into more negotiable forms for them. A serious land crunch to the west, where Kipsigis and Kisii live, sends a steady stream of settlers seeking a foothold, usually purchased, in the sparsely settled forest. A few large tracts of low-altitude forest have been rented for wheat farms.

Kipchornwonek were selling land even before they demarcated individual plots. Few sales were made before 1980, but the number grew quickly after that. In the earliest sales land cost only 2,000 Ksh an acre,[38] though prices quickly rose to 3,000–4,000 Ksh an acre and reached 5,000–6,000 by 1985 and 6,000–7,000 by 1988. Most sales were for two to ten acres and were made to Kipsigis from areas near Mulot and slightly beyond. Within a year or two, purchasers would arrive to begin clearing their land and build a home. When Okiek moved to live on individual plots, their Kipsigis clients became their nearest neighbors.

Kaplelach had made no sales contacts in 1982, but by late 1983 men were actively looking for Kipsigis clients despite the undecided subdivision ques-tion. Their first clients usually came from near Olmotiook or Mulot, not beyond like many Kipchornwonek ones. Land prices were more or less the same, but Kaplelach more readily accepted cows as partial or total payment (six cows per acre). By 1986, Kipsigis were settling in the Kaplelach area, though sales were technically illegal.

There are other difficulties with the sales. First, purchased cows often die after moving to a new, higher-altitude area; their Okiek owners lose both their land and their newfound wealth. Second, purchasers are usually not wealthy and move in to use the land after making only a down payment. Evicting people who have become neighbors becomes increasingly difficult as time passes without payment. Third, if Okiek receive the purchase sum in small, irregular installments, they tend to spend most of it right away. Sales are conducted by men, and Okiek men often spend payments on drinking binges. Several Okiek women have described the final irony of their husbands' sales for fast money: they can drink more not only because of the money they receive for land, but because immigrant Kipsigis women brew regularly, ensuring the liquor supply. Thus purchasers of Okiek land get their money back through liquor sales.

Many Okiek use capital from land sales to build a frame house with a *mabati* (iron-sheet) roof. Others plan to develop farms, open shops, or purchase a *matatu,* and do so. However, few Okiek in the area have coherent long-term plans for development of their land or capital. More often, most of the money is spent immediately. Social investment in consumption outweighs economic investment.

Okiek are not pleased by all the results of their land sales, but are unwilling to forego their sudden wealth, consumption, and development possibilities. A Kipchornwonek man whose brother had recently sold his land told me:

People feel bad now that there are people between them and it isn't just Okiek anymore. People also fear the people coming in; Kisii and Kipsigis bewitch people. [*CK: Why do they sell, then?*] Just for the money. And then people feel bad, too, when the money is gone. We felt good when it was just Okiek here.

At the same time, Okiek sometimes emphasize kinship with Kipsigis, noting that their gradual economic diversification has made them more like Kipsigis. The larger national context may also be helpful in understanding these shifts in identity towards Kipsigis and away from Maasai. While Maasai are still dominant in the Narok region, in a national context they carry the legacy of colonial romanticism and policies that branded them backward and resistant to change and isolated them from many colonial efforts at education, market development, and so forth. They are today among the ethnic groups (many of them pastoralists) they are considered 'least developed,' and are common targets of development programs. If Okiek participate in this system only in terms of familiar regional dynamics, then, they are not just at the bottom of the heap, but at the bottom of the bottom. Kipsigis, on the other hand, were regarded as a progressive, model tribe by the colonial administration (Manners 1967). As discussed earlier, they carry the legacy and experiences of that: a well-developed market system, smallholdings of tea and other cash crops, land pressures resulting from losses of land to the White Highlands, labor experience on those Europeans farms, and early incorporation into the educational system.

Okiek ethnic realignments, then, arise not only through their own redefined living conditions. More than that, they help define another avenue of national association and involvement within perceived political realities, one that stresses commitment to education and development rather than resistance to it.

If Okiek sometimes emphasize these avenues today, they are no more assimilating into a bounded ethnic group than when they incorporated Maasai dress and language into their cultural repertoire. Both are part of "the complex historical processes of appropriation, compromise, subversion, masking, invention, and revival . . . [that] inform the activity of a people not living alone but 'reckoning itself among the nations'" (Clifford 1988:338).

The contemporary Okiek situation has commonalities with the situation of other rural Kenyans, commonalities that are evoked in the rhetoric of national Kenyan identity, but other aspects of the Okiek situation are better defined more specifically and positively in ethnic rhetoric as Kipsigis. Okiek identity also continues to be an important distinction in local settings, carrying the positive side of their history and identity within the regional system of ethnicity.

Okiek history with Maasai, however, is also simultaneously carried forward in national and regional contexts. Generations of experience and interconnections with Maasai are not to be shed instantly. Rather, they are expanded with other possibilities that may lead more directly to participation in national economic networks and development efforts, and that may be more directly related to their current diversification. Many Okiek live in places still administered as Maasai areas, so the politics of that ethnicity will continue to be part of Okiek skill and experience.

When these negotiations of ethnicity are considered as individual subjective experience, the redefinition and reevaluation of signs of ethnicity that is such an Okiek forte also suggests a certain ambivalence. Okiek identity may include self-images of independent forest hunters and of accommodating bricoleurs, but being Okiek also includes being Torrobo. There is a simultaneous resistance to and integration of these derogatory images; as Bhabha says, it is "at once a mode of appropriation and of resistance" (Bhabha 1985:162). Bhabha's discussion of stereotypes and subject formation in colonial settings is relevant here, in another setting that "allows for the possibility of simultaneously embracing two contradictory beliefs" (Bhabha 1986:168). But in the Okiek case, the "officialness" of the self-understandings embraced may be more ambiguous, as is which of them might be "official."

The current situation and life of Kaplelach and Kipchornwonek Okiek is a far cry from that enshrined in the Golden Age image. With the developments of the past ten years, it is also quite different from the decades when Then became Now. Contemporary Okiek life and cultural identity are informed by these historical processes and modes of life, which serve as a broad background to the details of daily interaction and Okiek initiation. Yet initiation involves more than general aspects of cultural identity. Transforming Okiek girls and boys into women and men, initiation constitutes gender inflections and distinctions within shared Okiek identity.

Differences in work, rights, and abilities are central to Okiek notions of gender. In the final section of this chapter, I consider what some of these processes of diversification and transformation have meant on the domestic level. I outline the daily activities, responsibilities, and rights of the lives Okiek have known in the forest, both Then and Now, and related shifts in Okiek gender roles and relations.

Forest Lives: Work, Resources, Production, and Reproduction

In both the past and the present, different kinds of work, access to resources, and distribution and control of resources and products have been divided along gender lines, though the resources and products in question are now more varied. By considering their organization, this section characterizes "the multifaceted and partially contradictory configuration of relations between men and women in every area of their lives" (Godelier 1986:227), and how it has persisted and shifted.

I start by considering Okiek gender concepts and stereotypes, so salient and important in both the organization of daily life and the initiation process. Later analyses of initiation will fill out understandings of men and women with examples from ritual events. Gender concepts help to create and justify the shape of daily life and interaction, while simultaneously being created through those interactions and modes of organization. Systemic contradictions and interpersonal tensions that might emerge in gender relations are overruled or ignored within general concepts, or else taken as temporary or exceptional.[39] This preliminary sketch of roles, rights, abilities, and responsibilities attributed to men and women embarks from a recurrent Okiek analogy: women are like children.

This classificatory link is evident in common practices. For example, *laakokcu* (you children) is used to address a group of children, of women (by a male speaker), or of women and children (also by a male speaker); *laakok* (children) can refer either to children or to a man's family, including his wife. There are related differences in greeting. Children greet adults by proffering their head, as Maasai children do. After boys are circumcised, they greet all men by hand, even elders. Women, however, continue to give their head to men of their father's age-set or older, even if the women have married sons and daughters.

Women and children are first linked by association through maternal care. Women who have borne children, especially those with infants, are thought to have contagious dirt (*kereek*); this dangerous, unclean state comes from association with the blood and fluids of childbearing and the urine and feces infants shed on their mothers. This pollution renders childbearing women inauspicious for certain ritual roles. They are excluded as blessers in most cases, a role of some organizational prominence (as will be seen later). At the same time, childbearing brings women some esteem.

The essential point of the analogy, however, is to attribute to women a certain character and lack of certain "natural" abilities that are central to being an Okiek man. By the nature of things, so they say, men must be in charge of women and children. Women might disagree with certain particularities of the general stereotype at times, but accept its basic outline and results.

Women are said to lack restraint, always eating like children and doing whatever they want. Unable to listen to reason, to discuss and debate an issue together, to follow advice, how could women organize anything without dissolving into chaotic disarray and argument? Further, their knowledge of the world is far more limited than men's, as emphasized by a name for women and children together, *eemeet aap kaa* (the home country).[40] They stay home while men go to the forest, to meetings, to towns; men are *piik aap saang'* (outside people) or, individually, *ciit aap kaa* (person [man] of the house).

Indeed, women travel far less and less extensively than men. Wives visit relatives only with their husband's agreement, while husbands can come and go at will. There is also some structural truth to the organizational limitations attributed to women. As soon as she becomes adult a woman is married, leaving her family base to join her husband's. She lives in a junior position with women from different families, united through marriage to men of the same family. Meeting chiefly in small groups at the maize grinder or the river, or now during cooperative work groups, the ties and relations that grow among women are rather different from those of men who have grown up and been initiated together, continue to mature together, and come together for large meetings and in smaller groups to drink or work. The history of adult female ties in a neighborhood is sometimes shallower and is always mediated through the men who bring them together. The difference is relative; women might find relations or friends married into the same family or neighborhood. However, responsibilities restrict married women's movement and limit opportunities to come together.

Similarly, while women are incorporated into age-sets through male relatives, their structural assimilation lacks the experience of a shared postinitiation period. Female coinitiates go where their new husbands live. They may remain close friends but only occasionally stay close neighbors as well. Men's age-sets create a wider web of ties and influence, even outside one's immediate initiation group, and are not available to women in the same way.

This is not to say women have no strong ties or leave family links behind at marriage. The point is simply that Okiek social organization opens more possibilities to men than to women for wider, more extensive links. Male relations with a continuous history of coresidence and cooperation (or antagonism) are regularly re-created. In fact, men can roam widely and concern themselves with nondomestic affairs because their wives are home to care for things.

Responsibility is the other side of combining woman and child. Men are said to provide for (-riip) both, representing them as dependent even though the household is based on relations of interdependence. The forest life of Then provides one basis for this perspective, as will be seen below.

Both husband and wife can be rightfully angry at a spouse's failure to provide expected care, but their avenues of expression differ. A man shouts angrily if his wife is repeatedly away from home, hasn't prepared food, and so forth. He can also beat her. A woman is expected to respect her husband even in anger, not answer him back. When his negligence at going to the forest for food, helping in the garden, or squandering money on drink is at issue, however, his wife can only complain or start an argument that could again end in a beating for her. Her last and often most effective resort is to return to her relatives in protest, making their household dispute public.[41]

The analogy between women and children is more than a figure of speech condensing stereotypes about female abilities and character and Okiek gender relations. It is also a subtle, metaphorical denial of women's trials, demonstrations of bravery, and strength of will at initiation. It obliterates, or at least brackets, the essential process through which women become disposable to their natal lineage and appropriable to their marital one. In a sense, then, it erases the external source of women through which male links and patrilineal continuity are reproduced.

Yet the initiation process itself blatantly contradicts these assumptions and stereotypes, through individual displays of courage and through collective female organization of ceremonies. While no one denies this, it does introduce ambivalence and tension into the picture of gender relations and reveal another side of them in practice. This same ambivalence emerges in men's speeches during the first initiation ceremony, in their expressions and side comments, and in the very situation itself (see chapter 6).

The ambivalence is related to a structural contradiction between hierarchy in resource control and equality based on complementary interdependence. This equality is evident in the past, as Okiek recall it. The forest life based on meat and honey, loosely combined the basic household unit of consumption and production with family and neighborhood networks of cooperation in hunting and food sharing. The household was founded on the complementarity of men's and women's work, with men as the primary food providers and women providing the support of home, fire, water, prepared food, and the essential service of reproduction and child care. They also made household utensils from forest products and clothing from animal skins, including men's forest capes and leather honey bags. Women built homes when they moved. Most daily women's work centered on provisions for the individual household, as did men's honey-related work, trapping, and hyrax hunting.

Men hunted with their dogs and about three to seven nearby relatives and neighbors, dividing the meat to take home. In addition to hunting, trapping, and honey work, men also boiled hunting poison and made various tools and utensils: carrying straps for men and women, drills to make fire, bows, arrows, spear shafts, clubs, and carved snuff and tobacco boxes.

While both women's and men's work were essential, men's work was more culturally prominent and highly valued. Honey and hunting are central in Okiek identity, not just men's. It is of note that at this time, Okiek women could not maintain themselves and their children independently in the forest without male providers. Men, on the other hand, could and did maintain themselves on distant forest trips, sharing women's ordinary daily tasks of obtaining water and firewood, and building temporary shelters if needed. Of course, in the long term they could not maintain themselves and their family lines without women to bear children.

The material continuity of those family lines was also constituted by jurally defined ownership and control of two essential productive resources: hives and land. At the same time, this was the essential basis of hierarchy in gender relations. Okiek hives were their capital—their cows, as they often say.[42] The analogy is apt, for hives yield honey year after year like cows yield calves and milk, and a man could take more wives by making more hives and getting more honey. Hives were individually made and owned, inherited from father to son, and given as gifts in ceremonies and at marriages. While a woman might technically own a few gift hives, she had to get her husband, son, brother, or other male relative to climb it, though the honey was hers to eat, distribute, trade, or brew. However, men owned the vast majority of hives.

Surplus in the form of honey beyond that eaten and stored for future household needs was also largely under male control. However, honey brought home was distributed and stored by the woman of the house, so decisions about the surplus were mentioned and discussed. Accumulated honey could also be used to help a man's kinsmen celebrate ceremonies or look for wives, returning the surplus to reproduce culturally and physically the patrilineage from whose forest territory it was harvested.

Animals received in exchange for honey were eaten or kept with friends men made through trade and age-set relations (or perhaps through marriage). Though women did visit and travel to a limited extent, traded pottery, and met neighbors of other ethnic groups at home and at ceremonies, men were far more involved and influential in trade, travel, and wider interrelations among both Okiek and their neighbors. Men had the predominant interest and opportunity to build and call on sociopolitical resources in this way, though not an absolute monopoly.

Forest territories that gave access to honey were held patrilineally. The men of the family decided about outside uses or land transfers to another lineage. Similarly, men of the residential area handled legal cases or problems. The extent of their sociopolitical resources was not simply a question of establishing and maintaining such relations; they also had the ability and access to appropriate fora for their use. Women were excluded from meetings, the main official context for debate and decision. They were considered inappropriate actors there, in keeping with and perpetuating the notions of gender discussed above. Women are also like children because they are jural minors.

Women are the other "property" that passes from one lineage to another. Marriage arrangements control circulation of the complementary labor a man needs to establish and maintain his household, as well as the means to reproduce himself and his patrilineage. Women are given some voice, however small, in decisions about their children's marriages. But in theory, and to a great extent in fact, marriages are contracted by the men of the family. They also get and use most productive resources (hives or cows) given in marriage exchanges, while perishable goods, such as clothing, are shared by men and women (with women given less valuable and durable garments when purchased clothing was incorporated).[43]

Women influence the final outcome of their own and their children's marriages in other ways. Even if they are not quite docile pawns, though, agreement between patrilineages with property exchange is always the final ratification of a lasting marriage. Women are a vital resource embodying productive and reproductive labor, and are not given away for nothing. Labor is transferred jurally from one family to another, but women (and men) do not yield autonomy in more momentary disposals of their own person. Though widely recognized, that freedom is exercised and enjoyed in secret.

More than the jural side of marriage must be considered in gender relations. The bride plays little or no official role in the arrangements, yet her acquiescence is in the end necessary. Occasionally, young women refuse their prospective husband on the wedding day, with various results. They can also refuse later by continually returning home. It is not uncommon, nor was it in the past, for women to have one or two husbands before staying with one and bearing children for his lineage. Once she has children, other interests and constraints make divorce more difficult and rare.

Apart from marriage arrangements, a telling indication of gender relations is a woman's relative autonomy in regard to her own body. Sexual fidelity is expected of a wife, yet both men and women seem to relish diversions with lovers. Infidelity is widely recognized but well hidden; discretion is the rule. While encouraging a young woman to follow her husband, one older woman made it quite clear that responsibility was to the husband, but secret delight was found with the lover:

[D]o what your mother did and I did [i.e., agree to the marriage arranged] because that is the best. That is the best, better than all these other ways. We certainly give a woman away to be married. So then if you have some secret person that you have hidden, even so your husband is number one. Your husband is number one. You go and do that carefully so that no one sees it. So that he doesn't see, and your mother doesn't see, and no one sees it at all, not even a bird. *ii?* Haven't you understood now? Because we hide it. Women hide those things. *ii?* You hide it.

Okiek initiation is in some ways similar. Men are nominally the organizers of public ceremonies for both boys and girls, but men and women are each in charge of their own seclusion ceremonies. Each protects, defends, and celebrates their own secrets and the physical trial that earns them the right to adult knowledge and status. Usually, women simply assert the distinction between and the equivalence of male and female initiation, though they joke about the cowardice of males, who hide their operations in the forest.

Men, however, sometimes represent their trial as more difficult and their claim on shared secrets as prior, and disparage women's secrets simply because they are women's. At times, men approach the women's ritual house to ask for liquor, sometimes shouting impotently from a distance, sometimes coaxing a woman outside to bring it, or approaching teasingly or in joking aggression against the exclusion of men and their inability to call on their wives. To me, men have also interpreted women's secret songs and hoots as women getting out of hand and man-hungry.

Representation and practice of both marriage and ceremonies make evident the ambivalence and contradictions of Okiek gender roles; they resonate with the inherent structural tension between complementarity and interdependence, on the one hand, and imbalance in male and female access to and control of material resources, surplus, and sociopolitical position, on the other. The social and economic organization of forest life hinged on the continuity of male links, and gave men more structural and practical freedom and control. But women were the necessary lubricant, both the means of creating social continuity and its economic support. They could take some liberties to create more congenial places for themselves within that structure. If women are likened to impetuous, willful children in the patriarchal ideal of Okiek life, it is perhaps in part because an insistent autonomy remained in some matters that escaped official, male-oriented organization.

Okiek diversification gradually introduced important shifts in the nature of household interdependence. Ownership and control of land and hives, and control of marriage arrangements, all followed more or less the same pattern until quite recently, though cows became the standard bridewealth. Livestock are treated like hives, and largely in accordance with Maasai patterns. Most belong to men, and a woman's animals cannot be sold without consulting her husband, who would probably conduct the sale. Milking was added to women's work, though it takes little time with such small herds.

Trade continued to be largely in honey, though cash sales became more common as time went on and shop goods became more plentiful, even if they were still at Ololunga. Cloth and blankets replaced hide clothing; enamel utensils and aluminum pots largely replaced pottery ones. Shop goods meant that gradually women had to make fewer things, though they continued making honey baskets, hide capes, and some pottery. Shops also had tea, sugar, and salt, though even today many Kaplelach do not have sugar and tea on a daily basis.

The Okiek diet did broaden with the introduction of maize, and shifts in work patterns, most garden-related, began during the first ten to fifteen years of diversification. With the concurrent settlement, women were also freed from frequent house building. The more time-consuming construction of mud-and-thatch houses was undertaken less often and was done with men's help.

The first tiny gardens entailed no significant departure from the usual work patterns. Even now there is no clear gender ideology of garden work that divides tasks neatly between women and men, but one general pattern of agricultural work emerged that is related to the way diversification proceeded. Men generally did the heavy forest clearing necessary to start a new garden. Once done, they continued with hunting and honey collecting for the most part. Women took on most other work, with men helping on occasion and especially as needed at harvest.

Over time, people made larger gardens and maize became the staple. With more people doing directly productive work and, most important, with women now producing food almost by themselves, the pressure on men to provide forest food for their families' survival was reduced. Men did continue to hunt and collect honey; garden sustenance was not enough by itself and did not last the full year.[44] Besides, surplus honey was still sold and used to make wine, and meat was needed to eat with maize ugali until women learned more about gathering wild greens when men failed to provide.[45] Unless men, too, did garden work, what would they do but continue the past productive work they knew? Gardening not only relieved pressure on men to produce, but also provided an answer to that question—the maize the gardens produced could be brewed into beer, providing a steady supply for the men to drink.[46]

Unlike honey wine, however, maize beer is made by women. In addition to brewing for ceremonies and other formal occasions, women make beer for cooperative work parties and to sell. Cooperative parties entice men and women alike to work, not only for beer but for implicitly promised future help in their own gardens. They enable people to enlarge their gardens and give women an important way to recruit garden help if their husbands do not provide it. Similarly, illegal liquor sales let women earn small amounts of money for household needs, though much liquor goes to relatives on credit. The most successful women brewers are recent arrivals (few are Okiek) who try to refuse credit. Men then must pay for liquor with honey or sell some maize, depleting the small store for future months. Most Okiek men strike a fairly judicious balance between working in the fields and looking after herds, looking for honey and meat, and drinking or roaming. Yet extreme cases throw into sharp relief the implications of shifts in work and subsistence for gender relations.

Some twenty-five to thirty-five years ago, during forest life Then, women were indispensable and complementary reproducers and co-producers. Still equally indispensable, their contribution to household economy has become increasingly a matter of direct food production as well as daily support services. When husbands contribute only occasionally or are often absent, women increasingly approximate independent producers rather than co-producers. Their limited possibilities make that situation very difficult. Such limitations arise from a relative continuity in gender relations, with men still controlling access to and distribution of essential material and sociopolitical resources.

The land sales highlight both the worst and best of current household situations. A woman struggling to support her family chiefly through her own garden work can lose the very land she farms. Few people so far have sold their entire plots, but some have comparatively small plots left for their children to subdivide in the future. Households at the other extreme use property sales to develop their land and other capital with increasing prosperity.

The constraints experienced by women in the former situation are the same as in the past, but because of the land sales are felt more critically. Forced to be relatively self-sufficient economically, they do not have the autonomy to act independently of the man who administers family resources unwisely. Attempts through government authorities to prevent further land sales bring women up against the limits of their sociopolitical contacts, their inexperience in legal and official matters, and relative constraints on their mobility and hence their ability to pursue the matter, as well as the male officials' perception of women.

Women's experience with money, major sales, and the marketplace is often limited, but they would learn quickly if they were recognized as economic agents. However, their access to capital for development plans is limited. Women cannot sell livestock or land held by men, two main methods of raising cash. Cash crops are still new to Okiek, pursued only in minor form by even the most "innovative" Kipchornwonek men. As men, they can get and use resources to increase the amount of cultivated land with cooperative work or hired labor, purchase other seed, and make arrangements for sale or transport.

Thus while Okiek women now participate in production and household economy in ways that could lead to increasing economic autonomy, they are constrained by limited access to and control of material and social resources. The most unfortunate have husbands who contribute and work only erratically, appropriate the products as their own (which they are), and dispose not only of any surplus but of basic land resources, too, using the proceeds for their immediate consumption. Most households remain cooperative units combining productive activities in different balances—forest work, garden and herd work, and probably increasingly market work—with the man of the house controlling things and managing them with greater or lesser skill and care.

In this context, marriage and household arrangements are becoming more volatile and diverse as both men and women envision and try to exercise alternatives that were previously rare or virtually nonexistent. For instance, most Okiek men have only one wife, but the flood of capital from land sales has encouraged many to plan extended households with second wives.

Polygamous households were relatively rare among Okiek in the past, typically formed after the first household was well established. Many contemporary second marriages follow this pattern, involving men of the *eseuri* age-set or older. Yet few Kipsigis women who came to live among Kaplelach in a recent flurry of such marriages stayed. Two explanations were given. First, they found their new husbands irresponsible, negligent providers, and fled their drunken abuse. Second, some Okiek women refused co-wives and helped drive the new wives away.

Another set of newly polygamous households belong to relatively young men, *i rambau* or even *i rantai*. In these households the co-wives might be the same age, though from different ethnic groups. These men might take a second wife even before the first has two children. These young polygamous households seem to be establishing themselves more permanently.

For Okiek women, basic marriage arrangements continue as before. As discussed, Okiek women did and do manage to influence their final marriage arrangement to some extent. Childhood engagement is discouraged now, reportedly because one of the children involved might refuse the intended spouse at a point when the debt incurred by the prospective wife's family (that is, the gifts given by the prospective husband's family over time) is too large to repay. No Okiek women of the area to date have opted out of the marriage system entirely, nor had a real possibility to do so. For schoolgirls, however, marriage is being delayed beyond the usual age. This is still a new development, and it remains to be seen whether those girls will agree to be given to husbands as their sisters and mothers were, will find their own husbands and will have the unions ratified later with marriage payments, or might find and create other options.

When Okiek first began to diversify their economy, new practices and products were incorporated and accommodated within existing modes of social organization and work patterns, with some shifts and reorganization. As what began so simply has become a fundamental transformation in daily life, these same processes of diversification have continued, based on the same principles of sociopolitical organization and assumptions about gender roles and relations. Those assumptions and that organization contain contradictions that center around women's roles. With the transformations over time, the contradictions have become more pointed and, at times, have helped produce trying situations for Okiek women. Radical changes in the social and material basis of Okiek social groups—for example, dissolution of patrilineage continuity through shared land and the replacement of young age-mates' common period together by school—are too recent to allow predictions about the future shape of daily life or gender relations.

Although particular forms, concerns, and practices of daily life now differ considerably from what Okiek remember as their historical and cultural tradition, the same ceremonial occasions are still celebrated. Okiek schoolgirls might yet refuse the husbands selected for them, but they still insist on initiation into adulthood with their peer group.

Women and men continue to celebrate their own seclusion ceremonies and incorporate girls and boys into adult communities by sharing the secrets of their sex. Seclusion is another school, people often told me, a school where Okiek assumptions about gender are one lesson, taught in a context that reveals them to be often contradicted in practice. How the lessons of the two schools will combine to influence Okiek gender relations is another question for the near future. Of immediate concern here is how the ceremonies and process of initiation create Okiek women from Okiek girls, a process that both draws on and creates a continuity of past history and tradition within the life of the present.

4

Kepa Tuumto: The Journey to Adulthood

When they come out of seclusion, they just no longer want to be with those other children. They are shown secret things [in seclusion]. They make the difference. They change someone into an adult.

Kaina (Kopot Ntekwa)

Initiation is the climax of a series of three life-cycle ceremonies that punctuate Okiek maturation from childhood to adulthood. The first is a one-day ceremony, *kisile laakweet* (we're shaving the child), in which the heads of child and mother are shaved in the morning, and the child is given a new name in the evening. Some families celebrate it for a young child between three and five years old; others wait until the child is older, often just before initiation.[1] In the second ceremony, rare today,[2] children between twelve and fourteen years of age have their ear lobes pierced (*keeparpar iitik,* the ears are pierced), and later have them stretched with progressively larger ear plugs. Elongated lobes enhance the child's beauty. This ceremony also lasts a single day, from dawn to dusk.

The ear-piercing ceremony is like a preliminary initiation in both ritual form and physical trial. Its events closely parallel those of initiation, including morning processions from the forest, construction and blessing of a *mabwaita* shrine, parallel evening processions, and construction and blessing of a *toloocik* platform. The child's ears are pierced at dusk while he or she is sitting at the *mabwaita*—the same time and place of initiation head shaving and the same place of girls' excision the following dawn. A child demonstrates increasing maturity and ability to withstand pain during the ear operation, just as the more painful initiation operation must be endured.

Girls and boys are initiated separately at around age fourteen to sixteen, in a series of four ceremonies. The first is the most culturally emphasized and elaborate, entails the largest gathering and celebration, and is by far the most dramatic. Between the first and last ceremonies, initiates live together in seclusion from adults of the opposite sex. Initiation is later remembered nostalgically, and serves as a reference point of personal history for initiates and their age-mates, parents, and relatives.

People refer to this ceremonial transition to adulthood as *peentin tuumto* (they are going [for/to] initiation), using the central idiom of a journey, as discussed below. Unlike most ceremonies, initiation is usually done for several children together. Coinitiates might be classificatory siblings (for example, FaBrDa), maternal relations (for example, MoSi, FaMoBrDa), children of coinitiate fathers, or otherwise linked.

All parents of coinitiates invite guests for the occasion, but celebrations differ in scale and timing. Those who are able will celebrate the first ceremony by brewing liquor and slaughtering a cow to feed guests. The initial ritual events are repeated at each home that is celebrating. Others "borrow" (*-saam*) the ceremony from the family hosting the girls' excision. They might live too far away to cocelebrate, lack the resources to host a full initiation, or be unprepared because their child insisted on initiation before they had planned it. All initiates' families celebrate the final ceremony, but on a smaller scale than the first. Two secret seclusion ceremonies are held at the seclusion place, usually where the operation was done.

For men, initiation begins young manhood, formerly an exciting, adventurous time of roaming together, visiting girls, hunting, climbing for honey, and raiding cows. For girls, evening dances and nighttime flirting fill the time just prior to initiation, which culminates with the flashy display of fancy dance costumes the night initiation begins.

Maturation proceeds afterward through marriage, parenthood, and elderhood, but youth and initiation are a cultural high point in the life cycle. After marriage, life-cycle ceremonies, now experienced as parents and hosts, are still major occasions, especially those for one's first-born child.

Okiek call all three life-cycle ceremonies and each of the four initiation ceremonies *tuumto*. Most generally, *tuumto* means "ceremony," and was often defined for me through essential activities—singing, drinking liquor, eating. The occasions have a celebratory period and air, but there is ritual work to do, too. *Tuumto* is used in other important, more particular ways as well. As a more particular name, *tuumto* refers to initiation. The idiom of movement and travel using the verb meaning "to go" with *tuumto*[3] is used for the entire initiation process, but its most unmarked sense refers particularly to the first ceremony, whose ritual climax is girls' excision at dawn (or boys' circumcision).

Success in that public trial admits them to the company of initiated adults. Much of the subsequent seclusion process centers on the revelation of secrets known by initiated women (or men). This is the final, most specific sense of *tuumto,* and the most common sense for the plural, *tuumwek:* any secret, meaningful ritual procedure, including secret songs and especially secret things shown to initiates. As the woman quoted in the epigraph suggests, those secrets are central in transforming Okiek children into adults. Late in the first ceremony, when all the public events are over, the girls are taken for the first time into the women's house for secrets. This first initiation ceremony is indeed the first time they "go to the secrets."

Okiek life-cycle ceremonies are distinct celebrations of marked points in a child's growth, but are also a linked progression over time. The earlier ceremonies lead to initiation: "we shave them so that they can be initiated." Relations Okiek perceive among the ceremonies are supported by, and perhaps are partly based on, formal relations among them. Common principles of performance inform the different ceremonies, with common symbolic themes and semiotic resources combined in different ways.

In addition to common symbolic chords, other formal relations link constituent ritual events as progressions from one life-cycle ceremony to another. The events widen progressively in scope and contrast significantly in performance. These relations unite the ceremonial series over time and create both ceremonial continuity and difference as an important part of Okiek understandings of the maturation process. Some such relations will be discussed in the next chapter.

Initiation, Personhood, and Emotion

Initiation is a critical juncture, a process where children enter and adults emerge. Okiek understandings of this process are tied up with their concepts of personhood and of childhood versus adulthood, and are intimately related to assumptions about gender (reviewed in the previous chapter). Initiation combines high emotion, control, and knowledge, but in different ways for different participants over the course of initiation. Okiek understandings of emotion and its expression are also bound up with concepts of personhood and gender.

Girls' first ceremony focuses on the trial of excision. To endure it bravely, with no sign of fear or physical reaction to pain, takes great resolve and determination. To Okiek, this is both achieved and shown before the operation through the containment of powerful emotion and a tremendous concentration of will. Children make their own minds and hearts ready for the test. They sometimes insist, against their parents' wishes, on being initiated with friends.

While initiates demonstrate maturity through imperturbable emotional control during the first ceremony, adult participants present a variety of emotional displays in the day and night leading up to the trial. All are upset, uncertain, and anxious about the initiates' (their sisters, daughters, wife's sisters, and so on) strength and ability to succeed, and they describe their emotional state with one verb. Yet those strong feelings are expressed and shown in a variety of ways that are related to gender and age and which are seen as appropriate for different kinds of people.

Their emotional displays express the turmoil they feel, but are also specifically intended to influence initiates, to make them more determined to succeed. The sequence and progression of displays during the ceremony intensify the feelings of all involved, as discussed in chapter 2. The single verb -nereec describes the feelings of both initiates preparing for the trial and of the participants who show their emotional turmoil. It refers to anger as well as the determination, anxiety, and worry people at initiation describe. -nereec defines an emotional field difficult to translate by a single English word,[4] but "worked up" or "upset" suggest its wider sense.

Okiek also speak of emotion, will, and intellect in terms of a bodily idiom—in terms of heart, stomach (or intestines), and head. Thinking, pondering, and reasoning are related to the head (for example, ipwaat en meting' uung, you think [of a decision] in your head), and also entail listening with ears to other people. Unbalanced people are described as headless, with a turning head, or with a head that is not good (mamii metit; weentin metit; ma myee metit).

Heart and stomach phrases refer to general good character (myee mukuuleltany'iin, he's goodhearted/kind; cemyemaa, she of the kind/tranquil stomach). To take anger or jealousy seriously is to "put in the heart" or stomach (inten mukuulelta, inten maaeet). After an apology and blessing, angry words are no longer followed (-sip, that is, they are forgotten); one "unties the intestines" (-tyaac akutaanik) which had been spitefully "knotted" (-yuc).

An initiate's nereeket (from -nereec) is characterized in songs, speeches, and discussions in terms of both heart and head. She has determined in her head that she wants to go, and knows she can and will. People recall being extremely worked up as initiates, though theirs is an internal state that is as controlled as they will be externally at dawn. Songs urge them to squeeze their heart until all water is gone and it is hard, immovable, and unchangeable, that is, until will and head have controlled heart and visible emotional expression. Still, it can be seen.

He thinks, "I'll be initiated tomorrow." And he gets worked up thinking, "I'll go." [Said with force and emphasis.] . . . He is worked up. [CK: How does it show?] It's visible. He gets worked up until you see he's changed. He no longer laughs. The eyes get red. You see some whose body does this [quivers]. [CK: Can you see it in girls, too?] In some girls, too, you can see they are really worked up, but especially boys.

Men and women alike made comments like this, again articulating the Okiek view of "natural" differences in the constitution and abilities of men and women that both define and are based on their daily roles and activities.

Boys' and men's hearts are the same, as are girls' and women's, but those of men and women are quite different. Though both boys and girls brave initiation the same way, people say boys get *more* worked up. Neither flinches but boys are seen as *more* controlled; they can harden their hearts though determination alone, without encouragement through song and speech. A woman's heart is not as hard as a man's, though she, too, matures and learns through initiation.

Okiek find that quantitative difference underlines qualitative differences between male and female abilities to debate, make joint decisions, and control and manage resources. A young man's heart is hotter, but his head also becomes stronger with age. Strong-willed women, unable to listen to masculine "reason," confuse the mandates of head and heart, though they, too, can become wiser with age.

These notions of personhood and associated abilities and proclivities are also related to the ways in which women and men, old and young express strong feelings during initiation. Hot young men have physical fits, but nonetheless keep verbal control. Elders are the most controlled of all, showing their anxiety within the formal parameters of reasoned narrative form. Women's fits are physical and verbal. Older women might deliver emotional tirades, coherently structured but vehement, excited, and seemingly uncontrolled in style and delivery. Women also do most of the singing in initiation ceremonies, while men do most of the speaking, a fact considered further in later chapters.

The first success of initiation is a question of personal will and resolve—of having the heart for it and being encouraged and strengthened by powerful emotional displays by friends and relatives. Initiation in the larger sense, however, cannot be done alone. The real change of initiation involves knowledge and new ways of acting and interacting. Some Okiek explained the changes:

A child and an adult have the same heart, that doesn't change. It's the head that changes. Because they go and become clever. They're told to leave the playing of children and are shown secret things [*tuumwek*] so then they are no longer the same as children.

When they come out of seclusion, they just no longer want to be with those other children. They are shown secret things. They make the difference. They change someone into an adult. They are cursed in the seclusion house and told they will die if they tell the secrets. Then when they come out, they are just mature and still [not running about like children].

She becomes a woman. She goes into the women's house and then when she comes out, she no longer wants to go with children. She stays with women. There is no change in her heart, but you just don't go there with children anymore. You know other things when you come out.

After children display strong, mature will and emotional control during their initial trials, they are shown and taught the secret knowledge of the initiated. They are told how adults act. Their knowledge, customs, behavior, and ways of relating to people show they are adults when they come out of seclusion. Adult women, particularly the two ritual teachers, control the knowledge and reveal it to initiates.

Initiation prepares a girl for her adult roles as wife and mother, but despite her incorporation into the women's community of knowledge, Okiek do not regard her as truly adult until she has been given to a man in marriage and settled down to reproduce. "The wisdom of a woman comes when she has gotten older, after she has borne a child. . . . After she has had a child, she knows that [women] don't wander about [but stay at home]." The recognition of women's bravery, secret knowledge, and initiation as equivalent to men's and the simultaneous devaluation of these same things will reappear in later chapters. Structural contradictions emerge in a number of cultural idioms and events when Okiek assumptions about gender and adulthood are brought together in initiation, a time when it becomes especially clear that women, whom men represent as children needing direction, have essential productive and reproductive roles and independent ritual traditions.

Initiation at Ruruupto

The rest of this chapter describes the initiation of a particular group of girls in 1983, with minimal explanatory comments and interpretive asides. It was held in a low-lying area near the Ewaso Nyiru river, an area referred to as *ruruupto,* that included Okiek homes at Sukustoosyek, Ororuet, and Inkouuyuuy. The account provides a descriptive orientation and a chronological sequence to anchor and contextualize detailed analyses in later chapters. Those chapters focus on particular aspects of Okiek initiation in turn, dividing and discussing the process in different ways, attending closely to formal aspects and general patterns.

Describing a particular initiation gives a sense of the family relations and personal experiences involved, which can get lost in general analytical concerns. The personalities and politics of initiation, essential to interpreting performance particularities, come out clearly here. Though they fade into the background in the later formal analyses, general ceremonial structures and patterns must first be peopled with a richly textured, particular description. That experience is what anthropological analysis seeks to illuminate.

Initiation involves secrets. I was not allowed to attend women's secret ceremonies, but participated like other noninitiates, such as men, hearing songs at a slight distance and talking to women outside. However, some things are more secret than others. Women discussed parts of the ceremonies with me quite openly, stopping at the most guarded knowledge: *"Tuumto. Makimwai kiyaan"* (That's a ritual secret. We don't talk about that thing). Through

Table 2: Sequence of Initiation Ceremonies

---

1. *Kepa tuumto* (first ceremony)
2. *Kelap euun* (first seclusion ceremony)
3. *Ketuuitos suumoosyek* (second seclusion ceremony)
4. *Kelong'u en aineet* (coming out of seclusion

---

discussions with men and women, transcribing and discussing songs recorded outside, and time spent with secluded initiates, I put together a sense of sequence and procedure in seclusion ceremonies. No woman revealed *tuum-week* to me, but bits and pieces did come out. Throughout this work, I refer only vaguely to secret aspects of initiation in order to respect and protect their secrecy. Table 2 lists the four ceremonies of initiation in sequence.

Background and Preparations

When I returned to the forest in 1983, I was told that six Kaplelach girls would be initiated together later in the year: Tinkili, Nini,[5] Seraset, Lakwani, Tata, and Cepopoo. The first three were daughters of brothers. All of them were children of the same large, subdivided lineage, Arakiplet. Figure 7 shows relations between the nine girls eventually initiated, beginning on two different days three weeks apart. It also shows how they were separated into three different seclusion houses. In addition to seven Arakiplet girls (the six mentioned above plus one other), two others related through female links would eventually join the group, one of Kap Leboo family (Nampet) and the other of Kap Changoroi (Níní).

Within a month of my return, shaving ceremonies began for the girls and several small children. The first was for a small child of Kap Leboo on 28 January; Nini's was the next day. Three days later, her sister (FaBrDa) Tinkili was shaved. After a three week lull, it was Níní's turn. She was slightly younger, a daughter (FaBrDaDa) of the other two, and it had been uncertain whether she would be initiated that year or wait to go with her close friend Nampet (her "*maama*," one of a group of relatives traced through the mother [in this case, MoFaSiDaDa]).[6] (Nampet was one of my "daughters," then a schoolgirl at Ololunga in Standard Three.) Níní wanted to go that year; when her parents decided to join the ceremony, they shaved her.

Four days later, on 1 March, a ceremony was held for Tata, another "sister" (FaFaBrSoDa), combining shaving with delayed celebration of her earlier ear piercing. The three others, Cepopoo, Lakwani, and Seraset, had already been shaved. Shavings completed, the girls' families began concentrating on initiation preparations.

I was at Nkaroni most of April and May, following boys' initiations there.

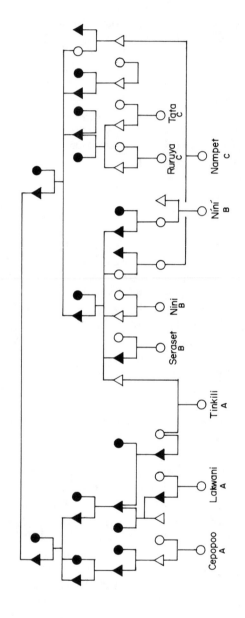

Figure 7. Kinship relations among initiates. A, B, and C indicate the seclusion houses the girls stayed in. Note: Nampet's father is MoBr to Tata's mother (relationship not indicated on diagram) and coinitiate with Tata's father.

When I returned on 23 May, the families were fully involved in ceremony arrangements. The girls, their brothers, and/or their parents went to the weekly Melelo market or the Ololunga shops several times to buy sugar, sweets, cigarettes, new clothes, beer ingredients, and the flag to be put up at each girl's home. The first initiation ceremony entails considerable financial investment, work, and planning. Table 3 estimates expenses for each host family in 1983.[7]

The girls' brothers went to Nkaroni or Nentolo several times to arrange dance costume rental. Brothers and fathers went to the forest hoping to get more honey for brewing, and some were still looking for a cow to feed their guests. The girls' parents discussed the choice of ritual leaders (*matireenik*); one Kaplelach woman of Kap Leboo, married and living at Nkaroni, had already been asked and had agreed.

On Thursday and Friday, 26 and 27 May, two host families (the parents of Nini and Tinkili) started brewing, leaving soaked maize meal to sour. They started making and storing honey wine, too. They planned to hold the ceremony the following Friday.

All the families involved had been consulting, planning to coordinate a single ceremony. But when those two families began to brew without agreement from all, Tata's father said he would have to hold his own ceremony. He didn't yet have everything that was needed. If Nini's father was going fast and would not wait, he would do his ceremony alone the next week. A ceremony can't be rushed, he said, especially for one's first-born child. Friends at Nkaroni advised him that his first child should be initiated at home, at any rate.

In what would be a related development, my "daughter" Nampet declared that she, too, would be initiated, since Níní was going to be. Her mother said they didn't have enough maize to feed her through the seclusion period and that she was still young, but the next week her father agreed, saying "I'm not the one to be cut, it's her. If she wants to go, it's up to her. Each person does what their heart tells them."

When it became clear that Nampet would join the initiates, her schoolmate Ruruya also began to insist. Her father, however, refused because he liked to hold his own ceremonies and wanted time to prepare. Ruruya was Tata's sister (FaBrDa). Tata's father tried to convince his brother to let Ruruya join Tata at his house. He did not succeed, and so he said Tata would have to be initiated with the others, even though she was his first-born, since there was no girl for her to go through initiation with.

Meanwhile, the families of Nini and Tinkili, who had soured maize meal, postponed the final brewing by a week; they were not quite ready. It was clear early on that all the girls would be initiated together but divided into two seclusion groups, but the two families disagreed about where the operation would be held.

Ordinarily there are several criteria that could be used to make the decision,

Table 3: Approximate Costs (in Ksh) of Girls' First Initiation Ceremony (in 1983)

Girl's Costume		*Specialists' Services*	
1 new khanga cloth	50/	payment to surgeon	25/
1 pair of shoes	40/	payment to *matireenik*	25/
beads for arms	50/	payment to *pitiintet*	10/
rental of dance costume	90/		
		Specialists' total	60/
Costume total	230/		

Food and Drink		*Other*	
can of Kimbo cooking fat	20/	flag	20/
potatoes (2 *debes*)[1]	40/	rental of record player	60/
salt	6/	cigarettes to give out	14/
tea leaves	7/	sweets to give out	15/
sugar (for tea and to mix	100/ (min.)	chewing gum to give out	15/
with honey during brewing			
case of soda	44/	Other total	124/
case of beer	181/		
honey to brew (1 *debe*)	500/		
millet to brew beer	50/		
maize to brew (2 bags)	500/		
cow to slaughter	850/ (min.)		
Food and drink total	2298/ (with average 2 bags of maize brewed)		

Total cost of hosting the first ceremony: approx. 2700/ (about $216 in 1983)

Note: All costs are not met in cash. Maize and honey are usually grown or collected. The cow is often from the family herd or gotten from a relative or friend. A boys' ceremony costs the same, less costume.

1. A *debe* is a unit of volume, roughly five imperial gallons.

but this case was ambiguous on every count. Neither Nini nor Tinkili was the first-born. Their fathers were the surviving brothers of a large family. Seniority was advanced to argue for Nini's home; her father was first-born by default, since their older brothers had died. Yet Tinkili's father was last-born, equivalent to first-born in some ways. Previous disagreements between the brothers may well have underlain this dispute; discord between their wives was also important. The wives carried the dispute into later initiation questions, too.

Each family insisted the operation would be at its house, but left the final decision to the ritual leaders. The effects of the disagreement were clear, however, during the final preparations. The girls' mothers got help from different women, did not help each other, and seemed at times unaware of each other's preparations. They gave the impression of deliberately proceeding with apparently independent plans rather than trying to coordinate for the same day.

A week before the ceremony, Ruruya's father agreed for her to join her sister Tata in initiation. It was certain, then, that there would be two ceremonies, held at different times; Ruruya had to be shaved first. Tata's father thus had extra preparation time, and would have the satisfaction of initiating his first child at home.

Nampet would also join this group as a "borrower." This meant that our family would have time to find a costume and other things. Her placement was not solely pragmatic, but based on closer relations between her parents and Tata's. Tata's and Nampet's fathers were coinitiates and had remained close friends. Nampet's father was *maama* to all the initiates because his mother was from their lineage, but a more closely related *maama* to Tata's mother since she was the daughter of his older sister.

In the final week before the ceremony, people worked and traveled constantly. The girls' fathers and brothers looked for more honey, went to finalize arrangements for dance costumes and then to bring back parts of them, or went to talk to possible ritual leaders. Women came to help roast sour mash (maize meal soaked and left to sour) and cut stacks of firewood, and were given beer or tea in return. Nini's married sister arrived to help, as did the mother of the future husband Nini was promised to. The other girls' suitors also visited, bringing things to help the girl's families.

On Tuesday, the first liquor was brewed for the young men who would decorate the houses on Thursday (a task that young men in Kipchornwonek began to take on about fifteen years ago) and the girls began to travel to invite guests. They wore new shoes and clothes, beads on their arms, and, as a preview, the bits of dance costume their brothers had brought. Leg bells and whistles announced them as the ceremony girls, even from a distance. They had been gathering almost every evening for the past week to sing and dance, as they would the night of the ceremony. On two nights, women took them into Nini's parents' house and began teaching them *kaiyantaaita,* songs they would sing daily while in seclusion.

Preparations for two separate ceremonies were final at this point, but Tata was not pleased. She told me she would sneak into the women's house Friday night, when her friends would be there, and steal the ceremony so she could be with them. (An uninitiated girl "steals" the ceremony by entering the women's house while secret ceremonies are being performed. She must then be initiated because she may have seen some of the secret.) If she did, Nampet and Ruruya would probably have to wait another year. They insisted that if she stole the ceremony, they all would; they didn't want to stay behind all by themselves.

On Thursday, the day before the ceremony, one of the girls' brothers made a final trip to Nkaroni about dance costumes.[8] Most things were ready by this time. The mothers of Tinkili and Nini brewed the last and largest batch of liquor, to celebrate on Saturday and Sunday after the girls' operation.

Young men turned up early Thursday afternoon to decorate the house in Nini's compound that would receive the majority of the guests; most of the young men were brothers to one or more of the girls. They created a canopy ceiling by tying the corners of five clean cloths to the rafters with bark string. After collecting acacia thorns, they unrolled and tacked around the walls two long rolls of heavy cardboard printed with green-and-white striped milk cartons. These rolls of unformed cartons belonged to a man from Nkaroni and made the rounds among his friends to decorate ceremony houses. (Those who didn't manage to get the milk carton rolls used sheets of newspaper.) The cartons made a high border around the walls. On top of them, the young men tacked up brightly colored travel brochures I had been asked to bring from Nairobi, and hung six to eight framed snapshots, some borrowed. In about an hour and a half, they made Nini's house a special place, ready for guests. They drank their beer, then split into two groups to go do Tinkili's and Kirutari's houses. The first guests arrived in the evening; the young and the old came early. The few older people were relatives who travel slowly, from some distance, and were wanted early to help with ritual events. Oldyo was one elder who arrived; he was the brother (FaBrSo) of Nini's father. Most of the early arrivals were young people. Girls from elsewhere came to sing with their friends on their last shared childhood days. Young men gathered to be with the girls and enjoy their own songs and chatter. For the first time a bonfire was made outside, and the girls danced around it.

The young people had been anticipating this with mounting excitement in the preceding months, especially as preparations quickened in the preceding week. On the eve of the ceremony they laughed, joked, sang, and danced exuberantly well into the night, finally settling down to sleep in Nini's brother's house, decorated for the festivities the next day. Ritual events of the first ceremony, described next, are summarized in table 4.

Morning Koroseek *Procession*

Arising early, the men sat by a small fire outside; women in the small house in Nini's compound where I slept sat inside talking. Nini's father and Oldyo discussed where to make the *mabwaita* shrine, and cleared brush from the site they selected. Níní's parents, who lived nearby and were "borrowing" the ceremony, arrived around eight in the morning.

After tea, young people prepared to go search the forest for *koroseek* saplings for the ceremony's opening procession. Only the three initiates to be secluded at a house in Nini's compound were present. The other three left from Tinkili's home, where they would be secluded, in a parallel search and

Table 4: Sequence of Ritual Events in Girls' First Initiation Ceremony (*Kepa Tuumto*)

Time	Event	
Early morning	Young people go to the forest for saplings	
	Elders build and bless the *mabwaita* shrine	
	Singing procession of young people with saplings to the *mabwaita*	
	Host mother anoints all present with fat	
	Elders bless	
Later morning	Girls give out sweets and chewing gum	General Focus
	Children eat honey	
	Elders drink one pot of beer	
	Girls sing and dance	
Early afternoon	Flag raised with names picked by girls	
Late afternoon/ early evening	Women go to the forest, return in singing procession with posts and vines, to the *mabwaita*	
	Elders bless procession, posts, and vines	
	Men of the girls' fathers' age-set build the *toloocik* platform (host father brews honey wine on it)	
	Elders bless *toloocik*	
Sunset	Girls' heads shaved by their mothers	
	Girls dressed in dance costume	
Evening	Girls sing and dance	
Night	Girls sing individual farewells	
Sometime between 12–2 A.M.	Men make encouraging speeches to girls (*ceerseet*) (Perhaps more dancing)	Girls as Central Focus
Between 3–5 A.M.	Girls confess their social debts (*pesenweek*)	
Between 4–5 A.M.	Girls taken into women's house for secrets	
Dawn	Girls excised	
Later	Girls begin seclusion and recuperation	
	Others begin to celebrate	

procession. As the initiates sang in their songs, it was time for farewell; the day had come for the brave ones to go.

Each initiate draped a beaded leather skirt (*ntetut,* pl. *ntetusyek*) around her shoulders; this is the costume of ritual actors in all Okiek ceremonies. They would wear the *ntetusyek* until they were dressed in dance costumes at sunset. Two young men also wore *ntetusyek.* One of them, good-hearted Sanare, also carried a hive adze. He would give the girls *koroseek* saplings to carry.

With costumes in place, off we went—eight young men, six girls, three initiates, and me. The trip was high-spirited, with much joking and laughter. Now and then a few people raced ahead in exhilaration, then rejoined the group. The initiates wore their legbells and blew dance whistles as we walked. After climbing through the forest for about forty-five minutes, people spread out to look for *koroseek.* The initiates and I stayed with Sanare.

Shouts announced saplings discovered. "Is it a good one?" Sanare called back. The first saplings were for the initiates and must have no torn or spotty leaves. Sanare also showed me that their saplings should have buds at the tip. When he found an appropriate one, he tapped it four times with the hive adze, then uprooted it and handed it to Nini, establishing her as first in the order the initiates would follow during their months of initiation.

With the initiates following, he looked for two more good ones, tapped and uprooted each the same way, and handed one to each in turn. The initiates would hold their saplings until the operation the following dawn. Once the first was found, other young people throughout the forest began gathering other *koroseek,* simply cutting them at the base. When everyone had saplings to carry, we started back.

In the last small clearing before the village, we formed a processional line. Sanare led, followed by the other young man in ritual garb, other young men, the initiates in order, and finally the other girls. I continued alongside, photographing and recording. Since I was laden with equipment and needed my hands free to work, we put a sapling down the back of my jacket; they insisted I carry one since I had come on the search.

Thus assembled, the procession started home with Sanare calling the first lines of *cepkondook ce leelac,* one of two opening procession songs for girls' ceremonies. The singing began before we could be heard at the houses, so people waiting there heard our approach through the song's increasing volume.[9] As we came down the hill, women came to meet us singing their own song, *celimen,* taking extra saplings to hold, and joining the processional approach to the houses.

The *mabwaita* shrine had not yet been built, though it is usually ready for the *koroseek* arrival. So instead of circling it four times to the right, the procession simply sang its way to the dooryard where it would be made and formed a semicircle open to the rising sun. Still singing, we stood until Nini's mother came with a small black horn of fat with a long sprig of wide green grass in it. She anointed each person's forehead with a dab of fat, beginning with herself, her husband, Oldyo, and Níní's father, and then moving around the semicircle. When she finished, Níní's mother did likewise. Ordinarily only the host mother anoints people, but Níní was her parents' first-born, so her mother did, too.

As they dabbed on fat, Oldyo broke off *koroseek* leaves to close the calabash of honey wine he was holding, making it a ceremonial container. Twice he took a mouthful of wine and sprayed it to the right around the semicircle. He then handed the calabash to another elder,[10] the father of Nini's future husband. He also spat honey wine around the semicircle twice. First Oldyo, then the other elder, blessed the ceremony; the gathering responded jointly to their lines. Both blessed in Maa. With that, the main ritual work of the opening procession was complete. All the *koroseek* saplings except the initiates' were leaned upright against the house, on either side of the doorway. Later, when the *mabwaita* was built, they would be added to make it full. At this point it was about nine-thirty or ten in the morning.

Daytime Activities

People dispersed to sit, talk, or busy themselves with different kinds of "food of the *koroseek*." Nini's father filled a small calabash with honey wine and put in its mouth the same broad grass that was in the anointing horn. As the host father, he held the calabash throughout the ceremony, a sign of his role.

The initiates gave sweets to children and chewing gum to women. As there was little honey, food was cooked for the young people who had gone for *koroseek*. Nini's oldest brother collected clubs, swords, and walking sticks from the men who had arrived and stored the weapons before bringing the first pot of liquor, the food the men were awaiting. When it was set down in Nini's parents' house, men filed in with long drinking straws. About fifteen men were there, including three or four Maasai friends. Others continued to arrive; it was still early. The eight to ten women outside got cups of liquor to drink.

While waiting for food, the young people gathered outside and sang. Girls stood in one circle, singing, while the initiates danced. To one side of them, young men made their own circle, singing age-set songs in Maa and jumping high in the air in pairs.

No ritual events were scheduled for some time, so I visited the other two host houses, that of Tinkili's family and that of Kirutari, Lakwani's father (FaBr). The scenes there were similar. In each compound *koroseek* leaned against the house, a sign of the earlier procession and blessings. Men drank a pot of liquor in the house, with a few sitting outside. Women were outside talking, inside finishing cups of liquor, or helping in various ways.

Only at Tinkili's was the *mabwaita* made. When I got to Kirutari's, between ten-thirty and eleven, things for the *mabwaita* had been brought and a few junior elders had just started it. They drove four thick base poles into the ground, pouring honey wine into the holes from a ceremonial calabash so they would go in deeply and easily. Just before they drove the poles in, Kirutari poured a libation around the base, inviting spirits of his deceased relatives to join the celebration. Poles firmly in place, they added leafy branches and then drank the wine remaining in the calabash. The final tying of the structure was left for later, around three-thirty, when four elers of Kirutari's age-set completed it, binding the base with *nyelwet* and *sinenteet* vines. After filling it out with more leafy branches and *koroseek,* they blessed the *mabwaita* while a larger group of men held the base and shared the prayer.

By early afternoon, all the initiates and young people had met at Kirutari's. By the doorway to the compound's main house, the initiates sang and danced with their girlfriends. Young men sang their own songs up the hill, some jumping high while others moved their heads and shoulders sinuously with the rhythm of the response. After some time, the girls joined them. They soon called me to photograph them together as a remembrance of the occasion (see plate 12).

Someone recalled the flag brought from Melelo market, and someone was sought to put it up in a tree near the house. Two names and amounts were sewn onto it. The first person would raise the flag and pay the first amount (which Lakwani would receive eventually); the second would take it down later and also would pay. Kimnyalul, *maama* to Lakwani (FaSiSo), was supposed to raise it but had not yet come, so another relative climbed high into a nearby tree to tie it in his stead, though Kimnyalul still paid the fee (one to two hundred Ksh, on average). Some weeks later, the husband of Lakwani's sister came to take it down and drink beer provided for him and his friends.

In the late afternoon I returned to Nini's parents' house, where elders were tying and blessing their *mabwaita.* I asked Nini's brother about their flag. He told me the names that were written on it, but so far they had forgotten to put it up. However, Nini's mother had by this time remembered her own ritual costume, the same kind of *ntetut* the initiates were wearing. The other girls' mothers also wore them. The owners of the girls' dance costumes arrived shortly after five o'clock in the afternoon and got their gear ready to dress the girls.

Toloocik *Procession and Shaving*

Meanwhile, four women had gone to the forest in search of *olerienit* poles and *sinenteet* vines for a platform (*toloocik*) inside the host house. Including Nini's future mother-in-law, they were mature women; all had several children. Two wore ritual garb and one carried a hive adze, as in the opening procession in the morning.

I did not go, but late-afternoon forest trips I took at other ceremonies were full of chatter, joking, laughter, and snatches of song. On reaching a suitable *olerienit* tree, the woman with the adze tapped the first branch four times before cutting it through and then continued to cut poles. Finally, they started back carrying the poles, the women adorned with coiled *sinenteet* wreathes on their necks or heads.

Still in the forest, they began to sing *celimen*, the same song women sang to meet the earlier procession. Hearing them approach, women at home also sang and came to meet them, taking wreathes for their own necks and swelling the foursome to a larger procession. They sang their way to the *mabwaita*, past the circle of girls singing their own songs, to stand in a semicircle open to the east. Two elders blessed them with honey wine, and the four women took the poles and vines inside to the hearth.

Two men would soon construct a tablelike platform (*toloocik*), driving its four legs down into the earth after having softened it with honey wine, and lashing crosspoles together with leafy ritual vines. On completion, two elders blessed their construction, and then honey and water were mixed in a leather bag on the platform and would be brewed into wine by the fire while the ceremony continued. The host father often brews this wine, but in this case his age-mate, the father of his daughter's future husband, did it. This honey wine would be the last consumed when the ceremony was about to end.

Meanwhile, outside the three initiates were seated in ritual order facing east on a cow skin, backs to the *mabwaita*, to have their heads shaved. Shortly before, they had been taken to the forest briefly by two young men, Nini's prospective husband and a brother to Níní (MoSiSo) who was also a son of (FaBrDaSo) Nini and Tinkili. There the young men prepared a secret charm (-*rat uusiik*) to ensure the girls' bravery the following day and lessen their pain.

In previous ceremonies, each girl had sat in a similar position to have her head shaved. A newly shaved head in those situations was part of a girl's maturation, which was also marked by new names, the gathering of relatives and friends, and other things. Hair growth regularly marks a change of status and ceremonial participation for Okiek, whether it is the full growth of hair worn by initiates and new mothers in their shared state of pollution, the trimmed perimeter of ritual teachers, or the newly shaven head of initiates coming out (see chapter 5). As their last childhood day ends, girls leave their childhood hair behind, preparing to enter the seclusion phase of initiation with their sunrise operation.

The sun was sinking at about five-thirty, when a small honey basket (*paleito*) of honey water was brought with which to shave the girls' heads. Nini was shaved by her married sister; Seraset and Níní were shaved by their mothers. Starting at the right side of the head, they scraped off the girls' hair and then their eyebrows while other girls stood behind the *mabwaita*, singing farewell and encouragement to the initiates. The initiates sat with their eyes cast down and their legs spread out straight so the hair and honey water would fall between them.

As the shaving continued and the initiates' girlfriends sang, women (mostly the initiates' mothers and sisters) came close and talked sharply to the initiates, telling them to be brave. Just as the shaving was finished, Níní's mother cried with Yaukwik, one of her sisters (FaFaBrDa), saying the time had come for young Níní to go. Yaukwik got increasingly worked up as she thought about it, and just after the girls sang a line mentioning Níní, she had a fit (*-tupuc*).

She cried, called Níní's name repeatedly, told her to go well, and swore she and the others in their family had proven their bravery.[11] Another woman came to hold Yaukwik, talking soothingly and wrapping her arms around from behind to restrain her from thrashing about, falling, and harming the baby on her back. She held her until she calmed down again. Níní and the other initiates simply stood up after being shaved, tied on head scarves, and rejoined their singing friends.

Nighttime Activities

Just about sunset, around seven o'clock, the three girls were taken around to the back of the house to be dressed in dance costume. The costume owners dressed them, starting with Nini, as usual. Over a man's shirt and a short skirt made from a khanga cloth, they wrapped a long striped cloth about three inches wide, around the girl's waist and crisscrossing her torso like bandoliers. A shiny back-apron tied at her waist hung over her buttocks.

Black and white colobus monkey skins sewn onto a frame were fitted on her arms. Finally, a tall miterlike hat was held in place with a face-framing headdress. She held fly whisks that would extend and accentuate her dance movements. Legbells and a whistle completed the costume with an aural accent (see chapter 5 and plate 18).

Okiek do not interpret individual costume elements symbolically, though any part left out would certainly be missed. Rather, the costume as a whole, with its flash and flamboyance, is the important thing. Its particular significance is threefold. First, as part of the temporal progress through initiation, it marks the evening threshold, when the ritual focus on the initiates intensifies and the dramatic tension heightens noticeably. Second, it dramatizes culturally recognized distinctions of song and encouragement between male and female initiation (see chapter 7). Finally, it is part of the aesthetic of song and dance integral to the ceremony and participants' experiences of it. Costumes are judged later in the evening, according to criteria combining overall style and dance movement.

By the time all three were dressed, around nine o'clock, a large bonfire lit the dance arena by the _mabwaita_. The girls danced a bit, testing the fit of their costumes, and paused for adjustments. They danced in the firelight, singing back and forth with their girlfriends, for about an hour and then rested, sitting on chairs at the _mabwaita_ to eat as an older woman stood by. She would be one of their ritual leaders, and subtly began taking charge of the girls she would guide over the next months. Metalala was the wife of Oldyo, the elder who blessed the opening procession and who was brother to Nini's father.

Though the girls continued to sing and dance, they were waiting expectantly for the other initiates to come join them from Tinkili's house with other young people. Around eleven o'clock, they gave matches and cigarettes to Nampet and another girlfriend to help them as they sang farewells to relatives and friends. They sang the same songs they had been singing all day with their girlfriends. But now, during this special musical encouragement (_ceerseet_), the initiates called individuals into the dance arena and addressed them in song.

The first singled out was Seraset's older brother (also Nini's brother and Níní's _maama_ [MoBr]). He stood silently as they sang farewell and reassurance; their last lines instructed Nampet to give him three cigarettes. One of Níní's brothers (MoSiSo) was next. As he listened, he was overcome with emotion, as Yaukwik was earlier, and fell down in a fit. Though it is described in the same term (-_tupuc_), a young man's fit is more physical than verbal, with none of a woman's pleas, curses, and cries. He, too, was held until he calmed down.

The girls continued singing farewells to their sisters, brothers, brothers' wives, and other maternal relatives (_maama_) until after midnight, pausing only for a dance interlude and then a rest. Many of the young men called up fell into fits, moved by the songs and the situation; several women sang answers in short dialogic exchanges.

Around one in the morning, the girls started to sing and dance again, though individual farewells had ended with the last of the cigarettes. They thought they heard the others whistling as they came through the forest, but were mistaken. Two young men argued and were admonished: people do not fight during ceremonies. Nini's married sister got worked up during the singing; she, too, cried and had a fit.

Since sunset, most older adult men had been in the outer room of Nini's parents' house, talking and drinking beer while the girls danced and sang outside with the crowd of young people and women. Many older women had also stayed inside, sitting in the inner room near the hearth or the doorway to the outer room. Shortly after one o'clock, people decided it was time to talk to the initiates. The beer pot was topped up, the men outside returned and resettled themselves, and three chairs were set near the doorway to the inner room.

The initiates danced in, blowing their whistles, and sat in order on the chairs. Nini's mother sat on the ground next to her daughter to receive gifts from speakers and store money for the girls' use after seclusion. Like the songs outside, the speeches were also *ceerseet,* encouragement. They shared themes and phrases, though they were developed quite differently, as befitted their performers' different social roles and statuses (see chapters 6 and 7).

Nini's father spoke first, to call for attention and open the way for others. He had a cold, was very hoarse, and was barely audible as he started. A man of few words, he was very succinct (see Kratz 1988c:634–41). He pointed to all the guests assembled and lay responsibility for the gathering squarely on Nini. She had debated and decided in her own heart that her initiation time had come; she had told her father to invite the guests. They had come and now it was up to her and the others to feed them with the ready food and drink by showing bravery. In closing, he gave a gift of twenty shillings, rising to present it to Nini and her mother. They received it together with cupped hands.

No speech followed immediately. Several men explained the speech procedure in case some did not understand. Then, through the low hum of conversation, Nini's older brother spoke. He stressed all his work on the girls' behalf, for example, in finding their costumes, and also pointed to the people who had come at the initiates' request. Encouraging them with twenty shillings, he told the girls to go bravely, not to shame all who had worked for the ceremony and all who had come to witness and celebrate it.

The speeches continued, each man speaking in order around the room. Some said only a few sentences. Others gave long, involved speeches to encourage the girls, showing acute anxiety by the way they talked (see chapter 6). At times, drunken conversation nearly overpowered the speeches, and the group's attention had to be refocused. I was the only woman to speak at this ceremony, and I used the same themes and phrases as others. When the men had finished, the girls rose and went back outside, whistling and dancing. An older woman told the men to leave and relinquish the house now to women's ceremonial work (though this was more a warning, as not all the men left right away).

Other girls who were singing with the initiates had gone to sleep by this time. The initiates sat on chairs by the fire while others chatted. Finally, around two-thirty, the other three initiates could be heard whistling as they came closer. They had waited until their own fathers and brothers had encouraged them at Tinkili's house. When they were near, the others began whistling and dancing. The two groups of girls joined with a new burst of energy in a long, strenuous dance to their whistle rhythms.

As their costumes were readjusted afterward, women came to take the girls, saying it had become late. The men refused to let them go, claiming it was still extremely early. Inside Nini's parents' house (now the women's ritual house), women began singing secret songs while the girls were changed into nighttime back-aprons to dance while their costumes are judged.

Around four in the morning, the dancing stopped and a discussion began about the girls' confession of social debts (*pesenweek*). A young Kipchornwonek man from Nkaroni, Tiongik, asked them about their wrongs and announced the arguments and the acts of disobedience that were confessed. Nini's brother assisted.[12] In the background, women were singing secret songs in their ritual house.

The young men lined the initiates up in order at the *mabwaita,* then handed Nini, the first, a *korosyaat* sapling to hold, enjoining her to truth and candor. Tiongik told the girls to describe times they had angered or cursed adults. Nothing was to be hidden, whether they had annoyed young men by refusing amorous advances or women by refusing to do errands.

With some prompting, Nini spoke, softly and hesitantly describing an argument with her mother. Tiongik turned to the crowd and repeated what she had reported, in slightly altered form. She named two more arguments with women, and after more prompting began to describe disagreements with young men. After each account, Tiongik turned to announce it to the audience, who could not hear her whispers or the interrogation that filled in details. Only when she insisted repeatedly that she could remember no more did Tiongik go on to the next girl in line.

When all had finished, people said the elders should curse anyone who still might be holding a grudge against the girls, since that person might charm the initiates and cause them to cry when cut. In this case, the curse was never organized; the excuse later was that people were too drunk to remember. They did, however, anoint the girls to show their good intentions toward them. Each person came forward, took a dab of fat from a small horn, spit into their hands, and then rubbed a blessing of fat and saliva down the girls' faces. The men began, and were followed by the women. With that, the last public ritual event before excision was finished.

The girls stayed in line at the *mabwaita.* As they waited, two young men stepped forward. One of them, Tinkili's boyfriend, took her hand and pushed a beaded bracelet onto her wrist, his last gesture of encouragement. It would be returned in a few hours, after her operation, if she demonstrated bravery. Several women came from their ritual house to claim the girls, this time without protest. They were taken into the house in ritual order.

Tata and the other two girls were said to be lurking nearby, planning to sneak into the house and steal the ceremony. Yalakwet, a man who may enter both men's and women's secret houses,[13] was put on guard to prevent this from happening.[14] It was five-thirty in the morning when the girls went in for their introduction to initiation secrets. The procedures of this first night included trials with stinging nettles (a physical trial with an anesthetic effect before the ultimate test).

Operation and Celebration

Less than an hour later, a number of women came back out. They moved *koroseek* saplings held in their right hands up and down slowly, singing two songs to announce dawn and the imminent operation. Men and women alike later told me they felt overwrought at the sound of those songs; it is a moment of great anxiety because the moment of truth has finally arrived. "You're crying [inside]. You just die, don't you? You don't know whether they will wait bravely or fear and cry out."

People who had been sleeping awoke and gathered again outside. More women emerged from the ritual house to join the waiting assembly. Those who would hold the girls from behind during the operation[15] broke *koroseek* leaves from the *mabwaita* for the initiates to sit on. One surgeon came from the house and told people to move back and not to crowd them.

At six-thirty, the girls' whistles started again inside the ritual house. Another surgeon emerged, wearing the beaded *ntetut* of a ritual actor. She struck the hide covering the doorway, and the senior ritual leader, also wearing an *ntetut* and holding *koroseek* leaves, came backwards out the door. The girls followed in ritual order, with the junior ritual leader, in the same attire, coming last. The whistles pierced the early morning as the procession slowly circled the *mabwaita* twice to the right. Suddenly, the girls sat on the ready leaves with their legs spread wide, each grasped firmly from behind, and the three surgeons began their work, excising each girl's clitoris and labia majora. The result, as Okiek see it, made their genitals "smooth" and "clean," as adult women's should be.

People edged forward until young men with switches forced them back from the women quickly cutting the girls' genitals. After what seemed to me a long time, the whistles began again. The operations were over, without a blink or a sound from the six girls. Men and women both rejoiced in song.

The girls were stripped of dance costumes by their mothers and the women they were leaning against. They lay collapsed, at least one looking as if she was in shock, but all the time blowing their whistles. Wrapped now in blankets, they got up with some assistance and stood, legs apart and blood dripping. Their leg bells were jingled until the costume owners claimed them; they were tied with *sinenteet* vines as a sign of the girls' success. Finally, the girls walked, awkwardly stooped and with their legs apart, to the small house in the compound where three of them would later be secluded. Some had to be carried.

Women sang "We want to rejoice," their song of celebration, with punctuating ululation and shouts of thanks for the girls' bravery and success. Men danced in a line, singing their own celebration song, *riret*. Nini's father looked like he had been crying a bit. The jubilant turmoil of this immediate celebration continued for some twenty minutes before people started to quiet down.

Nini's father would wear a necklace of heavy dark blue beads on his head all day, a lineage tradition that his younger brother, Tinkili's father, also followed. The girls' mothers would have the perimeter of their heads shaved the next day; their hair would then be left to grow until the girls emerged from seclusion (this head of hair is called *ol masi*).

Eventually preparations began for the sustained celebration with drink and food that would continue all day and night and into the next day. It was well after nine in the morning before tea was prepared for the guests at Nini's house, though the other two hosts had already served tea and started with maize beer by then. A special beer pot was reserved for the mother's relatives (*imaamook*) in each house. They alone drank that beer, with others they invited to share it. One of them tied the pot with *sinenteet* vines at the start and then gave a gift (such as a sheep) to the girl whose courage fed them. Another untied it later with a comparable gift.

On the first day of the celebration, each compound house had at least twenty to thirty men and fifteen to twenty women guests. Divided among the compound's houses by age as necessary, they sat drinking, talking, singing, and listening and dancing to a rented record player. The drinking was interrupted once or twice for food, ugali with bowls of beef stew. Many people drank all night long.

When the liquor finally began to run out the next day, the guests made short speeches thanking their hosts and presenting gifts intended for the initiate. Gradually people drifted off, heading home in the satiated exhaustion and exhilaration of a successful ceremony. What the girls promised in song, they had indeed fulfilled: "We will go until every person rejoices" (*kipeenti ot kosiim ciit tukul*).

The Healing Interval

While others rejoiced, the girls lay on their backs in the seclusion house, knees bent and legs wide apart. Their pain showed. A blazing fire kept them warm. When they came in they had been fed milk; porridge was cooked later as well. Close female relatives and other older women visited the girls soon after the operation. When they entered, they spat toward them lightly, as to a newborn child.

The girls were now *taarusyeek* (initiates), no longer children but not yet adult women. The first seclusion ceremony would be held after their wounds had healed. Until then, they could not hold things and did little for themselves. They could not touch food, but used leaves and sticks to eat. They could not stir the fire if it dimmed, or do any kind of work. In the early days, they were able only to sit in the sun, sleep, and eat. As their wounds healed, they gradually regained mobility. Throughout seclusion they would speak softly, refrain from washing, and hide themselves from adult men. *Taarusyeek* and their distinctive activities, prohibitions, and costume changes will be discussed further in chapter 5.

Immediately after the operation, the girls' health was a major concern. To help healing and compensate for blood lost, a sheep was slaughtered for them to eat meat and drink fat. Medicine was put on their wounds daily. I provided hydrogen peroxide and antibiotic ointments for these girls; usually it would be oil with powdered herbs.

When the ritual leaders left after the ceremony, they told the girls' parents to keep them together in one seclusion house. Displeased by that for various reasons, their parents took Tinkili, Lakwani, and Cepopoo to stay with Tinkili's mother three days later. They could still coordinate with the other girls' families and join them again for seclusion ceremonies, they said.

The initiates were in a relatively quiet healing period at this point, but their ceremony had been a clear sign that nubile young women would soon be available for marriage. Almost immediately, prospective suitors began to visit each girl's parents. Marriage proposals, politics, and negotiations became increasingly frequent during seclusion, until each family decided on their daughter's future husband.[16] The suitors' final visits to the girls' families and the weddings themselves were planned for shortly after the end of seclusion. Meanwhile, despite seclusion restrictions, the girls found ways to exchange messages of undying love with their boyfriends.

As these six initiates rested and gradually healed before their first seclusion ceremony, preparations continued for the remaining three who had yet to begin the journey to adulthood. Ruruya's shaving ceremony, which had delayed their initiation, was held ten days later. The same frenzied activity, travel, market visits, and preparation fill the next weeks for these families. Finally, on 1 July 1983, three weeks after the first girls went, the others followed in their footsteps. They entered a third seclusion house at Tata's the following day.

Seclusion Ceremony I: Kelap Euun

In late July and early August, I was away in other parts of Kenya. When I returned, the first seclusion ceremony, *kelap euun,* had already been held for each group of initiates, five to seven weeks after the first ceremony. I met initiates wearing the costume of the second seclusion phase and saw their seclusion houses with the bushy-fenced outside yards (*kaaptiryaang'et*), which had been built during *kelap euun.* This is a secret ceremony, and I could not have attended it. From discussions and outside attendance at other ceremonies, however, the following sketch emerges.[17] Table 5 outlines ritual events in the two seclusion ceremonies described here and in the next section.

For the first seclusion ceremony, the two *matireenik* (ritual leaders) come in the late afternoon, between five and seven o'clock, along with other women from nearby settlements and the initiates' female relatives from farther away. Some time after dark, after exchanging news, chatting, and tasting the liquor for the ceremony, all but initiated women are told to leave so that the house they are in can become the women's ritual house and the ritual leaders can begin their work. The men go drink in another house in the compound.

Table 5: Sequence of Ritual Events in Seclusion Ceremonies

First ceremony of seclusion (*Kelap euun*)[1]

Time	Event
Evening	*Matireenik* (ritual leaders) and guests arrive at house of family hosting ceremony
After dark	Men told to leave and drink elsewhere
Night (?)	*Matireenik* show initiates clay and charcoal body paint *Matireenik* give initiates costume, ornaments, and staffs
Night (?)	*Matireenik* show initiates to wash hands with bamboo containers
Night	*Matireenik* show initiates women's secrets ⌐ in some Initiates taught women's songs ⌐ alternation Secrets end with arrival of *ceemaasiit* (not revealed)
Around dawn (?)	Procession to river (?) and to circle archway built at crossroads
Morning	Initiates and *matireenik* build leafy enclosure outside *Matireenik* build the *mabwaita* shrine and miniature houses inside enclosure

Second ceremony of seclusion (*keuuitos suumoosyek*)[2]

Time	Event
Usually before the ceremony	*Suumuut* enclosure built
Evening	*Matireenik* (ritual teachers) and guests arrive
After dark	Men told to leave and drink elsewhere
Night	*Matireenik* show initiates women's secrets ⌐ in some Initiates taught women's songs ⌐ alternation Secrets end with arrival of *ceemaasiit* (not revealed)
Morning	*Matireenik* plaster and decorate doorway to *suumuut*

1. Order and timing of events is tentative. Some events may be missing.
2. Some events may be missing.

Kelap euun brings initiates into the more active seclusion period. With their painful wounds healed, they move about more freely and begin to use their hands again to eat, do beadwork, mud the inside walls of houses, and split firewood. This first seclusion ceremony shows the initiates all the activities allowed during seclusion and the prescribed ways of doing them. The most salient visual sign of the initiates' progress through initiation is the costume change that begins then, while the *kaiyantaaita* songs they are taught and begin to sing daily at sunrise and sunset are the clearest audible sign. Both are part of *kelap euun*.

Initiates are dressed in the new costume in ritual order by their *matireenik*. They are first shown how initiates apply white clay (*inturotoit*) and charcoal to their bodies, then are dressed bit by bit, with auspicious, ritual repetitions of four, in the skin clothing and ornaments they will wear until seclusion is over. Finally, they are given staffs to carry.

For the first time since excision, initiates wash their hands, learning a special way to be used until they come out. The *matireenik* give each initiate her own long, hollow piece of bamboo (about 75–90 centimeters long), filled with water and plugged with stiff *sekutik* grass. To wash her hands, she holds the bamboo between her legs and tips water out.

During the night, women periodically teach and test the initiates in *kaiyantaaita*, singing other songs in between while drinking. Some of their songs are secret ones the girls will learn eventually; others are ordinary ones sung anytime. Some secret songs are associated with the revelation of particular ritual secrets.

Also during the night, initiates are shown a series of these secrets for the first time. They are brought one by one in ritual order to where the *matireenik* have made the secret, asked about it, and shown what it is, sometimes with cryptic comments and directions about what they should do. Late at night, the song and frightening roar of *ceemaasiit* (wild creature) is usually heard, the only secret kept from initiates until the end of seclusion.

Kelap euun involves at least one procession.[18] The *matireenik,* or women they select, build an archway (*oormariicet*) in the bush at the nearest crossroads. Suspended above is a nest of biting ants. When the procession reaches the arch, the naked initiates are told to circle it four times while the nest is hit and ants fall on them. As with other ordeals, they must endure the bites without showing discomfort or pulling the ants off. Their fortitude is both further training and a demonstration of their capacity for adult control. At the same time, it is a lesson in obedience to and respect for their ritual leaders and elders.

Kelap euun ends with finishing the building of the seclusion area the next morning, when most guests have already left. Working with the *matireenik* and a few older women, the initiates make a fence of leafy branches at the side of their seclusion house. This small enclosure (*kaaptiryaang'et*) gives them a place to sit outside and still be hidden. Inside it, the *matireenik* build a small *mabwaita* shrine, consecrating the place of secret ritual as the other, larger one does the space of public ritual. Finally, they make miniature houses at its base, one for each initiate in order. They put sodom apples, representing the initiates' children, inside, concealed from the initiates. When the *matireenik* leave, they tell the girls to care for their houses, to keep them mudded well. When they return for the next seclusion ceremony, they will see whether initiates have done as they were told.

Seclusion Ceremony II: Ketuuitos Suumoosyek

The next seclusion ceremony, *ketuuitos suumoosyek,* brings few changes for the initiates. They continue the activities and restrictions started at *kelap euun,* still singing daily, smearing white clay on their bodies, hiding themselves from adult men, and so on. The ceremony takes its name from *suumuut,* the enclosure built inside the seclusion house (like a room within a room), and is in many ways a repetition of *kelap euun.* The initiates are again shown women's secrets, and their knowledge of songs is tested. The *suumuut* is often made before the ceremony, but the initiates' doorway (the enclosure has two, one for the initiates and one for other women) is plastered and decorated at its close.

Ketuuitos suumoosyek was celebrated for each initiate group, four to six weeks after *kelap euun* and eleven weeks after the first ceremony. Disagreements over the timing of ceremonies for the first six initiates continued to the end. In late August, both Nini's and Tinkili's households were brewing liquor.

Tinkili's mother said all six initiates would celebrate *ketuuitos suumoosyek* jointly at her house, where the beer would be ready first. Nini's group would come out of seclusion a few days later, when the other beer, at Nini's house, would be ready; those at Tinkili's home didn't yet have the clothes and beads needed to come out. Nini's mother, however, said the two groups would celebrate separately, with Nini's group combining *ketuuitos suumoosyek* and the final coming-out ceremony. That is, in fact, what happened, though the unpleasant feelings between such closely related households surprised and dismayed the ritual leaders and gave others a topic for gossip.[19]

Early on the evening of 25 August, women again came to Tinkili's. As each guest entered the seclusion area, the initiates broke into a *kaiyantaaita* song of greeting. They sat against the wall as they sang, covering their bodies with their hide capes in case new arrivals should find the singing inadequate and switch them. The *ceptoloolny'aat,* the young girl who eats the initiates' polluted (*kereek*) leftovers, also had white clay on her face for the ceremony, though she did not attend.

The ritual leaders arrived around six-thirty in the evening, and the men were chased from the house so that the girls could emerge from the *suumuut* enclosure or come inside from the yard. The leaders were given tea, food, and a taste of the liquor. At about nine o'clock, they prepared to make the first ritual secret over in the corner. Since they were ready to start their work, I, too, was asked to leave.

The women inside began their songs while the initiates sang *kaiyantaaita* in the enclosure outside. The women continued singing with short pauses until close to midnight, when a song usually sung for *ceemaasiit* began, punctuated with yelps and shouts. A woman who came out shortly afterward told me they had shown the initiates two out of the night's four secrets.

Men had meanwhile been drinking beer, talking, and singing about elephant hunts in a nearby house. As they got more intoxicated and their beer dwindled, some made joking forays to or mock attacks on the women in the seclusion house to try for more. They, as well as the women, would drink all night if there was enough beer.

Women resumed the ritual work and singing around one-thirty in the morning. Some four hours later, with all else done, the sound of *ceemaasiit* was heard, though it had yet to be shown to the girls. At dawn, the initiates greeted the day, by singing *kaiyantaaita*. Later, around seven-thirty, the women's rituals were over, and once the initiates had gone back into the *suumuut* enclosure or out into the yard, the men were allowed back into the house.

In the early daylight hours, Tinkili's mother raised several matters with the *matireenik* and other old women who were present. Some were disciplinary, for example, about initiates who had violated seclusion prohibitions by cooking food. She also mentioned that peculiar things had been found on the path, suggesting that someone wanted to charm the initiates. Such matters needed to be discussed openly when the women gathered for ceremonies; they could make initiates sick or barren if they were left hidden to fester.

Finally, around ten o'clock, the two *matireenik* closed the top of the initiates' *suumuut* doorway with sticks (the other door is for the women guests). After some secret procedures, they mudded the area and decorated it with three vertical rows of sodom apples joined by a horizontal bottom row. Two interpretations of the decoration were explained to me. First was an iconic relation: the initiates should have children as plentiful as the fruits. The second relates the fruits to chains on the initiates' headdresses; both protect them from bad eyes and evil wishes.

Coming Out of Seclusion: Kelong'u en Aineet

Two days later, the same ritual leaders go to Nini's house to celebrate the combined *ketuuitos suumoosyek* and *kelong'u en aineet* (coming out of seclusion, lit. coming up from the river) for the other three initiates. The coming-out ceremony I describe here continues to follow the initiates at Tinkili's house, who were the last to come out. Table 6 outlines its sequence of ritual events.

By late September, two of the three seclusion groups had emerged as young women, about three months after initiation began. The final trio waited another full month before their parents got the clothing, beer ingredients, and other things needed for their final ceremony. *Kelong'u en aineet* was held for Tinkili, Lakwani, and Cepopoo in late October.

Like the other secret seclusion ceremonies, this, too, began in the evening. The two *matireenik* arrived slightly earlier, around four in the afternoon, to prepare a structure that would be used at the river the following dawn. By dusk, the women had gathered in Tinkili's parents' house, where the initiates were secluded. The men were sent elsewhere to drink, the initiates emerged, and by eight-thirty, the ritual leaders were preparing the first secret to show the girls.

The initiates' knowledge of *kaiyantaaita* songs was tested again, and women again sang their secret songs through the night. For the last time as initiates, the girls were shown women's secrets. This time, none remained hidden. They were even shown women's secret *ceemaasiit,* and eventually each held it and produced its galumphing roar herself. From the outside, I heard *ceemaasiit* around two in the morning; after that a lull seemed to fall inside the house.

Late in the night, the initiates were lectured a final time about how adult women should behave, respecting people and staying at home, not roaming to look for men. The speech can be quite loud and abusive. They were also told not to tell women's secrets; a curse was said which would kill them if they did. The remaining secrets, including the "children" inside their miniature houses, were revealed to the initiates before they went to the river.

At the first light of dawn, between five-thirty and six in the morning, the *matireenik* took the initiates to the river with the other women. They led a final secret procedure using something reminiscent of a secret structure made the first night of initiation. Finally, the young women bathed for the first time since seclusion began. Then, wearing blankets as they did just after their operations, the girls were brought from the river in procession, hidden under other blankets.

While the women were at the river, the host father and other men collected materials to refresh the *mabwaita* and add an arch (*oormariicet*) onto it. Leafy sticks were put into the base of the *mabwaita*. More leafy sticks were put into the ground four to five feet away, and the two bunches of sticks were bent toward each other and tied together forming an arch. Two pairs of cross-sticks through the arch, meeting at the ground, would soon be used to open the way for the initiates.

Men also made a *sirtiityet* for each initiate and for the child who ate their seclusion food. The *sirtiityet* is an uprooted *korosyaat* sapling, like the one

Table 6: Sequence of Ritual Events in Final Initiation Ceremony (*Kelong'u en Aineet*)[1]

Time	Event
Evening	*Matireenik* (ritual leaders) and guests arrive at the house of the family hosting the ceremony
After dark	Men told to leave and drink elsewhere
Night	*Matireenik* show initiates women's secrets ⌐ in some Initiates taught women's songs ⌐ alternation Secrets end with arrival of *ceemaasiit,* finally revealed Initiates shown contents of miniature houses
Dawn	Initiates, *matireenik,* and other women go to river, pass through river structure, and then bathe
Early morning	Elders build archway onto the *mabwaita* shrine and make *sirtiityet* saplings
Morning	Women come from river in singing procession, circle the *mabwaita* for blessing, then go to nearby bush Initiates anointed and dressed in young women's finery Procession returns to circle the *mabwaita* while elders bless *Matireenik* and initiates kneel at archway facing east Way opened for each initiate by her brother Each initiate and the *ceptoloolny'aat* child given *sirtiityet* by her brother (father for the child) *Matireenik* and *piitintet* (blesser) receive payment from initiates' parents[2] Silent procession of *matireenik* and initiates to house where young women will sleep
Late morning/ early afternoon	People begin to celebrate
The following morning	*Matireenik* and initiates return to the *mabwaita* First initiate's father twists and cuts her *sirtiityet* First initiate's mother shaves daughter's head Secret done Initiates eat together in first initiate's home People drink and celebrate *Matireenik* and initiates continue in procession to each initiate's home in turn where cutting, shaving, and eating are repeated[3]

1. Some events during the secret part at night may be missing.
2. Payment is sometimes made before opening the way.
3. Sometimes done for several initiates at one home.

from the first day of initiation. For coming out, however, it has a bit of sheepskin on the bottom branch, propolis plastered to its bottom joint, and in some cases a spiral cut beneath the propolis.[20] The child's *sirtiityet* was short; she was like the smallest initiate. When all was ready, they awaited the women's arrival.

As they neared home the women started the two songs for young women coming from the river. Both stress the value and fertility of the now marriage-able women, calling them "heifers" or "cows." Women punctuated the songs with shouts, such as "For the quick one!"[21] When women at home heard their song, they went to meet them and join the song.

It was nearly nine-thirty in the morning when the procession approached. The senior *matiriyaat* led the singing group, followed by the initiates in order and the junior *matiriyaat* behind. The *matireenik* held blankets in place to hide the young women from men. The procession approached *mabwaita* and the arch, and circled it four times to the right while an elder sprayed a blessing of honey wine on them. Without stopping, the women went off singing to a nearby place in the bush.

There, the initiates removed their blankets and sat on skins. Other young women (such as their BrWi or Si) rubbed them liberally with fat until their bodies glistened, and adorned them with bead necklaces, bracelets, and ear-rings of many kinds. Their hair was full, having grown during the four months of initiation. The perimeter of their heads and their eyebrows were shaved at this time. A single strand of blue, white, and red beads was their simple headdress (*inkeeriiny'ot*). Finally, the other young women tied new cotton cloths over one shoulder of each initiate.

Ritual leaders took over then, putting a beaded leather skirt (*ntetut*) around each girl's waist and another over her shoulders. Their waists were wrapped in a ritual procedure during which a belt of *sinenteet* vines was put to the body four times before being tied. Gleamingly resplendent, the initiates were tucked back under their blankets as the procession reformed.

Singing the same songs, they returned to the *mabwaita,* again circling four times to the right and being blessed by two elders. This time they stopped. The senior *matiriyaat* knelt at the arch facing east, the initiates in line behind her under the tent of blankets.

Three things were done before the procession left again. First, the mothers of the initiates paid the ritual leaders and the blesser for their initiation services, passing money through the archway four times and spitting bless-ings.[22] Next, the "path" from seclusion was opened for each girl in order by a brother. Each brother stepped forward and named his gift for his sister, be it a sheep or cash money (20–40 Ksh). When she accepted it, he knelt opposite the ritual leader. Grasping the poles in the center of the arch with the ritual leader and his sister (who was still under the blankets), they moved them up and down while the *matiriyaat* led the song for opening the way (*yaatet aap ooreet*) (see chapter 7).

Finally, another brother gave each initiate, again in turn, a prepared *sirtiityet* sapling. That also entailed a gift similar to the first one. When she accepted, the initiate reached from under the blankets to grasp the sapling through the arch, guided by her ritual leader. The last sapling was for the little initiation girl; her father gave her a small gift (5–10 Ksh).

With the day's ritual work virtually finished by eleven o'clock, the ritual leaders and the initiates stood and walked silently in line, still hidden, to the nearby house of Tinkili's brother. The time for song was over. They entered and went to sit on the bed, where the senior *matiriyaat* ritually fed them honey. They would sleep there, with Tinkili's brother's wife as hostess, until the final acts brought them out of seclusion the next day.[23] The initiates spent the rest of the day talking and sitting with friends. Though no longer hiding, they were still hesitant when they came outside and shy about being seen even at a distance by men drinking at the other house.

This final ceremony is the second largest of initiation, with guests celebrating with beer throughout the day. When a daughter has "borrowed" initiation, the last ceremony is the major one, celebrated by her family when she arrives home.

The next morning, the initiates returned to stand by the *mabwaita* with their ritual leaders. The first girl's father took her *sirtiityet* and promised her a gift for cutting it; a hive, a sheep, or cash are all acceptable. He warmed the center of the sapling in a small fire of *olerienit* wood, twisted the sapling to the right, and then tapped it four times with a hive adze before cutting it through, putting both halves in the *mabwaita*. The other two initiates' saplings would be cut the same way when each reached her parents' home.

The initiates then sat on a cow skin, facing east with their backs to the *mabwaita*. The first girl's mother promised a gift of about 20 Ksh, and then shaved her daughter's head using milk from a small basket usually used for honey. Rubbing her clean head with fat, she replaced the beads (*inkeeriiny'ot*) from the day before with a multicolored beaded band with a projection (*enkishilit* <Maa) (see plates 30, 31). She also replaced the beaded skirt around her daughter's shoulders with a new cotton cloth, leaving the leather skirt around her waist.

The *matireenik* and the initiates then did something secret to let them leave their joint initiation home and go their separate ways. Then they filed into the home of Tinkili's mother to eat together for the first time as young adult women. Before feeding them, Tinkili's mother promised her another small gift (10–20 Ksh). Afterward, the young women waited outside until the *matireenik* were ready to proceed.

After drinking beer for some time, the ritual leaders reformed the procession. They continued to the second initiate's home, where her *sirtiityet* was cut and her head shaved. The initiates ate together again in that house; that mother gave her daughter a similar gift. Again the *matireenik* drank and ate while the young women waited outside, talking and sitting in the sun. The procession continued, repeating the same procedures at the last initiate's home. If it had been late, they all would sleep at the last house before dispersing to their own homes.

After four months together hiding from adult men and learning the secrets of adult women, the girls had become young women. Prospective suitors continued to visit their parents, though marriage arrangements were in the last stages and were expected to end as soon as possible with a wedding. Ideally, the young women would become new wives within the week.

This chapter has described a particular Okiek initiation in sequence, through time and space, to anchor the following chapters in which I begin to separate the ceremonies into different aspects for analysis. The next section looks at the initiation process in greater detail, analyzing ritual roles, costume, locations, and objects (chapter 5), the speech of initiation (chapter 6), and its songs (chapter 7). Tables in this chapter that outline the sequence of each ceremony can be used again for reference in those chapters.

Plates

This photo essay begins on the first day of initiation, as young people prepare for the opening procession. It illustrates the initiation process outlined in chapter 4, following the sequence of ritual events. The photographs show some of the many people who participated in those ceremonies and suggest the range of their feelings, experiences, and engagements. The essay stops on the final day of the last ceremony, when initiates have emerged from seclusion and become young adult women.

Whenever possible, I have used photographs taken during the specific set of ceremonies described in chapter 4. This includes all photographs taken from Sukustoosyek, Ororueet, Inkouuyuuy, Ng'apng'eenta, and Olesiny'a. In order to cover the full initiation process, however, I have also included pictures that I took at other ceremonies in 1983, 1984, and 1985.

Plate 1. NÍní, Seraset, and Nini (center, in headdresses) prepare for the early-morning *koroseek* procession that begins initiation. As the final touch, Seraset's mother ties a beaded leather cape (*ntetut*) around Nini's shoulders. Sukustoosyek, 10 June 1983.

Plate 2. After a lively search through the forest for the right saplings, young people in the *koroseek* procession return home, singing enthusiastically. Slowing down as they reach the home of the ceremony, these girls squeeze together in line, nearly enveloped by the leafy saplings they have brought. Sapoitit, 12 April 1985.

Plate 3. Nini's mother blesses all present, including Kopot Chepkeric, her oldest daughter, with dabs of fat. Sukustoosyek, 10 June 1983.

Plate 4. Absorbed in the ceremony, the young girls wait their turn to be anointed with fat. Sapoitit, 12 April 1985.

Plate 5. Kwampat Parmasai finishes a spirited blessing, spraying honey wine on the assembled group. The processional saplings will be used later to build a *mabwaita* shrine. Sukustoosyek, 10 June 1983.

Plate 6. After the opening procession, elders savor the first beer of the ceremony. Sipping from the beer pot through long straws, they exchange news and stories in the house that young men decorated with newspapers. Sukustoosyek, 1 July 1983.

Plate 7. Meanwhile, initiates sing outside with their girlfriends. Níní whistles a fast-paced rhythm for their energetic dancing as they begin the many moving good-byes to be said and sung. S̲u̲k̲u̲s̲t̲o̲o̲s̲y̲e̲k̲, 10 June 1983.

Plate 8. Nini grasps her sapling as she sings, promising to show courage when faced with the trials of initiation. Sukustoosyek, 10 June 1983.

Plate 9. Elders build the *mabwaita* shrine, site of many ritual events in Okiek ceremonies. The treelike structure is a sign of continuity, unity, and cooperation, as well as a marker of ritual space. Sukustoosyek, 1 July 1983.

Plate 10. Oldyo, Kwampat Lakweny'on, Kwampat Olderoni, and Meiboki chat as they bind the base of the *mabwaita* securely. The vines they use, like the branches and poles, all come from species with favorable associations. Sukustoosyek, 1 July 1983.

Plate 11. Parkesui, Indobiwo, and Magerer fasten a flag embroidered with two names firmly to a long pole. Magerer, a brother to one of the initiates, is named first. He will climb high in a nearby tree to lash the flagpole in place, advertising the joyful occasion. Sapoitit, 27 January 1984.

Plate 12. Lakwani (third from left) and Nini (with headdress) pose with some of the young male friends and relatives they are about to leave behind. Inkouuyuuy, 10 June 1983.

Plate 13. Twilight approaches as women from the *toloocik* procession arrive singing, bearing stout poles, and wearing leafy wreathes. As they come the initiates' heads are already being shaved at the *mabwaita* (right). Nkaroni area, 19 April 1985.

Plate 14. Seraset's mother shaves her daughter's head as other mothers work on their own daughters in the background. Sukustoosyek, 10 June 1983.

Plate 15. Níní's shaving is completed as her eyebrows are removed. At right, Nini waits, eyes cast down in controlled reserve. Soon all the initiates will be up singing again. Then their mothers will carefully dispose of the hair piled between the girls' legs and store away the small woven basket that held the honey water used in shaving. Sukustoosyek, 10 June 1983.

Plate 16. Kopot Lemeria led the women's procession, wearing a hyrax cape and carrying a hive adze. The song she sings continues the musical countdown to dawn. Her gravity shows the mounting concern of many of those gathered. Nkaroni area, 19 April 1985.

Plate 17. Sopiato finally wears the dance costume that she sang about and admired on others for years. The young Kipsigis man who owns the costume dresses her with care while young girls watch in awe and fascination. Sinentaaiik, 12 April 1985.

Plate 18. Sopiato is about to reenter the dance arena dressed in her evening dance costume. The man at left owns the costume. He and Kong'ang'ar, Sopiato's mother's brother, display the costume's two back aprons. Sinentaaiik, 12 April 1985.

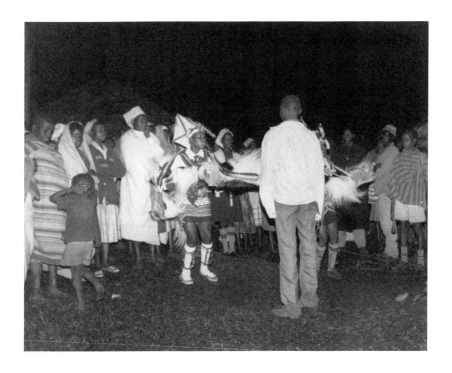

Plate 19. Fully adorned, Kironwa and Sibilon (partially hidden) dance and sing, their costumes tossing and swinging as they encourage the young man they have called forward. Others in the background enjoy the excitement. Nkaroni, 9 December 1983.

Plate 20. As men drink from the beer pot in front, James Rana encourages Sopiato and Jennifer to be brave. Arap Kilese (right) listens intently, but Sopiato's mother (next to initiates) must also attend to her infant. Sinentaaiik, 13 April 1985.

Plate 21. Initiates stand at the *mabwaita* as Benjamin starts to ask them about their social debts (*pesenweek*). Others relax by the fire, waiting for entertaining tales. Sinentaaiik, 13 April 1985.

Plate 22. Men celebrate the initiates' bravery at dawn with maize beer and convivial conversation. The house seems to echo their festive mood, festooned with milk cartons and framed pictures. In the rear corner, the young man in charge of music looks for the right song to play on his rented record player. Sinentaaiik, 12 April 1985.

Plate 23. Kironwa and Sibilon have finished their first seclusion period and been through the *kelap euun* ceremony, as their costumes show. Only in a wooded area, away from homes, could they stand openly to pose; usually initiates hide from adult men. Nkaroni, 12 April 1984.

Plate 24. Cepopoo has yet to blacken her eyes with charcoal, completing the "wild creature" (*ceemaasiit*) image appropriate to a secluded initiate. She smeared the white clay paint on herself, but her friend and coinitiate, Lakwani, traced the face designs for her. Near Ororueet and S̲u̲k̲u̲s̲t̲o̲o̲s̲y̲e̲k̲, 23 August 1983.

Plate 25. The day for the initiates' last ceremony has come. Shrouded from sight under blankets, they are brought home again, returning in procession to the *mabwaita* shrine. Flanked by their ritual leaders, they face Arap Senoi across the *mabwaita*'s new arch as he blesses them with honey wine. Other elders (including the initiates' fathers) watch at left, ready to advise on ritual procedure. Olesiny'a, 22 September 1983.

Plate 26. Ritual leaders Kaina and Kopot Semburi kneel at the *mabwaita* arch, the initiates behind them under blankets. When the right young man is found, he will offer a gift to "open the way" for the first initiate. Olesiny'a, 22 September 1983.

Plate 27. Initiate Semburi holds the special sapling (*sirtiityet*) given to her by Tulagan, her sister's husband. Kaina, one of her ritual leaders, stands by at right. Keeweet, 27 April 1984.

Plate 28. Oldyo twists the special sapling (*sirtiityet*) his child received on coming out of seclusion, having warmed it in a small ritual fire. Initiates receive gifts when accepting the sapling and when giving it up to their fathers the next day. Nkaroni, 8 May 1984.

Plate 29. Even little brothers want to get into the act on the last day of initiation. With this head-shaving at the _ma̱bwaita̱_ shrine, Nampet and Rururya will leave both the hair and the impurity of seclusion behind and enter adult life. Ng'apng'eenta, 23 September 1983.

Plate 30. Ruruya has already donned the *enkishilit* headdress of a young woman. Nampet pauses to hold her infant brother, Tutuna, before putting her own headdress on. Both young women returned to school for a time after initiation. Ng'apng'eenta, 23 September 1983.

Plate 31. Cepopoo's glistening beauty is crowned with her *enkishilit* headdress, sign of a young adult woman. She wears it for the first time in this picture, taken the day she completed initiation and left seclusion. Ororueet, 30 October 1983.

Part 3

Ritual Efficacy through Performance

5

What Goes without Saying: Coordination, Concentration, and Progressions through Nonverbal Means

Through the magic of a world of objects . . . a world in which each thing speaks metaphorically of all the others, each practice comes to be invested with an objective meaning, a meaning with which practices— and particularly rites—have to reckon at all times, whether to evoke or revoke it.

Pierre Bourdieu, *Outline of a Theory of Practice*

This chapter embarks on more detailed analyses of Okiek initiation, considering how the three key processes involved in ritual efficacy figure in ceremonial performances. Each chapter in this section focuses on particular communicative channels and media, which are all combined in performance. The analysis divides and separates what is joined in experience and practice, both by considering the multiple media separately and by distinguishing the three processes of semiotic movement, contextual re-creation, and emotional and experiential engagement. This facilitates understanding how the transformation of initiation works, but media cannot be entirely separated because they refer to, draw on, and combine with one other. Similarly, distinguishing the three processes above analytically separates cognitive and embodied understandings and experiences of initiation that are actually combined and crosscutting. In each chapter, then, I maintain the emphases required for analysis, but bring in other material as needed to understand the processes of ritual efficacy that are being considered.

I begin with nonverbal means that provide coordinated and intersecting itineraries for the journey to adulthood: ritual roles, costume, locations through space and time, and ritual objects. Nonverbal resources communicate a wealth of information throughout the process of initiation, and indeed help constitute the ceremonial experience. Both an essential means of performance and an essential context for speech and song, the appearance and use of these communicative media is scheduled, coordinated, and orchestrated to produce intended ceremonial effects.

The process of semiotic movement emerges especially clearly in nonverbal channels. Semiotic movement involves multiple, coordinated series of signs, each series within a channel and related by some further commonality, such as material or use. Differences and shifts between these related signs, sometimes only details, both represent and effect corresponding changes in the identity, state, stage, and other characteristics of those using them. Individually, each sign is an index of a particular role, place, ceremonial moment, and suchlike. Taken together as an ordered series through time, they define culturally significant progressions within and between ceremonies. Those progressions represent and help accomplish ceremonial transformation over the course of initiation in conjunction with coordinated semiotic movement in other channels. This process is fundamental to the synthetic cohesion that links different media and ritual events so that proceeding through their performative sequence *is* the ritual transformation. Specific progressions will be described below.

Many nonverbal signs of initiation appear in other contexts in slightly different ways, perhaps in other cultural progressions—in other ceremonies as well as in daily routines and practices.[1] Associations and cross-contextual resonances created by multiple, varied occurrences augment the meanings of those signs and also set initiation within the expanded contextual setting and scope of the life cycle, creating progressions that stretch from one ceremony to the next and span the life cycle.

These wide-reaching associations and experiential resonances are also critical to contextual re-creation, the process through which cultural assumptions that are premises for and essential background to initiation's transformation are represented and re-created. The use of particular objects, actions, or materials in particular ways evokes cultural knowledge and experience of other realms of practice and interaction, setting the transformation into adults within a larger world of Okiek society, history, and values. The life of the forest and gender relations are particularly salient in this process.

Repeated use of elements in similar contexts on similar ceremonial occasions can also create a sense of cultural continuity (or change) that both contributes to and draws on evocative and cognitive resonances. This adds another dimension to contextual re-creation, legitimating what is represented and evoked. The sense of continuity helps create "tradition" as a potential means of justifying cultural assumptions, values, and practices. Tradition becomes an adequate reason for doing things as they are done, a counter to questions or proposed changes.

Each nonverbal channel discussed here also contributes to different modes of experiential and emotional engagement in initiation. This is most obvious in ritual roles, but costume, objects, gifts, and so on are accouterments through which roles and events are defined and experienced, while different locations bring different sensibilities to ritual events. Ritual actors use acts and objects charged with associations and personalize general associations with particular individuals and relations. At the same time, new relations are created, or familiar ones amplified in ways that carry into the future.

Representative Roles, General Participation, and Special Relations

The people involved in initiation are central to every analysis that follows, so I start with the patterns and definitions of ritual roles, a sociology of ceremonial participation. It matters who wears costumes, holds objects, moves through different places, gives gifts to whom, consumes food, speaks, or sings. Modes of verbal participation, central in many ceremonial roles, are the focus of later chapters. Forms of ceremonial participation are not nonverbal in the same material sense as costumes or objects, but then the significance of all the ceremonial resources discussed in this chapter is constituted in some part verbally. I group them together because all are contextual background in similar ways. The repertoire of ritual roles for each ceremony is scheduled, just like the repertoire of objects appropriate to a certain ritual act, though who fills the roles in a particular performance must be decided. Similarly, patterns of ceremonial participation help constitute ceremonial structure and are involved in effective transformation in at least three ways that are similar to how other nonverbal media do the same things.

First, different roles constitute semiotic progressions over the course of initiation. Further, metaphorical relations are suggested and created between people in different roles who are formally linked and equated through shared connections in ritual activities, garb, and so forth. Such relations can be one basis of semiotic progressions and can also suggest iconic relations with other aspects of social organization. Finally, ceremonial sections and moments of the initiation process are distinguished structurally by patterns of participation and ritual roles that are coordinated with related patterns in other channels. These structural distinctions are integral to the orchestration of ceremonial experience and engagement.

Everyone at an Okiek ceremony participates in the ritual work, though in different ways. Three modes of participation can be distinguished analytically: representative roles, general participation, and special relations. The three differ in behavior, in relative duration, in whether actors are somehow marked, and in the ways Okiek refer to them. Social categories define appropriate actors in each case. Table 7 summarizes ritual roles and participation in initiation by ritual event.

A small number of people play special, continuing parts in initiation. Visually marked by costume or object for a long, continuous period, they take ritual roles in several events and are centrally involved in the entire initiation process. Apart from the girls themselves (who are marked by costume, objects, and acts throughout), these include their parents and the ritual leaders, both of whom are in special, close relations to the girls. Okiek give distinct names to only a few ritual roles, all of them special relations. I consider initiates and their ritual leaders more closely after examining other patterns of participation.

Representative roles call for a limited number of persons of a particular social category or relation to do specific acts in particular ritual events. The social category defines a large set of possible actors; those selected represent that social identity in the ritual role. Often marked by costume and objects as well as acts, the roles last only for the duration of that event. Okiek discuss these representative roles simply by referring to what people do, for example, the elders who put down the *mabwaita* (*paaiisyonik ce lumtoi mabwaita*), or the women who go for *toloocik* (*ceepyoosook ce peenti toloocik*).

In opening events, representative roles are defined in terms of broad social categories of age and sex. For example, those who lead the first of the two forest processions are young men, and those who lead the second are mature women. Those who actually take the parts are often close relatives of the girls. In the final ceremony, specific relations define the roles—for example, brothers open the way. Important relatives are involved in representative ritual roles, whether by definition or by choice, as well as in other, more widely shared activities. They play a central part in a process that affects them as well as the girls. As the girls' status and social identity are transformed, their relations with others change correspondingly.

While a few people are singled out in representative roles, usually numbering an auspicious two or four, others participate in the same events collectively. They follow, receive, and respond to other ritual actors, or simply watch, listen, and comment as a participating audience. At times, all act as a single group, such as when responding to a blessing. At other times, participants are again divided by broad social categories. In the opening procession, for instance, children and young men follow and sing with the two individuals who lead. They are met by women singing their own song. The leaders often blend into the group as the event proceeds and others join in. Thus, when theprocession circles the *mabwaita,* only costume and adze identify its leader.

The mode of general participation varies in different ritual events: joining processions, responding to blessings or songs, drinking beer and listening to speeches, and so on. Different kinds of general participation are as scheduled as representative ritual roles. The changing sequence of participatory modes is an expected, effective, and affective part of ceremonial experience.[2] It also contributes to the dramatic structure of initiation and the orchestrated framework of emotional and experiential engagement.

All present, for example, are involved in some ritual event of the first ceremony. Through this definition of roles and events, the effort and experience necessarily become collective, though not identical for all. Children, young men, young and mature women, junior and senior elders are all involved in particular ways. Over the course of the ceremony, their different modes and sequences of involvement separate, converge, and interact, the very sequence and patterns defining what the experience of initiation is. All coincide at the climax of dawn excision. Naturally, individual engagement also varies in intensity; people are most concerned about their own daughters, sisters, and girlfriends.

Temporary representative roles carry no special ritual power, though elders who bless and ritual leaders carry a certain weight and authority in those capacities. However, all these ritual activities, especially the ones that involve representative and special roles, entail an effort that needs to be reciprocated. The final column in table 7 shows the exchanges associated with each ritual event. Most participants are compensated with food. People in ritual roles that involve a special skill or continuing involvement are compensated in cash as well. Ritual leaders, the blesser, the circumcisor, and the mother who feeds the girls in seclusion are all paid for their work.[3] Simpole, an Okiek elder, explained:

They eat since they did work, so you have to give them food. Everyone who does work in a ceremony gets something. Those who do the *toloocik* get a calabash [of wine, which they use] to spit [a blessing] on it and then drink [the rest of it]. Anyone who works is given something. You can ask for what you want.

Most ritual work is temporary and enjoyable, not commoditized. As Simpole said, "The work of ceremonies is rejoicing, play, and song."

The consistent alternation of ritual acts and food is articulated in terms of work and compensation, but it is part of a continuing symbolic exchange—a general ceremonial reciprocity rather than the measured exchange of equivalence. The macrostructure of the ceremony replicates and reinforces this microstructural alternation in each ritual event; two or more days of solid celebration follow the first twenty-four hours of ritual work. This broad image

Table 7: Ritual Roles and Participation in Initiation

Ritual Event	Representative Roles and Special Relations (latter marked with *)	General Participation	Associated Exchange
I. FIRST CEREMONY			
Koroseek procession	Leader/follower (with initiates between) Mother* anoints 2 elders bless	Children and young men Women meet/sing All others anointed All others respond and are sprayed	Honey/sweets Chewing gum Pot of beer
Mabwaita shrine	2–4 elders build 2–4 elders bless	Fathers* and others hold	Calabash of liquor shared
Peenteereet (flag)	Raiser/lowerer (initiates select)		Money given Beer received
Toloocik procession	Leader and 3 others 2 of father's age-set build 2 elders bless	Women meet and sing	Calabash of liquor shared Calabash of liquor shared
Silet (shaving)	Mothers* Initiates	Girls/women sing and women might harangue	
Ceerset (farewell songs)	Initiates Those called up	Other young people/ women sing and watch	Cigarettes
Ceerseet speeches	Initiate, mother,* and speaker Father* starts	All elders can speak	Money given
Pesenweek (social debts)	Questioner Initiates Elders curse/bless	Audience listens and anoints	
Tuumwek (secrets)	*Matireenik* (teachers)* Initiates	Other women sing and can help	*Matireenik* paid later

Table 7: *continued*

Ritual Event	Representative Roles and Special Relations (latter marked with *)	General Participation	Associated Exchange
Excision (*tuumto*)	Surgeon Women holding backs 2 *matireenik** Initiates	Audience	Surgeon paid Gift given *Matireenik* paid later
II. SECLUSION CEREMONIES			
Tuumwek secrets, etc.	*Matireenik* (teachers)* Initiates	Other women sing and can help	*Matireenik* paid later
III. COMING OUT			
Yaatet aap ooreet (opening the way)	Brothers Elder *Matireenik* (leaders)* Initiates	Others talk, comment, watch, and might sing	Brother gives gift to initiate Parents pay *matireenik*
Giving *sirtiityet* sapling	Brothers Initiates	Others talk, comment, and watch	Brother gives gift to initate
Kiiilta (going to sleep)	Homeowner Initiates *Matireenik**		Homeowner feeds initiates and gives gift
Twisting *sirtiityet* sapling	Fathers* Initiates	The few present talk, comment, and watch	Father gives gift to initiate
Silet (shaving)	Mothers* Initiates	The few present talk, comment, and watch	Mother gives gift to initiate
Eating food	Mothers* Initiates	The few present pay no particular attention	Mother gives gift to initiate

of reciprocity is used to persuade and encourage the girls in songs and speeches (see chapters 6 and 7). They are made responsible for reciprocating the first day's ceremonial work; they provide the final food through their fortitude and bravery.

Patterns of participation also help structure other sections in the first ceremony, dividing the ritual period in two at sunset. Daytime ritual events are more general, setting the stage and initiating action. The second section of the ceremony focuses increasingly on the initiates, a change of focus that accelerates interactive intensification and begins to build to the dramatic and emotional dawn climax. The celebration for the guests is the third section.

The two ritual sections have structural parallels. Both begin with events in which the mother is prominent (first anointing and then shaving), and both include scheduled roles that involve people of all social categories—elders and young men, women and girls. The types of involvement scheduled— whether ritual acts, speech, or song—and their relation to enacting and re-creating gender roles are discussed below, along with blessings.

The transformation of initiation is represented and accomplished most intensely and immediately by acts and patterns of events during initiation itself, but semiotic movement also involves patterns that relate ritual roles, acts, and objects to the longer cultural process of maturation. The deployment of auspicious (_esiny'a_) pairs of two or four actors in ritual events creates some of these wider patterns and cultural progressions.[4] Similar ritual acts or sequences create dramatic, verbal, or material icons that link events within initiation, and also recall other ceremonies in the full life-cycle progression. This adds to their associational resonance, and can further suggest relations of equivalence, change, or transference. Some aspects of initiation have full significance only in relation to other ceremonies.

Processions are one example, with two ritual actors as leader and follower. As she matures, an Okiot travels in shifting ritual processions, each leading farther afield. As a child, she and her mother are sandwiched between ritual actors in a procession during her shaving ceremony, following the mature woman who shaved them both. The procession circumambulates her parents' home as a similar procession did three days after her birth, when she was first brought outside. The shaving ceremony is her first life-cycle ceremony and her social rebirth through naming.

Koroseek and _toloocik_ processions are included in ear-piercing ceremonies as well as initiation. In the ear-piercing ceremony, the girl alone follows a young man in the early procession, her peers farther behind. The procession is her first ceremonial separation from her mother, and traverses key locations in Okiek cultural geography (see below). She follows a young man again in the initiation procession, now joined with coinitiates. Later the initiates walk in procession between their ritual teachers, visiting a new landscape of adult secrets.

In wedding processions, each will once again walk in the middle, leaving her childhood home to follow her husband to his home. As her own children grow she herself takes the last or first place in ritual processions, guiding her offspring on the path of ceremonial traditions.

Several processions lead an Okiot into significant homes, ending at bed and hearth for ritual honey feeding (-*intolip*). This occurs in several ceremonies, and is also iconic to a mother feeding her infant. Significant progressions in who feeds her, and where, thread these different ceremonies together. At the shaving ceremony, child and mother are both fed in the child's home by the woman who shaved them. At the end of initiation, she is led to another house and fed by the ritual leader or the woman who lives there. Finally, in her wedding, she and her husband are fed at his home by his mother. She is later fed with her own children at their shavings, and eventually feeds her own sons and daughters-in-law at weddings.

At weddings, the ritual feeding on the bed equates a young woman's biological mother and her husband's mother. She joins the new household as a "daughter," in some sense replacing the daughters they give to others, and will bear children to perpetuate the family. Responsibility for the girl, as well as her labor and reproductive capacity, are transferred to her husband's family by the same act that incorporates her into it. The alternation between ritual work and reciprocating consumption is here given another wrinkle as it is linked into broader relations among work, social responsibility, and family nurturance. Many of these understandings and correspondences are explicitly recognized, but the mimetic progressions and repetitions in ceremonies make the links felt as well as known. Hence, understanding is "gained through seeing and drawing attention to connections or 'intermediary links' . . . rather than [only] by explaining acts in terms of preceding events, projected aims, unconscious concerns, or precepts and rules" (Jackson 1989:126).

A similar equation and transference within initiation creates a correspondence between the girls' mothers and their ritual teachers (*matireenik*). That link is an intermediate step in the transfer from natal home to marital home, and simultaneously brings initiates into the wider community of adult women.

Initiates' roles are elaborately defined, marked, and differentiated into a sequence of coordinated changes that is itself a central part of their movement toward young womanhood. The changes define their transformation from girls (*tiipiik; mebaysyek* "big girls") to *taarusyeek* (secluded initiates) to young women (*murereenik*), passing several other unnamed stages along the way. During their first ceremony, initiates begin to be marked off as a group by costume, by joint involvement in ritual events, and by the proxemics of events. Most decisively constituted at excision (after which they become *taarusyeek*), the initiates' group is ordered and theoretically inseparable until initiation is complete.

The order in which a group of girls go through initiation creates named, nonhierarchical distinctions within the group. The initiates sleep in that order, walk in that order, take song leads in that order, and are shown initiation secrets in that order during seclusion ceremonies.[5] These ordered positions are prominent in seclusion life, but do not obviously carry over afterward. Nonetheless, their ranked unity while sharing important experiences and changes parallels the organization of women's ritual community, where all are equal as initiated but ranked by seniority.

There are three positions in the group: *kipooretet, cerukween,* and *koyuumkoo/koyuumkok. Kipooretet* always goes first and shows (*-poor,* to show) others the way to follow. The second position, "those who sleep in the middle," includes any number of girls, though always in a fixed order. Okiek relate the final initiate's name to both *-yuum,* to gather up (for example, to bring up the rear and collect stray animals into safety in the evening) and *-yum,* to take shelter in.[6] Occasionally, ordinary birth order terms are used (*taaita,* first born; *toweet* last born); *cerukween* refers to birth order as well as initiate order. Finally, a young girl who is the "little initiate" is partner neither to the real initiates' restrictions and prescriptions nor to their trials. The *ceptoloolny'aat* child (from *tolooek,* remains) eats their leftover food during seclusion, containing their contagious, weakening filth (*kereek*). Often an initiate's sister, she takes no part in adult secrets, but receives a small *sirtiityet* sapling and a gift in the final ceremony.

Secluded initiates (*taarusyeek*) are marked as elaborately through behavior as they are visually by costume; strict initiate order is only one marking prescription. Part of the semiotic movement that shows (and is) their progress toward adulthood, these mimetic, verbal, visual, and spatial markings also change their experience, understanding, and perspectives, broadening them into those of an adult. "From an existential point of view, we could say that the bodily practices mediate a personal realization of social values, an immediate grasp of general precepts as sensible truths" (Jackson 1989:131). Throughout seclusion, initiates hide themselves (*-uny'kee*) from men and speak softly or whisper if men could sense their presence by hearing. They cannot bathe, cut their hair, draw water, or cook food. Other behavioral restrictions and prescriptions distinguish two stages of seclusion.

During the first part of seclusion, when their wounds are healing, initiates cannot touch food or fire. They eat meat with skewers and pick up ugali and cups with leaves. Someone else stokes their fire. Unable to move easily or far, they do little in the first healing weeks but sleep, sit chatting in the sun, and eat. Initiates should be fed well so as to emerge as lovely, healthy (*-ner*) young adults. At first, they especially need fat and meat to heal and to rebuild lost blood. The girls' brothers, fathers, or suitors should slaughter a goat or sheep for them, just as a husband should do for his wife after birth.

Though Okiek do not talk about initiation as either death or rebirth, as many other peoples do, other birth imagery is invoked at this point that relates initiates to both babies and mothers. Women spit toward initiates as they do to a newborn the first time they see it. That first day, they are also hand-fed like infants. Okiek liken *taarusyeek* to new mothers (*solootwik*) because of their food needs, confinement, specific restrictions on cooking, general inactivity, and their *kereek* (contagious filth). Some new mothers also smear white clay on their faces, as *taarusyeek* will during seclusion.[7]

Okiek characterize initiates at this point as sick people (*myani;* pl. *myantoos*). While they are out of sight and hearing, their presence is nonetheless recognized. Men and women alike inquire solicitously about their progress and recuperation until they recover. Recovery is officially marked and celebrated by the first seclusion ceremony, *kelap euun* (the hands are cleansed).

That ceremony defines activities for the rest of seclusion and gives initiates the use of their hands. They may now touch food after washing their hands in a special manner,[8] and may stoke (but not blow on) the fire. They also begin to sing their distinctive *kaiyantaaita* songs at dawn and dusk each day (see chapter 7), and can answer greetings by slapping their hide clothing or singing. They still do not bathe, cook food, or speak loudly; they continue to be vulnerable to *kereek* pollution; and they always take care not to encounter men. The initiates are more mobile and active after *kelap euun,* and *taarusyeek* work includes cutting firewood and mudding houses; both tasks have miniature representations in seclusion ceremonies. Above all, the initiates bead ornaments for the day they leave seclusion.

If *taarusyeek* are invalids at first, for the rest of seclusion they laughingly call themselves *ceemaasiisyek* (wild creatures, monsters). As they scurry into the bush to hide, with only a rustle of leaves, people passing might think them to be forest animals. Publicly silent all day long, they sing at dawn and dusk with the birds. But their costume, especially their body paint, really makes them *ceemaasiisyek*. Smeared in white, with striped markings and a racoon-like black mask around eyes and mouth, they say that even their mothers wouldn't know them (see plate 24). They are *ceemaasiisyek* until the last secret, the roaring *ceemaasiit,* is revealed to them in the last initiation ceremony. Then they emerge as *murereenik* (young women, brides). All seclusion restrictions and rules drop away, though seclusion habits and their shy self-consciousness when in male view take time to wear off.

Each rule and each change in costume that moves initiates toward adulthood is given to *taarusyeek* in ritual order by their *matireenik*. These two women, senior and junior (*ne oo ak ne serpin*), lead them through the ceremonies of initiation, while their seclusion mother is their daily companion throughout.[9] In principle, all initiated women can teach girls and lead them through initiation (*-matir*). In practice, a small number of women do the work; good *matireenik* are sought again by others.[10] Some are eliminated from consideration for the role because of bad habits, physical deformities, or tragedies in their lives.

Weeks before the first ceremony, the girls' parents begin to discuss possible candidates, citing the same characteristics I was told are important: a *matiriyaat* should be good, be peaceful, have children, and know the ritual work well. "*Sarurto ne kisipi*" (it is fullness/blessedness that we follow), one father said, a general principle that would indeed include many people.[11] The prospective *matiriyaat*'s husband must also agree since the job entails periodic absence from home.

Matireenik must be good-natured and even-tempered not only as a model for the initiates but also because their arguments would directly threaten the girls' well-being. Their husbands, who are always welcome to drink ceremonial beer, also figure in the choice. An obstreperous husband might spoil the ceremony even if his wife is a paragon of benevolence and wisdom. More seriously, a husband known to argue and beat his wife frequently might draw blood. This is dangerous, and also costly. If *matireenik,* initiates, or parents shed blood or tears during seclusion, a sheep must be sacrificed to wash it away.

Mothers, *matireenik,* and *taarusyeek* are also linked by hair growth. None shaves her head until seclusion ends, though mothers and *matireenik* shave the perimeter.[12] These common restrictions link mothers and ritual leaders, suggesting a correspondence in their relations to the girls. Similarly, host mother and *matireenik* wear ritual costume over the course of entire ceremonies. *Matireenik* don it when their secret work begins the first night, when most mothers have left theirs aside.

Spatially, initiates also pass from parental home to seclusion home and back, going from parents to *matireenik,* but not quite back again (they sleep and are ritually fed elsewhere the first night after they leave their seclusion house). *Matireenik* organize and lead ritual events during secret ceremonies, and have authority over other matters concerning *taarusyeek* that overrides the parents'. The girls have been given to them, but the transfer and associations do not create total identification. Mother and *matiriyaat* are explicitly compared and equated in the final lectures and advice to the girls, but *matireenik* do not have a nurturant maternal role. That is still played by one of the girls' mothers who feeds the initiates and becomes mother to them all. After initiation, initiates and *matireenik* address each other as *pamwaai,* like coinitiates, not as mother and child. *Matireenik* take over from mothers to lead initiates toward a new life; they are ritual mothers to them during this intermediate period between natal home and marital home. Yet they also bring them for life into new relations in the ritual community of women, where ranked equality rules rather than maternal nurturance.

Matireenik and parents are among the special relations of initiation—roles involved over some period of time, marked in several ceremonies, and connected importantly with the girls' transformation. The correspondence constructed between mother and *matiriyaat,* transferring girls from one to the other, is central in that process; it is one step in the larger semiotic movement of ceremonial maturation through the life cycle. In this larger context, which draws in other ceremonies, cultural progressions specific to initiation and those tying initiation into the general maturation process intersect and overlap. Patterns and associations of initiation become denser as more-textured contexts are re-created.

At the same time, these associative contexts inform the dramatic framework that outlines and creates the differentiated sequence of ceremonial experience and engagement. Patterns of ritual participation in the first ceremony help create dramatically important structural divisions, in coordination with other communicative channels discussed below. They also ensure that all present are involved. Members of every basic social category are given scheduled roles, whether their participation is representative or general. That participation is also a general agreement and ratification of cultural assumptions and categories that are implicit in and re-created by the performance.

A general notion of ritual work and reciprocity, if not recompense, informs that participation. This notion illuminates the alternation of ritual processions, prayers, talk, and so forth with eating and drinking. It also lays a cultural foundation for the obligation implicit in the requests and encouragement addressed to initiates—a grounding for the engaged emotional appeal and claim that helps girls begin the transformation that must take place first in their own hearts and wills.

People attend many ceremonies during their lives, experiencing them from a variety of viewpoints and with different degrees of engagement, but only once is a person the central focus of transformation. Initiates experience a series of roles during the transformative process, a semiotic movement specific to initiation that is elaborated and created in part with special behavioral prescriptions and prohibitions. They are led through the culturally defined sequence, from children to hidden *taarusyeek* who sing with the birds and are painted like wild creatures. The sequence is completed when the final ceremony reveals them to all as beautiful, marriageable young women who know what grown women know. The most dramatic and obvious manifestation of these roles, of where the girls are in their journey to adulthood, is visual: their costume.

Index and Invention in the Costume of Ritual

Costumes mark many ritual roles, and a particular sequence of costumes marks and creates initiates' progress through initiation. All are part of a larger indexical system of costume that shows distinctions of social identity in daily life, such as gender, age-set, ethnicity, and local group (Klumpp and Kratz 1992). In addition to clothing and ornaments, ceremonial costume can also include particular held objects. In initiation, all three are consistently specified only for initiates; coordinated changes in all together constitute the initiates' semiotic movement as produced through costume. Hair growth also marks ritual involvement, relating ritual actors and occasions through a three-way distinction: full head of hair, freshly shaved head, and perimeter shaved (-*kititi, -tudungi* [< Maa]).

The basic costume of ritual actors is the same in all Okiek ceremonies: a triangular beaded leather skirt (*ntetut,* pl. *ntetusyek*) worn around the shoulders, or a thigh-length hide cape (*injorubayt*), sometimes of hyrax skins. Once daily attire for adult women, beaded leather skirts are now used only in ceremonies. The cape is the corresponding male garb, and still is worn when men go to the forest to hunt or collect honey. In ceremonial contexts, the gender distinction is largely neutralized; men and women can wear either, though men complain that the skirt smells.

Ritual costume both distinguishes and unites ritual actors, linking them through the common skirt or cape but differentiating them by when it is worn and by objects held. The main representative actors who wear ritual costume during initiation are those leading *koroseek* and *toloocik* processions, one of whom also holds a hive adze (*kisincot*) in each procession to tap the first things collected. These actors wear ritual costume only for the event's duration, unlike those in special ritual relation to the girls.

Host mothers wear ritual skirts throughout the first ceremony (in practice, about half the day) and for at least part of the seclusion ceremonies, and might wear one again for the last ceremony.[13] *Matireenik* first don them when women's secret work begins late at night during the first ceremony. Thereafter, they wear them during seclusion ceremonies. As mentioned above, both mothers and *matireenik* grow their hair during seclusion, shaving the perimeter.

The host father holds a calabash of honey wine plugged with auspicious plants and is expected to wear a ceremonial cape throughout the first ceremony.[14] He does not wear ritual costume again, but uses the hive adze of processions to cut his daughter's sapling when she comes out. The *piitintet* (blesser) also holds a plugged calabash throughout the ceremony, a visual and material link between him and the father, who, it is hoped, will live to bless his own grandchildren's ceremonies. Use of such calabashes of wine further links the father and the *piitintet* with the adult men in representative roles who bless and build the *mabwaita* and the *toloocik,* though those men finish the wine in the calabash with the ritual event.

All these objects—beaded skirt and hide cape, hive adze and honey wine—carry an aura of tradition and times past for Okiek. People have used them in ceremonies for generations and also regard them as things that once were part of daily life but now have been replaced by modern equivalents. In addition to marking ritual actors, the objects also contribute to the aura of historical depth and constancy Okiek emphasize, value, and attribute to their ceremonies; they are material signs of continuity in ceremonial tradition. Associated with pursuits of forest life that have been enshrined as traditional, they also evoke modes of organization and assumptions that help reproduce that life, re-creating them in contemporary ceremonial contexts.

The girls' transformation into women is the heart of initiation, and specifically defined, detailed, and dramatic costume changes correspond with the sequence of named roles through which they pass. Costume changes also mediate between those roles, marking unnamed distinctions in the process. Table 8 summarizes initiates' costume changes over time; table 9 outlines the sequence of changes in more detail.

Initiates begin like all ritual actors, donning *ntetusyek* just before the morning procession. Like their parents, they wear capes throughout the day, but they change at dusk. Each girl is also to hold her *korosyaat* sapling until excision, though she leaves it when dancing. The prescribed daytime costume, *ntetut* and *korosyaat,* at once relates her to and distinguishes her from other ritual actors. The girls usually wear other special things as well, anticipating their nighttime dance costumes. They have, in fact, been wearing bits of that costume for days or weeks already, such as multicolored beads around wrist and forearm. As the ceremony approaches, these indices of attire increase. They wear the costume's leg bells and headdress days before the ceremony, and throughout the first day along with ritual garb.

Shortly after the girls are shaved at sunset, they are dressed in dramatic dance costumes (*muunkeenik*) (see plate 18).[15] The rented costume begins with a man's shirt, a cotton khanga cloth wrapped as a miniskirt, knee socks, and shoes. A red, white, or black striped band is wrapped around her waist and across her chest and back. Rows of leg bells (*muny'aawa*) go over her socks, jingling as she walks and ringing with her dance steps. On her head is a tall miterlike hat (*ceepkuuleet*), usually white or yellow cloth with green or red diagonal stripes and tassels at the top corners. A flat headdress (*keelteet*) strapped over the hat frames the girl's face with a semicircle of painted decoration. Those from near Nakuru have shiny tinsel and battery-operated flashlight bulbs on their headdresses.

Finishing touches are two. First, three black-and-white colobus monkey skins (*karaiitik*) are fitted to each arm, joined on wooden rods. One runs the length of the arm, while the others extend out front and back from the shoulder. Second, a stiff, oval back-apron (*ng'oisiit*) is attached, reaching to the knees. The one put on at dusk is usually white, with shiny bits of tinsel and metal. Later, it is replaced with a highly decorated black one that glitters even more brightly in the light of the bonfire.

Shine and flash in the firelight figure in Okiek judgments of the spectacular costumes, but the girls' dancing is also important since their light-catching movements create the flash. The hat tassels, apron, fly whisks (which are

• nonverbal Costumes tell us who is a girl & who is a boy.

Table 8: Initiates' Costume over Time

Preseclusion		Seclusion		Coming Out of Seclusion		Out
Kepa tuumto		*Kelap euun*	*Ketuuitos suumoosyek*	*Kelong'u en aineet*		
Ritual events	Celebration			*murereet #1*	*murereet #2*	
ntetut dance cape costume with sapling	blanket →→→	hide →→→→→→→→→→→→→ blanket clothing, ‖ white clay, →→→→→→→→→→→ etc.	→→→→→→→→→→→→→→ ‖ →→→→→→→→→→→→	(young woman #1) 2 *ntetusyek* capes, *inkeeriiny'ot* beads, etc.	(young woman #2) 1 *ntetut, enkishilit* tiara, etc.	ordinary daily clothes

Table 9: Sequences in Initiates' Scheduled Costume

Initiation and ceremonies → through time →	*Kepa tuumto* Ritual events (preseclusion)	*Kelap euun* Seclusion	*Ketuuitos suumoosyek*	*Kelong'u en aineet* Coming Out of Seclusion		Out
Basic clothing	*ntetut* cape/skirt khanga miniskirt knee socks shoes	blanket | *menekobeyt* (inner skin) *injorubayt* (outer skin)	↑ ↑ ↑ ↑	blanket | 2 *ntetusyek* 1 sheet	1 *ntetut* 2 sheets	ordinary daily clothing
Headdress	*keelteet* (face frame) *ceepkuuleet* (hat) (head shaved)	*lolashuriit* (hair grown)	↑ ↑ ↑ ↑ ↑ ↑	*inkeeriiny'ot* beads	*enkishilit* tiara (head shaved)	
Other ornaments	striped "bandolier" *ng'oisiii* (back apron) leg bells colobus skins *intoroogenik* beads on wrists	*topokwit* (metal band) *esuyayt* (copper coil) *intorotoit* (white clay) and charcoal body paint	↑ ↑ ↑ ↑ ↑ ↑ ↑ ↑	beaded ornaments *sinenteet* vine fat	beaded ornaments *sinenteet* vine fat	
Held objects	*korosyaat* fly whisks/*korosyaat* sapling	*kipteruaan* staff and beads	↑ ↑	*sirtiiyet* sapling	—	

held), and especially the colobus skins all carry and extend the dance motion visually, while leg bells and whistles punctuate it aurally. The girls display their youthful energy along with the dazzling glitter of their costumes throughout the evening, and are still in dance costume when they dance out at dawn for the operation. The moment they are cut, it is stripped from them. The *taarusyeek* are wrapped in blankets, which is their only clothing until they recover and *kelap euun* is held. Until then, they wear no ornaments and hold nothing.

During *kelap euun*, *matireenik* dress initiates in new costumes, which are worn until their last ceremony.[16] The daily costume of *taarusyeek* is nearly as elaborate as their dance costumes, though the effect is very different (see plate 23). Each wears a hairless, calf-length inner garment made of hide (*menekobeyt*), an outer cape, (also called *injorubayt*) of hide that still has hair, plain metal neck ornaments (*topokwit* and *esuyayt*), and a headband of dark blue beads with four chains hanging from the forehead to the bridge of the nose (*olashurtit*).[17] Initiates carry a stout staff (*kipteruaan*) with a thread of beads near the bottom.[18] The final component is considered the most distinctive, and is instrumental to their image as bizarre wild creatures (*ceemaasiisyek*): every day they smear themselves with white clay and blacken their eyes and mouth with charcoal.

Initiates' next costume change comes midway through the last ceremony when they go to the river and leave their *taarusyeek* costumes behind with their first bath. Wrapped in blankets and hidden from sight, they are brought back to their parents' *mabwaita* in procession, dressed as when they left it after excision. But they do not stop there. The procession continues into the bush nearby, where initiates are dressed in the finery of adult women. Their last costumes include the familiar *ntetut* again. As in the first ceremony and in seclusion, emergence also involves a two-costume sequence. In this case, however, distinctions are only in detail.

Her body well-oiled, each initiate is dressed with a new cloth sheet over one shoulder, one beaded *ntetut* around her waist, and another around her shoulders. She is adorned with a fine array of beaded ornaments. *Matireenik* tie her waist with leafy *sinenteet* vine. Finally, the perimeter of her head is shaved, and a strand of blue and white beads with red sections (*inkeeriiny'ot*) is worn at the trimmed hairline. Resplendently decorated, the initiates are again tucked under blankets, brought home, and given *sirtiityet* saplings, which they carry all day, much as they carried the *korosyaat* during the first ceremony.

Okiek explicitly relate the two uprooted saplings, a correspondence that brings the initiation process full circle, completing its semiotic movement. The last ceremony returns to objects with which initiation began, but in modified form, as the girls themselves return to daily life transformed in social identity, yet nonetheless the same people.

The following morning, the ritual costume shifts when their heads are shaved and *inkeeriiny'ot* beads are replaced with beaded tiaras (*enkishilit*), which are also worn by young Okiek and Maasai brides (see plates 30, 31). The *ntetut* at the waist is also replaced with a second new cloth, and they give the saplings to their fathers. The rest of the costume remains the same.

The costume worn at marriage is formally very similar; the new identity of young woman implies and is completed by becoming a wife and then a mother. Ideally a woman's husband takes her within days of coming out, so the costumes are also temporally close. On her wedding day, she again wears the costume that displayed her new adult status. She wears two leather skirts, tied with ceremonial vine, but her *enkishilit* tiara shows that she is not an initiate just come from the river, as does the sprig of auspicious grass tucked under it. Other important details make clear that she is a bride. She holds an oiled staff (as in shaving ceremonies and marriage talks) and carries special things (honey, fat, or milk) on her back—inside the cloth, as a baby is carried—for the procession to her new home.

Visual icons of costume also recall other occasions during initiation, creating associations and relations that are part of initiation's semiotic movement and contextual re-creation. Head ornaments, for instance, constitute another cultural progression that places initiation into the larger life-cycle context and that simultaneously operates as a detail within initiation. The internal progression is dance headdress, nothing, *taarusyeek* band, *inkeeriiny'ot* beads, *enkishilit* tiara. *Taarusyeek* headpieces are similar to those children wear during shaving ceremonies. The cultural sequence of ritual headdresses not only corresponds to points in the initiation process but also stretches further back with associations to shaving ceremonies and further forward to anticipate weddings.

Initiates' full costume sequence during initiation creates a more obvious visual sense of significant movement, contrast, and difference over time. In initiates' last public appearance before excision and their first one after it, they are magnificently adorned—a display of glowing youth and energy in dance costumes in the former, turned finally into the epitome of demure maidenly beauty, soon to be appropriated in marriage, in the latter. The splendor and beauty of both these costumes, their aesthetic power and pleasure, contrast sharply with the wildness and filth attributed to the seclusion costume and the plain roughness of old blankets, which are the transitional seclusion attire.

The costume sequence corresponds with initiates' sequence of named roles, but it also makes visible other distinctions in the process. Costumes of preseclusion, seclusion, and emergence—each a pair—change at decisive points. The preseclusion shift marks no role change, but occurs at the ceremony's structural divide of sunset shaving, reinforcing the patterns of participation and other media. The dramatic dance costume draws attention to the girls visually as other nighttime events focus on them verbally.

In seclusion, plain blankets mark transitions between hiding and displaying the initiates, and between named roles. They contrast with the costume the girls wear when actively learning the lore of initiated women. The first blanket-wearing period is extended; it is defined physically by the girls' healing and ends with the next ceremony. The final blanket transition is very brief, only as long as the procession home, where initiates wear the first coming-out costume.

As in the first ceremony, that costume changes when the initiates are shaved, this time in the morning. This shift of detail moves the costume closer to common ritual attire, removing the waist *ntetut* and replacing the head beads with the tiara. Again, the change comes at an important final turning point, when initiates are about to enter and eat in their parents' own home.

While the transformation of initiation draws on many media at once, then, movement through the process includes coordinated shifts in different media that are sometimes concurrent and at other times staggered, and that mark named distinctions at some times and at others structural divisions and periods not lexically distinguished. Initiation costume visually makes a greater number of distinctions than those recognized by the named roles of girl, *taarusyaat,* and *murereet,*[19] and details of costume re-create and modify Okiek characterizations and experiences of people in those roles.

Itinerary of Significant Places at Consequential Times

The dominant metaphor for initiation, the journey, includes both duration in time and movement in space.[20] Scheduled shifts in location, in both space and time, add another dimension to the transformative movement of initiation and to the experience of ceremonial occasions. The complexity of semiotic coordination and significance in the process is increased by the ritual construction of special places that are then included in the sequence of location changes. Once again, contextual re-creation, semiotic movement, and experiential engagement are entwined here. The time and space of initiation become significant through associations with other activities and contexts, through culturally defined sequences that create the process that turns children into adults, and through the personalized, immediate, and felt apprehension of those associations and sequences in each ceremony.

Locational shifts figure in initiation's transformation in three major ways. First, tours through significant locales of Okiek cultural geography are woven into ceremonies. This evokes and re-creates resonant chords of condensed association that can intensify ceremonial experiences. At the same time it reproduces cultural understandings of space and time that are enmeshed with social roles and relations, lending them different experiential and affective shadings (both through embodiment in practice and in explicit comments, discussion, and directions for ritual performance).

Some of those significant places are created during ceremonies; arenas of ritual space defined through special constructions. As discussed below, the materials used in them both condense associations with other places woven into ceremonies through procession and signify important cultural values and complementarity in gender relations and marriage. The ceremonies return again and again to these ritual centers; other events unfold in the presence of the founding constructions that re-create and affirm Okiek space and values.

Second, initiation moves the girls through different locations. That sequence of places is directly implicated in the transformative process, and the cultural definition of their seclusion place adds another strand to Okiek gender relations.

The proxemics of ritual events define the third mode of spatial shift in initiation's transformation. The spatial organization of participants during ritual events consistently moves initiates away from ordinary daily life as initiation proceeds, even before their physical removal from it.

Okiek cultural geography elaborates a central contrast between the forest and the home or settlement. At another taxonomic level, the forest category has an encompassing sense as the home of Okiek, something containing the settlement, just as settlements are part of the forest yet separate. The forest was the major source of Okiek subsistence in the past, with forest products carried home for consumption or use. *Tirap* represents the forest in this general, positive sense, emphasizing home, security, abundant food, peace, and refuge from enemies. *Tirap* is high-altitude, dense forest (see chapter 3), the home of giant forest hogs and bongo, hung with abundant hives, where non-Okiek neighbors are distant and through which they are unlikely to pass.

When settlements enter the spatial scheme, the forest whole is divided into home and forest. The *tirap* image persists, but the opposition brings out another sense of the forest, contrasting the uncertain, wild, and potentially dangerous outside world to the stable, warm safety of home. This binary division carries into the ritual representation of space, is replicated at different levels, and takes on related sets of dyadic associations. From different domains of traditional work comes the association of the forest with men and the home with women, generalized as those who roam outside (*piik ap saang'*) and those at home (*emeet aap kaa*).

In this spatial dyad, forest and home are weighted relatively equally; they are complements that are equally valued and equally essential for Okiek life, which entails regular traffic between them. Neither forest nor home is invested with greater esteem or priority; the forest's dangerous aspect is mitigated by the encompassing sense of the forest as Okiek home. Interdependence and unity are also stressed in spatial categories that divide the settlement. The forest/home pair is replicated in a series of divisions that become increasingly local and personal: male/female gathering places outside (*kok, pita*), dooryard/ house, outer room/inner room with hearth, other seats/hearth and bed, right/ left sides of the bed.[21]

Each of these carries a sense of being a male or female space relative to different contexts, but only the final division above—the right/left sides of the bed, which is in the most personal and private family space—explicitly articulates sexual divisions of space with the hierarchical categories of auspicious and inauspicious. However, other binary categories that are hierarchically ordered articulate with the categories of forest/home through shared male/female associations. In these pairs, used similarly all over the world to talk about and order other cultural worlds, one term is considered good, auspicious, senior, strong, and male, and the other bad, inauspicious, junior, weak, and female. These pairs include right/left, male/female, four/three, and east/west.

Okiek discussed these binary categories in terms of evaluative hierarchies both in conversations about ritual procedure and in interviews with me that posed them as hypothetical alternatives. There *are* occasions when three or left are ritually appropriate, but these are either in conjunction with a female actor (when another male actor uses four or right) or else invoke the inauspicious, for example in cursing.

Most of these spatial subdivisions come into play in Okiek ceremonies. Complementary ritual places are created that cross and combine the divisions of family space; ritual structures are built outside in the dooryard and inside at the hearth. Both structures are necessary, but there is an implicit hierarchy between them. The *mabwaita* is the dominant and more important one, built first in ceremonies and on various other occasions. It stands in the dooryard, which is male space relative to the hearth, where the interior *toloocik* platform is located. The *mabwaita* marks the central arena of ritual performance during initiation; it is where most public ritual events occur and where materials for the *toloocik* are first brought and blessed before being used.

In important ways, these two ritual structures condense the cultural world map. They reproduce the forest/home distinction domestically but also mediate it, since they are built of forest products brought home by women and children. The processions into the forest to gather the materials for them recall the excursions of men seeking and bringing home forest sustenance. Ordinarily, women receive what men bring, then prepare and distribute forest foods for daily use. In ceremonial contexts, men receive forest products and consecrate them for ritual use. Elders also construct both the *mabwaita* and the *toloocik;* this underlines and enacts their prominence and authority as organizers, and enables the occasion by creating and consecrating ritual space. But this capacity lasts only until seclusion begins. Though public performances and general representations refer only to the primordial *mabwaita* made by elders (Kratz 1987), women create their own ritual space in seclusion, constructing their own *mabwaita* within the girls' seclusion enclosure, the hidden dooryard of the house. They make no *toloocik*, but in the second ceremony they make an enclosure (*suumuut*) for initiates inside the house.

Thus Okiek spatial domains and associations are brought together to create ritual arenas. The initiates' journey weaves them all together; the girls pass through a sequence of significant locations, their itinerary for transformation. The journey combines actual movement through space in processions and figurative movement created by changing the initiates' living space. Table 10 summarizes the spatial progression of initiation.

As their procession winds through the forest, young people bring the noisy joy of ceremony there. Enlivening the forest with whistles, song, shouts, and laughter, they seek *koroseek* saplings that bring the forest home for the ceremonial *mabwaita*. The initiates' saplings join them to both forest and *mabwaita* throughout the ceremony. They leave childhood at the *mabwaita*, where forest and home are joined and the complementary union of men, women, and children is represented botanically. After the opening procession, the initiates stay close to home; evening events centered on them alternate between house and *mabwaita*. The initiates are not led in procession again until the *matireenik* claim them late at night.

Then they are led back into the house where people have socialized all day, but it is no longer the same. It has become the women's ritual house and the girls' seclusion house (*menceet*), another world of secrets though its physical location remains as before.[22] After excision, the journey continues in the wild forest domain, a domain separate but not completely isolated from daily life. The initiates travel and hide along forest paths, painting themselves as unrecognizable, wild-looking creatures. As women-to-be relative to men-to-be, however, even their wildness is more domestic. Their *menceet* is still within the bounds of home and settlement, while male initiates' seclusion place is in the bush. Until initiates (of both sexes) come out, ceremonial processions lead initiates away from the *menceet* and back again, always in the bush. Their semiotic movement continues as the seclusion place itself changes, increasingly domesticated and differentiated with ritual constructions.

The *menceet*, like the girls themselves in their blankets, remains physically unmarked until the first seclusion ceremony. Then a bushy enclosure is made and the women's *mabwaita* is built in that shielded dooryard, marking and making ritual space for the seclusion ceremonies. At the same time, the *mabwaita* marks the *menceet* as a residence, bringing it one step closer to ordinary homes.

When the initiates have regained their health, the procession of the first seclusion ceremony (perhaps to the river) makes them mobile. On the way back, the girls experience another trial at an arch (*oormariicet*)[23] built at a crossroads, marking the path of the *taarusyeek*. A forest path away from houses, it eventually leads home to another arch when they come from the

Table 10: Scheduled Spatial Progression of Initiates in Ceremonies

Initiation and ceremonies through time →

Kepa tuumto

Ritual events (preseclusion)

Locations: home → forest → mabwaita → → mabwaita → home → → mabwaita → home → mabwaita

Ritual Events: (koroseek procession) (shaving) (dancing) (ceerseet speeches) (pesenweek—social debts) (secrets) (excision)

↑ continued below ↑

Ketuuitos suumoosyek

Kelap euun

Seclusion

menceet → river (?) → oormariicet → menceet → → mabwaita → menceet → → → menceet with mabwaita and decorated suumuut enclosure
(seclusion house) | arch at crossroads | with mabwaita
(secrets) | | (secrets)

↑ continued below ↑

Kelong'u en aineet

Coming out of seclusion

Out

→ river → home mabwaita with oormariicet arch → bush → home mabwaita with oormariicet arch → nonparental home → home mabwaita → parental homes

(secrets) (passing only) adornment (open way and give sirtiityet sapling) (sleep at other house [kiiilta]) (break sirtiityet and shave) (eat food)

river. If indeed *kelap euun* takes initiates to the river, parallels to the final ceremony are quite strong, with its river bath and trip home to the arch at the *mabwaita*.

After *kelap euun*, the initiates' daily life follows prescribed rules of behavior, discussed above. *Taarusyeek* tread forest paths, but their home now has a *mabwaita*, like an ordinary home blessed with children. Their costume and activities are unchanged by the second seclusion ceremony, but their place of seclusion is not. Continued progress through initiation is marked there during the third ceremony (the second during seclusion), *ketuuitos suumoosyeek*, which is named after the two-door[24] enclosure built inside the *menceet*. The *suumuut* enclosure is the final elaboration, an internal modification like the *toloocik* of the first ceremony. With that, a domestic space complementary to the *mabwaita* is drawn into the ritual processes of seclusion. The *suumuut*'s decoration with small fruits by the *matireenik* is the visible sign of this next step in the *taarusyeek*'s spatial progression through initiation.

In the final ceremony, the significant space of seclusion residence is destroyed or abandoned, and the initiates' journey again moves in procession. Leaving dirt attributed to seclusion behind at the river, they make their way home again, returning to the *mabwaita* where their journey began. But neither shrine nor travelers are as they were before. An arch like the one in *kelap euun* is built onto the *mabwaita*, which is transformed like the initiates themselves and like the *sirtiityet* sapling that recalls the first ceremony's *korosyaat* sapling.

The initiates' path has finally led home, yet they still do not go there directly. The first return to public view is independent of their natal home, as the new adults will be when they establish their own homes. They go first to another home, to be ritually fed honey and sleep there before reaching the end of the initiatory trip. The ritual feeding relates initiation to the broader context of ceremonial maturation, showing a shift in and a widening of the scope of social relations.

Then, finally, the young women's journey ends at their parents' homes. Both father and mother mark their transformed relationship with their daughter with gifts as they finish the ritual work of initiation. Even feeding, the most basic act of daily nurturance between mother and child, begins again on a new footing with a small gift, recognizing the daughter's new adult status. No longer resident there, she only awaits her husband to take her to a new home, and is now like a guest in the home where she was raised.

Throughout initiation, the girls travel always in procession, in ritual order behind the senior *matiriyaat*, from the night of the first ceremony. Processional form is a dramatic icon, as discussed above, that links initiation to other life-cycle ceremonies, increasing social and spatial scope over time. The conventions of ceremonial processions are based on Okiek ideas of the auspicious, which in turn are based on the sun's movement and the passage of the day.

Both time and space are implicated and entwined in these notions. Auspicious divisions of space and time are combined with hierarchical complementarities of right/left and four/three to define fundamental principles of ritual performance that inform the scheduling, orientation, and procedure of ritual events and acts. These ritual practices also contribute to the hierarchical evaluation of the binary categories: right and four are always used in auspicious procedures, left and three in inauspicious ones (though these latter two inform some auspicious ritual practice with female associations as well) (Kratz 1989).

The principles of auspicious procedure might be summarized as: (1) do it four times; (2) go to the right; (3) face east; (4) men on the right; (5) start with the right or the male; and (6) start with the rising sun. These combine in various ways in ritual events. For example, the first morning procession of initiation circles the *mabwaita* to the right and stands facing the rising sun; blessings are sprayed on men first, beginning at the right if they are grouped together near the *mabwaita*.

The temporal scheduling of ritual events intertwines with these. Sunrise and sunset are the basis of ranking east and west as auspicious/inauspicious orientations; the rising sun is a recurrent image in blessings. Dawn and dusk are the scheduled times for public ritual events.[25] When elders build the *mabwaita* in the morning, creating ritual space, they simultaneously inaugurate the ceremonial time envelope. Between dawn and dusk, ritual activity lulls.

Other Okiek ceremonies last one day, with ritual activity scheduled in the morning and at dusk. Initiation, however, continues into the night in the first ceremony, pointedly turning attention then to the girls until the following dawn: displaying, addressing, moving, and beginning to educate them. Succeeding ceremonies all run from dusk to dawn. The revelation of special adult knowledge is a nocturnal activity. The temporal realm of seclusion, like the spatial one, separates initiates from daily, daytime life. When they leave seclusion, they emerge again to public daylight in the morning, the same time seclusion began. The final public ceremony of emergence continues from dawn to dawn, like the first one, though only celebration intervenes.

A proxemic progression gradually draws the girls into this nocturnal realm, beginning their transformation even before the *matireenik* take them away. This is the final spatial dimension of the initiates' journey to discuss. The use of space within ritual events progressively separates them from their place as children among other children. The nocturnal events of the first ceremony make this especially clear.

From the beginning of the first day, initiates are specifically placed— treated differently from their peers yet still among them. In the opening procession, they walk in ritual order for the first time, but they are still with their friends. Their rank order begins to constitute the girls as a special group who will be together for months in seclusion. At dusk, shaving pulls the girls from their peer group, but only temporarily. They soon join friends in song again. Similarly, they are removed and dressed in dance costume before returning again, highly marked by costume and taking the lead in song and dance, yet still in the midst of friends and relatives.

Their placement relative to others in ritual events gradually pulls them away, until in *ceerseet* speeches the girls are physically set apart from the men. They sit in line facing them, with the host mother at the end to mediate the reception of gifts. The communicative separation of the girls becomes more obvious here as well; men address them directly but no verbal response is allowed. In the last public event, *pesenweek* confessions, the girls again line up facing the crowd, this time at the *mabwaita*. The questioner mediates, standing between the girls and the crowd, not at the side like the mother during the speeches. There is no direct communication between the girls and others. The degree of communicative mediation has increased with the girls' physical separation: from direct address and exchange in song (never in speech), to direct address with silent response, to interpreted exchanges. After this event, the girls are led away to the women's house, where the separation will become total in seclusion and verbal communication is severed entirely with adult men and restricted in particular ways with others.

The spatiotemporal organization of initiation incorporates and creates significant places and times. Ritual locations both draw on and contribute to the import and affect of significant places of daily life and to their associations with social roles and relations, all contributing to contextual re-creation during initiation. The complex semiotic movement of the girls' journey through the locations and events of initiation is constituted not only by their movement through significant places but also by a creative construction that redefines places with ritual structures, and by subtle shifts of proxemic placement during ritual events as well. Those shifts, constructions, and changes of location help shape and orchestrate ceremonial experience and engagement over time.

Ritual Materials, Objects, and Substances from Forest Life

The concrete materials, objects, and substances used during initiation are the final media to be considered in this chapter. Most are drawn from or point to the life of the forest, incorporating into the ritual production of adult Okiek what Okiek stress and value in their history. Redolent with associations, the materials hark back to the forest as the essential place and basis of Okiek life and identity and are saturated with the social relations and values of that life.

These material media figure in ceremonial transformation most prominently through contextual re-creation. Nonetheless, they help define and give shape to ceremonial experience, and some are also incorporated into the cultural progressions of initiation's semiotic movement.

These evocative objects set apart people, places, and actions as ritually marked, creating ritual roles, acts, and space. Several are basic to the Okiek repertoire of ritual materials, being used regularly in other ceremonies and in new situations calling for ritual action. Leaving aside some of their ample associations, I review them here briefly,[26] considering first forest materials, then containers and other objects of daily life used in ritual, and finally auspicious substances.

The first are part of forest life quite literally, as well as recalling forest-based Okiek production. Saplings, vines, leafy branches, stout poles, and green forest grasses figure prominently in processions and constructions that define ritual space, as stoppers in ritual containers, and in the costumes of ritual actors. Forest materials are also used in initiates' secret trials and revelations. They come from a limited number of species. *Olerienit* is the most important tree for poles and branches used in ritual structures[27] and is the preferred wood for ritual fires. The ritual grass is *tankuriot*, greenly abundant throughout the forest, while leafy *sinenteet* is the primary vine of ritual.[28] Ritual saplings, of course, are *koroseek*.

In talking about costume, I mentioned the similarity of the *koroseek* and *sirtiitsyek* saplings held by initiates, which link and distinguish initiation ceremonies in temporal progression. The saplings are part of another iconic cultural progression that situates initiation within the ceremonial life cycle, recalling other ceremonial associations and stretching again to include shaving ceremonies and marriage. The series of held objects continues in each direction with a long thin staff (*olartatit*), which is carried by a bride in her wedding procession, used in shaving processions, and also carried to marriage discussions by the prospective groom's mother. The staff is made of *olerienit* wood or bamboo, and is rubbed with fat so the wood is not dry.

Most of these ritual species share natural properties such as hardness of wood, abundance, long-lasting greenness or moistness, apparent immunity to lightning strikes, and sweet fragrance. Ritual use invokes those properties for both the ceremonial occasion and its participants: strength, fertility, long life, freedom from catastrophe, and general good fortune. Other trees and plants are ritual materials simply by convention. The suitability of preferred materials is also reinforced by their repeated use in ceremonies; they all become ceremony things (*tukuuk aap tuumto*).

In combination these forest materials evoke associations of good fortune, prosperity, and blessedness, but the properties and uses of particular species also create gender-related accents. The *mabwaita* unites them all in a treelike icon of complementarity. The four stout center poles forming the base of the *mabwaita* are *olerienit*—hard, sweet-smelling, long-burning wood that is predominantly male through associations based on its strength and its use in hives and smoking out bees. The base poles are bound with *sinenteet* vines passed around the pole to the right and secured without knotting.

Sinenteet is abundant and resiliently green, with many delicate white flowers when in bloom. Its fertility—its abundance in the forest and its prolific blooms—suggests female associations, underlined by its white, milky sap[29] and confirmed by other uses. Tied on young women emerging from seclusion and at their wedding, *sinenteet* shows their nubility and untapped fertility. Women wear *sinenteet* wreathes during the *toloocik* procession and also (in an event added to initiation by Kipchornwonek) when being blessed at the *mabwaita* (see chapter 8).

The vine is further associated with marriage, the social means of incorporating women's fertility. It is tied on the special sheep (called *cepsinenteet*) a man gives his bride's mother, on the sheep brought after "stealing" a young woman (a first step toward marriage discussions), and also on the liquor pot reserved for mother's brothers at ceremonies.

Sinenteet and other vines bind and strengthen the *mabwaita* and other ritual structures as women weave together and perpetuate patrilineages through marriage and reproduction. The *mabwaita* is completed with leafy branches, the profusion of *koroseek* brought by young people making it luxuriantly bushy. The *koroseek* fill out the *mabwaita* as the children who carry them fulfill their parents' marriages.

The *mabwaita*, the *toloocik*, and the *oormariicet* are all made with these materials, which are also used for temporary constructions during secret ritual events; the forest is brought home to create ritual space.[30] In ceremonies, ritual forest materials embody the territorial realm encompassing Okiek life and identity and evoke the general values that Okiek pray for in blessings. Used in fundamental ritual structures that combine and mediate spatial distinctions and their associations, they also specify gender differences within Okiek identity in a way that unites them and stresses their complementarity within the framework of general ideals. The gender differences also recall the distinctions and relations between agnates and affines that underlie the reproduction of Okiek life and society.

Forest materials are used in combination with other ritual objects. For instance, when a young woman comes out of seclusion, her sapling has propolis, a black, resinous substance bees use to close holes in their hives, around the stem. Her father taps the sapling with a hive adze before breaking it. The adze and the propolis represent the remaining two groups of ritual objects to be discussed. The vegetal materials concentrate the associations and affect of the Okiek forest locale, but the activities of a hunting and honey-gathering life are drawn into ritual events by the second group of ritual objects, which includes the adze. Most are ordinary implements of daily life;

all are closely connected to honey and the Okiek sense of tradition. The two basic garments of ritual actors, the forest cape and the beaded skirt, are also consistent with these items.

The *kisincot* (hive adze) is the main tool of ritual events, used whenever forest materials are brought or cut, carried by the actor who leads processions to collect them. The primary hive-making tool, it was and is used by men to shape a honey-producing forest container and by men, women, and young people to act on and incorporate forest materials in ritual events. The connection between the *kisincot* and hives is salient in Okiek commentary.

Kisincot is used in ceremonies and to make hives. The honey from hives is used in ceremonies.

It is something we were using in the past, so we don't change it. You hit the sticks with a *kisincot* before you cut them with a panga. It is a thing of hives. In the past, when there were no pangas, people used just the *kisincot*. It was used to make hives and to cut *koroseek* and to do other ceremony works.

Most other ritual objects are small household containers for honey, fat, or honey wine. Okiek usually store honey these days in tin cans fitted with leather tops. Honey containers for ritual events, however, are those formerly in greater use, and are considered particularly Okiek objects, like the *kisincot*. Honey ritually fed to initiates—or to other ritual actors—is put into a tightly woven honey basket (*paleito*), or occasionally a small honey pot (*kesumeet*). Still made and used at home, both carry an aura of tradition and recall the forest life.

Fat for ritual anointing is held in a small black horn with a sprig of *tanguriot* grass in the mouth. While usually the tip of a buffalo horn is used, that of a sacrificed (and so auspicious) cow will also do. Fat and horn both incorporate the hunting side of forest life into ritual events.

The final ritual containers hold honey wine: small gourds plugged with auspicious plants carried by the host father and the blesser, calabashes of wine used in blessing and other ritual work, and the leather bag of honey wine brewed on the *toloocik* platform. Okiek use calabashes primarily to hold honey wine, though cow owners have some for milk. The limited range of uses identifies calabashes strongly with the wine, the men who use them, ceremonial occasions, and prayers.

As the *kisincot* recalls hives, the leather brewing bag points to honey collection itself. It is a larger version of the bag into which men put honey when high in the tree, surrounded by angry bees. Forest camps and convivial drinking sessions are also recalled, for a brewing bag is usually brought on long forest trips.

All the implements of daily life incorporated into ritual acts highlight activities central to the forest life Okiek see as their particular heritage, experience, and knowledge. They incorporate different moments of honey production, from hive making to collection to storage to consumption. The other definitive side of forest life, hunting and meat, is also incorporated through ritual objects, though in less-diverse and less-elaborated forms.

The final group of ritual objects includes products of forest life: honey wine, fat, honey, and propolis. Both honey work and hunting are represented, though bee products again predominate. These auspicious substances are incorporated into ritual events chiefly in blessing, anointing, and ritual feeding. As with mabwaita materials, they are also linked to particular social categories.

Honey wine is considered the male mode of honey consumption, and is most associated with elders and with ceremonies. Sprayed by mouth in blessing, the wine combines with the most concentrated and potent substance of blessing, the saliva of senior elders, to broadcast their benediction. Elders also use honey wine to consecrate mabwaita and toloocik structures as well as to help sink their base poles. Finally, men of the host father's age-set brew wine on the completed toloocik, thereby including preparation and process as well as product in the ritual proceedings. Consumption of that wine ends the first ceremony, as the blessing sprayed on the opening procession begins it.

The host mother's opening blessing is bestowed with fat. A concentrated animal substance recalling hunting and meat, it is a sign of prosperity, strength, good health, beauty, peace, respect, new births, and infants, combining male and female associations but emphasizing female ones in ceremonial contexts.[31] Fat is the more female substance of blessing, but it is also the balm of forgiveness during pesenweek, and makes finely adorned and newly revealed initiates gleam sleekly the day they come from the river.

Because fat is soft, white, sweet, and long-lasting, Okiek link the substance to honey. In its pure, undiluted form, honey is used only as food in Okiek ceremonies. This form of honey is considered to be for children, and is ritually fed to initiates when they leave seclusion. As already mentioned, this act of nurturance and welcome recalls similar ritual feedings at shaving and at marriage.[32]

Honey wine, fat, and honey become auspicious ritual substances that unite people, passing between them as benedictory spray, ointment, or sweet nourishment. These foods of forest prosperity bind them together in ritual action, incorporating the pleasures of forest life into consequential, ceremonially charged moments. The exchanges of food and ritual work here have another, ritualized form.

Propolis is also considered auspicious because it is a bee product. It is molded around initiates' saplings when they come out and on male initiates' staffs, and is also used in secrets. It seems a secret analogy likens propolis to something else, but people could comment explicitly only on its honey associations.

Ritual materials, objects, and substances firmly tie initiation to what Okiek regard as their distinctive history and tradition of forest life. Particular vegetal materials, specific implements of production and storage, and key forest products are material means by which that sense of tradition and its value are re-created in Okiek ceremonies. All highlight and concentrate associations and contexts related to the two activities Okiek emphasize in their forest life: honey gathering and hunting.[33]

Repeated use of the very same objects over generations simultaneously helps re-create a material sense of continuity in ceremonial tradition (see chapter 8). The ritual things discussed here further re-create that tradition by demarcating ritual space and time, by marking ritual actors and ritual acts, and by making those actors and acts recognizable. They also give particular form to ceremonial experience and facilitate various modes of ceremonial engagement. Yet most of these special ritual items come from daily life. The activities, social relations, and organizing assumptions of daily life thus are incorporated materially into ritual events, helping to re-create and represent a meaningful view of life that seems self-evident and natural.

The sense of place, history, and tradition so created is always a personal and social one. Social relations, especially those of gender, are entangled with distinctions of place, plants, and activities, all set within the overarching realm of forest life and its general ideals. The distinctions of roles, values, and assumptions so palpably present in the things of ritual are the background and setting within which and through which the children's transformation into adults takes place, and so are another facet of contextual re-creation. "The differentiating oppositions of everyday life [male versus female] both create those of ritual and ceremonial activities . . . and are created by them" (Wagner 1981:119). Some distinctions are at once made and mediated, as in the mabwaita's combination of forest materials.

Some ritual things are also implicated in the specific semiotic movement of initiation's transformation. In addition to creating ritual space, for instance, the saplings held by initiates are a visible part of their movement through initiation and through the longer ceremonial progression of maturation. The honey they are fed on reentry into public life is part of a similar progression defined through ritual feedings.

One final object figures in initiation events, confounding the neat forest concentration of the others: the flag raised to mark the place of the ceremony. A secular counterpart to the mabwaita and the toloocik, it marks the general location of the ceremony rather than a specific ritual center. Okiek note that this practice is a recent addition. The fabric is purchased at the market and the flag is sewn by a tailor there, and so the flag's associations stretch more toward the market and national economy and relate it to a set of changes in ceremonial practice that all involve increased expenditure, display, and consumption. Through the flag (and items such as the girls' dance costumes), a material sense of innovation and neotradition is also incorporated into the ceremonies, drawing in new contexts of daily life, giving contemporary form to ceremonial experience, and elaborating the assumptions of Okiek gender relations within these new contexts (see chapter 8).

Cultural Meaning, Movement, and Maintenance through People, Places, and Things

This chapter has discussed four media of initiation: patterns of participation, costumes, locations, and ritual materials. All figure in the key transformative processes of initiation: they re-create a culturally significant context for the change from child to adult, constitute semiotic movements that help effect that change, and create ceremonial structure and experience. There are patterns within each of these media-defined sets of signs, as well as interrelations and a coordination of patterns among media that are part of the complex orchestration of initiation's ritual efficacy.

Concentrated associations pack each set of signs discussed in this chapter. Unpacked and elaborated, the associations build a complex, multifaceted maze of significance leading to diverse contexts—some ceremonial, others not. They weave together a variety of social roles, relations, and activities, creating particular emphases and values in a rich, densely woven brocade of cultural meaning. This brocade is the backdrop of contextual re-creation.

Significant sequences of signs define cultural progressions in each medium, creating a sense of ritual movement and change and marking the movement throughout. Some progressions stretch widely, placing initiation within the longer process of growth and maturation; these include ritual processions, ritual feedings, head ornaments, and held objects. Other progressions are specific to initiation, such as the girls' sequenced roles, costumes, and spatial movement.

The complex coordination of these progressions and others to be described below are an important aspect of ceremonial structure. Shifts in a number of them concurrently can define structural divides and shifts of focus central to the dramatic development and emotional experience of a ceremony. Most semiotic movement discussed so far centers on the shifting locations of initiates within particular cultural progressions. This coordination highlights a broader, more general sense of semiotic movement that creates shared definitions and a shared experience of the ceremonies. For example, in the first ceremony, sunset brings a change of costume for the girls, a shift in participation patterns and event focus, and a shift in scheduled songs (chapter 7). When such shifts are not concurrent, they can distinguish other parts of a ritual process, as in the staggered and varied changes in initiates' named roles, costumes, and locations.

Though ceremonial structure includes coordinated scheduling of various media, this does not imply that a harmonious and unified message about social roles and values is conveyed through each of them. Media might be used to invoke the same roles or contexts in very different ways. Contradictions and paradoxes are not foreign to ceremonies, whether between media or within them. Indeed, they are sometimes central (V. Turner 1968; Karp 1986b); I will argue later that this is so in Okiek initiation.

For instance, the unifying complementarity represented in the *mabwaita* is reinforced by blessings but belied by encouraging speeches and verbal commentary (chapter 6). Similarly, the female *mabwaita* of seclusion and female organization of seclusion ceremonies silently contradict and offset the dominant message of men's priority and authority. Neither view is right or wrong; they present different, simultaneous, and sometimes contradictory interpretations of the same complex cultural reality.

The scheduling and coordination of different media in ceremonies create intersections and parallels, in which different media do similar things in different ways, as in the cultural progressions. Reiteration of themes and crosscutting associations reinforce both the sense of tradition and history and its seemingly natural order; they all seem to go together. Despite—and sometimes through—contradictions, multimedia repetition reveals different dimensions of the same relations and assumptions.

The concretization of ceremonial tradition is also fundamental here. Objects used and created time and again in ceremonies, acts repeated the same way in the same place—repetition creates an image of continuity, underlines a sense of history and unbroken tradition. That many ritual materials are drawn from ordinary activities, with associations stretching into other contexts of daily life is also important.

Ceremonial signs pull together many associations and contexts and help make explicit the relations between them. Their use and sequence in ceremonies also gives them an affective charge which then can often be traced in the contexts which contribute to their significance. In ceremonies, certain objects from daily life become material for sign vehicles, and receive an additional cognitive and emotional significance. (Kratz 1988b:246)

Material and mimetic continuity and the sense of ceremonial tradition also carry along, re-create, and justify cultural assumptions, values, roles, and practices. They are made to seem as natural, unchanging, and unchangeable as the ceremonial form that is re-created.

6

Prayer, Persuasion, Peace, and Prestation: Initiation through Speech

Articulated words are impregnated with assumed and unarticulated qualities . . . a poetic work is a powerful condenser of unarticulated social evaluations—each word is saturated with them.

V. N. Volosinov, *Freudianism: A Critical Sketch*

Many nonverbal aspects of initiation are not explicitly referred to during ceremonial performance; their significance is essential but much remains in the background. My account of their background of cultural assumptions in the last chapter sometimes led away from initiation through other contexts and experiences, where the associative resonances they bring to the ceremonies are elaborated and produced. This chapter and the next refocus more directly on the performance of ritual events—on the unfolding of the initiation process over time. They look closely at the verbal side of Okiek initiation, concentrating on speech in this chapter and song in the next.

Verbal resources are central to ceremonial analysis because they can shape particular emphases and textures of performance even in nonverbal media. Critically involved in the key processes of ritual efficacy, verbal resources are used and scheduled in ways that pick out and focus on particular parts of ceremonies, evaluate and define the ways ritual signs are to be taken, and influence and create the tenor and character of the experience for different participants. At the same time that other communicative media can be highlighted and evaluated verbally, verbal patterns and styles also define prominent and active modes of ceremonial participation in themselves, constituting other aspects of the contextual re-creation, semiotic movement, and experiential engagement of initiation.

As part of the essential context for making Okiek girls into women, patterns of speaking reproduce and reinforce assumptions about social roles, gender, cultural identity, and patterns of social relations. Distinctions of verbal mode and genre and their sequence in ritual events create a cultural progression that is entwined with assumptions about gender and identity and is critical to initiation's dramatic structure. This combines with progressions in other media to accomplish the girls' ceremonial transformation into women. Every scheduled kind of participation in the ceremonies includes a verbal component that helps shape the experience of initiates and other participants, implicating them in the framework of accepted assumptions as well as the particular transformation.

The convergences and interrelations of these three processes are particularly striking in the speech and song of initiation. For instance, the varied modes of encouragement (*ceerseet*) in the first ceremony define one of the most important cultural sequences of semiotic movement. Through definition of who encourages whom, in what way, and at what point in the ceremony, modes of encouragement simultaneously re-create central assumptions about gender and social relations. Assumptions are not only represented but also embodied, as people encourage in ways befitting their own identities. Modes of encouragement are also understood as displays of emotion. The encouragement sequence is thus further tied into the dramatic pacing of the ceremony, constituting the interactive intensification that helps orchestrate participants' experiential and emotional engagement. This semiotic movement is simultaneously emotionally moving.

While the speech of initiation helps recreate cultural assumptions and ideas about initiation, it concurrently contradicts and articulates alternatives to them in performance. The multiple roles and experiential perspectives combined in ceremonial performances make the emergence of other, unofficial viewpoints almost inevitable. At times, the very ritual events are defined and structured in ways that incorporate such ambiguities and tensions. Expressed within the formal and official dimensions of performance itself or in asides that comment on performance, unofficial viewpoints sometimes combine ambiguities related to both system integration and social integration.

Tensions related to the structural contradictions of Okiek age and gender relations are built into girls' *pesenweek* confessions and *ceerseet* speeches. The divergent interests and values of adults and children always emerge in the former; divergent understandings of women's abilities appear in the latter. In each case, performance of the ritual event reveals the contested and negotiated nature of authority and to some extent undermines official definitions. At the same time, individuals may also have contradictory feelings based on their personal relations with the initiates—at once proud of their lovely girls, anxious about their trial and pain, loath to lose the girls' presence at home, and pleased to anticipate their maturity and marriage. Ceremonial performance provides a forum for, and indeed brings out, multiple tensions among the typification of official representations, identification with personal relations (cf. Fortes 1987; Jackson and Karp 1990), and divergent unofficial views of social relations and gender identity. As these multiple ambiguities emerge in performance they, too, contribute to the tenor of experience, engagement, and heightening of emotion over the course of the ceremony.

In this chapter I consider scheduled ways of speaking in their sequential order (which is described in chapter 4). Some, such as blessings and curses, are Okiek speech genres included within larger ritual events. Others (encouraging speeches, confession of social debts, speeches of thanks, seclusion lessons, final gift-giving) are at the center of ritual events, with the event and the way of speaking often called by the same name. Two other modes of speech that are expected during the first initiation ceremony are neither explicitly scheduled nor necessary. Both are part of women's emotional displays. First, women overcome with emotion (-*tupuc*) often speak during their fits. Second, women sometimes harangue initiates.

I discuss how the communicative context, discourse structure, thematic patterns, and pragmatic force of each way of speaking figure in the efficacy of initiation and in the articulation of alternative perspectives and contradictions during ceremonial performance. Finally, I consider the speech of initiation with respect to overall ceremonial structure and general patterns of speech, silence, and verbal participation during the initiation process.

Blessing

Blessing punctuates Okiek ceremonies from beginning to end, and is an essential part of most ritual events.[1] During initiation, elders pray for good fortune and peace all along the way, blessing people and the ceremony, ritual materials and the products made from them. Blessings end forest processions, complete the ritual construction of the *mabwaita* and the *toloocik,* and often end girls' confession of social debts. Blessings continue to punctuate seclusion ceremonies, following each secret revelation. Finally, in the last ceremony, elders again say and spray blessings as the singing procession from the river circles the *mabwaita.*

Blessings re-create and perpetuate Okiek gender roles in the patterns of both performance and scheduling in the ceremonies. A pair of male elders pronounces public blessings, broadcasting their prayer materially by spraying honey wine from their mouths onto those blessed. Women very rarely perform public, spoken blessings. Initiation's main female blessing, the initiates' mothers' opening anointment of all present with dabs of fat, is silent. During seclusion these days, an old man or woman (*piitintet*) attends to bless secrets when needed.

Okiek identify male elders as the appropriate persons to bless on the basis of ideas about male and female abilities and roles. Men are capable of reasoned discussion and cooperation, and of organizing political life, the household, and ceremonial occasions; they are free of the inauspicious, polluting aspect of women's role as bearers and caretakers of children. The notion that elders can and do organize consequential matters is reinforced and in part created by their role as blessers. Their blessings mark the start and finish of ceremonies, establish the space for other ritual events, and finalize all ritual acts that mark major ceremonial divisions. Elders bestow blessings on each group of participants as well as on the ceremony as a whole. They thus ratify and complete the acts of other ritual actors. They bring young people and women under their aegis with final blessings on processions, and also encompass the work of initiates' fathers (usually junior elders) on the *mabwaita* and *toloocik* with final blessings.

Blessings are first and foremost prayers, but pragmatically they are also more than that. Their performance is a primary means of framing ritual events and the ceremony as a whole, reminding people of the nature of the occasion in order to invoke the appropriate key of harmonious cooperation. In other contexts, blessings frame the central focus of an occasion, for example, bracketing formal discussion at men's meetings or marriage discussions. In initiation, blessings frame entire ceremonies in this way, but are also performed during ritual events in between. The ability of ceremonial blessings to frame and key is more complexly embedded, marking sections and events as well as the ceremonial frame as a whole.

During the first day, for instance, an auspicious (*esiny'a*) foursome of blessings is said in two corresponding pairs. Blessings on the two forest processions and the two ritual structures built from the materials gathered during those processions unite all categories of social and ritual actors. Blessings define the appropriate key and enjoin all present to observe it as they are brought into the general ceremonial frame.

From dusk to dawn, during the nighttime section that focuses on the initiates, the only blessing comes after the girls' confessions. The last act before dawn, this blessing once again closes the section's public ritual events. The emphasis here is on reestablishing and displaying the appropriate key of peaceful cooperation in a way that concentrates good intentions on the girls. The confessions describe arguments and arrogant disobedience, revealing particular sources of ill will toward them that would be contrary to that harmony. Those are disarmed through naming, and elders curse any unspecified persons who still wish them harm. The final blessing reemphasizes the cooperative, peaceful attitude that should prevail, collectively ratifying the girls' absolution. As the last public act before dawn, it is the final guarantee that good will toward the girls prevails.

Each ceremonial blessing calls for peace, cooperation, and understanding and reminds people to act accordingly, to create the harmonious atmosphere expected during ceremonies. What blessings pray for and how wishes are expressed in them reveal and create an image of ideal Okiek life. Peaceful, cooperative harmony is one of four main themes and values expressed and combined in various ways in Okiek blessings. The others are fecundity, prosperity, and continuity.

Prayers for fecundity mention things associated with birth (such as *inkipa*, the slime of birth), ask for children, or focus on vast numbers (for example, asking that children be as many as locusts, swelling the family into an entire neighborhood). Prayers asking for children also pray for continuity, for offspring to continue the family line. Similar prayers ask for long life and continuity in terms of enduring natural objects and cycles: rocks, mountains, the moon. Invoking age-sets, particularly old ones, conveys a sense of continuity through the perpetuation of patrilineages, ritual cycles, and social relations.

Prosperity is represented in terms of property (especially cows), having many children and women, and being able to provide well for them. One recurrent line prays for ceremonies that never end, combining several themes: not only are never-ending ceremonies a sign of a home blessed with women and children, as well as the means to feed them and to entertain a houseful of guests, but ceremonies also create new adults to perpetuate the family line and swell its numbers.

Prayers related to the fourth theme, cooperation and peace, expand the family and lineage focus of other prayers to include relations between lineages and ethnic groups as well. These lines especially represent an image of the kind of interaction and tone appropriate for blessing occasions. Whether or not people fulfill that ideal, frequent blessings are regular reminders of it during the alternation of ritual events, drinking, and informal interaction that is involved in ceremonies.

These themes and images portray the ideal blessed life very much from a male point of view. Women's reproductive role is well represented inasmuch as women perpetuate male lines and create patriarchs' wealth and prosperity. Their productive role, however, is absent. Women's work in building houses, farming, cooking, carrying water and firewood, and raising children is the essential but silent background to the well-run, prosperous, ideal home. In much the same way, women's silent blessing with fat is the essential complementary act to elders' opening blessing in initiation. Women share the wishes and prayers expressed in blessings, but a different image would emerge were a female viewpoint represented instead.

The gender roles acted in ceremonies and represented in blessings are hardly a complete or accurate picture of daily life, but they are directly related to Okiek gender ideology. Okiek notions and assumptions about gender roles and abilities are applied not only in ceremonies but also in legal cases, marriage negotiations, and other public arenas of responsibility and control. The notions are represented, re-created, and reinforced by the images of blessings, as well as by their performance.[2]

Blessings represent ideal Okiek life from the viewpoint of the elders who say them, then, and their scheduling in ceremonies reproduces and represents the image of elders as organizers and ratifying overseers. As performers, too, elders themselves embody the values for which they pray. Coming from the oldest age-set present, blessers have already lived a long life during which they have fathered children and sometimes grandchildren. The honey wine available for blessing shows some modicum of prosperity and luck. Finally, the _esiny'a_ pair of elders who bless are linked in cooperation to start the occasion with good wishes and harmony.

The performance draws in the others present as well, so the cooperative agreement wished for in the prayer is indeed realized, at least for its duration. Blessings are antiphonal, resembling the call-and-response form of most Okiek songs. After each line called by an elder, those gathered answer with a short word, such as _nai, sere_ (amen), or _Enkai_ (God < Maa). Elders lead the prayer and ratify the ritual work, but everyone present agrees, responding with their own ratification of the blessing and of the elders' position as spokesmen and organizers. The coproduction of blessings engages people in the ritual event of the moment and in the assumptions and social relations implicit in blessings and ceremonial organization.

As elders iconically embody values prayed for and the blessing performance re-creates an image of desired cooperation, the verbal structure of blessings similarly incorporates principles and images iconic to those central values in the texts themselves. Their poetic structures are consistently based on lines grouped in auspicious twos and fours, groups combined and interwoven in ways as diverse as the ways people come together in joint purpose and fellowship.

Okiek bless in three styles, each associated with a different ethnic group and language: Okiek, Maasai, or Kipsigis. At times, elders change language and style in midblessing, for example, from Maasai to Okiek and back again.[3] Table 11 shows the two Maa blessings from the initial procession of the ceremony described in chapter 4. Other ceremonial blessings are included in appendix B.

The lines of Okiek and Maasai blessings share a basic grammatical structure. Lines are of three kinds: (1) verb phrases with imperative or subjunctive forms, introduced by the particle _ot_ (in Okiek) to mark the optative mood;[4] (2) descriptive continuations of verb phrase lines, clearly linked to other lines with connectives or other phrases; and (3) enumerations of groups who concur in the wishes of the blessing, most often a list of age-sets. Pragmatically, imperative and subjunctive verb phrase lines both count as requests or wishes expressed in prayer. Most Kipsigis-style blessings have two similar line forms: (1) the form *X ole X* (X, say, X) for adjectives and verbs; and (2) *mii X ole mii* (there is/are X, say, there is/are) for lines using nouns.[5] The final phrase after *ole* is the expected response.

Blessings and lines both vary considerably in length. They are not narrowly defined by metrical conventions of syllable length, verse structure, or rhyming patterns. Nor is there clear narrative or pragmatic progression through the entire blessing. Rather, the overall poetic structure of blessings consists of a combination of smaller line groupings linked by exact and partial repetition, grammatical parallelism, or semantic continuity.

Most commonly, lines are in *esiny'a* groups of two or four, but variations in repetition and ways of expanding and varying lines introduce many line groups within groups, some of three and five lines. Some successive line groups are related through semantic, formal, or sonic transitions. Single lines occur most often between line groups, demarcating them. Single lines might also be linked in larger patterns of two or four repetitions threaded through the entire blessing. The overall effect is a dense interweaving of formal and semantic relations not only between successive line groups but between groups spread over the full blessing as well.

The succession of dense, localized poetic patterns is further consolidated by general similarities of line structure that emerge from the small set of basic grammatical constructions and semantic themes used in blessings. In Okiek-language blessings subjunctive forms introduced by *ot* are particularly important in producing more general aesthetic coherence, while in Maa-language ones repeated assonance of the *ent-* verb prefix, which introduces imperative and subjunctive forms, is prominent. These features bind blessings together sonically and pragmatically, as blessings themselves temporarily unite the event's participants.

To clarify these poetic patterns, here I examine closely the first blessing in table 11, which in table 12 is rewritten to show line groupings and linked groups. In both blessings listed in table 11, successive lines are related by grammatical parallelism, repetition, sound similarity, and semantic continuity, which group them into clusters (usually pairs or foursomes), sometimes broken with single intervening lines. The first blessing has similar complex interrelations between nonadjacent lines and line groups, creating a tightly woven poetic structure within the overall cohesion produced by common syntactic forms and verb form assonance.[6]

Kwampat Sembui (Oldyo; Kwampat Sembui means "father of Sembui." The equivalent title for a woman is Kopot, "mother of") begins with four lines based on the verb *-rropil* (to smell sweet). The first two are linked by the initial *tiaaki*, though the verb form changes from subjunctive in the first to imperative in the second. The second pair carries the imperative form to the initial position and specifies in the second line what should be fragrant (*ol-orere*, the crowd of people).

Table 11: Blessings for *Koroseek* Procession

A. Blessing in Maa by Kwampat Sembui
(Rana family, Kap Oldyo lineage, *il terito* age-set)

A. Kwampat Sembui's blessing

1.	tiaaki metorropilo	(sere)	Tell [them] may you be sweetly fragrant	(amen)
2.	tiaaki entorropil	(sere)	Tell [them] be sweetly fragrant	(amen)
3.	entorropil	(sere)	Be sweetly fragrant	(amen)
4.	entorropil ol-orere	(sere)	May the people be sweetly fragrant	(amen)
5.	entagil	(sere)	[Marry each other, multiply, and] spread[1]	(amen)
6.	entubul	(sere)	Flourish	(amen)
7.	entubul	(sere)	Flourish	(amen)
8.	entoisho	(sere)	Give birth	(amen)
9.	entoisho	(sere)	Give birth	(amen)
10.	nirikiriki	(sere)	And continue to marry [each other]	(amen)
11.	entubul	(sere)	Flourish	(amen)
12.	entaa ol-maati	(sere)	Be as many as the locusts	(amen)
13.	Enkai na ejo	(sere)	God [is the one] who says so	(amen)
14.	entaa ol-orere	(sere)	Be a community	(amen)
15.	entubul	(sere)	Flourish	(amen)
16.	entaa ol-Torrobo	(sere)	Be Okiek[2]	(amen)
17.	entaa ol-Maasai	(sere)	Be Maasai	(amen)
18.	entaa ol-Torrobo	(sere)	Be Okiek	(amen)
19.	entigil il-oshon	(sere)	Divide into sections[3]	(amen)
20.	entigil il-oshon	(sere)	Divide into sections	(amen)
21.	entagol	(sere)	Be strong	(amen)
22.	entubul	(sere)	Flourish	(amen)
23.	entubul	(sere)	Flourish	(amen)
24.	entoisho	(sere)	Give birth	(amen)
25.	in-tomonok	(sere)	Women	(amen)
26.	nirikiriki	(sere)	And continue to marry	(amen)
27.	il-asho liny'i	(sere)	Your calves[4]	(amen)
28.	enjuru	(sere)	Prosper	(amen)
29.	too in-kipa naa melok	(sere)	Be [like] the sweet slime of birth	(amen)

B. Blessing in Maa by Kwampat Parmasai
(Kap Leboo lineage, eseuri age-set)

B. Kwampat Parmasai's blessing

1.	meiruko Enkai ole-dukuya	May God agree to the first [blessing]	(amen) (sere)
2.	meiruko Enkai	May God agree	(amen) (sere)
3.	meiruko eseuri	May eseuri age-set agree	(amen) (sere)
4.	meiruko il tareto	May il tareto age-set agree	(amen) (sere)
5.	entaa— ento— entorropil	Be—be sweetly fragrant	(amen) (sere)
6.	entubulo	Flourish	(amen) (sere)
7.	entubulu	Flourish	(amen) (sere)
8.	entoisho naa katoisho	Give birth, [those] who should bear[5]	(amen) (sere)
9.	min4oki la kayama kuna o nkulie	May you talk of those who marry these and others[6]	(amen) (sere)
10.	in-tomonok metagolo ink-oriong'i	May the women have strong backs	(amen) (sere)
11.	naa metoisho	And may they give birth	(amen) (sere)
12.	il-arin mikitasho e-lukuny'a	May the head be always creative[7]	(amen) (sere)
13.	e-lukuny'a le enk-aji	The head of the home	(amen) (sere)
14.	il-arin mikitasho e-lukuny'a	May the head be always creative	(amen) (sere)
15.	meeta e-naikuti	May there be ceremonies	(amen) (sere)
16.	incoo eilepu	Let them rise [like the sun]	(amen) (sere)
17.	metaiborro en-aisho	With no one cursing the liquor[8]	(amen) (sere)
18.	metaiborro en-aisho	With no one cursing the liquor	(amen) (sere)

1. Literally, to break, divide, or distribute. Okiek translated it as meaning "marry each other and have children," so that the family spreads through procreation and through intermarriage.

2. I.e., be as many as an entire people.

3. I.e., be so many that you are like an entire section (il oshon, Maasai territorial subgroups).

4. I.e., children.

5. I.e., women should have many children.

6. I.e., have your own children so that you talk about the marriages of the children you have now and those of your future children, rather than about other people's children and their marriages. An alternative translation given for this line is "May you stay and endure for many years."

7. I.e., creative, cool, clear, and level-headed thinking.

8. I.e., the liquor for the ceremony. Let no one argue or shout or otherwise spoil the peace and good will of the occasion.

Table 12: Poetic Structure and Line Groupings in Kwampat Sembui's Blessing

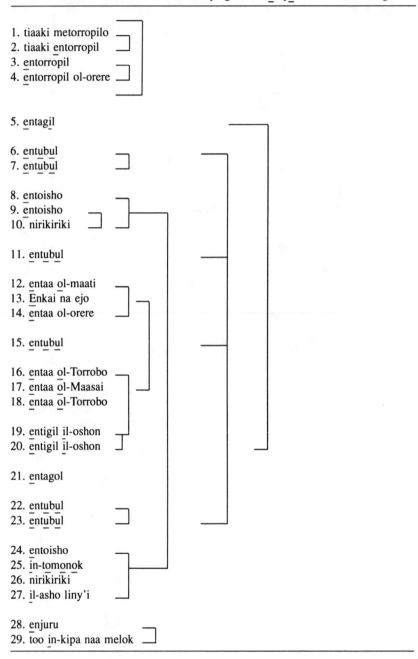

1. tiaaki metorropilo
2. tiaaki entorropil
3. entorropil
4. entorropil ol-orere

5. entagil

6. entubul
7. entubul

8. entoisho
9. entoisho
10. nirikiriki

11. entubul

12. entaa ol-maati
13. Enkai na ejo
14. entaa ol-orere

15. entubul

16. entaa ol-Torrobo
17. entaa ol-Maasai
18. entaa ol-Torrobo

19. entigil il-oshon
20. entigil il-oshon

21. entagol

22. entubul
23. entubul

24. entoisho
25. in-tomonok
26. nirikiriki
27. il-asho liny'i

28. enjuru
29. too in-kipa naa melok

Entagil, line 5, stands alone in local line structure, but combines with lines 19 and 20, if this pair of exact repetitions is taken as a unit. That unit creates a formal-semantic pair with the same verb, and a semantic foursome with lines 16–18 (see below). Line pairs with exact repetition combine as a single unit in other cases as well, forming groups of two or four with other lines. For example, line pairs 6–7 and 22–23 repeat *entubul,* as do two single lines (11 and 15) between other groups. Together, there are four *entubul* occurrences, two of single lines and two of repeated pairs.

Lines 8–9 are another pair of repetitions, with line 10 a semantic continuation. This group about giving birth is echoed in lines 24–27, where the lines 8–10 are repeated and filled out.

After the intervening single *entubul,* lines 12–14 consist of a pair linked by semantic and grammatical parallelism separated by a single line. That line specifies God as the speaker of imperatives that would otherwise be neither reasonable nor felicitous; prospering and increasing are not within ready human control. After another single *entubul* (line 15), another trio replicates the structure of lines 12–14, separating two exact repetitions with a line that parallels them grammatically. The two trios (12–14 and 16–18) are also linked by semantic and grammatical parallelism, all based on the verb "to be" (*a-ra;* pl. imperative *entaa*) and praying for increase and strength in numbers.

As noted, lines 16–18 also form a semantic quartet with the following paired repetition (19–20). *Il-oshon* (section, group), *ol-Torrobo,* and *ol-Maasai* are semantically related. Okiek and Maasai are distinct ethnic groups, but in some circumstances are talked about as related sections. The pair also develops the sense of the first group of lines (16–18): becoming as large as an entire ethnic group, the family will subdivide into sections, intermarry, and continue to increase. Though the size metaphors are poetic exaggeration, that is the process of lineage expansion, with eventual intermarriage between subbranches.

Line 21 is again a single line, very similar in sound to both the verb in the preceding lines and the final pair of *entubul* lines immediately after. Finally, after the four lines about birth (24–27), which echo and expand lines 8–10, a final line pair closes with a general prayer for prosperity (28–29). This pair is linked to the birth theme of the preceding foursome by *in-kipa* in the final line. *In-kipa*'s general sense here is "goodness and blessing," but it also refers specifically to the slime of birth on newborn children or animals.

Specific textual patterns differ in other blessings but are based on similar relations between lines and groups of lines. The poetic structure of Okiek blessings varies, produced not through narrowly defined formal rules but by combining a relatively small set of poetic principles, aesthetic tendencies, and thematic foci in a variety of ways in different contexts. The relatively free combination of line groups and the varied links between them are structural complements to the absence of linear narrative or pragmatic progressions in blessings.

The poetic structure of blessings has much in common with that of songs, as will be seen in the next chapter, but there are important differences. For instance, the poetic structure of song emerges only with extended performance. Their poetic principles may be similar to those of blessings, but the difference in performers is critical and informative. Call-and-response songs are coproduced to a far greater extent than blessings, with constant shifts of lead singer as well as dialogic exchanges between call and response. Song is considered a potential vehicle of emotional expression and, at times, escalation; the singers in ceremonies are women, young men, and above all, the initiates.

When elders bless, the poetic structure of blessings shows once again that they know how to organize things, this time verbally. They control the performance; others follow with agreement (-yan). They create relations between lines—predominantly in patterns of two and four, sometimes intricate and dense—that are icons of the auspiciousness and cohesion for which they pray. Structural and poetic similarities with song assimilate and incorporate a certain affective energy into blessings, but under the elders' influence. Subjunctive and imperative verbs that ostensibly address God and/or exhort people on God's behalf are also the appropriate means through which elders simultaneously enjoin those present to take the wishes to heart themselves. Elders' authority is persuasive, not coercive; the persuasion of blessings is simultaneously semantic, formal, poetic, and performative.

The structure and performance of blessings is involved directly in the semiotic movement of initiation chiefly as part of the scheduled events and acts that create the ceremonial sequence defined as transformative. Blessings in the first ceremony also share the change of focus that is part of the general movement of that sequential structure, concentrating more attention on the initiates during the nocturnal events.

Blessings are much more centrally implicated in contextual re-creation, establishing and carrying on the cultural understandings within which the initiates' transformation takes place. Blessing themes, images, and expressions portray a particular set of values and picture of gender roles, representing assumptions that inform the life and social relations initiates will join as adults. Blessings re-create, legitimate, and perpetuate those relations and assumptions not only through their content, but also by the definition and enactment of blessing performance.

Elders whose central place of authority and respect is portrayed in blessings step into that place as auspicious, appropriate spokesmen who pray for everyone. They appear to organize the ceremony, simultaneously approving and completing ritual events with their benediction, and controlling and creating poetic icons with their persuasive influence. Through cross-contextual associations, blessings combine political, jural, and religious authority and become genres of power (Kratz 1987, 1989). "[T]he specifically symbolic power to impose the principles of the construction of reality—in particular, social reality—is a major dimension of political power" (Bourdieu 1977a:165).

Similarly, ceremonial blessings create a sense of continuity and tradition as a legitimating backdrop to the ceremony as a whole (Kratz 1987:89, 1993). Blessings display, re-create, and reaffirm the ideal picture by combining different refractions of it within their structure; all make cultural practice into tradition and the natural order. They create an impression of continuity, maintenance, and affirmation, not one of change, movement, or development. Blessings create a framework of tradition and draw all present into it together.

Contextual re-creation and experiential engagement overlap here. As other participants are implicated in the values and tradition conveyed in performance, tacitly accepting them through their response, they simultaneously affirm a proposed outlook on the occasion. Blessings invoke the appropriate key for the ceremony, and ideally influence ceremonial comportment to help establish that key. United in participation and agreement, people are urged and reminded to carry that harmony (evident even in blessings' verbal structure) throughout the ceremony. In fact, people usually disperse from the blessing laughing and joking, while elders linger to finish the blessing liquor. Blessings thus also initiate the affective and experiential texture of ceremonial involvement.

Ceerseet

The next major scheduled mode of speech comes much later, during a nocturnal event focused on the initiates that impresses on them collective expectations and their own obligation. When men speak to the initiates at this time, both the event and the speeches they make are called encouragement (ceerseet).

After dusk, the girls' vigorous dancing and singing is the center of attention outside; a tumultuous crowd gathers to watch the costumed initiates. While young men, girls, and women talk, joke, and shout comments, the initiates sing farewells. Some are addressed personally to individuals, who might respond by falling into emotional fits (see below and chapter 7). The scene is lively, full of noise, flash, movement, and an increasing excitement that combines high spirits with anxiety.

The songs outside also encourage (-ceer). What Okiek mean by "encouragement" here is the creation of an inescapable net of social pressure, thrown at the girls from many directions at once through repetitive urging, claims of unfulfilled responsibility, provocative challenges, and reiterated requests. All of this plays on the emotional ties of their closest relationships of kinship and friendship. Encouraging speeches and songs have a common purpose and share many themes and idioms, though different participants express them in different ways, forms, and contexts.

As initiation unfolds temporally, the sequencing of different forms of encouragement entwines the semiotic movement of ceremonial structure with the interactive intensification that shapes its dramatic contours and the experiential and emotional engagement of participants. Okiek notions of male and female are also re-created and reinforced by the organization and order of modes of encouragement, bringing contextual re-creation into the mix of drama, movement, and engagement as well.

While the initiates dance outside, most of the men are inside drinking beer. As the night wears on, the conversation becomes animated and can get riotously heated if the more boisterous drunks become argumentative. Respectful comportment is expected of all, but some may lack or lose self-control. Thus the host also tries to keep order with directives and reminders—stay seated, talk quietly to your neighbor, keep quiet during speeches, don't shout, don't argue, don't wander about the house, and so on. Though the scene may dissolve into a noisy ruckus now and then, it usually approximates the model of a quietly sociable and amicably tipsy houseful of drinkers. The initiates leave the animated crowd and spirited dancing outside to dance into this very different atmosphere for the *ceerseet* speeches.[7]

They enter a house of elders who are apparently enjoying their beer in a controlled, amiable way. These men give the final encouragement with judicious, measured, and heartfelt words. And heartfelt they are. Though the unbridled excitement of the dance arena is suddenly cooled and calmed, a similar anxious concern and penetrating emotional tension comes out in the men's talks as well. There are no tears or fits, which would be unseemly for elders. Instead, a man conveys emotional involvement in the tone and delivery of his speech. He may "feel his heart constrict and pound in his chest when he talks to his girls," as one man told me, but he shows it in a more restrained manner.

The elders' encouraging speeches convey the same anxious anticipation, doubt, and urgent requests for bravery as do encouraging songs, but in a controlled, organized way, each elder speaking in turn, repeating the same message. As elders' blessings finalize other ritual events, so, too, men's speeches finalize and make unanimous expectations of the girls. Through their ratification, the encouragement intensifies and focuses an increasingly coercive pragmatic force on the initiates.

Yet the speeches contribute more to the persuasive unanimity than just the legitimation and authority of the elders. The elders in question are the girls' fathers, which underlines the poignant pull of personal relations. Most men particularize their addresses, reminding the girls of their relationship, of some specific meeting, or of how *they* have done things the girls asked for. Their personalized appeals affect the other listeners and heighten their own emotional involvement as well as their influence on the girls.

The intensification is also produced from a certain tension between contextual re-creation—the men are enacting the part of contained, imperturbable men of authority—and emotional and experiential engagement—these are their own daughters. As that tension emerges in the restrained but unmistakably emotional tone of some speeches, both the ideal typification of men and their personal engagement can be emphasized. Small but repeated contradictions of gender ideology nonetheless confirm its typifications. The men are so controlled that their high anxiety emerges only in small signs (small compared to women and young people). At the same time, they show that their worried involvement is such that the usual male self-control is threatened.

Who actually speaks to the girls, then, and how? People described *ceerseet* as the time when the girls' fathers, that is, all the men categorized as fathers through kinship and age-set links, talk to them; in a more general sense, elders (*paaiisyoniik*) or men were named as speakers. The host father speaks first. After him, speakers may go by seating order or age-set order (beginning with the host father's age-set), or may self-select. Ten to fifteen men usually speak, though there may be twice as many; the last few speakers might be women. Talks range from one to about eight minutes in length.

Though all the men might speak, the paternal relation is prominent, emphasized by the host father's lead role, the age-set sequence, the speeches themselves, and Okiek commentary.[8] It carries great rhetorical and pragmatic power for encouragement in part because fathers are considered responsible for organizing the ceremony, feeding the guests, and bearing the financial burden, though the work and cost are actually shared among family members. By linking himself to the father, a distantly related speaker or infrequent visitor draws himself into the web of obligations that makes encouragement compelling.[9]

Metaphorical extensions of kinship are usually made through the paternal relation, but other relations also bind. *Imaamook* (relatives in the mother's lineage), brothers, and sisters' husbands all have strong rhetorical claims as well. Familiar relatives commonly talk about their work to prepare the ceremony the girls asked for, leaving the kinship link implicit and obvious; distant visitors often note their relation explicitly as they begin.

The girls' demeanor during the speeches contrasts with the scene outside just as sharply as the atmosphere in the house does. They dance into the house and sit in line, facing the drinking men, with the host mother at one end to help receive gifts. During the talks, the girls sit silently, eyes downcast.[10] Men call them by name and by relation terms. They use interrogative constructions, words, and markers that usually call for a response. Yet the girls respond in no way. At the end, they silently receive the money given. The young Kipsigis man whose record player was hired might play a snatch of music. A brief dance is the only response girls might then make to the talk that is sometimes gently earnest and sometimes a vehement diatribe, but always pointedly directed to them.

On the one hand, the girls' silent, passive manner is exaggerated respect before their fathers, a respectful demeanor belied later by their *pesenweek* reports. On the other, the constraint on any response strengthens their obligation to respond at dawn with bravery. The girls' immediate response to encouragement is internal; they harden their hearts and concentrate their wills for the painful test that is their true response.

As *ceerseet* proceeds, several different, sometimes contradictory, definitions of what is going on operate simultaneously, sometimes at cross purposes (cf. Karp 1987:138). No one disputes the official definition: the speeches are men's encouragement to the initiates. But the multiple participants present and different perspectives on the effect of encouragement introduce other aspects and understandings that question and sometimes undermine that definition. Alternative definitions emerge especially in the comments and conversation that precede, interrupt, and intervene between speeches. If only the speeches are considered, the official definition is largely confirmed.

Initiates are the acknowledged addressees of the talks, but the speakers are certainly aware of the others present. Given the setting and situation, it could hardly be otherwise. When the speakers begin, they call repeatedly for quiet over the hum of drunken discussion, and suffer interruptions as others heckle or break in to add something they have just remembered. Some men are quite drunk and cause serious disturbances. The house is dark or dimly lit by kerosene lamps. Unable to see well, people must direct the speaker to the mother to give his gift, or fumble in the dark with flashlights to make change for a hundred-shilling note, holding up other speeches.

The audience for the speeches can be disruptive, but there are also concerned witnesses and listeners. Speakers are conscious of both, and in fact take those other roles and perspectives themselves before and after their own address. Details in the speeches show that there are other addressees (see below). Speeches are not only encouragement to the girls but also indirect displays for the audience. A description of the efforts and resources expended for the ceremony, for instance, obligates the girls but also shows others what a responsible brother one is. At the same time, this public display strengthens the girls' obligation, for their implicit promises are witnessed.

Personal display may be part of the speeches, but it is camouflaged within and enabled by adherence to the official definition of the event. Drunken hecklers represent another interpretation that challenges the "serious" definition from a different perspective. Side conversations, joking asides, and heckling all emphasize the presence of an interactive audience that is not always affirming or attentive. They may find the persuasive force and intent seriousness of the speeches affecting at times, but that is sometimes less relevant for them than their own side interactions or deflating the speaker (and his display). Their other involvements and interruptions suggest another viewpoint that elevates a definition of the event as drunken sociability and contest, in some ways undercutting the official definition.

The official definition is not undermined only by audience hecklers, however. Even when the surrounding hubbub is controlled and a man is well into his earnest appeal, there are still breaks in delivery and persuasive momentum as the girls, the ostensible addressees, are discovered dozing, or the mother (who should be listening, ready to receive gifts) is found to have slipped out. Speakers are often told to carry on whether the initiates are asleep or not, in part foregrounding the talks' unacknowledged audience and display aspects.

Comments made at these and other times also reveal a contrary attitude that denies the speeches' efficacy, thereby questioning the basis and rationale for the entire event and the assumptions that sustain it. Speakers are told to continue whether or not the girls are listening. After all, words alone won't give the girls brave hearts if they haven't got them already. Some speeches also emphasize that success depends on determination hardened well before the ceremony starts.

This idea is also familiar from the songs in boys' ceremonies (see chapter 7), but boys are not encouraged in speech as girls are. The difference is explained by the contrast between boys, who can encourage themselves, and girls, who are considered intrinsically weak-willed and changeable, like women. Without the extra spoken encouragement of *ceerseet,* girls might not succeed. The event is necessary to keep their intention unwavering, even if their strength comes ultimately from within.

This official definition is contradicted in several ways, highlighting a problem of system integration. First, the gender-based justification is directly opposed to the basic premise of initiation for both girls and boys, which is that initiates show maturity by drawing on their own strength and inner resources for personal, physical self-control. If speeches are superfluous to initiates' inner determination, then perhaps there is yet another dimension to the speakers' display and persuasion. Those gathered might also be showing and convincing themselves that they are in control in the face of evidence to the contrary.

The second contradiction arises from the notion that women follow their whims without listening to advice, an idea that strikes at the heart of the *ceerseet* event. At one particular event (described further below), one speaker who recognized this stopped during his ardent plea, struck by the futility of encouraging girls who were incapable of listening to oratorical reason. Again, either speakers are speaking to themselves or certain assumptions about women must be false.

The simultaneous presence of all these varied interpretations during *ceer-*

seet produces tensions between perspectives and alternations between emotional appeals, heckling jokes, and other interruptions. In some cases different interpretations are foregrounded by different participants; in others they coincide in the performance of a single participant. The personalized sense of *ceerseet*'s double bind contributes to the emotional tenor of the experience for speakers and listeners alike: they can only help their girls through encouragement, yet those efforts are inevitably ineffective, whether because the children must succeed on their own or because it is futile to reason with women.

Drunk or not, men deliver talks that are recognizable speeches of encouragement. *Ceerseet* speeches vary in elaboration, but all have a common discourse structure, a basic sequence of thematic-cum-pragmatic sections. In addition to the common structure, there is also a rhetorical-poetic repertoire of ways through which speakers make their talks encouraging, incorporating the intended pragmatic force into the form and delivery of speeches. Appendix C contains a selection of speeches.[11]

The basic structure of encouraging speeches consists of a short opening vocative section followed by the longest, most variable section where encouragement is produced through persuasive argument and implied obligations. A short transitional section, usually with a metastatement about the speech or the situation, leads to the closing. Finally, verbal encouragement is underlined with an encouraging gift.[12] After that, speakers often declare themselves finished, for example, *Ko caan. Mamwaun ng'aleek ce caang'* (That's it. I don't tell you a lot of words). This general structure is illustrated below in the briefest, most skeletal of speeches:[13]

(vocative)	*Laakokcu*	You children
(encouragement)	*akemuru kiet// ko makimuru ko len/*	we've come [from] far away]// but we didn't come for nothing/
	Okweek inko kuureec// makimace kemuru/ keip kiayny'uun edoishoit/	You're the ones who invited us// We don't want to come/ and take shame home [with us]/
(transition)	*Kaayaat anee kurkeet/*	I've opened the door [started]/
(gift)	*kumi//*	ten [shillings]//

The closing gift-giving section often makes a final request for celebratory food and includes one of the themes common to encouraging speeches and songs. The girls are challenged scornfully to run, if they fear, to Kisumu or another land where people are uncircumcised.[14] A revealing alternation in the use of person sometimes occurs in this section, an alternation that returns to the question of unacknowledged audience and display. The following excerpt from a speech by A.N. (see table 14 for the entire speech) illustrates the "take the money and run" theme and the shift of person:

I have one cow myself/ I'll sell it tomorrow-*i*/ for all those three// I'll add it for you all to those other cows I sold [to hire your costumes]// So that if, um—/ you cheat, um—/ the guests you invited [by running away from initiation]// [then] you go off and go get into a [public transport] car with that money, and go to whatever country you end up going to// So it's a sheep that I'll sell for you tomorrow/ a female// Each of you will take twenty [shillings] twenty [shillings] twenty [shillings]// I add it for you to those cows that I sold/

Throughout his speech A.N. uses first person or second person; third person is used only once (to refer to the guests) until the final section (quoted above). There, in the opening lines, he refers to the girls in third person before switching back to second and first person to give the gift. The temporary switch highlights the dual sense of display in the speeches, noted above. A.N. simultaneously demonstrates and flaunts his generosity and responsibility to those gathered and calls on them to witness what the girls implicitly owe him.

There are other dimensions of display here as well. Both men's emotion and their great emotional control are clear in the interjections and the deep sighs that are interspersed through the talk. The display of this hairline boundary between controlled reason and emotional outburst helps men maintain their reputation as controlled and also enhances the persuasive, binding power of their talks (the fits of younger men and women similarly enhance their persuasive effect).

Finally, the gift itself is part of encouragement's binding persuasion, for a gift is a claim, but it is also display. Gifts vary in amount according to the guest-host relation and the giver's means. During *ceerseet,* normally individual, personal claims and negotiations of material assistance have a public expression and are collectively witnessed. As indications of prosperity and/or closeness, gifts display what everyone knows, to the advantage of the girls receiving them.[15] At some ceremonies someone acts as bookkeeper, intervening after the speeches to clarify the record. This not only makes display explicit, but adds a more calculating, businesslike accountability to it (seemingly discounting the emotional quality of the speeches), suggesting yet another perspective on and definition of the event.

Each man develops the same general discourse structure, repeating the same sequence, argument, themes, and images, but never in the same way. The narrative sequence of speeches, which build an argument and an appeal, illustrates men's "natural" reason and ability, compared to women's harangues (see below). In a circular reinforcement, men speak judiciously in part because they speak within discourse conventions; they can and do speak within conventions (defined as judicious speech) because they are men and elders.

Each speech demonstrates the speaker's knowledge and ability in this reasoned male way of speaking, but is also a personal and emotional appeal. The speeches are a series of personal, particular expressions that nonetheless repeat the same message and thereby gain an increasing force of unanimity.

The total combination creates a compelling sense of obligation and determination for the girls, and a sense of general expectation and anxiety for the others.

Speakers develop their arguments and create their rhetorical, emotional, and pragmatic effects with various devices—formal and grammatical means combined with thematic emphases and variations. They include various kinds of repetition, grammatical and thematic parallelism, interrogative constructions and rhetorical questions, phatic prompts, controlled emotional outbursts, lexical intensifiers, and quoted and reported speech. I examine this poetic-rhetorical repertoire with examples from two speeches. The first speech by P. is transcribed and translated in table 13.

First, diverse kinds of repetition emphasize certain themes, elaborating them to develop their persuasive power. Patterns of repetition also define and link structural subdivisions in speeches, particularly in the second section, the encouragement per se. Phrase repetition (sometimes with variation), repetition through parallel syntactic structure, and thematic repetition are most important.

Examples of phrase repetition from P.'s encouragement show how the varied repetition of key phrases, elaborated and evaluated from different angles, draws a compelling picture of inescapable obligation, and how skilled variation makes transitions between key refrains that both develop and lend cohesion to discursive argument. P. opens his second section with a virtual chorus of varied repetitions of the phrase *kaiwe tuumto* (you've gone *tuumto*). The pragmatic context for the refrain is created by short phrases interspersed with it. Simple descriptive phrases first place the onus for the occasion on the girl: *she* wanted it, as her quoted speech attests irrefutably. P. then builds a sense of the trial's imminence and inevitability; his use of the recent past tense in the repeated verb (*kaiwe*) for a future but impending event adds to the urgency.

The next refrain is (*[meinken] tuumto ko nee* ([you don't know] what *tuumto* is), introduced with a transitional permutation of the first refrain (*tuumto ne kipeentin*, it's *tuumto* that we go to) and repetition of the central shared word (*tuumto*) fronted in the permutation. The first phrase, *kaiwe tuumto,* is repeated once again after the refrain change, adding one more cohesive element. Discourse contexts for the new refrain develop the initial theme and pragmatic effects in several directions. First, P. underlines the distinction of experience and knowledge between a child and an initiated adult with his implicitly challenging suggestion that the girl didn't know what she was getting into and may not be up to the trial. Second, he alludes to his own memory of the experience, presenting the thought as upsetting by clucking, sighing, and swearing in emotional disturbance. An emotional display is considered strong encouragement; the girls themselves are disturbed because they are upsetting their relatives so much, and this hardens their will to be brave.

Finally, P. elaborates the second refrain with a seemingly kind, concerned effort to teach (or warn) her what she is in for, an elaboration as pragmatically loaded as the simple descriptive development of the first refrain. A blunt warning of tremendous pain ends in the challenge to the girl to declare her fear if she cannot endure it and another emotional outburst, which is calmed by his friend and initiation-mate. Of course his daughter neither answers nor leaves. Again she obligates herself by silence. Refusing the "chance" to run when it is "offered," she implicitly pledges courage.

Parallel syntactic structure and thematic repetition, often combined with refrain phrases, can create similar effects, as seen in A.N.'s speech in table 14. After calling the children, A.N. begins with a four-phrase series composed of two pairs that each end with *tako anee ni* (it's still me). The second pair challenges the girls sharply through its interrogative form. A.N. twice repeats the syntactic form of negative question, also challenging. Each repetition of the negative question ends a set of phrases that begins with *ayu ne* (when [rel.]). *Ayu ne* starts another, interlocking series of parallel structures: relative clause questions.[16] Syntactically, these questions are also related to the relative-initial construction in the first statement, *anee ne* (I'm the one who). All these relative clauses are also in marked order in the sentence, fronting and emphasizing "I" and "when."

Each relative-initial phrase creates a different hook for the girls, based on a subtle interplay of presupposition and focus that arises in part from their construction. The first phrase focuses on A.N.'s self-identification, presupposing that *someone* had to exhaust himself for the girls ("I'm the one that went [running] about, getting tired . . ."); they would be obliged to *someone*. The second, *ayu ne,* focuses rhetorically on when exactly they asked him to help, taking as given that they did. Their quoted speech gives evidence of that, portrays his efforts as fulfilling their request, and thus intensifies the obligation; they *asked* him to do it. The third relative again focuses on "when." Here the assumption is that the elders would not come to the house without invitation. Who is responsible? Once again, of course, the girls are named in the negative question that follows.

Parallel phrase structure integrates the comment on the assembled elders at this point, which otherwise would be thematically intrusive to the focus on A.N.'s exertions. Yet their inclusion broadens the obligation, relating his concerted efforts to the efforts all the elders made to come; all have the same expectations. When A.N. gives his gift later, he refers to these guests, not to his own work, to invoke shame on girls who run.

These patterns of repetition and parallel syntactic structure mark the first subsection of A.N.'s encouragement, closed structurally in two ways. The first is the final *ii?,* which would evoke response in ordinary conversation: an answer to a question, a denial, or some indication of attention. The girls' silence implicitly accepts the responsibility laid on them, as in P.'s speech when they ignore the chance to run away. Second, two metacommunicative phrases follow and demarcate the section. They too include parallel phrases

Table 13: P.'s Encouraging Speech
(P. is host for the ceremony, father to one girl, sister's husband to the other)

P.: ... aleincin/ iweenti// amu nee si maiwe/ ko kiawe anee// itepaati ipaarei
in—/ kiapakaace itepaaten iny'ee/ ko kiawe anee?
hi?
ko/
aleincinin/
aleincinin/

kaiwe-ai tuumto/
kaiwe tuumto/ ne kiimace/
tapala ne kiisaamu/ kiipaarei in— "amace awe tuumto"// ko kainy'on iwe
tuumto/
kaiwe ra tuumto// ai inta nee? ko kainy'on kaiwe ra// amu apwaate ale//
meko tena seruut-i ak kuutiit/ s'iwe tuumto// ako tuumto ne kipeentin//
tuumto// ko meinken ile tuumto-i/ ko nee// ikase kityo kemwai/ [cluck]
Meinyikake/
menken tuumto ile nee/ ikase kityo// amu/ ake— kopaarei in—/
[sigh and cluck] mankooikee cu kooce/ kimwa— kimwai/ amu tos iyon
akomung' ng'aleek kimwau koitiita/
tuun kowo kopaarei-i/ "tuumto ko nee"// ako maink— meinken iman
amakineet/ ko kaaneetiin anee aleincin-i/ akoik kaiwe-ai tuumto/ ko
tuumto-i// ko tuumto/ kiy ne kikiilcinkee/ imuite kabisa// ko yuu
kinamuite/
[cluck] ko yuu kinamuite// imuite/ amu kiy ne ng'waan ne kikwang'e/
ne kiyayuun/
ne mapoci iwe/ i— i— itey kiy/ itulatul//
ile amu kong'waaniit/ ko kaikai aneetiin anee aleincin/ ng'waan kiyaan
kiyayuun// amace imwaiwaan paani/ ko in— imwauwaan paani ko inikeer
ile/ maimuuce/ imwaiwaan/ asic acunten paani iwe/ ko mac-i/ ii— in—/
iyay ko yuu naan/
[cluck] Kap Apaiye/ matin ikeeraan ang'alaani muutya ako aa ng'eetat
kabisa// kabisa/
ko yuu/

Table 13: P.'s Encouraging Speech (Translation)

P.:   . . . I tell you/ you're going [for initiation]// Why shouldn't you go/ and I went myself// You sit and think, um—/ I've left you to stay yourself/ and I went myself?

Hi?

So/

I tell you/

I tell you/

You've gone *tuumto*, then/

You've gone *tuumto*/ [the one] that you wanted/

Never mind the one that you asked for/ You said, um— "I want to go *tuumto*"// So [now] you've come to go *tuumto*/

You've gone *tuumto* today// And no matter what, Well, you've come and gone *tuumto* today// Because I'm thinking that// it's no longer as long as the distance between nose-*i* and mouth/ before you go *tuumto*// But it's *tuumto* that we go to// *Tuumto*// So you don't know *tuumto-i*/ is what// You just hear it said/ *[cluck]* Meinyikake/

You don't know what *tuumto* is/ You just hear [of it]// because/ but— saying, um—/

[sigh and cluck] She didn't give herself the other one/ she sa- she said [she wanted]/ Because when words have come out we should say them truly and well/[1]

When she goes tomorrow, she thinks/ "What is *tuumto*?"// But you don't— truly you don't know because we don't teach [you about it]/ So I've taught you myself, I tell you/ it's become [time] and you've gone *tuumto*/ So *tuumto*/ is *tuumto*/ Something that we really try to do our best at/ You stay completely still// Like I stayed still/

[cluck] Like I stayed still// You stay still/ because it is something astonishingly painful/

that is done to you/

If it's not possible for you to go/ [well and] you— you— you do this/ You squirm around//

You say, "Because it hurt"/ So it's better I teach you myself and tell you/ It hurts, that thing that is done to you// I want you to tell me now/ so if— you tell me now if you see that/ you can't [do it]/ Tell me/ so that I can leave you now quickly and you [can] go/ when you haven't [yet]/ you— um—/ done that [i.e., shown fear by squirming]/

[cluck] Kap Apaiye/ There's no seeing me talking quietly [calmly], though I'm truly a man/ completely/

Like/[2]

---

1. I.e., when a matter comes up, it should be spoken of clearly. He refers here to his mention of "the one that you asked for." The initiate (his daughter) had wanted to be initiated on another, earlier occasion, but he refused to allow it.

2. After swearing by his lineage with the name Kap Apaiye, P. comments on the controlled way a man should speak and his own emotion. This phrase, *ko yuu*, which translates as "like," is the beginning of a phrase commonly used in conversational oaths (see Kratz 1989:644–46). This is another demonstration of his emotion; it moves his good friend A.M. to try to calm him down.

Table 13: *continued*

A.M.: muutya/ muutya pakule/

P.: paani koi// ni// momii ciit ake ne kimaany' en Kap Larusi/ Kap Larusi/
kabisa// oi iyoo ceepyoosook maile manke— in—/ ki mii ko
maikopeentin ceepyoosook/ amu kaaroon ne opeenti/ ko makimii/
eceek ng'eetotik// ce pa koi/ kake se ng'eetat ake tukul ne pa kai/ inko
makikany' kiit ake tukul/ peeleek anan anan ko saaeenik anan ko
nee/akipwaat kele/ kicuurunaati weeriik aap kai pa Kap Larusi/ kikipe
komyee/ [*cluck*]

[*sigh*] inkeri akot iny'on ikoonaan mosiket ake ne oo/ ne manamuuce/
kaikoonaan mosiket ne oo/ ko mosiket ne kaikoonaan ko pukootyet/

pamuru/
pukootyetny'uun kabisa/ nai ile/ imii paani koi/ maimiitii koing'waang'/
imiitii Kap Larusi// Kap Larusi ne imii/ s'inken ile/ miitii kaing'waang/
ko yuu inko mii tosi/ kaaitaap/ piik alak tukul/ Kap Larusi ne imii/ ko
kiimwai iman ile opeenti ak Nini/ oi inkeeron Nini omii tuwai/ ko inee
n'opwaa opeenti tuwai// maikenteraan pamuru kabisa// meikenteraan/
amu maakenteriin anee// maakenteriin/ ko koale/ lelesta ake tukul ne
ayaycini Nini/ ayayuun/ okerkeiit ot kokeer ciit ake tukul/
mm?
ma tuun akot kole— mwai ciit ake tukul in—/ ciit ake tukul ne siirtai
kole/ "ikeere/ kowo kolaac laakweeny'iin/
kopakaac niin/
amu mamaken kiy// amu pa koin"/ akot ai n'ii pa inee eemeet ake/ ne
mananken/ ot opwaan otepaaten ak laakwaniny'uun/ ko ayayuun lelesta
ake tukul/ ne kaayaycin// maikenteraan pamuru kabisa amu si
ikenteraan/ amuuci akot anee awe rokoeet kabisa/
rokoeet ot ko mekekasaan en koi/
s'anken ale matin kaawe/ ko many'aliiltos laakok ce miitii kai/
hm?// many'aliiltos/
many'aliiltos apwaati/ matin kopa awe/ aiku ng'uuny'uny'eekcu ikeere
ityece/ ipaare tyaana piik ko kikopa iyu/ ko many'aliiltos laakok/

Table 13: (Translation) *continued*

A.M.:   Calm down/ Calm down, initiation-mate/

P.:   Now this family// This one// There is no other person in Kap Larusi that
        was whispered about/ Kap Larusi/ None at all// Or unless there were
        women, don't say we don't— um/ we're there when women are
        usually going/ Because tomorrow when you go/ we won't be there/
        ourselves, the men// of this family/ But every man of this family/ If we
        fear anything else/ elephants or buffalo or what/ we remember that/ the
        boys of this Kap Larusi family were really brave at initiation/ We went
        well/ [cluck]

        [sigh] And there again you come and give me another big [heavy]
        burden/ that I couldn't have/
        You've given me a big [heavy] burden/ and the burden that you've given
        me is my wife's sister/

        Wife's sister/
        Truly, my wife's sister/ Know that/ you are in this house now/ You're not
        with your family/ You're at Kap Larusi// Kap Larusi is where you are/
        So know that/ your family is there/ Like— if they are [there like]/ the
        family of/ any other people/ Kap Larusi is where you are/ So you said
        truly that you would go with Nini/ and there's Nini, you're together/
        She's the one that you've come to go together with [for initiation]//
        Don't cheat [shame] me, wife's sister, at all// Don't cheat me/ because
        I didn't cheat you myself// I didn't cheat you/ I said/ any lovely thing
        that I do for Nini/ I'll do for you/ You will be [treated] the same until
        anyone can see [it]/
        Mm?
        [So that] tomorrow no one even says— any one says afterwards um—/
        anyone who passes by says/ "You see/ he went and dressed his child
        [well]/
        and left that one/
        Because he doesn't care a thing/ because she's for that family"/ Even if
        you yourself are for another country/ that I don't know/ if you come
        and sit with this child of mine/ then I'll do for you any lovely thing/
        that I've done for her// Don't cheat me at all, wife's sister, because if
        you cheat me/ I can even go and hang myself completely/
        Hang myself until I am not heard again in this house/
        So I know that there's no problem when I'm gone/ that the children [and
        wife] of this house will not have trouble/
        Hm?// They won't have trouble/
        They won't have trouble, I think/ there's nothing [to worry about if] I go/
        and become this soil that you see you step on/ How many people do
        you think have died here/ and the children have no trouble/

Table 13: *continued*

[cluck] Meinyikake// meikenteraan kabisa/ tepaaten itepaaten ko yuu ciita//
meipwaati ak iny'ee ile/ "amii— kokuuraan tosi koi// any'o awe tuumto
ko yuu iyon in—// ko kiaale any'on aweenti en kai"/

ko momii ng'aleek alak tukul ne taamwaiwaak-i/ aleincinaak kityo omuiten
pamuru kabisa// omuiten// kesulwaak ak okweek pooruekwaak ko yuu
iyon akesulci piikcu tukul/

ko/
aa pa Kap Apaiye// matin ikase ikeeraan ang'alaani muutya ak aa ng'eetat
kabisa ng'eetat inne naan ipaarei ng'eetat kabisa// hm?// ak maakencinaak-
e anee// inkeri sumunit ne katiny'e/

[unfolding hundred-shilling note] pakalini/ pakalini akeenke ne kaaceeraak
tuwai// opce/ manko—/ ale amu Nini ni/ koip sumunit// opce tuwai en
kweeneet/ momii kweeneet iyu? opce tuwai en iyu// iip kepeeper/ iip
kepeeper// mankowo sumunit akot taba—/ tongolo akot tongolo akot
intururu manko— ko— ko— kowo— kowong' ake tukul niin/
kowong'en ake tukul/ kiy kaakoonaak/
[cluck] papaiyet ak kwaanta/ aa pa anee ing'edo soyua/ *[sigh/grunt]*

Table 13: (Translation) *continued*

[cluck] Meinyikake// Don't cheat me at all/ Sit, you sit like a person// Don't you think yourself/ "I'm here— this household called me, then// to come and go *tuumto* like when, um—// I said I would come and go in this house"/

So there are no other words that I still [want to] tell you-*i*/ I just tell you, you stay still, wife's sister, completely// Persevere// [and] your bodies, too, will be made good for you just as [their bodies] have been made good for all these people/

So/

I'm for Kap Apaiye/ There's no hearing [or] seeing me talking calmly, and I'm a man completely, very much a man, the one [about whom] you say [he's] a man completely// Hm?// And I didn't cheat you myself// Here is the small coin that I have/

[unfolding hundred-shilling note] This hundred shillings/ It's this one hundred shillings that I encourage you both with// Divide it/ Not to—/ I say because this is Nini/ to take fifty cents// Divide it together in the middle/ Isn't this the middle? Divide it together here// You take half/ You take half// Not even fifty cents should go, let alone—/ ten cents, even ten cents, even five cents shouldn't— to— to— go to— increase the share of that one/ to increase the share of either/ in the thing I've given you/ *[cluck] Papaiyet ak kwaanta/* I'm for the red open forest area/ *[sigh/grunt]*

Table 14: A.N.'s Encouraging Speech
(A.N. is brother to the girls, member of the host family)

laakokcu/

anee ne kiang'etaate aceeng'aati kurpeetng'waang'-i/ ko tako anee ni/
kaopaarei kiamei-i?/ ma tako anee ni?// ayu ne kiopaarei in—// ne kiopwaan
oleincinaan, "oi ceeng'— ceeng'aatenweec tukuuk"?// maawe aceengaat?
toomasic-i? ayu ne kopwa kosyepaaten kityo paaiisyaanik en iyu?/ moosue
paani— ma okweek inko kuurei-i?// ii?

ko mainte kiy inko amwauwaak anee paani/
aleincaak anee paani/

koang'et/ akopa okweek// ameta kaasiit— wakati yangu// kaasiisyekyuuk tukul/
akopa okweek// okasei-i?
ko koacokan/ akot taacokani paani/ aalte tuukyuuk/ akopa okweek/
ko ta atese taai-is kora// hm?//

ko se en anee paani inko amwauwaak-i//

aceer— atiny' anee teeta akeenke/ aaltai kaaroon-i/ en laakokcaan tukul ko
somok// atesunaak en tuuk cu kaace ko aaltai// si ing'aap in—/ okenter in—/
taeek inko kaokuuraati// oipaati opa ocut eropiyiasyekcaan kariisyek opeene
eemeet inko opa opeene// ko aarteet ne aaltewaak kaaroon/ supeenta// koip ake
tukul ishirini ishirini ishirini en okweek// ateswaak tuuk cu kaace aaltai/

Table 14: A.N.'s Encouraging Speech (Translation)

You children/

I'm the one that went [running] about, getting tired looking for your things-*i*/ So this is still me/

Did you think I died-*i*?/ Isn't this still me?// When was it that you all said, um—// that you all came and told me, "Oi, look for— go and look for things for us"?// Didn't I go and look? Haven't I gotten them yet-*i?* When is it that elders have simply come to sit here [in this house]?/ Don't you see now— isn't it you all that called them-*i?// ii?*

So there's nothing that I tell you now myself/
I say to you now myself/

I was exhausted/ because of you all// I leave my work— my time// because of you all// All of my works/ because of you all// Do you hear-*i?*

So I was tired/ I'm still tired even now/ I sell my cows/ because of you all/

So [but] I'm still continuing// hm?//

So this what I tell you now myself-*i*//

I encour— I have one cow, myself/ I'll sell it tomorrow-*i*/ for all those three children// I'll add it for you all to those other cows I sold [to hire your costumes]// So that if, um—/ you cheat, um—/ the guests you invited [by running away from initiation]// [then] you go off and go get into a [public transport] car with that money, and go to whatever country you end up going to// So it's a sheep that I'll sell for you tomorrow/ a female// Each of you will take twenty [shillings], twenty [shillings], twenty [shillings]// I add it for you to those cows that I sold/

with synonymous verbs (*amwauwaak anee paani/ aleincaak anee paani*, I tell you now myself/ I say to you now myself).

The second subsection reiterates A.N.'s exhausting efforts. It parallels the first section's start thematically, also using the same initial verb, *-ng'et* (to be tired).[17] A new refrain, *akopa okweek* (because of you [pl.]), punctuates a catalogue of his efforts, repeatedly hammering the girls with their responsibility for his sacrifice. This subsection is divided with the phrase *okasei-i?* (do you [pl.] hear?) and a pause similar to the *ii?* ending of the first. After a third and final reprise, using another synonymous verb (*-cokan*, to be tired < Kiswahili *kuchoka*), A.N. ends the subsection with another phatic prompt, *hm?*

In reviewing the ways these speakers use repetition plus grammatical and thematic parallelism to structure their encouragement and create persuasive force, other poetic-rhetorical devices came up as well. For example, both A.N. and P. use interrogative constructions, which in that context further implicate girls in their commitment. "The most general thing we can say about a question is that it compels, requires, may even demand a response" (Goody 1978:23), yet none is allowed. All questions are necessarily rhetorical when no response is allowed or expected. Thus the girls' silence is an implicit agreement, accepting the responsibility to perform well. Rhetorical questions are really challenges that will be answered at dawn.

Phatic prompts (such as *ii?, hm?, hi?*) are similar to rhetorical questions in their pragmatic function and are extremely common in encouragement. All have question intonation and some are referential questions, such as *okasei?* (do you [pl.] hear?). These questioning sounds are part of an adjacency pair (Sacks and Schegeloff 1974) that calls for response in most contexts, but the girls cannot respond to them either. Phatic prompts can also play structural discourse roles. A.N. marks and closes subsections of his talk with them; P. uses them similarly, though less consistently.

Finally, phatic prompts contribute to the emotional tenor and impact of talks in ways related to other discourse contexts. Prompts are often used when giving commands (especially to children but also by men to their wives). In directives, prompts elicit a sign that a command has been heard and will presumably be heeded. Silence indicates annoyance or sullenness. *Ceerseet* encourages by making initiates annoyed (*-nereec*); their prescribed silence is appropriate to the state.

Repeated nonreferential prompts, such as *ii?,* can also show annoyance, for example, when speaking accusatorially. Repeated use of these prompts in encouragement, then, displays the speaker's own heightened emotion (which would also be described with *-nereec*). Part of the interactive intensification central to initiation's efficacy, this emotional display, like others, is considered a powerful intensifier of the girls' own annoyed determination. What sounds like aggressive, challenging speech helps rouse their resolve, which is shown by their nonresponse.

However, the true cast of speakers' emotion is shown as anxiety, not anger, by other frequently used devices that show the intensity of their emotion. They cluck in annoyance at strong, evocative moments, or break off to swear (-*waal*) by an elephant or buffalo they killed or by a hive, an ox, a child, or their family. P.'s encouragement is a perfect example. His is punctuated with deep sighs, clucks, and repeated swearing by his lineage under various names (Meinyikake, Kap Apaiye). He breaks his talk with emotional displays when struck by particularly hard thoughts, such as his own circumcision experience or the devastating shame if she squirms. This last is so upsetting that his friend and coinitiate must calm him.

All this clucking, sighing, and swearing displays *controlled* emotional outbreaks, befitting men and unlike other emotional fits. By contrast, an uncontrolled, inappropriate, and shameful outburst came at the end of another speech (Kratz 1988c:646–67); the speaker reviled women abusively (*kaarkeet aap pieek*, shitty woman) and had to be hushed.

Two final rhetorical-poetic devices of encouragement should be mentioned. First, lexical intensifiers heighten the tenor of *ceerseet*, for example, the repeated use of *kabisa* (completely, utterly < Kiswahili). Exaggerated emphases are rhetorical overstatements, related to poetic exaggerations. Second, quoted and reported speech also figure importantly in *ceerseet*'s rhetorical effects. A.N. and P. both use quoted speech, for instance, to establish and underline the girls' responsibility for the ceremony: they *asked* for it, she *told* him she wanted it. P. also develops his encouragement through quoted speech.

Quoted speech can portray thought and deliberation as inner dialogue or dramatize later reactions to the ceremony through imaginary conversations. Quoting the initiates' inner dialogue allows the speaker to address doubts he feels they may have. P. shows his daughter wondering what *tuumto* is, her ignorance leading to a frightened squirm at unexpected pain. He creates the context of her inner uncertainty so he can "teach" and warn her challengingly. In his own quoted inner dialogues, a speaker may deliberate about going to the ceremony, pondering constraints and responsibilities involved. These exaggerated difficulties demonstrate how seriously *he* regards *his* obligation to the girls. Their burden of obligation and expectation thus becomes heavier still.

Quoted reactions to the ceremony often focus on the gossip and shame that follow public disgrace, magnifying the stigma to affect the girl's family and even her father's entire age-set. Here quoted speech at once dramatizes, particularizes, personalizes, and externalizes the shame.[18]

Many poetic-rhetorical devices of *ceerseet* carry such hooks and challenges. The basic rhetorical strategy is to encourage through obligation and provocation, to create a situation where the girls are so hedged in by responsibility that it is virtually impossible *not* to respond to the requests, challenges, and commands. Emotional fervor binds them further.

Requests, challenges, and commands punctuate encouraging speeches. Structurally they provide both starting points for elaboration and succinct summary appeals that close the persuasive sections. They are also central to encouraging songs, a trio of dialogic call-line groups that share the illocutionary force of directives.[19] Speeches and songs also share a number of themes and even exact phrases (cf. Kratz 1987:85–88, 1990a). Men often develop shared themes further, particularizing and personalizing the summaries of song.

For example, girls sing, "Don't shame my brother to work for nothing." A.N.'s speech is a brother's monologue giving that message personal force— detailing the work he has done, reiterating his exhaustion, and then upping the ante of obligation further with his final gift. "Don't shame the guests. Run to Kisumu if you fear. No one in this family has cried. Go [*tuumto*] and we will rejoice for you." These and other song themes recur in speeches, fleshed out and often delivered with a display of emotional fervor and restraint by those expected to be both controlled and in control.

Men refer to preceding speeches, citing their consensus to underline the truth of what they all say. Themes and phrases are repeated over and over, and diagrammatic iconicity in discourse structure also contributes to the repetition that creates men's growing consensus in *ceerseet*. It is, in fact, a larger consensus, which is finalized in these encouraging speeches: the ceremonial sequence includes an intensifying progression of encouragement in different forms by different people, coordinated with the semiotic movement of other media.

As the last encouragement, speeches are a powerful elaboration and reiteration of what has come before in song, in harangue, in emotional fit. Final legitimation comes from adult men in ways that re-create cultural notions of gender. The power of emotional displays, binding expectations, gifts, and the now-unanimous consensus is concentrated on the girls, who must in turn concentrate their will for dawn. All that remains is to remove any unknown obstacles to their success. The last public event before dawn, *pesenweek*, is intended to do just that.

Before going on to that event, however, two aspects of *ceerseet* must be noted that were passed over in looking at the verbal creation of encouragement and obligation. First, the delivery of the speeches contributes to the emerging constitution of the girls as a group of initiates. The spatial and proxemic dimensions of this semiotic movement were discussed in chapter 5. Speeches also begin to treat the girls as a group verbally, addressing them together with the second person plural. In principle, men encourage all girls equally, even though particular girls (such as a speaker's relatives) are singled out at times. This alternation between second person singular and second person plural highlights a tension between the individual and the incipient group just before group unity becomes fundamental to seclusion life.

The communicative pragmatics of the situation mark and contribute to the semiotic movement of the girls' transformation in another way as well: they are treated as adult agents in the speeches. Speakers exhort, encourage, and rhetorically oblige the girls to act bravely, yet the obligation *is* only rhetorical, and the directives are as much appeal and request as order. Speakers are anxious and uncertain about the outcome.

This is not the usual situation between parents (adults) and children. Children are expected to listen, though they might disobey. They are not given the right of choice, though they might take it. Further, if they obey or disobey, they affect only their own household, or perhaps neighboring and related ones. At the threshold of adulthood, though, girls are charged in *ceerseet* with the adult responsibility of assembling an expectant public of witnesses. Equally important, they are addressed as people with adult prerogatives of choice, though only compliance will prove their maturity. They are treated as adults, and asked to prove that they are indeed worthy of it.

The second aspect returns to the re-creation of Okiek gender roles and relations, along with their tensions and contradictions. These speeches include passages and asides that represent and perpetuate stereotypical views of men and women, sometimes in strong emotional terms, as in the abusive example above. At times, speakers disparage women almost unthinkingly, using idiomatic phrases based on stereotypes. Denigration can also be a deliberate rhetoric of encouragement through scornful challenge.

For instance, the abusive speaker contrasted men and women: men honor responsibilities and do what they say, while fickle women do what they want without thought for other people or commitments they have made. Others used male identity as evidence of honesty (for example, "I'm not fooling you, I'm a man") or knowledgeable experience (for example, "if we [men] don't know, do you think you do?"). And as mentioned earlier, another speaker finally broke off in frustration: girls just can't be encouraged.

Yet other perspectives that undercut those very stereotypes are also voiced in the speeches, and can equally be part of the rhetoric of encouragement. Women's own strength and their independent ritual tradition and knowledge are explicitly recognized in speeches. Women's abilities, bravery, and strength are at once devalued and acknowledged by men. Such tensions and ambivalence, intrinsic to Okiek gender relations, emerge particularly clearly here in the overt content of *ceerseet*. Along with the contradictory premises about gender and initiation that underlie the entire *ceerseet* event, discussed above, these tensions and ambivalence also contribute to an atmosphere that is already emotionally charged.

For example, P. admits men don't know about lineage women's bravery. Another man notes that women's appearance of ignorance is false: "[Y]ou see (them) and think they're foolish because they are here, but they know something. These ones have become women." He later stresses women's strength and will in initiation: "[D]on't they remember their own initiation? Do you all think you will give them hearts, my friend? Their own hearts are there."

Cultural stereotypes and assumptions about women and men meet contradictions in the face of girls' initiation, the realm of women's control, organization and ritual knowledge from which men are excluded and about which they are kept ignorant. Yet the stereotypes and assumptions still provide an important idiom through which to prepare girls for that trial.

The last word before girls enter women's ceremonial realm, men's encouragement is not just a final plea for bravery. It is also a parting shot emphasizing the male-dominated view of the world even as they give control of the children to women temporarily. By relinquishing them for the initiatory sojourn in the women's world, the men ensure that these girls will return again to be organized in a new way, by a new set of men: their husbands' families. But the girls will also have new knowledge and a new community that reassembles at each subsequent girls' initiation.

Still organized through men in a sense, that community is nonetheless a constant counterpoint. The comparable experiences of men and women during initiation, including their comparable courage during the trials and secrets, do not undermine the predominant picture of Okiek gender relations, yet the fact of their comparability is always a challenge to it. Women's ability to organize and maintain their own ceremonial tradition may be acknowledged here, but its implications for greater equality and authority are ignored in other contexts.

Encouraging speeches, then, are implicated in creating gender identity through contextual re-creation in complex ways. No simple reproduction of stereotypes, they draw on and contribute to assumptions about men and women, yet subtly deny them as well. The context, definition of the event, and verbal expression all show the inherent tensions of gender relations. Contradictions and ambiguities within assumptions about gender are highlighted in *ceerseet* by juxtaposition with contrary assumptions about initiation. Multiple perspectives and diverse participants contribute further to the complex tensions within the event, as speakers cite personal understandings of these assumptions and contradictions as lived. Elements of the girls' adult-life-to-be are constantly reinserted into the ceremony, their contradictions and ambiguities infusing the ideology of gender that is the official view.

The speeches give girls the strength to be cut without a twitch by stirring them emotionally. But the speeches and the situation move the speakers and listeners as well; this is an important part of ceremonial experience and engagement for all. This is especially true for mature adult men, for whether the girls are strengthened or not, *ceerseet* is *the* event through which they participate as individuals in the ceremonies of their daughters, sisters, and sisters' children. Men's other scheduled participation is limited mainly to building ritual structures and blessing, but they are no less concerned or emotionally involved in the occasion. However, their engagement is appropriately expressed only in this controlled, reasonable forum of discussion.[20]

The display of emotion barely under control is rhetorically effective, but it is also felt. Each speech is an effort to steel the girls' hearts, but is also a meditation on the relationship between the girls and the speaker, often recalling particular interactions in ways that personalize and intensify emotional engagement. Other listeners are sometimes moved as well, clucking in annoyance or commenting on the poignancy of a passage. In this way, too, the audience reached is wider than just the addressees specifically identified.

The fathers' final emotional addresses add the last intensification to the searing emotion that strengthens the girls' resolve. *Ceerseet* moves the girls to fulfill the wish that is by then unanimous, and simultaneously implicates them in accepting the cultural assumptions that underpin and are re-created in the ceremonies. Other participants reaffirm and re-create them as well through their own participation and involvement, despite the ambivalences and contradictions that emerge at the heart of the event.

Pesenweek and the Curse

After *ceerseet,* everyone at the ceremony is united, with one unanimous request and expectation concentrated forcefully and persuasively on the girls. That single-minded desire accords with the girls' sung promises to brave their painful trial and, it is hoped, with their strong-willed resolve. All seem intent on a single purpose, yet sinister obstacles, such as hidden resentment, residual anger, or jealous envy, could still thwart the girls' efforts at unflinching courage. To disarm these potential threats, the girls are asked to tell their *pesenweek* (social debts) to expose any possible grudge against them. In addition, a curse is usually said to counteract other, unknown evil intentions to ruin the ceremony.

We curse the evil person [*caalwaakintet*]. That is a bad person who curses the children. Someone who doesn't follow what other people do and is usually alone. It's someone who hates to see a lot of children since perhaps they have none themselves or have no cows.

Ceerseet climaxed the interactive intensification that engaged all participants in a significant sequence of differentiated forms of encouragement. Following that, *pesenweek* is a change of mood, in some ways an anticlimax. It is also a parting of ways. The trajectory of transformation proceeds for the initiates; their semiotic movement continues through the spatial, proxemic, and communicative sequences already discussed. The emotional effects of encouragement are also given an additional twist during *pesenweek* (again the name for both ritual event and its central verbal exchanges). But the initiates leave the others behind here. For other participants, *pesenweek* presents a radical change in tone, a moment of hilarity after compelling speeches and songs. For them, the event creates a certain distance from intense emotional engagement. Though it does not discount their concern or anxiety, their remaining role is simply to wait, witness the girls' trial, and if all goes well, to celebrate.

But tension of contrary definitions is constitutive of the *pesenweek* event, a tension essential to the girls' continuing transformation and to the narrative transformations that are part of the event's immediate purpose. From the girls' perspective, the event is serious, its paramount purpose removing the threat of outstanding *pesenweek*. This is the event's official definition. While not overtly contested, the way the threat is disarmed through public confession has other dimensions that take precedence for some audience participants. They are most interested in the entertainment value of the announced transgressions, which provide an opportunity to tease, embarrass, and joke with those named by the girls. This is also an official definition of how *pesenweek* proceeds, but from a different perspective. The two definitions produce a tension between notions of reportability in *pesenweek* accounts (that is, notions of what should be included in confessions) and between distanced and dramatized accounts. The simultaneous hilarity and seriousness is integral to the event's role in the efficacy of initiation as a whole, as well as to its immediate intended effect: absolution effected through amusement.

The double definition of this situation recalls the contrast of earnest, serious appeal in *ceerseet* speeches and the sometimes drunken, heckling audience. As with *ceerseet,* the two simultaneous interpretations bring out tensions and ambiguities inherent in the event and the assumptions it draws on. Side exchanges in *ceerseet* pointed to contradictions in Okiek concepts of gender. Contextual re-creation in *pesenweek* again highlights some assumptions about gender relations, but relations of age and the contradictions of child/adult relations come especially to the fore, as discussed below.

In other contexts, *pesenta* refers to a monetary or material debt, but here *pesenweek* are social debts, outstanding promises of retaliation issued in anger. Not all arguments are reportable *pesenweek,* only those in which someone angrily tells the girl, "*Aya.* Just wait, you'll see at the *mabwaita*," or more simply, "*Aya.*"[21] Nor do arguments with all people count. Only initiated adults can threaten the girls; disagreements with children are harmless. While such comments may well be idle threats, they cannot be dismissed because they could equally well be real. Anger alone can have the effect of a curse in some cases (Kratz 1989).

As this preamble suggests, young men and young women are the main debtors, each associated with a typical kind of disagreement.

There's nothing that remains hidden [now]. There's no longer anything hidden—someone that cursed you, or that you cheated, or that— that you, um—or a woman you cursed, telling her, "*Aya,* may such and such [happen]." Nothing at all is hidden. Even [someone] that you pulled him out, um—if you were sleeping together and you pulled him out so he would stop-*e,* stop—and he told you, "*Haya.*" So, uh—everything is said. Hm. Someone that you cursed, or a woman that cursed you, or a young man that cursed you, we name all those. There is no longer anything hidden now. Hi? You hear?

The young men who are named usually became annoyed during flirtations when the girls refused their advances. Young women were most often provoked when girls refused to do errands, get water, grind maize, or perform other tasks.[22]

These public disclosures can be acutely embarrassing for the girls, but their embarrassment is overcome in order to recount the incidents. A young man acts as interrogator and announcer, mediating between girls and audience, taking part in two quite distinct exchanges. In the background, women are singing and shrieking in the ritual house the girls will soon enter. The booming growl of secret *ceemaasiit* might be heard as well. With the final moment of truth audibly closer, the questioner asks each girl's *pesenweek* in ritual order at the *mabwaita.*

The questioner tells the girls to reveal all, presses them repeatedly to tell more, and accuses them of hiding things. Each girl tells him her *pesenweek,* whispering or speaking very softly. To her, he is sometimes a sympathetic listener simply getting the story straight and sometimes sharp and insistent, pushing her to tell more. He might seek details or clarify the *pesenta* with questions. The questioner can also guide confessions, suggesting kinds of people or incidents to name, particular people, or things that *he* remembers. For instance, if a girl begins naming young men, he prompts her to remember women, and vice versa. He can also guide a girl to end, changing his insistent question from "And what else?" to "Say one more and we'll finish."

After each *pesenta,* the young man turns from his whispered tête-à-tête with the girl to face the talking, laughing audience. Getting their attention, he announces it loudly, often to bawdy, joking comments. After answering their questions or comments, he turns back to press the girl for the next *pesenta.* This exchange sequence recycles with each girl until all finish.[23]

In this split-screen scene, the girls still do not speak publicly or communicate directly with the guests; that happens only in song. Two contrasting interactions are united in this event, meeting in the man who is both questioner and announcer. His earnest dialogue with the girls contrasts with his joking banter with the listeners during his announcements. The mercurial shifts of this double definition are one facet of *pesenweek* absolution through amusement. The questioner might tell listeners not to laugh, projecting the grave tone of one into the other, but the admonition is not serious. An air of levity, almost burlesque, is created, akin to the reversal or carnival described in other cultures (Babcock 1978; Bakhtin 1968). Here it is less a momentary inversion of rank and authority than a saying of the unsaid, a revealing of the hidden.

The levity trivializes the incidents recounted, in contrast to the consequential nature of the *pesenweek* event. When strung together, all these daily dramas about the same small things seem laughable. Important conversational exchanges are recounted, but the interactional context is too sketchy for angry outbursts to seem reasonable. *Pesenweek* display childishness, which is to be left behind as adults. Yet the adults involved are also childish, and dangerously so; they must leave behind their resentment through revelation, forgiveness, and anointment. "So those people, men and women, come and bless the boys [or girls], putting fat on them to show they are happy now, and hold no grudge."

All known persons who might harbor grudges are revealed and disarmed through *pesenweek*. The curse goes one step further, to collectively condemn anyone still with sinister intentions. A blessing might follow as well, distinguishing between the benefits that are wished on good guests and the death that is invoked on those who are hidden and evil. This formal curse is a collective guarantee of the event's key:

While blessings help to define the cooperative and peaceful key appropriate to ceremonies, the anointing and formal curse demonstrate publicly that it has in fact been achieved individually and collectively. Explicitly scheduled and related to blessings by poetic structure, the formal curse invoked in ceremonies is linked to them as a kind of guarantee of key at a point when the initiates' trial of circumcision or excision is imminent. (Kratz 1989:643)

Curses reverse the blessings described earlier. The antiphonal performance and line structure of curses are similar to those of blessings, but their themes are opposite. Curses similarly evoke the inauspicious in performance, being said by one or three elders who are removed from the gathered people and who face west, where the sun goes down. Appendix D includes curses said after *pesenweek*.

Pesenweek and the curse end public ritual events leading up to excision, finishing between three and five A.M.. Afterward, the girls sit at the *mabwaita* until women claim them. Begun with blessings calling for peace and cooperation, the events end by officially demonstrating its accomplishment. The guests' wishes and the girls' wills are in accord and jointly focused. Unsuspected obstacles have been removed. Only dawn remains to end the anxious waiting and start both the celebration and the girls' seclusion.

In many ways unlike preceding ritual events, *pesenweek* nonetheless continues initiation's transformative processes. *Pesenweek* topics and themes seem to differ from those of the preceding songs and speeches, yet the angry encounters transpose and recast a very familiar theme. All of the girls' *pesenweek* were incurred when the initiates refused to comply with directives or requests. Thus the *pesenweek* confessions and announcments report these angry exchanges with the same overriding pragmatic force as the encouraging speeches and songs that concentrate directives urging the girls to bravery. If directives and requests, trivial in retrospect, were refused in the past because of childish obstinance, all is forgiven. The most consequential request is now in the balance—the chance to prove adult maturity by satisfying this single unanimous directive.

The verbal form and discourse structure of *pesenweek* confessions and announcements are critical to the event's pragmatic effects. *Pesenweek* are short, summary narratives about the girls' interactions, told and retold;[24] Appendix E includes a selection of them.[25] The girls tell them as first-person narratives, and then the questioner reframes them as reported narratives by announcing them. Through verbal form and performance, minor incidents and squabbles are first made into serious threats, and then trivialized and disarmed.

These confessional narratives differ from other narratives in several important ways.[26] First, the content is remarkable. *Pesenweek* are not about incidents that ordinarily count as publicly reportable in personal narratives (Labov and Waletzky 1967). To be sure, a good argument is reportable as gossip, but *pesenweek* recount petty incidents, not juicy scandals or dramatic scenes. The topic of dispute often makes them nonreportable as well. Girls might talk privately about the sexual advances they rebuffed, but they normally hide such adventures from general notice.

Pesenweek violate normal contextual limitations on reportable topics, ignore usual statutes of reportability, and substitute an alternative, ritually specific notion of what is reportable. This official notion of reportability corresponds to the serious interpretation of *pesenweek* as threatening social debts, and helps delineate the essential structural elements of *pesenweek* narratives. Yet it hardly justifies the interest and hilarity of the event. An ordinary notion of reportability coexists and competes with the context-specific one, especially during announcements in which a humorous interpretation prevails. Through these coexistent interpretations, squabbles that were made serious are once again made ridiculous. The two notions of reportability call for different emphases and information in the accounts, however, which the questioner/announcer must balance.

Formally, *pesenweek* are also notable formally as relatively unelaborated, often skeletal accounts, compared to other personal narratives. The essential thing is simply to say that something happened with someone and thereby clear the air. Only two key components are invariably included in both confession and announcement: an identity and a threat. If the girl omits one of these pivotal components or whispers indistinctly, the questioner elicits it.

The girl's identity is initially obvious, as she is the speaker. The other person involved is the one who must be named, usually in a prominent initial position. The prominence of the other person is maintained subsequently when the *pesenta* is announced, and is emphasized by transformations in announcements. Girls' identities thus fall to the background, since they are no longer obvious as speakers. Indeed, audience members sometimes must ask which girl is involved.

This is an initial indication of how absolution takes place—that is, through a kind of social assimilation (Kratz 1991). *Pesenweek* confessions create an anonymity in which individuals seem to meld into a larger, representative group. Jackson describes a similar process in Kuranko mourning, "the transformation of person into persona, of an individual into a category" (Jackson 1989:84). With the girls' identities more shadowy, the growing list of *pesenweek* takes on a collective sense, their very similar faults blending them together. Particularities of involvement merge into a common narrative position; the identity of others is foregrounded. This change of focus is one way that particular, personal incidents are distanced, made into a class of encounters, and recast as trivial and unthreatening. The dynamic is quite the opposite of *ceerseet,* where particularization and personalization enhance the speeches' encouraging effects.

The other key component, the threat that constitutes the *pesenta,* is an ominous but known ending, often quoted verbatim. Announcers sometimes tinker with the girl's own ending, changing it, expanding it, or adding an absent final quote. *Pesenweek,* then, are end-oriented narratives, like the comic punchline narratives discussed by Bauman (1986:68–73). Far removed from Bauman's Texas stories, *pesenweek* endings are nonetheless pragmatically similar in important ways.

First, the punchlines are part of the closing couplets that mark the narrative's end. Final *pesenweek* quotes are also conventional, formulaic markers of closure, as well as the threats that define *pesenweek.* Conventionalizing changes in the final quote provide clearer endings and help constitute *pesenweek* as a recognizable narrative group.[27] This also helps make *pesenweek* into a class of incidents rather than personal events, contributing further to absolution through social assimilation.

Second, the Texas punchlines rekey what came before, giving it another, ironic interpretation that is humorous. Multiple rekeying, reframing, reinterpretation, and narrative transformation are the essence of *pesenweek.*[28] The angry final quote rekeys the preceding interaction so that it is suddenly a threatening *pesenta.* Humor, irony, and a second reinterpretation are then created through the divided performance context and the double interpretation of reportability. The *pesenweek* form, and the changes between the personal narrative that is confessed and the reported versions that are announced, are central to these interpretive transformations. A more detailed look at them will show how the process works and how it contributes to initiation's ritual efficacy.

To begin with narrative form, the contest of reportability and interpretation means that what comes between the opening identification and the final threat is in constant negotiation. Skeletal "punchline narratives" are sufficient to expose and defuse *pesenweek,* but juicy details give more amusing entertainment. The *pesenta* below shows how the questioner/announcer can play to the audience, embellishing a reluctantly reported incident. Italics indicate an announcement.

Girl: Indobiwo/ [laughing]
Qs/Ann: hee?
Girl: Indobiwo/
Qs/Ann: I say/ I say, tell me those words of yours/ I say, words aren't hidden now/ Talk!/ These words I'm asking you now, what are they like? [i.e., it's no big deal]/ You just say the words that you have to say/
Girl: I say, he thought he would take down my underpants/ I refused/
Qs/Ann: You refused? What did he tell you?
Girl: He told me, "You still will name me [someday]"/
Qs/Ann: Just that? Or is there something else? Talk!/ We don't hide [things]/ Move down here, then/ Move down here, then, where the others are/
Girl: Just that/
Qs/Ann: *Hoo!/ quiet!/ Listen again! Indobiwo—/ Where is he?* In whose house?
Girl: In my house/ my house down there/ where we usually slept/
Qs/Ann: *Listen again! Indobiwo, it's said/ He thought, it's said, he would look for*[29] *this child and this child refused/ He grabbed her underpants and took them down by force, it's said/ and when her underpants reached, it's said, her feet-i/ the child returned them/* [girl moans "ooooooiii"] *She told him, "Go away because I don't want you"/ He told her, "May you tell this yet at your ceremony"/ Hoo!/ And what else?*

The announcer turns the girl's brief, hesitant report into a battle between girl and suitor, complete with quoted exchanges. The audience finds the announcement hilarious in part because it exposes private matters, the changed notion of reportability creating a ribald humour. The image of an amorous adventure as a tug of war is also funny. The laughter of *pesenweek,* however, is complicated, as much a matter of social positioning, expression of authority, and means of distancing and dismissal as simple amusement.

Just how skeletal *pesenweek* can be is seen in the range of orientation that is provided in different cases. The identification and characterization of the dramatis personae, the setting, and the initial circumstances that set the story in motion are usually basic orienting narrative elements (Labov and Waletzky 1967). *Pesenweek* are quite variable in background information, as table 15 shows.[30] Some are full-blown narratives with partial background (#1); others give only bits of background, often as afterthoughts or later interjections (#2).

Still others give only essential information and are virtually contextless (#3). An alternative sense of reportability may be operative during *pesenweek,* but the redefinition carries through to varying extents in different accounts. It is rather limited in the last two *pesenweek* of table 15, where reportability is confined to identity and threat alone. Their implicit narratives maintain their original unreportablity.

Whichever notion of reportability is ascendent, a minimal orientation is not problematic because they *are* about ordinary interactions. The people involved are known and the settings are familiar. Furthermore, the outcome is predefined since the story is told as a *pesenta.* Thus unlike narratives where orientation is critical to telling, understanding, and effect, *pesenweek* orientation is treated as a marker of specificity, adding the mark of truthful evidence. The narrative's central interaction is also treated differently. The conclusion is the climax of most narratives, the denouement to which action leads or the punchline that caps the story. *Pesenweek* endings, however, are already known. In this case, the central interaction claims attention and comment.

All these structural contrasts between *pesenweek* and other personal narratives begin to show how discourse structure is joined to ritual function in performance. Minimal narrative elements are integral to the event's absolving task; minimal orientation pulls narrated incidents from the fullness of interactional context and helps distance them. The anger portrayed in the narratives seems pointless without contextual justification, so forgiveness becomes the only reasonable action. The contested balance of detail in the middle that is the center of interest underlines the importance of the specific mode of *pesenweek* performance, with its competing notions of reportability, in redefining girls' social debts. Their mode of presentation and the subtle shifts from confession to announcement move toward the social assimilation central to absolution.

The reinterpretative effects of decontextualization and disorientation are enhanced and completed by a number of changes in the announced versions that create a contrast between the girls' telling and those of their questioner. The devices that disarm *pesenweek* threats are a small set of simple formal changes. Some of these changes, such as those marking a change of speaker from girl to announcer, result from the *pesenweek* performance context. Others have more room for creative manipulation by skillful mediators who play the announcements for greater hilarity. These consistent narrative transformations begin with the initial identification, regularizing a tendency to emphasize the other person involved that is found in the girls' own accounts.

Because girls' accounts are often quite skeletal, they can seem more like a narrative list than a series of personal narratives. In fact, *pesenweek* are often cast in list form by the way girls provide the critical initial identification: *ak X* (and [name]). Like conventionalizing final quotes, this syntactically marked list form helps collectivize the incidents being recounted as a class of encounters. Girls start other accounts with the person's name, making the identity prominent, as the list form does. But they begin some *pesenweek* with ordinary sentences in unmarked word order (inflected verb followed by the name), with no particular syntactic or morphological marking.

When the questioner announces the social debt, he consistently uses initial constructions that front the name, bringing it into a position of emphasis, and usually setting it off by a brief pause as well. In addition to the list form and name-fronting, another regularly used initial construction, based on the verb *-ng'eet* (to get up) also emphasizes the name, similar to the colloquial English phrase "he up and [verb]": *kole king'eet* X (she says X up and [verb]). Name-fronting can also be combined with a call for audience attention: *kas akile* X (listen, she said X).

The announcer also makes the other's name prominent by repetition during the *pesenta* and/or by mentioning it at the end of the announcement, before he turns back to the girl, as the name of Kopot Lakweny'on is repeated at the end of *pesenta* 3 of table 15. Similarly, he specifies by name people whom the girls identify indirectly; for example, someone a girl identifies as "that young man for Sebaya [a younger brother] and them" is clarified and made explicit by the announcer as Kimany'e. The girls, on the other hand, are only occasionally called by name in announcements, usually being referred to simply as "the child" or "this child."

In announced *pesenweek,* then, a focus and emphasis on the other person is developed in several ways. Simultaneously, the identity of the girls themselves is subtly backgrounded and collectivized through shifts in speakers and modes of reference. The shift in narrators automatically turns personal narratives into reported ones, and necessitates not only referential clarifications such as "the child" but inflectional changes as well.

The personal pronouns and inflection in girls' personal narratives are first and third person, with "I" and "s/he" sharing the stage. Announced, reported narratives use only third person, "she" and "s/he," a shift in narrative perspective that accompanies the one in narrative focus. In combination, these simple changes remove the narrative pivot from the individual girls. The resulting shift in character prominence verbally distances the girls from the angry interactions. As they are removed from the foreground and an adult is placed center stage, the anger begins to seem triflingly inconsequential and less threatening.

The consistent framing of announced *pesenweek* as reported speech is also integral to the performance context. Prefaced with "She says . . ." or the equivalent, *pesenweek* become reported narrative and reported quoted speech, which explicitly mark their removal from the immediacy of personal narrative and directly quoted speech. The distancing role of quotative frames has frequently been observed (Bauman 1986:66; Sherzer 1983:204), as has their role in portraying different interpretations of reported speech and events.

Table 15: Differences in Contextual Background in Three *Pesenweek*
(Qs/Ann = Questioner/Announcer)

Pesenta 1

Girl:	ata iny'ee kora Partoti ira/ si . . . iny'ee/
Girl #2:	peesio kikipeenti Mbokishi/
Girl:	aa— acup/ alein-i/ kikipe ak akot Michael/ . . . ko weeriik akot William/ ale anam Michael euut-i/ a— anam Partoti/ alein "ot iborr-e"/ koleincaun "mayuutwaan"/

Qs/Ann:	*akile in—/ laakweet ake naan-ayn/ laakwa ni kaan in—/*
Qs/Ann #2:	*tako Tinkili-ai naan-ai/ aketuc /*
Qs/Ann:	*kole in—/ kile konam in—/ kile konam in— manken ale/ . . . manken ale kikuuren/ konam euut/*

Qs/Ann #2:	ile ng'aa?
Girl:	Michael/ kale anam euut—/
Qs/Ann #2:	*kole Michael/*
Qs/Ann:	*Michael/ ko— koparei Michael ne kanam-i/ ko Partoti ne kanam euut/*
Girl:	acup/
Qs/Ann:	*koleinci "ot iborr" /*
Girl:	ko ki tako weeriik akot Michael paanaan/
Qs/Ann:	*ko ki tako weeriik/ hmm/ akot Michael/*

Pesenta 2

Girl:	ak Nutuuta
Qs/Ann:	hnn?
Girl:	ak Nutuuta kora ne kinereecei ayeeso keru tuwai/ kipa akot ee Mau/

Qs/Ann:	*kole Arap in—/*
Qs/Ann #2:	*ak Nutuuta kile kiyeeso kile koru tuwai am—/ kikipe akot kaameet Mau/*

Pesenta 3

Girl:	ak Kopot Lakweny'on ne kialenci "yuu ng'aa?"
Qs/Ann:	eh?
Girl:	Kopot Lakweny'on ne kialenci "yuu ng'aa?"/ kilencaun "aya"/

Qs/Ann:	*kole ak Kopot Lakweny'on ne kileinci kile "yuu—"/ kilenci in— "yuu ng'aa?"/ kilenci-i/ kole "yu ng'aa?"/ kolenci "aya"/ Kopot Lakweny'on/*

Table 15: Contextual Background in Three *Pesenweek* (Translations)

Pesenta 1

Girl:	Even Partoti, too, [for me]/ so . . . you/
Girl #2:	That day we were going to Mbokishi/
Girl:	I— I cursed [him]/ I told him-*i*/ We went with Michael and them/ . . . when William and them were [still] boys/ I thought [I would] take Michael's hand-*i*/ I— I grabbed Partoti/ I told him, "May you turn white-*e*"/ He told me, "I won't forget this"/
Qs/Ann:	*She says, uh—/ This is another child now/ that other child, um—/*
Qs/Ann #2:	*It's still Tinkili-ai, that one-ai/ She left [some out]/*
/Ann:	*She said, um—/ She thought [she would] take, uh—/ She thought [she would] take, uh— I don't know / . . . I don't know his name/ to take [his] hand/*
Qs/Ann #2:	You say who?
Girl:	Michael/ I went to take [his] hand—/
Qs/Ann #2:	*She says Michael/*
Qs/Ann:	*Michael/ So— she thought she had grabbed Michael-i/ but it was Partoti's hand she had taken/*
Girl:	I cursed [him]/
Qs/Ann:	*She told him, "May you turn white"/*
Girl:	So Michael and them were still boys then/
Qs/Ann:	*So they were still boys/ hmm/ Michael and them/*

Pesenta 2

Girl:	And Nutuuta/
Qs/Ann:	Hn?
Girl:	And Nutuuta, too, that was annoyed [when] I refused to sleep together/ [when] Mother and them went to Mau/
Qs/Ann:	*She says Arap in—/*
Qs/Ann #2:	*And Nutuuta, it's said, she refused, it's said, to sleep together, um—/ [when her] mother and them had gone to Mau/*

Pesenta 3

Girl:	And Lakweny'on's mother, that I told, "Honest to who?"
Qs/Ann:	Eh?
Girl:	Kopot Lakweny'on that I told, "Honest to who?"/ She told me, "Aya"/
Qs/Ann:	*She says, and Lakweny'on's mother that she told, it's said, "Honest—"/ She told her, uh— "Honest to who?" / She told her-i/ "Honest to who?" / [Then] she told her, "Aya" / Kopot Lakweny'on/*

The change in narrative attitude implied by quotative distancing becomes even clearer in announcements that lack the encompassing frame of reported speech. These usually include occurrences of *kile* (it's said; supposedly), a modal modifier that produces similar distancing. Instead of marking the announcement as reported speech, however, *kile* marks it as something the speaker heard, not indicating where or when. By implication, *kile* conveys the speaker's doubt about, or at least lack of commitment to, the statement's truth. These announcements remove the girl still further from the *pesenta,* not even attributing the report to her specifically.

Apart from quotative frames encompassing the *pesenta* as a whole, the announcer might also alter the way girls handle particular bits of speech and action. Changes go both ways, making a girl's quoted speech into a less immediate reported speech or action as well as turning a girl's reported speech or action into more dramatic quoted speech. These bidirectional switches illustrate the tension between notions of reportability in *pesenweek* and the questioner-announcer's contradictory impulses to at once distance and dramatize social debts.[31]

The tension between gravity and humour is also underlined by the final set of changes made consistently in girls' narratives. The announcer's delivery breaks the girl's version into more measured, marked word groups,[32] introduces prosodic changes of volume, tempo, and intonation, might reorder orientation she provides, and adds or deletes details.[33] The overall effect of these changes and other contextualization cues (Gumperz 1982) is to dramatize the *pesenta.* The announced delivery is far more effective than the girls' rapidly mumbled versions, which are filled out gradually and haphazardly by questioning.

The announcer's dramatization might seem to work against distancing and trivializing the *pesenweek.* Yet these dramatized versions are the ones from which the initiates have already been removed by other formal devices and by the very performance context; the interaction is now between the announcer and the audience. They thus highlight the reinterpreted versions of the incidents, accommodate the audience's appetite for the laughable, and reinforce changes in narrative perspective, focus, and attitude with public pronouncement, comment, and acceptance. The audience becomes a coauthor only with these transformed narratives, which have already been reframed for reinterpretive absolution through amusement (Duranti 1986).

When the announcer retells each *pesenta,* then, his repetition incorporates a series of changes. Individually, each alteration is minor. Several result necessarily from the *pesenweek* performance context; shifts in perspective that alter the threatening nature of *pesenweek* will result with most any announcer. Yet the most entertaining *pesenweek* show that there is still an element of artistry and showmanship in juggling different definitions of the same event.

The announcer takes the initiates' voices away in more than one sense. He not only speaks on their behalf and mediates interactions with the audience, but also alters the narrative perspective and attitude they presented. He adroitly shifts them into the background and recreates them verbally as a collective group while focusing attention on the others involved. Girls are distanced from their social debts, and the incidents related in the *pesenweek* are further assimilated by being portrayed as failings common even to adults.

The final result is a series of skillful framings and reframings that transforms interpretations of *pesenweek* until there is no alternative for responsible adults but to absolve the children. A nonreportable ordinary interaction turned serious threat is in turn changed back into a laughably minor event through the combination of changes in discursive details and the particularities of performative context. The events of girls' *pesenweek* are not only "retroactively constituted by the narratives" here (Bauman 1986:51); they are constituted and then reconstituted again in the course of the ritual event.[34] At the same time, changes in the definition of the girls themselves continue to take them toward adulthood and responsibility.

The difference in social identity between child and adult is a radical one, but its creation through initiation includes a number of gradual processes in which *pesenweek*'s place as the final public event before excision is significant. It completes the gradual separation of the initiates from their childhood lives, a semiotic movement that has been traced in the spatial and communicative organization of ritual events. As they are separated they are also created as a cohesive group—the initiates—which stays together until initiation is over.

As a ritual event, *pesenweek* also figures, perhaps more tellingly, in the semiotic movement and associated dramatic and emotional orchestration that emerge from the sequence of ritual events that defines ceremonial structure. Semiotic movement, contextual re-creation, and experiential engagement are closely intertwined here. *Pesenweek* increases the building burden of obligation for the girls, but simultaneously breaks from that engaging momentum for the other participants. Encouragement expresses support for the girls, but also makes clear to them the unanimous expectations of their friends and family, creating increasingly intense pressure to perform bravely. For the girls, *pesenweek* builds on what encouragement began, but in other ways.

For instance, *pesenweek* guarantees the sincerity of encouragement, revealing adults who might seem to encourage but actually seek revenge. Absolution, anointment, and the final curse neutralize all threats. As usual, male elders lead the curse's collective ratification, exercising and creating their own social and ritual prominence in this final event. The girls really are on their own at that point, with no obstacles remaining but their own childish weakness of will. Their challenge stands out all the more starkly; the pressure on them mounts still further.

Pesenweek also underline the challenge by revealing the girls' childhood history of disobeying, reneging on promises, failing to live up to expectations, and ignoring directives—precisely the kinds of statements that have dominated the speech and song of the ceremony to this point. There is more to be transformed here than just the interpretation of *pesenweek;* the girls' past history must also be rewritten. That transformation does not take place during *pesenweek,* however. The burden is simply laid on them, like that of encouragement. Their bravery under the blade is again the only answer, the watershed that turns that embarrassing childhood history into an adult beginning through compliance with the ultimate directive. The *pesenweek* split in interpretation, key, and reportability parallels the growing split in responsibility. For the girls, none of this is a laughing matter.

However, there is another dimension to the *pesenweek* exposure of childish willfulness, a dimension that is again two-sided. Coming after *ceerseet* speeches, when the initiates were first addressed as if they were adult agents with the right of choice in a consequential matter, *pesenweek* also show that children prematurely appropriate the right of choice, as if they were adults. Further, they show that some adults involved in *pesenweek* are themselves less than reasonable and responsible.[35] Some examples, in fact, show that the child refused a demand quite legitimately and reasonably. Ideal assumptions about children, adults, and their interactions, then, are also contradicted by these tales of daily life.

What creates a *pesenta* is an interaction between child and adult gone awry, but with something wrong on the part of *both* participants. The child is disobedient and disrespectful, and the adult is angry and vengeful. Through this breach *pesenweek* re-create and illustrate the expected and moral norm for child-adult interactions, but something else also happens. When so many *pesenweek* are strung together, they begin to define an alternative norm in the midst of laughter. That norm is described from the child's perspective rather than the adult's. An unofficial view comes to the fore to vie with the official view of appropriate interaction (Volosinov 1987), but only temporarily. This unofficial, child's perspective is controlled and dismissed by the adults' laughter along with their joint *pesenweek* blame.

These interpretive modulations on morality and responsibility also incorporate a flickering perception of the girls' identity at precisely the point when they leave ordinary society as children for good. When shared blame is shifted onto the foregrounded adult, the child is herself treated more like a responsible adult in a joint relation. When her relations with adults start anew with *pesenweek* absolution, then, a narrative image also begins to project the more equal adult relation to come.

Reported *pesenweek* portray contraventions of ideal relations between children and adults, which should be characterized by respectful obedience. That portrayal simultaneously reinforces cultural assumptions about relations of age and authority, shows that they are often ignored, and also challenges them. There is more here than a simple contrast between ideal and real, between what people say they should do and their practice. These accounts chronicle acts of resistance to adult authority, which is sometimes misused as coercive power; their proliferation confers a certain fleeting legitimacy on the individual acts. The split between girls and others, between their two definitions of the event and their correspondingly opposed notions of reportability, are all critical to *pesenweek* and to initiation's dramatic and effective progression. Yet at this very point of separation, the concurrent rupture of perspective that necessarily emerges simultaneously introduces a glimpse of resistance and an undermining alternative. The repeated framing and reframing of events, reinterpretation, and shifting of blame introduce complexities of real life and perspective into assumed moral dicta and their ceremonial re-creation.

The laughter of *pesenweek* recalls the Rabelaisian laughter that Bakhtin found to be such a telling sign of social heteroglossia (Bakhtin 1984). In an event that is at once consequential and anticlimactic, the alternative narrative perspectives of the initiates and the announcer coincide with the alternative moral perspectives of children and adults to evoke laughter. The laughter both dismisses the girls' wrongs and disguises blame, adult ambivalence, and the questions the child's perspective raises for official morality. This adult laughter simultaneously combines authority and powerlessness, acute involvement with and deliberate disengagement from the girls.

This laughter of contradiction may subvert the serious tone and interpretation of the event, but it does not subvert the event itself. Dismissal and disguise are modes of domestication. Social assimilation is a disarming appropriation of dissent that bestows absolution. These dissident alternatives are rooted in the child's perspective. The transformation of initiation is part of a grown child's reach for the power and participation of an adult, a reach that entails acceptance of the perspective that constrains her as a child. Children's opposition may continue, but its locus of concentration is now younger children who have yet to face initiation. Nonetheless, this picture of resistance in the midst of ceremonial compliance raises the possibility of future resistance against differences of adult authority and power defined by gender.

The challenges embedded in this re-creation of notions about adults and children are also implicated in the other participants' involvement and experience of initiation. Adult laughter at *pesenweek* embodies these contradictory perspectives and contains a touch of nervous laughter as well. Adults have given children a choice that affects adult honor, and those children have just shown a collective challenge to assumptions about adult authority.

Audience participation and response are as essential for absolution through reinterpretation as the announcer's narrative transformations (cf. Brenneis 1986:343). Those transformations make the girls into a more anonymous group, removing the individuality of their involvements. Social anonymity is part of the audience side as well. In the darkness, individuals are hard to pick out visually, and the girls and the audience face each other as two groups. Adults collectively hear and forgive the initiates; they ridicule one another as well as the girls.

For the girls, *pesenweek* carries forward the momentum of other ritual events and the urgency of encouragement. For the others, the momentum flags. They, too, became intensely and emotionally involved through encouragement, but they can do no more for the girls. The exposure and humor that absolve *pesenweek* reshape the audience's engagement. The laughter of *pesenweek* is also a device that distances the audience and sets them up for their dawn role as witnesses to bravery.

Collective adult action is central to *pesenweek,* but individual relations between initiates and others are also involved importantly in ritual efficacy. At the same time that the event separates the girls from others, it also lays the basis for their reunion in future transformed relations. Ritual efficacy involves not only the transformation at hand, but the way it is embedded in and later carries into daily life. *Pesenweek* forms the basis of future adult relationships between the initiates and other adults by clearing away past wrongs and misunderstandings.

Final Thanks

The dawn climax of the girls' operation relieves the anxious tension and begins the hoped for celebration. After two or three days of virtually nonstop drinking, interrupted occasionally for food, the liquor runs low. The host tells guests that the ceremony will soon end, opening the floor for guests to give him gifts of thanks with short presentational speeches. The speeches mark the end of rejoicing and the first ceremony, a secular end to the frame that began with blessings days earlier.

My attention stays with the girls, for whom seclusion is just beginning, and follows their transformation through other ceremonies of initiation. Thus, I do not discuss the final speeches fully here. A summary description of their form and performance will provide closure on the important first ceremony and point to interesting relations between these speeches of thanks and the earlier encouraging speeches.

In some ways these final speeches and gifts parallel and complete the earlier speeches, but in other ways the two are explicitly differentiated. The physical context and setting are similar; the final speeches are again delivered in a houseful of drinkers. Again, most speakers are men, though women are welcome to give thanks.[36] The general form of a presentational speech ending with a gift is also similar.[37] Nonetheless, these speeches are quite different in purpose, delivered to the host rather than his daughter, and differ thematically, as would be expected. Men might introduce their thanks with references to the gifts given earlier, during *ceerseet,* but the connection is sometimes belittled and dismissed by others in interrupting side comments (for example, "Those are yesterday's words").

Speeches of thanks resemble encouraging speeches in their general form. They, too, often open with a vocative statement, leading into a second section of thematic development, in this case centered on gratitude, the guests' satisfaction, and more praise for the girls' bravery. As in encouragement, the speaker might dwell here on how he came to be at the ceremony, establishing himself as a bona fide guest, not a gate-crasher. The speaker may point to the host-guest relationship, one facet of other ongoing relations of kinship, age, residence, and friendship that are also part of the text here.

The third section of *ceerseet* speeches, the regular metacommunicative transition comment, is less consistently included in speeches of thanks. In this case, presenting the gift is not an abrupt change of topic from the themes of gratitude developed in the second section. Similar metacommunicative comments are nonetheless included as disclaimers or to mark the conclusion at times. The brief final section of thanks presents the gift and describes the object or amount, much like encouragement.

Apart from obvious and expectable thematic differences, then, these final speeches of thanks are quite similar to encouraging speeches in general discourse structure. Unlike encouraging speeches, thanks may leave out the vocative opening, the transitional section to gift presentation, or both, but the same four sections still define the basic structure.

The two events are closely parallel, but final thanks have none of the controlled passion of *ceerseet* and far less emotional investment. These differences result from differences in pragmatic intent and scheduling in the ceremonial sequence. Further, final thanks is less focused as an event than *ceerseet* in several related ways. First, it is often very difficult to establish and maintain audience attention for thanks, sometimes delivered in the midst of loud talking and singing. Second, the host, as addressee, has none of the girls' dramatic power to attract attention during *ceerseet*. Encouragement contributed to a mounting concern and emotional crescendo that is no longer relevant; gifts of thanks are not always interesting enough in themselves to command attention.[38] Finally, thanks can be less focused in a literal sense. When guests are divided into several houses for celebratory drinking, speeches take place in each house, not at one time and place with all the guests together.

Speeches of thanks may not be dramatic, but they nonetheless contribute to ceremonial structure and the efficacy of initiation's transformation. Thanks are a matter of final obligation and formal closure for the first ceremony, an anticlimax that brings the ceremonial days of ritual action and joyous celebration to an end. The initiates themselves are elsewhere; the semiotic movement of initiation continues for them in seclusion. Thanks are not directly involved in that continuing movement, but they release other participants from the parts they have played in it. The split between the initiates and others that was dramatized in *pesenweek* is completed here as the guests disperse and return to daily life.

The cultural premises of gender relations, central in the girls' change of identity, are not explicitly mentioned in these talks. Nonetheless, they are incorporated and re-created in the definition of the performance context: who announces the end of the ceremony, who makes most of the speeches, men's gifts compared to women's. The speeches are more specifically concerned with social relations between guests and hosts, which are part of an ongoing series of obligations and counterobligations.

It is these relations and assumptions about modes of participation and experience during ceremonial celebration that become the focus of contextual re-creation here. The roles of host and guest are the two sides of experience most clearly drawn in the speeches, including the sense of satisfaction, pleasure, and mutual respect that is considered part of an ideal ceremonial experience. Final thanks are the only regular formal context in which guests' and hosts' expectations are clearly and explicitly articulated. The shared experience of coguests, in which friendships are renewed and strengthened in joint drinking and conversation (or disrupted in drunken argument), is referred to occasionally, but more often left implicit in these descriptions of enjoyment.

Guests expect to be fed fully and fairly and to leave well-satisfied, though many try to influence the distribution of food and liquor in their favor. The host tries to keep the liquor flowing and balance the guests' demands. He expects guests to drink peacefully and respectfully, and also to show appreciation with final gifts. Hosts often complain, in asides during speeches or in comments afterward, about those who drank and left without thanks. Guests often grumble later about favoritism in liquor distribution.

Final speeches of thanks, then, are also a moment of mutual evaluation, when people compare their own experience at this ceremony with what they think it should be and with the representations in the speeches. Their judgments can influence both what they expect at other ceremonies—what "satisfaction" means[39]—and the sense each has of the current relations between the guests and the host. Gifts of thanks express in material form the guests' satisfaction, appreciation, or disgruntlement with the way the host treated them, simultaneously giving their relations a final accent as they proceed again in the midst of daily concerns.

The Unscheduled but Expected

Before going on to the rest of the initiation process, it is important to consider two unscheduled modes of speech that I have referred to repeatedly. They occur when people have emotional fits (-*tupucu*) and when women harangue the girls. Neither is necessary to the ceremony, neither essential to formally scheduled ritual events. Some ceremonies proceed without them. Nonetheless, when people do yell or fall, showing intense anxiety and emotion (-*tupucu*), it is no surprise. Similarly, no one is taken aback if a woman berates initiates in the evening at the *mabwaita*. The occurrences of these two modes are almost as patterned as if they *were* predictably scheduled, and they figure in the semiotic movement of initiation's sequence and interactive intensification as if they were.

I consider the two together for a number of reasons. Both fits and harangues are unscheduled but expected occurrences that express and display great emotional upset. As verbal forms, they are expected only of women, intended to "encourage" initiates, and might share themes with encouraging speeches and songs. Finally, both contribute to initiation's efficacy and experience in similar ways, much like the speeches in scheduled events.

Considered unpredictable individual reactions, fits can occur at any time. Occasionally, someone might have a fit during the first morning procession or just before girls emerge at dawn. Most people, however, have fits at two times. When girls sing farewells at night, fits are a frequent reaction to their individual messages (see chapter 7). Likewise, fits are common in the early evening, when the women's procession returns and the initiates' heads are shaved. Then, too, girls' songs might provoke the intense emotions, though some people react strongly when the progression into the evening events makes them suddenly recognize the operation's imminence.

Afterwards, people say their fits resulted from thoughts about the girls' trial, the implications of their failure, and anxiety about their ability to face it. Some add that they did it to encourage the girls. Initiates are an intended audience even though they may be some distance away, involved in something else. Fits show the girls how upset their relatives are, so they become annoyed (-*nereec*) themselves and determined to succeed. As part of initiation's interactive intensification, this form of encouragement is an explosive leap compared to the gradual stoking of *ceerseet* speeches. Fits are individual expressions and displays of anxiety and concern, but they simultaneously heighten and charge the emotional atmosphere of the ceremony for other guests as well, helping to build the dramatic progression and intensify the emotional tension of the ceremony over time.

People who have fits might yell, cry, fall to the ground, and thrash convulsively until someone calms them. As might be expected, male elders are virtually never involved in emotional fits. Older women might have fits, but more usually it is young men and women who have fits, with a telling sexual dichotomy in their displays. Young men (for example, the girls' brothers) fall and throw themselves around without coherent speech; their verbalizations are typically incoherent. They might fall during the evening without apparent provocation, but most do so during the girls' farewell songs.

Women, on the other hand, often work themselves into a fit verbally (though not during farewell songs); they may or may not fall over. A woman yells about the initiate, her family's bravery, the shame of failure, and other familiar encouraging themes. At the height of the fit, she repeats particular phrases over and over again. At the same time she might start to fall, put her hand behind her head and bend from the waist in a bobbing accompaniment, cry, or bump into people and things until she is held. Table 16 shows what one woman shouted at the ceremony described in chapter 4 during her fit.[40]

When women harangue initiates, they speak quite clearly and specifically to the girls, sometimes shouting in their faces. Harangues are usually delivered in the evening, as the girls' heads are shaved, by older women (the age of the girls' mothers or senior sisters). Women say very similar things whether they have a fit or harangue, but harangues say more, without the seemingly uncontrolled repetition of fits. In addition to invoking individual relations and telling girls not to shame them, harangues also include general statements of conduct meant as imperatives, like song lines such as "We don't move."

Harangue delivery is loud, vehement, and sounds very angry. As in men's speeches, the appearance of anger contributes to the encouraging effect. The dynamic of intensification is also similar. Again, girls are unable to respond with word or gesture, sitting with downcast eyes as they are shaved and abuse is poured on them. However, there is an important contrast in these encouraging emotional displays. Men (fathers) keep a delicate balance, showing control of strong emotion in an orderly forum and incorporating reasoned persuasion in their speeches. This women's (mothers') verbal display seems the picture of uncontrolled anger, freely expressed in a tumultuous scene with singing, movement, talking, and other activities all going on at once.

Though considered unpredictable, fits and harangues are very much part of the culturally organized pattern of persuasive encouragement, emotional display, and interactive intensification found in formally scheduled ceremonial events. Using the same themes and phrases of encouragement, they are addressed to the girls by young and old women, their sisters, brothers' wives, and mothers. Young men's fits are physical, without coherent verbal messages.

While fits and harangues are intended to influence the girls to steel themselves internally for their test, they simultaneously re-create and reinforce Okiek assumptions about gender and age. Women are overcome, unable to control either emotions or words, but older women nonetheless channel intense feeling into a form of connected, continuous discourse. Older men keep both in rein, though with a display of difficulty that underlines their control. Young men are also overcome, but without impetuous verbal outbursts. No contradiction to their identity as young men (*murenik*), their fits are related to the highly emotional state evoked in former times before cattle raids and elephant hunts. The total array of encouraging displays of emotion, then, shows an increase of personal control with age for both men and women, but an absolute difference in verbal control and ability between men and women of all ages.

Fits and harangues are intended to have effects (and do), but the emotions displayed are neither sham nor independent of "internal states" (cf. Appadurai 1990). Okiek also understand them as a sign of the intense experiential engagement of initiates' close relatives. That intensity is matched later with the overwhelming relief and joy expressed in running, shouting, song, and ululation after the girls prove themselves. It is a palpable emotional power that brings tears to the eyes of observers as well.

Seclusion and the Final Formalities

This final section considers the speech of the rest of initiation: seclusion ceremonies and the final ceremony that brings girls back into public life as adults. Chapter 5 discussed the verbal restrictions and prescriptions of daily seclusion life and how they continue initiates' semiotic movement and help create their role and experience as *taarusyeek* (secluded initiates). They do not greet visitors verbally, speak loudly, or call coinitiates by name, even after seclusion. Initiates also sing special songs daily after the first seclusion ceremony (see chapter 7). The songs, too, help create the girls' *taarusyeek* status and show that they have moved beyond that ceremony.

Those songs and others are also part of the secret knowledge learned during seclusion ceremonies. The ceremonies have two other major components: a series of trials and a set of secrets that are revealed to the girls. I will not consider the discourse of these secret ceremonies in detail, but a sketch of the broad patterns involved will nonetheless suggest how it figures in the continuing initiation process.

Seclusion trials are borne silently and unflinchingly, as in the first ceremony, though none are as severe as excision. It seems little is said in connection with these additional tests. Initiates know by then to do whatever they are told and not to complain or squirm if they experience discomfort as they follow the ritual leaders through ceremonies. The trials continue to test and strengthen the mature self-control initially proven by excision. They also continue to test initiates' willingness to adhere unquestioningly to instructions and to follow ritual leaders with absolute trust and obedience. Thus, the theme of directives heeded and ignored carries into seclusion.

According to adults, trials make initiates clever (*-ng'aamiitu*). Some young people with fresh memories of them also said the painful tests were just to trouble them. Trials make initiates clever *by* troubling them. Lessons that remain unspoken are learned through experience: initiates learn to control

Table 16: Y.'s Emotional Outburst (*Tupucu Y.*)

Y. is a sister to the initiates. This occurs at dusk, just after the girls have been shaved and are singing again with their friends. Y. also exchanges a few lines with them. Shortly after, a visiting girl sings, "ak iwe ne mining', o lina, ma mining' mukuulel, o lina," referring to the smallest girl in the group, Níní ("You go, then, small one, *o lina,* the heart is not small, *o lina*"). Y. says, "O Níní!" and then goes into her outburst:

Kigo Níní/ Kigo Níní/ Kigo Níní/ Kigo Níní/ Kigo Níní/ Kigo Níní/ Kigo Níní/
Kigo Níní/ Kigo Níní/ Kigo Níní/ Kigo Níní/ Kigo Níní/ Kigo Níní/ Kigo Níní/
Kigo Níní/ Kigo Níní/ Kigo Níní/ Kigo Níní/ Kigo Níní/ Kigo Níní/ Kigo Níní/
nono/ nono/ nono/ nono/ nono/ nono/ nono/ nono/ nono/ nono/ nono/ nono/ nono/
nono/

[someone tells her during these repetitions of "nono":] meipar laakweet

oye s'oye eyiony'uun/ s'iwe kiririani/ s'iwe s'inkomwauwuun kang'waang' kile
kiawe yuu koonuut/ mankopiriiriitu koony'eek ko len kiririani/

[someone tells her:] makiwiirtaikee

oye/ inko manaweenti ko yuu iny'ee/ ko yuu iny'ee/

[someone tells her:] cakten . . . / inko yamin caan/ kaiwiirten laakweet?/ nee kaasiit
ni?

iwe Níníny'uun/ iwe keeltany'uun serpin/

[someone tells her:] maiwiirtai *[and she answers:]* maawiistai

kaikas-i?/ mankoperperiitu koony'eek ko len Níní/ amace itepaaten/ itepaaten . . .
komyee/ . . .

Table 16: Y.'s Emotional Outburst (*Tupucu Y.*)
(*Translation*)

Kigo Níní *[repeated 21 times]*/
dear *[repeated 14 times]*/

[someone tells her during the repetitions of "dear":] Don't kill the child [which she is carrying on her back]

oye oye my child/ you go then, you awful thing/ you go, let your mother tell you that I went, I swear by your father/ don't make [your] eyes red for nothing, you awful thing[1]/

[someone tells her:] We don't throw ourselves about [and get hurt]

oye/ if I didn't go [for initiation bravely] I swear by you/ I swear by you/

[someone tells her:] "Be quiet . . . / Let those [words] be enough for you/ Have you tossed the child off [your back]?/ What kind of work is this?

you go, my Níní/ go, my little leg [i.e., small girl]/

[someone tells her:] Don't throw [the child] off *[and she answers:]* I'm not turning about

have you heard-*i*?/ don't make your eyes foolish for nothing, Níní/ I want you to sit [still and bravely]/ you sit . . . well/ . . .

1. Red eyes are considered a sign of being worked up or angry. Here she means Níní shouldn't get worked up and show such outward signs, only to be a coward in the end.

their reactions and impulses, to defer to and heed those older and wiser, and to recognize their own position within the community of initiated women. Bodily experience re-creates and reinforces definitions of appropriate adult behavior. As self-control becomes a habit, turning into self-mastery, relations of authority based on age and gender are inculcated simultaneously, in a way that makes them felt as well as known.

Most initiation secrets include cryptic constructions, set up one at a time by the ritual leaders and other old women. When one is ready, the initiates are brought in one by one in ritual order and shown the secret (which might be covered with a cloth) while adults make a particular "showing noise." The girl is asked what it is, and responds that she doesn't know or identifies one object in it. Whatever her answer, the next comments or questions emphasize her ignorance. The ritual leader continues to question her, tells her about the secret, then tells her to do something with it before letting her sit off to one side. The leader's tone and manner are stern and brusque; the initiates are often questioned quite sharply. After the last initiate takes her turn, the ritual teacher leads the initiates in a short song that marks that secret's end and affirms the revelation and the initiates' agreement with the ceremony and their part in it.[41] The secrets are shown again in later seclusion ceremonies. Initiates felt this was a test of their first learning; the ritual leaders were still harsh. Initiates are taught secret songs in a similar way. Their knowledge of songs is also tested when women teach them at ceremonies.

At the very time initiates are given secret knowledge to make them adults, then, they are also tested and intimidated. Initiation establishes the equality of all women, but simultaneously establishes a hierarchy of authority and age within that equality. Initiates are brought into the ritual community of initiated women, but at the lowest rank. The ways they are conducted through seclusion ceremonies and shown women's secrets are essential to this.

The hierarchy is re-created and enforced by initiates' obedience to ritual leaders and others, and by their exaggeratedly quiet and slightly fearful respect of the women who test their singing and lecture them. They are shown secrets in a way that enhances their uncertainty as neophytes. Each comes naked and alone before older women who fire questions she cannot answer. The girls also know they can be switched for mistakes or slowness—for example, when they sing badly.

Initiates do not understand all they are shown, told, and taught to sing. Their essential lesson is simply to agree, pay attention, repeat, and do as they are told. Continued compliance to ritual orders is essential to the forging, enactment, and re-creation of relations of influence and authority. Some relations re-created in seclusion ceremonies emphasize female and ritual links, but these are linked to notions of gender, age, and authority in general (notions also included in seclusion songs). As initiates continue through seclusion ceremonies, their semiotic movement and experience merge with these assumptions, re-creating them in an embodied way. As initiates, much of the cleverness they are taught is obedience and self-control. Having endured the ceremonies as initiates, they will participate more equally in the community of initiated women. With time and repeated participation, they may become wise as well as clever.

One final aspect of the speech of seclusion ceremonies (which may not be a regularly scheduled event) must be also mentioned. Late on the night of the last secret ceremony, women again harangue the initiates abusively. They are lectured on respect, on how to treat their husbands, relatives, and the women who are now their ritual kin (mainly the *matireenik* and the seclusion mother). The loudest, most abusive harangues concern sexual fidelity, the primacy of wifely responsibilities, and the dire consequences of revealing initiation's secret ritual knowledge. A conditional curse is pronounced to kill anyone who tells the secrets.

As with the revelation of secrets, the harangues teach but also intimidate. Their advice and instruction are practical rather than esoteric, but in delivery the lectures are at one with the sharp questioning, again re-creating and enacting ceremonial relations of authority. These lectures help re-create other cultural assumptions as well, explicitly discussing Okiek ideas about the relations of man and wife, a woman and her affines, and so on, much as seclusion songs do more obliquely. The vehemence of their delivery, however, suggests that in practice some of the ideals emphasized might be flouted as often as they are respected. Other perspectives may emerge in performance to undercut or coexist with official ones.

Meyerhoff's discussion of and excerpts from secret Pokot initiation instruction are of special comparative value here because I could not record or observe secret Okiek instruction (Meyerhoff 1981:175–84). She notes that Pokot initiates are questioned, provoked, perhaps beaten, and "made to kneel over in a completely servile and subordinate position so that they listen to what the old mothers are saying" (Meyerhoff 1981:176). Both social instruction and ritual secrets are essential to make them adult women and wives. Yet their mode of performance shows that the knowledge sharing that completes initiation is done in a context of authority.

The dominant and official message of Pokot instruction concerns the ideal behavior of married women. However, while these notions are re-created and foregrounded through referential content, they are simultaneously contradicted, implicitly and explicitly, by details of context, performance, and modes of expression. Such details show the "actual complexity of their marital situation, at times revealing the sources of power and strategies they have as a group and as individuals in difficult marital situations" (Meyerhoff 1981:176). An unofficial women's view emerges as individuals recount personal situations and examples, a view that counters the male-dominant official perspective much as the female-organized ceremony itself contradicts assumptions about women. At the same time, the hierarchy of age is mitigated slightly by the explicit recognition that "in time, these girls will grow older and be in a position of authority over the next generation of girls" (Meyerhoff 1981:176).

Seclusion instruction becomes heated and emotional. As in the most intensely emotional events of the first Okiek ceremony, dramatic *ceerseet* and serious/hilarious *pesenweek,* both cultural ideals and contradictions emerge in performance through this moving discourse. The official view may be stressed to initiates, but the experiences related and affirmed in this female forum show it is not the only view and not always right. The tension of their simultaneity is essential to the girls' experience of initiation, expressing and validating ambivalences they may feel about the changes they are experiencing and their imminent married lives (Kratz 1990c). The community of women is reforged for the other women present as well, incorporating the initiates at the same time. The community meets only for ceremonies, but this collective locus of unofficial perspectives can be a source of support in daily life, too.

During the first two seclusion ceremonies, one secret is kept back from initiates, maintaining their inequality of knowledge: *ceemaasiit.* This secret is first a noise that frightens them throughout initiation; it is said to be a wild animal or monster. In the final ceremony it, too, is revealed. With all the secrets shared and the equality granted by this secret knowledge finally established, the initiates are taken to the river in preparation for coming out.

Still hidden from view under blankets, the newly washed girls are brought from the river in procession. The women who bring them sing that the girls have become mature, valuable, and available heifers. After blessings and adornment, the singing procession returns again with the initiates finely dressed but still hidden. They stop at the arch built onto the *mabwaita* and begin the final formalities that end seclusion and display the beautiful young women after months of hiding. These formalities continue until the next morning and include the first night away from their seclusion house.

The spoken aspects of the final ceremony are all short, straightforward statements that accompany ritual actions. That morning, two main things are done before the initiates are taken silently to another house. The first order of business is *yaatet aap ooreet* (opening the way or path); the way is opened for each girl by one of her brothers.[42] The initiates kneel behind their ritual leader; the blessing elder kneels on the opposite side of the arch, facing them.

The first young man begins by promising his sister a gift—a sheep, a hive, or money (about 20–40 Ksh, US$1.50–$2.50). From under the blanket, the initiate might refuse through the ritual leader, making him raise the amount or change to money. Once she agrees, the way is opened. On one side the blessing elder and the brother hold the poles that come through the arch; the ritual leader and the initiate (from under the blanket) hold them on the other. Together they move the poles up and down while the elder sings a short song to open the way. This is repeated for each initiate in ritual order, with intervening discussion and confusion while a brother is found to give the opening gift.

The second ritual task is to give each initiate a *sirtiityet* in a similar way. A *sirtiityet* is an uprooted sapling with attached bits of propolis and skin from a slaughtered sheep, and is made from the same species as the *korosyaat* sapling held during the first ceremony (see chapter 5). Again, it is brothers who give the saplings, again accompanied by a gift. Initiates carry their saplings until the next day. After the ritual leaders and the blessing elder are paid (usually the initiates' mothers pay them, passing the currency through the arch four times and blessing the payment) the initiates are led away to the house where they will sleep.

The next morning, they return to the *mabwaita* and its arch, with no singing and no longer hidden from view. The girls' siblings began their official reincorporation into daily life; today their parents finalize it. The first initiate's father promises her a gift, then takes her *sirtiityet*, warms it over a small ritual fire of *olerienit* wood, twists it four times to the right, and cuts it with a hive adze, first putting the blade to it four times. Next her mother (or suitable substitute) gives a gift and shaves her head, removing the hair of seclusion (*ol masi*). The initiate removes one beaded leather skirt and puts on clean new clothes and a beaded tiara (*enkishilit*). Then all the initiates eat food together in the first iniate's mother's house after she gives her daughter another small gift. After the *matireenik* drink beer prepared for them, the procession continues to each initiate's home, where the cutting of the sapling, the shaving, and the eating are repeated. After the last home, the ceremony is over and the initiation is complete.

Verbally, the ritual acts that bring initiates out of seclusion are quite simple; all are promises of gifts. These final gifts are different in several ways from the encouraging gifts of the first ceremony, when the girls were constrained from response and felt mounting coercive persuasion. Individual relations, rhetoric, and reiteration were vital to the persuasion of encouragement. The gifts of coming-out, however, are representative of the giver's status, and are accompanied by ritual acts rather than speeches. Here, a single person acts for a category of people in a similar social relation to the initiate. Though the ritual acts seem to be done casually, without a lot of preparation and with much joking, the acts and the objects used in them are deeply resonant with associations from Okiek history and other ceremonies. These gifts and acts finish what the first ceremony began, accepting and completing the change that has been accomplished. The representative mode of ritual participation and resonant acts and objects recall and return to that ceremony's daytime events, with contextual re-creation focused again on Okiek identity and the range of social relations to which the initiates are returning.

The first gift explicitly "opens the way," being given by someone from whom the initiates have been hidden, but each of the others in turn also "opens the way" to other social categories of actors. The initiates are formally received back into ordinary interaction, the promised gifts reopening temporarily suspended relations in their new adult status. The definition of the ritual actors who give the final gifts distinguishes key family relations, emphasizing patrilineal links. The initiates are ritually fed honey, however, in a house that is not their natal home, an act that links initiation's semiotic movement into the larger ritual progression of the life cycle and shows how the initiates' relations as adults widen through marriage (see chapter 5).[43] The semiotic movement of initiation ends soon after.

The girls' experience of their initiatory journey has made a difference that is immediately apparent in these final acts of initiation. These young women are not the same girls who could not respond. When coming out, they can actually refuse gifts, quibbling over form and amount. They do so through their ritual leaders; their first adult communication is mediated, as was the last childhood one in *pesenweek*. Nonetheless, this is a communicative exchange, not a one-sided monologue. Not only do the initiates have a say as adult communicative agents, but also the givers must satisfy them for the ceremony to proceed. Acceptance here is an active response, as an initiate finishes each ritual act jointly with a gift-giver. Her response both resumes ordinary relations with kin and begins a change in them. Her kinspeople's gifts recognize and complete the initiate's change of status verbally, mimetically, and materially. In the process, the gifts redefine the experience and expectations of the initiates' kin as well.

Efficacious Patterns and Processes in the Speech of Initiation

As this chapter has shown, intricately interlinked patterns of speaking are central to the effects of Okiek initiation. These patterns contribute to the three key processes of ritual efficacy, which combine in a complex and shifting mix over the course of initiation's ritual events. In performance, patterns of speaking also combine with patterns in other communicative media (examined in the previous chapter) and with the songs of initiation (to be considered in the next). Some patterns of speaking are most relevant within particular ritual events; other patterns stretch across events to create larger structures within and across ceremonies.

These interrelated patterns of speaking figure importantly in initiation's efficacy. Each ritual event and its associated ways of speaking are understood both in terms of an immediate purpose and efficacy, related to the event itself, and in terms of the overall ceremonial structure and progression of initiation. Within each event, communicative exchanges, context, and specific formal and thematic patterns of discourse structure contribute to the event's immediate, recognized purposes; those purposes in turn figure in the larger aims of initiation as a whole. The repertoire of verbal resources and poetic-rhetorical devices are similar in several events (for example, different kinds of repetition, grammatical parallelism, and quoted and reported speech), but they are used in quite different ways, are combined with other resources, and have quite different effects.

Blessings are central in the general structural framework of ceremonies, constituting an occasion and location as ceremonial and setting the ideal tone participants should create in cooperation. Basic cultural assumptions and values are embodied in the actors, settings, and objects of blessings, as well as represented in verbal imagery, themes, and structure. Blessings are scheduled relative to other ritual acts in a way that also helps re-create the same assumptions and reinforces the sense that cultural order is natural.[44]

The main event in which men are directly and personally involved in the girls' semiotic movement is *ceerseet*, which is explicitly intended to enable the girls' transformation by encouraging them. The performance and persuasive force of the speeches are based on cultural premises about gender roles and abilities. The speeches also draw on the strength of emotional ties and shared experience in personal relations of kinship and friendship to solidify the girls' commitment to silent, unmoving fortitude. The tensions and complexity of gender relations emerge in several ways during *ceerseet*. These speeches of encouragement simultaneously portray gender stereotypes and recognize women's ritual knowledge and tradition, a recognition that blatantly contradicts and undermines the stereotypes. The speeches are intended to have an emotional effect, to work girls up (*-nereec*), but emotional involvement is not theirs alone. Men display controlled emotional intensity, heightening their own participation in and experience of the ceremony as well as that of other listeners.

In contrast, *pesenweek* is a scene of hilarity and release whose immediate purpose is to hear the girls' social debts in public confession and absolve the girls. An entertaining time of sexual joking for all but the initiates, the revelry also exorcises evil wishes, lingering resentment, and stubborn grudges. The embarrassing revelations also contribute to the girls' inner transformation, putting subtle pressure on them (like the speeches) by exposing past childish obstinance. The episodes recounted also present vignettes illustrating cultural values and social relations. *Pesenweek* reinforce and legitimate these values since they show contravention to be a serious threat. Yet they also show that relations of authority and respect are often violated. As a result, this event also bears contradictory interpretations and possibilities.

Secrets are revealed during seclusion ceremonies in ways that constitute other relations of respect and authority: ritual relations between the initiates and their teachers, and a hierarchy of age and experience within the community of initiated women. The teaching of secret songs and the showing of secret sights are, of course, central to the girls' continuing transformation into women, as women who have already been initiated share with them the secrets of that community.

Finally, the gifts that accompany ritual acts when girls come out of seclusion both finish their semiotic movement into womanhood and resume and emphasize important kinship relations in that new status. Girls complete initiation and emerge immediately into the same field of central family relationships of which they were part before initiation. At the same time, they are poised on the brink of new relations through marriage, relations that will extend and reshape familiar agnatic ones.

The patterns of speaking within ritual events can also be part of larger patterns that span the course of initiation, part of the general structure and dramatic orchestration of the multifaceted experience of ceremonial transformation. For instance, wider patterns of speech help divide the first ceremony structurally into sections that focus first on the general ceremonial setting and cultural values and then on the initiates themselves. Blessings are the main kind of speech scheduled during the general first section, where they alternate with ritual songs and processions. The second section includes *ceerseet* and *pesenweek,* events that concentrate on affecting initiates and draw heavily on personal relations and interactions to do so. Most of the emotional displays of encouragement are concentrated in the second section; the transition between the first and second sections at dusk is the first time at which emotional fits are expected. Dramatic tension mounts through the second section, and interactive intensification heightens emotional and experiential engagement, leading to the climax and release of the dawn operation and the subsequent celebration. The verbal aspects of ritual events are essential in creating both the tension and the intensity of this second section. Poetic devices and different discourse structures also work toward the intended pragmatic ends in each event.

Various forms of directives and requests have arisen repeatedly in this chapter. They constitute a critical verbal motif, which figures in a number of specific analyses, that combines formal, semantic-thematic, and pragmatic dimensions. The more general patterning of directives and requests is one example of a verbal pattern that is crucially synthetic to the transformative ceremonial progression. Over the sequence of ritual events, directives and requests are reiterated in various ways and modes and from various perspectives, creating a progression of semiotic movement that is essential to the definition and intensification of Okiek initiation and its efficacy. A girl's role and responsibility in relation to the directives and requests that occur over the course of initiation show her shifts of status from child through girl beginning initiation and initiate in seclusion, finally ending as young woman.

Imperatives are common from the very beginning, first in blessings and later in curses. Though imperatives are taken as prayers and requests, they also include a degree of influence and implied assent, thereby shaping the way people will act during the ceremonial occasion. Questions of authority and control are more explicitly involved in the directives addressed to the girls during the first ceremony. However, even those include a strong sense of persuasion and compliance, rather than simple command and blind obedience. This is both a subtle indication of the girls' incipient change in identity and social relations and one foundation of the anxiety and interactive intensification that builds experiential and emotional engagement during the first ceremony. It further suggests that the normative picture of social relations, authority, and obedience has other sides.

Encouraging speeches are replete with directives and requests. Those who speak should command respect and obedience, yet they address the girl as one who can and must *choose* to comply, one who must find the inner strength and maturity to do so. Women's harangues address her in much the same way, as one with the capacity of choice. Limited though her actual choice may be, the girl's position as one who *agrees* to give her body bravely redefines her position vis-à-vis her adult relatives. Her freedom to choose is the root of the anxiety that sends other people into emotional fits, uncertain that she will be steadfast. Fits are further encouragement in the spiral of interactive intensification, with additional directives and requests. *Pesenweek* reveal that, in fact, girls have broken promises and refused to comply in the past, when still supposedly dutiful children. The onlookers' anxiety may well be warranted, and so the girls' determination to rewrite that past is further hardened.

After demonstrating her maturity and powerful will, an initiate suddenly loses all freedom of choice again during seclusion. She does as she is told, following wherever her ritual leader goes in seclusion ceremonies.[45] When she comes out of seclusion, though, the change hinted at in encouragement is realized. She responds and accepts gifts as an adult. She is a responsible person, one who must be taken into account, even if she is a woman.

The importance of directives and requests throughout initiation also suggests that Okiek relations of power and authority have a large component of persuasion and influence. Respect (-*kaany'it*) is the foundation of such relations, and is based on age, experience, kinship, or ritual relations. But respect is largely a matter of heeding and listening, that is, of agreeing to be influenced, rather than blatant coercion and outright control.

In addition to these patterns of verbal form, other patterns in the definition and scheduling of communicative roles and contexts also stretch over the course of initiation. The significance of general patterns of speech and silence will be considered in the next chapter in relation to song. Here it is enough simply to note again that who speaks and who doesn't, when particular people are scheduled to speak, and how they are expected to speak are all important aspects of initiation's contextual re-creation. These patterns are also central to initiation's dramatic pacing and the process of experiential and emotional engagement. The differentiated modes of encouragement are the best example of how these processes converge: distinct forms of encouragement are appropriate to gender and age, and their sequential scheduling is critical to initiation's interactive intensification.

Contextual re-creation through spoken media involves a range of interconnected assumptions and notions that inform Okiek life. These include assumptions about personhood, cultural identity, and relations of gender and age. Such notions are important means through which people make decisions, interpret, understand, evaluate, and experience the changing situations and interactions of their lives. Relations of gender and age are the dominant foci of initiation's contextual re-creation, but assumptions about cultural identity, guest-host relations, kinship relations, and other realms are also touched on. Different assumptions are foregrounded in different ritual events in ways related to initiation's structural divisions and emphases.

For instance, the blessings that predominate in the opening section of the first ceremony are a kind of summary, touching on aspects of cultural identity, social cooperation, gender, and age. The contextual re-creation that occurs during the evening events focuses more specifically on gender and age. *Ceerseet* emphasizes gender, while *pesenweek* concentrates on age, though notions of age are incorporated in *ceerseet* and notions of gender are found in *pesenweek* as well. The final speeches of thanks foreground relations of hospitality. Seclusion ceremonies continue to center on relations of gender, but also introduce more elements of intragender hierarchy and authority. The contextual re-creation in the final ceremony of initiation returns to many of the notions combined in the opening events of the first ceremony, giving close patrilineal relations an extra accent as well.

As initiation reproduces Okiek social organization by creating new adults, then, it also incorporates and re-creates a wide range of assumptions that are central to Okiek life. This is so not only for initiates but also for other participants. Beginning in a way that links many of these assumptions together simultaneously, contextual re-creation then plays variations on that chord through these shifts of focus and emphasis. The overtones of notions dominant in one event carry through others, too, as new dominant notes are sounded.

Semiotic movement would be more like melodic line, to continue with the musical metaphor, tracing a continuous progression from initiation's start to its finish in multiple channels simultaneously. The discussion of semiotic movement in the speech of initiation has highlighted an important distinction between two types of semiotic movement. The first is created by cultural progressions of particular sign series, usually within channels. This kind of semiotic movement featured prominently in chapter 5. The initiates' gradual removal from and eventual return to direct communication is one speech-related example. This kind of semiotic movement usually centers on initiates, who are physically or metaphorically moved through the process of initiation through these multiple, coordinated sign series.

The second type of semiotic movement is related to the temporal progression of ceremonial structure itself. The ceremonies and ritual events of initiation are themselves defined as a cultural progression that, when appropriately performed, changes girls into women. This type of semiotic movement is the framework within which the first type takes place. At the same time, however, the semiotic movement of ceremonial structure is made up in part of these other cultural progressions. The two are closely intertwined and mutually implicated, but the distinction is analytically useful. The patterning of directives and requests discussed above and the ordered succession of forms of encouragement both are tied to and contribute to the sequence of ritual events and the semiotic movement of ceremonial structure. This semiotic movement creates not only a specific propulsion for the initiates, but draws other participants along as well, blending with experiential and emotional engagement.

The semiotic movement of ceremonial structure accelerates and slows as the drama of the progression of ritual events intensifies and subsides. Various modes of experiential and emotional engagement are scheduled into and also fostered by the progression. Though such engagement is neither automatic nor uniform among participants, the contexts, performance, discourse structure, and poetic-rhetorical devices of the various ritual events work together to encourage and facilitate such engagement. They are also means through which such engagement is expressed, displayed, and further heightened. These dramatic rhythms help make initiation's semiotic movement effective and affecting.

The focus on performance in this chapter has shown how contextual re-creation, semiotic movement, and experiential engagement fuse in the speech of each ritual event and throughout the initiation process to create ritual efficacy. In addition, it has shown that multiple perspectives and contradictions emerge during ceremonial performances, though they may not figure in Okiek explanations and ideal representations of what goes on. Contextual re-creation may emphasize ideal pictures, but at times those pictures are simultaneously questioned or undercut. Alternatives are also voiced. "The very process of attempting to legitimate a social order by idealizing it always provides its subjects with the means, the symbolic tools, the very ideas for a critique" (Scott 1985:338). In performance, then, contextual re-creation has more than one face; contradictions and alternatives are reproduced simultaneously with ideal notions and types. Questions of power and authority are raised and the notions themselves contested throughout this central ceremonial process of initiation. Different participants may find different questions and contradictions most salient and personally relevant, for those participating in initiation are at different phases in their own life cycles and experiences. Similarly, they have different perspectives on and attitudes toward resistance and toward the alternatives voiced and reproduced through the ceremonies.

These inconsistencies and discrepancies result in part from the multiple and diverse participants involved in every initiation ceremony, with their intrinsic differentiation of outlooks and interests. This differentiation is also implicit in the very change initiates undergo. They leave familiar childhood perspectives for adult ones that they have at times opposed and subverted. As they are socially resituated and incorporated into adult standpoints, the perspective that is urged on them and presented as ideal is one that favors men in many respects. The alternative perspectives that emerge most conspicuously during initiation performances are those of women and children. Alternative representations of women surface most consistently, along with modes of women's resistance to general assumptions about their nature and roles. Women's seclusion ceremonies themselves constitute "a social space in which the definitions and performances imposed by domination" do not necessarily prevail (Scott 1985:328).

However, Okiek initiation is not simply another example of separate situations where hegemonic and counterhegemonic definitions and discourse prevail.[46] Women's seclusion ceremonies teach and reinforce ideal representations of Okiek gender relations at the same time that they expose and counter them. Furthermore, contradictions in and alternatives to Okiek notions of gender do not emerge only in such separate, "unmasked" situations. They are equally manifest in *ceerseet* performance, a central and climactic event that features speeches by men. Is this an acknowledgment of false assumptions or of discrepancies of power and authority between men and women? Is it a recognition of alternative perspectives?

That may well be the case, but there is more to the inconsistencies revealed in initiation performance than multiple perspectives and participants. Contradictions are also multiple and diverse, related to questions of both social integration and system integration. These contradictions appear at various times over the course of initiation, differentially foregrounded in much the same way that contextual re-creation emphasizes different foci in different events (and often in coordination with those foci). *Ceerseet,* for example, is the moment during which contradictions between the premises of initiation and assumptions about gender crystallize, while gender-related contradictions continue to be important throughout seclusion. Contrary guest-host expectations and actions are central to the final speeches of thanks during the first ceremony of initiation. Official and unofficial perspectives on adult-child relations come to the fore during *pesenweek.*

This analysis of the multiple perspectives and contradictions of Okiek initiation adds a new dimension to several views of initiation and ritual. First, it suggests that while initiation is indeed a critical moment in the maturation of a person, a point at which personhood officially changes, it may not be sufficient or entirely correct to regard initiation as a sociological adjustment to appropriate social roles. Initiation may not always make exactly the kind of people desired. Just as ideal values and norms are simultaneously contradicted in performance, so, too, the ideal outcome is not always perfectly achieved.

Second, the analysis questions the view that "there is, in ritual, a strain to internal consistency of action and meaning. . . . The resolution of contradiction and inconsistency constitutes a transformational process which, when completed, leads to the re-establishment of consistency within a new form" (Kapferer 1979a:5). Not all contradictions are resolved, and continuing inconsistencies are inherent in the multiple perspectives and heteroglossia of ceremonial performance. The "strain" to consistency is simultaneously countered and combined with other tendencies to inconsistency. A monocular view that sees only one side and takes only one perspective cannot do justice to the complexity, polyvocality, and multidimensionality of ceremonial performance.

These new dimensions in ritual analysis can help illuminate other work on ceremonies. To take an example that remains within eastern Africa, Gisu initiation has been much studied, but scholarly interpretations differ. The differences are not as great as they seem, however. Debates between La Fontaine and Heald on Gisu initiation appear to emphasize different aspects of a similar, monocular "official" view. Initiation ceremonies do re-create social categories and status distinctions (La Fontaine 1977, 1985), just as they do "shape self-understandings and attitudes" (Heald 1989:200). Yet neither scholar explores or explains how the ceremonies do so, how their effects are produced by those involved. La Fontaine recognizes that analyses of ritual efficacy must take all participants in initiation into account (1985:104), yet dismisses Gisu understandings of the effects of initiation as irrelevant to explaining ritual efficacy (1977:422). Neither Heald nor La Fontaine considers Gisu initiation from multiple perspectives. Further, neither one recognizes the possibility of "unofficial" views arising in the midst of ceremonial performance and questioning both status distinctions and self-understandings. Heald identifies the dilemma of Gisu life as arising from conflicting values of individualism (for men) and kinship interdependence (Heald 1989:77), yet fails to consider the ways these different values are simultaneously incorporated into Gisu initiation, just as she fails to consider female actors in initiation and in Gisu life more generally.

These failures at gender analysis and at considering multiple perspectives in initiation also reach the core of disagreement between these two scholars concerning authority in Gisu life. Heald can argue for a lack of real authority in Gisu life only by ignoring gender relations. Gisu convictions that if they were to "initiate women, relations between spouses would be a continual battle, for women would be able to exercise a power equal to their husbands'"

(La Fontaine 1977:423) certainly suggest that initiation helps to re-create relations of inequality and authority along lines of gender as well as age. La Fontaine pays greater attention to the elders involved in initiation, while Heald focuses on initiates' own initiative in the process. They come up with divergent analyses of authority that differ by emphasis and perspective, though both focus on intergenerational relations. La Fontaine may over-emphasize elders' power and influence in daily life, but Heald constructs an overly Hobbesian Gisu world. Some kinds of authority may be fragile—perhaps relying on persuasion, influence, consent, and shifting relations, and not always acknowledged—but they are nonetheless claimed and sometimes exercised. Further, the debated authority of age seems to intersect with much clearer relations of authority and power in other realms that are not considered (for example, in gender relations).

The analysis of the patterns of speaking in performance has shown how processes of ritual efficacy are necessarily combined with multiple perspec-tives and contradictions in Okiek initiation. The speech of initiation is also essential in three general processes, which I consider in closing. First, as discussed in chapter 2, language plays a crucial creative role in establishing the significance of other signs in ceremonies. Through language, aspects of the ceremony are picked out, their meanings and associations in part created and highlighted through references in the speech or song of ritual events. At the same time, they are given particular evaluative slants and emphases. Reiteration of particular themes and expressions in the speech and song of initiation is one example of the way certain aspects of ceremonial perfor-mances are picked out, emphasized, interpreted, and evaluated (cf. Kratz 1986). In many cases, however, discussions and comments that contribute to the multifaceted significance of the acts, objects, places, songs, ways of speaking, ritual roles, and other details of ceremonies occur in other contexts, dispersed throughout other occasions and daily interactions. Explicit exegeti-cal commentary, whether for a researcher or for others, is one special case of this.

Second, speech extends the moment of a particular initiation ceremony through time, calling aspects of the past into the present and projecting the present occasion into the future. Encouraging speeches, for example, bring the history and significance of past ceremonies and of particular relations to bear on the present situation. They present one view of the history of social relations that justifies the speaker's position in encouraging the girl and laying his expectations on her. At the same time, this enhances the persuasive power of his claim and the obligation the girl should feel.

In the final ceremony, on the other hand, gifts are often promises. They resume the central patrilineal relations the girls grew up with, with new wrinkles for the future. The ceremonial form of renewal also projects into the ensuing interactions between initiates and those who give the gifts, creating a ritual relation that becomes a new facet of their continuing relationship (though often a minor one).

The third process also relates to time and history in initiation, but in an even more general way. Speech is a central resource through which Okiek incorporate changing circumstances, relations, and experiences into their ceremonies most directly and immediately. For instance, the usual themes may be given different expressions or other languages may be incorporated into various events. Further, new interpretations in keeping with new experiences might be given verbally to objects, acts, and materials that continue to be part of ceremonial performances. Chapter 8 discusses at greater length adaptations and changes in Okiek initiation over time.

Some of these general processes are found in the song as well as the speech of initiation. In the next chapter I continue to look at verbal resources in initiation, concentrating now on song. Song weaves together the ceremonial structure and process of initiation like the processions that bind forest and homestead, alternating with speech and defining another kind of ritual participation.

7

The Musical Molding
of Initiation

So too, music has power to ease tension within the heart and to loosen
the grip of obscure emotions. . . . From immemorial times the inspiring
effect of the invisible sound that moves all hearts, and draws them together, has mystified mankind.

I Ching

Song permeates Okiek initiation, from the opening forest procession to the
final river procession. It is indispensable for some ritual events, a primary
means of initiation teaching during seclusion, a type of adult secret to be
learned, and a source of enjoyment and entertainment in all ceremonies. Many
kinds of songs are sung during initiation. I discuss only those specifically
scheduled as part of the ceremonies, the required, necessary songs that *must*
be sung at certain times by certain people for initiation to be accomplished.[1]

Scheduled initiation songs are themselves differentiated, with important
distinctions of singer, scheduling, purpose, theme, and verbal and musical
form. The distinctions between song types and the definitions of who sings
what, how, and when are central aspects of contextual re-creation, experiential
and emotional engagement, and semiotic movement through song.

Song figures in the work of initiation in many ways, again combining the
key processes of ritual efficacy both within events and in larger configurations
across longer temporal expanses. These musical patterns are linked with those
of the other media discussed, creating different refractions, density and redundancy, and contrasts and counterpoints in performance. Together the different
media establish the possibility and means of effective transformation from
childhood to adulthood.

The first part of this chapter maps the diversity of song types, verbal
structure, and call line types that are the musical means of initiation. These
formal resources incorporate assumptions and understandings that are mobi-

lized toward ritual efficacy in performance. The detailed description of the first half is also a necessary background for the second part, where I consider different song types in turn to see how their performative, thematic, pragmatic, and poetic patterns figure in initiation's transformation. Before beginning these detailed analyses, I set them in the context of Okiek understandings of song and musical experience.

"To sing" and "to dance" are both -tien in Okiek; the senses are often combined, as people dance or move rhythmically while singing. Okiek songs have a call-and-response form; individuals sing short call lines (-kuuru tienta, call the song) and are answered by a group of singers in chorus (-yan, respond, agree).[2] Okiek categorize songs with various distinctions, such as call singer, common occasions of performance, topic, and ethnicity, often combining them.[3] Many song types are also differentiated by musical and verbal form, though formal aspects are not the basis of Okiek categories.

The main nonceremonial contexts of song are drinking parties for older people and evening gatherings of young people. The drinking might be during marriage talks, after cooperative work, or for some chance occasion, as well as at ceremonies. Songs adults sing when a bit drunk include elephant hunting songs, age-set songs from their youth, and other songs learned from Kalenjin-speaking neighbors.[4] Age-set songs were once the principal songs of youth, sung especially by young men in the evenings, sometimes with girlfriends, after hunting, raiding, and visiting. Young people still sing them, but now less commonly. They prefer to gather, when they can, for dances with a battery-operated phonograph. Girls also practice their initiation songs together in the evenings.

While group singing is entertaining and enjoyable, Okiek also take it as evidence of sociability, satisfaction, and at least temporary harmony. More than that, though, they consider the experience of the singing itself as able to produce and intensify those and other feelings at times. Interactions with and between call singers are part of this, expressing friendship and creating fellowship through specific exchanges. Two people might sing together, for instance, alternating call lines that praise husbands or age-mates, talk about common experiences, and comment on their joint singing and obvious enjoyment. When someone sings well or reminds others of powerful shared experiences (for example, an exciting hunt), the singer is greeted with a warm, sliding handshake.

The ordered arrangement of song is also part of the way it inspires and represents congeniality. Call and response turns alternate regularly, with length and overlap determined by the song's verbal and musical structure. This model of communication is sometimes invoked quite pragmatically to curtail obstreperous disruptions of formal discussion. People are enjoined to sing, that is, to replace the chaotic shouting that prevents discussion with the exaggeratedly regular turns of communication in song. Group singing first drowns out and then hopefully diverts troublemakers. Restoring the form of respectful interchange encourages a corresponding affective shift.

Song not only exaggerates regular turn-taking compared to speech; it is also seen as amplifying affect. As a communicative mode, song is considered capable of inspiring strong feelings in singers and listeners alike. In addition to fostering a general sense of sociability, its combination of sound, rhythm, interaction, theme, and poetics somehow touches off memories, thoughts, and feelings in ways that can grip or sometimes quite literally entrance performers and audience. Men are said to feel worked up (-*nereec*) on hearing the elephant song, roused by memories of former hunts. Singing the night before a hunt made them fearlessly anxious to hunt again. Similarly, age-set songs about cattle raids and courting beautiful girls gave men courage for such exploits. Some initiation songs are experienced as similarly encouraging and provoking. The evocative potential for arousing affect that Okiek attribute to song is central to the interactive intensification of initiation and the girls' transformation.

Most initiation songs are not performed expressly for the appreciation of those who hear them, but as ritual actions, emotional expressions, dramatic intensifications, or advertisements of social role. Many ritual events and songs are virtually ignored by those not directly involved, since they are performed when different people are doing different things. During the first ceremony, for instance, different songs can be sung simultaneously; the close proximity of different activities produces overlapping sounds. Women sing in their afternoon procession as they pass the initiates, who are singing near the *mabwaita;* young men amuse themselves with yet other songs nearby. The initiates' song and costumed dance at night *is* a practiced aesthetic display, but it is also far more. Interaction between singers and spectators is essential as personal messages, farewells, and encouragement are sung.

Ritual songs and girls' songs are only part of the repertoire of initiation songs; the full repertoire for both boys and girls includes roughly sixty songs. The following section first considers song categories within that repertoire, and then the basic verbal structure of song. Both are important to understand how initiation becomes effective through song.

Songs of Initiation: Categories and Call Lines

Okiek categorize the songs of initiation on the basis of call singers and performance contexts, often in combination: ritual songs (songs tied to and scheduled as part of particular events), girls' songs (encouraging songs sung by girls during initiation), *cepketilet* (songs for boys' initiation and secret men's songs), *kaiyantaaita* (songs of secluded initiates), and women's secret songs. Table 17 shows distinctions within these song types; it covers both girls' and boys' initiation, which share only some songs. Distinctions between song types are one basis of broad musical sequences in initiation over time, and are material through which cultural progressions of semiotic movement are defined. The song sequence is a musical outline of ceremonial structure that can be experienced as compelling and emotionally moving. The second half of this chapter follows these Okiek groupings to look at the songs in performance. This first part of the chapter also uses other, analytical groupings to consider patterns of ceremonial participation and verbal form that might otherwise be obscured.

Okiek song categories encapsulate and fuse notions about different kinds of singers and occasions. Tables 18 and 19 separate these crosscutting Okiek criteria in order to consider contrasts in patterns of scheduled ceremonial participation in song during girls' and boys' initiations.[5] These patterns are based on and re-create notions of age and gender, and also show how singing interweaves with the patterns of participation that have already been discussed.

Table 18 indicates how distinctions of gender and age are incorporated into the scheduling of song during initiation. Adult men (*paaiik*) take no part in scheduled song during girls' initiation, except for one song of rejoicing.[6] Even their rejoicing song is one for which young men (*murenik*) sing the call lines in the morning forest procession, and is more usually associated with them. Young men, too, are musically silent after that procession until the celebration.[7] Scheduled song pertaining to the ceremony itself, performed unfailingly, is sung chiefly by women or by the girls themselves. This reverses the situation reviewed in the last chapter, for the scheduled speakers of initiation are predominantly men. Even girls' social debts are announced by a young man.

During boys' initiation, however, men are active singers. Their *cepketilet* songs accompany or replace women's in the morning procession,[8] are sung throughout the day and evening, and are sung in rejoicing (when both men and women respond). Men also sing in boys' seclusion ceremonies and when young men come from the river, leaving seclusion.

It is not surprising that men lead songs for boys' ceremonies, but the radical gender distinction in singing during girls' ceremonies is not reversed. Women sing for boys as well as girls. They still sing in the two forest processions, converse in song with boys as with girls, and rejoice with their own songs as well as responding to men's. Okiek women's verbal role is intimately bound up with song in all ceremonies; in boys' initiation it is virtually limited to song. Men, on the other hand, play an important verbal part in all initiation through speech: blessing, cursing, questioning, and encouraging daughters. For their sons, they also sing.

The general connection Okiek recognize between song and emotion is implicitly extended here to link communicative modes with gender.

Table 17: Okiek Initiation Songs by Type of Song

Ritual Songs
  A. forest processions
    1. young people
    2. women
  B. predawn songs
    1. women
  C. songs of rejoicing (*siimet*)
  D. songs of seclusion secrets
  E. river processions
    1. women
    2. men
  F. song to open the way (*yaatet aap ooreet*)

Girls' Songs

Cepketilet
  A. public
    1. men
    2. boys
  B. secret (at *menceet*)

Kaiyantaaita
  A. female
    1. initial dawn/dusk series
    2. others
  B. male
    1. initial dawn/dusk series (*kipawes*)
    2. others

Women's Secret Songs

Ceremonies are seen as organized by men. They do that principally through speech, whether in procedural discussions or formal ritual events. Okiek women make their presence felt and feelings heard in the official ceremonial realm especially through song. Men's speech is represented as reasoned, influencing others through logic and knowledge. This contrasts with song's ability to sway through emotion, a link that extends to incorporate parallel notions about women. Notions about speech and song as contrasting communicative modes thus become part of Okiek ideas about gender.

In fact, men and women make similar appeals and use similar themes during initiation in both speech and song. The image of men as managing ceremonies is countered in several ways, not least by women's prominent role in making their daughters into women and directing the secret portions of

Table 18: Okiek Initiation Songs by Social Category of Singers

A. Girls' Initiation (number of songs in parentheses)
Women
   A. public ritual
      1. forest procession (2–3)
      2. predawn (2)
      3. rejoicing (*siimet*) (1–2)
      4. river procession (2)
   B. secret
      1. during seclusion (12+) (also kaiyantaaita)
      2. ritual (1?)

Young People
   A. public ritual
      1. forest procession (2)
   B. girls' (12+)

Initiates
   A. *kaiyantaaita*
      1. girls'
         a. initial dawn/dusk series (3)
         b. others sung with women (at least 6–10)

Men
   A. public ritual
      1. rejoicing (*siimet*) (1)

Old man or woman
   A. ritual: *yaatet aap ooreet* (1)

B. Boys' Initiation
Women
   A. public ritual
      1. forest procession (2–3)
      2. rejoicing (*siimet*) (2)

Young People
   A. public ritual
      1. forest procession (1)
   B. boys' *cepketilet* (1)

Initiates
   A. *kaiyantaaita*
      1. boys'
         a. initial dawn/dusk series (*kipawes*) (2)
         b. others sung with men (about 3–5)

Table 18: *continued*

Men
   A. public ritual
     1. *cepketilet* (2)
     2. rejoicing (*siimet*) (1 *cepketilet*)
     3. river procession (2)
   B. secret (at *menceet*)
     1. *cepketilet* for *menceet* (at least 2–5) (also *kaiyantaaita*)
     2. ritual (1?)

Old man
   A. ritual: *yaatet aap ooreet* (1)

initiation. Yet women actually enact other ceremonies as well; they sing ritual songs that are indispensable to ritual events. Though not explicitly acknowledged as such, their songs and ritual acts are a structural web comparable to men's blessings and overt organization. If they refused to sing certain songs, the ceremony would be derailed.

Men sing in boys' ceremonies as one way to begin claiming jurisdiction over boys leaving childhood. They challenge women's musical monopoly of ritual events, asserting their organizational priority in song as well for boys' ceremonies. Men's musical claim is also testimony about emotion and gender, related to that incorporated in encouraging speeches to girls. Men and women alike encourage boys in song; there are no speeches for them. Differences in men's and women's call lines, however, represent, embody, and sustain notions of gender, as seen below. Boys should need no encouragement or promises, particularly from women. Nonetheless, they can be urged on to bravery. This more austere encouragement is sung, the medium itself a sign of emotional engagement and an appeal from men to boys. Men's songs set an example for how boys should respond to women, in song, since their lines are more like statements than emotional appeals. Boys' singing begins to show their manly self-control; they begin to disengage themselves from women's and children's domains through song.

While young men (*murenik*) who participate in initiation ceremonies consider themselves to be separate from women and children, they are not yet fully included with older men; their scheduled verbal role in initiation is limited. Moreover, they help bring forest materials in singing procession, as women do later, and are received with the same women's songs (table 19) and then with elders' blessings. Women and young people jointly contrast with elders—those who bring and sing versus those who receive and speak. The common grouping of women and children in daily life, which is a partial

Table 19: Okiek Initiation Songs by Context/Event

Songs for Public Ritual Processions
  A. morning procession from the forest (*kepa koroseek*)
    1. young people
    2. women's answer (same as *toloocik* ones)
    3. men's *cepketilet* answer in boys' ceremony
  B. afternoon procession from the forest (*kepa toloocik*)
    1. women (women in procession and women meeting them sing the same song)
  C. final procession from the river (*kelong'u en aineet*)
    1. women
    2. men

Predawn Ritual Songs
  A. women

Songs for Rejoicing (*siimet*)
  A. women's for girls and boys
  B. men's for girls
  C. men's (and women's) for boys (*cepketilet*)

Other Ritual Songs
  A. opening the way (*yaatet aap ooreet*)

Songs of Encouragement
  A. girls'
  B. *cepketilet*
    1. men
    2. boys

Songs of Seclusion
  A. *kaiyantaaita*
    1. female
      a. initial dawn/dusk series
      b. others sung with women
    2. male
      a. initial dawn/dusk series (*kipawes*)
      b. others sung with men
  B. Women's secret songs
  C. Men's secret *cepketilet*
  D. secret songs for *tuumwek*
    1. men
    2. women

justification of elders' role as blessers, is enacted in the roles and performance of ceremonies as well. Notions of age and gender are thus reinscribed as part of ceremonial tradition through their performative implications.

The two processions, so similar in structure and enactment, bracket the first day with corresponding events. As table 19 shows, specific song types are scheduled during specific sections of the first ceremony. This indexing combines with other framing devices already discussed, including costume and modes of ritual participation. Ritual songs of procession start and end the daytime section, where the focus is on general Okiek values, social roles, and social relations. During the nighttime section, focused on initiates, girls and their songs take center stage. Ritual songs reconcentrate attention at dawn, reemphasizing the general frame of the ceremony just before the girls are cut. Exultant singing and ululation then start the final celebratory phase.

As different songs and types of song help define ceremonial structure, they also describe a temporal sequence; they are signs of ceremonial process and of initiates' semiotic progression. The sequence of songs is just one musical index of ceremonial movement through initiation. As seen below, temporal movement through initiation is also indexed by a progression in the kinds of call lines sung. Yet another progression within individual singers' call turns parallels that one, anticipating and reiterating in microcosm the dramatic movement of the ceremony as a whole.

Song is also implicated in the spatial organization and movement of initiation. Over half the ritual songs are processional; the significant places of Okiek life and ceremonies are woven together with song and procession: forest and village, river and seclusion house, and finally river and village (see chapter 5). The first procession goes to each home hosting the ceremony, binding them together with song and saplings for each *mabwaita*. The journey of initiation is full of musical movement and progressions.

These indexical patterns of song, sung and heard in sequence through time, are critical to experiential and emotional engagement. People anticipate and anxiously await songs that accompany or precede events in which they are emotionally involved. The full sequence of the first ceremony, of course, is a countdown to the children's operations, but there are other moving moments along the way. Anticipation and experience of the songs can spark rising emotions that intensify with dawn's approach. For instance, when women break the silence with ritual songs to announce dawn and reassemble the gathering, they also evoke the heightened excitement and anxiety of the final wait.

Verbal Form of Initiation Songs

Women's dawn songs are distinguished by their line structure and chantlike melodic form. Similarly, some processional songs include unique song words or a special, distinctive set of call lines. These and other formal aspects of the songs of initiation are essential material, some of the nuts and bolts through which ceremonies are made effective. This section reviews the verbal forms and resources used in initiation songs, with attention to relations between song and speech.

The language of Okiek song and the language of Okiek conversation are alike in many ways, but at every level of linguistic organization there are systematic distinctions. Even common resources are used differently and have a different structural organization. In song, sounds are added to words, and there are unique "song words," uncommon morphological forms, patterned repetitions, and conventional restrictions on line combinations and syntax. One result of these differences is that compared to speech, the referential flow of communication is slowed down, interrupted, and rearranged in song. The patterning of interaction in song performance introduces similar interruptions, regularizing the rhythm of exchanges that in speech often follow the referential flow more closely.

Poetic form and pragmatic effect are prominent in both the song and the speech of initiation. The alternations and timing of speech and song in ceremonies play on and exaggerate culturally relevant contrasts and similarities of form, message, and context. This play of form and content is central to the pacing and experience of initiation. The verbal resources of Okiek song are instrumental to its effect.

Initiation songs are sung in Okiek and include loan words from Maa, Kipsigis, and Kiswahili, like conversation.[9] Words common to speech and song are usually pronounced the same way, but words at either end of a call line might be extended in song. Vocative syllables are commonly added at the start or end of lines, serving as structural markers as well as melodic material. Few Maa words occur in the songs, but Kipsigis words and phrases are more common in song than in speech, especially in girls' songs.[10] Used formulaically in song, the phrases are akin to other song words, but are also in daily use by some Okiek. Girls' songs also include many Kiswahili words common in conversation.

Special song words included in initiation songs are only sometimes taken as referential. Referential ones, especially common in seclusion songs, are often interpreted in terms of similar sounding conversational counterparts. For instance, a common phrase of seclusion songs, *pampa muut*, is interpreted as "to go respectfully," its components likened to *panta* (trip) and *muutya* (slowly, respectfully). There is usually considerable consensus about the meaning of such words, but some have several interpretations. For example, some people understand *lemuto le cinca* to refer to a green necklace (cf. Maa *emurto narok*, black necklace), while others emphasize the sense of cutting suggested by other sound similarities (*kemuut*, to cut; *kuchinja*, to butcher < Kiswahili).

Nonreferential song words can be inserted in call lines to split and extend them over two turns; some call lines consist entirely of such words, such as repetitions of *laleygo,* the most common one. Certain song words, both referential and nonreferential, are tied to particular songs. For example, *sonaya* (nonreferential) is associated with a women's procession song, and *riret* (referential: a deep place in the river) is associated with a young people's procession song.

Morphologically, Okiek song and speech differ chiefly in their most frequently used noun forms. Kalenjin nouns have two forms (called primary and secondary on the basis of formal criteria [Tucker and Bryan 1964–65] or inclusive and exclusive in an effort to specify their enigmatic semantic distinctions [Toweett 1979b:93–94]). Secondary forms are primary forms with suffixes. The shorter primary form is far more frequent in song; secondary noun forms are most common in conversation.[11]

Primary Form	Secondary Form	English Gloss
muusar	*muusareek*	porridge
keeciir	*keeciiryet*	sheep
mooi	*mooyta*	calf
kuumin	*kuumiik*	honey
tyaany'	*tyaanta*	animal

The syntax of speech is modified in song by relations between phrase length and formal call line structure. Phrases that are clearly linked semantic continuations and would follow each other directly in speech might be separated in songs by inserted song words or response sections, with phrases repeated after the break. These patterns of repetition contribute to the songs' poetic structure, at times creating the incremental semantic progress and elaboration characteristic of "strict" parallelism (Jakobson 1968; Fox 1977; Silverstein 1981; Kratz 1990a).

While song and speech share their basic linguistic material, the added sound syllables, special song words, morphological markedness, syntactic breaks, and repetitions of song draw attention to the differences between speech and song. Indeed, song does not flow like the ideal speech of reasonable men. It is full of interruptions and unusual sounds and shapes, and is far closer to Okiek notions of emotional speech. The broad effect of these differences is to draw out communicative exchanges in song and in the process to reorient communicative emphases and expectations. To use Jakobson's distinctions, the poetic and metalinguistic aspects of communication are projected forward within the referential, propelling the pragmatic effects of attention to other contextual aspects of communication.

Referential communication *is* pivotal in many initiation songs, but in song the referential function is also regularly downplayed, overridden, undermined, or at least played with. Referentiality is always somewhat less prominent in song than in speech simply because of musical form, but other communicative functions are particularly emphasized in certain songs or in certain contexts. Even lines with straightforward referential meaning often mean more than they say. Allusion and metaphor are the stuff of Okiek song, important devices of indirection and edification by puzzlement (Fernandez 1987). Further, most information explicitly conveyed by song in initiation is not new, in contrast to what is commonly expected in referentially oriented conversation. What is emphasized, rather, is who is involved, their relationships, how they sound, how the song proceeds—in short, the context and the experience of sung communication. In initiation, this calls attention to diverse aspects of the ceremonial change taking place; by doing so, song can effectively intensify that very experience.

These linguistic contrasts between speech and song are organized within songs in terms of call and response turns and line structure. Songs are divided into sections by the alternations of an individual singer's call and the group's response. A caller's turn might consist of a single solo call line or might continue for several lines, with a group response between them. Call lines are the most prominent structural units of song, meaningful kernels that are combined to convey messages and appeals and from which larger poetic-pragmatic structures are created in performance.

Most call lines are six syllables long.[12] The end and/or beginning of the line is often marked with an added vowel (usually -*e* or -*o* finally and *o*-initially); certain words demarcate call lines in some songs.

(1) *kimace laalta koong'-o*   we want glowing eyes-*o*
(2) *sonaiya-e kimace laalta koong'-o*   *sonaiya-e* we want glowing eyes-*o*
     sonaiya-e laalta koong' uu taait-o *sonaiya-e* glowing eyes like a lamp-*o*
     sonaiyany'uun   my *sonaiya*

In some songs, such as the ritual song *riret* (example 1), a singer's turn consists of a single call line at a time. In other songs (such as example 2), singers put two or three six-syllable lines together, with a short interlocking response between them. The six-syllable segments are framed by melodic contour (which falls at the end and rises at the next section) as well as the vocative syllables or words. Three-line combinations are especially common in girls' songs, the triad set off by a longer response section. Example 3 is from a girls' song; the lines are marked with melodic contour and the framing word *cooroonook* (friends). The song's response is also framed with *cooroonook* and a corresponding final melodic fall.

(3) *kencin ng'aa kipaako cooroonook*   who fools young men *cooroonook*

put koroos ne pa puuc cooroonook	[to] break koroosik saplings for nothing *cooroonook*
tuun kaaroon ko hasara cooroonook	tomorrow morning it's a loss *cooroonook*
[response] Elis Elis cooroonook, ka-liya s'ipeel laakweet cooroonook	*[response]* Alice Alice *cooroonook,* what's wrong that you burn the child *cooroonook*

At times, six-syllable lines are split, filled in with a three-syllable song word, name, or relationship term, and sung over two sections. Example 4 adds the song word *laleygo:*

(4)   *o-s'akong'et raaresyot-o*   *o*-so the laughter is over-*o*
       o-laleygo kong'eeten-o   *o-laleygo* beginning-*o*
       o-laleygo inkuuni-o   *o-laleygo* now-*o*

Three-syllable names and relationship terms can also be the main referential matter of call lines, usually combined with nonreferential syllables or one of several three-syllable frames, such as *amwaun X* (I tell you X).

Catalogue of Initiation Call Lines

When call lines from all initiation songs are considered together, the songs form three groups in terms of shared call lines: preseclusion, seclusion, and coming out of seclusion.[13] Within each group, call lines can also be categorized on the basis of grammatical form and thematic content, distinctions that often correspond to pragmatic differences as well.[14] Each category has initial lines and expansion lines. Initial lines can occur singly or expanded, usually with two or three expansion lines, but more rarely with four or five.[15]

(5)   *meikenter kariik aap*   don't cheat/shame the costume of
       kariik aap kuukany'uun   the costume of my brother
       ce kakwer maeelik   that has logged many miles
       kosukan Nkaroni   going round Nkaroni

These categories are useful for considering general thematic distributions, progressions, and transformations in song over the course of initiation. They also allow comparison of songs in terms of themes and line constructions.[16] Call line types and distributions emphasize commonalities among songs that are instrumental in creating processual continuities within and across ceremonies. The rest of this section reviews different types of call lines, noting continuities of theme and idiom among groups. Equally important, however, are differences among songs,[17] distinctive and diverse ways of handling common themes, their specific content and imagery, and different contexts of performance. These facets of initiation song will be discussed in the second half of the chapter.

Preseclusion Songs Girls' songs, the corresponding *cepketilet* songs of boys' ceremonies, and all ritual songs except the final river procession songs are sung before seclusion. They include eleven kinds of call lines, summarized in table 20. The first five are mainly indexical, highlighting the occasion, location, time, and people involved in initiation.

1. Index of Occasion Few in number, these lines occur mainly in ritual procession songs, where they help constitute the occasion's ceremonial frame. Most are declarative statements referring to the assembled guests, the circumcisor, or other things as signs of the ceremony. The following example, citing the processional saplings as a ceremonial index, also has a locative sense from the possessive pronoun, that is, the ceremony is in *our* place:

(6) *neny' aan resiontet-e*   the ceremonial sapling is ours-*e*

2. Index of Time Call lines that index time are more numerous. Also signs of ceremonial occasion, they are concerned chiefly with the imminence and approach of initiates' physical test. Interspersed throughout girls' songs, these lines are a steady countdown to the operation. Practicing before the ceremony, they sing about the day to come (7). However, at the ceremony, they mention evening and dawn (8).

(7a) *ng' orietng' waang' Jumamos*   Saturday is your demise
(7b) *komure wiikiitni*   when this week finishes

(8a) *akoimen inkuunaan*   it's become evening then
(8b) *akoeeci poorwekwaak*   it's dawn for your bodies

Time lines predominate in some women's ritual songs, and are prominent as the women sing to announce dawn, the end of the countdown.

A number of these lines portray time running out as a function of truth:

(9a) *o meko pa kiplenke-e*   *o*-it's no longer deception-*e*
(9b) *akopoit iman-e*   it's become true-*e*

Time and truth are related through the difference between word and deed. When the ceremony is distant, girls can boast about their bravery in songs. As it approaches, however, so does the time to fulfill their promises; words alone cannot prove their maturity. The girls' performance at excision will reveal their words as truth or as children's deception. The contrast of truthfulness and fraudulent cheating is developed further in dialogic lines described below.

Table 20: Types of Call Lines in Preseclusion Songs

1. Index of Ceremonial Occasion
   o laleygo tuumaan neny'aan   o *laleygo* that ceremony of ours

2. Index of Time
   komure wiikiitni, akong'et oljankar   when this week finishes, the lies will
                                            be over

3. Index of the Initiates
   laakokcaak   our children

4. Index of Singer
   koonkoi kwaany'iik aap syabanik   thank you, women of the necklaces

5. Locative-Identifier
   eceek cu menotik, caan pa Kamaeec   it's us the brave ones, those of
                                            Kamaeec

6. Directive to Initiates/Assurance from Initiates (dialogic)
   tuun iwe s'asiimuun araaweet ak nusu   go tomorrow and I'll rejoice for you a
                                            month and a half

7. Challenge to Initates/Assurance from Initiates (dialogic)
   kencin ng'aa paaiisyek kilabu ne pa   who cheats the elders with useless
       puuc   [undrinkable] liquor

8. Request to Initiates/Promise from Initiates (dialogic)
   kimace muusareek ce lalang' uu   we want porridge that is warm like
       caaiik   tea

   s'iriiku karibu s'akonin resiondet   then you come near and I will give
       n'inamtoi Nkaroni   you a ceremonial sapling to take
                                            home to Nkaroni

9. Nonreferential Lines
   laleygo laleygo laleygo   *laleygo laleygo laleygo*

10. Metapragmatic Comment
    oonkeesiimcin-e   let's rejoice for them-*e*

11. Song-specific Lines
    oo riretny'uun   oo my *riret*

3. Index of Initiates   These lines index initiates as a collective group in various ways: as children (*laakokcaak,* our children; *wareekcaak,* our pups/ kids), as an age-group of peers (*cooroonook,* friends; *marembu,* lovely girls < Kiswahili), or as a group constituted by shared initiation (*tolooek,* initiates).[18] Other lines pick out individuals, calling them by name, by relation (*kuukany'uun,* my sibling; *cepmwander,* husband's sister), or by affectionate terms that refer to birth order (*toweetny'uun,* my last-born). These lines might occur as direct or indirect objects to a preceding line, but more often they are either vocatives preceding or following dialogic lines or modifiers in apposition.

(10)   *o-laleygo atyece*   *o-laleygo* I will step
       o-iye kityec kuukany' uun-e   *o*-where my sister stepped-*e*
       o-kaameet aap Risanoi-e   *o*-mother of Risanoi-*e*

Lines indexing individuals also focus and direct dialogic lines to one singing girl, temporarily establishing a more particular connection within the general musical communication.

Many of these lines are three syllables long, and can be used to split and extend longer six-syllable lines of other types (11a). When a three-syllable line is sung alone, the remaining time in a six-syllable turn is filled with nonreferential syllables or a three-syllable frame that makes its vocative function explicit (11b):

(11a) *o-s'ikooneec wei-Ruci*   *o*-so give us *wei*-Ruci
       o-s'ikooneec resiontet-o   *o*-so give us a sapling-*o*
       o-naan mung'tai mbali-o   *o*-one which will go far-*o*

(11b) *o-amwaun wei-Jeni-o*   *o*-I tell you *wei*-Jeni-*o*
       ak iwe mamei ciit-o   go, no one dies-*o*
       o-tos kipek ce pa keny'-o   *o*-else those of the past would have
                                            perished-*o*

4. Index of Singers   Though extremely common in other kinds of songs (Kratz 1981b), lines that index singers other than initiates are rare in initiation. Call lines in this very small group are usually sung by women, pointing to their ceremonial participation and thereby indexing occasion as well as singers:

(12)   *kaptiikee-ye*   women-*ye*[19]

5. Locative Identifiers   These call lines are also rare in initiation, though very common in other songs (Kratz 1981b). They identify a village or place in the forest, indexing the lineage or families associated with it. At times the link of people and place is explicit, as in example 13. Like lines that index singers, these also point to the occasion, specifying ceremonial location:

(13)   *eceek cu meenotik*   it's us, the brave ones
       caan pa kamaeec   those of the place where the sun
                                             doesn't rise

These five types of indexical lines begin to show how initiation songs augment and interlock with the processes of ritual efficacy discussed in other chapters, adding accents, modulations, and elaborations with related effects. Indices of occasion and time help declare and create the ceremonial frame of initiation. More common early in ceremonies and at the start of songs, they are musical complements to elders' blessings. Time lines interpolated throughout the first ceremony are a detail integral to its dramatic development, an explicit marker of semiotic movement through time. Lines that link time and truth are also coded for gender, as seen below.

Lines indexing initiates as a group support and reinforce their gradual spatial and proxemic movement during the ceremonies, helping to create their collective sense by calling attention to them and addressing them as one. Vocative lines to individual girls in dialogic exchanges personalize formulaic lines, directing them to particular friends and relatives much as men's encouraging speeches draw on personal appeals to obligate girls to be brave. The scarcity of lines that index other singers or locations is striking because they are so common in songs outside initiation. Their absence suggests and strengthens the ceremonial focus on the occasion and on initiates; lines of these types that *do* occur are related to these foci. Other singers take a more prominent place in initiation songs in lines that emphasize their relations with initiates, as in the next three types of call lines.

All three of these types are dialogic, their illocutionary force changing according to the singer in sung exchanges. Pragmatically, the lines are of a kind. All are directives when addressed to initiates, though not all are expressed directly. When sung by initiates, they become assurances or promises instead. Two of the three groups show this with morphological changes in verb inflection. Among the most numerous and diverse types of call lines, these dialogic groups are also the most descriptively elaborated. They include almost as many secondary expansion lines as initial lines; directives and challenges also have a good number of tertiary expansion lines. (Secondary and tertiary expansion lines occur in the second and third slots in a turn.)

6. *Directive to Initiates/Assurance from Initiates*   Most explicitly phrased as directives, this group has the largest preseclusion repertoire. When addressed to initiates, they are usually imperatives (singular or plural, positive or negative).

(14)   *tuun iwe s'asiimuun*   go tomorrow and I'll rejoice for you
        s'asiimuun araaweet   so I'll rejoice for you a month
        araaweet ak nusu   a month and a half

Most negative imperatives center on cheating and honesty with the verb *-kenter* (to fool or cheat, with the sense of shame here). All of the decorations, food, and work done will become evidence of shameful deception if the initiates fail (see example 5).

Directives sometimes use more coaxing, or polite imperatives phrased with the subjunctive verb form and introduced by *ak* (and) (15a). They can also be phrased indirectly, like the general statements of conduct with a first person plural subject (15b) that are admonitory directives to children.

(15a) *ak iwe Kishuayon*   go Kishuayon
(15b) *kiciil mukuulel*   we squeeze the heart
         koik ciilayuot-e   to become a squeezed [hard] thing-*e*

Initiates sing the lines as indicative statements, usually inflected for a first-person subject. They assure others that they will perform as expected. Changes in person and illocutionary force sometimes entail related changes in agreement and form (compare example 15):

(16a) *kipeenti ot kosiim*   we will go till [they] rejoice
         ot kosiim araaweet   till [they] rejoice a month
         araaweet ak nusu   a month and a half

(16b) *ma potaan kikenter*   it isn't for me to cheat/shame
         tukuuk aap kuukany'uun   my brother's things

A few of these lines also occur in rejoicing songs, undergoing another pragmatic change to become celebration. As singers announce the girls' successful fulfillment of directives and promises, a consistent tense change to recent past tense makes the context and intent clear:[20]

(17)   *katii ot kony'aal*   they sat till it's right

The full line inventory in this group is large, but it involves a small set of verbs and semantic fields. Many lines build on the verb "to go" (*kepa*), for instance, developing initiation's central journey idiom. They tell initiates to go (or initiates promise they will go), describe how the girls should/will go, or talk about the proud reaction that will follow. Such line sets built on single verbs are essential to the poetic form and pragmatic effects that emerge in performance, as seen below.

7. Challenge to Initiates/Assurance from Initiates   Most challenging call lines are rhetorical questions: who does X? The lines are phrased in terms of unspecified third persons, and there are no morphological distinctions by singer; the illocutionary force is clear only if the singer is known. Sung to initiates, they are directives, indirectly stated, telling them *not* to do X. Sung by initiates, they dissociate the girls from such acts, reassuring friends and relatives that they will not do them:

(18)   *kencin ng'aa paaiisyek*   who cheats elders [with]
       kilabu ce pa puuc   useless [undrinkable] liquor

These lines also emphasize a small set of central verbs. Many rhetorical questions build on *-kenter* or *-kencin* (to fool, shame, cheat), as negative imperative lines do. A smaller group are based on the verb *-ik* (to become), with song-specific words for those who squirm, squawk, or run:

(19)   *iku ng'aa kiluilui*   who becomes a squirmer
       kinte let kinte taai   put last put first
       ko mainai sababu   and you don't know why[21]

Other rhetorical questions mention encouragement as both challenge and praise:

(20)   *ceere ng'aa ne maimuuc*   who encourages one who cannot
       ne maimuuc koceerkee   who cannot encourage herself

No encouraging words will give the girls the heart and will to succeed; it depends on their own strength. These lines anticipate and echo the contradiction between notions about gender and notions about initiation that surfaces in men's speeches.

Challenges that are not cast as questions might set initiates against the success of others before them. Lineage pride and reputation, for instance, are at risk with each initiation:

(21)   *mankotiny' kainy'aan*   our family has not had
       cepicep entotua   someone who ran away in fear

Others scornfully advise them to go live with Luo in Kisumu, who do not circumcise. This is another theme shared with men's speeches.

(22)   *ne ikas meikany'e*   if you feel you fear
       ko neekit ooreet aap   the way is near
       ooreet aap Kisumu   the way to Kisumu

8. Request to Initiates/Promise from Initiates   Sung to initiates, these lines request proper behavior during the operation or a sign of the initiates' success, either celebratory food and liquor (called fermented porridge [*muusar*] in song) or a botanical sign (usually a sapling). A few make direct requests, using the verb "to give," but most are indirect, saying "I/we want X." All the requests are indirectly phrased directives, telling initiates what they should do.

(23) *amace resiontet*   I want a sapling
      naan yapu poortang' uung'   that comes from your body

When initiates sing them, the lines are promises: "I'll give you X." Like the explicit directive lines, inflection changes according to singer.

Lines about food and saplings carry into celebration, again announcing fulfilled promises. In rejoicing, people can simply combine nouns from these lines with *koonkoi* (thanks). Other lines are changed to recent past tense, like the directives:

(24) *kakooneec muusareek*   they gave us porridge
      ce lalang' uu caiik   that's warm like tea

All three types of dialogic lines are centrally involved in the interactive intensification of sung encouragement and the dramatic pacing of the first ceremony. They are a vital means through which people become experientially and emotionally engaged in initiation. Furthermore, the themes, idioms, and very phrases of these lines anticipate and echo those of encouraging speeches and women's harangues. Their shared directive force resonates with the themes of the girls' confessions as well. The varied repetition of themes in different media by different people creates a density and texture of performance and experience. Coupled with the social definitions of the participants, this establishes a unanimity that underlines assumptions embedded in the ceremonies about relations of gender and age, and about initiation itself.

The final three preseclusion line groups—nonreferential lines, metapragmatic lines, and song-specific lines—are small. Nonreferential lines are vocative syllables that fill the time of a call line. Many are vocalic, combining *o* and *e* with transitions and onsets articulated with *y* and *h*, for example, *oyee oo eee* (from *celimen*). By far the most common nonreferential line, however, repeats the song word *laleygo*.

Metapragmatic lines comment on what the song itself does or the performance context.[22] They can effect a change of call singers (25a), but more often exhort people to sing together well (25b).

(25a) *maing' ete pamwaainy' uun-o—*   don't be tired, my age-mate-*o*
       n'anamuun pamwaainy' uun-o   let me take over for you my age-
                                           mate-*o*

(25b) *oonkeesiimcin-e*   let's rejoice for them-*e*

Finally, song-specific lines are lines unique to particular songs. They often include a song word from the response section, as in this example from the processional song *riret:*

(26)   *oe riretny' uun-e*   *oe* my *riret-e*

Song words are only one factor that makes song-specific lines more referentially opaque than other call lines. In lines from another processional song
(*cepkondook ce leelac*), for instance, a series of nouns are strung together;
they are not obviously related and have different interpretations.

Many song-specific lines feature in ritual songs in which performative and
indexical aspects are at least as important as referential communication. The
songs have very small line repertoires and song-specific lines that deemphasize or problematize referentiality. The unique lines index and accentuate the
specific and limited performance contexts of the songs. Singing the song *is*
performing the ritual event; the specificity of both the performance context
and the lines makes the songs highly marked indices of the ceremonial
occasion and the ritual event in which they are sung.

Seclusion Songs   Songs sung in seclusion include men's and women's
secret songs and *kaiyantaaita* songs sung by initiates. The following line
groups are based largely on *kaiyantaaita,* which differ for male and female
initiates, though performance contexts are similar.[23] *Kaiyantaaita* are regarded as secrets hidden from the opposite sex. Nonetheless, male and female
songs have similar types of lines and even share certain lines. Lines fall into
several types thematically; thematic differences are often reinforced by grammatical differences and the use of different key verbs.

Seclusion call lines build on three- and six-syllable units, like preseclusion
songs. A seclusion line's full semantic extension is usually nine syllables,
sung as two turns of six and three syllables, six and nine syllables (repeating
the first six in the second phrase), or six and six syllables (repeating the last
three of the first phrase to start the second). Like preseclusion songs, call lines
are demarcated with vowels, framing song words, call-and-response pattern,
melodic shape, or some combination of these.

Line combinations vary little in *kaiyantaaita*. Initial six-syllable lines
usually have a single conventional completion, unlike lines in girls' songs,
which can be followed by several expansions.[24] The completion is usually
linked to the first line by repetition:[25]

(27)   *kipeenti pampa muut*   we act respectfully[26]
        pampa muut mace keel

Similar verbal resources and structural forms are used in preseclusion and
seclusion songs, but their specific shapes and conventions of use differ. These
contrasts and the distinct line types are all related to the different performance
contexts and pragmatics of *kaiyantaaita*. Time themes are no longer elabo-

rated, and lines that call individuals by name or personal relation are no longer appropriate. Initiates are an indivisible group in seclusion, called simply *taarusyeek* (secluded initiates) or by position within the group. Singing *kaiyantaaita* helps make *taarusyeek* what they are. Learning the songs *is* initiation into adult ritual knowledge.

Much of what they learn involves respectful relations, and most *kaiyantaaita* lines are about respect. Others refer to the initiates' present identity as *taarusyeek* and future identity as adult women or men. There are four general kinds of *kaiyantaaita* call lines.

1. Lines about General Conduct   Based on the verb "to go" (*kepa*), these lines carry on the journey idiom that permeated the first ceremony. In these songs, however, *kepa* lines talk about respectful behavior that should be general adult conduct, especially during ceremonies. Other lines consist of images and allusive references. They include song words and idiomatic uses specific to *kaiyantaaita* as well as ordinary Okiek words.

In some contexts, these lines are dialogic, with appropriate inflectional changes. When adults teach initiates, they often sing lines as polite imperatives with a subjunctive verb form introduced by *ak* (and); initiates repeat the line in the first person plural:

(28a) *ak opa pampa muut*   so you [pl.] act respectfully
(28b) *kipeenti pampa muut*   we act respectfully

Male initiates sing a somewhat greater variety of lines about general conduct, including lines sung by female initiates. They also add an extra three syllable extension to lines in some songs. Men sing a number of these same *kepa*-based lines in their *cepketilet* songs before boys' circumcision. They consider them theirs, even though women also sing them in secret ceremonies.

2. Lines about Ritual Respect   The next two groups elaborate who should be particularly respected. This one concentrates on the ritual relations created by initiation, for example, naming ritual leaders and co-initiates. Both groups are constructed on the verb *-teec*, which means both "to respect" and "to build." People interpret the lines in terms of both meanings, one "inside" the other, more obvious one. For example, when initiates sing "We build our seclusion place [that] doesn't leak water, it flows with honey and milk," they mean more than careful construction of the enclosure. The second, "inside" meaning is that one should have respect for one's fellow initiates, who share the enclosure. Similarly, lines about respecting ritual leaders have an "inside" meaning about creating ritual leaders through participation in the activities of initiation.

These *-teec*-based respect lines also undergo dialogic changes in teaching contexts. Most lines in this group sung by female initiates are sung by male initiates as well. Males also sing about the initiates' particular order; these lines are less common in girls' *kaiyantaaita* but are sung in women's seclusion songs.

3. Other Lines about Respect   While the first two groups include a number of lines sung by both female and male initiates, male and female lines diverge in the last two line groups. This group of *-teec*-based lines specifies nonritual relations that require respect. Female initiates sing about a wide array of persons, including husband, father-in-law, mother, and fellow women. Boys name mainly age-mates and their mothers. One assumption implicit in their array is spelled out in the line "Respect is an important thing, as important as a cow and a man."

4. Lines about Initiate and Adult Roles   Most of these lines allude to activities associated with women's or men's adult roles. Female initiates sing of unending work that continues even after sunset, such as going for water, grinding maize, and chopping firewood. Male initiates usually refer to tall trees in the forest, recalling men's forest work and the trees used in ritual, and suggesting sexual interpretations as well. Men also sing of trees during seclusion ceremonies, with similar associations, for example, "We're people of that tall *saptet* tree [with the] waving head" (*ki piik aap saptaan kaai ny'elny'el met*).

The gendered patterning of seclusion lines suggests how these songs help teach initiates about adulthood and gender roles and re-create, evaluate, and naturalize gender distinctions at the same time. Many general lines and lines about ritual respect are shared, but more specific lines about daily life differ for male and female initiates. Differences in men's and women's labor are inscribed in those lines, as are different definitions of key respect relations, relations that also entail authority and power. Female initiates sing of respect for husbands and in-laws, for instance; male initiates have no such lines about wives and affines. They stress relations among men more, such as respect for age-mates, and also sing about the preeminence of men in general.

At the same time, song lines define contested ground. Both men and women regard their respective *kaiyantaaita* as part of their own secret knowledge. Indeed, they have different melodies, many different lines, and some different ways of handling the same lines. Nonetheless, some lines are shared. Only men sing shared lines in contexts where both men and women are present, and only men made claims of ownership when I mentioned the commonalities. Less concerned to establish their priority, women simply asserted that they use them as well.

Yet there is a sense of contention within some lines sung by female initiates. When they sing about women's endless work, for instance, there are "inside" senses that question gender roles even as they teach girls to fill them. Ambiguities and multiple interpretations are expected of lines in these songs, and are implicated in the multiple, sometimes contradictory views represented in ceremonial performance. Ceremonial experience and engagement are forged in part through puzzlement and uncertainty in seclusion, but differences of authority and age are an integral part of the puzzlement.

Postseclusion Songs   Postseclusion songs are few, including only the ritual songs of the final initiation ceremony. Like other ritual songs, they are tied to a particular ritual event: the procession that brings initiates home from the river. Boys' and girls' ceremonies each have two procession songs with different call lines. As in the initial procession songs, singers repeat a few lines many times. There are two kinds of call lines, as well as song-specific and nonreferential lines.

   1. Index of Transformed Status   The singing procession from the river is initiation's second moment of rejoicing and ululation. Many lines announce the reason for celebration: the initiates are now adults. The single referential line shared by men's and women's processional songs claims initiates for the company of initiated men or women, as appropriate: "They've become ours" (*akopunceec*).

   Other lines in women's songs speak metaphorically of young women as cows: *akoik roor* (she's become a heifer), *akoik tany'* (she's become a cow). The marriageable young women are valuable and desirable property that will indeed bring cows home. Men's songs proclaim the initiates' arrival from the river and identify them as men with various epithets: lions, those of the sounding voice, those of the hunt.

   2. Relation to the New Adults   Other lines in river procession songs are about relations to the new young adults. Women carry on the cow metaphor, declaring that the initiates should be stolen. One women's song consists entirely of such lines. Men sing mainly about relations between young men and their mothers (and other women), telling women to rejoice again.

   Postseclusion songs and their call lines are few. They simply declare the finish and successful results of initiation's journey. The end of the initiates' semiotic movement is then distinctly marked by the absence of song in the very last procession of initiation. Some lines in the river procession song hark back to the first ceremony, stressing the contrast of beginning and end. Young men are now lions (*ng'etuuny'ik*), not lion cubs (*wareek aap ng'etuuny'ik*), as they were at the start. Young women are cows and heifers, not calves, as girls and boys both were called.

   These different images and epithets are the final sung component of contextual re-creation, summary representations of men versus women. The songs are also the signal for renewed ululation and celebration of the initiates' return, the final moment of emotional power and engagement as fathers receive their daughters back and sons are restored to mothers.

Songs of Initiation: Context, Form, and Performance

Okiek recognize singing as a way to show, evoke, and potentially intensify emotion and involvement. Reviewing the verbal resources of song in the first part of this chapter suggested that singing is integrally involved in the efficacy of initiation. The evocative, intensifying potential of singing materializes in performance. The culturally understood amalgam of musical material, call lines, social interaction, and context synthesizes and becomes part of initiation's transformative processes through performance. The rest of this chapter looks more specifically at song performance and ritual efficacy, concentrating on the contexts and pragmatics of performance. To do this I follow Okiek song categories (see table 17), considering each kind of song in order through initiation.

Ritual Songs

Ritual songs are sung first, last, and at various other points during initiation. Each one is scheduled quite specifically at a particular time, during particular ritual events. All are sung as ritual actions. There are about fifteen ritual songs in total during initiation, virtually all tied to events that are considered old and traditional. Songs of ritual performance are also expected to represent unchanging tradition, but a closer consideration reveals innovation (see chapter 8).

Okiek emphasize the uniqueness and specific contextual definitions of ritual songs, but the songs can be grouped by type of ritual event (table 21). Table 21 names specific songs to clarify distinctions and correspondences between girls' and boys' ceremonies. It also shows that many ritual events have a small repertoire of songs, often auspicious pairs. Men's rejoicing songs (*riret* for girls, *kaikai kesiim* for boys) are a notable exception, another aspect of gendered patterns of singing during initiation.

While ritual songs share important aspects of contextual and functional definition, it is difficult to generalize about their musical form or verbal themes as a group. Their formal diversity reinforces the distinctiveness and contextual specificity Okiek emphasize within ritual songs. Each ritual song uses a small repertoire of lines, often about six.[27] Of these lines, a number are specific to the particular song; these recur frequently in the song. This, too, emphasizes the particularity of each song. However, there are patterns of call line use in several subgroups of ritual songs, as well as links of musical form within three subgroups.

Women's dawn songs, women's river procession songs, and men's river procession songs each have certain musical correspondences in tonal material, intervalic relations, phrase contours, and call-response relations (Kratz 1988c:407–9). In each group, songs echo and expand each other melodically

Table 21: Ritual Songs

Processions
    A. from the forest (girls' and boys' ceremonies)
        1. morning (*kepa koroseek*)
            a. young people's songs
                (1) *cepkondook ce leelac*
                (2) riret[1]
            b. women's answering songs (see afternoon procession)
        2. afternoon (*kepa toloocik*—women's songs only)
            a. *celimen*
            b. *matimwaitan tuumaan*
            c. *sonaya*
    B. from the river (*kelong'u*)
        1. women's songs for girls
            a. *akoik roor*
            b. *takiyuupe*
        2. men's songs for boys
            a. *suyet*
            b. *ooyeoo*

Predawn
    A. women's songs for girls
        1. *yoesyosi*
        2. *akorirci*

Rejoicing (siimet)
    A. women's songs for girls and boys
        1. *kimace eceek kesiim*
        2. *kisiim en koros*
    B. men's songs for girls
        1. *riret*[2]
    C. men's and women's songs for boys
        1. *kaikai kesiim*[2]

Other
    A. opening the way (*yaatet aap ooreet*)
        1. *orio*

1. Only in girls' ceremonies. Doubles as young people's song in forest procession and men's rejoicing for girls.

2. An encouraging song that is also sung in boys' first forest procession and to rejoice for them.

as well as verbally. Melodic and tonal parallelism between songs is reinforced with linguistic and thematic parallelism.[28] Each group is from a climactic ritual event, immediately before rejoicing (either before initiates' operations or on their final return home). Each uses a very small number of thematically linked call lines. Unlike other ritual songs, where the lines that are sung gradually shift over the course of the song or contrast markedly between linked songs, the calls of these three groups are repeated from start to finish, the variations in the lines elaborating the same few themes. Combined with analogous patterns of musical form in each pair, the songs are a way to call attention to and help heighten climactic moments by seeming to slow or extend time through this density of musical and verbal interweaving.

Other subgroups of ritual songs have no apparent musical relations, but are marked by clear patterns of call line use. Each group is defined by specific scheduling during initiation, and becomes part of the semiotic movement that defines ceremonial structure. The groups' line patterns often reflect the gender and age of their call singers, at the same time supporting Okiek assumptions about gender and adding to initiation's contextual re-creation.

For instance, young people's procession songs have largely song-specific lines, and are perhaps the most referentially limited and opaque of ritual songs. No dialogic lines are included. The young men who call the songs might later speak their encouragement. They sing, like women, but seem to say little or nothing; they do not use the feminine mode of song to encourage girls. One of their procession songs (*riret*) is also sung later, to celebrate. At that point they do sing dialogic lines about promises fulfilled. The verbal dichotomy between men who speak and women who sing is neutralized when all rejoice in song.

Women's procession songs have a high proportion of lines that index ceremonial occasion and time. This is especially true of *celimen,* their first processional song. *Celimen* also encourages exuberant singing with many metapragmatic lines. Songs early in the ceremony are particularly involved in establishing the ceremonial frame. Like elders' blessings, these sung exhortations make explicit the involvement and participation that are considered appropriate. Later in the procession, women sing directives, challenges, and requests. Women's songs progress from lines that frame and index the ceremonial occasion—lines that are primarily ritual action—to lines that begin the encouragement that becomes central in girls' songs.

Rejoicing songs (women's and men's alike) all include a small set of challenging and directive lines in recent past tense, showing that promises have been fulfilled. They also refer explicitly to their rejoicing intent, whether with metapragmatic lines (for example, "let's rejoice for them-*e*") or words in the response. Given the usual distinctions between men's and women's line patterns, their similarity in these songs is significant. Orchestrated differences in men's and women's modes of encouragement over the course of initiation gradually build to consensus before the initiates' operations. That unity is demonstrated in this exultant singing. At the same time, the songs also mark a shift in ceremonial structure. The joint engagement in song is the culmination of ritual events and the start of the final celebratory phase of the first ceremony, which continues with food and drink.

Each of the musically related song groups is also linked verbally, increasing the density of interreference and cohesion in each contextually defined group. The two women's river songs sing about girls' transformation into heifers, a metaphor of marriageability, and share unique call lines about stealing the new heifers. Men's river songs have a distinctive predominance of calls that identify young men with various names (lions, those of the hunt, and so on). At the same time, the strong gender marking of the songs is combined with a few phrases used in both men's and women's river songs (and only in those songs), indicating the final moment when new adults (of either gender) are brought home. Thus, both men and women declare, "They have become ours," though meaning men in one case and women in the other.

Finally, dawn songs contrast with other initiation songs in a number of ways that involve time. They have a prevalence of time lines, a three-syllable call line structure, and a unique sequence of lines about dawn that develops incrementally over three turns, with the last turn using one of several terms that refer to initiates:

akorir	it's dawn
akorirci	it's dawn for
mooeekcyaak	our calves

The play of temporal contrasts in musical form between these songs and others is a counterpoint to the explicit temporal emphasis in the lines. Time is both emphasized and manipulated at dawn, which is the end to the countdown, heightening the moment's drama and affect.

These patterns help distinguish and create subgroups of ritual songs, emphasizing their unique scheduling in initiation and their association with particular ritual events. This also makes the songs unmistakable temporal indices of ceremonial structure and semiotic movement through the ceremony. Gender-related line patterns are another thread in the process of contextual re-creation, corresponding to and supporting notions about gender, communicative mode, and ceremonial participation. Ritual songs are also implicated in initiation's emotional and experiential engagement, especially through line patterns over time.

Referential call lines in ritual songs take two points of view; their alternations are one facet of the sung shaping of ceremonial engagement. The first expresses singers' involvement and concern with the performance directly, as in metapragmatic exhortations to sing and the directives in women's songs. Directives are not dialogic here, but more distanced, as if singers are simply letting their wishes be known, watching, and waiting. The other involves declarative statements of time and place (for example, "it's dawn"), yet these seemingly observational statements are not detached. They not only mark the ceremony's progress, but also register and affect its emotional tempo, the quickening of anxious expectation and the joyous relief after dawn. To further explore this aspect of experiential engagement, I examine the sequence and call line patterns in ritual songs of the first ceremony.

Young people open the ceremony musically, the playful exuberance of their forest trip maintained in performance but contained in single-file procession as they come home. Their processional songs include indices of place and occasion, with no clear line development over time. They sing mostly song-specific lines, themselves indices of narrowly defined performance contexts.

Song-specific lines in both of their songs are given affectionate connotations by certain words and suffixes. One song (*cepkondook ce leelac*) has lines framed with the phrase *coorueeny' uun* (my friend). Though not usually taken referentially here, connotations from ordinary usage carry into the song. The other song (*riret*) uses suffixes that are a sign of affection or solidarity in conversation. *-wei* (a particle connoting friendliness) and *-ny' uun* (my) are used in parallel ways in these song lines, marking the tenor of relations. Conversationally, both suffixes show affection when added to a proper name or relation term in address. *-wei* is also a verbal suffix in conversations between men of one age-set, especially those initiated together, indexing solidarity and friendship (for example, *kalei-wei,* I say, friend).

Pragmatically, the processional songs are performative. As ritual action, they accomplish the event to be performed, establishing and indexing the start of the ceremonial frame. The call lines are central to this. The poetic pattern that emerges from the small number of lines is a varied repetition that repeatedly displays the occasion and frame, often with unique (and indexical) lines. Repeated affectionate suffixes in lines help channel the young people's companionship and excited gaiety into the song and procession. They also help set the tone for the ceremony as a whole, which is ideally congenial and cooperative.

When women meet the procession singing *celimen,* more lines refer explicitly to occasion and time. Young people frame the occasion unthinkingly with their song-specific lines; adult women announce it more self-consciously and referentially. Metapragmatic lines urge women to join together in song, introducing another image of amicable unity appropriate to ceremony. These lines anticipate and support the blessings that follow processional songs.

However, a more consequential message also begins to appear in women's songs, with directive, request, and challenging lines addressed to initiates. Time-as-truth lines also start the challenging countdown to dawn.

Dialogic lines increase as women continue singing. Their song starts as performative ritual action, full of framing lines, but gradually begins the encouragement that will be central to the ceremony. This sequential development of call lines parallels and foreshadows the dramatic movement and shifts of focus in the ceremony as a whole. Women begin the shift from the opening ritual action, narrowing in on the initiates and focusing ritual action on affecting and transforming them. At this point, the implications of the ceremony are just beginning to be highlighted musically.

A corresponding pattern occurs in calls sung by individual singers. Many open by indexing the occasion or calling for participation and cooperation. They then launch into a short series of directive lines, interspersed with lines that index initiates, identifying them as the intended audience of the directives. All these musical icons of ceremonial structure at the opening subtly remind those participating of what is to come, evoke past ceremonial experiences, and begin to enmesh them in the present ceremonial experience. At the same time, the singing women begin to develop the density of interreference that contributes to that experience.

During the day, the adult guests relax, talking and drinking. The initiates dance and sing intermittently with their girlfriends. Thus far, their singing is still like the sociable evening gatherings of the past months. However, now they are expected to sing; women prompt them if they seem lackadaisical. The dialogic lines women began in procession are central here. Encouraging themes are reiterated in girls' songs during the day, but are as yet without the emotional intensity of the coming evening performance. Largely peripheral to adult activities, the constant sounding of daytime performance and the young people's excitement help maintain the ceremonial atmosphere. As evening approaches and attention turns to the girls, their singing affects some people more strongly, prompting them to emotional displays.

Scheduled ritual song also reappears at dusk. The second procession refocuses the ceremony, starting the section centered on the initiates. Women repeat their procession song (*celimen*), reestablishing and reinforcing the ceremonial frame again, marking the passage of time again. The context-specific song is itself a prime index of ceremonial sequence; its time lines underline the continuing countdown to dawn. Recognition of that progression, which is highlighted through the songs, can heighten involvement and intensify its experience.

After sunset, the only scheduled public songs are the girls' poignant final farewells, danced in costume. The songs are the same as before, but now they are the central event, involving not only fellow children but young men and women, significant relatives and friends. Directives and appeals are activated in these interactions, which are no longer children's play. Time continues to pass, as the call lines note. These songs, too, end after the girls' confessions; the initiates sit silently until the ritual leaders finally claim them. Eventually, even the secret songs emanating from the women's house quiet down.

At first light, some women emerge. They announce dawn and the impending operation with two songs, the first public ritual songs since sunset. Once again, women refocus the ceremony. People reassemble for the final wait in heightened excitement and anxiety. Dawn songs are full of time lines, the imminence of the test the inescapably urgent message.[29] They also sing the last directives and requests, often the most explicit, as final encouragement. The moment of truth has come, as these songs emphasize, amplify, and dramatize in a number of ways.

The ceremonial sequence so far has been marked by musical progressions, both in song types and call line patterns. As experienced through performance, the progression is a dramatic buildup as well. At this critical climax, the ceremonial sequence is also marked and underlined in the pair of dawn songs with a departure from standard call line structure. Calls of the first song (*akorirci*) are the usual length and are delivered quickly in a declamatory manner. After that song, women have a choice between two songs. One parallels the first melodically, while the other contrasts sharply, with a chantlike form and a syncopated response.

Verbally, both contrast with the first, with clearly articulated three-syllable calls and little melodic ornamentation or tonal alternation. Their opening time lines are developed incrementally; the three-syllable structure also draws out directive lines. This slows down the delivery of call lines splitting them over two or three short turns, and musically draws out the climactic tension of the moment as well. At the same time, the songs also contrast sharply with the first one because they are less songlike, particularly the near-chant one. The moment is tremendously emphasized; time seems to slow down as drama and emotion intensify.

As women finish the short, insistent call and response alternations of the second song, more women emerge from the house. The crowd waits. Women may repeat the songs. People wait with mounting anxiety. The crowd grows and jostles. Young men race in with switches, threatening to beat those who push and block the wide path between the door and the *mabwaita*. At last, the ritual leaders dance out with the girls between them. After they circle the *mabwaita* the initiates suddenly sit and are grasped from behind, and the surgeon begins to cut. The crowd surges, women cry, and soon it is over. Women grab *koroseek* saplings and run east, singing jubilant songs of rejoicing. Men celebrate in song as well.

In some cases, women celebrate with entirely nonreferential calls. Many men's calls are also referentially limited. Song itself is celebration; referential meaning becomes inadequate and almost irrelevant. Even song is inadequate for women, who punctuate it with joyous ululation. The referential lines included announce the girls' truthfulness and their fulfilled promises. The main metapragmatic line sung makes the celebratory intent clear: "Let's rejoice for them" (oonkeesiimcin).

This sequential review of ritual songs in the first ceremony has shown how they figure in the experiential and emotional engagement of initiation. The songs help set the tone of the ceremony, being used to repeatedly reinvoke the ceremonial frame at important points. Women are strikingly responsible for this aspect of initiation, acting like ceremonial timekeepers doing the countdown to dawn. If men are the organizers, as they say, women are the ceremonial conductors.

Different patterns of line use in ritual songs create song groupings associated with particular ritual events. The performance of the songs in sequence then marks the progress of the ceremony, but line patterns over the course of the ceremony also contribute to its dramatic contours. Women's musical countdown is clearly part of this, particularly the dawn songs. Similarly, patterns of line use create musical icons of ceremonial structure on several scales, from sequential patterns across the entire ceremony to sequences within individual turns. Such patterns are a way to replay previous ceremonies and forecast the present one, recalling past experiences and linking them to the current one.

Finally, some of the songs are the primary expression of joy and relief at initiation's climax. The ritual songs that lead to that tumultuous musical jubilation sometimes address initiates, but always keep a somewhat distanced viewpoint. In girls' songs, discussed next, the musical interaction between initiates and others heightens the ceremony's emotional intensity. Their provocative challenges and dialogic exchanges in song develop dramatic tension in the progression to dawn marked by ritual songs.[30]

Girls' Songs and Cepketilet

Initiates sing with their friends for months before the first ceremony, but initiation ceremonies are the ultimate occasion for girls' songs and dances (tientaap tiipiik). That first night they wear resplendent costumes, are the center of attention, and dance girls' dances for the last time, hopping and twisting inside the circle of singers. In costume, their motions are extended and exaggerated by colobus skins on their arms, fly whisks in their hands, tassels on their hats, and flashing aprons at their waists (see plate 19). Leg bells are an aural accompaniment to whistles as the girls dance, adding an accented rhythmic pattern in more than half of the songs and regular, isometric beats in the others.

The songs are also a crucial mode of encouragement, the girls' only direct exchanges with others in ritual events, and their only chance to answer others verbally and encourage them in turn. As such, they are pivotal in the ceremony's dramatic orchestration and central to experiential engagement and semiotic movement. Boys' ceremonies have no such spectacle, but *cepketilet* are the corresponding songs for them. Men sing two *cepketilet* before the boys are circumcised; one other is sung by the initiates and their female relatives.

Girls' song repertoire is large compared to the three *cepketilet*. In the period from 1982 to 1985, girls in my research area sang about fifteen songs, with a "hit parade" of half that number being sung most often (table 22), and several two-whistle dance songs without words. In musical form, girls' songs are the most cohesive and consistent of initiation songs, with clear commonalities in tonal organization, rhythmic patterns, melodic phrase contours, and call and response organization.[31] In contrast, the few *cepketilet* songs of boys' ceremonies are divergent in musical form, differing both from each other and from girls' songs (Kratz 1988c:424–25). Nonetheless, girls' songs and *cepketilet* correspond closely in performance contexts and verbal themes, but with important differences in who sings, how and how much they sing, and the call lines used. These distinctions exemplify and help re-create Okiek notions about men and women, another rendering of gender in relation to encouragement.

Girls' singing is more than socializing, play, and display. The songs have explicit communicative intents and effects, though their phrases and expressions are formulaically familiar. They are farewells as the girls leave their accustomed daily life, but the songs also encourage them and reassure friends and family (-*ceer*). *That* effect is at the heart of their evening performance. Initiates make themselves brave through the songs, as with their fathers' speeches:

We listen to the songs and get worked up [-*nereec*].

We listen to the songs. We hear them and are encouraged, and we also encourage people, singing to tell them, "I'll be brave. I'll wait. I won't cry out."

Emotional displays and reactions to song also harden their determination:

They fell down [-*tupuc*] because they were worked up, because we've gone to be initiated. [*CK: How do you feel when you see people falling down?*] We get worked up as well. We sit completely still [during the operation] so that they didn't fall for nothing and then we don't sit still.

Girls' song performance becomes increasingly focused and emotional as the ceremony proceeds. At first like sociable dances with their friends, sung exchanges become more pointed as time passes. Young women begin to join in, exchanging calls with the girls. When the initiates are shaved at dusk, their friends sing to them as their separation begins. Mature woman might harangue

Table 22: 1982–1985 Repertoire of Girls' Songs

Kitare ng'aa*	Cepet*
Elis elis*	Kiroopan roopta*
Iya iya marinda*	Mary mary mary*
Lina*	Raang'cin
Jaina*	Kwaheri Mulot
Ndegeit	Taim ng'aa
Siisenkee kelyeekcu	Kisukan en tapoot

*Songs sung most often

the initiates with phrases similar to call lines, sounding angry and upset. The initiates are silent, answering in song when they rejoin the group. Younger girls get upset now; the initiates' sisters and closest girlfriends sometimes sing in tears.

After sunset, the initiates sing and dance continuously by the light of the bonfire. The costumes they sang about for months are finally theirs for one night of glory. They still sing to and for each other but also call friends and relatives for personal farewells. Women who are called often answer in song; young men neither sing nor speak, but many fall, showing their strong emotional reaction. The crowd, continuous dancing, flashing costumes, sung exchanges, shouted comments and emotional displays—all contribute to the mounting emotional tenor during the night. The excitement is increasingly tinged with anxiety, however, as dawn approaches.

Dialogic call alternations personalize sung exchanges and combine several rhetorical approaches to encouragement. First, they encourage with praise and promises: the girls will be celebrated for their bravery. Second, they encourage by provocation. Lines promise shame for the cowardly and disgrace for her entire family. Challenging lines dare the girls, hardening determination by ridicule and abuse. One girl described various modes of encouragement:

[Our fathers] gave us money [as encouragement] and told us to die if we don't wait [for the operation]. [CK: And women?] They sing, too, and some gave us money and cursed us, told us to go marry our father.

Finally, other lines encourage with the hook of commitment, as men's speeches do, describing all the work and expense of preparing the ceremony. Others did their part in good faith; now it is up to the girls. Requests sung by people the girls care about are answered with promises, committing themselves yet more explicitly. The urgency of encouragement is emphasized by the many time lines.

Cepketilet songs are also intended to encourage in boys' ceremonies. As discussed in the last chapter, men do not make encouraging speeches to boys; they should have the strength and determination to encourage themselves because boys are like men. Men say they encourage boys through song: "We encourage the young men so they get worked up, so they will wait for the circumcision." The encouraging role of the songs, however, is simultaneously admitted and denied. As one line puts it, "Who encourages those who should encourage themselves?"

One way that encouragement is simultaneously accomplished and denied is through the definition of singers and the way they sing. Adult men sing two *cepketilet* to initiates; the boys do not respond, but simply wait bravely for the knife. They do exchange calls with their mothers and sisters in the third song (*laleyo*), standing by the *mabwaita*. Occasionally young men sing that song as well, including lines that discount encouragement and women's role in it even as women sing. Boys are encouraged in part by repudiating their need for women's encouragement and denying women's right to encourage young lions (for example, *meikoocin koceeraak, kaariik aap sepepe,* don't let houses of gunny sacks [women] encourage you). By centering the rejection on women, the fact of boys' encouragement through song is obscured. These lines also challenge and taunt the boys, claiming they are unworthy of manhood because they still listen to women. They are white-eyed like their mothers, not red-eyed like angry lions.

What emerges here is another face of the same contradiction between concepts of gender and assumptions about initiation, the contradiction that arose most sharply in the encouraging speeches discussed in the previous chapter. When girls are the subject of encouragement, the strength of will they prove with initiation and the effectiveness of encouragement are both problematic because women are supposed to be weak and unable to listen to reason. With boys, the need for encouragement is the difficulty; men are supposed to harden their own hearts, but all children need encouragement.

Like girls' songs, *cepketilet* are sung at various times. Sung when the first procession arrives, during the day, and most continuously in the evening, they are part of men's greater participation in song for boys' ceremonies, part of their appropriation of male children into their own adult realm. Women and big girls often sing while boys are shaved at dusk, marking that transition and beginning their farewells, as girls do when their girlfriends are shaved.

Cepketilet and girls' songs are similar in performance contexts and intent, but Okiek stress their differences as much as their similarities, also emphasizing definitions of gender. Indeed, encouragement is less elaborated and emphasized in speech and song for boys: there are far fewer *cepketilet,* only one of which is sung by the boys themselves, and *cepketilet* are sung only at the ceremony. Boys wear no elaborate costume and don't dance at all. They have no scheduled event for farewells like the girls' good-byes that are sung with cigarettes. My Maresionik assistant commented on the difference, also noting that girls receive more gifts than boys.

A girl sings to men and people, says "'I've called you, my uncle," and so on and you feel like you want to cry, so you give out anything you have with you. Girls have a lot of words. The boys don't sing and dance, but just stand there until morning. [*CK: I thought the* cepketilet *songs said the same thing.*] No, they say something like, "We're going to be circumcised. We'll wait for everything. Mother, I won't shame you." [. . .] Women say those things, too, but then they add more. They talk about you and your character, saying things like "You're a good person and I've called you." Boys don't have many words.

As he points out, *cepketilet* share a number of call lines with girls' songs. However, there are telling differences in other lines, in line frequencies, and in themes developed. Furthermore, even though *laleyo* is sung by boys and female relatives, much as girls' songs are, his observation is borne out by the patterns of call turns and lines used by different singers.

For instance, lines that index and address initiates differ significantly for men and women singers. Girls and women sing about initiates as children, relatives, and girls (using the Kiswahili word *marembo,* pretty ones), and call them by name. When women sing with boys, they use a similar range of lines but with boys' epithets, for example, "young lions" (*wareek aap ng'etuuny'ik*). Men, however, include other kinds of indexing lines in their songs. They still occasionally call boys their children, but more commonly point to their youth as ignorance, calling them "those who are still foolish, who lick porridge like babies." In line expansions they refer to the lessons to come, when boys will see men's secrets. This contrast of childhood ignorance and initiated knowledge is missing from girls' songs. They, too, learn secrets, but public understanding places women with children. Women's words do not have the weight, wisdom, and consequentiality of men's.

Men also include many lines that advertise initiates' maleness with various words for boys (for example, *weeriik meng'eec,* "young boys," and the Kipsigis *ng'eetik,* "boys"), or by identifying men with shining spears, hunt and battle, leather hive straps, and great pain, for men claim their circumcision is the more painful.[32] These last lines also proclaim the singers' maleness and begin to identify the boys with men rather than children and women.[33]

Directive, challenge, and request lines are central to the encouragement of both girls' songs and *cepketilet.* Again, lines and themes are shared, but there are differences. All develop the journey idiom for initiation. But lines about truth versus cheating are far more common and elaborated in girls' songs. The song boys sing with women has some such lines, but they are virtually absent when men sing to them. A parallel difference appears in directive and challenging lines based on the verb "to cheat" (*-kencin, -kenter*). In girls' songs, this is a well-elaborated and common theme of challenge. In *cepketilet,* however, such lines are extremely rare. Lines using *-kenter* are absent from men's *cepketilet* and those in *laleyo* are usually sung by women. Men just tell boys to go, and challenge them with unblemished lineage records.[34]

Once again, this rhetorical difference expresses and perpetuates conceptions of men and women and expectations based on them. Girls tend toward playful cheating; they might change when faced with a severe test. Not only do they need encouragement, they depend on others for it. The commitments of their friends and loved ones must be pointed out to oblige them and work them up.

Girls' songs also include many promises to celebrate their success and descriptions of the joy it will create. Boys' songs have far fewer promises and elaborations, mostly in the song with women. Again, men do not promise to rejoice; they simply tell boys to be brave. Young lions need no promises; they set their own hearts to the test. *Laleyo* lines tell boys not to let women encourage them; it is practically an insult to be treated like girls.

These line differences all help reproduce Okiek notions of gender, a process so overdetermined that it emerges even in the details of initiation song. The cumulative effect of these details again fosters Okiek suppositions about gender and emotion. Men sing to their sons, but their lines are seemingly straightforward, without women's emotional appeals. For their part, boys show their masculinity by restraint in singing, especially compared to girls.

Men also extend their image as organizers and decisionmakers when they sing certain directive lines that are more common in the *kaiyantaaita* (seclusion songs) of both boys and girls. These obliquely phrased directives continue the journey idiom to talk about tradition and respect. Only men sing them publicly, showing that they know and use women's lines. In fact, they consider them theirs: "Women may sing it, too, but if so they do it softly so men don't hear them, since it is men's." Nonetheless, the lines are part of women's secret songs; it is apparently a "secret" from men that women know part of *men's* songs.

The use of metapragmatic lines in girls' songs and *cepketilet* points to other performative differences in turn-taking and line combinations. Girls often sing them to each other, saying, "Let's play, let's sing loudly"; neither boys nor men sing metapragmatic lines before circumcision. Girls' song is truly a group performance, with each initiate and each musical interlocutor taking very short turns, usually changing after a single call. This is true even during girls' farewells.

There is no clear sequential pattern or obvious progression in the lines that are sung over girls' short turns. Some dialogic turns follow each other directly, immediately answering a request, directive, or promise, but many are answered only in later turns, if at all. Yet through this rapidly changing, seemingly random combination of lines, the assembly of singers jointly produces a rhetorically powerful poetic structure in performance: emergent parallelism (Kratz 1990a). Poetic structure and pragmatic purpose merge in performance. Based on the structure of dialogic lines, emergent parallelism helps give stronger persuasive force to singers' encouragement. It is also one way through which singers affect and intensify the ceremony's dramatic progress and participants' engagement in it.

Each dialogic line group has a few basic patterns, described earlier in the chapter. Lines vary in their precise development, but many are based on a small group of initial verbs. This creates structural-semantic sets of lines related in form by partial repetition and also by content. Directive lines, for instance, have sets built on the verb "to go" (*kepa*), expansion lines built on the phrases *si kong' et* (so that [it] ends) and *ot kosiim* (until they rejoice), and a set of negative imperatives using the verb "to cheat" (-*kenter* or -*kencin*). Challenging lines share the structure of rhetorical questions, many built on three verb phrases: "who becomes," "who tells," "who cheats/shames" (*iku ng'aa, leincin ng'aa, kenter* [or -*kencin*] *ng'aa*). Most request lines build on the verb "to want," with a few using "to give."

In performance, correspondences among these structural-semantic line sets create complex cross-weavings between lines and line segments, based on different degrees of repetition and different kinds of variation. These inter-twinings are set within the common, unifying pragmatic thrust of the lines as directives, with a common thematic repertoire and common figurative phrases and images. The result is a poetic structure akin to the canonical parallelism described for other societies (Gossen 1974; Fox 1977; Jakobson 1966; Traube 1986; Kratz 1990a), but in these songs it is an emergent parallelism, apparent only as performance proceeds.

A limited variety of parallel structures are combined in virtually any order, interspersed with other lines related pragmatically or semantically. Each directive line of each group is an individual hook with a particular rhetorical barb and phrasing, but all have a single pragmatic focus, encouragement, and a specific temporal focus, the operation at dawn. They come at these foci from different directions, with arresting images of bravery and joy, fear and shame, personalized with lines that index and address initiates, praising, taunting, and exhorting them. The songs convey a many-sided but unanimous wish; one after the other, each singer says the same thing. The unanimity of the message and the emotional force of the songs grow simultaneously as their poetic structure emerges. Dialogic exchanges personalize and intensify that message and effect through sung interaction with close relatives and friends.

The result is a poetic net rather than the tightly woven fabric of canonical parallelism, with its consistent, extended development of particular metaphors (cf. Malinowski 1978; Tambiah 1968; Weiner 1984). This poetic net enmeshes initiates in insistently demanding directives and taunting challenges from friends and loved ones. Whatever the distractions of crowd and performance, its barbs are sharply prominent: repetitions of "go," "give us," "we want," "shame," and "rejoice." Many friends and relatives, too, are moved by the songs; they are worried, anxious, and sad, with some in tears and some in emotional fits. The kaleidoscope of varied but insistent repetition intensifies encouragement for all concerned, underlines its urgency and unanimity, and weaves a persuasive net with condensed images that come from many singers and many directions but have a single focus.

The lack of linear, discursive development in girls' songs is significant. What might be seen as an uncontrolled poetic structure is appropriate to the interactive mode of performance, to the atmosphere of mounting excitement and apprehension, to song as a mode of communication as Okiek see it, and especially to the gender of those who sing. The untamed intensification of female song is contained and concentrated immediately afterward in men's encouraging speeches, which use the same themes and phrases. There they are elaborated and discursively developed in the reasoned but still heartfelt male form of encouragement. *Cepketilet* in boys' ceremonies also have a poetic structure woven from parallelistic line sets, but they differ from girls' songs on precisely those dimensions. Men take longer turns than those found in girls' songs, addressing several initiates at once or developing a theme.

The full repertoire of *cepketilet* lines is comparable to that of girls' songs, but there are striking differences in the lines sung by women and initiates in *laleyo* and those sung by men. Men call surprisingly few directives, mainly those shared with seclusion songs. They challenge boys more often early in the ceremony; directives, requests, and challenges are used more equally as singing progresses. These specifically encouraging lines are embedded within a large number of lines that index initiates as boys and the singers themselves as men, and call on boys by name. The poetic net in this case is not only persuasive but also strongly marked as male.

The mix of lines sung in *laleyo* is quite similar to girls' songs, again with many directives. Turns are still longer, like men's turns in *cepketilet,* but combine rhetorical modes of encouragement, like a series of short turns in girls' songs. Boys' turns are the exception. Though *laleyo* is identified as the song that they sing, initiates actually take relatively few turns. Often three, four, or five people sing to them before one is moved to respond in song. When they do, their turns are very short, using a very small number of lines repeatedly. Boys say little beyond "I/we will go, a young man/men, so that you rejoice."

Truly, as my assistant observed, boys don't have many words. They are encouraged by *cepketilet* but respond little in song. There is no need to repeatedly promise the expected, but the expectations incorporated in these different ways of singing do help reproduce Okiek notions of gender. Further, the boys' impassive manner in song is part of the way they move from the realm of women and children to that of men. In song, they no longer answer women's words like children, but because they are still boys they have no right to answer or join the songs of men. The very songs and the way they are sung begin to make them, and show them to be, men. Similarly, girls' and women's way of singing accentuates related notions about women.

The songs are important encouragement for both boys and girls. The concept of encouragement is one thread that draws participants together in initiation. Differentiated in terms of gender and age, the diverse modes of encouragement also produce settings in which contradictions between gender and initiation emerge. They appear most clearly when men encourage girls in speeches and when women sing encouragement to boys.

In both cases, men deal with the contradictions by denigrating women, emphasizing ideal gender types that justify their own preeminence and authority. Yet at the same time they still proceed in terms of assumptions basic to initiation. They encourage girls and boys alike even though the former supposedly will not heed and the latter supposedly do not need it. Women do not comment publicly on the contradictions in either case, whether in side comments or song; not all voices are heard in every context. Who is heard and what is said when such contradictions emerge are political matters that involve power.

The scheduling of the modes of encouragement also outlines the dynamic of interactive intensification in the first ceremony. The emergent parallelism co-produced in encouraging songs heightens the emotional tenor of the situation, but there is more to the persuasive power it creates than repeated bombardment with requests, challenges, and directives. The co-production of the songs, with many singers taking calls, also creates a fusion of perspectives that develops dialogically. The dialogic nature of the song lines consolidates all present into two group viewpoints, initiates versus others. This nascent verbal separation develops further and is realized spatially in the encouraging speeches that follow. Yet both groups still focus jointly on a single outcome at dawn. The co-produced songs thus unite all present, yet in such a way that the major division between the initiates and the others present is emphasized. As well, singers can still evoke the pull of personal relations in the calls that are exchanged. People are increasingly engaged in the ceremony, even as the semiotic movement of initiation takes initiates closer to adulthood.

Kaiyantaaita

Having earned the right to learn and sing adult songs through their bravery, initiates begin with *kaiyantaaita* after the first seclusion ceremony. *Kaiyantaaita,* the songs of secluded initiates, are not called by the usual word for song (*tienta*) or referred to with the usual verb for singing (*-tien*). Initiates sing (*-yanta*) them every morning at dawn and every evening at sunset as daily announcements of their new status as secluded initiates. As part of the musical progression of initiation, *kaiyantaaita* continue to move initiates into women's (or men's) adult community. The teaching of the songs, the lessons of conduct encoded in them, the creation of shared experience as women, and the understandings of women's lives that the songs can open up all play a part in the efficacy of initiation.

Not all of the teaching is straightforward and obvious, nor is it all gentle. The puzzlement, questions, ambiguities, uncertainties, and intimidation of initiation teaching simultaneously re-create concepts of gender and relations of power, authority and hierarchy between men and women, among women, and among men. The ambiguities and uncertainties also create a space for multiple interpretations and views.

Initiates' daily kaiyantaaita are part of the regimen of seclusion; they always sing at dawn and dusk and take call turns in ritual order. First they sing three songs outside in their seclusion enclosure. After spitting to both sides against pollution, they go inside to sing two or four more songs, again spitting at the end. The first songs outside are sung only at that time, in specific order, with distinctive call lines. Male initiates have two different initial songs during which they rap together sticks (kipawes). Kipawes songs (The term refers to both the songs and the sticks) are similarly restricted in performance and also have unique call lines.[35]

The inside songs are sung at other times as well. Initiates sing to greet visitors to the seclusion area and during seclusion ceremonies, when they are taught and tested. Female initiates learn at least six songs with shared call lines, in addition to the initial trio. Male initiates sing at least three kaiyantaaita in addition to kipawes. Male and female songs share lines about respect but are completed differently. The songs also differ in patterns of line use, in other lines sung, and in musical form.

Men and women each claim ignorance of the other's kaiyantaaita and of their allusions and referents.

I don't know what they mean. They're women's words. The kaiyantaaita let people know that the girls have been initiated and are no longer children. Men also sing kaiyantaaita, but they are different. They are sung to let people know they've been cut. All I know about women's ceremonies is that they are there teaching the initiates. I go and drink with the men [in the men's house] and just hear the songs, but I don't know them.

I know women's kaiyantaaita. I hear them [singing in the men's house] just like women hear men's [during their ceremonies], but neither knows the words of the other's songs.

Even if some parts are shared and some ritual events might be similar, the differences are more encompassingly important. What is significant is that men and women have their own secret ritual traditions and knowledge. Emphasized by secrecy, this knowledge and difference helps produce a sense of sexual solidarity, identity, and autonomy.

Unlike most songs, _kaiyantaaita_ are explicitly and deliberately _taught_ to initiates. The song lessons, like the revelation of secrets, are part of the continuing formation of the community of adult women (or men), re-creating the difference and knowledge that they share, a baseline that is not part of shared childhood experience. Lessons drill initiates in _kaiyantaaita_ but also test their learning, simultaneously teaching them unquestioning respect for the authority and knowledge of older women.

In principle, any initiated woman can teach the songs and show initiates the secrets. One song line conveys this, emphasizing the equality of initiated women: "We respect/ construct ritual teachers, ritual teachers are a hundred" (_kiteece matireen, matireen ko pakal_). In other words, every initiated woman is a ritual teacher because she knows women's secrets and songs. In fact, however, the tacit division of ritual labor reproduces the hierarchy of ritual knowledge and authority. _Matireenik_ and older women take care of secrets (_tuumwek_) and younger ones teach _kaiyantaaita_. The youngest are largely silent observers who continue to learn.

Most of the teaching is done during seclusion ceremonies. Women sing a call line and each girl repeats it, going down the line in ritual order. If an initiate sings poorly or makes a mistake (for example, mixing up parts of a call),[36] she might be berated or hit with a switch to "make her wiser" and learn to sing properly. Call lines are to be repeated exactly, so mistakes are readily recognized.

Lines may make referential sense as they stand, but are often allusions, their meaning not transparent. For example, _kipeenti king'uruuk uu keeciir_ (we go bending over like sheep) alludes to the way initiates traverse open areas, in a stooped run with capes over their heads. Initiates must learn to repeat lines verbatim, perhaps before they understand them. Some words are familiar; others are obscure, used only in song.

The allusive, semidisguised reference of _kaiyantaaita_ is not indirection for the sake of politeness, saving face, or avoiding argument, as it can be in political discourse when direct, straightforward discussion would be disruptive (Bloch 1975; Brenneis and Myers 1984). Indirection and disguise in _kaiyantaaita_ are in the service of control, at least in part. Knowledge of _kaiyantaaita_ is one basis of the initiated's ritual authority over initiates. Just as using a particular speech style can limit participation in discussion to those practiced in it (Bloch 1975; Brenneis and Myers 1984), the allusive metaphors of song keep initiates uncertain about the songs' significance and reluctant to assert themselves. One issue that can be influenced by this hierarchical control will arise soon after initiation: initiates' marriages and whether they will agree to follow the husbands selected for them. Initiates' choices about husbands, which are defined in terms of respect and responsibility, much as initiation itself was through encouragement and during seclusion, can have far-reaching effects through the cultural politics of marriage (Kratz 1990c).

Even when initiates can repeat call lines precisely, the ceremonial teaching context continues to create a situation of authority and control, emphasizing their lowly position. When testing initiates, initiated adults might sing indistinctly, hiding lines to frighten initiates into uncertainty, or find fault where no fault exists. They trouble initiates to make them realize that even though they are no longer children, they still know nothing compared to older adults, who should be respected. As initiates learn and perform *kaiyantaaita* the ritual authority of age is reproduced, along with the secret ritual traditions of each sex. Paradoxically, those traditions also create an equality within the community of initiated women or men, and help constitute gender identities.[37]

As in girls' songs and *cepketilet,* a poetic net of emergent parallelism is produced in *kaiyantaaita* by the combination of parallelism in structural-semantic sets of lines, use of a small number of verbs (mostly *-teec* [to respect, to build]), and repetition of parts of the line as sung in performance.[38] Compared to preseclusion songs, the line sets have less variety and very little variation in the completion of particular lines. Yet however similar formally, the poetic structure has very different pragmatic effects in *kaiyantaaita.* Before seclusion, emergent parallelism is part of the persuasion that encourages girls to act appropriately in a unique context. *Kaiyantaaita* convey precept rather than persuade; they are allusive explication rather than encouragement. They are concerned with creating new adults who know the general principles of appropriate (respectful) behavior. A closer look reveals differences that help produce these distinct pragmatic effects.

Many dialogic lines before seclusion depict actions and their corresponding consequences (for example, "I'll go and you'll rejoice"; "Fear and you shame your family"). In contrast, most *kaiyantaaita* lines name or allude to social roles or relations after the common verb *-teec.* Various aspects of these roles are highlighted by veiled images or by juxtaposing the initial object of *-teec* with another noun phrase, to equate and elaborate them. For instance, the line below is among those that elaborate women's work responsibilities:

(29) *kiteece ceepyooseet, kiteece*   we respect the mature woman,
          ceputkween moorionket   we respect she who splits fire-
                                                             wood and logs

This poetic net is a palimpsest of partial images, each expanding and altering the other and collectively projecting guidelines for proper behavior. These injunctions are not news to initiates, who have long observed and taken part in social interaction. However, *kaiyantaaita* overlay their general understandings of respect with specific images and selective examples from adult roles. At the point when initiates' own position in such interactions is changing, the teaching of initiation highlights cultural expectations and understandings of their new social relations. *Kaiyantaaita* say what has been seen and heard, but the interplay between hiding and revealing in words and images also leaves room for obfuscation and multiple meanings.

Veiled allusions in call lines make multiple interpretations possible. There can be "inside" meanings, and different people can have different understandings. This indeterminacy and ambiguity means that specific "applications" of a line's "rule" are progressively elaborated in the experiences the initiates will have after seclusion, and also as their experience of initiation secrets increases. But it can also mean that the very indirection that helps re-create ritual hierarchy carries the seed of alternative understandings that might question or subvert notions about gender relations or the hierarchy of age.

In the following line, for example, most people understood *sakai soi* to mean a man or husband searching for food in the forest:

(30) *kiteece sakai soi ko loo tyaan*   we respect searching in the open
                                                forest, the animal is far

Initiates suggested that it also meant ritual teachers, who gather materials in the forest for their secrets, with the animal being the secret *ceemaasiit*. The acts and agency of male and female teachers can be equated through the same oblique characterization, bringing to attention the contradiction of women, who supposedly cannot organize things, managing their own ceremonies and safeguarding their own secret knowledge.

Call lines shared by male and female initiates might also have divergent meanings. Both sing *kiteece siraa loong' loitiko* (we respect the shield striped [like a] zebra). Sung by men, the line refers chiefly to respect for members of one's age-set, a principle highlighted in other lines as well. "Inside" it also praises the age-set and area, pointing to the differentiation of warrior groups by shield designs (Winter 1977). Sung by women and taken literally, referring to a real shield, the line suggests respect for men and an acknowledgment of women's own position in many contexts as subordinate. Yet it also refers to female coinitiates. Girls secluded together make a small painted shield to guard the doorway when they are out. The shield is a sign that joins them as coinitiates. Yet again, this interpretation equates male and female initiates and their experiences through appropriation of a male sign, tacitly undercutting the literal sense.

More detailed examples of multiple, sometimes subversive interpretations require more detailed secret knowledge, but these lines show how such double entendres work. Meyerhoff (1981:175–84) and H. Moore (1986:174–77) discuss the ways that both Pokot and Marakwet women represent a dominant image of social relations in their seclusion ceremonies and at the same time contradict it. All signs point to similar contradictions in Okiek seclusion songs and ceremonies.

At each dawn and dusk, the sound of *kaiyantaaita* is a daily reminder of the presence of the initiates, who are otherwise hidden and silent. Learning to sing *kaiyantaaita* and submitting willingly, obediently, and respectfully to lessons from initiated women is an important part of seclusion life and of initiation's efficacy; it continues their progress and semiotic movement toward adulthood. Performing *kaiyantaaita* creates, enacts, and advertises girls' role as secluded initiates. Central to seclusion experience, the singing is part of the pleasant congeniality that can develop within a group of initiates as well as part of the intimidating instruction of seclusion ceremonies. The songs also help constitute a community of initiated women with distinct, secret ritual traditions, including these songs and common experiences. Their allusive, oblique lines and the way they are taught also reproduce relations of ritual authority within that community, thus combining contextual re-creation and experiential engagement.

Kaiyantaaita are intended to teach proper social relations and gender roles; this is their more explicitly recognized contextual re-creation.[39] Their special words, allusions, and poetic structure are part of this, giving initiates lessons that will continue to edify and become relevant in situations they meet as adult women. Multiple line interpretations give them other senses as well, including unofficial perspectives that might oppose the official view.

Song, Efficacy, and Time

Threading through Okiek initiation from start to finish, singing is fundamental to the task of making children into adults. Song-specific forms of cultural processes integral to initiation's efficacy interpenetrate and blend in ceremonial performance with other media. As with other media, some effective patterns that unfold in initiation song are focused locally, within particular ritual events, while others interlock with local patterns to stretch across events and ceremonies.

For instance, distinctions among types of song, call lines, and the scheduled patterning of singing all help differentiate the experience of initiation into ceremonies, events, and so on, defining the coordinated progressions that are necessary to accomplish initiation. Some patterns in the use of call lines are closely related to the specific purposes of ritual events, as in women's dawn songs, girls' encouraging songs at night, or rejoicing songs. At the same time, other line patterns over the course of the first ceremony and all of initiation create larger structures and processes; specific content, central themes, and pragmatic force change over the course of initiation. Song simultaneously differentiates and makes continuous the experience, acts, and events of initiation, binding them into a ceremonial whole and drawing participants in through experiential and emotional engagement. Continuities of idiom, figures of speech, basic call line structure, and dialogic and poetic patterns unite initiation songs, making their musical sequence a larger coordinated whole despite significant internal differentiation.

Call lines and song themes are based on and help re-create cultural assumptions about gender, age, authority, social relations, and the stages of initiation. The same assumptions are also encapsulated in Okiek categorizations of initiation song, which are based on who sings them and when. To appreciate the multiple ways contextual re-creation works through song, both boys' and girls' initiation must be considered; the song sequence in each case is gender specific. Songs are sung at corresponding times and with similar line repertoires, but the particular songs, singers, and uses of lines differ. Contrasts between patterns of singing re-create Okiek distinctions of gender as much as the songs' themes do. The contrasts appear both in general patterns of ceremonial participation and in the details of call turns taken by men, women, boys, and girls.

The scheduled patterns of speech, song, and silence in ceremonial participation are related to Okiek notions of gender and age and are also implicated in the dramatic orchestration of ritual efficacy. Ritual song is women's equivalent to men's blessings; also, they sing the encouragement men speak to girls. Acknowledged organizers, men have the power and the recognized ability to speak, be heard, and bless, but women's songs and processions actually perform much of the ceremony that men's blessings ratify.[40] The multiple contrasts between encouragement in song and speech encapsulate Okiek representations of men and women: contrasts in expected protocol and organization, general tenor and key, mode of emotional expression, poetic structure and organization, and contrasts in the participants and their use of speech versus song. Okiek ideas about gender relations are extended and represented in these different kinds of ceremonial participation, and are bound up with ideas about the power and expression of emotion.[41] An inherently affecting medium full of repetitions and interruptions (like emotional speech), song is women's mode of verbal participation. Even when men do sing for boys, their call lines are more contained, with few of the challenges and directives common in girls' songs. Boys' own sung response is taciturn compared to girls, befitting young men.

In the speech of initiation, different assumptions are foregrounded in different events in ways related to structural divisions and emphases in initiation. In initiation song, assumptions about gender and personhood are consistently important, but ritual songs especially foreground and frame the ceremonial occasion. Hierarchical differences of power and authority come to the fore more in seclusion songs. A hierarchy of power is always implicit in distinctions of gender, but intragender hierarchy is also of explicit concern in seclusion. Seclusion songs help constitute relations of respect and authority within adult communities of men and women, as well as relations between women and men. As they learn and sing, initiates become equal to adults of their gender, yet they are junior members of the company, without a full understanding of all they see, hear, and sing.

During seclusion, when women finally take over, certain alternatives, contradictions, and tensions in gender representations also emerge. In the first ceremony, before seclusion, multiple views were expressed in song, but they merged into a single opposition between initiates and others, who are yet united in one desire: that the initiates be brave. Cross-gender encouragement was perhaps the principal site then for the emergence of contradictions related to gender, whether in men's speeches to girls or women's sung encouragement to boys. Such contradictions are not resolved but rather overtaken by ceremonial momentum and concentration on the impending operations. Nonetheless, men focus on what they see as women's deficiencies in both situations, not really blaming them for contradictions between ideologies of gender and initiation, but thus maneuvering through the moments.[42]

In seclusion songs, allusion and indirection simultaneously re-create ritual hierarchies of knowledge and open up an interpretative range. _Kaiyantaaita_ thus create a discourse of possibility at the same time that they teach precepts of propriety. Other songs that women sing during seclusion ceremonies shape the directions of possibility, presenting images that undermine some ideals the initiates are being taught and lampooning men and the niceties of courtship that cloak sexual desire. Initiates have come a long way before they see and hear such antics, however, and have some way yet to go before they participate in them themselves. Song is critical in the semiotic movement of that journey, both in defining the itinerary through ceremonial structure and in constituting a more specific musical progression that defines initiates' progress.

The initiates' musical progression proceeds in the first ceremony from singing girls' songs during the day to evening singing in dance costume with a wider and more intently involved audience (for boys, there are _cepketilet_ songs). Their initial seclusion period is marked by silence, which is broken after the next ceremony with _kaiyantaaita_. Initiates' daily singing of these songs maintains and proclaims the continuity of the initiation process between ceremonies, up to the end of the process. Initiates do not sing in the final ceremony, their silence breaking the daily seclusion routine. But for the first time they do speak, through the intermediary ritual leader, to accept gifts. At any point in time, initiates' progress is clear from their song. Their musical progression marks and makes their identity as children, _taarusyeek,_ or new adults, identities that are amplified and reinforced by coordinated progressions in other media.

The progression specifically linked to initiates, of course, is interspersed with other kinds of song by other singers, and is part of the larger sequential structure of initiation. Different kinds of initiation song form a sequence of temporal, processual landmarks. Yet those landmarks are not just processual signposts. Taken together, they *are* the process. Initiation *is* going through the sequence of songs and associated events, combined in performance with other media. Ceremonial texture, drama, movement, and effect are created through microlevel shifts within media (for example, sequential line patterns in women's procession songs, or shifts in line form in dawn songs), macrolevel changes within media (for example, changes of song and song type over time), and culturally defined contrasts and progressions between media (for example, the sequence of encouragement in various modes). All proceed simultaneously; they are synthesized through joint participation and experience to make the girls into women.

The sequence of song types also elaborates the density of marking that divides initiation into phases and sections, a phenomenon that has come up with every media involved in ceremonial performance. Ritual songs, with their narrowly defined performance contexts and unique call lines, are important markers of temporal and dramatic junctures between ceremonial sections, as well as especially clear markers of ceremonial structure and progression. The first ceremony is refocused and reassembled through ritual song three times: at dawn, dusk, and again the following dawn. Each time, ritual song continues the countdown to dawn. A final public reassembly, the auspicious fourth ceremony, takes place months later when initiates come from the river in the last singing procession.

The ritual songs are more than landmarks of ceremonial structure; they also heighten the dramatic and emotional tenor of these moments. The role of singing in defining ceremonial structure and process is integrally bound up with dramatic orchestration and emotional and experiential engagement. The musical sequence becomes emotionally charged through previous experience, so that people anticipate songs and events to come. People are moved by their understanding and experience of the music itself, the words sung and heard, the context of performance, their relations with the singers, the structural and sequential messages of the song, and the thoughts and memories stirred by all of these. Poetic form and call line progressions intensify anticipation and engagement, as does repetition of musical phrases (Zuckerkandl 1956:175, 212).

For Okiek, song is a means to facilitate and express emotional engagement. Girls' songs and *cepketilet* are explicitly intended to encourage initiates and reassure others, and are felt as particularly moving. At various points, especially during those songs, initiates' relatives and friends show the power of their feelings and thoughts with fits. They say they are overwhelmed by emotion when they take lyrics to heart. As they reflect on the lyrics, images in them are particularized and peopled with initiates who are their sisters, sisters-in-law, or *imaamook* (relatives linked through the mother), and also with their own memories of pain. These emotional displays are evidence, to Okiek, of the evocative potential intrinsic to musical experience. Such displays not only arise from but also add to the interactive intensification of song, and serve as additional encouragement to the children.

Detailed analyses in this chapter showed that formal and thematic distinctions and progressions are central to the ways that song contributes to ritual efficacy. Related to different performance contexts and purposes, they are critical means through which the differentiated musical sequence and process of initiation is created. Various reiterated themes reflect changing concerns, relations, and purposes over the course of initiation; referential communication in song is important to Okiek. What singers say is significant, but how they say it is also important. When people communicate in song, emotions are always a subtext featured in part by distinctions between speech and song.

The contrasts between Okiek speech and song that were described in the first half of this chapter recall special forms of language that have been recorded in ritual contexts throughout the world. While similar kinds of resources and distinctions might be used in different places, however, the particular formal aspects combined in ritual language in a particular culture vary tremendously. Efforts to characterize ritual language in any general formal sense may simply be unproductive. As the last chapter showed, no single formal characterization can describe even Okiek ritual language; discourse structure and style are not the same in different ritual events and genres. The same is true of language in initiation songs.

The formal differences between conversational Okiek and song occur in varying degrees in various kinds of songs. This is part of the differentiation of Okiek initiation song. As initiation proceeds into seclusion, the frequency of esoteric words and phrases increases, primary noun forms are used more consistently, the range of verbs and grammatical constructions in call line sets are more narrowly defined, and variations in wording and call line combinations become virtually negligible. Greater formal marking in seclusion songs is part of their secret nature, obfuscating with unfamiliar words and veiled images.

This formal trajectory in the language of song is rather different from the more striking, often event-related differentiation of speech during initiation, yet both are bound up with pragmatic effects. This suggests that pragmatic or formal-functional generalizations about ritual language might be worth investigating, even if general formal characterizations are problematic. Malinowski was one of the first to explore this path in his account of the language of Trobriand magic. His "ethnographic theory of the magical word" discussed the combination in Trobriand magic of ordinary conversational language and what we might now call the nonreferential and poetic aspects of the spells. Malinowski argued that nonreferentiality and formal distinctions (in phonetic form, patterns of repetition, special vocabulary, chanted delivery, and so forth) in magical language must be understood within a larger, pragmatic theory of language and meaning. He suggested that the apparently "weird" and "intelligible" aspects combined in magical spells are more alike than they might seem (Malinowski 1978:248). Both are meaningful because both have effects critical to the magical act intended, but this is apparent only when language and communication are considered pragmatically and in context. Trobrianders themselves are quite explicit about this:

Repetition, shifts in rhythm, specialized vocabulary, and changes in pronunciation . . . are believed to be necessary to achieve successful results. . . . Repetition of the spell, accompanied by changes in rhythm, is believed to be the effective force in causing the words to enter the appropriate object. . . . The repetition acts as verbal persuasion. (Weiner 1984:183–84)

Later scholars have developed Malinowski's understanding that poetic structure and nonreferential aspects of ritual language are essential to its pragmatic effects and constitutive of ceremonial transformations (Weiner 1984; Tambiah 1968; Silverstein 1981). However, this recognition of pragmatic effects has thus far remained focused on ritual speech; there are further theoretical and methodological implications when the language of ritual is considered within a broad communicative approach to ceremonial performance. Speech and song alternate and mix in performance, combining in the total verbal progression of initiation that synthesizes analytically separable sung and spoken progressions. Alternations and contrasts between speech and song are another important part of the scheduled ceremonial structure and sequence through which ritual efficacy is produced, and are central to its orchestrated intensification of experience. Relations between verbal modes, such as song and speech, and between verbal and nonverbal media in ceremonies must be considered in order to understand not only the form and effect of ritual language but also the nature and processes of ceremonial occasions. Such study of the media combined in performance should follow leads from local idioms to explore specific formal-functional relations and their pragmatic effects.

The contrapuntal synthesis of song and speech in performance can be illustrated by looking at a few of the themes and formal poetic resources of Okiek initiation. Thematic and formal distinctions among the songs of initiation are set within continuities of idiom, image, and structure already mentioned, but some of the distinctions and continuities also stretch into the speech of initiation to forge an overall verbal progression.

For instance, the pervasive directives and requests discussed in the last chapter are just as ubiquitous in initiation songs. The journey image and idioms of obligation and challenge appear in speech and song alike, often using the very same phrases. As a leitmotif in speech, directives outline the shifting position of initiates, as children becoming adults, in relations of power and authority. The directives' varied contexts and pragmatic force suggest that those relations are based on persuasion and influence to a considerable degree, often articulated in the idiom of respect.

In songs, the frequency of directives, requests, and challenges increases as the first ceremony proceeds, but they initially appear in the opening event, an episode that is otherwise concerned with establishing the ceremonial frame and key, thereby beginning the various semiotic progressions. These song lines also launch the campaign of persuasion, interactive intensification, and pragmatic redefinition of initiates. The women who sing these first directives foretell a direction in which both speech and song will develop, with audible images that will become increasingly conspicuous. Increasingly abundant and insistent in song, these dialogic lines become the only means of direct interaction with initiates, their intensifying capacity first culminating in the emergent parallelism of sung evening exchanges.

Between the first sung directives and that evening bombardment, initiates have heard the same message in harangues. After the evening song, they hear it again in men's speeches. Interactive intensification can be traced within speech and within song, but also builds on contrasts between verbal modes combined sequentially in performance. Repeating common themes and idioms, encouraging songs and speeches have very different persuasive developments and formal organization. Evening singing is a highly charged time emotionally, full of flash, noise, and emotional fits. The singing is powerfully moving, and the entire scene intensifies initiates' encouragement and others' engagement. Men's speeches after that, with their controlled, heartfelt emotional displays, rein in the emotional pitch, as initiates must harness this intensification to harden their own will to self-control. Women have the final encouraging word in song, however, when they reconcentrate attention at dawn, producing the final moment of dramatic tension with their songs and drawn-out directives. The difference between song and speech in encouragement is intrinsic to the ceremony's dramatic development and is also bound up with conceptions of gender.

When the main theme of initiates' singing changes to respect in seclusion, connections between relations of power, persuasion, and respect emerge perhaps more clearly than in speech. They are connected through the shared form of directive lines and continuities of idiom that link preseclusion songs and *kaiyantaaita*. Lines based on the verb "to respect" and the journey idiom "to go" dominate in seclusion, but continue the form of encouraging directives in girls' songs. Persuasion becomes teaching, which is itself another kind of subtle persuasion to accept and acquiesce to relations of power and authority based on gender and age. The common poetic form of emergent parallelism also links the two kinds of songs.

Poetic devices in blessings and in men's encouraging speeches are also akin to emergent parallelism. The poetic structure of blessings is similarly based on lines using only a few grammatical structures; assonance from modal markers corresponds to the repetition of framing verbs in song lines. In performance structure, too, both are antiphonal. Men use grammatical parallelism and varied repetition in their speeches to organize sections and create persuasive refrains. Yet in both cases, the spoken male mode is structured more regularly than song. Speeches have elaborate linear developments of persuasion through discourse structure. Blessings have line groupings in auspicious numbers, sometimes with complex poetic interweavings. Again, formal and performative continuities and differentiations that create the verbal progression of initiation and make it work also contain and re-create the assumptions about gender relations on which it is based.

Central themes, idioms, phrases, and formal patterns, then, are varied and dispersed in the different media and different settings used by different people in initiation. Certain relations between song and speech can be recognized through common verbal resources, but they are also closely interconnected with the patterns and processes in nonverbal media that were described in chapter 5. All are interwoven through joint scheduling over the course of initiation, but also through reference to certain objects, places, and persons in the song and speech of initiation. Song and speech both point to and describe selected nonverbal media and help create their significance and associations by pointing beyond the ceremonial context as well. During the first ceremony, for instance, dance costume is picked out verbally; girls are constantly told not to shame the costume and how much work it represents. Attention is also drawn to dance costume by the preparation, travel, and expense it entails, by the people who come solely to attend to the costumed girls, and by interest and comments when the girls dance. Verbal emphasis in this case underlines an already highly marked and visually striking sign, but it also instills greater significance by making the dance costume a sign of success and bravery.

An initiate's sapling also receives extensive verbal attention in song. Without verbal emphasis, it would seem like any other sapling brought in procession, and the fact that an initiate holds it would be a minor detail of ritual procedure. Far more insignificant visually and far less noticeable in performance than dance costume, the sapling is equally important verbally. It carries equal weight as another sign of success; some guests may also carry *koroseek* saplings home to broadcast the joyful news.

By contrast, no mention is made of the beaded leather skirts that are worn as ritual costume or the calabash that is carried by the host father. All are part of ceremonial protocol and performance, but only some are highlighted verbally and given particular significance during the ceremony. During each stage of initiation, certain aspects are singled out for verbal comment, evaluation, and emphasis while others equally necessary and fundamental are not. In some cases, aspects picked out verbally become condensed, central images in gender distinctions, such as the dance costume, which is worn by girls, not boys. Language plays a similar constitutive role with respect to aspects not specifically mentioned during ceremonies, but their significance, value, and associations are created verbally in other contexts that are more dispersed in daily life.

The multiple media of ceremonial performance, then, are replete with interreference, are interwoven through multiple refractions of similar images and messages, and are mutually elaborating and enriching as their orchestrated combination unfolds. This might point to a high degree of redundancy in ceremonial performance, but what might seem like repetition in a referential sense is in fact a richly varied and pragmatically powerful construction in time. Notions of redundancy and repetition stress the cognitive aspects of understanding, but there is more to ceremonial performance and experience. Its multimedia nature has as much to do with apprehending experience through engrossment, doing, feeling, and social interaction as with cognitive understanding. Musical experience particularly underlines this inseparability. "Techniques of the body must be compared with musical techniques, since both transport us from the quotidian world of verbal distinctions and categorical separation into a world where boundaries are blurred and experience transformed" (Jackson 1989:132).

Yet this dense interweaving of dispersed repetitions, refractions, and variations in different media in performance is not like a tapestry or a rug, however much the weaving analogy speaks to crosscutting structural interconnections. As Zuckerkandl (1956:217) points out for music, the patterns of tapestry rely on space and simultaneous presence, while the patterns of ceremonial performance and music alike are directional, oriented in time, and involve dramatic orchestration and patterns of intensification.

Looking at initiation song has made ceremonial alloys of time, memory, and experience especially salient. The sequence of initiation songs marks time on a macro scale while the sequence and structure of call lines can create temporal variations on a micro scale, as in women's dawn songs.[43] "Music is a temporal art because, shaping the stuff of time, it creates an image of time" (Zuckerkandl 1956:259). This musical capacity is incorporated into ceremonial performance, where it is joined and deployed with other communicative resources to play on past, present, and future as lived experience and to enlist memory and anticipation in the dramatic orchestration through which participants effect ceremonial changes.

But initiation is a joint production, incorporating the experiences of many people at once. When aspects of the past are brought to present experience, evocations and memories are partial, selective, and not fully shared. In the present, ceremonies are themselves always experienced in multiple ways, fragmented through different perspectives. Anticipations of the future can reveal different hopes, intentions, and values with respect to the immediate future of the initiates involved or to broader projections of the present and past into the future. Initiation cannot but bring these multiple personal pasts, presents, and futures into ceremonial experience, but such a mix also means that multiple and contradictory voices will be raised within the structured whole. Cultural assumptions, social relations of power and authority, and personal interpretations can be simultaneously re-created and problematized.

Another joint product also underpins and emerges from this shared but multiple experience, as well as from other discussions about it. Okiek also interpret and situate initiation broadly in time, coproducing an image of ceremonial tradition that blends differences of memory, anticipation, and experience. To say that Okiek tradition is continually re-created and mutable, however, is not to say that there are no continuities and shared memories that resonate anew with ceremonial performances, but instead to raise the question of how Okiek create images of continuity. The dance costume and sapling discussed above are verbally equal in importance as signs of success, but there is a more subtle, implicit temporal leveling going on as well. The sapling is regarded as part of ancient Okiek ceremonial practice, while the dance costume is a recent innovation. In the song and speech of initiation, they are indistinguishably merged. Chapter 8 will consider changes in initiation over time and the verbal re-creation of ceremonial tradition.

Part 4

Conclusion

8

Initiation through Time: Historical Conditions, Structural Constraints, and the Image of Tradition

Everyone has their own tradition [work].

Kopot Sampuri

If we don't do what our grandfathers were doing, it is like we are doing nothing.

Simpole Mapelu

We've come and changed some words [practices] [in ceremonies].

Kacaca

Okiek invest initiation and their other ceremonies with a very definite sense of ceremonial tradition and continuity through time, but the practice that constitutes and carries the force of tradition has considerable scope for individuality and change as well. Older Kaplelach and Kipchornwonek certainly recognize changes in initiation within their memory. Some contemporary variations and alternatives in ceremonial practice may be incipient structural changes or the bud of thematic reinterpretations in times to come.[1] On a longer time scale, creative variations, elaborations, or circumstantial modifications can together develop into more general and striking changes in ceremonial form. Okiek ceremonial tradition is based on extensive and specific structural identities, but these identities are broadly defined. This creates a tradition with room for variation, change, reinterpretation, and redefinition;

291

alterations do not undermine the overwhelming sense of continuity attributed to initiation.

This chapter may seem an odd interruption, pulling back from the close analyses and details of ceremonial performance in the preceding section to consider how Okiek construe and construct their initiation practice through time, a consideration that necessarily remains open and somewhat inconclusive. However, it is not enough simply to summarize my exploration of how ritual efficacy is produced in Okiek initiation and sketch its theoretical implications—though I will try to do just that in the last chapter. The progressive narrowing of scope characteristic of monographs—going from broad theoretical questions to general ethnographic setting to focused topic—must be broadened again not just by returning to theory, but also by another historical recontextualization through Okiek reflections on initiation. This chapter, then, reconstitutes the broader contextual and historical frame of chapter 3, which receded to the background during the close synchronic analyses of subsequent chapters. The last chapter will then return to the theoretical frame opened in chapter 2, which was exemplified and explored in detail in the last part.

Ceremonial history is closely related to changing circumstances and developments in other domains of Okiek life. A historical perspective on ceremonial practice reveals specific ways Okiek have interpreted, incorporated, and influenced their changing historical circumstances. This chapter reviews changes Okiek remember in their initiation practice and then considers the locations of these changes in ceremonial structure and sequence, their particular shapes, and differential Okiek emphases and evaluations of them in accounts of ceremonial history and tradition.

My historical discussion of initiation encompasses two time scales, distinguished epistemologically by different combinations of evidence. The first is the relatively narrow and recent period circumscribed by my own experience with Okiek, from 1974 to 1991. My attendance and participation at and documentation of Kaplelach and Kipchornwonek ceremonies were the basis of many discussions with Okiek, some about differences that developed over that period. Blackburn's 1968–69 research slightly extends the time for which detailed notes, photographs, and tape recordings of initiation ceremonies are available.[2] The period for which Okiek recollections are supplemented by our shared experience and detailed documentation of particular ceremonies, then, covers roughly twenty years.

A longer, somewhat variable time scale is defined by Okiek comments and memories alone. The historical image that emerges from them is more a general sketch than a detailed picture, and accounts of ceremonial practice before *il ny'angusi* (roughly the 1950s) are sometimes contradictory. I have found no written accounts of Kaplelach or Kipchornwonek initiation from colonial or precolonial times to supplement current Okiek memories of their earlier practice.

The oldest Okiek alive today were initiated in the 1930s, but the oldest age-set with substantial living representation (*il ny'angusi*) was initiated in the 1940s and 1950s. The earliest personal memories of initiation ceremonies today, then, including late childhood experiences, might reach back to 1915 or 1920. Even with accounts remembered from the stories of parents and grandparents, the period covered here hardly reaches 1900, and information on early decades in the century is tentative.[3] Changes in ceremonial style and practice are not prominent topics in Okiek conceptions of history; I will return later to how Okiek regard ceremonial history, traditions, and changes in ceremonial practice.

Reconstruction of Okiek ceremonial practice before 1968 is based on discourse of three kinds. First, spontaneous Okiek comments to me or to other Okiek noted differences from initiation in earlier times. Second, I specifically asked older men and women about particular components of initiation. They identified aspects of ritual events, costume, songs, and other details that had changed or remained the same since long ago (*keny'*—but the perception of what counts as long ago varied with age). We talked about when changes began (in terms of specific age-sets), what people did before, possible influences in the changes, and what people thought of them. People also recounted what they had heard from their parents and grandparents about earlier ceremonial practice. I had these general historical discussions with people of *eseuri* age-set (most in their forties in 1985), *il ny'angusi* (in their fifties and sixties), *il terito* (in their sixties and seventies), and the few living members of *il tareto* (most in their eighties) (see table 1 for a list of Okiek age-sets).[4]

The third type of discourse about past ceremonial practice also took place in interview contexts. I asked a sample of Okiek men and women of different age-sets about their own initiations, including who had taken ritual roles, who their coinitiates and *matireenik* had been, what ritual events had been performed, what songs sung, what kind of food prepared, and so forth. Personal histories usually confirmed trends and changes identified in the general discussions. A larger sample of men and women identified only their coinitiates and *matireenik* for me. This often led to general discussions about their own ceremonies and the history of Okiek ceremonial practice. In describing ceremonial changes and continuities, I maintain these discourse distinctions as much as possible, as they figure in later discussion of the imaging of tradition.

A Summary of Ceremonial Changes and Continuities

Between 1900 and 1991, Okiek changed their initiation conventions in ways that affected ritual roles, ritual events and materials, costumes, songs, and even the entertainment of guests. During this same time, it should be remembered, they also diversified their economy, shifted their patterns of work, residence, and interaction with their neighbors, encountered the effects of colonization in various ways, and became increasingly incorporated into a money economy. Interrelations among these sets of changes will be considered later; first I describe changes in different aspects of initiation and consider their chronological clusters and patterns.[5]

Ritual Roles

Ritual roles in initiation have increased in number and shifted in several ways since the beginning of the century, though only slightly. First, *piitintet* (sprayer/blesser) has become a standard, named, and compensated role. Blessings were always essential to ceremonies, but now an elder is singled out for each initiation to bless every step. He receives 10 Ksh per initiate for the work. The formalization of the role seems to have gone hand in hand with a proliferation of blessings. "There was no blesser who got paid. They weren't spraying all the time, just for *koroseek* and for the *mabwaita*." The formalization elaborated an already important and repeated ritual act, and accompanied other kinds of materialization in ceremonial practice, but it is unclear whether the increased prominence of men as blessing ratifiers might have been related to shifts in gender relations.

People were unanimous that Okiek had no paid *piitintet* before *eseuri* (1955–1974). Some thought it started late in *eseuri*, picked up from Kipsigis. However, the role may have taken its present form (or at least become more prominent) more recently. My notes from 1974–75 do not refer to the *piitintet*, nor do Blackburn's earlier ones. I first encountered a *piitintet* at ceremonies in 1983; people told me then it had started recently. If Blackburn and I both overlooked it earlier, "recent" (a relative term) could indeed refer to *eseuri*. If the paid role did crystallize after 1975, to locate it during *eseuri* is to assimilate a recent development to other changes said to have begun then. That placement gives it a neotraditional sense by shifting it back to a time of recognized ceremonial innovations.

As for the Kipsigis source, Okiek might have found a model there, but they gave it their own interpretation and name. Kipsigis initiation includes an elder (*paayaat aap tuumto*) who blesses and also acts as general ritual organizer and administrator.[6] The official role of the Okiek *piitintet* is only to bless. Old people who are present at the ceremony discuss and decide ritual procedure in conjunction with members of the host family; the blesser may take part, but not in an official capacity. The *matireenik* also determine procedure during seclusion ceremonies.

The second change in named ritual roles concerned the *matireenik* themselves; only some Okiek acknowledged it. General historical discussions affirmed the role's continuity from the earliest times, and individuals of every age named their ritual teachers.[7] The change involved the number of teachers, and was mentioned chiefly by people of *il ny'angusi* or older. According to the oldest woman alive in 1982, when she was initiated (during the *il meiruturut* subset), Okiek might have only one *matiriyaat*, not two.[8] Others of the same *il tareto* age-set said they had a single teacher; *il terito* identified their age-set as the first one for which two *matireenik* was standard practice. Only two younger people claimed a single teacher; both were Kaplelach initiated early in *il ny' angusi*.[9]

Matireenik have long been part of Okiek initiation, then, but before *il ny' angusi* it seems their number could be one or two. The current conventional pair, firmly established for both Kipchornwonek and Kaplelach by the end of *il ny' angusi*, is largely unquestioned by younger Okiek. They have no personal memory of earlier variability and rarely if ever hear it mentioned.

Ritual Events

Other changes in the roles of initiation concern general modes of participation and are tied up largely with new ritual acts or events. Farewells sung to individuals who are given cigarettes and individual encouraging speeches with gifts have both been added to girls' initiation; they are new elaborations of earlier practice. Similarly, raising a flag emblazoned with two names was adopted within memory. In all these, participation has shifted in ways that temporarily focus on and emphasize individual relations within a larger group. All also involve money or other gifts, and are thus part of the increased materialization of initiation.

People talked most readily about these three changes in the events of the first ceremony of girls' initiation: the personalized flag, the individual sung good-byes, and the encouraging speeches. These recent shifts in Okiek ceremonial pracice are widely recognized and often remarked upon; all three are said to have been learned from Kipsigis. All are said to have begun at the end of *eseuri* or the beginning of *i rambau*, dates that are confirmed in women's personal histories. Kipchornwonek initiated during *il tiyoko* subset are the first to remember them; Kaplelach girls followed suit during *i rambau*. Girls began to wear elaborate dance costumes at these same times, when important economic changes begun in the previous age were spreading and their implications were developing. Only the flag was incorporated into boys' ceremonies, but individual histories show that boys adopted it somewhat later. No *eseuri* men remembered a flag; only later *i rambau* men had flags naming chosen relatives.[10]

The amount paid by those named on the flag has gradually escalated, as have other ceremonial costs. Blackburn records the 1969 fee as 20 Ksh. In 1975, the flag raiser paid 40 Ksh and the dropper 50 Ksh. By 1983–84 the raiser averaged 160 Ksh (ranging from 80 Ksh to 280 Ksh) and the dropper 180 Ksh (ranging from 100 Ksh to 300 Ksh). Personal histories seem unreliable on this point. Current practice inflates memory; most people recall 100 Ksh as the fee for the first flags of *il tiyoko* and *i rambau.*

Sung encouragement was part of Okiek initiation well before *eseuri.* The *eseuri* additions of dance costume and cigarettes, with a change of songs, elaborated existing practice, and also increased participation by young people and materialization (see below). Earlier songs were also dialogic, it seems, but it is not clear whether individual messages were sung, as they are now; older woman did not remember calling on individuals.

Individual speeches of encouragement may have been the earliest of these changes incorporated in their present form; a few people dated them as far back as early *eseuri,* during *il terekeyani.* Reports on previous practice differed; some said they spoke to initiates outside at the *mabwaita,* while others said they just sang outside with no speeches. Monetary gifts of encouragement were initially very small, perhaps a few shillings; some gave honey instead. These, too, inflated over time: in 1969, the average gift was 5 Ksh (with the largest about 10 Ksh), while in 1975 it was about 12 Ksh (close relatives gave a cow or sheep). By 1983, encouragement averaged 25 Ksh; virtually no man offered less than 10 Ksh.[11]

It seems that soon after these changes were incorporated into girls' initiation, another common practice was dropped. I was told in 1975 that young men had once had evening competitions, at the point in the ceremony when girls now sing individual farewells. Calling out big animals they had killed or cows they had raided, they threw down spears. The men became quite worked up (*-nereec*) and could fight; my assistant at the time described such a fight from 1971. A public exhibition of bravery and emotion, this verbal competition was another kind of encouragement to initiates. Seemingly spontaneous but expected during ceremonies, like emotional fits, this encouragement was too dangerous, too potentially explosive in its physical and emotional display. People decided to discontinue the practice.

When we talked about added or altered ritual events in the first ceremony, people often pointed out enduring events as well. The two processions, *koroseek* and *toloocik,* were most often cited. Such contrasts were loaded with unspoken implications, emphasizing a continuity that both balanced and countered the changes discussed. *Koroseek* and *toloocik* processions are not the only ritual events that stretch back to the beginning of memory. Even the oldest Okiek also remember *pesenweek.*[12]

The first ceremony of seclusion, *kelap euun,* is also long-abiding in Okiek initiation, but not so the second, *ketuuitos suumoosyek.* The oldest Okiek affirmed their own experience of *kelap euun,* its changes of costume and activities, and daily *kaiyantaaita.* Women of *il tareto* said that their age had neither a *suumuut* enclosure nor the associated seclusion ceremony. Building the enclosure was not feasible in the traditional Okiek houses they were living in at the time. An *il tareto* man marked *il kalikal* (early *il ny'angusi*) as the start of *ketuuitos suumoosyek,* though some women suggested an *eseuri* start, assimilating it to later changes. All men and women of *il ny'angusi* I spoke with, with one exception, remembered going through the ceremony, as did virtually all younger people.

Constraints of secrecy prevented discussion of most of the specifics of seclusion ceremonies. Most people simply affirmed the secrets as being the same as their grandparents', but several Kaplelach women said some secrets today are different. A Kaplelach man of *il ny'angusi* said in particular that miniature houses for female initiates and cattle enclosures for male initiates were new to Okiek with his own age-set, the same one when Okiek began to settle and keep herds at home. All attributed these changes, like others, to Kipsigis influence via Kipchornwonek.

These secrets are under the authority of the *matireenik,* so directional patterns in the selection of ritual instructors might illuminate these claims of influence. Networks of ritual relation suggest that the oft-cited Kipsigis inclinations come not simply from Okiek and Kipsigis attending each other's ceremonies, but at times from active participation in central roles. One of the oldest Kipchornwonek woman in my research area, of Kap Geemi lineage, was taught by Kipsigis *matireenik.* Most other Kipchornwonek women of *il tareto, il ny'angusi,* and *eseuri* had teachers from a small number of families, all of them Kipchornwonek from the western side, near areas where Kipsigis had moved in earlier. They include lineages with families at Oltikambo, the Okiek settlement closest to the Amala River.[13] The Okiek women most frequently invited to teach Kipchornwonek girls today are from different families, but were themselves taught by women of the western lineages. They began to teach during *i rambau.*

The ritual networks of Kaplelach women do not stretch as far initially, but the direction is similar. The only living Kaplelach woman of *il tareto* whom I knew claimed a single Kipsigis *matiriyaat.* The local ritual network then jumps to *eseuri* age.[14] Most Kaplelach girls of *eseuri* and early *i rambau* were instructed by Kaplelach women from their own area and by one Kipchornwonek (Kap Kwonyo lineage) woman married into Kaplelach. In some cases, a Kaplelach woman taught along with one of the regular Kipchornwonek *matireenik* of the time. From late *i rambau* to the present, however, Kaplelach began to invite the same Okiek who teach Kipchornwonek girls, bypassing nearby women who have taught other Kaplelach girls.[15] Networks of ritual filiation for both Kaplelach and Kipchornwonek, then, have a west-east directionality at precisely the times that people identify as the main periods of ceremonial change. This offers support for claims of Kipsigis influence, and suggests some of the avenues through which it was conveyed.

To return to changes in ritual events, what remains to consider is the final ceremony. Its public aspects—opening the way, giving the *sirtiityet* sapling, sleeping at another home, head shaving, and cutting the sapling—are all considered to be enduring Okiek ceremonial practice. However, there are two recent additions to the ceremonial sequence. The first, already mentioned, is another transaction inserted just after initiates are given saplings: the *matireenik* and *piitintet* are paid. *Matireenik* have always been accorded the recognition, respect, and compensation of a gift for their work, though previously it was in nonmonetary form. Money is the only method of payment today, but the amount is small (about 20 to 25 Ksh). Incorporating payment into the ritual sequence seems relatively recent. The coming out ceremony I attended in 1975 had no public payment; from 1982 onward, every one I attended did.

Ritualization of the transaction has two important effects. Pragmatically, *matireenik* are assured of payment when it is scheduled in the ceremonial sequence. Conversational banter at the time centers on the need for full payment on the spot; debts and promises are not acceptable. If some parents are unprepared, the ceremony waits until they borrow money from someone there. Ritual relationships newly forged in initiation should not begin with resentment at debts repeatedly claimed but unpaid. Continuing debt would reduce the ritual relation and job to an ordinary transaction. An important change in the economic structure of initiation, monetary payment is incorporated and organized in a way that maintains the special character of the relation.

That is the other effect. Ritualization distinguishes an otherwise ordinary financial transaction, momentarily separating the currency from the realm of commodity transactions. The money is held jointly, passed through the arch four times, and blessed. Drawing on standard ritual patterns, financial remuneration is made into a suitable substitute for a transaction previously marked with "a medium of exchange with the capacity to objectify and transform identities and social relationships" (Comaroff 1985:69), such as a hive or a cow.

The second addition is included either at coming-out or during the second seclusion ceremony. The initiates' female relatives kneel at the *mabwaita,* facing east. With the blesser, they hold a pile of *sinenteet* wreathes while he spits wine on the garlands and blesses. He then puts a wreath over each woman's head, completing the action on the fourth time. The women drink from a pot of maize liquor by the *mabwaita* with straws usually reserved for men, and finally the elder blesses each woman, using fat on a stick usually used for cleaning milk gourds. At the end of the ceremony, women leave their wreaths on the *mabwaita.*

This event incorporates things that were not regular parts of Okiek life until they began to cultivate maize and keep cattle. This women's blessing, a very recent change that is again identified as Kipsigis in origin, had become a regular event for Kipchornwonek by 1983. It was not yet Kaplelach practice and was regarded as a local variation. Yet one Kaplelach elder saw that it was beginning to spread:

Before people were only putting [the wreathes] on when they went to bring things for the _toloocik_, but now people copy Kipsigis, who put them on during the seclusion ceremony. My people, Kaplelach, don't know that work, but some are starting it now. Kipchornwonek and Kipsigis are the same, they do the same things.

Ritual Materials and Costume

These women's wreaths bring into focus ritual materials, an aspect of ceremonial continuity and change that has already been touched on. The central ritual plants, objects, and substances used in initiation, including the _mabwaita_ and _toloocik_ constructions, are regarded as _pa kuuka_ (for grandfather), icons of continuity in Okiek ritual tradition (cf. Kratz 1987, 1993). As one _il tareto_ man said,

When I was young, I heard elders saying that they had done _mabwaita_ and _koroseek_ since the beginning, so I don't know anything about its start. We've always done it.

Indeed, these ritual materials are often used to demonstrate the permanence of ceremonial tradition; the hive adze, honey-related products, and the _mabwaita_ itself were pointed out to me repeatedly as old things Okiek have always used. Yet alongside materials that seem to tangibly perpetuate their grandparents' practice, Okiek have added other materials that became regular parts of their life with economic diversification. Without forsaking familiar substances, they incorporated others as alternatives. Discussions of ritual procedure make explicit equations between old and new, with preferences ordained by historical priority.

For example, if there is no honey wine, maize beer can be used for blessings. Ritual shaving can be done with milk if honey water (_lukuumiik_) is lacking:

Lukuumiik is the old thing that was used before milk, the old thing that our fathers used. It's like honey, and honey is like milk. If you don't get one, you can use the other.

They're the same, they're both used in ceremonies and either of them can finish the ritual work.

New and old ritual materials alike are incorporated into new ritual events, like the payment of _matireenik_ or the blessing of women and wreathes. In this way, changes in ceremonial practice are woven into the familiar sequence of events through common materials and practical patterns. They also share in the sense of tradition carried by some materials.

If people represent ritual materials as prime examples of ceremonial continuity, they identify costume prominently with innovation, usually citing the example of dance costumes. Yet costume, too, shows an interplay between continuity and change. Spectacular dance costumes were first worn by girls in my research area during _eseuri_. Kipchornwonek sought them first, renting them from Kipsigis to the west. As with other innovations, costumes became part of Kaplelach ceremonies somewhat later, but by *i rambau* Kaplelach, too, were going west in search of them.[16] Rental cost has risen, like everything else: in 1969, Blackburn records it as 30 Ksh; in 1983, rental cost 100 Ksh or more. By 1983, costumes were available nearby. A few Okiek at Nkaroni had purchased them, joining the young Kipsigis men who outfit initiates.

Previously, girls did not change from the basic attire of ritual actors. They simply danced in the beaded leather skirt (*ntetut*), strapping dance bells made of seed pods to their thighs. The leather skirt and cape (*injorubayt*) have been ritual costume through the years, in contrast to dance costume. People emphasized that their grandparents used them not only for ritual but also as daily clothing before cotton cloth was available; this provides another material link with the past.[17] Initiates' costumes in seclusion and on coming out are also part of earliest memories of ceremonial practice. The white clay and skins of seclusion are specifically noted as unchanging Okiek practice. The heavily adorned costume of young women coming out is also affirmed as longstanding.

Modes of Entertainment

At about the same time that girls started to wear dance costumes, young Okiek also began to decorate the homes hosting the first ceremony. This ornamentation was just one part of the increasing elaboration in the entertainment that is provided for guests. Initiates of *il ny'angusi* are the first to remember painting red-brown and white bands on the outside of mud-walled houses; such decoration couldn't be done on the leafy walls of earlier Okiek houses. People began decorating inside with cloth, newspaper, and pictures late in *eseuri*, according to women of that age-set. As with the flag, house decoration began somewhat later for boys' ceremonies. In personal histories, only one man older than *i rambau* recalled a decorated house; he was initiated at a Nandi home.

Over the same period, celebration in the first ceremony was also extended and diversified. Before *il ny'angusi*, celebration was shorter and involved much smaller quantities of liquor and food. Since then, hosts have added many types of food and drink, increased the quantities they serve, and extended the celebration to several days. In general discussion, people all remarked on the gradual diversification and increase of amounts over time. Personal histories, however, only confirmed this diversification. Estimates of how much maize beer and honey wine was brewed in times past roughly matched the quantities brewed today, no matter what age the speaker was. Details of contemporary practice seem projected onto past memories here, as with the flag fees discussed above.

Before *il ny'angusi,* parents brewed only honey wine and provided honey and game meat to eat. During *il ny'angusi,* most Okiek also made maize beer. A few remember slaughtering a goat or cow to feed guests then, but most remember eating the meat of giant forest hogs. Some people noted that guests ate only meat then; ugali (today's polentalike maize staple) was not cooked, as gardens were small and it was still new to them.

During *eseuri,* slaughtering a cow became general practice, though some people from both halves of the age-set remember none at their own initiation. By *i rambau,* every host slaughtered a cow and provided ugali. Hosts also began to buy distilled maize liquor (*wutekiik*) then, giving it to special guests privately. Ceremonies I attended in 1975 included all these: honey wine, maize beer, distilled maize liquor, ugali, beef, honey, and of course sweet tea. By 1983, hosts were expected to provide soda and bottled beer as well, usually a case of each, and to buy potatoes to boil with the beef. Some hosts also bought biscuits or flour to make chapati bread for younger guests. When the assistant chief initiated his daughter, he slaughtered an extra goat to feed guests the first day.

Guests also welcomed one additional mode of entertainment and accepted certain scheduling changes introduced over the same period. Beginning in the mid-1960s during *eseuri* and (for Kaplelach) *i rambau,* renting a battery-operated record player became a common practice, one borrowed from Kipsigis initially. Records were good for ceremonies, I was told, both to entertain guests and to control loud conversation and singing that might lead to drunken argument and mar ceremonial peace.

The scheduling changes accommodate wider Okiek involvement in education. The timing of initiation was previously determined chiefly by parents' preparations and readiness, but those with schoolchildren now try to adjust their preparations to coincide with school holidays. Similarly, those who take schooling seriously try to condense the entire process into that holiday month.[18] As Okiek participation in education increases, contemporary differences in timing will probably be supplanted by the school-based norm, already common with Kipsigis and Nandi.[19] Though very few Okiek are engaged in external wage labor, the standard work week also figures here. The first ceremony now begins invariably on a Friday, with celebration through the weekend.

Speech and Song

Discussions with Okiek painted the general historical picture of initiation so far reviewed—with changes in ritual roles, events, materials, costume, and modes of celebration. Tracing specific shifts in the speech and song of initiation, however, is another matter. Current reports on past speech patterns, if available at all, may not be very reliable. Comparison of formal structures, specific phrases, and thematic idioms are virtually impossible without verbatim texts recorded at different periods.

Blackburn did not tape encouraging speeches or *pesenweek* in 1968–69, nor did I in 1974–75. He summarized themes in his notes on *ceerseet;* my own early notes recorded a running translation of both events. We both recorded some songs. I know of no other records of speech or song in earlier Okiek ceremonies, so only limited comparison is possible. Thematically, the speeches of 1969, 1975, and 1983 and the confessions of 1975 and 1983 are quite similar. Some early speeches comment specifically on the novelty of speeches, though the major shifts in ceremonial practice had already taken place before the available summaries.

Creative textual variations often refer to the changing material circumstances of daily life. Such improvisations simultaneously incorporate those circumstances thematically into ceremonial action and relate ritual events to contemporary Okiek life. Over time, apt expressions and incorporations become part of the common thematic repertoire. Later, however, particular phrases and figures of speech can be tied to a particular time only if they mention datable things. For instance, speeches and songs tell fearful initiates to run away in a *matatu* (public transport vehicle), a reference that began after 1950.[20] Contemporaneous reference to both enduring and changing aspects of ceremonial practice confers a sense of continuity on both, with cross-references between communicative channels weaving them more tightly together into a holistic image of time-honored tradition. This historical leveling occurs in encouraging songs as well.

Contemporary initiation songs are another complex synthesis of continuity and change. Only some songs are seen as persisting from earliest remembered times. The repertoires of some old types of song have been expanded with new additions or in some cases entirely replaced by recent adoptions. Okiek commented on the history of different initiation songs but did not talk about particular song lines or images and could rarely remember older songs that had been replaced.

Some initiation songs are expected to change regularly. Each age has its "hit parade" of girls' songs with different melodic patterns and refrains, though many themes, phrases, and the general structure of call lines carry from one age-set to another. On the other hand, according to Okiek, the corresponding *cepketilet* songs of boys' ceremonies have not changed in melody or refrain. But both the girls' songs and the *cepketilet* sung today are regarded as recent adoptions from Kipsigis. Girls' songs were learned when they began to wear dance costume, during *eseuri*. Before that, people said, boys and girls alike had *cepketilet,* but not those sung today.

The two *cepketilet* men now sing are also attributed to *eseuri;* the third one, sung by boys with female relatives and friends, was learned later in *eseuri*. Kaplelach date them a bit later, during *i rambau*. As a genre of song, however, *cepketilet* is regarded as deeply rooted in Okiek ceremonial tradition, previously sung at points when different songs are sung today. Several people commented, "We didn't have a lot of [different] songs." *Cepketilet* were once sung in a greater variety of initiation contexts and included a more differentiated repertoire. Their performance contexts now are narrower and more specific.

Old women usually insisted they could not remember the old songs, but when they sang brief snatches for me they used the same themes as today's songs.[21] There are no texts of early Okiek *cepketilet,* but phrases and themes in 1930s Kipsigis girls' songs attest to considerable continuity in the tradition from which Okiek drew contemporary songs (Peristiany 1964:267–72). The *cepketilet* song Orchardson recorded in the 1920s shares less with those of Okiek today, but includes phrases that are part of boys' seclusion songs (Orchardson 1961:133–34).

Ritual songs might be expected to stretch far back in Okiek memory, like central ritual materials and many events that involve the songs. In fact, only some ritual songs do, but historical distinctions in ritual songs are usually deemphasized, being neither spontaneously identified nor commented on. These musical changes come out only in discussions with older people about ritual details, discussions they often find tedious. This historical representation contrasts significantly with the accentuated innovation of girls' songs. Indeed, because of this contrast I did not realize at first that old Okiek consider some ritual songs recent. Similarly, younger Okiek rarely recognize such musical changes.

Opening procession songs are a good example. Both of the processional songs sung by young people (*cepkontook ce leelac* and *riret*) are identified as songs learned from Kipsigis and incorporated into initiation during *eseuri.*[22] Before then, they sang *cepketilet* songs and were met by women singing the same song as now (*celimen*). During today's boys' ceremonies, the procession switches to *cepketilet* on arriving home.

Celimen, women's ritual song, *is* regarded as long-enduring. Part of the refrain was used in Kipsigis initiation early this century, but Orchardson describes the song as sung daily by female initiates in seclusion (Orchardson 1961:62, 133). Along with *celimen,* several other songs are regarded as having been sung since the earliest Okiek age-set: the dawn songs before girls' operations, the processional songs for leaving seclusion, and the chanted opening of the way.[23]

Initiates' seclusion songs (*kaiyantaaita*) are like *cepketilet:* considered old Okiek practice, yet with repertoire changes included under the general term. Shifts in *kaiyantaaita* are recognized only by the oldest Okiek. An unbroken heritage is claimed for girls' first three songs outside and boys' daily *kipawes* songs.[24] The rest of the repertoire, however, includes songs that were added at other times.

The temporal tracing of initiation songs, then, reproduces the paradoxical intricacies of initiation history in general. An encompassing assertion of continuity is applied to the multifaceted process of initiation as a whole, but within there is a complex differentiation, combining differences of historical circumstances and attitude. The broad continuity is a mosaic of practice for which there is no memory of alternative or origin, new practice that has well-known beginnings that are widely recognized and discussed, and practice whose novelty people pass over silently unless questioned. The last, rarely noted or questioned, is well on its way to becoming practice whose origin and previous alternatives are lost to memory. I consider these processes of continuity and change in Okiek initiation and their representations further after a final chronological summary by age. The summary will bring into focus temporal conjunctions in changes just reviewed (see table 23).

Il Tuati *(1896–1917) and* Il Tareto *(1911–1929)*

Information is sketchy at these limits of remembered history, but there is no evidence of differences in ceremonial practice between the age-sets of *il tuati* and *il tareto*. Although there was undoubtedly much more to it, clear images of initiation then include a *mabwaita* shrine and an opening procession blessed with honey wine, with the *cepketilet* songs current at the time and women's *celimen* song. Initiates wore the usual costume of ritual actors, with thigh bells for girls. Many, if not all, families had an afternoon procession and a *toloocik* platform. In the evening, girls sang their *cepketilet* songs, may have been encouraged outside, and were asked about their *pesenweek* before entering the women's house. Guests celebrated with honey wine and game meat, giving thanks with honey and hives before departing.

Initiates were taught by one or two *matireenik* in seclusion. After *kelap euun,* they sang at least three of today's *kaiyantaaita*, smeared themselves with white clay, and wore skin clothing. The final ceremony was much like today's, though initiates were typically given hives rather than money or livestock.

Il Terito *(1926–1948) and* Il Ny'angusi *(1942–1959)*

People suggested that having two *matireenik* was becoming regular practice during *il terito,* but recount no other changes in ceremonial practice at the time. A few changes were introduced during *il ny'angusi,* mostly in celebration conventions and seclusion. Guests began to expect maize beer to drink, and some hosts slaughtered domestic animals for them as well. Initiates began painting houses' outer walls for decoration. People noted no ritual changes in the first ceremony, except that a new song, *riret,* might have been sung in some ceremonies then.

A pair of *matireenik* had become the rule for Kipchornwonek by the first half of the age-set and for Kaplelach by the second half. Another seclusion ceremony, *ketuuitos suumoosyek,* was also added to the ceremonial sequence at this time. Okiek may have begun to use miniature houses in seclusion training during *il ny'angusi,* and also to teach initiates some secrets that differed from those of their grandparents.

Eseuri *(1955–1974)*

Eseuri saw many shifts in initiation practice, the majority concentrated in the first ceremony. Kipchornwonek girls began to wear fancy evening dance costumes rented from Kipsigis. Flags were raised at their ceremonies, and houses were decorated inside and out. This age also saw a musical transformation of initiation. The *cepketilet* of the opening procession were replaced by other songs, girls began to sing Kipsigis songs of encouragement, different *cepketilet* were adopted for boys, and men and women alike learned new rejoicing songs. Most of these changes became regular Kipchornwonek practice in the second half of *eseuri;* they might have started intermittently during the first half.

Encouraging speeches were also becoming more prominent in the first half of the age-set; they were delivered inside the house, with gifts. Sung encouragement was embellished materially during the second half, when Kipchornwonek girls began to give cigarettes in individual farewells. It might have been *eseuri,* too, when the activities of the blesser (*piitintet*) became a regular, paid role. Finally, hosts during *eseuri* almost always slaughtered a cow to feed guests, and hiring a record player to entertain guests became standard. Some also diversified the liquor provided, adding distilled liquor to the usual beer and wine.

I Rambau *(1967–1984)*

I rambau saw only minor shifts in Kipchornwonek practice. Boys began to have flags and decorate houses inside and out, as girls had already begun to do. The larger set of changes that Kipchornwonek began during *eseuri* became the Kaplelach norm, too, during this age. Young men's verbal competitions in the evening were also discouraged at this time to prevent fights.

From late *i rambau,* Okiek recognize few changes. During this period, payment of both the *piitintet* and the *matireenik* was incorporated into the final ceremony, and a paid blesser might have become standard (or at least began to be a more prominent role). Guests at the first ceremony came to expect still more, calling for soda and bottled beer in addition to everything else, and potatoes mixed into the usual beef stew. Finally, Kipchornwonek also incorporated an additional blessing of women using *sinenteet* wreathes, an event shared with Kipsigis but not yet part of Kaplelach ceremonies.

Table 23: Okiek Initiation: Ceremonial Changes Discussed

Ceremonies are referred to by number for simplicity. This table only summarizes ceremonial changes discussed and does not list the full sequence of ritual events and activities. For names and full descriptions see chapter 4. The earliest age-set shown here lists objects and events clearly remembered, but is only a partial description of ceremonies at that time. Items listed only under that age-set had no changes noted.

Age-set	Ceremony I	Ceremony II (seclusion)	Ceremony III (seclusion)	Ceremony IV (ends seclusion)
il tuati/il tareto (1890s–1920s)	mabwaita shrine procession with song blessings ritual costume only evening song by initiates encouragement outside confession guests fed honey wine, game meat guests give hives and honey	1 or 2 ritual leaders	not practiced	gifts of hives to initiates
il terito (1930s–1940s)	no changes noted	2 leaders becoming standard	not practiced	
il ny'angusi (1940s–1950s)	new processional songs? paint houses outside guests given maize beer and perhaps sheep/goat meat	2 leaders standard some changes in secrets?	second seclusion ceremony added	

eseuri
(1950s–1970s)
	new processional songs
	dance costume for girls
	flags raised for girls
	paint houses inside too
	girls sing new songs and give
	   cigarettes
	boys sing new songs
	new rejoicing songs
	encouragement inside with gifts
	blesser role formalized?
	guests: cow slaughtered, some
	   distilled liquor, phonograph
	guests give money and livestock
		other gifts to
		   initiates too
		   (money and
		   livestock)

i rambau
(1970s–1980)
	flags raised for boys
	houses decorated for boys
	verbal competition discouraged
	blesser role formalized
	guests: soda, bottled beer, potatoes
	guests give money and livestock
		payment included
		   in ritual
		   sequence

Structure and Situation: Cultural Processes in Initiation History

Okiek identify the changes in initiation just reviewed and simultaneously affirm the unchanging continuity of their ceremonial tradition. This seeming paradox raises the fundamental questions of what Okiek mean by "tradition" and how they re-create and maintain the image of tradition in the face of such adaptability (Kratz 1993). The first step in exploring these questions is to consider the circumstances and contexts of this innovation and continuity in initiation.

Okiek have reshaped their ceremonial practice in relation to at least two kinds of conditions. First, the Okiek initiation process itself defines certain structural conditions and constraints on ceremonial transformations. These conditions are especially pertinent to questions of form and location: why did Okiek introduce changes in particular ways and at particular points in the ceremonies? The second kind of conditions is defined by the broader historical situation outlined in chapter 3. These conditions can illuminate questions of motivation, content, and linkages beyond initiation.[25] Analytically separable, sociocultural structure (here more particularly ceremonial structure) and particular historical situation are always combined in the ways people act and interact; they are both conditions and consequences of people's actions. People's lives and decisions simultaneously produce and are produced through particular structures and situations (cf. Comaroff 1985:78, 252; Karp 1986b; Ortner 1984; Sahlins 1981:79).

I first consider ceremonial changes in terms of formal patterns, using markedness theory as one way to interpret them. The changes cited in my historical profile involve a relatively small number of formal processes, which are sometimes combined: addition, deletion, substitution, repetition, expansion or elaboration, and simplification. More important and interesting than formal typologies, however, is an understanding of the locations and patterns of such shifts over time within the ceremonial sequence and communicative repertoire.

The changes made during *il ny'angusi* were in two areas: modes of celebration (food and house decoration) and seclusion. The first entailed addition and elaboration within the most secular part of the ceremony, while the second added another seclusion ceremony and possibly more seclusion songs. By all accounts, the added ceremony largely repeats the first seclusion ceremony; its distinctive event is making an internal enclosure parallel to the outside one built in the first. The addition also brings the ceremonies of initiation to a culturally resonant total of four.

Innovations during *eseuri* were concentrated in the first ceremony, largely in its nocturnal events. New songs were substituted for old, girls' costume was elaborated, and other ritual events were either added or elaborated (for example, individual farewells with cigarettes and individual speeches with gifts). The only addition in the daytime part of the ceremony was the flag, though songs were also substituted in the first procession. Hosts continued to elaborate modes of celebration. Gifts and payment for services shifted increasingly to money.

Early *i rambau* saw a consolidation and spread of the *eseuri* changes. Since then, the few changes in ceremonial practice have centered on the final ceremony and, once more, in modes of celebration. The two additions to the final ceremony recapitulate and elaborate ritual events long included. Payment of ritual workers is incorporated into the series of exchanges between initiates and their relatives; *matireenik* repeat the same acts, but receive payment now on their own behalf. The additional blessing of women repeats other blessings with a more specific focus and elaborate form, extends the contexts and uses of standard ritual materials, and combines them with others incorporated more recently.

In the contemporary form of initiation, then, this gradual accretion of shifts over the past ninety years has a cumulative concentration in the first ceremony. Its nocturnal section has the most changes—a diverse set, most of which were added during *eseuri*. Its final celebration has undergone a single diversification process that has been virtually continuous from *il ny'angusi* onward. The daytime section has remained more or less the same in sequence, though with different songs and a somewhat expanded set of possible ritual materials. The flag is its only new event, an event whose particular location can be related to the sequence and focus of the daytime section.

The ceremonies and practice of seclusion have changed little since *il ny'angusi,* so those cumulative shifts are specific to that age-set. If other changes have been introduced, their secrecy prevented me from learning and asking about them. Comments suggested that some secrets may have been added or substituted for others. The final ceremony again has little cumulative change, only shifts introduced quite recently. One addition to the ceremonial sequence is related to the new monetary mode of compensating ritual workers. No isolated shift, this is related to historical circumstances.

In addition to patterns within the ceremonies and sections of initiation, patterns of change over time include cases where girls' ceremonies were modified earlier than boys' (flag, house decoration) and others where changes occurred only in girls' ceremonies (cigarettes, encouraging speeches, costume). These differences and the temporal order of Kipchornwonek and Kaplelach shifts are considered below.

What can be made of these clusters and temporal orders in a formal sense? Within the limits of ceremonial structure and sequence, the concepts of markedness developed from Trubetskoy (1969) and Jakobson (1971; Jakobson and Waugh 1979) can help interpret the formal patterns. Markedness theory predicts and explains the location and order of changes within a formal system in terms of relations of markedness among its elements. Specifically, it predicts that where systems can be defined in terms of a hierarchical series of markedness relations, distinctions will be added first within the unmarked sections, introducing new elaborations through further modes of marking. The term "markedness," however, is used for a number of different notions that do not always go together: formal markedness, semantic markedness, and distributional or functional markedness (Lyons 1977:305–11).[26] In looking at different aspects and levels of ceremonial structure, a multifaceted notion of markedness that draws on these several senses is most useful.

Here I consider markedness relations among different phases and ceremonies of initiation, among the three sections of the first ceremony, and among ritual actors. This perspective suggests that shifts in Okiek ceremonial practice since 1900 began in ways that correspond to the constraints of markedness. However, some later changes are directly contrary to "the tendency to non-accumulation of marks" (Waugh 1976:91), that is, the tendency for markedness to be elaborated and superposed on unmarkedness. Other structural principles also come into play, neutralizing the relevance of markedness relations in certain cases. In general, these other principles involve repetition or regularization of productive contrasts and patterns in the ritual idioms.[27] The cumulative history of these ceremonies, themselves specially marked occasions, shows that at times markedness relations are not simply neutralized by other structural conditions; rather, the usual tendencies of markedness are reversed.

All the initiation ceremonies are full of specifically defined, distributionally marked activity, but the first ceremony is the most marked of all formally—in elaboration of events, number of participants, cultural emphasis, and obvious investment of resources.[28] The dawn climax divides the first ceremony into two sections, one ritually marked (with a defined sequence of events and actions), the other a less defined celebratory period.

The ritual section divides further into a daytime section (centered on framing events and the reiteration of general cultural assumptions) and a nocturnal section (in which ritual events focus on initiates). Of the two, the nocturnal section can be considered marked because its events occur only during initiation; the daytime processions and shaving occur also in ear-piercing ceremonies. Further, the nocturnal focus on initiates might be considered another kind of marking. Initiates are undoubtedly the most highly marked ritual actors in terms of costume, involvement in ritual events, and specification of their communicative modes, spatial locations, and so on.

Looking at changes in initiation within this framework, the overall pattern of shifts centers on the most formally marked and elaborate first ceremony. They begin, however, in unmarked sections: first a shift in seclusion, and then concurrent changes in seclusion and in the unmarked celebratory section of the first ceremony. As noted, seclusion changes also brought practice into line with culturally resonant oppositions and patterns, balancing outside with inside seclusion enclosures and bringing the number of teachers to a consistent two and the total number of ceremonies to four. Later changes proliferated during one age-set. They entail an ever-increasing elaboration of celebration (again in the unmarked section of the first ceremony) and increasing distinctions clustered around initiates, either on their person or in the ritually marked section focused on these most marked actors.

In essence, these later shifts make what is already marked more highly marked: the first ceremony becomes more involved and lavish, the place of ceremony is marked again with a flag, initiates already marked with saplings and ritual costume wear multiple and more elaborate costumes, and poignant farewells are given material as well as musical form. The structural principles of markedness and the logic of ceremonial sequence combine here: an increasing formal and material elaboration of the most marked actors in the most marked ceremony is concentrated during the section when the ceremony's focus on initiates helps to build dramatic tension to a dawn climax. That increase of markedness exaggerates differences integral to the dramatic orchestration, perhaps even heightening the emotional intensity. Tendencies identified by markedness theory in ordinary situations are reversed on these marked occasions, with the intensified markedness contributing to the ceremonial process.[29]

Although Okiek have changed many aspects of initiation practice, they have maintained the same fundamental structural sequence and cultural logic in the overall process. As with Merina circumcision, discussed in chapter 2, these processes should be seen in relation to the pragmatic functions of initiation: the crucial transformation of children into adults and its corollary, the gender-specific constitution of that change of identity. Both have remained integral to Okiek initiation, with the ceremonial structure through which the change is effected in performance correspondingly persistent. The specific understandings of Okiek gender relations have, however, shifted somewhat; changes within the structural continuity should also be seen more particularly in light of this.

Given this pragmatic continuity, there must be certain structural constraints on changes in ceremonial practice if the transformative process is to maintain its coherence and efficacy. However, this is not at all to say that ritual is timeless, uncreative, and unchanging. Particular changes in ceremonial practice and the ways they are incorporated depend very much on the particular historical situation. The Okiek situation does not involve the radical and sometimes sudden socioeconomic transformation and disjunction that often are common where revitalization movements develop. Nor have Christian churches served as yet as a central opposition or complement to Okiek cultural tradition. Nor did direct, close contact with a white settler population impinge in an abrupt way.

Precisely because of this, Okiek are an important case, one where the initial conjunction and interaction of different social and cultural orders associated with colonialism have been mediated to some degree through other neighbors long familiar to Okiek. In earlier times Kipsigis, who have since become more influential neighbors, lived at some distance from Okiek. Thus, the Okiek situation since 1900 has been one that simultaneously involves this mediated interaction, related shifts in direct interaction with various neighbors in the region, some relatively limited but direct colonial interaction, and increasingly direct interaction with the postindependence national government.

Situating Ceremonial History

Within the constraints of structural stability, Okiek have incorporated important changes in ceremonial practice since 1900, changes related to their specific historical circumstances. As contexts, associations, and experience shift over time, radically or subtly, those changes are incorporated into and influenced by ceremonial contexts among others. Ceremonies are thereby implicated in broader processes through which cultural meanings and sociocultural structures and relations are re-created in different circumstances. The central question here is how those processes emerge in ceremonial experience—whether in changes in the specific associations of familiar ritual materials and events, in changes where new ritual materials and events are incorporated into familiar ceremonial sequences, in innovations in ceremonial contexts, in shifts in sociopolitical interpretations and implications of ceremonies, or in some combination of ways.

Chapter 3 reviewed a wide set of historical changes in Okiek life. The most obvious ones involved economic diversification: the start of farming, followed by several roughly concurrent changes including an increase in garden size, the adoption of maize, increased settlement, a change of house type, and the introduction of home herding. All took place during *il ny'angusi* for Kipchornwonek and early *eseuri* for Kaplelach. Related shifts that have since developed, most importantly in the organization of forest work and in other gender-related patterns of work and interdependence, also trace their origin to these changes.

Patterns of Okiek interaction with their neighbors were subtly shifting at the same time, having begun somewhat earlier, as Kipsigis gradually moved closer. Kipsigis were also important mediators in Okiek experience of various colonial interventions related to land, market development, and encouragement of the very kinds of economic changes Okiek were adopting. Direct Okiek experience with colonial enterprises also began through limited labor migration during *il ny'angusi* and slight involvement in education during *eseuri*. Monetarization runs as an undertone through all of this. At first it was minimal, mostly involving occasional trips to purchase shop goods and the occasional sale of honey for money. By the 1980s, Okiek were well integrated into the larger market and consumer economy.

Changes in Okiek initiation practice must be seen in light of these changing circumstances. There is clearly a temporal connection. Okiek recall that, beginning in early *eseuri* (*il terekeyani*), there were at first a number of minor shifts in ceremonial practice, then a rash of changes; these spread and proliferated during the second half of the age (*il tiyokoni*). As well, central themes and patterns in the ceremonial changes can be related to the historical circumstances of their beginnings. First, there are several analogous shifts in participation. Farewells with cigarettes, the provision of dance costumes, personalized flags, and encouraging speeches with gifts all pick out and highlight individual personal relations. Most of these changes also increase initiates' own involvement with decisions about ceremonial particulars; this is part of a general increase in scheduled participation by young people (seen also in house decoration and other changes).

This increased personalization in initiation took place during *eseuri*, the same time that direct involvement with town and market life was on the increase. The correspondence hints at two things: first, processes of individuation that have been described repeatedly as accompanying so-called modernization, and second, one of the central tensions associated with individuation in the context of modernization—the directing of resources toward personal economic advancement versus the use of them to further community-based social relations.[30] Here these incipient processes are incorporated into the central ceremony of community social organization.

Shifts in other domains of experience that correspond to the participation shifts are also worth noting, beginning with differences defined along lines of age. Historically specific experiences of successive Okiek generations become institutionalized and summarized in terms of age-sets. In some cases, such experiential differences can exacerbate tensions inherent in socioeconomic and political organizations (Kratz 1988b; cf. Lonsdale 1988).[31] This is relevant to the more prominent place of young men in the first initiation ceremony.

With few exceptions, young men of *il ny'angusi* were the first Kipchornwonek and Kaplelach to take temporary paid employment, largely in police or game department service. The proportion employed was relatively small and their employment periods relatively short. Nonetheless, these young men encountered ways of life quite different from forest life, and came home with different knowledge and experience. Gained not from their fathers and grandfathers through the wisdom of age, that knowledge was still acknowledged and drawn upon when appropriate. Differences of experience and access to different kinds of resources also became part of the divisions of age.

In some ways, it was quite fitting for young men to expand their usual roaming and adventuring to include town and job for a time. Cultural notions about gender also suggested men should be the first to learn about such things. This experiential difference also led to differential access to the new opportunities and resources for men and women, parallel to other gender distinctions.

There was a similar situation during *eseuri* with the first Okiek sent to school (again mostly boys). Few of them stayed there long either, but the experience was in some respects remarkably different from life at home. Those who did stay came home with skills and knowledge that could give them access to other employment opportunities, though those were taken up temporarily if at all. Accommodating initiation scheduling to school holidays recognized the importance of this alternative education.

Though young men have taken on a more visible role in girls' first ceremony, they remain peripheral to most ritual events and procedural decisions. Bringing in the trappings of modern town life, they embellish the ceremonial sequence, perhaps also claiming public recognition of their wider and different experience. Reinforcing rather than undermining the sociopolitical organization that initiation helps re-create, their role as "modern" has thus been conventionalized. Young people of *eseuri* first incorporated modern decorations and other innovations into initiation, but now they are junior elders and host parents. Costumes, pictures, decoration, cigarettes, and similar details remain the province of young adults, the constant changes and fashions of modernity given a regular place in initiation through them. Okiek in the mid-1980s were not yet break-dancing to Michael Jackson and sporting punk haircuts (like young people in Nairobi), but their equivalents may well be found in future initiations.

Initiates' prerogative for decisionmaking in initiation, though of limited scope, is part of a general shift in young people's experience. For flags and farewells, girls usually select relatives who have long been important for Okiek women: brothers, relatives through their mothers, and sisters' husbands. Yet if the relations that are emphasized have changed little, preferential personal closeness is highlighted in a way that links them to understandings of personal relations with more open material and financial components.

Girls' dance costumes provide an example where personal relations, young people, a modernizing style, and initiates themselves have all become more importantly involved in ceremonial preparations and display, but where the basic tenor and conduct of gender relations remains the same. Costumes are sought and brought in a way that perpetuates assumptions about gender relations and incorporates them into ceremonial practice in another way particular to young people. Young men travel to bring costumes home; girls' access to wider networks of interaction and exchange through which they are found are once again mediated by men.

The minor shifts in the ritual roles of *matireenik* and *piitintet* are probably best considered part of the general increase in material outlay. But they are also connected with the other participation shifts (such as in farewells, flags, and speeches) as part of a tendency to regularize and formalize ceremonial relations, and to mark ritual relations and ritual work monetarily. Also in line with increased involvement in employment and market transactions, formalizing the roles assimilates them to a more clearly defined "job" and to the kind of exchange transaction associated with employment. Yet ritual relations are not really commoditized here. Incorporating payment into the final ceremony suggests a certain tension working against commoditization. Cash payment may assimilate ritual work to other employment, but the fairly nominal amount,[32] the actual practice, and the ritual incorporation of the transaction all seem to counter such a simple equation.

Emphasis on personal relations in initiation was modified at a time of changing settlement patterns and subtle modification in patterns of daily interaction. Previously, possibilities for assembling men into (largely patrilineal) work groups and their access to forest resources were major factors in decisions about residence and relocation. Wider neighborhood relations were constituted through the same work groups, as well as through visits, special occasions, and men's meetings. Settlement composition, neighbors, and the particulars of daily interaction changed with seasonal movements, though some core family relations were regularly nearby. Such shifts were especially salient for women, who did not participate in forest work and the wider networks that lent broad continuity to the changes.

As Okiek began to keep more permanent base settlements during *il ny'angusi* and *il terekeyani,* settlement and neighborhood ties became more enduring. For women, one thing this meant was more time to develop other abiding personal relations. Other work patterns eventually developed that facilitated this further, with cooperative garden work by women as well as men, and women staying home while their men went to the forest.

The economic and productive potential that women developed with economic diversification, then, went hand in hand with a situation where their other personal relations might be enhanced. Settlement and solidarity were still largely organized in terms of patrilineage and age-set, but women began to have more possibilities for the kind of personal relations based on enduring patterns of daily interaction, work, and shared life that had long been part of men's experience. Many of the ceremonial changes that emphasize individual personal relations have been incorporated only into girls' initiation, except for the flag, which was also added later for boys. While this difference may be related to other circumstances and assumptions about gender, it also corresponds to concurrent shifts in patterns of work and residence in women's lives.

Finally, the interrelated shifts of economic diversification involved one more important realm of individual decisionmaking and action. Garden work was a household concern and its products household property. Individual holdings were not foreign to Okiek socioeconomic organization; hives were individually owned, as was their honey yield. But garden work and produce was organized, allocated, and appropriated rather differently than honey. Honey was still a male product from lineage land resources, its collection enmeshed in networks of male work groups and its surplus open to lineage demands and needs such as marriage and ceremonies. In addition to involving women more centrally in production, gardening also increased and strengthened the domains of individual and household decisions about work, ownership, and distribution.

Fernandez suggests that revitalization movements create a sense of "returning to the whole" through their ceremonies, a sense of relatedness and viability (if not complete coherence) in diverse domains of experience. They provide a "more open opportunity for creative ritualization . . . than is characteristic of most human situations, committed as they are to well-worn routines and the inertia of institutions" (Fernandez 1986:183; cf. Fernandez 1982). Revitalization movements typically emerge in situations that combine a sense of cultural bankruptcy and ineffectiveness with increasing differentiation of formerly overlapping and diffuse relations, often with commoditization and an increase in scope.

The Okiek case shares some aspects of that situation. In the period under review Okiek have become involved in other modes of experience, other relations with fewer dimensions, greater commoditization of exchange, networks and knowledge of wider scope, and greater differentiation of experience by age and gender. However, the Okiek case differs in that there is no sense of cultural bankruptcy; as well, initiation is a ceremony with the very kind of routine Fernandez contrasts with the greater openness of revitalization movements. Okiek initiation shows how creative ritualization goes on in the other, more routine situation. Innovations in Okiek ceremonial practice bring some of the new and differentiated domains of Okiek experience into the initiation process, relating them to those of continued relevance and power from times past. They add more parts to create a more encompassing whole of a slightly different configuration, one that creates a more extended sense of relatedness.

This aspect of ceremonial innovation is central to understanding the general escalation and elaboration in Okiek initiation. Escalation is most obvious in the steady increase in the amount and varieties of food and drink for guests. At first it involved mostly the new products of diversified productive activities, but over time there has been an ever-greater monetary expenditure not only to feed guests but also to entertain them with records, decorate the girls, and compensate those assisting in ritual roles. Correspondingly, material transactions involving money, cigarettes, or other gifts have also been incorporated into ritual events. Guests' financial contributions have also expanded; now they give encouraging gifts. These increasing monetary expenditures can be correlated with the increasing incorporation of Okiek into the money economy. Again, the same age-set is a key transitional time for both these ceremonial changes and the associated economic and social changes—cash honey sales increased in the 1950s and after, and purchased goods became increasingly common and diverse, facilitating essential shifts in women's work. These market processes have continued and expanded up to the present, when land sales provide more capital than ever to build *mabati* (tin-roofed) houses, buy clothing and furniture, and, of course, drink beer.

Chapter 3 examined the way Okiek economic diversification exacerbated a central tension in gender relations, a tension between complementarity and interdependence in household production, on the one hand, and hierarchy in access to and control of material resources, surplus, and sociopolitical influence, on the other. Women had an increasing capacity for direct production as farmers and were increasingly viable as independent producers. There was a concomitant decrease in the pressure on men to produce. Women's new potential, however, was constrained by sociopolitical organization and its underlying assumptions about gender roles.

The introduction of more formal encouraging speeches and gifts can be interpreted in light of these dynamics in the relations between production and gender. Speeches increase men's explicit verbal role in women's key ceremony, in a way that emphasizes the controlling link between men and property (in its new monetary form as well as in the form of livestock and hives). Scheduled as the final encouragement, it gives men the last, ratifying word, like blessings. Their speech style also recalls legal-political meetings (which exclude women), a prime forum for the formal expression, exercise, and re-creation of their sociopolitical authority. The new event thus foregrounds key areas where the hierarchy of control and access come into play. Further, it underlines the legitimation of that hierarchy through the essential and "natural" differences between men and women—men who need no encouragement and unpredictable, weak women who must be spoken to, challenged, and obliged to stand their ordeal.

At the same time that women's social and economic potential was shifting toward a greater capacity for independence, then, an event that reiterates the key legitimating assumptions of gender relations and the socioeconomic hierarchy was incorporated into girls' initiation, the central occasion that contradicts those assumptions. This makes even more telling people's side remarks during *ceerseet,* comments that point out the contradiction inherent in the situation. The speeches also include some of the most blatant expressions of men's ambivalence towards women.

The various parallels I have traced suggest that Okiek have interpreted and incorporated changing circumstances and transformations in various domains of life in their initiation practice. I have concentrated so far on interrelations between shifts in ceremonial practice and Okiek economic diversification, and on the timing of direct Okiek experience with employment in colonial service, schooling, and the money economy and market system more generally. Still to consider are simultaneous regional developments, intermediate in scope between these most local daily concerns and involvement in larger national networks and developments. They sometimes involve intermediary connections and interpretation between the local and the national.

Kipsigis have made a number of cameo appearances so far and seem always to be in the wings as the direction and source from which diverse new practices, both ceremonial and economic, came. Okiek consistently remember a time lag, too, roughly an age-set, between the changes of Kipchornwonek, who are nearer Kipsigis, and Kaplelach, who are farther away. What is to be made of this?

Kipsigis neighbors had been gradually moving into Okiek areas since at least *il ny'angusi,* settling in greater numbers as years passed. At the same time, Okiek were settling down and moving operatively closer to Kipsigis subsistence practice. Kipsigis were not only the source of seed for early Okiek gardens; they could also show them how they managed their own agropastoralism by example and through discussion. Physical and practical convergence have together meant increasing Okiek-Kipsigis interaction over time, and a gradually greater integration that has drawn on a shared Kalenjin language and tradition. Networks of ritual relations, already discussed, are one facet of these processes.

Changes in Okiek ceremonial practice are not simply chameleonlike switches in which the Okiek take on whatever their neighbors do. Rather, they are a selective incorporation and adaptation of those elements of their neighbors' practice that are responsive to Okiek experience as well, an Okiekization. Their neighbors' presence is part of that experience. The apparently chameleonlike nature of these shifts, however, is the superficial impression conveyed by a signal attitude to cultural difference that is central to Okiek cultural identity. In this case, Okiek place different ceremonial practices on an equal footing rather than devaluing one with respect to another.[33] Incorporating aspects of their neighbors' practice, then, is neither desecrating nor demeaning, nor does it especially glorify their neighbors. Rather, it makes use of available cultural resources for Okiek purposes. This is consonant with similar Okiek attitudes about language use, costume, interaction with other ethnic groups, and different modes of production (Kratz 1981, 1986; Klumpp and Kratz 1992). In addition to the regional shifts in population that were the immediate context, then, this bricoleurlike openness and ability is one more facet to include in understanding changes in Okiek ceremonial practice.

The question remains, however, why Okiek have incorporated aspects of Kipsigis initiation practice as their own. Several factors figure here, including structural and broad situational appropriateness. As seen above, Okiek ceremonial changes accord with the structural logic and constraints of the ceremonial process. They can, in fact, be partially understood as intensifying its constituent contrasts. At the same time, many of these changes resonate with shifts in other domains of Okiek life and experience, other refractions of similar cultural processes.

Kipsigis, too, experienced the different kinds of relations and constraints that colonialism brought, but their experience began earlier than that of Okiek in this area and was often more direct and intensive. By the time Kipsigis came to the area in larger numbers, some aspects of these experiences had already become part of their ceremonial practice, practice that was already shared with Okiek to some degree. This meant that the similar ceremonial practice of their increasingly close neighbors was already responsive to the similar new encounters and experiences in which Okiek were becoming involved. Okiek made most of the changes in initiation during the time when their economic shifts were most profound and new experiences were first encountered. However, further developments both in these economic processes and in Okiek circumstances more generally have continued to be incorporated in initiation at the same time as the basic ceremonial changes that have already occurred continue to produce elaborations and variations through their own momentum.

Kipsigis have often been mediators of modernity for these Okiek. For example, colonial land policies affected Okiek through Kipsigis movements in response to land pressure that they felt more directly. The introduction of maize and hand-operated mills followed a similar route, reaching Okiek as their diversification became more far-reaching, and contributing to it. For Okiek, Kipsigis have come to be associated with a "modern" lifestyle and practices in many ways. They were, then, an appropriate source of changes in initiation that were responsive both to that mediated colonial experience and to the changes in daily life that accompanied new productive activities. Further, the new practices already had a genealogy in the parallel Kipsigis "tradition." A source of innovations in both initiation music and maize-growing, Kipsigis' mediating role and consequent associations were summed up by an Okiot of *il ny'angusi:* "It was just these words of *maendeleo* (development, modernity) that came like the ones that come today, so we did it, too."

Imaging Tradition and Protection through Numbers

This section considers Okiek conceptions of ceremonial tradition (Kratz 1993), a sense of history in which continuity and repetition are of the essence. Clearly, tracing the history of ceremonial practice is not a simple or "objective" comparison of form, but an evaluative endeavor. Questions that can have different answers are central to re-creating a sense of ceremonial tradition:

what counts as difference, change, continuity, and repetition? Different Okiek responses and reactions in the discussions I had with them about ceremonial history impressed on me that these questions are necessarily ideological. Past becomes present in part through a projection of present practice into the past. Furthermore, assertions of the continuity of tradition vary in scope and detail.

When I began to discuss initiation history, I noted that accounts of ceremonial practice before *il ny'angusi* were fuzzier and more contradictory than those concerning later practice. This implicit, discourse-created periodization coincides with and re-creates the double image Okiek have of themselves and their past, their idealized distinction between Then and Now. Memory has its limits; earlier memories might well be vaguer and perhaps collapsed, condensed, idealized, or projected into a more unified "past." Yet such processes are selectively uneven: some things are remembered in great detail and clarity, others constitute a general and ideal past, and others are not remembered at all. "Both forgetfulness and memory are apt to be inventive"(Borges 1972:38)—the past becomes present in different ways as people create multiple images of both, commenting on and framing current practice, politics, and their sense of identity through history.

Okiek presented an overall image of ceremonial tradition that consistently asserted and affirmed a broad sense of enduring continuity with previous generations. R. Wagner admonishes:

The contexts of culture are perpetuated and carried forth by acts of objectification, by being invented out of each other and through each other. This means we cannot appeal to the force of something called "tradition" . . . to account for cultural continuity, or for that matter cultural change. (R. Wagner 1981:50)

Nevertheless, for Okiek it does have explanatory power. They use the continuity of tradition as both explanation and justification for doing things and for the way things are. At the same time, people can take recourse in that continuity to dismiss questions of difference and change, claiming that such questions are rendered irrelevant or trivial by the more encompassing sense of tradition. Within the overall continuity, however, changes in ceremonial practice are also accommodated, changes which emerge in more specific and narrowly focused discussions.

The question now is how Okiek create such a forceful image of ceremonial tradition through discourse and through performance (though people do not see themselves as creating either the ceremonies or an image of them [cf. White 1973; Bloch 1986:168, 194]). Imaging tradition incidentally images a sense of cultural identity as well; the continuity of tradition and a distinctive sense of being a collectivity—those who follow the tradition—are closely related.

First I consider some ways Okiek talk about ceremonial history. Changes in initiation are cast in the image of tradition through five main rhetorical techniques: back-projection and concentration in time, canonization through silence, shifts of emphasis and balance through selective attention, synechdochal encompassment, and assimilative generalization. While none of these is falsification of history or intentional obfuscation, their joint use in imaging Okiek ceremonies through time produces a picture of overriding continuity, and creates a tradition that enshrines and justifies ceremonial practice.

The most simple and dogmatic examples of back-projection are straightforward assertions of continuity since time before memory: "We've always done it." Practice known becomes original practice; current memory becomes primordial. Back-projection can also reshape changes in ceremonial practice. For instance, some accounts projected the recent formalization of the blesser's role further back than warranted, which is possible in part because an earlier version of the role could receive the projection. This back-projection, which places formalization into the *eseuri* age-set, is also an example of temporal concentration. Some people put more-recent changes back to *eseuri* or brought those of *il ny'angusi* age forward. By concentrating changes that might have covered several age-sets into one widely recognized as an age-set of change, continuity during others is enhanced.

Concentration also creates a kind of neotraditionalism, establishing a unified period of concurrent changes that can be taken as the starting point for a new continuity in some aspects of ceremonial practice. The Kipsigis source of changes also contributes to this. Not created ex nihilo, changes come rather from a parallel tradition with its own continuity. Whether or not they might be recent changes in Kipsigis practice as well is irrelevant; their incorporation is sanctioned, in a way, since they have already become part of the parallel practice.

Simple silence is a most effective and versatile way to deemphasize ceremonial changes and eventually erase memories of the transition. As alternatives drop from memory, silence canonizes changes as enduring tradition. Young Okiek, for instance, were often unaware that there had once been a single ritual leader and no second seclusion ceremony. Silence shrouds more than additions and alterations. Abandoned events and acts also disappear from memory if they go unnoted. Verbal competition among young men, mentioned to me in the mid-1970s, was discussed in the 1980s only if I asked about it. How does one learn about such forsaken practice unless one already knows to ask about it?

Silence is just one mode of selective attention. Continuity or change can also be emphasized or diminished with directed shifts of attention. When we talked about added or altered ritual events, people often pointed out enduring ones as well, such as the processions of the first ceremony. Loaded with unspoken implications, such comments never curtailed discussion of changes, but they rebalanced them to stress continuity in the overall complexion of initiation. Certain comments volunteered to me during ceremonies effected a similar foregrounding, pointing to particular ritual materials as having been used by Okiek for ages. Such material embodiments, they seemed to suggest, were particularly convincing demonstrations of continuity.

Ceremonial changes are neither denied nor ignored, but selective attention also defines those most commonly noted and emphasized. Almost without exception, the changes that were emphasized intensified or elaborated existing distinctions. Further, the most widely recognized and readily discussed shifts were in the first ceremony: the personalized flag, individual good-byes with song and cigarettes, and encouraging speeches at night. All three are neotraditional changes dating from *eseuri* and were said to have been learned from Kipsigis. This was true of initiation songs as well. Girls' songs were often noted as being innovations; changes in ritual or seclusion songs were more often passed over in silence.

Selective emphasis weighted the scales in favor of continuity (or evened them up). Often, examples also implied a further extension of continuity through synechdochal encompassment or assimilative generalization. For instance, naming processions as exemplars of tradition implies the same of everything in these ritual events: the *mabwaita* shrine, spatial organization, blessings, songs, plants used, costumes, and so forth. Citing such a ritual event encompasses the complex combination of communicative resources in that event, and so shifts in some details can be subsumed within the continuity of general practice.[34] The image of continuity and tradition is enlarged and extended. Questions I asked about particular details often bore this out, but not always.

The totalizing process thus accomplished implies, by enthymemic reasoning, a common continuity for all aspects of the event. For example:

These songs are part of the opening procession.

The opening procession is something we have done since the time of our grandfathers.

The songs have been sung since the time of our grandfathers.

The first and third statements are not explicitly stated. The first is assumed and shared knowledge, the last the conclusion implied by the shared knowledge together with the explicit statement.[35]

Other examples accomplish the same effect in the opposite way, again using enthymemic reasoning but in assimilative generalization. Picking ritual materials to demonstrate continuity suggests that the status of tradition should be further extended to the way the materials are used, those who use them, and so on. Continuity can be generalized from part to larger context in many ways, assimilating the whole into the image of tradition. For instance, new materials are incorporated into a repertoire canonized as *pa keny'*, "ancient" (for example, using maize beer as well as honey wine in blessings), or new acts fit into standard patterns with standard materials (for example, incorporating payment into the final ceremony).

Old and new can also be assimilated verbally through co-occurrent phrases in song and speech. Examples already mentioned include the evocation in encouraging speeches of the seemingly immutable ceremonial saplings and the recently adopted dance costumes, both now signs of bravery and success. Likewise, it seems that speeches and songs of initiation have long included a chalenging theme that tells initiates to flee if they fear the operation. Current phrasing of the challenge in terms of catching a *matatu* to Kisumu, however, clearly updates the theme.

The ways Okiek speak about ceremonial history create a discourse-based image of tradition that supports the assertion of continuity. Similar assertions are common in other cultures, but are demonstrated differently and with different images of tradition. In areas of Indonesia, for instance, people demonstrate continuity in part through verbatim repetition of ritual texts. Mambai on East Timor represent and protect continuity for their ceremonial tradition not by indefinite projection into the past, but by identifying archetypal origins with acts of the deities. "The efficacy of symbolic action is held to rest upon the continuity between an original archetype and an inherited tradition. . . . Ritual forms are the tangible link with original time" (Traube 1986:183). Mambai tradition is also represented as something to be safeguarded, a special knowledge and pracice carried on by some on behalf of others. This aspect of the Mambai image of tradition is created in part through role distinctions; ritual specialists are entrusted with esoteric knowledge and texts.[36] At this point, Mambai discourse-based imaging of tradition merges with conventions of ceremonial performance.

Okiek produce continuity of ceremonial practice through the structure and conventions of performance itself, rather than through trained specialists. This is the second way that continuity and its image as tradition are created: through performance. Performance reproduces ceremonial practice that largely conforms to that remembered from the past, even if it does not conform as exactly as verbatim repetitions. Further, it creates a context to attest and confirm the continuity of what people do now. Some structural arrangements that create continuity in Okiek practice also protect initiation secrets.

The duality of ritual roles is a good example. There are two blessers (or blessings), two ritual instructors, and a leader and follower in processions. With two actors undertaking a joint task or decision, they must agree on procedure and on whether changes are consequential or simply variation. The dualism also embodies what are for Okiek auspicious numbers. But auspiciousness is also security at times, especially with ritual instructors (*matireenik*). The teachers take immediate responsibility and authority for the way things are done at that particular time, but they are embedded in the wider network of ritual knowledge and authority that is formed through initiation instruction. Ritual filiation through instruction is both hierarchical and egalitarian; both aspects come into play here. First, ritual teachers can refuse to introduce significant difference, claiming recourse and deference to their own teachers. They can claim consultation is necessary with those more senior and knowledgeable (and absent), and so effectively negate change at that time. Second, all adult women (or men) share the knowledge of the initiated and are potential *matireenik*. General participation at ceremonies, then, is a further check and constraint on change in initiation practice. Radical changes or omissions would be witnessed; the initiated company could object if they felt something was amiss.

I encountered this web of constraints when I sought permission to attend secret ceremonies. At times I met with unanimous refusal. At others, one *matiriyaat* agreed but needed her colleague's approval to admit me. As time passed, more women thought I should be allowed into their rituals. A pair of Kaplelach *matireenik* finally agreed, but in the end claimed they could not admit me without talking with their own teachers and with Kipchornwonek women. Both continuity and secrecy are protected in a way that also emphasizes sexual solidarity (Kratz 1990b).

Yet changes are introduced, and two general forums (the initiated and the elders), gathered in performance, are essential in affirming the result as nonetheless continuous and unchanged in essence from the past. If those whose memory and experience stretch furthest back can agree on appropriate procedure, even if it differs from other ceremonies, the whole is thereby canonized as appropriately reproducing the tradition of their grandparents. The important thing is consensus among those present about proper ceremonial practice, which is virtually guaranteed if things reach the point where people are assembled, beer brewed, and so forth. This means the image and primacy of tradition is necessarily confirmed, upheld, and maintained, but *not* that the ceremony continues in exactly the same form.

Over time, cumulative changes in ceremonial practice appear to be fairly extensive, but they are encountered incrementally. Each is dealt with locally and specifically, lending each in turn the legitimating aura of continuity and tradition from other aspects of practice. Okiek initiation *does* have a basic pragmatic continuity during time within memory; that enduring effect and its associated structure are a crucial foundation for imaging tradition. Okiek understanding of ceremonial tradition includes but is not undermined by changes responsive to shifting social and material circumstances. Ceremony and daily life are inseparably linked, mutually engendered and transformed. Produced both in practice and in talk about practice, this sense of continuity and tradition is intimately involved in Okiek cultural identity, their own continuity through time as a people who encounter new circumstances and neighbors with incorporative creativity and integrity.

9

Untamed Heifers and Gentle Lions: Ceremonial Transformations and Performative Efficacy

Single explanations of ritual behavior, however satisfying to the ob-
server, seem to me to deny the nature of symbolism itself and its use in
human society to express the accepted and approved as well as the hidden and denied, the rules of society and the occasional revolt against
them, the common interests of the whole community and the conflicting
interests of different parts of it.

Audrey Richards, *Chisungu*

The unifying concern of this book has been to understand the ways Okiek
make their children into adults through initiation and what that metamorphosis
means, particularly when girls become women. Exploring these questions has
meant taking a number of different perspectives, and has led through multiple
analyses and interpretations. The transformation of initiation is accomplished
within and through ceremonial structure and performance. I have argued that
this involves three key processes operating simultaneously, processes that are
differentially foregrounded and emphasized in various events and channels
but which all involve multiple media. First, through contextual re-creation,
critical cultural assumptions are represented and re-created as setting and
background to the transformation. In the process, those assumptions can be
affirmed, legitimated, sometimes reshaped, and questioned. The broader understanding and representation of initiation, cast as ceremonial tradition, helps
naturalize these assumptions as well, even if what tradition is considered to be
changes through time. In Okiek initiation, notions about cultural identity and
relations of gender and age are central to this process.

325

Semiotic movement concerns changes within the "natural" order represented and reproduced through contextual re-creation. This second key process centers on the overtly recognized and intended transformation that is accomplished by initiation. Semiotic movement is the means through which a specific change in cultural definition is accomplished, in this case from girl to woman. One social skin is stripped, as it were, and replaced by another (cf. T. Turner 1980) by changing signs associated with one culturally defined position (girl) to those associated with the other (woman), often moving through intermediate positions (for example, secluded initiate). Costumes, locations, acts that signify social relations, and ways of speaking can all figure in such significant cultural movements. Taken individually, such signs of costume, song type, and so forth are indices of particular points in the process of initiation. Taken in series, over time, they produce significant movement. In Okiek initiation, many of these progressions are specific to initiation ceremonies. However, some are also part of wider and longer progressions that stretch outside the initiation context, tying initiation to other life-cycle ceremonies and to the broader cultural context of maturation.

Semiotic movement is also critically involved with ceremonial structure, the scheduled sequence of events and combinations of media. Within events, identities are deconstructed into a number of signs in different media. The semiotic movement of initiation is carried simultaneously in different channels, in different cultural sequences that converge at the end to complete the transformation. Some shifts in those sequences are synchronized, jointly constituting and demarcating structural sections of the ceremonies. The sequence of ritual events is itself another cultural progression. Each event becomes an index of temporal and social progress through the initiation process. The transformation of initiation is accomplished by moving through these sequences.

In constituting ceremonial structure and sequence, semiotic movement dovetails with the third key process through which ritual efficacy is produced, experiential and emotional engagement. Ceremonial sequences are dramatically orchestrated, drawing participants into events of different tenors and building to emotional climaxes. The ceremonies of initiation are felt in a range of ways by different people—initiates, parents, siblings, girlfriends, boyfriends, *matireenik,* and various other guests. It is a potentially moving experience for all, at times anxious, heart-wrenching, jubilant, and intense, often combining many feelings at once. It is a test of determination, a time for convivial enjoyment and companionship, and for all a momentous change, though each person experiences it differently.[1]

Ceremonial structures and procedures that are common to every initiation are personalized and particularized through experiential and emotional engagement. At the same time, each person's particular formative experiences of initiation are universalized, becoming part of the experience of all Okiek adults (and, more generally, part of what it means to Okiek to be an adult). Individuals are joined to the collectivity of adults through the common (yet different) experience of initiation, and are involved in different initiations in different ways throughout their lives. Emotional and experiential engagement is created and shown in a variety of culturally specific ways related to ceremonial structure and performance and to different participants.

At the same time, experiential and emotional engagement incorporates and highlights the implicit and practical dimensions of ceremonies, dimensions that add evocative associations with other occasions and sensibilities to ceremonial experiences. Such "overdetermination through indetermination" (Bourdieu 1977a:110) links initiation with other contexts, drawing in other experiences and contributing to the sense of coherence and universalization that is at once felt, affirmed, and given value. Such cross-references within and beyond the initiation context are material, practical, and verbal. While they help create a sense of coherence, of tradition, and of the givenness of basic cultural assumptions, they also help concentrate and heighten individual and collective involvement.

The three key processes of ritual efficacy are separable only in analysis. Indissolubly merged in practice, they are combined in various ways in different events over the ceremonial sequence. These processes are the fundamental ways through which the transformation of initiation is jointly effected. The workings of these processes became clear through an approach that privileges communication and performance in ceremonial analysis. This approach offers a more nuanced understanding of ritual efficacy, but also contributes more generally to studies of ritual and symbolism, performance studies, and work on gender and ethnicity.

Most processual analyses of ceremonies have built on the base provided by van Gennep, either stressing major ritual phases (as in his distinctions of separation, liminality, and reincorporation) or elaborating on the social significance of particular phases (for instance, communitas and liminality). Examining the communicative modalities of ceremonies closely in performance provides a more fine-grained sense of such general phases, and also reveals other processes and accentuations that are simultaneously part of ceremonial experience. This emphasis on communicative modalities shows how actors organize meaning and experience in ceremonies. It draws attention to cultural idioms through which ceremonial transformations and effects are represented, to the ways actors use those cultural idioms, and to the different media involved, their interrelations, and their differential and combined contributions to the power and efficacy of ritual. The emphasis also encourages and facilitates explorations of other important questions: how frames and keys are created, how the contradictions and ambiguities of multiple perspectives are accommodated in performance, and how the texture and density of performance is produced and made effective through multiple media.

Methodologically, close attention to communicative channels and resources in ceremonial analysis makes clear the constitution of ceremonial structure (what might be called ceremonial structuration, to adapt Giddens's term [1979, 1984]), revealing diverse and intersecting scales of structure that range from ritual acts, events, and ceremonies to patterns of language use in particular speeches and events and over ceremonial sequences. Crosscutting, coordinated, and sequential interrelations among these different structural levels and elements create a complex orchestration that incorporates the potential of efficacy into ceremonial structure in ways that are realized in performance and are understood and felt in various ways by those involved. The interrelations are both macrolevel and microlevel ones; they are forged within and between media and within and between events, through aspects such as poetic structure, thematic patterns, and aspects of communicative context. Regard for interweavings among communicative media can demonstrate how poetic patterns dispersed throughout ceremonies are joined with other modes of ceremonial structure in creating ceremonial effects. Ceremonial phases are more than progressions of symbols and themes; they simultaneously involve pragmatic progressions, dramatic orchestration, and different modes of engagement that are created through multimedia performances.

To understand those modes of engagement and the working of that orchestration entails attention to the intentions and viewpoints of various participants. Such attention to "the sophisticated way that performers and audiences use poetic patterning in interpreting the structure and significance of their own discourse" is intrinsic to an approach that concentrates on ceremonial performances, taking an "agent-centered view of performance" (Bauman and Briggs 1990:69–70). This attention to performers, audiences, and performances brings out several important points about efficacy and agency in initiation. First, Okiek initiates appear to have greater capacity for influencing and making certain choices in ceremonial proceedings than is acknowledged in most analyses of initiation. More generally, analyses of performances show that participants' involvement and the influences they have on others participating are an integral part of ritual efficacy. Their choices and involvements are part of the orchestration of experiential and emotional engagement, their influences part of interactive intensification.

Second, it becomes clear in looking at particular performances not only that meaning is emergent, but also that the understandings that emerge in ceremonial performance are multifaceted and sometimes contradictory, and can include a certain ambivalence on the part of those involved. In several cases, ambivalence and contradictory, unofficial views are apparent only by listening to side channels and comments from a participating and engaged audience. Contradictions between official and unofficial versions of gender relations emerge perhaps most heatedly during encouraging speeches; in the burlesque of *pesenweek* confessions, contradictions related to age are part of the event's very structure. These multiple meanings, multiple purposes, and contradictory interpretations contribute to the tenor of the events and also figure in the larger ceremonial orchestration of ritual efficacy. Yet they would be lost in analyses that do not consider actual performances and multiple perspectives.

Two further points arise from listening to the unofficial voices and contradictions that emerge in ceremonial performance. Ceremonies are indeed ways through which important social transformations are achieved, but they are not always (or perhaps ever) successful in ideal terms. Ideal images of gender roles and relations are central to Okiek initiation, but the unofficial views that are simultaneously part of ceremonial performances suggest that initiates and other participants alike may also have perspectives that counter or contradict assumptions that inform those images. Those perspectives may arise from simultaneous locations within multiple social relations or from multiple desires and intentions (both matters of social integration), or may be associated with other ideal assumptions and structural principles (matters of system integration). The clearest example of the latter in Okiek initiation is the incompatibility of assumptions about gender and those about adulthood and initiation. Contradiction and conflict are not the same, however, and do not necessarily go together (Giddens 1979:144–45). Contradictions that emerge in ceremonial performances do not always entail open confrontation or contest.

Ritual events always proceed with more than one definition because they always involve more than one perspective. Nonetheless, one perspective (or set of perspectives) becomes recognized as the "official" one (at least for some particular time and context). The establishment of an official perspective implies that differences of power and authority are also re-created during ceremonial performances. The key processes of ritual efficacy are entwined in the dramatic orchestration of ceremonies in ways that privilege certain interpretations and perspectives and help persuade participants of the naturalness and traditionalness of certain relations of power and authority.

In Okiek initiation, relations of power and authority are defined and represented principally in terms of gender, age, and ethnicity; most contradictions emerge at the intersections of these social dimensions of power and authority. The temporal and processual outlook inherent in performance analyses helps to show how different definitions and issues of power, authority, and inequality arise and become linked in ceremonies. Over the course of initiation, gender, intercultural relations, and age are differentially highlighted in the events, sections, and ceremonies of initiation, but even when emphases shift, issues represented in other parts of initiation continue to resonate. One way they continue to resonate is through the use of related poetic resources and patterns built on the use of corresponding communicative means.

Questions of Okiek cultural identity especially come into focus when initiation is set within a regional context and a longer temporal span, manifested in how Okiek represent tradition. Okiek concentrate their notions of tradition in two central domains, which interconnect in multiple ways: ceremonies (particularly initiation) and their forest abode and life as hunters and honey-gatherers (Kratz 1993). The two become entwined in Okiek cultural identity. The tradition of forest life also entails representations of gender and age, representations that reverberate with and support those central to initiation. In initiation, the two domains of tradition unite in seclusion, when initiates enmeshed in the ceremonial process live a forest-centered life. A liminal forest- or bush-dwelling period during initiation is common to many cultures, but in this case it is also overlaid with notions of cultural identity. Representations of ceremonial tradition help create a sense of continuity through history, with a forest-resonant life in the present that recalls the more forest-reliant life of the past.

Both arenas of Okiek tradition incorporate an essential dialectic and tension. First, Okiek forest life is inextricably set within the regional network of interethnic relations with their neighbors, where Okiek are placed by others on the bottom rung of a hierarchy of status and prestige. Okiek understandings reinterpret and invert these views, at the same time recognizing and in essence acquiescing to them through the inversion. They redefine the tension of complementarity and hierarchy as one of similarity and difference. Nonetheless, hierarchical views still inform wider Okiek relations and possibilities.

With an antihierarchical, relativistic attitude toward cultural difference, Okiek have incorporated elements of their neighbors' lifeways into their own. The incorporations are part of an intricate cultural bricolage through which they reshape or redefine the elements in an Okiek idiom, both facilitating their interactions and perpetuating the attitudes of their neighbors toward them. Kipchornwonek and Kaplelach are at once uniquely themselves and yet somehow resemble their neighbors. Their contemporary lives are in part the product of their past histories and present engagements with close Kipsigis and Maasai neighbors and, on a broader scale, of their direct and mediated involvements with colonial interventions and modern national development. These processes of bricolage, representation, and ongoing reinterpretation are not unique to Okiek, but are among the ways people in every culture understand, shape, re-create, and modify their sense of themselves, their lives, and their changing circumstances.

Ceremonial practice is the second domain of tradition and cultural identity. It includes the same dialectic between similarity and difference and the same tolerant attitude toward variation. Indeed, Okiek initiation incldes that very cultural bricolage, incorporating elements of Kipsigis initiation practice, new products, and so on. For Okiek, tradition in initiation is defined by a broad similarity and continuity that has room for individual differences, family variations, and the incorporation of changes over time. The image of tradition emerges from a joint dialectic, between similarity and difference, on the one hand, and between past and present (projected toward the future), on the other. Okiek cultural identity weaves together their own experiences and history with their neighbors' cultural traditions and practices as part of both experience and history.

From Calves to Wild Cows

The analyses in part 3 concentrated on particular ritual events, looking at the arrangements, workings, and effects of the key processes of ritual efficacy in each part of initiation. While I regularly related these focused analyses to broader processes throughout initiation, some closing comments are needed on several wider, linked patterns that are also related to initiation's ritual efficacy: (1) a larger sort of parallelism in performance that draws together a number of ritual events; (2) the shifting emphases on gender, age, and cultural identity over the course of initiation; and (3) a related progression of dominant metaphors that can be traced throughout initiation's transformative process.

The focused analyses identified a diverse range of formal devices, thematic repertoires, and poetic structures in different media, all of which contribute to the efficacy of ceremonial performances. Some are common to a number of ritual events, though their particular functions and effects vary. In the speech of initiation, for instance, relatively few resources were involved, including semantic and grammatical parallelism, thematic repetition and variation, syntactic fronting, interrogative constructions, quoted and reported speech, sound similarity and assonance, varied displays of emotion, and strategic silence. People use and combine them in different ways, however, in different events and ways of speaking. Those patterns of use help define ritual events and the ceremonial progression through their differences.

At the same time, common forms and themes bind different events together into a whole. Relations of poetic structure, cross-reference, and shared idioms create a framework of continuity spanning the ceremonial progression. Within that framework, thematic shifts help reorient and shape the central concerns of different parts of initiation, for example, as thematic shifts in the initiates' songs do, going from girls' songs to *kaiyantaaita* (seclusion songs). Similarly, thematic narrowing and concentration within parts of the progression can influence and contribute to dramatic quickenings and affective tensions. Such relations, along with multiple thematic references and invocations (both verbal and nonverbal), contribute to the abiding sense of coherence that emerges from Okiek initiation, providing a kind of refractive repetition in different communicative modes. The particular scheduling of these refractive repetitions is essential to dramatic pace and affective meter and is central to ceremonial experience and effect. The overall combination into ceremonies and events scheduled in relation to one another creates the transformative movement of initiation over time.

That combination is organized in part as a kind of emergent parallelism writ large, in a performative sense. In chapter 7 I discussed emergent parallelism in initiation songs, a poetic-pragmatic form that results from the combination in performance of call lines drawn from a small set of thematic-pragmatic groups that are themselves built with a limited range of grammatical constructions and root verbs. A related kind of organization links ritual events across Okiek initiation, contributing to the production of ritual efficacy through performance. This is most obvious in the first ceremony. As in the song parallelism, a small number of themes are repeated, dispersed through a number of events with minor shifts from one event to another. These common themes are raised and addressed by different participants in each event, often in common idioms, though not identically. To extend the analogy with song parallelism, the varied participants would correspond to the varied call lines of songs. In fact, initiates' sung good-byes, during which the emergent parallelism of song appears most clearly and insistently, are part of the larger performative parallelism.

The themes that are most consistently foregrounded give the ceremony as a whole an urgent and predominant force that concentrates on the initiates in the form of a directive, a unanimous request-command-exhortation awaiting their single decisive response in dawn bravery. Different sets of participants are drawn into the ceremony in turn, in different events, each expressing and responding to the common themes in their own ways. The different events and participants emphasize various facets of this directive, with persuasive pulls appropriate to each relationship with the girls. Throughout, initiates are always represented in a position of willful choice, and are ever the focus of everyone's directives.

What emerges over the course of the first ceremony is precisely that increasing unanimity, which becomes clearer over time as each person joins in the differentiated chorus, speaking, singing, and acting in ways that are appropriate to their age, gender, and relationship to the initiates and are also appropriate to the ritual event. In girls' songs, the poetic form and pragmatic force of parallelism emerge over time and can continue and repeat indefinitely. The performative parallelism also emerges over time, over the course of the ceremony, but its trajectory is more directionally defined; it emerges through and is part of the orchestrated movement through the ceremonial sequence, taking the girls forward toward the moment when there is no longer any real choice. The changes of participants and the order in which they add their voices are also part of the pragmatic effect of the performative parallelism, adding to the growing force of expectations focused on the girls and the engagement of other participants. This performative parallelism traces the broad trajectory of interactive intensification during the first ceremony. Again, this broader parallelism is simultaneously part of the poetic-dramatic form of ceremonies and critical to their pragmatic effects.

Similar kinds of emergent performative parallelism can be traced across events in the other initiation ceremonies as well, though different themes are foregrounded in seclusion and at coming-out. In each case, the central themes are part of the permutation of emphases in the process of contextual re-creation discussed above and also part of a progression of dominant metaphors over the course of initiation. These broader structures are produced through the ordered combination of ritual events, each event having complex and interconnected communicative patterns. The result is a ceremonial whole that is greater than its parts, an effective structure through which Okiek work the transformation of initiation in performance.

The differential foregrounding of gender, age, and cultural identity goes hand in hand with related shifts in the unofficial views and contradictions that emerge at different moments during initiation (for example, views of women as courageous and competent, or of children as righteous rebels; contradictions between gender differences and common adulthood through initiation, or between the equality of initiated adults and hierarchies of age). As gender, age, and intercultural relations are each highlighted in turn during initiation, the interlinkages among modes of authority, power, and hierarchy that are related to these themes of initiation are represented and re-created. The shifts in foregrounding show that each of these three themes—gender, age, and intercultural relations—involves a central tension between representation as equality and complementarity and representation as hierarchy and differential authority. Each theme presents a different permutation, but one basis of their interlinkages is the structural similarity of these different relations of inequality. The different representations mentioned above can be coordinated simultaneously or sequentially in the interplay through different media and perspectives, and appear in ways that may seem either consistent or contradictory. The contradictions themselves remain unresolved, emerging in other contexts as well. The different perspectives that come together in contradiction are continuing sources of diverse interpretations, interests, and motivations informing social life.

Interethnic relations and cultural identity emerge as themes in the opening section of initiation's first ceremony, but they are more muted in actual performances than themes of gender and age. Cultural identity becomes critical, however, in broader Okiek understandings of initiation, history, and tradition. The dialectic of Okiek ethnic identity relies on the trick of perspective. Okiek interrelations with their neighbors can be seen in terms of hierarchy, denigration, and dominance on the one hand, and on the other hand in terms of equality and complementarity, relativity, and accommodation. Their neighbors see only one side of the coin, but both perspectives are included in the Okiek view of things.

Gender-inflected versions of cultural identity are at the core of Okiek initiation, with a related contradiction characterizing Okiek gender relations. Initiation's first ceremony especially emphasizes Okiek notions of gender, with a later stress on relations of age that carries through seclusion. The process ends with an accent on gender again as young women emerge from seclusion and enter the sphere of adult gender relations through marriage. Unlike interethnic interactions, which are often intermittent even if regular, gender relations are centrally constitutive of daily Okiek life. What might be seen in the realm of interethnic relations and cultural identity as an interplay of contrary views becomes here a more critical tension, one in which age is implicated as well. That tension has further ramifications for the way discrepancies in power and authority are played out and felt in Okiek life.

The complementarity and interdependence of men and women in production and reproduction is set against a gendered hierarchy in access to and control of material and sociopolitical resources. The hierarchy is established through a social organization based on patrilineages and age-sets. The cultural basis and legitimation of this skewing lies in an essentialist argument about the nature and capabilities of men and women, an argument that is justified and made self-evident through the restricted possibilities of that social organization.

In both boys' and girls' initiation, norms of conduct consonant with the male-oriented hierarchy are articulated and inculcated, but women's initiation is also a context that blatantly contradicts the assumptions on which it is based. Contrary to the image of women as incapable of decisionmaking, cooperation, or collective accomplishment, their seclusion ceremonies demonstrate their ability for independent organization and action. The idea that women conform unfailingly to the norms they are taught is belied by the vehemence of some seclusion lectures to female initiates, especially regarding sexual fidelity and unquestioning obedience to their husbands.[2]

Initiation is the primary occasion when the unity of women is constituted and reaffirmed in a ritual community, and it is also a singular challenge to the received view of gender roles and relations. For men, the gathering for boys' initiation is one among many. Challenged with women's ritual community and ceremonial organization, men sometimes try to evaluate the trials and secrets of initiation hierarchically as well, introducing a male priority. The attempt is joking or halfhearted, however, in partial realization of the inherent contradiction between assumptions about adulthood and assumptions about gender. This contradiction, along with related ambivalences, also emerges in initiation ceremonies—in speeches to the girls, side comments, joking attacks on women's ritual house, and other places. The situation highlights the contradiction and brings out tensions ordinarily defused by the dispersal of women among households. Women's abilities and strength of will are at once recognized and denied.

The experience and knowledge of elders and ritual leaders give them an authority of age that is incorporated into ceremonial structure and also recreated by their ceremonial roles. Clefts and contradictions of age first become salient during the uproarious confession of social debts (*pesenweek*). The norms prescribing respectful obedience from children and reasonable behavior from adults are simultaneously countered and supported by accounts of willful independence, petty arguments, insistent coercion, and refusals by children that are often quite reasonable.

Throughout the seclusion ceremonies—and beginning on the night of the first ceremony, when *matireenik* conduct the girls into women's house of ritual—interconnections between authority based on age and gender are foregrounded, with a permutation in the principal contradiction of gender relations. In seclusion, the focus is on the dialectic between intrasexual equality and the hierarchy of authority based on age. Within the ritual communities of initiated women and initiated men, sexual solidarity is forged and focused through shared trials and secrets that exclude the opposite sex. It is consolidated through continued ceremonial participation throughout their lives. Initiation is a formative experience, the grounding of an irrevocable equality among women or among men; all share equally in the ritual knowledge of the initiated.[3] Solidarity created through shared experience and knowledge is fundamental in creating the ritual community. Yet that basic equality is differentiated and hierarchical as well, with distinctions of authority created through differential control and access to initiation secrets. A hierarchy of ritual knowledge is defined within each sex by the correlated dimensions of age and experience, which are also relevant to Okiek social relations more generally.

As initiates are shown initiation secrets and taught secret songs, their equality with other adult women is built within the hierarchical relation between initiates and ritual teachers. Even as they near the end of seclusion, however, and are increasingly familiar with the secrets, a disparity of knowledge remains, concentrated and embodied in *ceemaasiit* (the wild creature).

The last secret, *ceemaasiit* remains hidden until initiation is virtually complete, held back but present through its threatening roar. This final distinction of ritual knowledge is removed only at the last secret ceremony of coming-out, when each initiate sees it, holds it, and herself produces *ceemaasiit*'s roar. This completes the shared experience of secrets that is the basis of sexual equality and solidarity within their ritual community. All secrets at last are shared as initiates reach the juncture of adulthood, leaving the seclusion world to reenter ordinary daily life in their new status. *Ceemaasiit* is an appropriate finale to the constitution of new adults not only because it combines secrets of sight and sound but also because of the associations and double entendre of its name.

Initiates are painted like wild forest creatures (*ceemaasiisyek*) during seclusion, and this other wild creature is disclosed just before the initiates themselves are to be shown publicly. Their new adult roles are closely bound up with marriage, legitimate sexual relations, and reproduction. In other contexts, *ceemaasiit* can be a joking euphemism for either male or female sex organs (but more commonly men's). Both men and women have their own secret *ceemaasiit*, each iconically appropriate to the sexual innuendo of the name. The name and form of the final secret, then, play on the imminent unleashing of young adult sexuality; for young women, it is unleashed and at once bridled reproductively within the confines of marriage.

The hierarchy of knowledge is leveled with the revelation of this final secret, but the authority of age and experience is disarmed only temporarily. When initiates come from the river, gender again becomes the focus that is advertised and celebrated. At last shown publicly as young adults, wearing the ritual costume of Okiek women, initiates are reunited with adults of the opposite sex through ritual acts and materials that recall the history of Okiek forest life.

Just as different sections of initiation highlight different cultural assumptions and social relations, each resonant with particular contradictions and ambivalences, so, too, a related sequence of dominant images or metaphors characterizes movement through the ceremonial sections. At once an overarching feature of the progression of initiation and inscribed in the particulars of speech and action during the ceremonies, these metaphors are already familiar from my detailed analyses of ritual events, where they were encountered in a variety of forms. As initiation proceeds, the dominant metaphor shifts: children (calves) begin their journey to adulthood, become wild creatures, and then return as heifers (women) or young lions (men). Metaphors prominent in earlier sections do not disappear, but carry through as linked undertones.

The opening ceremony highlights the journey metaphor, which informs the entire initiation process. The opening procession prefigures the odyssey initiates will travel, from home to forest and back again, an odyssey of identity that leads them through the most Okiek of spatial domains to return as adults. The dangers of the journey and the bravery it requires are emphasized in the songs and speech of the first ceremony; fear of the knife and its pain are most immediately pertinent. Ritual events lead up to the journey's difficult and painful start, when initiates leave their childhood home, friends, and familiar life behind. Their decisive bravery at dawn is the last farewell, showing that they are indeed ready for the journey. As children, initiates are called calves in song; male initiates are called both calves and lion cubs, epithets that will come up again later.

During seclusion, the journey continues with a sojourn in the forest, a domain often represented as potentially dangerous, with frightening wild creatures. Yet the forest is also the nurturant, familiar home of Okiek. The forest and the secrets of seclusion dominate this second section of initiation, combined in the hidden wild creature, *ceemaasiit*.

Leading hidden lives like wild creatures, at ease only in the forest (and living there if male initiates), initiates become *ceemaasiisyek* in seclusion. Costume and body paint camouflage their humanity and identity. They compete with birds in morning and evening songs, and stay together like animals in a pack or flock. In songs, the journey continues in esoteric verbal form. A journey of flash and noise, of violent and sudden danger, becomes a slow, silent journey of respect. Along the way, the hidden initiates are shown the secrets that confer the adult equality and status they claimed as they started the journey.

Initiates demonstrate adult ability through their concentration of will at the cut of the blade, and thereby earn equality. Yet the force of will demonstrated equally by each adult introduces a social wildness of absolute equality that is tamed through hierarchical distinction. The central dynamic of this section of initiation establishes that hierarchy within equality, inculcating obedience and respect in initiates and controlling them as junior members. The secrets are the central means through which this is done, with *ceemaasiit,* the wild creature, always held back to maintain and reinforce the initiates' inexperience and ignorance until the end.

The "natural" differences between men and women and appropriate gender relations are also part of seclusion teachings. When initiates come out of seclusion, processional songs summarize these distinctions with different metaphors for the new adults. Girls become heifers to be given in marriage or stolen through elopement, while boys prance as young lions. Men always retain something of the wild and the forest—roaming more widely, encountering the unknown, finding food from the forest, and enjoying a social power and position that is in some ways predatory on the complementarity of household production. Yet (ideally) they bring home the yields of their travels and of the forest. The power and strength of the lion and his productive promise are tempered to a gentler nurturance, contributing to complementary production.

When they emerge at the end of the journey, the wild creatures of female seclusion are domesticated and desirable, with reproductive promise. Women are far more valuable than any real cow, but men nonetheless exchange women for cows. The bovine idiom continues into the negotiation of marriage arrangements. Yet marriage is not a peaceable kingdom. The heifers are indeed soon taken by lions, but their continued domestication is always an ongoing process, and sometimes a struggle.

Appendixes

Appendix A discusses the political debate over excision and circumcision and frames it within the broader realm of culturally specified notions of identity and maturity. Appendixes B through E consist of selected transcriptions from tape recordings made during Okiek initiation ceremonies between 1983 and 1985, with facing English translations. Key examples are also incorporated into tables in the main text for convenient reference. These transcriptions provide more complete contextualization, additional examples, and material for considering other questions related to the language of Okiek ceremonies. They also constitute the first extensive published collection of Okiek texts and one of the few published collections of African-language texts to include language recorded in use in a variety of contexts. Conventions of transcription are in each case those noted in the main text.

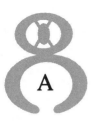

Initiation and Circumcision

This book is about Okiek initiation, which includes circumcision for boys and excision for girls. For Okiek (and for the Kenyans who share the practice), the operations are a central initiation trial, creating a permanent physical sign differentiating adults from children. It is also a critical sign that marks them off from East African peoples who do not associate adulthood with circumcision. While this book is not about circumcision or excision per se, I do want to address some of the many issues that have been raised about circumcision practices.

Currently, most debates center on female circumcision. While a number of constituencies and influences have contributed over time to the ways in which these debates are formulated, most recently they have been taken into and associated with feminist politics. The contemporary debates concern political action: what (if anything) can and should be done about female circumcision, and by whom? In much of this literature, circumcision is treated as the same phenomenon in all places, and is redefined as "genital mutilation"; male dominance and oppression are the proposed explanations for the practice. Political discourse about circumcision, however, is much older and more widespread than many contemporary writers seem to realize, and the current debates have roots in other issues and controversies.

Discourses about both male and female circumcision are located more generally within histories of the body and understandings of the body as a site of signification. These discourses are connected at different times and in different places with specific understandings of other realms that might include reproduction, sexuality, adulthood, motherhood, power, religion, and diverse kinds of identity. The ways in which circumcision articulates with those understandings can be very different, making any single interpretation of circumcision everywhere both elusive and misleading. Boon notes the difficulties of universal interpretations of circumcising practices: "circumcision/noncircumcision, much more than a logical opposition, could be made to represent rhetorical, religious, and political antitheses." For instance, "in the sixteenth century, [male] circumcision at times separated Christian/ Muslim in Europe and Muslim/Hindu in Indonesia" (Boon 1990:58–60).

Just as there is no single interpretation of circumcision, neither is there a single political solution to "the issue of female circumcision." Birth complications and other long-term health problems that have been linked to some form of female circumcision are real, but the rhetoric through which female circumcision has been constituted as an issue is often so problematic that the associated strategies and their consequences must be questioned and examined closely. For instance, graphic descriptions of "genital mutilation" (Hosken 1979, 1981; Sanderson 1981) figure prominently; they are sensationalistic images intended to help mobilize political action. They are given little or no contextualization, however, and are used without careful consideration of the power relations assumed, the results of the representations disseminated, or the repercussions of failed campaigns. Such images make it difficult to bracket the referents they describe (and so disarm some critical impulses), but such bracketing is necessary to examine the rhetorical strategies in which they figure.

The rhetorical argument against female circumcision is presented most clearly by international action groups; it proceeds as follows. First, the mode of defining the issue simultaneously constitutes two singular, monolithic objects out of many different situations and circumstances: "third world women" and "female circumcision." In creating the latter, the objectifying form of scientific language is wedded to graphic images and strongly worded evaluations. A set of reasons and justifications for female circumcision are then reported and countered, with a call to international action on behalf of women throughout the world. Each of these rhetorical moves needs to be considered, but first some of their historical antecedents should be identified.

The recent resurgence of anticircumcision activity began in the 1970s, buoyed by the United Nations Decade of Women (1975–1985), but it continues a much longer tradition of missionary and colonial opposition. In Kenya, for instance, debates about circumcision began almost as soon as missionaries arrived, and were framed within the question of whether (and which) local customs violated standards of Christian behavior and had to be condemned and eliminated. Female circumcision became the center of controversy in Kikuyu areas in the 1920s and 1930s, the debates formed as much by interests and efforts in England as by local factions (Murray 1974). Current feminist campaigns may not recognize the continuities, but their rhetoric depends on arguments and images that were also central to colonial and missionary projects, complete with implicit evolutionary scales and notions of "progress" defined by their own criteria and values. Looking at the burgeoning of American evangelical women's associations in the post–Civil War period, Brumberg outlines a movement with an essentially middle-class spirit and a rhetoric very similar to that of contemporary anticircumcision literature. Those women focused their condemnation on a slightly different list of "characteristic atrocities" toward women in other countries, but they too "revitalized cultural stereotypes that were either dormant or had never really disappeared" (Brumberg 1982:349). While anticircumcision campaigns today may not illustrate their arguments with an actual " 'moral map' of the world," (a colorful graphic device and popular teaching aid in the antebellum evangelical women's groups) (Ibid.:354), the hierarchical mental map is still implicit.

Images of third world women in circumcision campaigns often combine notions of progress with feminist values defined in Western contexts. Mohanty (1988) and Stephens (1989) discuss the constitution of third world women as an object of contemporary feminist scholarship. The concept is formed by homogenizing divergent circumstances and assuming women to be a preexistent, coherent group with shared interests and desires. This also requires removing the concept of "woman" from any specific cultural context, and isolating it from related notions that help form understandings of gender. Erasing differences based on nationality, class, ethnicity, religion, or age, the average third world woman emerges as a contrast to elite women, largely but not exclusively Western. This average woman lives in a village, carries heavy loads, bears many children, and "leads an essentially truncated life based on her feminine gender (read: sexually constrained) and being 'third world' (read: ignorant, poor, uneducated, tradition-bound, religious, domesticated, family-oriented, victimized, etc.)" (Mohanty 1988:65). A great divide lies between these women, who are the victims of practices redefined as genital mutilation, and other women born in the third world who have joined the campaign against it. The latter are seen as being self-conscious, making choices, and having agency, while the former are portrayed as powerless, constrained by a tradition defined by men, unable to think clearly, and having only problems and needs, not choices. Their oppression joins them into one group—spanning several continents, and myriad religious, political, economic, and social situations—though they do not yet recognize it.

This rhetorical creation of third world women emerges in literature on several topics. In this case, what defines and unites the oppressed group is its shared victimization through "female circumcision." Female circumcision is the second discursively created object, constituted by extracting fragments from many different cultural practices. The fragments all concern genital modification but may share little else, being taken from diverse sociopolitical contexts. In other versions, an even broader category (for example, crimes of gender) is used to link female circumcision, purdah, rape, dowry deaths, arranged marriage, preference for male births, and domestic violence (Heise 1989). Thus isolated and combined, the fragments are reconstituted into "female circumcision" through a seemingly objective, universal discourse about women's bodies that is defined through scientific, medical language. Clinical descriptions rearrange the fragments into three types of operations (circumcision, excision, infibulation) and map them geographically. In the process of being isolated and medicalized, the fragments are redefined not only as female circumcision but judged and revalued into mutilation. This move defines and assumes a universal moral high ground, and simultaneously relocates female circumcision into an international arena for condemnation and political action.

The notion of "third world women" is relevant to this redefinition. Only women who have no choice, agency, or consciousness—precisely the third world women image that is created—would submit to such practice. Because they are unable to act for themselves, international action is intended to deliver them from mutilation. (This language brings to mind parallels to the rhetoric of Operation Rescue's antiabortion campaigns, as well as that of missionary evangelists.) Yet related Western practices such as breast reduction or enhancement, multiple ear piercings, and body piercings (including genital piercings) are "modifications" that are seen as ways to "take control" (Gladsjo 1991; cf. di Leonardo 1991d:151; Reed 1992:26, 33–34 notes similar double standards in U.S. poverty research and policy). These self-definitions are much closer to some local definitions of circumcision in initiation as a sign of self-control, change, and maturation. Like circumcision, the Western practices are also linked to understandings of the body, sexuality, and gender relations, but the understandings are rather different, as are their social and institutional settings.

Defining circumcision as mutilation also has a longer history and wider distribution, and is not limited to female circumcision. Male circumcision has also been a political issue in cross-cultural contests of definition; arguments about male "mutilation" sometimes parallel those about female circumcision. In the first century, for instance, male circumcision practiced by Jews was the center of controversy. "In direct contrast to Roman accusations that circumcision was a mutilation of the body that made men ugly, the Rabbinic texts emphasize over and over that the operation removes something ugly from the male body" (Boyarin 1992:496). The Rabbinic emphasis is echoed by Sudanese women in the 1980s who "assert that [circumcision] is performed on young girls so as to make their bodies clean (naẓīf), smooth (nāᶜim), and pure (ṭahir)" (Boddy 1989:55). The two stances toward circumcision—as ugly multilation or as beautifying cleansing—often recur when people with different understandings of the body encounter one another. Such opposed views (external versus internal; allegedly universal versus particular) often dominate political confrontations, but cross-cultural encounters also entail the possibility of informed critique. Critiques may be directed to the categories of discussion and analysis as well as to institutions and practices, and may be generated internally as well as through intercultural experiences. To be an effective basis for change, however, critiques need to address and engage the understandings and interests of those involved.

Using decontextualized fragments to create the medicalized notion of female circumcision obliterates local explanations. A set of universally applicable reasons and justifications are advanced instead to explain the widespread practice that has been constituted. Local understandings of adulthood and marriage are "erroneous beliefs" to be challenged (Sanderson 1981:113), and the real root cause of female circumcision is clear:

Female circumcision has its origin in the male desire to control female sexuality. Throughout time, men have contrived various means to accomplish this end: the early Romans slipped rings through the labia majora of their female slaves to prevent impregnation; the Crusaders in the 12th century designed the chastity belt to thwart unsanctioned sex. And in present-day Africa, young girls are mutilated to dampen their sexual desire and ensure their virginity until marriage—an absolute necessity in most traditional African and Muslim cultures. (Heise 1989:18; cf. also Sanderson 1981:48–52)

Evidence for these assertions and information on the means through which "traditional African and Muslim" men "contrived" and have perpetuated this state of affairs are absent—which of Africa's diverse cultures are included? at what period? Systematic information about a variety of topics that bear on such claims is also absent—for example, different contexts and representations of circumcision, ways in which marriages are contracted, alternatives to marriage, women's supposed and actual sexual autonomy within marriage, attitudes that different people take towards sex, and so on. All these are highly variable in Africa, however, and a single cause for female circumcision would be difficult to suppport in the face of detailed information.

A parallel argument about male circumcision and control of sexual passion was once advanced just as insistently by theologians and philosophers:

Philo offers four standard explanations and defenses of the practice, all of which promote rational and universal reasons for being circumcised. . . . [In one, he] argues that circumcision both symbolizes and effects the excision of the passions— that is, it symbolizes the reduction of all passion by effecting in the flesh of the penis a reduction of sexual passion. (Boyarin 1992:486–87).

I doubt that many circumcised men today would agree that the operation reduces sexual passion. What is often ambiguous and unclear in the linkages asserted is whether circumcision is supposed to affect sexual desire, sexual pleasure, sexual activity, or some combination of these.

Sex is a topic that Okiek men and women alike speak of with relish, indicating that they enjoy it. Before initiation, girls can sleep with their boyfriends, but childhood pregnancy is considered shameful. Women mentioned no differences in their sexual experiences before and after initiation, but I did not explicitly ask them about it. While some other Kenyans told me initiation is a way to "keep women at home" (again ambiguous), Okiek did not talk about initiation or circumcision in terms of dampening sexual pleasure or desire (whether for men or for women). Rather, they spoke of women's excision in terms of cleanliness, beauty, and adulthood. They saw genital modification and the bravery and self-control displayed during the operation as constitutive experiences of adult Okiek personhood. The larger initiation process, intended to teach children proper adult behavior, certainly has implications for adult sexual activity because it helps define appropriate partners. Nonetheless, though extramarital affairs are officially met with disapproval, both women and men noted that such affairs are not uncommon.

Purported universal explanations for circumcision that portray it as a means of sexual control assume a single (Western) understanding of sexuality for all women. The same picture of third world women as passive, oppressed creatures also undergirds the explanations at the same time that the assumptions about sexuality help confirm it. Boddy identifies some of the difficulties with this in her work in northern Sudan:

[I]t is only partially correct to view the operation and the context it reproduces as vehicles of women's subordination; circumcision and its social implications are strategically used by women as bargaining tools with which to negotiate subaltern status and enforce their complementarity with men. Most view circumcision less as a source of oppression (after all, none has experienced adulthood intact) than one of fulfillment, however difficult this is for Western readers, imbued with Western notions of sexuality and self-realization, to comprehend. And women saw men's attempts to regulate their activities [by reducing the severity of circumcision from "pharaonic" (infibulation) to "sunna" operations] as trespass on women's preserve. . . . [T]here was considerable debate of the issue among women, and a tacit condemnation of the suggested innovation. (Boddy 1989:319)

Neither women's roles in perpetuating practices that include circumcision nor the ideological complexities involved in each case can be overlooked if political action aimed at eradicating circumcision is to have any effect. Rather, they are important loci from which analysis, critique, and action might be generated. The decontextualized fragments from which the concept of female circumcision was created must be recontextualized, and their places within specific social, political, and economic circumstances considered. There is no single "solution," despite international conferences, recommendations, and calls for legislative abolition.

What is called female circumcision is part of numerous and diverse cultural practices and ceremonies, each differentially embedded in specific institutional and social structures. While an international campaign of consciousness-raising may be worthwhile, no single strategy and no simple legal abolition of female circumcision will work. The different forms and locations must be taken into account, and the women involved must help define as well as make choices and strategies for eliminating or replacing the operations. "It is on the basis of such context-specific differentiated analysis that effective political strategies can be generated" (Mohanty 1988:74–75).

In identifying the "multiple constraints and agencies" involved (di Leonardo 1991d:152) in cultural practices that include circumcision, some political actions can also be recognized as having other, adverse consequences that are contrary to broader goals. For instance, were Okiek girls' initiation to be abolished because it includes excision, the primary context in which women come together as a group, constituting a ritual community and a forum for social critique, would also disappear. Criticisms voiced during women's secret rituals may not change the gendered structures of power and inequality, but the forum is still an important model through which women can explore and define their experiences (cf. Cott 1977:201).

The longer political history of female circumcision in Kenya is another factor that influences contemporary national actions. Kikuyu female circumcision became a prominent symbol of anticolonial sentiment when the Church of Scotland Mission and some segments of the Church Missionary Society tried to prohibit the practice in the 1910s and 1920s (Murray 1974, 1976). Jomo Kenyatta, later president of Kenya from independence in 1963 until 1979, was involved in the controversy, opposing colonial intervention in Kikuyu custom. The antiabolition movement became an impetus for starting independent schools and churches. Locally, this controversy was also related to changing notions of the body and shifting social relations (for example, marriage patterns and the waning of *ngweko* [sexual play between young people]) (Luise White, personal communication). Since 1979, the Kenyan government has periodically conducted campaigns against female circumcision with Christian and colonial overtones, sometimes banning female circumcision but with little success (for example, in 1982).

In other areas of Kenya currently, women and families often decide not to circumcise their daughters in the context of Christian evangelization and conversion. This linkage raises additional questions of ideology, social and political context, and other gendered power relations. The decision is sometimes associated with education as well. To appreciate and address the questions raised by female circumcision in Okiek initiation, then, requires an understanding of Okiek notions of gender and adulthood, of Okiek history and social organization, of their sociopolitical relations in regional and national settings, and of Okiek ceremonies of initiation and the ways they figure in those notions and relations. This book pursues those issues and understandings.

Blessings

Transcriptions of Blessings*

1. Girls' ceremony at Arap Oloso's, 1 July 1983.
Blessing of *mabwaita* by Korodo (Kap Kwonyo lineage, *il terito* age-set) and
Kwampat Sembui (Rana family, Kap Oldyo lineage, *il terito* age-set). The first
is in Okiek, said in Kipsigis style. The second is in Maa.

A. Korodo

kiim	(kiim)
kiim	(kiim)
kiim	(kiim)
tuumto	(tuumto)
ne pa saantetny'uun	(. . .)
ne pa saantetny'uun	(kiim)
kiim	(kiim)
kiim	(kiim)

[pause] ara kaaleel? *[someone answers him]* maacileel

kiim ol— tuumto— kiim ole kiim	(kiim)
kiim ole kiim	(kiim)
laakwaani, iyayei tuumto iyayei	(yayei)
inkoron laakok	(sere)
igilei tuumto ata	(sere)
kiim ole kiim	(kiim)
kiim ole kiim	(kiim)
kiim ole kiim	(kiim)

[Mentegai] akoyam-ai toi/ kutkuut-ai/

*See table 11 for additional blessings.

348

Translations of Blessings

1. Girls' ceremony at Arap Oloso's, 1 July 1983.

A. *Korodo*

Strong	(strong)
Strong	(strong)
Strong	(strong)
Ceremony	(ceremony)
Of my brother-in-law	(. . .)
Of my brother-in-law	(strong)
Strong	(strong)
Strong	(strong)

[pause] [Korodo asks if he has made a mistake and is told he hasn't]

Strong you— ceremony— strong, say strong	(strong)
Strong, say strong	(strong)
You child, you do the ceremony, you do [it]	(he does [it])
There are children	(amen)
Repeat ceremonies [for children] many times	(strong)
Strong, say strong	(strong)
Strong, say strong	(strong)
Strong, say strong	(strong)

[Mentegai comments] That's enough, then, friend. Finish it [the wine], then.

B. Kwampat Sembui

ee sere metorropilo	(sere)
ink-oishuaa eno kiteng'	(sere)
enta— en— inca— incoo iyiook Enkai ol masi	(sere)
meilepu anaa enk-olong'	(sere)
meilepu anaa enk-olong'	(sere)
entagolis satiman	(sere)
entagol kiriman	(sere)
entagol kiriman	(sere)
entagol	(sere)
entubul	(sere)
aisho intai ink-amulak	(sere)
entaa i-latimi	(sere)
ilo in-toyie	(sere)
ilo il-ayiok	(sere)
ni ishorere	(sere)
ena kipa ake	(sere)
noo en-kishon o il-tung'anak	(sere)

2. Boys' ceremony at Nkaroni, 9 April 1983.
Blessings said while drinking by Simpole (Kap Mapelu lineage, *il tareto* age-set), Arap Musigoini (*il ny'angusi* age-set), a Kipsigis man, and Arap Miyon (Kap Larusi lineage, *eseuri* age-set). The first two are in Maa. The third is in the Kipsigis language and style. The last one starts in Okiek, then switches to Kipsigis and back again.

A. Simpole

metorropilo	
metorropilo e-naikuti	(ai)
meilepu anaa enk-olong'	(ai)
meneja ena aji ketotonie	(sere)
tiaaki eilepu anaa enk-olong'	(ai/sere)
meibaa ol-tiren	(ai)
naa mikincoo Enkai in-kishu	(ai)
mikincoo Enkai il-ayiok	(ai)
mikincoo Enkai in-toyie	(ai)
taa eipoturi	(ai)
mikincoo Enkai ene kipuonu ne	(ai)
metejo ol Maasai pookin oo netuo ena aji, etooko en-aisho, ee etuo	
metorropilo	(sere)
nai metorropilo	(sere)
nai metony'orra en-aisho	(sere)

B. Kwampat̲ Sembui̲

Ee amen, may you be sweetly fragrant	(amen)
Wombs of a cow[1]	(amen)
Be like— God give you locusts [many children]	(amen)
May you rise like the sun	(amen)
May you rise like the sun	(amen)
The place of men be strong	(amen)
The place of men be strong	(amen)
The place of men be strong	(amen)
Be strong	(amen)
Flourish	(amen)
I give you my saliva	(amen)
Be [as strong and abundant as] *i-latimi* trees[2]	(amen)
Go [with] girls	(amen)
Go [with] boys	(amen)
That you bear [so there are more ceremonies]	(amen)
Of birth slime	(amen)
And of blessed life and people	(amen)

2. Boys' ceremony at Nkaroni, 9 April 1983.

A. Simpole

May you be sweetly fragrant	(amen)
May the ceremony be sweetly fragrant	(amen)
May you rise like the sun	(amen)
May it [always] be like this in the house with people sitting [and drinking in ceremonies]	(amen)
Tell [them] rise like the sun	(amen)
May there be many at the hearth	(amen)
And may God give you cows	(amen)
May God give you boys	(amen)
May God give you girls	(amen)
Be prosperous and respected people	(amen)
May God give you a place [where] we come	(amen)
May all Maasai who came to this house and drink beer say,	
May you be sweetly fragrant	(amen)
Amen, may you be sweetly fragrant	(amen)
Amen, may you eat honey	(amen)

1. I.e., may you come from the womb of a cow, be borne well, and stay well.
2. Also, have ceremonies. *I-latimi* is a tree Maasai use in ceremonies, like *koroseek*.

metony'orra en-aisho   (ai)
metony'o— metony'orra en-aisho   (nai)
naa te nepuo enk-ang' eny'e meinepu in-kishu eiguran   (nai)
meinepu eiguran in-kishu   (nai)
meilepu anaa enk-olong' in-kishu   (ai)
meilepu anaa enk-olong'   (ai)
metalang'a in-gumet   (ai)
metalang'a in-gumot   (ai)
metalang'a— ilo— ilo ijo

B. Arap Musigoini
tiaaki ejo ole-dukuya
meiruko Enkai   (sere)
meiruko Enkai   (sere)
tenaa etoomono en-daa o en-kishon, mikincoo naa Enkai   (sere)
mikincoo ena na etoomono   (sere)
tenaa in-kishu, tenaa in-tomonok o in-kera, mikincoo naa
   Enkai   (sere)
meiruko iyiook Enkai   (sere)
metaa ena aji ene il-mosor   (sere)
metaa ena aji ene il-mosor   (sere)
naa il-ayiok o in-toyie   (sere)
o noo in-kishu   (sere)
metii . . . il-mosor
ne medung'oo ai kata   (sere)
tiaaki entobik   (sere)
entobik   (sere)
. . . iyiook
namelok   (sere)
ne metii ol-kirobi   (sere)
ne metii ol-tikana   (sere)
. . .

C. Kipsigis man
kaale tuumto
paipai ole paipai   (paipai)

May you eat honey	(amen)
May you eat— may you eat honey	(amen)
And when they go to their homes, may they find the cows	
playing	(amen)
May they find the cows playing	(amen)
May the cows rise like the sun	(amen)
May they rise like the sun	(amen)
May they avoid holes[3]	(amen)
May they avoid holes	(amen)
May they avoid— what— what was said	

B. Arap Musigoini

Tell [them] what the first one said	
May God agree [to it]	(amen)
May God agree [to it]	(amen)
Whether he prayed for food, or blessed life, may God give it	(amen)
May [God] give you what was prayed for	(amen)
Whether cows, whether women and children, may God	
give it	(amen)
May God agree to you	(amen)
May this home be a place of ceremonies[4]	(amen)
May this home be a place of ceremonies	(amen)
For boys and girls	(amen)
And for cows	(amen)
May there be . . . ceremony	
That never stops	(amen)
Tell [them] endure	(amen)
Endure	(amen)
. . . you	
Sweet	(amen)
That has no flu	(amen)
That has no malaria	(amen)

. . .

C. Kipsigis man

I say ceremony	
Happy, say happy	(happy)

3. I.e., not step into them and go lame. The word for "hole" is mispronounced in this line and corrected in the next.

4. _Il-mosor_ means "eggs," but here refers to the food eaten during ceremonies, i.e., the calabashes of beer.

ny'ooru kaa ole paipai	(paipai)
pa . . . tuumto ole pa	(ai)
pa ole pa	(pa)
se laakokcaan ak iceek euunekcuak, purkei ole purkei	(purkei)
akot itookutny'uan ko paipai ole paipai	(paipai)
paipai ole paipai	(paipai)
akot— akot caaiik ce kikooin, iis ole iis	(iis)
iis ole iis	(iis)
tintai tomonok ole tintai	(tintai)
paipai tany'aan uuy ole uuy	(uuy)
uuy ole uuy	(uuy)
paipai pa ole pa	(pa)
pa Kebeni pa ole pa	(pa)
pa kapsambuut pa ole pa	(pa)
pa ng'etuuny'ik pa ole pa	(pa)
lein eemooni, akot paaiisyek ak ceepyoosook, kaasiin ole kaasiin	(kaasiin)
kaasiin ole kaasiin	(kaasiin)
kong'etei laakok ce pa embarnotik, kaasiin— kaasiin ole kaasiin	(kaasiin)
ng'elyepta ko any'iny' ole any'iny'	(any'iny')
akot koong' asiis kesai kele-i, ceepang'olo, taareteec ak eceek ak ikeer en kaat, ko ai n'isase ko itaac naan ko yuu itaace piik alak	
ko ng'elyepta ko— ne kooni paaiisyek, any'iny' ole any'iny'	(any'iny')
any'iny' ole any'iny'	(any'iny')
tiny'e inkoryeet ole tiny'e	(tiny'e)
tiny'e ooreet, tiny'e ole tiny'e	(tiny'e)
ng'aap Kipkaiykee pa ole pa	(pa)
pa Kebeni pa ole pa	(pa)
pa ng'etuuny'ik pa ole pa	(pa)
lein eemooni any'iny' ole any'iny'	(any'iny')
lein akot itookut aap laakok, purkei ole purkei	(purkei)
purkei ole purkei	(purkei)
kasyep taai paar ole paar	(paar)
kasyep kataam paar ole paar	(paar)

Meet [your] home [on return as] a happy place   (happy)
For . . . ceremony, say for   (amen)
For, say for   (for)
Those children, too, their, hands, warm, say warm   (warm)
Even their bed [should be] happy, say happy   (happy)
Happy, say happy   (happy)
Even— even the tea they are given, may it cause them to (cause to
   prosper, say cause to prosper   prosper)
Cause to prosper, say cause to prosper   (cause to
                                                          prosper)

Come having childbearing women, say come having   (come having)
That cow is happy,[5] hard, say hard   (hard)
Hard, say hard   (hard)
Happy, for, say for   (for)
For Kebeni[6] for, say for   (for)
For a place of ceremonial capes for, say for   (for)
For lions[7] for, say for   (for)
Tell this country, even elders and women, agree, say agree (agree)
Agree, say agree   (agree)
Starting from the children of young male initiates,
   agree . . . agree, say agree   (agree)
The tongue is sweet, say sweet   (sweet)
Even we pray to the east and say, God, help us too and
   see this house, and even [someone] you dislike, wel-
   come her/him as you welcome other people
So the tongue is— that elders give [in blessing] sweet, say (sweet)
   sweet
Sweet, say sweet   (sweet)
Have clothing, say have   (have)
Have a clan[8] have, say have   (have)
Of Kipkaiykee for, say for   (for)
For Kebeni for, say for   (for)
For lions for, say for   (for)
Tell this country [the gathering] sweet, say sweet   (sweet)
Tell even the children's bed, warm, say warm   (warm)
Warm, say warm   (warm)
[If they] lay on the right [side], prosper, say prosper (prosper)
[If they] lay on the left [side] prosper, say prosper   (prosper)

5. The cow referred to is identified as the ritual leader.
6. Kibeni and Kipkaiykee (see later line) are both divisions in Kipsigis warrior groups.
7. The ceremony was for boys.
8. People identified the meaning of *ooreet* here as "clan," not "path."

mabwaaitany'aan ko uuy ole uuy   (uuy)
yaas ang'wan yaas ole yaas   (yaas)
yaas ole yaas   (yaas)
tiny'e kipny'a— tiny'e ceepny'apayit, tiny'e ole tiny'e   (tiny'e)
tiny'e ole tiny'e   (tiny'e)
tiny'e kapyukoi tiny'e ole tiny'e   (tiny'e)
taisaai tany' ole tany'   (tany')
kiim ole kiim   (kiim)

D. Arap Miyon
ot koonaak Mungu sapaanto   (sere)
ot koonaak Mungu sapaanto   (sere)
ot taaretaak   (sere)
ot taaretaak   (sere)
taaretei laakok   (sere)
kotaaret solootwek   (sere)
kotaaret tuuka   (sere)
ot koonaak tuuka Mungu   (sere)
ot koonaak laakok   (sere)
ko koonaak kiit ake tukul   (sere)
kepar— kipaarei— sere ole sere   (sere)
ki— sere ole sere   (sere)
pa laakok pa ole pa   (pa)
pa laakok ole pa   (pa)
pa laakok ole pa   (pa)
pa tuuka ole pa   (pa)
pa piik ole pa   (pa)
kipwaane ole kipwaane   (kipwaane)
ot kooneec Mungu kora   (sere)
kiit ake tukul ne kimace   (sere)

Our *mabwaita* is hard, say hard   (hard)
Spray four [times] spray, say spray[9]   (spray)
Spray, say spray   (spray)
Have the— have the cow given for feeding initiates in
   seclusion, have, say have   (have)
Have, say have   (have)
Have affines have, say have   (have)
You should still remember a cow, say cow[10]   (cow)
Strong, say strong   (strong)

D. Arap Miyon

May God give you a blessed life   (amen)
May God give you a blessed life   (amen)
May [God] help you   (amen)
May [God] help you   (amen)
[And] help the children   (amen)
[And] help the childbearing women   (amen)
[And] help the cows   (amen)
May God give you cows   (amen)
May [God] give you children   (amen)
[And] give you everything   (amen)
We say— we say— amen, say amen   (amen)
We— amen, say amen   (amen)
For children for, say for   (for)
For children, say for   (for)
For children, say for   (for)
For cows, say for   (for)
For people, say for   (for)
We're coming, say we're coming [for ceremonies]   (we're com-
                                                          ing)
May God help you again   (amen)
[With] everything that is wanted   (amen)

---

9. *-yaas* was identified as the Kipsigis word for *-piit* (to spray, to spray a blessing with honey wine).

10. Interpreted to mean that when initiates come out, they should remember how to find cows to make themselves prosper and gain a wife.

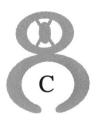

Ceerseet (Encouraging Speeches)

The following are the first four encouraging speeches made to initiates at a girls' initiation held at Kewet. The first speech also appeared in table 13. It is repeated here to set it within the larger context of the ritual event, to present it as it was delivered (in sequence with other speeches), and to make a longer sequence of *ceerseet* speeches from a single ceremony readily available for analysis. Sequential speeches are marked off by full lines of *****. Some speeches are interrupted for a time by side conversations. These are indicated by partial lines of *****.

The pause structure of the speeches is shown here in the following way: the longest pause (about four seconds or so) is shown by the start of a new line at the left margin; the next longest is marked with //; the shortest is shown by /. Skipped lines within a speaker's turn indicate changes of sections and transitions to new sections within speeches, as discussed in chapter 6.

I maintain the pause structure marking in the English translations of the speeches. To make the translations easier to follow and understand, however, I have also used capitalization and commas within the pause marking in a way that approximates English phrasing. The capitalization and commas do not indicate other pauses; they are intended simply to clarify the sense of the speeches. I have also retained emphatic and affective Okiek particles—such as *-is, -ais, -i,* and *-o*—in the English translations. These particles are important to the performance and to the mood of the event but are very difficult to translate. They can also serve as structural markers. Translations in appendix E also use capitalization and commas and retain these particles.

Transcriptions of Speeches

Ceremony at Kewet, 9 December 1983.
Recorded by Simion Sena.

P.:   . . . aleincin/ iweenti// amu nee si maiwe/ ko kiawe anee// itepaati
            ipaarei in—/ kiapakaace itepaaten iny'ee/ ko kiawe anee?
            hi?
            ko/
            aleincinin/
            aleincinin/

            kaiwe-ai tuumto/
            kaiwe tuumto/ ne kiimace/
            tapala ne kiisaamu/ kiipaarei in— "amace awe tuumto"// ko kai-
            ny'on iwe tuumto/
            kaiwe ra tuumto// ai inta nee? ko kainy'on kaiwe ra// amu apwaate
            ale// meko tena seruut-i ak kuutiit/ s'iwe tuumto// ako tuumto
            ne kipeentin// tuumto// ko meinken ile tuumto-i/ ko nee// ikase
            kityo kemwai/ [cluck] Meiny'ikake/
            menken tuumto ile nee/ ikase kityo// amu/ ake— kopaarei in—/
            [sigh and cluck] mankooikee cu kooce/ kimwa— kimwai/ amu tos
            iyon akomung' ng'aleek kimwau koitiita/
            tuun kowo kopaarei-i/ "tuumto ko nee"// ako maink— meinken
            iman amakineet/ ko kaaneetiin anee aleincin-i/ akoik kaiwe-ai
            tuumto/ ko tuumto-i// ko tuumto/ kiy ne kikiilcinkee/ imuite ka-
            bisa// ko yuu kinamuite/
            [cluck] ko yuu kinamuite// imuite/ amu kiy ne ng'waan ne
            kikwang'e/
            ne kiyayuun/
            ne mapoci iwe/ i— i— itey kiy/ itulatul//

Translations of Speeches

Ceremony at Kewet, 9 December 1983.

P.:   . . . I tell you/ you're going [for initiation]// Why shouldn't you
           go/ and I went myself// You sit and think, um—/ I've left you
           to stay yourself/ and I went myself?
           Hi?
           So/
           I tell you/
           I tell you/

           You've gone *tuumto,* then/
           You've gone *tuumto*/ [the one] that you wanted/
           Never mind the one that you asked for/ You said, um—"I want to
           go *tuumto*"// So [now] you've come to go *tuumto*/
           You've gone *tuumto* today// And no matter what, Well, you've
           come and gone *tuumto* today// Because I'm thinking that// it's
           no longer as long as the distance between nose-*i* and mouth/ be-
           fore you go *tuumto*// But it's *tuumto* that we go to// *Tuumto*// So
           you don't know *tuumto-i*/ is what// You just hear it said/ [*cluck*]
           Meiny'ikake/
           You don't know what *tuumto* is/ You just hear [of it]// because/
           but— saying, um—/
           [*sigh and cluck*] She didn't give herself the other one/ she sa—
           she said [she wanted]/ Because when words have come out we
           should say them truly and well/[1]
           When she goes tomorrow, she thinks/ "What is *tuumto*?"// But you
           don't— truly you don't know because we don't teach [you
           about it]/ So I've taught you myself, I tell you/ it's become
           [time] and you've gone *tuumto*/ So *tuumto*/ is *tuumto*/ Some-
           thing that we really try to do our best at/ You stay completely
           still// Like I stayed still/
           [*cluck*] Like I stayed still// You stay still/ because it is something
           astonishingly painful/
           that is done to you/
           If it's not possible for you to go/ [well and] you— you— you do
           this/ You squirm around//

---

1. I.e., when a matter comes up, it should be spoken of clearly. He refers here to his mention of
"the one that you asked for." The initiate (his daughter) had wanted to be initiated on another,
earlier occasion, but he refused to allow it.

ile amu ko̱ng'wa̱a̱niit/ ko kaika̱i a̱neeti̱in a̱nee aleincin/ ng'waan
kiya̱an kiya̱yuun// amace imwaiwaan pa̱ani/ ko in—
imwauwaan paani ko inikeer ile/ maimuuce/ imwaiwaan/ asic
a̱cunte̱n paani iwe/ ko mac-i/ ii— in-/ iya̱y ko yuu naan/
[cluck] Kap Apaiye/ matin ikeeraan ang'a̱laani muutya ako a̱a̱
ng'eeta̱t kabisa// kabisa/
ko yuu/

A.M.:   muutya/ muutya pakule/

P.:   paani koi// ni// momii ciit a̱ke ne ki̱maany' en Kap Larusi/ Kap
Larusi/ kabisa// oi iyoo ceepyooso̱ok maile manke— in—/ ki
mii ko maikopeentin ceepyoosook/ amu kaaroon ne opeenti/ ko
makimii/ e̱cee̱k ng'eetotik// ce pa koi/ kake se ng'eetat a̱ke̱
tu̱ku̱l ne pa ka̱i/ inko ma̱kikany' kiit a̱ke tu̱kul/ pee̱le̱e̱k a̱nan ko
saaeenik a̱nan ko nee/ a̱kipwa̱at kele̱/ kicuurunaati weeriik a̱ap
kai pa Kap Larusi/ ki̱ki̱pe̱ komyee/ [cluck]

[sigh] inkeri akot iny'on ikoonaan mo̱siket a̱ke̱ ne oo/ ne man-
amuuce/
kaikoonaan mo̱siket ne oo/ ko mo̱siket ne kaikoonaan ko
pu̱ko̱o̱tye̱t/

pamuru/
pu̱kootyetny'uun kabisa/ nai ile/ imii paani koi/ maimiitii
koing'waang'/ imiitii Kap Larusi// Kap Larusi ne imii/ s'inken
ile/ miitii kaing'waang/ ko yuu inko mii tosi/ kaaitaap/ piik a̱lak
tu̱ku̱l/ Kap Larusi ne imii/ ko kiimwai i̱man ile opee̱nti ak Ni̱ni/
oi inkeeron Nini omii tuwa̱i/ ko i̱nee n'o̱pwaa opeenti tuwa̱i//
maikenteraan pamuru kabisa// me̱ikenteraan/ amu maakenteriin
a̱nee// maakenteriin/ ko koale/ le̱lesta a̱ke tukul ne ayaycini
Nini/ ayayuun/ o̱kerkeiit ot kokeer ciit a̱ke tu̱kul/
mm?

You say "because it hurt"/ So it's better I teach you myself and
tell you/ It hurts, that thing that is done to you// I want you to
tell me now/ so if— you tell me now if you see that/ you can't
[do it]/ Tell me/ so that I can leave you now quickly and you
[can] go/ when you haven't [yet]/ you— um—/ done that [i.e.,
shown fear by squirming]/
    [cluck] Kap Apaiye/ There's no seeing me talking quietly
    [calmly], though I'm truly a man/ completely/
Like/[2]

A.M.:   Calm down/ Calm down, initiation mate/

P.:   Now this family// This one// There is no other person in Kap
    Larusi that was whispered about/ Kap Larusi/ None at all// Or
    unless there were women, don't say we don't— um/ we're there
    when women are usually going/ Because tomorrow when you
    go/ we won't be there/ ourselves, the men// of this family/ But
    every man of this family/ If we fear anything else/ elephants or
    buffalo or what/ we remember that/ the boys of this Kap Larusi
    family were really brave at initiation/ We went well/ *[cluck]*

    [sigh] And there again you come and give me another big [heavy]
    burden/ that I couldn't have/
    You've given me a big [heavy] burden/ and the burden that you've
    given me is my wife's sister/

    Wife's sister/
    Truly my wife's sister/ Know that/ you are in this house now/
    You're not with your family/ You're at Kap Larusi// Kap Larusi
    is where you are/ So know that/ your family is there/ Like— if
    they are [there like]/ the family of/ any other people/ Kap
    Larusi is where you are/ So you said truly that you would go
    with Nini/ and there's Nini you're together/ She's the one that
    you've come to go together with [for initiation]// Don't cheat
    [shame] me, wife's sister, at all// Don't cheat me/ because I
    didn't cheat you myself// I didn't cheat you/ I said/ any lovely
    thing that I do for Nini/ I'll do for you/ You will be [treated]
    the same until anyone can see [it]/
Mm?

2. After swearing by his lineage with the name Kap Apaiye, P. comments on the controlled way
a man should speak and his own emotion. This phrase, *ko yuu,* which translates as "like," is the
beginning of a phrase commonly used in conversational oaths (see Kratz 1989:644–46). This is
another demonstration of his emotion, and moves his good friend A.M. to try to calm him down.

ma tuun akot kole— mwai ciit ake tukul in—/ ciit ake tukul ne
    siirtai kole/ "ikeere/ kowo kolaac laakweeny'iin/
kopakaac niin/
amu mamaken kiy// amu pa koin"/ akot ai n'ii pa inee eemeet ake/
    ne mananken/ ot opwaan otepaaten ak laakwaniny'uun/ ko
    ayayuun lelesta ake tukul/ ne kaayaycin// maikenteraan pamuru
    kabisa amu si ikenteraan/ amuuci akot anee awe rokoeet kabisa/
rokoeet ot ko mekekasaan en koi/
s'anken ale matin kaawe/ ko many'aliiltos laakok ce miitii kai/
hm?// many'aliiltos/
many'aliiltos apwaati/ matin kopa awe/ aiku ng'uuny'uny'eekcu
    ikeere ityece/ ipaare tyaana piik ko kikopa iyu/ ko many'aliiltos
    laakok/
[cluck] Meiny'ikake// meikenteraan kabisa/ tepaaten itepaaten ko
    yuu ciita// meipwaati ak iny'ee ile/ "amii— kokuuraan tosi koi//
    any'o awe tuumto ko yuu iyon in—// ko kiaale any'on aweenti
    en kai"/

ko momii ng'aleek alak tukul ne taamwaiwaak-i/ aleincinaak kityo
    omuiten pamuru kabisa// omuiten// kesulwaak ak okweek
    pooruekwaak ko yuu iyon akesulci piikcu tukul/

ko/
aa pa Kap Apaiye// matin ikase ikeeraan ang'alaani muutya ak aa
    ng'eetat kabisa ng'eetat inne naan ipaarei ng'eetat kabisa//
    hm?// ak maakencinaak-e anee// inkeri sumunit ne katiny'e/

[unfolding hundred shilling note] pakalini/ pakalini akeenke ne ka-
    aceeraak tuwai// opce/ manko—/ ale amu Nini ni/ koip
    sumunit// opce tuwai en kweeneet/ momii kweeneet iyu? opce
    tuwai en iyu// iip kepeeper/ iip kepeeper// mankowo sumunit
    akot taba—/ tongolo akot tongolo akot intururu manko— ko—
    ko— kowo— kowong' ake tukul niin/ kowong'en ake tukul/
    kiy kaakoonaak/

[So that] tomorrow no one even says— any one says afterwards,
um—/ anyone who passes by says/ "You see/ he went and
dressed his child [well]/
and left that one/
Because he doesn't care a thing/ because she's for that family"/
Even if you yourself are for another country/ that I don't know/
if you come and sit with this child of mine/ then I'll do for you
any lovely thing/ that I've done for her// Don't cheat me at all,
wife's sister, because if you cheat me/ I can even go and hang
myself completely/
Hang myself until I am not heard again in this house/
So I know that there's no problem when I'm gone/ that the children [and wife] of this house will not have trouble/
Hm?// They won't have trouble/
They won't have trouble, I think/ there's nothing [to worry about
if] I go/ and become this soil that you see you step on/ How
many people do you think have died here/ and the children have
no trouble/
[cluck] Meiny'ikake// Don't cheat me at all/ Sit, you sit like a per-
son// Don't you think yourself/ "I'm here— this household
called me, then// to come and go *tuumto* like when, um—// I
said I would come and go in this house"/

So there are no other words that I still [want to] tell you-i/ I just
tell you, you persevere, wife's sister, completely// Persevere//
[and] your bodies, too, will be made good for you just as [their
bodies] have been made good for all these people/

So/
I'm for Kap Apaiye/ There's no hearing [or] seeing me talking
calmly, and I'm a man completely, very much a man, the one
[about whom] you say [he's] a man completely// Hm?// And I
didn't cheat you myself// Here is the small coin that I have/

[unfolding hundred-shilling note] This hundred shillings/ It's this
one hundred shillings that I encourage you both with// Divide it/
Not to—/ I say because this is Nini/ to take fifty cents// Divide
it together in the middle/ Isn't this the middle? Divide it together here// You take half/ You take half// Not even fifty cents
should go, let alone—/ ten cents, even ten cents, even five cents
shouldn't— to— to— go to— increase the share of that one/
to increase the share of either/ in the thing I've given you/

[cluck] papaiyet ak kwa͟a͟nta͟/ aa pa a͟ne͟e i͟n͟g'e͟d͟o soyua/ *[sigh/
grunt]*

****

R.:   iru-o? ruoten/

A.S.:   i͟nk͟o͟pa͟ kipaako en koi/ mekopaaci ra/

P.:   cutaati keriinkaanik/

****

Kw. L.:   a͟ne͟e/ a͟ne͟e se— wei/ ka͟s-ai/
           pa͟— pa͟pa͟/ Nini/

           ipwaati iny'ee in—/ kiapookit-ai peesiet ki͟iny'e͟/

           . . . ata toi ko͟ra-i/ kitwekcin toi laakok-e mookoocini toi
           mukuulelweekcukwaak/ ata oame kot/ omuuci akot o͟kwe͟e͟k o͟am
           okaske͟e͟/

           ka͟s-ai/
           pa͟pa͟/ peesiet ki͟inye— kiany'on/ kiaiku ki͟ma͟ya͟a͟t-is/ kiapookit
           ot— kabisa// pe͟esiet ki͟inye͟ s'akuuriin en— en o͟o͟re͟e͟t/ asue
           akiinte tuwai ko͟ra͟// a͟mu kile kiawe aru ki͟ma͟yaat peesionaan/
           ale any'on-i/ ko kiany'on— asue ko akuuraak komyee/ kolen-
           caan Kopot La͟kweny'o͟n-i/ "kuure ne͟e͟ laakok" aleinci "hapana/
           akuure ko͟ra͟"/ alei—

           ee ra-i/ ai piikcu tukul-i/ se isue piikcu tukul/ maikointe koi pa
           kang'waang'? inta— kiy ne te͟no͟ weeri͟ik a͟ap koi pa
           kang'waang' ana ko kiy ne te͟no͟/ laakok ko͟ra͟/ laakok tukul-ais/
           ko weeri͟ik ak kang'waang'-i/ tos inken ile͟/ a͟kopa ak M͟ungu/
           se piikcu tukul tena kiy/ se piikcu tuk— tukul// iny'ee ne kaikuure
           ra// iny'ee ne ka͟ikuuru/ an masooman ka͟a͟siini// ko kiicam iman/
           ko kiimwai iman ile/ "ka͟a͟ca͟m i͟ra"// ikase? ko maiko akemwai
           ko͟ra "kaaca͟m ira"// ma͟ia͟m ko len/ s'imwai in—/ maam ko le͟n
           tosi/ ko mankoamunen ko͟keny'/

[cluck] Papaiyet ak kwaanta/ I'm for the red open forest area/
[sigh/grunt]

****

R.: *[to the girls]* Are you sleeping-*o*? Sleep/

A.S.: Let young men leave this house/ It's no longer possible today/

P.: They're going about falling into holes/

****

Kw.L.: Myself/ Myself then— friend/ Listen, then/
My— my child/ Nini/

You remember, um—/ I was drunk, then, that day [when we met]

. . . even so, friend-*i*/ We talk, then, to the children-*e*. You don't
give them your hearts, friend/ even if you get worked up/ You
can even get very worked up/

Listen, then/
My child/ That day— I came/ I've become a drunkard-*is*/ I was
so drunk— really [drunk]// that day and then I called you um—
on the path/ I see you two are together again [now]/ Because I
went and slept as a drunkard that day/ I thought, I'll come-*i*/ So
I came— [and] I see [you two and] I called you loudly/ Kopot
Lakweny'on told me-*i*/ "What are you calling children for?" I
told her, "No/ I'll still call [them]" I say—

And today-*i*/ And all these people-*i*/ So you see all these people/
Are they usually in this house of your mother's? If— is this the
number of boys [sons] for this house of your mother, or is this
the number/ of children even/ All the children-*ais*/ Whether
boys and your mother-*i*/ Then you would know that/ she went
with God/
So all these people like this/ So all— all these people// You['re
the one] that called them today// You['re the one] that called
[them]/ And they didn't study this work// But you truly liked
[agreed to] it/ So you truly said/ "I've liked [agreed to it,]
then"// You hear? So once it's said again "I've liked [it,] then"//
Don't say it for nothing [and then be afraid]/ and then you say,
um—/ Don't fear for nothing, then/ [for] you won't be feeling it
again [after this time]/

amwaun ng'aliaat akeenke kityo anee Kwampat Lakweny'on-i/
ma— matanken toi ochei anee ang'alaan komyee/ ng'aleek inko
caang'// amace kityo aleinciin nee/ papa/

akoik iman-a// kimace-i/ ikooneec ak iny'ee amtit/ kabisa kiam
komyee/ kiam komyee amtit kabisa// . . . kiam komyee amu/
kiam amtit komyee/ amu akerooteci ak eceek/ si inko— amu se
piikcu tukuuul-i/ ko iny'ee ne amtaati// amu-i/ se in— ot
kony'ooruun ng'aliaanaan/ komung'te Mau/ komung'te akot/ en
kieet ko makinken en Ntoror akot/ kieet aap ikwopik/
kepwaa Ntoror/ kipaarei kipunu akot/ ikwopik iyuuno/ piik alak/
kikase kipaarei Ntoror ko makinken/ ai asa makinken ayny'un
eceek ipaarei iny'ee ne inken?// komung'te ng'aliaantanaan/
kole-i/ "kony'o koreeny'ci kwaanuusyek laakwani/ en iyu"/
laakweet aap ng'aa?
ng'aa?/ ilterekeyani//

kimace ak eceek ee papa/ kimace ikooneec iman amtit kabisa//
kimace ikooneec kabisa/ amu inta kipaarei kemwai ng'aap
ng'eetotik-i/ ko mainken ak iceek eemeet aap kaa// mainken ka-
bisa/ mainken/ ceepyoosook/ ng'aleek aap ng'eetotik//
amu iman/ omii tuumto/ ko— se tuumto/ kany' tuumto/ kooneec
amtit amu akoit-a tuumto/ ko kimace/ akoit-ai ra/ akoit kabisa//
ko kaiwe metabaiki/ ko meipaarei kitena kiy/ ee suen-o/ cu
tukul-o/ akot ceepyoosook ko inte kaa/ amu se cu tukul toi-i/
komwai kole koyaaktai— ko ipaarei komwai kiy pa ng'aliaani
isue ipaarei perpereec amu inte iyu/
ko inken kiy/ kokoik ceepyoosook cu// ko-ais-i/ ko itin-e kaasii-
naan ra/ ra ra ra ra/ ipaarei piikcu tukul/ ipaarei maipa tuumto-
i? ipaarei kipek cu tukul-i? maipek// koik iny'ee n'ipaarei ale
in-/ "awe amei"// ata—/ ai iny'ee— ee met-i/ ata koipiin
korooita-e/ ko met kora// ikase? matin kele nee/ ko met kora/
inko ipiin korooita ko met kora/ ko-a/ ikasei/ ko met kora/
matin kele "maamei/ amu korooita ne koipaan"/ kile maitutu/
meipaarei "ale atutu amu koipaan korooita"/ ikasei?// ko ak
ootar tuumto papa//

I just tell you one word myself, Kwampat Lakweny'on-*i*/
I— I don't usually speak a lot myself, friend/ a lot of words// I
just want to tell you what/ My child/

It's true now// We want-*i*/ you to give us food too/ so that we eat really
well/ So that we eat food really well// . . . we eat well because/ we
eat food well/ because we've come to the ceremony [with gifts], too
/ So if— Because all these people-*i*/ You're [the one] that they will
leave here talking about/ because-*i*/ So, um— if that [shameful]
word gets you/ it will come out at Mau/ It will come out even/ in
countries that we don't know, even Ntoror/ that country [where]
Maasai [originated]/ They came from Ntoror/ We say they came
from/ Maasai came from there/ [They're] other people/ We hear it
said "Ntoror," but we don't know it/ And now if we don't know
[about it] ourselves [i.e., men], then are you the one who knows?//
That word will come out [in far off places]/ They say-*i*/ "This child
came and shamed her fathers/ here"/ Whose child?
Who?/ [A child of] *il terekeyani*//

We also want, my child/ We want you truly to give us food
well// We want you to give [it] to us completely/ Because if we
thought we were saying [words] of men-*i*/ Well, women don't
know themselves// They don't know at all/ They don't know/
women/ men's words//
Because truly/ you're in *tuumto*/ and— this *tuumto*/ Wait for
tuumto/ Give us food because *tuumto* has arrived-*a*/ So we want
[it]/ It has come today, then/ It has really come// And when you
go tomorrow/ don't think it's [just] like this/ So look-*o*/ All of
these-*o*/ Even the women in the house/ Because all of these,
friend-*i*/ that send you on errands— So they want to say a little
word [errand] and you see them and think they're foolish because they're here/
They know something/ These have become women// So then-*i*/ So
you have that work [to do] today/ Today today today today/ You
think all these people/ you think they didn't go *tuumto-i*? Do you
think all these died-*i*? They didn't die// So it becomes you that says,
um—/ "I'll go and die"// Even—/ and you— And death-*i*/ Even if
disease takes you-*e*/ it's still death/ You hear? No matter what/ it's
still death/ If disease takes you, it's still death/ So-*a*/ you hear/ It's
still death/ There's no saying, "I didn't die/ because disease is what
took me"/ You think you'll rise from the dead/ Don't say, "I think
I'll rise from the dead because disease took me"/ You hear?// So
you finish *tuumto*, my child//

ko mekonte lokooiya— amwai kityo anee Kwampat Lakweny'on ale nee?/ ale/ Nini/ okooneec okooneec nee?/ okooneec
ak eceek/ kiamiisyen kabisa/ kiamiisyen komyee/

ko ak iny'ee laakwani kora// amu laakwani kora// saait ake ko—
in pukootyetny'uun/ pakiteng'ny'uun/ ako in— kaimuti kora/ se
kai— kainy'on kora/ ko iman// opwaan ope suen-o/ se
laakwani— suen-o/ se laakwani/
yuu oi paani entasataani Kopot Nini// kang'waang'— se Kopot
Nini/ ootuupce/ laakweeng'uung' toi ni/ ne kaopwaan opa tuwai
kabisa/ laakweeng'uung'// kaikas-i? laakweeng'uung' kabisa//
ko maipaarei paani/ laakweeng'uung'/

opa tuumto kaope ira tuumto ra/ se kaaroon-i/ ipaarei s'osue ni/
s'osue ni otay kiy otay kiy otay kiy otay kiy/ osue ciit ake
tukul/
isu— isue ni/ isue ni/ itay kiy itay kiy/ ko petuun na kaisue//
okooneec amtit kabisa/ okooneec amtit komyee/ kiam komyee//
kooneec amtit kiam komyee//

amu kaatil Kwampat Lakweny'on okooneec amtit kiam komyee/
kiyaan toi ne kaamwauwaak ak anee/ aleincaak/ okooneec amtit
kiam komyee/
kooneec kabisa/ okooneec laakokcaancuuk/

[unfolding money] ee taac/ siling tamanisyek cu/ amu in—/ amu
inta ipaarei okweek omweiyo paani ole opeenti ano-i/ mainte
iyet opeenti paani/ tukuuk kityo ne kimace eceek/ ne kaano ne
kopa taai/ ne pa taai// takonamtecin kaameet iny'eekee/

****

Sm.:   siling ata?

P.:   kimwai kele—

Kw. L.: siling taman caan kaakoon ak anee in— Kwampat Lakweny'on/
        Kwampat Lakweny'on-ais/

So there is no other word— I myself, Kwampat Lakweny'on, just say, I say what?/ I say/ Nini/ Give us— give us what?/ Let us too/ eat well/ eat fully/

So, and you too this [other] child// Because this child too// perhaps she's my WiSi/ my SoWi/ But, um— you brought her here also/ You came to this house too/ truly/ You've come to go [for initiation], look-*o*/ this child— look-*o*/ this child/
It's like— and now this old woman, Kopot Nini// your mother— This Kopot Nini/ you're siblings [with her]/ This one is your child, friend/ [The girl] that you've come to be initiated together with, really/ she's your child// Have you heard-*i*? She's really your child// Though you don't think [so] now/ she's your child/

Go *tuumto*, you've really gone *tuumto* today/ So in the morning-*i*/ You think you'll look at this [person]/ So you look at this [one], you do this, you do this, you do this, you do this [i.e., looking all around]/ You look at everyone/
You look— you look at this one/ You look at this one/ You do this, you do this/ until you don't know what you've seen/ Really give us food/ Give us food well/ so we [can] eat well// Give us food to eat well//

Because I've stopped, Kwampat Lakweny'on, give us food to eat well/ That's what I tell you myself, friend/ I tell you/ Give us food to eat well/
Give [it] to us completely/ Give [it] to us, you children of ours/

[unfolding money] Here receive/ these ten shilling notes/ because um—/ because if you think yourselves that you're scared now and say you're going wherever-*i*/ There's no place you're going now/ We just want things [to eat] ourselves/ [Do it like] that first one/ the first one// The mother is still holding it herself [i.e., he directs them how to receive the money]/

****

Sm.: How much?

P.: We say that—

Kw.L.: That's ten shilling that I gave too, um— Kwampat Lakweny'on/ Kwampat Lakweny'on-*ais*/

Kw. I.:   kimwai eropiyiasyek es si onai/

Kpt. N.: kale siling taman ak muut/

Kw. L.: kale taman ak muut/

M.:   siling tomonuni/

Kpt. N.: ipaarei kaaleel-o?

Sm.:   se tosi— yaani maanai-is ineetei/

Kw. L.: konereece ng'aa-in ceepy— ceepyoosook maipwaati iceek pan-
             tany'uaan opaarei okooini tukul mukuulelweek-iwei/ mii
             mukuulelweekcuaak/

****

Smb.:   eeee—/ yuu kele laakokcu ko—/ ma— manken anee ng'aleek-
             caan caang' kipaarei kiteytaati kiy/

             laakwani iyon kaile iweenti/ ko/ akot en kasari koapaarei akot
              anee in—/ saait ake in—/ mara ko ko ra ayay ing'aap taai/ al-
             ein kityo/ tos ko amut akot— ko kaaroon akot ne any'onei/
             ko yuu paani ale/ "inait"/
             ko/ komace kityo// okas kiy ne akemwaiwaak paaiisyaanik-i/
             keleincaak nee?

             paani/ kiy ne yuu piik tukul/ ko kimuuc tuumto// kimace iyon kai-
             le kirimac tuumto papa// itar/
             itar tuumto kabisa/
             ko mailein paani in'ikeer piikcu— kaaroon/ anan ko ceepyoosook
             ce miitei/ anan ko kipaako/ momii ciita ne mo— ne mainken/
             hm?
             kimuitoi in— ketar kaasiit ne akemakcinkee-i/ en—/ en kasarta ne
             okai-s ile/ "kaatar"/ kasaraan/
             anan ikwange-o?// ii?

Kw.I.: Say it [using the old system of money] in rupees so you'll know.

Kpt.N.: I said fifteen shillings/

Kw.L.: I said fifteen/

M.: Thirty shillings *[counting in rupees, but saying "shillings"]*/

Kpt.N.: You think I'm wrong-*o*?

Sm.: So then— that is, I didn't know-*is*, you tell [it]/

Kw.L.: Who get's worked up wom— women. Don't they remember their trip [initiation]? Do you think you'll all give them your hearts, friend/ Their hearts are there/

****

Smb.: *Eeee*—/ It's like, you children, so—/ I don'— I don't know how to say a lot of words when we think of doing this/

Child, when you've said you're going/ well/ Even at this time, I thought even myself, um—/ maybe, um—/ Maybe today I do the first/ I just tell you/ Otherwise it should be yesterday even— be tomorrow even that I come/[3]
But it's like now I said/ "Let me go there"/
So/ they just want// Do you hear what these elders have told you-*i*?/ What did they tell you?

Now/ It's what everyone is like/ that can do *tuumto*// When you've said you've wanted *tuumto*, my child, we want// you to finish [it]/
You finish *tuumto* completely/
And don't say now when you see these people— tomorrow/ Or if it's the women who are there/ or the young men/ There's no one [no adult] that doesn— that doesn't know/
Hm?
We just sit still, um— and finish the work that we've chosen for ourselves-*i*/ en—/ In the time that you know that/ "I've finished"/ That time/
Or are you dozing-*o*?// *ii*?

3. I.e., ordinarily he would have come just for the celebration period, beginning the following day.

Kpt N: marue/

Smb.:   ko paani papa in— n'isue paani in—/ ai n'ikeer paani kapwaan
         paani-i/ maikomii piikcu tukul-i?// iny'ee ne koikuure/ ot
         kopwa/ komace kaaroon koam amtit-i// in—/ ne koikuurcini//
         matian paanaan koik peaati piik-i/ kepakaac mayueekcu isue mii
         koi-i/ ipaarei tarei Incore ineekee mayueekcu?
         inta kepakaace/

         kimace kityo kiy ne akile in—/ ketare kasarta ne akole in—/ ak
         ketare ketar kopek// ii? momii ciita ne mainken en Kenyaini/ ata
         ceepyoosook momii ciita ne mainken/

         en— Semburi/
         ko-i/ ale apaarei inkenaan anee// kaikas-i?/

         mace iyon kariny'on-i/ koi/ ma kap pukootyetng'uung'-i?
         ko/ mamace in—/ ng'aleekcu pa nee? cu pa aibu/ iipu koi//
         ng'aap ko maitalaikin in— kap opule koyayuun tuumto en kau/
         iny'on ano? kap pukootyetng'uung'// ko mace— ale imuki? itai
         kiy metit/

Kw. L.: mwaicin iny'ee/

Smb.:   ale amwaun-o/

Kw. L.: mwai/ pakaac ata kora komuk/ inkorue koru/ mwaicin iny'ee
         ng'aleekuuk/

Smb.:   komace keero—/
         itar kasarta ko yuu akot amu— kwang'ut akot in—/ in kai— en
         kap pukootyetng'uung' akot/
         eh?

Kpt.N.: They're not sleeping/

Smb.: So now, my child, um— if you see now, um—/ And if you see
now [they've] come now-*i*/ Are all these people usually here-
i?// You're the one who called [them]/ until they came/ They
want to eat the food tomorrow-*i*// um—/ that you called them
for// So that it shouldn't be people are going off then-*i*/ and
leaving this beer that you see in this house-*i*/ Do you think In-
core will finish this beer by himself?
If we leave it/

We just want what I said, um—/ to finish the time that was said,
um—/ And we finish [it], finishing [it] until it's done// *ii*?
There's no one that doesn't know [about it] in this Kenya [i.e.,
this crowd gathered]/ even women, there is no one who doesn't
know/

En— Semburi/
So-*i*/ I say, I think you know me// Have you heard-*i*?/

They want when you've come-*i*/ to this house/ Isn't it your
SiHu's house-*i*?
So/ I don't want, um—/ these words of what? Of shame/ You
bring [them] to this house// If it wasn't too much, um— for my
MoBr's house to do the ceremony for you at home/ Where do
you come? To your SiHu's house// So they want— I say, are
you nodding off? [Her] head is doing this/

Kw.L.: [Just] talk to her/

Smb.: I say, I tell you-*o*/

Kw.L.: Talk/ Let them nod even/ Let those that sleep sleep/ You just tell
her your words/

Smb.: So it's wanted, look—/
You finish the time like all [the others] because— it [would be] a
surprise [shock] even, um—/ in this house— in your SiHu's
family even/
eh?

ile akile ko̱li̱ya̱n/ ng'aa ne mainken ata ceepyoosookcu tuku̱l kai-
pwa̱ iyu/ ng'aa ne mainken/ ata piik tuku̱l/ i̱tar in— ka̱sa̱rta ne
akilencaak in— ko ka̱sari̱/ i̱tar kopek// ko mailen— miki—
makimei toi/ oi cu paani mii koi tuku̱l-i/ tos tomokonai-o?
oi Rana/

ko yuu kele in—/ ka̱sa̱ra̱n n'amwaun/ S̱embu̱ri̱/
ko aleincin in—/ ki̱mui̱ta̱/
ko̱ko̱cakte// yuu paani a̱kopek ce̱cu̱u̱k-ai amu mamace a̱nee ng'al-
ee̱k ce ca̱ang'/ aleincinaak kityo— amace kityo okooneec ne̱e̱?
mu̱u̱sa̱ree̱kcu kiam kaaroon laakokcuuk/ ki̱a̱m a̱mtit// kaaroon/
okooneec a̱mtit kiam-i/
moosor toi/ oo/ o̱cakten/ akile o̱cakten/ kimace okooneec a̱mtit/
ki̱a̱m/ a̱mti̱t// kaaroon kipeenti kepaarei "ariririri̱ri̱/ laako̱kcuuk
in—/ kokooneec a̱mti̱t ne a̱keam"/

kowo ano Kopot I̱nco̱re-o?

****

Kpt S: inkiri a̱nee/

Smb.:   e-e toi/ e̱ntasata ne ka̱a̱n ne kaakuure Kopot I̱nco̱re̱/

Kw. L.: kale kowo ano e̱ntasatanaan iny'ee/

Kpt S: ko mii— ko mii ki̱y ne kowo ko̱ny'i̱m si kony'o/

Kw. L.: aiye ng'alaane-i/

K.:   ta̱a̱ci̱n laakok/ kony'o kokoocin ka̱a̱mee̱t/ ma̱ra̱any'ra̱a̱ny'ci̱/

P.:   mataacei laakok/ . . . ko iny'o iny'ee iyu ko— in—/ maikinam-
         cinke̱e̱ ka̱a̱si̱i̱t ake/ . . .

You say what's wrong/ Who doesn't know, even all these women
that came here/ Who doesn't know/ Even everyone [knows],
you finish, um— the time that you were told, um— this is the
time/ Finish it to be finished// And don't say— we don— we
don't die, friend/ And all these now who are in this house-*i*/
wouldn't they have known-*o*?
Oi Rana/[4]

It's like this, um—/ that time that I told you about/ Semburi/
So I tell you, um—/ we sit still/
And just be quiet// It's like now, mine are finished-*ai* because I
don't want a lot of words myself/ I just tell you— I just want
you to give us what? This porridge to eat tomorrow, my chil-
dren/ We'll eat food// tomorrow/
Give us food to eat-*i*/
Don't all talk at once, friend *[to others there]*/ yes/ Be quiet/ We
want you to give us food/ We'll eat/ food// Tomorrow we'll go
[home] saying "Aririririri/ our children, um—/ they gave us
food and we ate"/[5]

Where has Kopot Injore gone-*o*[6]?

****

Kpt.S.: Here I am/

Smb.: No, friend/ It's that [other] old woman that I call Kopot Injore/

Kw.L.: I say, where did that old lady go anyway/

Kpt.S.: There's— there's something she went to get and then she'll come
[back]/

Kw.L.: [She does that] and he's talking-*i*/

K.: The children can receive it/ and then come and give it to the
mother/ Don't delay people/

P.: Children don't receive [gifts]/ . . . so you come here um—/ We
don't start another work [when in the middle of one]/ . . .

4. He swears by his lineage, Kap Rana.
5. *aririririri* is the sound of ululation.
6. The mother who is to receive the money.

Kw. L.:   inkeeron tosi akony'o/ akony'o/ oi inkiri akony'o/ maikooik̲e̲e̲ ase/
          . . .

Sm.:   o̲c̲a̲k̲t̲e̲n̲-a/ se caan toomko— ko— ko̲ng'a̲l̲a̲a̲n̲ kosic/ . . .

Smb.:   siling a̲r̲t̲a̲m̲/ in// ce komiitii/ koip l̲a̲a̲k̲w̲a̲n̲i̲ tiptem koip ni tiptem/
          . . .

****

A.M.:   Nini/
          oo-oo/ ii?

Kpt. N.: makiyanei/ akile ee—oo/

A.M.:   inkeneec-i?
          inkeneec a̲n̲a̲n̲—/
          tuun— pe̲e̲siet ko kituuiye en o̲o̲reet in—// taipaarei pa̲p̲a̲ ni a̲n̲a̲n̲
              taipaarei inken kang'waang— ai mainken kang'waang' mainken
              a̲k̲e̲/ imace inaieec-i? ee?

          ko// kiy ne kamwai paaiisyaanik kamwai i̲m̲a̲n̲i̲t̲// kimwauwaak ciit
              a̲k̲e̲ t̲u̲k̲u̲l̲/

          se paani/ ikasu iny'ee/ iny'ee ne makiwaale/ momii ciit a̲k̲e̲/
          ikase-i?// oi y̲a̲ iyon k̲i̲w̲a̲a̲l̲i̲i̲n̲/ i̲k̲e̲n̲t̲e̲r̲e̲e̲c̲ iny'ee//
          ikase-i?
          se ko yuu a̲n̲e̲e̲ paani/ ame— maa— me— ma/ akot toi inko
              koma̲c̲e̲ k̲o̲w̲o̲ k̲o̲w̲a̲a̲l̲ iyet a̲k̲e̲-i/ kosic k̲u̲u̲t̲i̲i̲t̲ en— iny'ee// ii?
          ne sice k̲u̲u̲t̲i̲i̲t̲ ko iny'ee/

          inai pa̲p̲e̲ ile/

          tuumto ko ni// kale kiimace/ ile ki— ki— kiina̲m̲e̲n̲ akot ko ta
              kimii L̲o̲l̲d̲a̲m̲a̲/ i̲n̲e̲r̲e̲e̲c̲e̲// kimace ayny'on ra i̲n̲e̲r̲e̲e̲c̲/
              kimani̲n̲e̲r̲e̲e̲c̲ peesionaan toi/

Kw.L.: There she is, then. She's come/ She's come/ O there she is, she's come/ Don't delay then/ . . .

Sm.: O quiet-*a*/ So those who haven't yet— talked can get [a chance]/ . . .

Smb.: Forty shillings/ um—// is what there was/ This child takes twenty [and] this one takes twenty/ . . .

****

A.M.: Nini/
oo-oo [be quiet]/ *ii*?

Kpt.N.: We don't respond/ saying *ee*— yes/

A.M.: Do you know us-*i*?
Do you know us or—/
Tomorrow— That day we met on the path, um—// Do you still think this is father or you still think you know your mother— or you don't know your mother and you don't know [who] another [person is][7]/ Do you want to know us-*i*? *ee*?

So// the thing all these elders said, they've said the truth// Everyone told you/

So now/ you get up [and run off in fear]/ You're the one we usually swear by[8]/ There's no other person/
You hear-*i*?// *Oi*, it's bad when we swear by you/ and [then] you cheat us yourself//
You hear-*i*?
So like me now/ I didn— no— no—// Even, friend, if you want to go and swear by something else-*i*/ you're what the mouth finds// *ii*?
What the mouth finds [to swear by] is you/

You know, my child, that/

this is *tuumto*// I say, you wanted [it]/ You say you— you started even when we were still [living] at Loldama/ to get worked up// Today we want you to be worked up indeed/ You weren't worked up that day, friend/

7. I.e., do you still respect your parents and recognize and honor important family relations?
8. A common phrase to swear truth with is "first-born of my coinitiate," which is what Nini is for A.M.

M.W.:   kitientos oi inkitwekci?

?:   mailuulci kityo tereet aap paaiisyaanik/

A.M.:   ale—/ koruya/ oruitosi-o?

Kw. L.: omwai kityo laakok ata inko muku ata inko luule . . . omwai kityo
        okweek/ . . .

A.M.:   ai peesiet/ kikimii Loldama/ kimainereec/ ipaarei inereec kityo itay
        kiy itay kiy/ ii tooma/ ko kitoomakoik kasartang'uung'/ tos
        kikaiwe keny'// inkiri akoita ra panta// inko iitieu ne kiairo/ in-
        kiri/ akekooniin// amu kiisaame// ii?// ii?// amu kiisaame/ ii?
        ma isar ne kiiny'e ne kikipaarei/ iny'ee ni/ ko kikile akot koonuut-
        i/ kasari ko ni/
        ko in—// iny'ee ayny'on ni/ ko inko iitieu inkiri akekooniin/
        ko inko ne kiiny'e ne kiimakene iny'ee safar— en— kas—
        mukuuliltang'uung'-i/ ko akekooniin asiny'e ne kimakuun
        eceek/ ko iny'ee ni/ aketamayianuun// inkiri-ais akekooniin/
        akeleinciin/ kwaantany'uun/ "iweenti"/ iya/ kopureniin kityo/
        iny'eekee// momii ake tukul ni— pa Kap Larusi ni— kiikase
        kele kikoliyan?/ ee? ale apaarei inken amu in—/ tos ikasaati/
        hmm?// aoi ni meyb— meybaisyek tukul-i/ kele/
        tos ikasaati/ aini Cepkosa ne kopa amut-i/ tos toi maikas ile/
        kitepte kole/
        tos ma iny'ee ne karup-o/ ma iny'ee ne pa aeeng' paani?/ ak
        Kironwa-i? amu ooc aeeng'// hm? momii ne kikekas/ kikekas en
        iyet ake/ ipaarei toomkokasan— kiy tos ikasei ko maang'aati
        ceepyoosook// momii kiit ake ne kitiny'e/ ake tukul/ tekuunik ce
        kitiny'e//
        momii kabisa/

M.W.: Are they singing when they're talked to? [i.e., nodding off, asleep]

?: Just don't fall over into the elders' [liquor] pot/

A.M.: I say—/ They're asleep/ Are you asleep-*o*?

Kw.L.: Just speak to the children even if they're nodding, even if they're falling . . . You all just talk/ . . .

A.M.: And the day/ we were at Loldama/ you weren't worked up/ You just thought you were worked up, doing this, doing this/ You weren't yet/ So your time had not yet come/ else you would have gone [for initiation] long ago// There it is, today the trip has come// If you dare [to do] what was said/ there it is/ We've given [it] to you// because you asked for it// *ii*?// *ii*?// Because you asked for it/ *ii*?
You didn't get that one that you said[9]/ This is it/ So all your fathers said-*i*/ this is the time/
So, um—// This is indeed it/ So if you dare, here it is. We've given [it] to you/
So if it was that past one that you wanted yourself, the trip— um— fee— your heart-*i*/ Well we've indeed given you the one we wanted ourselves/ and this is it/ We've blessed it for you// Here it is, then, we've given [it] to you/ We've told you/ my child/ "you're going"/ *iya*/ Unless it defeats you/ yourself alone// There's no other that— in Kap Larusi that— did you hear [anything] said [about anyone, saying] something bad happened [when they were initiated]?/ *ee*? I say, I think you know because, um—/ otherwise you would hear about it/ hmm?// And the gir— all the big girls-*i*/ Let's say/
Else you would hear it about/ And Cepkosa, who went recently-*i*/ Otherwise, friend, wouldn't you hear that/ she did such and such/
Isn't it you that should follow [her]-*o*/ Aren't you the second [next one] now?/ with Kironwa-*i*? Because you two are together [being initiated on the same day at different places]// Hm? There is none that has been heard/ that has been heard of elsewhere [because of cowardice]/ Do you think it wouldn't have been heard— otherwise you would hear women whispering [about it]// There is no other [such] thing that we have [in this family]/ None at all/ [No] cowards that we have//
There are none at all/

---

9. This speaker also refers to the time earlier when the girl wanted to be initiated but was not allowed to be.

aleincini kityo/

akekooniin kiy kiimace/ kiisaam koria/ akoik kasartang'uung'// ko
ake— akele ak eceek "ot taaretiin Mungui"/ ii ya kaikentereec
kaaroon/ ikeere piikcu— kiikeere piikcu en Kewet-i?// keer
piikcu tukul-o/ inken amu ceepyoosook cuno/

kiikeer ceepyoosook som— ang'wan, muut/ ce mii Kewet-i?

iny'il itay kiy koang'ta en iyu// kiikeer paaiisyaanik ce iite taman//
ce mii Kewet?// ii?

ko ma iny'eekee-ais/ ak Semburi/ kiikeer-o Semburi?

mii ne kokeer? amu omii tukul/ kooroni/ kiokeer in—/ piik ce
teno kiy-i?// kaaroon-ai osice kiy kiomace// kiomace nee/ ko osice kaaroon/

ko/ [cluck]

[long pause]

aleincaak ma cu— makiceere cu ng'eetotik/ inkoceer ceepyoosook
cu pa aeeng'/ [laughs]

Smb.:   kitwekcin kityo kokas/

A.M.:   ale oo/ kiy ne yuu iman/ . . .

Kpt. N.: kale koruitos/

Kpt. S.: kele laakok ce ruitos-o/

Smb.:   pakaac koruiya/

P.:   ma kang'et/

Kw. L.: ale pakaac koruiya/

A.M.:   inkoruya/ ata inko ruiya okweek/

Kpt. S.: koruya ma ya koruya ko mii kaa ne mii paaiisyaanik?

I'm just telling you/

We've given you what you wanted/ You asked for it this time/
Your time has come// So we— we've also said, "may God help
you"/ You're bad if you cheat [shame] us tomorrow/ You see
these people— have you [ever] seen these people at Kewet-*i*?//
Look at all these people-*o*/ You know [them] because those
there are women/

Have you [ever] seen thr— four, five women/ that are at Kewet-*i*?

Do the same thing with your eye again here [i.e., look around]//
Have you [ever] seen so many elders, up to ten// that are at
Kewet?// *ii*?

And not you alone-*ais*/ Semburi/ Have you [ever] seen [it]-*o*,
Semburi?

Is there any [one] who has seen [it]? because you're all together/
in this place/ Have you [ever] seen, um—/ this many people-*i*?//
Tomorrow-*ai* you'll get what you wanted// What you wanted/
you'll get it tomorrow/

So/ *[cluck]*

[long pause]

I tell you it's not these— we men don't encourage these/ Let other
women encourage [them]/ *[laughs]*

Smb.: We just talk to them to hear/

A.M.: Right/ That's what the truth is like/ . . .

Kpt.N.: I say they're asleep/

Kpt.S.: We have sleeping children-*o*/

Smb.: Let them sleep/

P.: Aren't they tired/

Kw.L.: I say let them sleep/

A.M.: Let them sleep/ So what if they sleep/

Kpt.S.: They sleep. Isn't it bad [for them] to sleep when [they are] in a
house where elders are?

Kw.L: ata koruiya/

A.M.:   pakaac koriip tereet/ osi koruiya/ ot koik kaaroon/

Kpt. S.: araakenaanit-ai ne akopar/

A.M.:   kimakene nee-o os kiinte kora tuun/

Kw. L.: momii ne koocini mukuulelweek en cu tukul/

Smb.:   takigile keriec-o?/

Kpt. S.: ko ng'aa ne takoriecei?

Smb.:   pakaac lempeita/

Kpt. S.: kimayiaat . . .

A.M.:   momii papa kiy ne atinaanu/

Kpt. S.: kotienipak ko pa puunik/

A.M.:   atin siling taman/ isi—/ iwe ialaaten/ soda// iwe eemoniino/

S: siling ata/

A.M.:   taman/

S: taman, oo/ ne pa Arap Miyon/ kokooci Sembui siling artam koipce
         tuwai/

A.M.:   ko ma cu ce arootunen koi/ ce kaapaarei ipun/ iyet kaiwe matatu/
         ma cu arootune anee/ ilein/ kaarootu en koi/ kaaroon ne arootu/
         ko cu ne akooniin s'iween iny'ee/ mailein ce arootunen en koi/
         ce ipune kityo/

****

Kw.L.:   So what [lit., even] if they sleep/

A.M.:   Let them guard the pot/ and sleep/ until morning/

Kpt.S.: Anxiety-*ai* [is the thing] that has killed them/

A.M.:   What do we care-*o* and we're all still here tomorrow/

Kw.L.:   There's no [one] in all of these that gives them hearts/

Smb.:   Will we brew again-*o*?/

Kpt.S.: Who is still brewing [again]?

Smb.:   Stop fooling [cheating]/

Kpt.S.: Drunkard . . .

A.M.:   I came with nothing, my child/

Kpt.S.: Let them sing [doze], these cursed enemies/

A.M.:   I have ten shillings/ so—/ you go buying soda with it// [when] you go to that [far] country [fleeing in fear]/

S.:   How much/

A.M.:   Ten/

S.:   Ten, yes/ for Arap Miyon/ And Sembui gave forty shillings for them to split/

A.M.:   But these are not [the shillings] that I came with [to give] to this house as a guest/ [They're the ones] that I thought you would go with/ wherever you go in a *matatu*/ These are not what I came with as a guest/ You say/ I came to this house as a guest/ It's tomorrow that I give my gift/ but these are what I give you so you can go using them yourself [if you run away in fear]/ Don't say [these are] what I came with as a guest to this house/ [They're] just what you can use going [if you run away]/

****

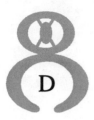

D

Curses Said during *Pesenweek* Confessions

Transcriptions of Curses

1. Boys' ceremony at Nkaroni, 8 April 1983.
Curse for *pesenweek* by Kwampat Koibitat (Kap Larusi lineage, *il terito* age-set) before blessing.

ileincin-a ng'emintet
inka ng'emei laakweet aap ciito
an inko sua ko ya
ot ipin isoonet
ot iraraktoien araaweet
ot iraraktoien isoonet
inko inteyen inko yucei mukuulelta
inko inte inko yucei maaeet
oooo
ot isip asiista
ileincin olobarakisyek aap tuuka, ko loong'
kotorooceec
kotorooceec
puunik
ileincin otalameec
ileincin ot ipok isoonet
ileincin ot paraak eng'apeysyek
ot wecaak
eekoonet

Translations of Curses

1. Boys' ceremony at Nkaroni, 8 April 1983.

Tell the spoiler
That bothers someone's child
Or sees that [a child] is bad
May the wind take you
May you go down with the moon
May you go down with the wind
If there is [someone] who knots [his] heart
If there is [someone] who knots [his] stomach
Oooo
May the sun take you
Tell the kind people of cows, rise
To come and meet us when we come
To come and meet us when we come
Enemies
Tell them to keep away from us
Tell them may the wind take you
Tell them may the sticks on the path hurt you
May the light of dawn hate you

2. Girls' ceremony at Arap Oloso's, 1 July 1983.
Curse for *pesenweek* by Korodo (Kap Kwonyo lineage, *il terito* age-set),
Kwampat Sembui (Kap Rana lineage, *il terito* age-set), and Kwampat Kirogu
(Kap Mengware lineage, *il terito* age-set). All three speak at once, not in turns.

Korodo	*Kwampat Sembui*	*Kwampat Kirogu*
ng'emintet		
caalwaakentet	caalwaakentet	caalwaakentet
ciicaan ne panei	tuumin	tuum— saapwet
ot— oooo	ot imei	
ot iraraktoi araawaani	ot rarakten araaweet	raraktoi
rarakten tabooyantoni	ot rarakten olakirai	raraktoi
ng'emintet ake tukul	kipteng'kekcyot	
kipteng'kekcyot	inko ng'emei tuumin	
ko ceepyoosook	inko ng'emei tuumin	ileinci
ko ng'eetaat	ko ng'eetaat	ot iemaati tapooyan-tonin
petin tuumin	ot ng'emin Mungu	
ooooo		
ot iemaati asiista	ot iemaati asiista	ot iemaati kityo iny'ee
ot iemaati asiista	ot iemaati araaweet	ot iemaati araaweet
ot iemaati araaweet	ot irarakte	ot irarakten tapooyanta-naan
ot irarakte	kipteng'kekcyot	
ot irarakte	inko ng'emei laakok	
ciita inko ng'emei laakokcu	ko ng'emin tuumin	ol arruoni
ot ng'emin sapaanto	ko ng'emin sapaanto	ileinci ot ng'emin sa-paanto
ko ceepyoosa	ot petin korosyaat	ot wecin korosyaat
ot wecin kapkorosyaat	ot petin ol masi	ot petuun korosyaat kai

2. Girls' ceremony at Arap Oloso's, 1 July 1983.

Korodo	*Kwampat̲ Sembui*	*Kwampat̲ Kirogu*
Spoiler		
Evildoer	Evildoer	Evildoer
That person who be-witches	The ceremony	Cere— ceremony
May— oooo	May you die	
May you go down with the moon	May you go down with the moon	Go down
Go down with this star	May you go down with the star	Go down
Any troublemaker	Evildoer	
Evildoer	That troubles this ceremony	
Be it a woman	That troubles this ceremony	Tell her
Be it a man	Be it a man	May you go off with that star
[May] ceremony be lost to you	May God trouble you	
Ooooo		
May you go off with the sun	May you go off with the sun	You just go off
May you go off with the sun	May you go off with the moon	May you go off with the moon
May you go off with the moon	May you go down	May you go down with that star
May you go down	Evildoer	
May you go down	That troubles children	
The person that trou-bles these children	That troubles this ceremony	Spoiler
May blessing trouble you	Blessing troubles him	Tell him may blessing trouble you
If it's a woman	May *korosyaat* sapling be lost to you	May *korosyaat* hate you
May the place of *korosyaat*	May the hair [that marks] ceremonies and birth be lost to you	May *korosyaat* be lost to the house

. . .

	inko ng'emei laakok	
inko ng'emei laakok	kipteng'kekcyot	ol ang'emaanit
petin kereek	ko petin kereek	
petin kereek	petin sapaanto	petuun tuun korook
ng'eet- ng'eetat ne ng'emei tuumi	ot namin	
petin sapaanto	ot wecin	intarruoi
wecin sapaanto	wecin sapaanto	. . .
petin sapaanto	petuun mabwaita	
petin maat	petei maat	petei
petei maat	petei	petei
petei tuuka	petei	petei
petei paanteek	petei	petei
ng'emintet	ng'emintet	ng'emintet
ne ng'emei tuumi	ng'emintet	ng'emintet
ko ceepyoosa	ko ng'eetaat	ko ng'eetaat
kong'emei tuum- tony'aan	ot ng'emin Munguin	ot ng'emin Munguin
ot namin— ot namin— irarakte tapooyat		
oooooooooooiii	ooooo	hooo
	akomei	akomei

Bas . . .

	That troubles children	
. . .		
That troubles children	Evildoer	Evil person
The dirt of children be lost to you	The dirt of children be lost to you	
The dirt of children be lost to you	Blessed life be lost to you	The dirt of children be lost to you
Man— a man who troubles this ceremony	May [it] get you	
Blessed life be lost to you	May [it] hate you	Be spoiled
Blessed life hate you	Blessed life hate you	. . .
Blessed life be lost to you	*Mabwaita* be lost to you	
Fire be lost to you	Fire is lost	[It's] lost
Fire is lost	[It's] lost	[It's] lost
Cows are lost	[They're] lost	[They're] lost
Maize is lost	[It's] lost	[It's] lost
Spoiler	Spoiler	Spoiler
That troubles this ceremony	Spoiler	Spoiler
Be it a woman	Be it a man	Be it a man
That troubles our ceremony	May God trouble you	May God trouble you
May [it] get you— may [it] get you— go down with the star ooooooooooiii	Ooooo	Hooo
	S/he has died	S/he has died

Okay . . .

8
E

Pesenweek

Transcriptions of *Pesenweek*

These *pesenweek* are from the first two girls to speak at the ceremony described in chapter 4. The following initials are used for the main speakers involved: T. = questioner/announcer; Tn., L. = initiates; A.N. = brother to some initiates, standing with T. and helping to ask *pesenweek*. Ellipsis points indicate inaudible or indistinguishable words. Announcements of *pesenweek* are shown in italics.

Ceremony at Sukustoosyek, 10–11 June 1983.

T.:   . . . paani ikasei? Momii kiy ne ta kiuny'ei/ mankomii kiy ne kiuny'ei/ ciita ne kicupin/ anan ne kiiken/ anan ko ne ki—/ ne kiing'eet en— anan ceepyoosa ne kiicup/ kolenjin "Haya ot ko kole"/ momii kiy ne kiuny'ei ake tukul/ ata ne kiing'usune in— inko orue tuwai ing'usune si kong'eet-e/ ng'eet ko—/ kolenjin "haya"/ ko in— kimwai ng'aleek tukul/ hm/ ciita ne kicup anan ko ceepyoosa ne kicupin anan ko muren ne kicupin/ kimwai caan tukul/ inta mekomii ne kiuny'e saa hii/ hi? ikasei?

[silence and a prompt while he waits for Tn. to start; background discussion overlaps (in part A.N. saying Y. is a woman since he can go into the women's ritual house), as does the sound of women singing in their ritual house]

A.N.:   ui kaarkoni koinaang'waang/ kaarkeet-ai ciicaan aketun/ pa koi/
?:   oo
A.N.:   pa koi/
?:   inkaainoon/
A.N.:   inkeri toi/

392

Translations of *Pesenweek* Confessions*

The following initials are used for the main speakers involved: T. = questioner/announcer; Tn., L. = initiates; A.N. = brother to some initiates, standing with T. and helping to ask *pesenweek*. Ellipsis points indicate inaudible or indistinguishable words. Announcements of *pesenweek* are shown in italics.
Ceremony at Sukustoosyek, 10–11 June 1983.

T.: . . . now you hear? There's nothing that remains hidden [now]/ There's no longer anything hidden/ Someone that cursed you/ or that you cheated/ or that—/ that you, um— or a woman you cursed/ telling her "*Aya*, may such and such [happen]"/ Nothing at all is hidden/ Even [someone] that you pulled him out, um— if you were sleeping together and you pulled him out so he would stop-*e*/ stop—/ and he told you, "*Haya*"/ So, uh— everything is said/ Hm/ Someone that you cursed, or a woman that cursed you, or a young man that cursed you/ We name all those/ There is no longer anything hidden now/ Hi? You hear?
[silence and a prompt while he waits for Tn. to start; background discussion overlaps (in part A.N. saying Y. is a woman since he can go into the women's ritual house), as does the sound of women singing in their ritual house]

A.N.: You woman, go to your house *[said to a man who can also attend women's rituals]*/ That person is a woman-*ai;* he's been married/ He's for this [women's] house/

?: Yes

A.N.: [He's] for this house/

?: Which one/

A.N.: Here he is, friend/

*For explanations of the uses of capitalization, commas, and Okiek particles in these translations see the introductory note to appendix C on page 359.

Tn.:   . . .

T.:   hi?

Tn.:   momii . . .

T.:   momii akot ciita ne kicupin?

            [silence between them, background talk elsewhere]

T.:   aini akot in—/ akot in—/ tom—/ tooma akot in— opol ak
            kang'waang? eh?

┌A.N.:   ai maiuny' toi apaarei maiopol ak kang'waang'/
├T.:   momii kiy ne kiuny'ei/
└Tn.:   maikipole ak ee/   maikipole ak ee/

T.:   eh? kolein nee?

Tn.:   . . . momiitei/

T.:   eh? kolein nee?

Tn.:   . . .

T.:   eh?

Tn.:   . . .

T.:   koleinjin "aya"?

Tn.:   *oo*/

A.N.:   o-o omwai inko tukul/

T.:   *kole kipol ak kaameet-i/ kolenci "aya"/ kolenci "ta tuun im-
            wauwaun peesio"/*

?:   ng'aa? ainoon ni?

T.:   *in— Tinkili/ kipol in— ak kaameet kolenci "aya ta tuun im-
            wauwaun peesio en kaa ne kituuiyecin"/*

A.N.:   *ko ma ra-o?*

T.:   *ko ma ra-i?* aini ciit ake/ momii ciita ne kicupin piikcu pa kooroni
            tukul akot Arap Ntete ne mapetei ko telelei/

A.N.:   pakaac anee inyee/ momii mamwaian en cu tukul/ kicupan
            laakokcu tukul/

T.:   eh?

A.N.:   kicupan laakoicu tukul anee/

Tn.:   ak Kopot Nasyeku ne kialenci "ot komutin koouut"/

T.:   *akile ak Kopot Nasyeku-i/ ne kilenci "ot komutin koonuut"/
            Kopot Nasyeku*

A.N.:   *kaikase ra kakonte in—/ akile in— . . . laakwe— kile "ta tuun
            tuun ketuuiye en— kimwai tuwai-i"/*

Kopot Tn.: ak ng'aa ira?

Tn.:   . . .

T.:   Hi?

Tn.:   There's no . . .

T.:   There's not even someone that cursed you?

          [silence between them, background talk elsewhere]

T.:   And even, um—/ even um—/ Haven'—/ haven't you even, uh— argued with your mother? eh?

A.N.:   Hey, don't hide [things], friend. I think you usually argue with your mother

T.:   There's nothing hidden/

Tn.:   I usually argue with Mother/

                           I usually argue with Mother/

T.:   Eh? What did she tell you?

Tn.:   . . . there's nothing/

T.:   Eh? What did she tell you?

Tn.:   . . .

T.:   Eh?

Tn.:   . . .

T.:   She told you, "*Aya*"?

Tn.:   Yes/

A.N.:   Hey, tell it all/

T.:   *She says, she argued with [her] mother-i/ and she told her, "Aya"/ She told her, "You still will name me someday"/*

?:   Who? Which one is this?

T.:   *uh— Tinkili/ She shouted, um— with [her] mother [and] she told her, "Aya, you still will name me someday in the house where we will meet"/*

A.N.:   *So isn't that today-o?*

T.:   *So isn't it today-i?* And another person/ There's no one in all these people [that live in] this place that cursed you, even Arap Ntete? Never mind if he's standing here/

A.N.:   Never mind me/ There's no one in all these [girls] that won't name me/ All these children cursed me/

T.:   Eh?

A.N.:   All these children have cursed me/

Tn.:   And Kopot Nasyeku, that I told, "May your father marry you"/

T.:   *She says, and Kopot Nasyeku-i/ that she told, "May your father marry you"/ Kopot Nasyeku*

A.N.:   *Have you heard today there is, um—/ She said, um— . . . the child said, "We still will meet, um— we'll say [this] together-i"/*

Kopot Tn.: With who, then?

A.N.:   ak laakweeng'uung'/

Kopot Tn.:   aa Tinkili-a?

T.:   *ool kole kole maikipol ak eel ileinci-il ale "ta tuun kituuitosi*
               peesio"l

A.N.:   . . .

Kopot Tn.:   ko ma ra-i? ko peesiet ake?

T.:   *kokiipol ak Kopot Nasyeku-il manken anee ne kikuuree kiyaanl*

A.N.:   Kopot Tapsinkil/

T.:   *kolenci ale "ot komutin koonuut"l mwai ni . . . ineentetl*

A.N.:   kiicupe?

T.:   eh?

Tn.:   kipirkee ak ee/

T.:   kipirkee ak kang'waang'-i?

Tn.:   kipirkee ak ee iny'ee/

T.:   kipirkee ak kang'waang'-e/ *kole kipirkee ak kaameetl*

Kopot Tn.:   kole kolenji nee Kopot Nasyeku?

T.:   *kiopirkee-i? ak Kopot in— ak Kopot Nasyeku*

Kopot Tn.:   oo/   oo/

A.N.:   *kolenci "ot komutin koonuut"l*

T.:   *kolenci "ot komutin koonuut"l* kaliya s'opwan o— opirkee ak
               ee?

Kopot Tn.:   ileinci iny'ee "tan imut ira kwaanta"/

T.:   aini ake/ ai makiuny'e-ayn/

A.N.:   kale maiuny'e ata kipakosyekcukwaak/

T.:   ai kipakosyekcu/

A.N.:   ai maiuny'aatekee tukul-i/ ipaarei tooma okenkee?

Tn.:   ak Kopot Lakweny'on ne kialenci "yuu ng'aa?"

T.:   eh?

Tn.:   Kopot Lakweny'on ne kialenci "yuu ng'aa?"/ kilencaun "aya"/

T.:   *kole ak Kopot Lakweny'on ne kilenci kile "yuu"—/ kilenci in—*
               "yuu ng'aa?"l kilenci-il kole "yuu ng'aa?"l kolenci "aya"l
               Kopot Lakweny'onl

?:   ileinci "toom ng'aleek"/

A.N.:   With your child/

Kopot Tn.: Aa, Tinkili-*a?*

T.:   *Yes/ She said, she said, "We usually shout with Mother"/ [and]*
            you tell her-i/ I say, "We still will meet one day"/

A.N.:   . . .

Kopot Tn.: So isn't it today-*i?* Is it any other day?

T.:   *And she argued with Kopot Nasyeku-i/ Myself, I don't know who*
            is called [by] that [name]/

A.N.:   Kopot Tapsinkil/

T.:   *She told her, "May you marry your father"/ This one said . . .*
            herself/

A.N.:   Did she curse you?

T.:   Eh?

Tn.:   She was fighting with Mother/

T.:   She was fighting with your mother-*i?*

Tn.:   She was fighting with Mother, [I tell] you/

T.:   She was fighting with your mother, then/ *She says, she was*
            fighting with [her] mother/

Kopot. Tn.: She says, what did she tell Kopot Nasyeku?

T.:   *Did you fight-i?   with Kopot, um— with Kopot Nasyeku?*

Kopot Tn.:   yes/   yes/

A.N.:   *She told her, "May your father marry you"/*

T.:   *She told her, "May your father marry you"/* What's wrong that
            you come— and fight with Mother?

Kopot Tn.: You tell her, "May the father marry you, then"/

T.:   And another/ And we don't hide [incidents], indeed/

A.N.:   I say don't hide [them], even [if they involve] these young men of
            yours/

T.:   And these young men/

A.N.:   And you all usually go about hiding yourselves [flirting?]/ You
            think you have yet to cheat each other?

Tn.:   And Kopot Lakweny'on, that I told, "Honest to who?"

T.:   Eh?

Tn.:   Kopot Lakweny'on that I told, "Honest to who?"/ She told me,
            "Aya"/

T.:   *She says, and Kopot Lakweny'on that she told, it's said,*
            "Honest—"/ She told her, uh— "Honest to who?"/ She told her-
            i/ "Honest to who?"/ [Then] she told her, "Aya"/ Kopot
            Lakweny'on/[1]

?:   Tell her there are still words [to be said]/

1. This is a challenge, asking who Kopot Lakweny'on would swear by to show she is not
lying.

A.N.:   mwai ake/

Tn.:   ak/ ak-i/   ak Sanare/ kilencaan "ankeeru en timta"
         ayeese/

T.:   hm/ *ale ak Sanare ne kilenci "ankeeru en timta" koyeeso*/

Y.?:   *inkaaino naan?*

T.:   *Sanare*/

Y.?:   *an laakwaan-o?*

T.:   *Tinkili*/

Y.?:   *oo*/

T.:   *kilenci Sanare "ankeeru en timta" koyeeso*/ *kolenci "aya"* /

?:   omwai-a ng'aleek tukul/

T.:   makiuny'e asiny'e/

A.N.:   ale mainte inko kiuny'e/ meiraarisyei/

T.:   an— an mekeraariye paani/ aki ya Mungu/ mwai iny'ee// aini
         akot Coel akot/

A.N.:   ata ko Coel/ ma maicupe iny'ee Coel-i?

T.:   tooma opol ak Coel?

Tn.:   ee/

A.N.:   aini anee?

T.:   petei kotelelei tosi/

A.N.:   ale— ata toi ateleli i— maiuny'e/

Tn.:   hm-mm/ tooma . . .

T.:   akopek-i?

A.N.:   ee/ kale aini anee-i? toomaticupaun-i?

T.:   momii ciita ne kiriken? eh?

A.N.:   mwai toi/ maiuny'/

T.:   ne kikiiken ileinci s'oru ko mataa-iso/

Tn.:   hm-mm momiitei/

T.:   eh?

Tn.:   momiitei/

A.N.:   ata kipakosyekcu tukul-i?

Tn.:   mm-mm/

?:   uny'ei ak iny'ee/ . . .

A.N.:   uny'ei/

T.:   iuny'cini nee-o?/

Tn.:   ciicikaan kityo/ inte . . . ne kiyay kokeny'/

A.N.:   ng'aa?

Tn.:   in—/ ne pa Kap Senoy naan serpin naan tuupca ak/ iceek/

A.N.:   Say another/

Tn.:   And/ and-*i*/ [T.: Hm] And Sanare/ He told me, "Let's sleep in the forest," and I refused/[2]

T.:   *I say, and Sanare who told her, "Let's sleep in the forest," and she refused/*

Y.?:   *Which one is that?*

T.:   *Sanare/*

Y.?:   *Which child*-o?

T.:   *Tinkili/*

Y.?:   *Yes/*

T.:   *Sanare told her, "Let's sleep in the forest" and she refused/ He told her, "Aya"/*

?:   You tell all the words/

T.:   We're not hiding [any], you hear/

A.N.:   I say we don't hide anything/ Don't laugh/

T.:   An— there's no more laughing now/ Honest to God/ You talk// And Coel [T.'s older brother] and them, even/

A.N.:   Even if it's Coel/ Don't you usually curse Coel-*i*?

T.:   Haven't you [ever] argued with Coel?

Tn.:   No/

A.N.:   And me?

T.:   Even if he's standing here, now/

A.N.:   I say— even if I'm standing here, friend yo— don't hide [it]/

Tn.:   No/ not yet . . .

T.:   Are they finished-*i*?

A.N.:   No/ I said, and what about me-*i*? Haven't you ever cursed me-*i*?

T.:   There's no one that you cheated? Eh?

A.N.:   Tell [it], friend/ Don't hide [it]/

T.:   That you cheated, telling [him] you would sleep [together] and then you didn't/

Tn.:   No, there aren't any/

T.:   Eh?

Tn.:   There aren't any/

A.N.:   Even among all these young men-*i*?

Tn.:   No/

?:   She's hiding, you [know]/ . . .

A.N.:   She's hiding [some]/

T.:   What are you hiding [them] for-*o*?

Tn.:   Just that person/ There was. . . . that did it, too/

A.N.:   Who?

Tn.:   um—/ The one for Kap Senoy, the one sibling to/ them/

---

2. In *pesenweek*, references to sleeping (such as this one) are often sexual suggestions when they involve a young man and one of the initiates.

A.N./T.:	mailen—
Tn.:	mailein kopiraan kila en kainy'aan koyeeso/
┌A.N.:	*akile ak/ ak Toto/ Toto/*
├T.:	*kole ciicaan pa Kap Senoy-i/* ni ko
	serpin-i?
└Tn.:	mm-mm/
Tn.:	naan tuupce/
A.N.:	hoo Inkutukay/
T.:	*kole mace— maikolein kopir kila/ ne koleinci iny'ee kile*
┌	*"inkeeruyen-e"/ koyeesyai/*
└A.N.:	*koyeeso/*
?:	*inkaainoon ni?*
A.N.:	*Inkutukay/*
?:	*an laakwa?*
A.N.:	*Tinkili/*
?:	*oo/*
T.:	aini ake?
Tn.:	ak Samson kokeny'/
T.:	Samson-i?
Tn.:	Samson ne kiakeeraat ko kilencaan/ "nee ne kaapirkee ak ikeeraataan"/
T.:	*kale ak Samson kilei/ ale ne kiikeer-e/ ale ak Samson ne kikeeraat/ kolenci in—/*
A.N.:	*"kaikeeraat? ipaarei nee ne kaapirkee?"*
T.:	*koleinci "maikeeraataan ipaarei nee ne kaapirkee?"/* [some laughter] *keero/ an makiraarcin-ayn/ kisisenkee/ oonken ole tuumin-ais okweek ko ng'aleekcu ce/*
?:	ocakten/
A.N.:	*oyeep iit// oyeep iit// oyeep iit okweek/*
T.:	*ale makitweku/ an makiraarie/ kikase kityo kiy ne akikas kisisenkee/* hm/ aini ake/
Tn.:	ak . . . ne pa Mbokishi Naneu/
T.:	Naneu?
Tn.:	hm/ kole/ kole ki . . . Kiramatisho/
T.:	akiile kiliya/
Tn.:	kikile/ kikile kile ki . . . Kiramatisho ko kimaimwai/

A.N./T.: He usually tells you—

Tn.: He usually says he'll beat me in our home and [I] refuse/

┌─A.N.: *She says and/*   *and Toto/ Toto/*

├─T.:   *She says that person of Kap Senoy-i/*   The young one?

└─Tn.:   No/

Tn.: That one that is [his] brother/

A.N.: Hoo, Inkutukay/

T.: *She says he usu— he usually says all the time he'll beat her/* when

┌─   *he tells her, it's said, "Let's sleep"/*   and she refuses/

└─A.N.:   *and she refuses/*

?: *Which one is this?*

A.N.: *Inkutukay/*

?: *Which child?*

A.N.: *Tinkili/*

?: *Yes/*

T.: And another?

Tn.: And Samson, too/

T.: Samson-*i?*

Tn.: Samson, that I watched and [he] told me/ "What have we fought about [so that] you watch me [like that]"/

T.: *I say, and Samson that said/ I say, that she watched-e/ I say, and Samson that she watched going about/ and told her, uh—/*

A.N.: "Are you watching me? What do you think I'll fight?"

T.: *He told her, "You want to watch me, what do you think I have fought?"/* [some laughter] *Look/ Now, we don't laugh at her, indeed/ We just are quiet [when these things are said]/ You know that it's a ceremony*-ais *and it [has] these words/*

?: O, quiet/

A.N.: *Listen// Listen// You all listen/*

T.: *I say, we don't talk/ and we don't laugh/ We just listen to what we hear and are quiet/ Hm/ And another/*

Tn.: And . . . the one for Mbokishi, Naneu/

T.: Naneu?

Tn.: Hm/ She said/ she said . . . Kiramatisho/

T.: So what was wrong?/

Tn.: We said/ It was said [that] we said . . . Kiramatisho, but we didn't say it/

[A.N. laughs]

T.:   *akile in—/ ak in—/ ne pa in—/*

A.N.:   *Arap Nonkuta/*

T.:   *ne pa Arap Nonkuta-i/ ale ale in—/ ale/*

A.N.:   *kitaakot kile Kiramatisho/*

T.:   *kale kitaakot Kiramatisho/ kowo komwai/ ako mamwai kile*
            laakokcu/ raait/ nee ake?

A.N.:   *[to other]* Tinkili toi naan/

?:   tooma ke—/ tooma ketar/

A.N.:   mwai iny'ee/ keesun/ ikeesun/

?:   mwai-ipak an makiuny'ei/

T.:   makiuny'e toi/

Tn.:   ak Parkesui ne kilencaan "ankeeru tuwai ankeeru tuwai" ayeese/
            koleincaan "kila ikenaan . . . ko mamace keru tuwai"/

T.:   *akile ak Parkesui kile-e/ maikoleinci kila "ankeeru tuwai ankeeru*
            tuwai" koyeesoi/

A.N.:   *ko mamacei kile/*

T.:   *ko mamacei-is/*

?:   *ko ng'aa ciici macei laakwa ak . . . /*

T.:   *sss keero/ osisenkee okweek/*

A.N.:   *ale ocakten okweek/*

?:   ale koraarisyen Coriin liye/

T.:   nee ake/

Tn.:   momiitei/

T.:   hm?

Tn.:   momiitei— ak Raili ne kolenci/ usho . . . Raili/ "camekee Raili"/
            kale "kikokwang'so laakok aap kooroni . . . meileincaun
            ocamekee/ iyay . . . tukul"
            [side conversation going with AN and others also]

T.:   *akile ak Raili/ akile Raili/ akile Raili kile/ kileinci in—/ kileinci*
            laakokcu in— "ocamekee"/ kalei "kikokwang'so laakokcu pa
            kooroni/ mookatyaan-i? eheh/
            . . .

R?:   inawo-o/

[A.N. laughs]

T.:	*She said, uh—/ and, uh—/ the wife of, uh—/*
A.N.:	*Arap Nonkuta/*
T.:	*The wife of Arap Nonkuta-i/ I say, I say, um—/ I say/*
A.N.:	*It's said Kiramatisho was involved/*
T.:	*I say Kiramatisho was involved/ And she went and said* [aya]/ *But it's said these children didn't say* [anything about her]/ *Right/* What else?
A.N.:	*[to other]* That's Tinkili, friend/
?:	Not yet—/ They're not finished yet/
A.N.:	You say [them]/ Finish/ You finish/
?:	Tell [them] indeed, and we don't hide [them]/
T.:	We're not hiding [them], friend/
Tn.:	And Parkesui, that told me "Let's sleep together, let's sleep together" [and] I refused/ He told me, "You always cheat me . . . Don't you want us to sleep together?"/
T.:	*She says, and Parkesui, it's said-e/ He usually tells her all the time, "Let's sleep together, let's sleep together" and she refuses/*
A.N.:	*So she doesn't want [him], it's said/*
T.:	*So she doesn't want [him]-is/*
?:	*So who does the child want and . . . /*
T.:	*Sss, look/ You all just be quiet/*
A.N.:	*I say you be quiet/*
?:	I say Cory is laughing, friends/
T.:	What else/
Tn.:	There aren't [any more]/
T.:	Hm?
Tn.:	There aren't— and Raili that I told/ *usho* . . . Raili/ "Hello, Raili"/ She said, "The children of this place have become foolish . . . You don't tell me hello/ you do . . . all of you"/ *[side conversation going with A.N. and others also]*
T.:	*She says, and Raili/ She says Raili/ She says Raili, it's said/ she told them, um—/ She told these children, um— "Hello"/ She said, "These children of this place have become foolish/ Don't you greet me-i?" eheh/*
	. . .
R.?:	Let me go-*o*/

T.:	aini ake/
Tn.:	ak ne pa Arap Ncoe/
T.:	ne pa Arap Ncoe?
Tn.:	hnn/
A.N.:	Arap Ncoe koyayei nee?
⌐T.:	ne pa Arap Ncoe/
└Tn.:	ne pa Arap Ncoe/
A.N.:	ooo/
T.:	kolein nee?
Tn.:	ko— kopaarei kile "kitei" ko kimakimwai/ kole "kany' kityo tuuming'waang"/
T.:	*akile in—/ ak ne pa Arap Ncoe-i/ akile in—/ akile kile kile laakokcu kile kole "kitei"/ ko maimwai/*
A.N.:	*kole "tako omwauwaan"/*
T.:	*koleinci "tako omwauwaan"/ ne pa Arap Ncoe/ s'okeesonu/*
?:	makitile akeenke/
??:	ata akeenke/
T.:	kaituc/ ee?
Tn.:	manken ake/
A.N.:	ale ata— ata kipakosyek cu serpen/ ipaarei tooma ti—/
R:	oo/ lein tako loo komwauun/
Tn.:	ak Nutuuta
T.:	hnn?
Tn.:	ak Nutuuta kora ne kinereecei ayeeso keru tuwai/ kipa akot ee Mau/
T.:	*kole Arap in—/*
A.N.:	*ak Nutuuta kile kiyeeso kile koru tuwai am—/ kikipe akot kaameet Mau/*
T.:	*[laugh] nee ake?*
Tn.:	ak Arap Tue/
⌐T.:	kolein nee?
└A.N.:	kolein nee?
Tn.:	koleincaun "oonkeeru tuwai" ayeese/
T.:	*akile ak Arap Tue ne pa Nkaroni-i/ ne kileinci "oonkeeru tuwai" koyeeso/ koleinci "mankeeru tuwai"/*
?:	ne pa Kap Silipa?

T.: And another/

Tn.: And Arap Ncoe's wife/

T.: Arap Ncoe's wife?

Tn.: Hnn/

A.N.: Arap Ncoe, what did he do?

   ⌐T.: The wife of Arap Ncoe/

   ⌊_Tn.: The wife of Arap Ncoe/

A.N.: Ooo/

T.: What did she tell you?

Tn.: She— she thought it was said, "She cried out [at circumcision]," but we didn't say it/ She said, "Just wait for your ceremony"/

T.: *She says, uh—/ and the wife of Arap Ncoe-i/ She says, uh—/ She says, she said, it's said, these children said, "She cried out"/ but they didn't say it/*

A.N.: *She said, "You still will name me"/*

T.: *She told them, "You still will name me"/ Arap Ncoe's wife/ So finish/*

?: Not even [a single] one is cut [out]/

??: [Not] even one/

T.: You've left some/ Ee?

Tn.: I don't know another [to say]/

A.N.: I say even— even these small young men/ You think you haven't yet—/

R: Yes/ Tell her it's still far [a long way to go before she finishes] telling you/

Tn.: And Nutuuta/

T.: Hnn?

Tn.: And Nutuuta, too, that was annoyed [when] I refused to sleep together/ [when] Mother and them went to Mau/

T.: *She said Arap, uh—/*

A.N.: *And Nutuuta, it's said, she refused, it's said, to sleep together, um—/ [when her] mother and them had gone to Mau/*

T.: *[laugh]* What else?

Tn.: And Arap Tue/

   ⌐T.: What did he tell you?

   ⌊_A.N.: What did he tell you?

Tn.: He told me, "Let's sleep together," and I refused/

T.: *She says, and Arap Tue from Nkaroni-i/ that told her, "Let's sleep together," and she refused/ She told him, "We won't sleep together"/*

?: *The one for Kap Silipa?*

A.N.: ne pa Kap Silipa? hi?

Tn.: hmm/

A.N.: *oo/ ne pa Kap Silipa/*

?: oo/

T.: hm-hmm/

Tn.: ak Indobiwo kora ne kituuiyaan/ kimiitei ak William/ ak silanaan ne pa akot Sebaya/ koleincaun "oonkiiyee"/ aleinci "mayeye/ anken anee iye iwe irue"/ aleinci "awe aru kap Nabaru"/ koleincaun "ui iru kaat aap Arap Ntete/ maikokenaan laakok tukul/ kepe keru kap Arap Ntete"/ aleinci "ui"/ akeer koleincaun "awe aru anee en timta meamace laakok aap kooroni"/ awe aru kap Nabaru/ tuun ko ny'ooruaan "iny'ee—/ ak iny'ee las . . . awe aru"/ aleinci "mace . . . kipako eceek . . . / mairu kityo?"/ kopaarei ko yey-is kainy'uaan/

T.: . . . sawasawa/ kaituc-i?

Tn.: hmm-mm/

T.: sawasawa/

A.N.: mwai-a/ kekeesta/ mwai toi naan kekeesta/

T.: *akile in—/ ak in—/* kikuure nee?

Tn.: Indobiwo/

T.: ile Indobiwo? Indobiwo/ *akile ak in— Indobiwo anan kikuure nee-e/ ne kileinci in—*

A.N.: *kituuiye en ooreet/*

T.: *kituuiye en ooreet/*

A.N.: *koleinci "oonkiyee"/*

T.: *koleinci "ookiyee/ kepe keru kaat aap Arap Ntete"/ koleinci "awe aru in— kaat aap in—/*

A.N.: *Nabaru/*

T.: *"kaat aap Nabaru"/ koleinci "kilya iny'ee s'ikenaan kila/ oi ta tuun imwaiwaun peesio"/ akot peesio-is/*

A.N.: ta imwai ake/

Tn.: mekomiitei ake/ caan kityo/

A.N.:   The one for Kap Silipa? Hi?

Tn.:   Hmm/

A.N.:   *Yes/ the one for Kap Silipa/*

?:   Yes/

T.:   Hm-hmm/

Tn.:   And Indobiwo, too, that met me [on the path]/ We were with William/ and that young man of [the household of] Sebaya and them/ He told me, "Let's go back"/ I told him, "I'm not going back/ Do I know where you will go sleep"/ I told him, "I'm going to sleep at Nabaru's place"/ He told me, "Go sleep at Arap Ntete's house/ All the children [i.e., girls here] usually cheat me/ Let's go sleep at Arap Ntete's place"/ I told him, "Go [away]"/ I saw him tell me, "I'll go and sleep in the forest myself. I no longer want the children of this place"/ I went and slept at Nabaru's place/ The next day he met me, "You—/ you, too . . . I go and sleep"/ I told him, "[what] do young men want . . . themselves . . . / Can't you sleep alone?"/ He wanted to ret— [make me return] to their house/

T.:   . . . Okay/ Have you left any-*i?*

Tn.:   Hmm-mm/

T.:   Okay/

A.N.:   Tell [it]-*a/* and we'll finish/ Tell that one, friend, and we'll finish/

T.:   *She says, uh—/ and, uh—/* What's he called?

Tn.:   Indobiwo/

T.:   You say Indobiwo? Indobiwo/ *She says, and, um— Indobiwo or whatever he's called-e/ that told her, uh—*

A.N.:   *They met on the path/*

T.:   *They met on the path/*

A.N.:   *And he told her, "Let's go back"/*

T.:   *And he told her, "Let's go back/ Let's go sleep at Arap Ntete's house"/ She told him, "I'm going to sleep, uh— at the house of" um—/*

A.N.:   *Nabaru/*

T.:   *"Nabaru's house"/ He told her, "What's wrong that you cheat me all the time/ You still will name me someday"/ Even someday-is/*

A.N.:   Say another [one] still/

Tn.:   There are no more/ Just those/

A.N.:   mekonte? ta ipwaat/

T.:   ta ipwaat/ an makiuny'-ayn/ kit . . .

A.N.:   mainte inko kiuny'ei/ kimwai/

T.:   mwai-ipak/

T.:   ai makiinten mookwek/ kimwai/

A.N.:   ai maikas— maikas ko makiuny'ei-o // ipwaat-a— ipwaat-a ak
         iny'ee paanaan/ alak/

T.:   ne kauutuun/ ata en Nkaroni-s/ ata en Sinentaaik-is/
         [silence]

Tn.:   ak Arap Sindiye/ kiayeese kora keru ak Arap Sindiye/

T.:   hm?

Tn.:   kiayeese kora keru ak Arap Sindiye/ ko kimii ak akot Cepkosa/

T.:   kolein nee?

A.N.:   [to others] kale makiraarisyei/

Tn.:   ki— kileincaun-i/ kileincaun "kole Arap Sindiye opa oru tuwai"/
         aleinci "maaweenti"/

T.:   mwauun ng'aa?

Tn.:   mwai akot Cepkosa/ "kole Arap Sindiye opa oru tuwai"/ ayeese/
         kikimii ak Sopiato/

T.:   hmm/ ale in—/ kikoleinci— ki— in— kikoleinci Arap Sindiye
         "oonkepe keru tuwai" // koyeeso/ komii— ko kimii— ko kimii ak
         Sopiato/ koyeeso kopa koru tuwai/
         . . .

A.N.:   mwai ak iny'ee/ paanan ko takopwaati niino/ imwai/

T.:   s'inaman-o korosyaat en euut/ eh?

L.:   . . . kiany'on en kaain/ kiayeeso . . . lang'at . . . Nutuuta/ kony'on
         Nuuta-e/ kile ". . ."/ ayeesoi/ kong'araany' metit kowo/ ko
         ing'aap komung' kityo/

A.N.:   an silan-o?

L.:   Nutuuta/

A.N.:   Nutuuta?

L.:   oo/

T.:   kole in—/ kole king'eet in—/ kole king'eet kile Nutuuta-i/ ko
         ing'aap komung'/ kole koleinci "kepe keru tuwai in—"

L.:   en timta/

T.:   en timta/ koyeeso/ kong'araany' metit kowo/

A.N.:   laakwaani pa in—/ ne pa ipiitoniino/

A.N.: There aren't any more? Keep thinking/

T.: Keep thinking/ And there's no hiding, indeed/ if . . .

A.N.: There's nothing hidden/ We say [everything]/

T.: Talk, then/

T.: And don't swallow it in your throat/ We say [it out loudly]/

A.N.: And don't you hear— don't you hear that we don't hide-*o*// Think then— you think, too, then *[to next girl]/* [of] others/

T.: That you forgot/ even from Nkaroni-*s*/ even from Sinentaaik-*is*/ *[silence]*

Tn.: And A͟ra͟p Sindiye/ I also refused to sleep with A͟ra͟p Sindiye/

T.: Hm?

Tn.: I refused to sleep with A͟ra͟p Sindiye, too/ when we were together with Cepkosa and them/

T.: What did he tell you?

A.N.: *[to others]* I say we don't laugh/

Tn.: They— they told me-*i*/ They told me, "A͟ra͟p Sindiye says, you go sleep together [with him]"/ I told them, "I'm not going"/

T.: Who told you?

Tn.: Cepkosa and them said/ "A͟ra͟p Sindiye says, you go sleep together [with him]"/ I refused/ We were with Sopiato/

T.: Hmm/ *I say, uh—/ A͟ra͟p Sindiye told her— uh— told her, "Let's go sleep together"// and she refused/ They were— they were— they were with Sopiato/ and she refused to sleep together/*
 . . .

A.N.: You talk then, too/ And meanwhile that one can still be thinking [of other things to say]/ Talk/

T.: And you hold the *korosyaat* in your hand/ Eh?

L.: . . . I came from that house/ I refused . . . evening . . . Nutuuta/ Nutuuta came-*e*/ He said, " . . . "/ I refused/ He shook his head and went/ It was just after he had come out [of seclusion]/

A.N.: Which young man-*o?*

L.: Nutuuta/

A.N.: Nutuuta?

L.: Yes/

T.: *She says, um—/ she says he up, uh—/ She says, it's said, Nutuuta up and-i/ just after he had come out [of seclusion]/ She says he told her, "Let's go sleep together, um—"*

L.: In the forest/

T.: *"In the forest"/ and she refused/ And he shook his head and went [away]/*

A.N.: *This child for, um—/ for that side across there/*

?:   *tako Tinkili ni-o?*

A.N.:   *aa-aa/*

?:   *ne pa Kirutari/*

A.N.:   *oo/*

T.:   eh-huh/ momii kiy ne kiuny'ei an makiraarcin asiny'e/

A.N.:   mainte— matakiuny'ei/ kimwai toi . . . /

T.:   momii kiy ne kiuny'ei/ kimwai wazi/ akot kokasei piikcu/
            kiparaastoi akot in—/

A.N.:   aini kiinte eceek/ ko inte eceek ko inte intasatutik iyu/

T.:   iyayaate nee-o Cory iny'ee?/

L.:   ak . . . ne maikoleincaun kila "ankeeru tuwai" ayeesoi kila/

T.:   an muran?

L.:   ne pa akot Sebaya/ maikoleincaun kila "oonkeeru tuwai"/ ayeese/

T.:   *kole Sebaya ne maikoleincin—/* [L. starts laughing]

A.N.:   *e-ee/ kole Kimany'e ne maikoleincin kile in— "oonkeeruyo" kile
            koyeeso/*

Y.?:   *ale akwang'/ kile kiyeete iman Sebaya?/* [laughter]

T.:   mwai/ . . . tukul/ aki ya Mungu/ ai ne kiing'usune tosi/ orue tuwai
            aki ya Mungu/

L.:   mekomii/

T.:   oo-oo/ uny'ei . . . lakini makiuny'e-is/

┌─A.N.:   ale makiuny'e toi mainte inko kiuny'e kimwai wazi/
└─T.:   ale momii kiy ne kiuny'e/ aki
                                            ya Mungu

L.:   ki . . . Partoti ak Tinkili en ipiitoniin-i/ koleincaun "ankeeru en . . .
            oonkepe keru koi tukul"/ aleinci "maaweenti"/ koleincaun . . .
            kila "aya"/

T.:   ng'aa? Partoti?

L.:   hmm/ en Mbokishi . . . /

T.:   *kole king'eet Partoti in—/ kole koleincaun "kepa keru koin-i"/
            koyeeso/ koleinci "aya"/*

Tn.:   ata iny'ee kora Partoti ira/ si . . . iny'ee/

L.:   peesio kikipeenti Mbokishi/

?:	*Is this still Tinkili-o?*
A.N.:	*No/*
?:	*The one for Kirutari/*
A.N.:	*Yes/*
T.:	Eh-huh/ There's nothing hidden, and listen, we don't laugh/
A.N.:	There's nothing— that's still hidden/ We say [everything], friend . . ./
T.:	There's nothing hidden/ We say [everything] clearly/ even so these people can hear/ We even announce [it], um—/
A.N.:	And we're here/ And we're here and old women are here/
T.:	What are you doing, Cory-o?/
L.:	And . . . that usually tells me all the time, "Let's sleep together." I refuse all the time/
T.:	Which young man?
L.:	The one for Sebaya and them/ He usually tells me all the time, "Let's sleep together"/ I refuse/
T.:	*She says, Sebaya that usually tells her—/* [L. starts laughing][3]
A.N.:	*No/ She says, Kimany'e that usually tells her, it's said, uh— "Let's sleep [together]," it's said, and she refuses/*
Y?:	*I say I'm astonished/ She really said she refused Sebaya?/* [laughter]
T.:	Talk/ . . . all/ Honest to God/ And [what about someone] you pulled out, then/ [when] you were sleeping together, honest to God/
L.:	There aren't any more/
T.:	Oo-oo/ She's hiding . . . but there's no hiding-*is*/
A.N.:	I say there's no hiding, friend. There's nothing hidden. We say [everything] openly
T.:	I say there's nothing hidden/ honest to God/
L.:	It— . . . Partoti and Tinkili from that side-*i*/ He told me, "Let's sleep in . . . let's all go sleep in this house"/ I told him, "I'm not going"/ He told me . . . always, "*Aya*"/
T.:	Who? Partoti?
L.:	Hmmm/ At Mbokishi . . . /
T.:	*She says Partoti up and, uh—/ She says, he told her, "Let's go sleep in that house-i"/ and she refused/ He told her, "Aya"/*
Tn.:	Even Partoti, too, [for me]/ so . . . you/
L.:	That day we were going to Mbokishi/

3. T. has named the younger brother, about ten years old at the time, through which L. identified the older brother, Kimany'e.

Tn.:   aa— acup/ alein-i/ kikipe ak akot Michael/ . . . ko weeriik akot
William/ ale anam Michael euut-i/ a— anam Partoti/ alein "ot
iborr-e"/ koleincaun "mayuutwaan"/

T.:   *akile in—/ laakweet ake naan-ayn/ laakwa ni kaan in—/*

A.N.:   *tako Tinkili-ai naan-ai/ aketuc/*

T.:   *kole in—/ kile konam in—/ kile konam in— manken ale/ . . .
manken ale kikuuren/ konam euut/*

A.N.:   ile ng'aa?

Tn.:   Michael/ kale anam euut—/

A.N.:   *kole Michael/*

T.:   *Michael/ ko— koparei Michael ne kanam-i/ ko Partoti ne kanam
euut/*

Tn.:   acup/

T.:   *koleinci "ot iborr"/*

Tn.:   ko ki tako weeriik akot Michael paanaan/

T.:   *ko ki tako weeriik/ hmm/ akot Michael/*

?:   *makimwai caan pa weeriik/*

T.:   *ee-ee/ yaani-o/ Partoti asiny'e ne akemwai/*

A.N.:   *Partoti/ kinam euut/ kopaarei konam in—/*

?:   *Michael/*

T.:   *oo/ konam Partoti euut/ koleinci "aya ta tuun omwauwan"/*

L.:   ak ciiciino/ nin pa Kap Senoy/ paaiintet aap Esta/ kiny'o kile in—/
kile "akoparpar Esta kiyaan inkomut kwaanta cu pa aeeng"'/

T.:   ng'aa ni?

L.:   niino pa Kap Senoy/ paaiintet aap Esta/

T.:   *akile in—/ paaiintet aap Esta-i/ koleinci ne kile in—/ kole
"akoparpar Esta in—/ akoparpar— akoparpar—"*
[others talking]

T.:   *kole/ kolein/ kole "akoparpar Esta ciicaan ko inkomut kwaanta
in— laakok aap aeeng"'*

A.N.:   *kiiny'imu iny'ee koek-e/*

T.:   mwai . . . /

L.:   ak ciici kiiny'e kora/ Inkutukay/ kole kotwekweec en koiin ak
Nini keyeese/ konereec paanaan/ kole ". . ." / kiinte ak Nini en
kaainy'uan/

Tn.: I— I cursed [him]/ I told him-*i*/ We went with Michael and them/ . . . when William and them were [still] boys/ I thought [I would] take Michael's hand-*i*/ I— I grabbed Partoti/ I told him, "May you turn white-*e*"/ He told me, "I won't forget this"/

T.: *She says, uh—/ This is another child now/ that other child, um—/*

A.N.: *It's still Tinkili-ai, that one-ai/ She left [some out]/*

T.: *She said, um—/ She thought [she would] take, uh—/ She thought [she would] take, uh— I don't know / . . . I don't know his name/ to take [his] hand/*

A.N.: You say who?

Tn.: Michael/ I went to take [his] hand—/

A.N.: *She says Michael/*

T.: *Michael/ So— she thought she had grabbed Michael-i/ but it was Partoti's hand she had taken/*

Tn.: I cursed [him]/

T.: *She told him, "May you turn white" /*

Tn.: So Michael and them were still boys then/

T.: *So they were still boys/ hmm/ Michael and them/*

?: *We don't say those [that involve] boys/*

T.: *No/ That is-o/ Partoti is the one that was named/*

A.N.: *Partoti/ She took [his] hand/ thinking she had grabbed, um—/*

?: *Michael/*

T.: *Yes/ She took Partoti's hand/ He told her, "Aya, you still will name me" /*

L.: And that person/ That one for Kap Senoy/ Esta's husband/ He came and said, um—/ He said, "That thing has pierced Esta, let the father marry these others"/

T.: Who is that?

L.: That one for Kap Senoy/ Esta's husband/

T.: *She says, um—/ Esta's husband-i/ told her, it's said, uh—/ he said, "pierced Esta, uh—/ pierced— pierced— "*
[others talking]

T.: *She says/ he told her/ "That person has pierced Esta, let the father marry, uh— the other children"*

A.N.: *He took out stones [heavy matters?]/*[4]

T.: Talk . . . /

L.: And that person, too/ Inkutukay/ He wanted to talk to us in that house with Nini, and we refused/ He got annoyed then/ and said, ". . ."/ We were with Nini in their house/

---

4. This incident seems to be about Esta's husband's suspicion of a tryst between his wife and someone else. He cursed the girls while angry about that.

A.N.:	*ale koleinci Inkutukay in—/ "oonkepe keru koiino" kile koyeeso/ en kaainy'uan/*
L.:	koi tosi/ kiinte ak Nini/
?:	*tako Tinkili ni ana ne pa . . . /*
T.:	*koi/*
A.N.:	*en koi/*
T.:	*kointe ak— ko mii ak Nini/ ale koyeeso/ koleinci-i/ "tepi kot tako omwauwaun"/*
?:	*tako laakwa ni kaan ni-o?*
AN/T.:	*ee-ee/*
?:	*ainoon?*
T.:	*ni pa in—/ kap Kirutari/*
A.N.:	ketin iny'ee/
T.:	momii kiuny'e asiny'e/
A.N.:	ata ceepyoosook/
L.:	kimii kora Kilowan/ kimii Kilowan kora-e/ kimii Kilowan/ . . . kiny'o kepol kweemai ak Prisilla/
T.:	Kilowan?
L.:	oo/ ko ki . . . kweemaaaai/ koyey paanaan/ konereecta/ en Sapoitit/
T.:	*kole kiny'o kile Kilowan/ kweemai koruyo laakwaani-e/ kony'o ko kiting'aanu toocit/ kiny'onei kweemai kony'o kityo kole koleinci "ankeeru tuwai"/ koyeeso/*
?:	*ainoon-o laakwaanaan-iwe?*
T.:	*ne pa kap Kirutari-o/ kony'o Kilowan koting'aanu toocit kweemai kole koleinci "ankeeru tuwai" koyeeso/ kole kong'aar metit konereecta/*
A.N.:	oyei laalweec mai/
T.:	mwai-ipak/ mwai alak asiny'e ata ceepyoosook toi/
A.N.:	ata ceepyoosook komwai/
T.:	ciita ne kicupin ana kilya/
L.:	kileincaun Ruci/ "koonaan impiiroit/ naan tikiik inka amacei naan tuui iny'ee utko"/ aleinci "kany' en kaany'aan"/ kole "moo-yeesoi?/ okenaan? aa laakweeng'waang-i?"/ ne pa Samson/
T.:	*kole king'eet Ruciin kole kosaam impiireet-i/ kole kosaam impiireet in—/ Ruciin/ ne tikiik-e/ koleinci in—/ "kilya ocei s'okenaan okweek kila/ aa laakweeng'waang?"/*

A.N.:   *I say, Inkutukay told her, uh—/ "Let's go sleep in that house," it's*
          said, she refused/ In their house/

L.:   It was this house/   We were with Nini/
?:   *Is that still Tinkili or the one of/*
T.:   *This house/*

A.N.:   *In this house/*

T.:   *They were with— they were with Nini/ I say she refused/ He told*
          her-i/ "Just wait, you still will name me"/

?:   *Is this still that child-o?*

A.N./T.: *No/*

?:   *Which one?*

T.:   *This one for, um—/ Kirutari's household/*

A.N.:   Repeat [tell me another]/

T.:   There's nothing hidden, you hear/

A.N.:   Even women [are named]/

L.:   There was also Kilowan/ There was also Kilowan-e/ There was
          Kilowan/ . . . he came and shouted [late at] night with Priscilla
          [?]/

T.:   Kilowan?

L.:   Yes/ So . . . [late at] niiiiiight/ and returned then/ and went away
          angry/ at Sapoitit/

T.:   *She says, Kilowan came, it's said/ [late at] night when this child*
          was sleeping-e/ He came with a flashlight/ He was coming at
          night/ He just came and told her, "Let's sleep together"/ and she
          refused/

?:   *Which one-o is that child, friend?*

T.:   *The one for Kirutari's household-o/ Kilowan came with a flash-*
          light [late at] night and told her, "let's sleep together" and she
          refused/ He shook [his] head and went away angry/

A.N.:   Hey, light this fire for us/

T.:   Talk, then/ Say more, you hear. Even women, friend/

A.N.:   Even women are named/

T.:   Someone who cursed you or whatever/

L.:   Ruci told me/ "Give me a plastic water container/ It's the blue one
          I want, that very dark one"/ I told her, "Wait at our home"/ She
          said, "Won't you refuse?/ You're cheating me? Am I your child-
          i?"/ The wife of Samson/

T.:   *She says, Ruci up and asked to borrow a plastic water container-*
          i/ She says, um— Ruci borrowed a water container/ the black
          one-e/ She told them, um—/ "What's wrong so [that] you usually
          cheat me all the time/ Am I your child?"/

L.:   ata kora Ruci/ kima— maikolein asiny'e "oonkeeru tuwai"/
any'oor laakok aap aeeng' kepe-is tukul koleincaun "leelintaap
koong' ne ii pa/ kipako/ makooneec koru"/

T.:   Ruci?

L.:   Ruci ne pa Samson-ira/

A.N.:   ketin-ais-iwe/

T.:   . . . mwai/ mwai-ipak/ ata koonuut asiny'e ata iyon koicup
koonuut ciita/

A.N.:   . . . maicup Arap Kurando? ii?

L.:   oo/

T.:   ko maimwai caan tukul/   iuny'ei?

A.N.:   ko maimwai— ko maimwai caan/ ak
                                                 kinken
                                               eceek/

T.:   tuk ce paarei ciicii makiuny'ei aki ya Mungu/

L.:   kimwai ceepkisas/

T.:   kiliyai?

L.:   kiyape muuita . . . /

T.:   kiisus-i?

L.:   ee-ee/ *[laughing]* kiake— *[laughs]*

A.N.:   kiiyeete?

T.:   kiiyeete muuita?

*[side conversation of A.N. w/ other: who do you refuse a skin to? Arap
Remboi]*

T.:   *king'eet-e/ kole kikiyeet— kiyeetei in— Arap Remboi muuita/*

L.:   kaale maac—/ kale kopirkee ak ee/ kisuupkee ak ee/ kisuupkee
ak ee-i/ *[laughs]* kisuupkee ak ee/ aleinci "amunee s'isuup"/
aleinci "amunee s'ikwer ee?" kole "maakwer"/ ak kile paanaan
"kiakwer"/

T.:   *akile in—/ akile kisuupkee Arap Remboi/ ak kaameet-i/*
[laughter]

?:   *mwai-o/*

T.:   *kisuupkee Arap Remboi ak kaameet-e/ koleinci "amunee s'isuup
ee?/ kepa kelalei (?) kikwer ana akwer"/ raait/ mwa— opakaac
raariyat okweek/ keesun-a tosi/ ana ko takotepaat akot Arap
Ntete/*

A.N.:   ata eceek toi/ ipaarei . . . /

L.: Even again Ruci/ usu— She usually tells me, you hear, "Let's sleep together"/ I meet other children [and] we all go-*is* [sleep elsewhere together]. She tells me, "Flirting is all you want/ [with] young men/ They don't let us sleep"/

T.: Ruci?

L.: Ruci, Samson's wife now/

A.N.: Repeat [it] then, friend/

T.: . . . talk/ Talk then/ Even your father, you hear, even if [one of you] cursed your father/

A.N.: . . . didn't you curse A̲rap Kurando? *ii?*

L.: Yes/

┌T.: So you don't say them all/   Are you hiding [some]?

└A.N.:   So don't you say— don't you say those/ and we [already] know [about] it ourselves [i.e., how could you hide that?]/

T.: [Those are] things that kill someone, we don't hide, honest to God/

L.: He said *cepkisas* [hated girl]/

T.: What was wrong?

L.: We argued about the [sleeping] skin . . ./

T.: You bit him-*i?*

L.: No/ *[laughing]* I— *[laughs]*

A.N.: You refused [him]?

T.: You refused him the [sleeping] skin?

[side conversation of A.N. w/ other: who did she refuse a skin to? A̲rap Remboi]

T.: *[He] up and-e/ She says she refused— she refused, uh— A̲rap Remboi a [sleeping] skin/*

L.: I s̲ay, I̲ didn't—/ I say, he fought with Mother/ He was wrestling with Mother/ He was wrestling with Mother-i/ *[laughs]* He was wrestling with Mother/ and I told him, "Why are you wrestling [her]?"/ I told him, "Why do you hit Mother? I told him, "Don't hit [her]"/ and he said then I hit [him]/

T.: *She says, um—/ she says, A̲rap Rembo̲i was wrestling/ with [her] mother-i/*

   [laughter]

?: *Tell it-o/*

T.: *A̲rap Remboi was wrestling with [her] mother-e/ and she told h̲im, "Why d̲o you wrestle Mother?/ Let's go . . . we hit or I'll hit [you]"/ Right/ Talk— You all stop laughing/ Finish then/ or let Arap Ntete and them stay [without being named]/*

A.N.: E̲ven us, friend/ you think . . . /

T.:	ata anee/
L.:	kiki . . . ak William/ ko kile . . . /
T.:	hee?
L.:	. . . / ki kile kile kiaken kile/ . . . William "kalya s'isasaan?"
A.N.:	ng'aa?
L.:	William/ ko makimwai/. . . komuunceec kweemai ak sikonyet/ . . .
T.:	William?
L.:	oo/
T.:	kolein ". . . isase?"
L.:	oo/ kepe eceek kepe . . . / *[laughing]* kole ". . . isasaan"/
T.:	*kole king'eet William-e/*
A.N.:	*kaale kaimwei/*
T.:	*king'eet William kile in—/*
A.N.:	*kaalapat/* [laughing]
T.:	*king'eet William in—/ komuunci kweemai/ ak sikonyet/ kopaarei kony'o kopir/ kole "amunee si kony'onei in—/ si kopaarei kisase"/ mwai alak/*
?:	pakuleny'uun?
A.N.:	naan ne kaimweiene? inken kiy ciici/
T.:	ta imwai ake/ ne . . . kora/ ne . . . /
	[other side comments]
L.:	Tinkili/ ng'aa ne kicupe . . . peesiet kiiny'e-ai/ aa/ kile peesiet kiiny'e kiinte koi kiiny'e tukul/
Tn.:	oo-ira/ akicup Michael ak William/ kiyeese keyaatu/ kile "ma-yaataksei paani"/ "omeelkee—"/ mamwai komeelkee?/
L.:	manken/
Tn.:	"ak omeelk— ot omeelkee en koi"/ ot— ko tukul/
T.:	Samson?
L.:	Michael/
T.:	Michael?
L.:	oo/ kimii akot Tinkili/ . . . akot Tata/
Tn.:	kikimiitei kaainy'aan tukul/
T.:	kioyeese oyaatu-e?
L./Tn.:	oo/

T.: Even me [you name me]/

L.: We . . . and William/ so he said . . . /

T.: Hee?

L.: . . ./ He said, it's said, I cheated him, it's said/ . . . William "What's wrong that you hate me?"

A.N.: Who?

L.: William/ But we didn't say it/ . . . he came to us very early in the morning with a stick [to beat us]/ . . .

T.: William?

L.: Yes/

T.: He told you, ". . . you hate?"/

L.: Yes/ We went ourselves to . . ./ *[laughing]* He said, " . . . you hate me"/

T.: *She says William up and-e/*

A.N.: [to William] *I say you're frightened/*

T.: *It's said William up and, um—/*

A.N.: *He's run [off]/* [laughing]

T.: *William up and, uh—/ came very early in the morning to them/ with a stick/ thinking he would come and beat [them]/ They said, "Why is he coming, uh—/ that he thinks we hate [him]?"/ Say more/*

?: My coinitiate?

A.N.: That's what you're frightened of? This person knows something [else to be named]/

T.: Say still another/ that . . . again/ that . . . /
[other side comments]

L.: Tinkili/ who cursed. . . . the other day-*ai/ aa*/ It's said, that day we were in that house together/

Tn.: Oh, right/ We cursed Michael and William/ We refused to open [the house for them to come in]/ saying, "It can't be opened now"/ [They answered] "You lick one another— "/ Didn't they say to lick one another? [i.e., cursed them]/

L.: I don't know/

Tn.: "And you lick— may you lick one another in this house"/ May— all of you/

T.: Samson?

L.: Michael/

T.: Michael?

L.: Yes/ We were with Tinkili and them/ . . . Tata and them/

Tn.: We were all at my house/

T.: You refused to open [the house for them]-*e?*/

L./Tn.: Yes/

T.:   kikuure Samson?

L.:   Michael/

Tn.:   Michael-is/

T.:   Michael?

L./Tn.:   oo/

T.:   *kole kiny' on Michaelin-e/ kole kowo in—/ kopaarei kowo koleinci*
              "oi yaatwaan"/ ko matakoyaatci ciit/ koleinci "ot omeelkee tukul
              en koi"/

Tn.:   any'onei kong'erat/ Ink— Inkutukay en aineet ko miitii ak Mich-
              ael/ kowo iny'ee Michaelin/ komaa— koleincaan iny'ee "an-
              keeru en aineet"/ ing'aap komung' kityo/ ayeese keru tuwai
              konereec/

T.:   ng'aa ni?

Tn.:   Inkutukay/

T.:   *kole king'eet Inkutukay-e/ ing'aap kokamung' kityo/ kowo kolein-*
              ci in—/ kolein Tinkili kole "ankeeru tuwai en aineet . . ."/
              [Tn. laughs]

?.:   *oo met/ ng'aa pa aaineet kokeny'?* [laughter]

A.N.:   *Inkutukay/*

T.:   *Inkutukay/*

Y.?:   *en oriit aap pek/*

T.:   *en oriit aap pek/ ko ing'aap ko mung'/ koleinci "mamaciin"/*
              karokeesu?/

Tn.:   hm?

T.:   karokeesu anan tako mii alak/ keero/

T.:   ale aini— ale aini ceepyoosookcu ce okatgee/ ma maicoo—/
              opiraategee tukuuk?

Y.?:   moomwai-o ceepyoosookcu kopar kiy?

T.:   kale mamwai ceepyoosook// tako mii akeenke ne imwai-i?/ ii? ii?

L.:   mm-mm/

⌐T.:   bas/
└A.N.:   kaiuny'/ kaiuny' kityo/

L.:   maauny'ei/

⌐A.N.:   ile maiuny'ei? nam iyu/ nam tosi iyu/ *[giving korosyaat to next*
              girl]
└T.:   ata ne ing'usune/ ata an— ata inta anee ne ing'usune anee/
              omwai olein "ang'usune/ maampait"

T.:   ng'alaan-ipak/ . . .

T.: He's called Samson?

L.: Michael/

Tn.: Michael-*is*/

T.: Michael?

L./Tn.: Yes/

T.: *She says Michael came-e/ She says he went and, uh—/ He thought [he would] go tell them, "Oi, open [the house] for me"/ [but] no one opened [the door] for him/ He [then] told them, "May you all lick one another in this house"/*

Tn.: I was coming at dusk [and met]/ Ink— Inkutukay at the river together with Michael/ Michael left/ So didn— so he told me, "Let's sleep in the river"/ Just after he had come out [of seclusion]/ I refused to sleep together and he was annoyed/

T.: Who is this?

Tn.: Inkutukay/

T.: *She says Inkutukay up-e/ Just after he had come out/ he went and told her, um—/ He told Tinkili, "Let's sleep together in the river . . ."*

[Tn. laughs]

?: *What a killer [lit., what a great death]/ Who's this for the river now?* [laughter]

A.N.: *Inkutukay/*

T.: *Inkutukay/*

Y?: *In the water/*

T.: *In the water/ Just after he had come out [of seclusion]/ She told him, "I don't want you"/ Have you finished?/*

Tn.: Hm?

T.: Are you finished or are there still others [to name]/ Look/

T.: I say, and— I say, and these women that you greet/ don— didn—/ do you argue about things?

Y?: You don't name-*o* these women, and there are many here?

T.: I say, name [some] women// Is there still one you'll tell-*i?/ ii? ii?*

L.: Mm-mm/

⌐T.: Okay/

└A.N.: You've hidden [some]/ You've just hidden [some]/

L.: I'm not hiding [any]/

⌐A.N.: You say you didn't hide [any]? Take this/ Take this, then/ *[giving korosyaat to the next girl]*

└T.: Even [someone] you pulled out/ even, um—/ Even if it's me that you pulled out myself/ You tell it and say, "I pulled out/ the crocodile [i.e., his penis]"

T.: Talk, then/ . . .

Notes

Chapter 1

1. I discuss some of the issues that have been raised about circumcision in appendix A.

2. Kipsigis began moving into Kaplelach areas before that time as well, but were chased out by Maasai in the 1960s.

3. These marriage negotiations will be the basis of a future book, in many ways a companion to this one: *Looking for the Hairless Cow: Arranging Okiek Marriage.*

4. More extensive transcriptions have been deposited with the Kenya National Archives in Nairobi and can also be found in Kratz 1988c.

Chapter 2

1. This study focuses on how to make people who are biologically mature into socially mature people as well. Discrepancies and contradictions between social and biological maturity and the cultural recognition given to these processes are another important dimension of this entwining, discussed in Fortes's works *Religion, Morality and the Person* (1987) and *Oedipus and Job* (1959).

2. Turner himself notes the distinctions: "I had brought into the field with me two distinct theoretical orientations, and these determined the kinds of data I collected and to some extent predetermined the sorts of analysis I expected to make. On the one hand, following in the tradition of the Rhodes-Livingstone Institute research, I collected the kind of data that would have enabled me to analyze the structure of the social system in which *Mukanda* occurred. . . . On the other hand, I recorded ritual details, their interpretation by experts and laymen, and those items of secular behavior directly related to the servicing and maintenance of the ritual complex" (Turner 1967:261).

3. A comparison of index references in *The Forest of Symbols* is one simple indication of this: there are fifteen entries for "dominant symbol" versus a single entry for "instrumental symbol."

4. Compare the emphasis on referential meaning at the expense of indexical and pragmatic meanings in language analysis (Silverstein 1976).

5. Singer (1972:70–72) outlines a similar methodological concern for significant association. He takes different performance components as the basis of associations, and also considers associations made through vernacular names and categorizations of ceremonies.

6. Audrey Richards's *Chisungu* (1956) is a notable exception. It includes songs and information on mimetic aspects of Bemba initiation in an appendix, and distinguishes between comments made to her during the course of the ceremony, comments made by any woman present, subsequent interpretations by three named Bemba experts, and her own descriptive account.

7. Giddens is right that actors can have different orientations vis-à-vis social norms—different interests that do not coincide—and that interpretation and significance can be contested. His sense of all this, however, makes actors seem not only knowledgeable but perhaps overly rational. Giddens might benefit from a dose of Bakhtinian heteroglossia, in which multiple interpretations are simultaneously part of an exchange and superimposed in the same communicative forms, and different orientations are possible simultaneously for the same actor. Giddens's understanding of language in social use is also insufficiently varied and insufficiently multifunctional. His review of American scholarly work on language in social use is oddly limited to ethnomethodology and some early sociolinguistic studies, missing much that bears directly on his interests. Thompson (1984:chapter 3) replicates his teacher's shortcomings in his own consideration of language.

8. Karp's paper on Iteso marriage ritual (1987) is a notable and welcome exception that focuses on irony and draws explicitly on Bakhtin.

9. Talal Asad's papers on medieval Christian ritual (1983, 1987) are an important exception. They suggest that historical studies of ritual may well emphasize questions other than those about ceremonial functions and meanings, which have dominated anthropological work.

10. Irvine 1979, the introduction to Brenneis and Myers 1984, and Parkin 1984 are all telling and cogent criticisms. They criticize him for many things, including a concept of "traditional societies" so broad as to be useless, with no distinctions of sociopolitical structure; a vaguely defined and misleadingly conflating concept of "formality"; confusion of belief in the fixity of oratory with actual fixity; and forgetting the analytical nature of dichotomous reductions that are united in lived experience.

11. Feeley-Harnik notes similarly persistent institutions of the Sakalava monarchy but stresses the many fundamental changes they have gone through. She suggests that the nature of political legitimation has shifted, coming to rely more on links to dead ancestors than on the vulnerable living, in order to protect "the very principles on which their actions were based" (Feeley-Harnik 1984:12). The effects of corvée and taxes, prominent in her account, are curiously underplayed in Bloch's work on the Merina, who dominated the Sakalava. He simply notes the use of the ritual as a mode of corvée recruitment (Bloch 1986:159) and "traditional forms of taxation and corvées on an unprecedented scale" (Bloch 1986:14).

12. R. Wagner also stresses multiple sign use and multiple contexts, but he debunks the idea that any context of use is more important than another:

The various contexts of a culture get their meaningful characteristics from one another, through the participation of symbolic elements in more than one context. They are invented out of each other, and the idea that some of the recognized contexts in a culture are "basic" or "primary," or represent the "innate," or that their properties are somehow essentially objective or real, is a cultural illusion. (R. Wagner 1981:41).

Wagner also credits people with greater creativity in shaping cultural understanding and actions, what Bourdieu calls habitus.

13. Thompson says Bourdieu concentrates on style at the expense of content, but his own narrow reading in sociolinguistics prevents him from recognizing what an impoverished sense of style Bourdieu works with. For him, style means only register or dialect rather than the wider range possible in communicative repertoires, and he emphasizes diglossic situations in particular.

14. Scotton's recent work (1983, 1988) significantly refines the study of code-switching.

15. Beidelman's analysis of Swazi ritual, however, is based on published material. Though he used rich sources, such details were most likely unavailable to him. His is a remarkably nuanced

reinterpretation in light of this, and very useful in conjunction with Lienhardt's focus on sacrificial rites for its attention to another type of ritual purpose and form.

16. This interpretation of physical control in terms of capacity for adulthood, changes in comportment, and development of moral personhood is not unique to Okiek, though the specific idiom may differ in each case. Compare Jackson's (1989:41) discussion of Kuranko initiation where "mastery of one's reaction to pain . . . is regarded as the paradigm of all self-mastery."

17. Like many Okiek words that describe emotion, -nereec is a verb, describing an emotional process more than a state. Compare Rosenberg 1990, which notes similarities between ethnose-mantic approaches and the nominalizations prominent in anthropological studies of emotion.

18. This interpretation of initiation and power extends a view on Swazi royal ritual and power presented in Beidelman 1966 and discussed in the introduction to Arens and Karp 1989.

19. These elements are often purged from anthropological accounts of ceremonies, though there are exceptions such as Handelman 1979, Kapferer 1979b, and Karp 1987. Still, humorous aspects of ceremonies are treated as a phase in the ritual process, an element of a ritual of rebellion, or some other type of escape valve. Humorous asides and side channels have rarely been included in analyses of the formal ceremonial proceedings.

20. Despite broad structural similarities, however, easy equations of "oppressed" groups raise problematic questions—for instance, who makes the equations, for what political purposes, and for which component of the equation? What specific difficulties, historical developments, and local alliances does the broader equation elide? These equations can also run into the same kinds of difficulties as the broad category of "third world women" (see appendix A).

21. "While actual expressions of women's culture ideology vary greatly, the following is an ideal-typical description. There is an entity, women's culture, which represents an Ur-form of women's nature and has the same characteristics across time and space. These characteristics include moral superiority to men; cooperative rather than competitive social relations; selfless maternality; and benevolent sexuality. Thus women's culture embodies the notion that there is an authentic feminine selfhood that has been distorted, accreted over by male domination. While many of these tenets are parallel to those said to be characteristic of radical or cultural feminism, I would distinguish between women's culture and these theoretical strands in feminism. Women's culture is not a political or theoretical perspective but a protean set of claims that may be . . . used to construct varying arguments concerning women's rights and duties" (di Leonardo 1991b:244).

22. Ingrid Sischy, then the photography critic for the New Yorker, provided another example in a lecture at the Getty Museum: "Remarks on Gender in Art and Photography" (6 December 1990). Into haunting photographs by Lady Hawarden, Sischy read female bonding and mother-daughter relations. To her, only a woman could have taken the photographs; Lady Hawarden "photographed like a woman." In light of what she saw as overwhelming evidence of female subjectivity and essence, Sischy ignored (as irrelevant) conventions of theatrical photography, upper-class costume play, portraiture, and painting that were current at the time Lady Hawarden worked.

23. The assumed sense of continuity and history (often glossed as "tradition") is also negotiable and changing (Hobsbawm and Ranger 1983; Kratz 1993).

24. Kitching 1980 is of interest and help in this task, but a longer historical trajectory is needed.

Chapter 3

1. Most of my research has been with these two Okiek groups, though I have visited others (Omotik, piik ap Oom, Kapsapulik, and Kipsang'any' in Kenya, and Akie in Tanzania), talked and worked with Maresionik assistants, and visited northern Torrobo groups near Mount Nyiru

and the Mathews Range. I will not survey scholarly work on Okiek or Torrobo here. Literature reviews can be found in Kratz 1977, Kratz 1988c, and Rottland and Vossen 1977.

2. Waller (1984, 1985) contributes significantly to regional studies with histories of different Maasai sections and their interactions. Galaty (1986) also calls for a regional approach.

3. Blackburn's 1968–69 research is another comparative baseline for some topics. Living in Narok, he visited various Okiek groups, including Kaplelach and Kipchornwonek. Dr. Blackburn has generously shared material on ceremonies he attended in my research area.

4. Perhaps most significant for Okiek was the colonial creation of reserves and the movement of Maasai. Kaplelach and Kipchornwonek were not involved in the actual population shift, but the moves shuffled Maasai sections, replacing old neighbors. Later, some Okiek were conscripted as labor with Maasai age-mates to construct the road over the Mau. In the 1950s, during Mau Mau, Okiek from this area were collected into a camp.

5. Kratz 1988c discusses Okiek and Torrobo groups further.

6. However, systems of interaction between Okiek groups in the western highlands and Torrobo of the north and east might have come together in the Leroghi area.

7. Huntingford wrote about Kipkururek Kamelilo-Kapchepkendi, who live north of Nakuru (Huntingford 1929, 1942, 1951, 1954, 1955). Blackburn 1974 discusses early Okiek history and movements on the Mau. Blackburn regularly includes Cheranganyi in his Okiek lists, but I leave them out here. His first list (Blackburn 1970) marked them "reported but not confirmed." Rottland found none in this area who called themselves Okiek, and notes that only Blackburn has called people there Okiek (Rottland and Vossen 1977). The question is whether highland Marakwet who hunt and collect honey more than others are simply called Okiek, or are related through history and practice to Okiek farther south. Similarly, Rottland (personal communication) reports no evidence of Okiek in the Elgon area. I leave aside Blackburn's Kony' on that basis; they were also among the groups originally "unconfirmed." Blackburn's lists of Okiek include most groups who have been called Torrobo, including El Molo on the shores of Lake Turkana. I make finer distinctions and limit the use of the term Okiek to those who now call themselves that and to others who formerly spoke Kalenjin and have a history of interaction with Okiek. Presumably, they would have called themselves Okiek before they changed languages.

8. Herren (personal communication) recently confirmed that Mukogodo Digiri formerly spoke a Kalenjin language.

9. Kipchornwonek say Omotik lived to their west, but Rottland says Omotik claim to come from Mutarakwa, considerably farther west.

10. Linguists classify Omotik either as a branch of Southern Nilotic that is coordinate with Kalenjin and Datooga (Heine 1973), or as being closer to Datooga, jointly forming a single branch coordinate with Kalenjin (Ehret 1980; Rottland 1977, 1981).

11. Kratz 1986 discusses differences in linguistic repertoire as well, including trends in multilingual ability over time.

12. Kratz 1988c discusses tentative patterns of intra-Okiek interactions more extensively. I use past tense to speak of visiting networks because people seem no longer to keep them up but rather maintain contact chiefly with Okiek in nearby groups. Young men particularly used to roam widely and visit different Okiek groups after initiation and before marriage.

13. A critical example of those historical differences and their results today relates to land: some Okiek find themselves squatters on their own land (declared forest reserve or demarcated to others), were evicted or moved into Forest Department settlements to work in exchange for temporary use of a small plot of their own land, or were moved elsewhere during colonial times. The most fortunate of Okiek, Kaplelach and Kipchornwonek among them, now own and will receive title to portions of what was formerly their land.

14. Distefano's work in historical linguistics (1985) also suggests such different networks of interaction. His linguistic classification subdivides the Mau-Tinderet group of Highland South Kalenjin into North Mau and South Mau. The former includes Tinet, Ravine, and Tinderet as examples; the latter is represented only by Kipchornwonek, for lack of comparative material.

15. The Tanzanian Akie, separated from Kenyan Okiek long before this time, suggest that the term Akie (or Okiek) existed before the formation of the current regional system of ethnicity, but what kind of ethnic sense it carried at that earlier time is unclear.

16. The characterization might be more appropriate for other Okiek who stayed near Maasai settlements. In hard times, however, some Maasai moved closer to Okiek, and again relative clientship is a question.

17. The description of the forest and the other language spoken suggest Ole Kulet is talking about Okiek.

18. Waller 1984 traces the history of Uas Nkishu and other Maasai sections in the Trans-Mara.

19. This summarizes the Maasai ideology of Torrobo and Maasai. Galaty is the best source on Maasai images of Torrobo, and the only one based on field research (Galaty 1977a, 1977b, 1979, 1986; cf. Chang 1982). Kenny 1981 uses early literature to discuss the Dorobo category as pastoralist "other."

20. See Blackburn 1971, Blackburn 1982, and Ambrose 1986 for more detail on forest zones and ecology.

21. *Hamamelidaceae Trichocladus ellipticus Eckl. and Zehy. ssp. malosanua (Bak.) Verdc.*

22. *Celumpuut = Araliaceae Schefflera volkensii (Engl.) Harms. Tikeltit = Acanthaceae Acanthus eminens C.B.Cl.* Dried *seketeetik* berries are a medicinal forest product sought by Maasai.

23. Other Okiek groups held hunting rights by *konoito*, too. See Blackburn 1986 for more detail.

24. Kratz 1988c:72–73 names honey-producing species.

25. *Latyet* (cf. Maa *e-latia*) refers to a group of houses relatively close to one another.

25. Okiek generally follow the naming and timing of Purko Maasai ages; Kipchornwonek have begun to learn Kipsigis correspondences, too. This is a highly simplified description of Okiek age-sets. Prins 1953, Baxter and Almagor 1978, and Stewart 1977 provide leads into the extensive literature on age-set systems; the latter two have bibliographies for further investigation.

27. Donovan 1987 describes changes in land use and settlement at this time for Kipsigis north and west of Kaplelach and Kipchornwonek. Extensive clearing of forests continuous with Okiek ones began there in the 1940s. My visits to areas north of his research site suggest that the same general processes covered the area all along the western edge of the Mau.

28. Okiek state these preferences many years later, though perhaps the animals they got depended as much (or more) on what animals Maasai and others made available to them.

29. Though there is no obvious connection, this also coincided with Mau Mau freedom fighting.

30. Mulot, the southernmost market on his map, lies at the eastern edge of the former Kipsigis Reserve (Manners 1976:334). Mulot was one large market where Kipchornwonek at Nkaroni sold honey and bought goods in 1974. It was an overnight trip then, but today one can walk an hour, catch a *matatu* at Nentolo, and return in the evening.

31. Manners describes traders' influence in the Reserve around Kipsonoi, Bomet, and Litein, which provided a double incentive for planting maize as a cash crop. The traders bought the maize and then sold manufactured goods for the money earned. A similar relation probably held for other markets created farther south and east, such as Mulot, though it has yet to be documented.

32. Okiek consumption patterns and aspirations have developed along lines similar to those of other rural Kenyans (and other developing nations), though somewhat later (Hay 1988; Wilk 1990). Yet relatively recent Okiek economic diversification and incorporation into development efforts introduces a wrenching disparity, not unique to Okiek, between consumption desires and what their current production can provide and sustain. As discussed below, land sales offer a temporary but often devastating solution. The sales dispose of large proportions of an essential production factor and use proceeds in a way heavily (sometimes exclusively) weighted toward

social investment and consumption with little or no economic investment toward future production and maintenance.

33. In 1982, Sogoo had two shops (one Okiek-owned), one tea shop, a butchery, a bar, and a maize mill. By 1988, there were fifteen shops open—three tea shops, four butcheries, three maize mills, two tailors, a carpenter, a medical store, and of course the bar. Kipsigis owned fifteen buildings and ran twenty-one establishments; Okiek owned six and ran seven (some buildings house more than one business).

34. Ololunga school first opened in 1943.

35. Children herd, care for younger siblings, and help in the gardens. Girls also help their mothers with household work.

36. Galaty 1980 and 1991 discuss the history, structure, and internal conflicts of Maasai group-ranches and subsequent land sales.

37. By claiming land where people had been living, he appropriated an area with a clear-water source, which has been quickly developing into the next Okiek center, with a school, shops, and a planned road. He also benefited from previous work that cleared forest for gardens and houses; he could then plant large areas, develop better pasture, and so on.

38. About $120 in 1984; closer to $160 at the time of the sale.

39. For instance, the dependence of men on women for social reproduction, that is, the perpetuation of patrilineages with offspring, is ignored. Women's independent organization of seclusion ceremonies is considered a temporary exception to normal roles.

40. Women and men alike use *eemeet aap kaa*.

41. See Kratz 1990c on portrayals of marital responsibilities and disputes in the advice given to a bride and groom at their wedding.

42. Comaroff 1985:124–29 and Comaroff and Comaroff 1990 discuss the concepts of capital and commodities as applied to cows.

43. In another book, *Looking for the Hairless Cow: Arranging Okiek Marriage,* I will look at Okiek marriage arrangements and the issues discussed here in detail. The property mentioned here is contemporary. Okiek were giving cows in marriage even before beginning to diversify, getting them from Maasai and slaughtering them to eat. Long ago, they gave honey, hives, and hyrax capes. The basic distribution was similar; male relatives took most hives, with one for the mother.

44. Even now, most Kaplelach maize is gone months before the new harvest. More Kipchornwonek harvests carry through the year. Some have surplus that they can sell, trade, or use to help Kaplelach relatives who run short.

45. The variety of greens eaten seems related to gardening itself. A number of wild greens Okiek have learned about from Kipsigis are secondary growth in former gardens.

46. Kratz 1977 describes Okiek liquors, brewing, and drinking occasions in detail.

Chapter 4

1. Okiek shaving ceremonies are similar to Maasai ones (*enkitupukunoto enkerai ti aji*, bringing the child out of the home); certain aspects correspond even in detail.

2. Okiek still celebrated the ceremony in 1974, but by 1985 children no longer wanted long ears.

3. For example, *kepa tuumto* (to go [for] initiation); *peentin tuumto* (they are going [for] initiation); *akopa tuumto* (they have gone [for] initiation).

4. There are similarities to the Ilongot concept of *liget* (M. Rosaldo 1980) and the Gisu *lirima* (Heald 1982), but also important differences. For instance, Okiek men and women both become worked up (*-nereec*), though each sex shows it differently; Gisu consider *lirima* a male capacity.

5. Two of the girls eventually initiated are named Nini, distinguished by tone (high-high versus low-high). To differentiate them in the English-language text, I use Níní for Nini (hh) and an

unmarked Nini for the other, whose parents hosted the ceremony. Seraset was about seven during my first research period; she was the daughter of the Kaplelach family I stayed with at that time.

6. I use quotations for kin terms only when the classificatory use gets more extended, as *maama* (MoBr, Si child, etc.) is here.

7. Ceremony costs have risen over the years not simply because of inflation, but because of increases in what is considered standard and necessary for every initiation. Many, but not all, of the increases involve longer, more elaborate entertainment for guests. Chapter 8 discusses these changes in relation to changing circumstances of Okiek life. Table 3 shows average 1983 ceremonial costs, but households also vary in how much more than this they can provide. For instance, the most lavish ceremony I attended in 1983 was hosted by the assistant chief of the area. In addition to what is shown in the table, he also provided bottled beer and some whiskey miniatures as well as an enormous amount of honey wine and maize beer, had slaughtered a sheep as well as a cow, and had more of almost everything else. He also had his daughter's costume brought at greater expense from farther away by Maresionik Okiek, from near the area where stylistic innovations in costumes begin. Some of the special items brought for guests were not distributed equally to all, but allowed him to make distinctions among his guests. Among his special guests were several Administration Police, who stayed in a private room by themselves during the celebration. Families who cannot meet the basic host expenses become "borrowers," initiating their children at another home. Tata's father did not want to let her be initiated at his brother's home because it might give this impression.

8. He refers to this later in his encouraging speech (see chapter 6 and table 14).

9. The central point of view in this account is my own participation in this ceremony, but I include other perspectives and observations from ceremonies where I took part in other ways.

10. On elders and their ceremonial roles, see chapter 5 and Kratz 1988b.

11. See the first example in table 16.

12. See chapter 6 and appendix E.

13. Because of his birth history as a single man among sisters.

14. They said later they *were* hiding there but couldn't enter the carefully watched house.

15. They are related to the girls in various ways, such as MoSi, or FaSi, or Si.

16. Decisions are influenced by property, past relations between the two families, politics within the bride's family, and assessment of the future husband's personality and ability to provide for the bride (this will be discussed in my forthcoming book on Okiek marriage). Weddings are planned for soon after girls come out so that their chances to elope are limited; the best way for a girl's family to control and profit from her now-legitimate reproductive capacities is to give her away quickly.

17. The following outline describes only aspects of the ceremonies that people were willing to discuss with me; it does not reveal the secrets of seclusion or violate the confidence of any Okiek with whom I spoke.

18. It is unclear to me if it occurs early the next morning or sometime earlier. I also received conflicting reports on whether *kelap euun* includes going to the river, with this procession as the trip home.

19. There were surely a number of things animating this rankling, including continued bitterness from the dispute over the circumcision location. Reputation and economics were also involved. A long seclusion period can indicate wealth, since it means feeding initiates for a longer time, but seclusion can also be prolonged if some parents have difficulty getting things for ceremonies. The delay at Tinkili's house was not enough to interpret as real poverty. Nor did Tinkili's mother suggest that all the initiates wait, so she might simply have been offering peace, recoordinating and reuniting the initiates as they should have been. Nini's mother wanted to end the seclusion; her own daughter had been shaved prematurely because of illness. By combining the two ceremonies, they cut the initiation process short, but no shorter than if they had followed Tinkili's mother's suggestion. Their insistence on independent ceremonies suggests a deeper resentment.

20. Propolis is a dark, malleable substance with which bees close cracks and holes in their hives—a kind of bee glue.

21. *Cepcep* (quick) has two interpretations: a young man who is clever and quick enough to marry a girl by eloping ("stealing") or quickly coming for marriage talks, or someone who is sexually adept.

22. More commonly, payment is last.

23. This part of the ceremony is called *kiiilta* (lit., to anoint away), like the wedding day when a young woman is taken to her husband's home.

Chapter 5

1. See Kratz 1986 on cross-contextual relations, especially iconic similarities between signs.

2. I concentrate here on roles and participation in ritual events; later celebratory feasting includes other differentiations. The most salient division then is host/guest, which is also part of the division of labor and activities on the day of ritual events. Both host and guest include further distinctions (Kratz 1988c:183).

3. Each *matiriyaat* receives 20–25 Ksh per initiate (about $1.50 in 1983), as does the circumcisor. The seclusion mother receives 100 Ksh or a calf for each girl. The blessing elder receives 10 Ksh per initiate.

4. Ritual participation patterns that single out a pair of representative actors from general group participation also parallel in some ways the call-and-response pattern of Okiek song. As with song, any appropriate person can take lead roles (though situational peculiarities affect choices); leaders meld into the group later, much as lead singers rejoin the response group when another caller begins.

5. The order is sometimes determined by fathers' age-sets, though the initiates' age and size are also cited in explanation in conjunction with other factors. Consistent principles of order are: (1) the child at whose home they are cut is first, and (2) siblings of the same biological parents should not be adjacent. The last initiate has often "borrowed" the ceremony, might be more distantly related, and could well be a bit smaller or younger than the others.

6. At times, people relate these positions to character and destiny. My cowife, for instance, cited my sojourn with them to show how her husband's position as *koyuumkok* was consistent with how he lived. He gathered people together (*koyuumis piik*), and people came to him for shelter.

7. Compare also pictures of new Maasai mothers (Adamson 1967:226–27). Both male and female *taarusyeek* are likened to *solootwik*.

8. Male and female initiates each have their own way to wash their hands (Kratz 1988c:192).

9. All the mothers visit regularly, but the one in whose home they stay becomes "mother" to all, and is addressed as *kopot taarusyeek* (mother of the initiates) during seclusion.

10. No particular relation of age or kinship determines who will be *matireenik*, though the two must not have been in the same seclusion house during their own initiation. Married women older than the girls, they might in fact be a sister or a mother's sister.

11. A rough estimate, based on personal ceremonial histories, suggests that less than a quarter of the women who could in principle be a *matiriyaat* (and perhaps far less) actually serve in that role at least once. Between one third and two fifths of the girls initiated in an area share at least one *matiriyaat*. It is also interesting to see where *matireenik* come from, if they are not local. Kaplelach bring Kipchornwonek, but Kipchornwonek at Nkaroni bring *matireenik* from Nentolo, where there are other Kalenjin-speakers as well as Okiek (see chapter 8).

12. New mothers also grow their hair. In all cases, the hair is called by the Maasai term *ol masi*. The hair bond is also articulated in terms of contagious danger (*kereek*); if the mother kept her hair after her daughter came out, it would harm the daughter.

13. Other initiates' mothers can, too, but rarely do. Other women wear *ntetusyek* during secret seclusion ceremonies when they go for the forest things needed in ritual secrets. This suggests temporary roles associated with ritual events in those ceremonies as well.

14. This is most strictly observed for the first child's ceremony. Subsequently, fathers often only carry the calabash, like a blessing elder.

15. Okiek adopted these elaborate dance costumes during *il terekeyani* (after 1960); see chapter 8.

16. Male and female initiates have very similar costumes. Gender differences are prominent in where they stay, what they do, and their seclusion songs, but except for small differences, costume shows their shared status and experience as *taarusyeek*.

17. Similar headdresses are worn by female Maasai initiates. The Maasai initiate shown in Adamson 1967:218 has other ornaments similar to Okiek ones: a wire neck ring and linked rings of blue beads and brass on a chain.

18. The staffs of male *taarusyeek* have one pointed end and a propolis ridge above it; male *taarusyeek* also hold blunt bird arrows.

19. Disagreements among Okiek as to when the terms *taarusyaat* and *murereet* become appropriate bring in the unnamed distinctions marked by costume. Some say girls are *taarusyeek* immediately after excision, taking their physical state as decisive. Others say they become *taarusyeek* when they start to sing, that is, after the first seclusion ceremony and its costume change. Disagreements about the term *murereet* pick out two points of decisive change: when initiates are first seen on coming out, and when they are shaved the next day, with the final costume change.

20. The journey idiom is common cross-culturally, often bringing myth and ritual together in various ways for mutual exegesis. Ritual is sometimes considered a metaphoric reenactment of a primordial journey recounted in myth, with myths as legitimating origin stories for ritual practice. The Okiek ceremonial journey weaves in procession through culturally significant places, though not specific named locations, as do some Australian cultures and Mambai of Timor (cf. Traube 1986).

21. See Kratz 1977:214-16 on these and other spatial divisions, and Kratz 1988b on the *mabwaita* and the hearth as places of blessing and libation.

22. Spatial distinctions are clearer in boys' initiation because they are removed to a seclusion house in the bush. Girls' movement is less in physical space than in cultural definition and use of space; an ordinary home becomes the women's seclusion house. Symbolic movement in rites of passage often moves from inhabited social space, through liminal residence in a wild nonhuman domain, and back again to the social world (van Gennep 1960; Droogers 1980; Turner 1969).

23. Kipsigis word lists gloss *oormariicet* as "gate for cattle" (Toweett 1979b:21) or "entrance." I have heard Okiek use the word only for ceremonial arches, but the arches mark the path of the *taarusyeek*, in keeping with the sense of the glosses. Toweett's gloss is of interest in light of the final songs which declare girls heifers as they are brought from the river (see chapter 7).

24. In the forest *menceet*, male initiates use the left door, men and boys the right one. This gives *taarusyeek* the female, less auspicious entrance, in line with their association with childbearing women through their shared *kereek* uncleanness.

25. Even so, delays from "official" times are practically inevitable. By contrast, Rendille in northern Kenya begin their ritual clock at midday rather than sunrise (Geoffrey Clarfield, personal communication).

26. See Kratz 1988b for more detail.

27. *Oleaceae Olea africana Mill.* Other species used in ritual structures include *masaita* (*Oleaceae hochstetteri Bak.*), *tepeng'wet*, and *ketuuyuet* (the tree *koroseek* saplings grow into). *Tepeng'wet* (*Compositae Veronia auriculifera Hiern*) is used mainly for ceremonial arches.

28. *Compositae Veronia auriculifera Hiern* and *Asclepiadaceae Periploca inearifolia Dill. and Rich.* Other vines combined with *sinenteet* in ritual constructions are *ny'elwet*, *moyuet*, and occasionally *toropcyat*.

29. In contrast to the clear "water" (sap) of other trees and plants.

30. Another group of forest materials figures in the harsh secret trials of initiation, primarily two varieties of stinging nettle.

31. Compare the *sinenteet* vine, which has strong female associations but also introduces the idea of patrilineal alliance through marriage. For contexts, uses, and associations of fat, see Kratz 1988b.

32. On both occasions, handfuls of honey are also given to children just after the ritual feeding. They run around the house four times, licking honey and crying "waa waa" like infants. At shavings, these children are said to represent children who should follow the one shaved. At marriage, they represent the children that should bless the union. If available, honey is the preferred food for young people and children after the *koroseek* procession.

33. Compare Wagner 1981:37: "These elements are meaningful to us only through their associations, which they acquire through being associated with or opposed to one another in all sorts of contexts. Meaning is therefore a function of the ways in which we create and otherwise experience contexts."

Chapter 6

1. See Kratz 1986, 1988b, and 1989 for further discussion of Okiek blessings and curses.

2. The representation of women in ritual might also reverse or contradict their recognized status in contexts of daily interaction, as Bloch finds in Merina rituals. His observation on this, however, is equally true of Okiek: "These roles are part of a drama that creates an image . . . that needs to be created because in many ways it contradicts what everybody knows" (Bloch 1986:45).

3. The style most commonly used varies by Okiek group, by context, and also according to the elder's history and experience. Kipchornwonek recently learned Kipsigis style, but it is still rarely used by Kaplelach.

4. Maa blessings have no such modal marker. First- and third-person subjunctive forms in Maa have an initial *m-;* second-person subjunctive and imperative forms are usually the same. Second person plural imperatives have the form *ent-* + stem. Most subjunctive Maa blessing lines are third-person, often referring to Enkai (God). When Okiek translate such lines (for instance, *metorropilo*) they often make them second-person subjunctive forms in Okiek, which are introduced by *ot* (for example, *ot ong'omdutiitu,* may you [pl.] become fragrant).

5. Kipsigis who have been recorded at Okiek ceremonies use the same line structures, but with a wider variety of verbs, another variation of structure, and often with more extended spoken line prefaces.

6. The second blessing, examined in Kratz 1988b:260–61, is less densely crisscrossed with relations between nonadjacent line groups, consisting rather of a straightforward stringing-together of groups, with some adjacent groups linked by sound similarities.

7. Arrangements are made for the event before they dance in, thus restoring the picture of peacefully drinking elders if there had in fact been shouting, singing, complaining, or staggering about.

8. For instance, one man told the initiate that all present were of *il terekeyani* age-set, assimilating everyone to her father. His slightly drunk SiHu couldn't resist heckling, taking the other man's comment literally and pointing out members of other age-sets.

9. Maasai guests may stress longstanding friendship with the father, for instance, or paternal relation based on age-set. They also note that they are unaccustomed to such speeches, which are not part of their own ceremonies.

10. And sometimes dozing. After days of hectic preparation and hours of dancing, the tired girls often nod off and are told to wake up. This is one contrast between official versions of *ceerseet* as serious, portentous speeches that harden the girls' will and unofficial versions apparent in performance.

11. Transcripts of all the speeches recorded at each ceremony are too extensive to include. Appendix C includes the two opening speeches and two later ones from one ceremony, including interruptions and conversations between or during addresses. For further examples, consult Kratz 1988c:602–49.

12. To be more specific about these structural sections, the vocative section calls the girl(s) by name, by relation term, or simply "you children," as in the example. Often a single word, it might also (1) link with and affirm preceding speeches (e.g., "Listen to what K.N. said"); (2) introduce the speaker (e.g., "I'm K.N."); or (3) comment on the relation claimed (e.g., "Aren't you truly my first-born child [i.e., the first-born of a member of that age-set]?") or the event itself (e.g., telling the girl to listen). Some speeches have a second vocative section later, when the speaker focuses on another particular girl.

The main section of encouragement varies in length, in tone, in the number of themes drawn in and developed, and in the ways they are woven together. Some are further divided into subsections, perhaps set off by metacomments or related formally, for instance, by parallel grammatical structures. Detailed examples below illustrate structural variations.

Like the first section, the third transitional section is quite short. Some men include a summary reprise of encouragement and appeal here. Others omit a transitional statement, marking it instead with a pause, by moving forward with the gift, or with similar gestures. The transition frequently includes a concluding metacomment: the speaker declares himself finished, winds up for his final summary appeal, or leads into the final gift with a disclaimer of poverty.

In the final section, the encouragement gift is announced, presented, and received. At its briefest, this is simply a statement of the amount or a handing over with the comment "Here." When the gift is not money, the specific animal or hive promised is described to show the promise is serious.

13. Three relative pause lengths are shown in transcription: shortest (/), medium (//), and the longest (about 4 seconds), shown by skipping to a new line and starting with a capital letter. Skipping to the middle of the next line indicates that the words followed each other with pause.

14. Kisumu is a city in western Kenya, where many Luo people reside. Luo are one of the few ethnic groups in Kenya who practice neither circumcision nor excision.

15. For instance, an Okiot assistant chief gave his daughter an unprecedented 500 Ksh encouragement in 1983 (about $31), five to ten times the usual amount.

16. The two *ayu ne* questions are also linked by use of the plural form of "to come" (*-pwa*).

17. The first uses ambulative form, *ng'etaati*, stressing A.N.'s running about and looking for the girls' things.

18. The quoted speech in P.'s encouragement to his wife's sister reports imaginary gossip about his unfulfilled promises to her. This is rhetorically like inner speech that shows a speaker's decision to honor obligations. P.'s gossip emphasizes the public, visible evidence that he does for her what he promises. The unspoken implication is again that *her* chance for a similar public display of responsibility is soon to come.

19. Expressed in various ways in speeches, in song they take three principal forms: direct and indirect requests, challenges such as rhetorical questions, and explicit directives in various imperative constructions (see chapter 7).

20. I already noted the discrepancy between this ideal representation and the drunken and often disorganized reality. I have not discussed here an interesting contrast made in side comments between *ceerseet* speeches and oratory (*-ruaac*) during men's meetings. Discussion during marriage talks is a third context and way of speaking related to these two.

21. The distinctive thing is not the word *aya*, but the angry tone and exchange at the end.

22. When young married women's children are still young, big girls are an important source of help for them in household labor.

23. The basic sequence can be characterized formally as: Press + {prompt} > {reject prompt} + Pes. + {qs} > Ann. + {qs}. (Key: { } = optional; > = is followed by; Pes. = confessed *pesenta;* qs = question(s); Ann. = announcement of *pesenta*). This basic dialogic sequence varies in many

ways. For instance, if another man helps the questioner, they have interchanges. The questioner might clarify something with the girl while announcing. Some sequences cycle several times before the exchange continues; for example, there may be a series of prompts and rejections before the girl tells a *pesenta*. In fact, when a girl rejects a series of presses and/or prompts, her *pesenweek* sequence ends and a new girl's begins.

24. Each girl's series expands until she insists she remembers no more. Older girls sometimes have more sexual *pesenweek* to report, but the balance of *pesenweek* is weighted toward young men, even with younger initiates.

25. Appendix E includes the *pesenweek* of two girls, including the interrogating interchanges and audible audience comments. A larger selection is in Kratz 1988c.

26. Foucault 1980 discusses the historical emergence, sociopolitical location, and uses of confessional narratives in European culture. Kratz 1991 compares Okiek and Catholic confession.

27. A review of *pesenweek* endings shows that all of the transformations in announced final quotes are formally motivated in part (Kratz 1988a:321–24).

28. My focus is on how their verbal forms and devices contribute to the structure and process of initiation, but they are also of general interest in showing how changing perspectives are created, and how narrative can "be an instrument for obscuring, hedging, confusing, exploring, or questioning what went on, that is, for keeping the coherence or comprehensibility of narrated events open to question" (Bauman 1986:5–6).

29. "To look for" is a euphemism for "make sexual advances to."

30. The announced *pesenta* is in italics. These *pesenweek* were named by the same girl, who was first in line. Analysis of the sequencing of *pesenweek* would show that some girls add more background information in their later *pesenweek*, as they warm up and as the questioner coaches them on what kind of information he wants. This pattern is not consistent, however, and calls for closer situational analysis. Similarly, the sequencing of kinds of *pesenweek* (with men and with women) varies considerably, but does not affect the narrative transformations or the overall effect of *pesenweek* in initiation.

31. It is worth noting that neither girls nor questioner-announcers ever begin to reenact the *pesenta*, assuming voices as their own in direct quotation, without framing quotative verbs. Perhaps this is not surprising given the ultimate interpretation of *pesenweek* as absolved and removed.

32. Word groups are marked by slight pauses, by an emphatic or clarifying final *-e*, or emphatic or listing final *-i* with a jump in pitch on the last word in the group. Some quoted exchanges are broken into smaller word groups by introducing more quotative verbs. In *pesenta* #3 of table 15, the announcer begins to rush through his account without extra breaks, then stops and overcorrects with extra breaks, repetitions, a final *-i*, and yet another final repetition of the other person's name.

33. Added detail usually plays to the audience's demand for humor and embarrassment. Deleted detail usually reduces a very full *pesenta* to a more regular form, omitting what adds little to the account (for instance, others who were present or extra quoted exchanges) and telescoping the time covered into a single event (Kratz 1988c:320).

34. *Pesenweek* have prospective effects on narrative and experience as well as retrospective ones, flagging certain incidents as "to be reported" (William Murphy, personal communication).

35. It is worth noting that the adults who are most commonly named are close to the initiates in age and status, that is, young women and young men.

36. How do men's and women's gifts compare? At the most lavish ceremony I attended, one men's house gave 1,170 Ksh (about $73 in 1983), while a slightly smaller house with many women totaled 317 Ksh (about $19).

37. Speakers self-select, often after a conversational lull. Monetary gifts range from five shillings to over a hundred (30¢ to $6 in 1983). Larger gifts and livestock are generally from close relatives and friends, though gifts are also related to the donor's prosperity and to whether one felt

well fed and satisfied. The host usually arranges for someone to record these transactions in writing, including promises to be claimed later.

38. Compare Irvine's (1979) dimensions of "formality." Thanks and encouragement also contrast in the extent to which "public" or "social" identities are invoked along with "personal" identities, (another of Irvine's dimensions). Ideal audience behavior is more or less the same at both events, but during thanks it is harder to get people to approximate what they "should" be doing.

39. The expectations of "satisfaction" have escalated steadily over the years, first adding maize beer, then bottled beer and soda (see chapter 8).

40. Two other examples are in Kratz 1988c:339–41.

41. This is so for male initiation. General ceremonial structure and practice are so closely parallel in male and female initiation that I would expect a similar song or sign of closure.

42. Or a male relative of comparable age, such as MoBrSo or SiHu. When boys come out of seclusion, their sisters open the way; their brothers give them *sirtiisyek* saplings. The "path" opened is the one that was closed to initiates while in seclusion, the people they could not see. Some Okiek also interpreted "path" as the one for suitors who want to marry the girls, though a different sense would have to apply to the same event in boys' initiation.

43. Boys are also fed in another house when they leave seclusion. At marriage, both bride and groom are fed by the groom's mother. The groom maintains his central patrilineal relations in marriage; the wife gets a new mother in her husband's mother.

44. While the sense of tradition associated with ceremonial structure and patterns helps make such assumptions seem natural, it does not necessarily make them automatically seem legitimate as well (Scott 1985:322). The challenges and contradictions that emerge in ceremonial performance show that both the legitimacy and the naturalness are contested in some contexts.

45. Okiek use -*sip* (to follow) to talk about more than initiates' compliance with ritual leaders (sometimes quite literally following them). It also refers to continuing their ceremonial tradition ("following" grandfather and grandmother) and to following people's advice. The key political slogan of President Moi (also a Kalenjin-speaker) draws on the same imagery in Kiswahili to emphasize continuity with the ideals and policies of Kenyatta, his predecessor: *fuata nyayo* (follow the footsteps).

46. Genovese 1974 is a classic analysis of such a situation, looking at American slavery. Scott 1985:328–30 reviews other examples and generalizes these social dynamics in terms of "mask" and "non-mask" situations.

Chapter 7

1. People sing other songs as the spirit moves them, in exuberance or camaraderie. "It is through such participation that a large number of people identify themselves with the aims and purposes of a social event and interact with one another" (Nketia 1974:30). While such singing certainly contributes to the experiential and emotional engagement of initiation, nothing is considered amiss if people do not sing.

2. A good singer, to the Okiek ear, calls solo lines loudly and audibly. A loud, clear delivery shows confidence and knowledge of the song. Good singing is also a matter of timing and delivery. When I replayed tapes, people often laughed at singers who mistimed their entry, forgot words, or mixed up phrases. Instruments accompany a few songs: girls use whistles and leg bells during their first initiation ceremony, men beat a hide during boys' first ceremony, and male initiates use sticks during two seclusion songs. A widespread association between percussion and transition suggests that relations of sound quality, psychological, cultural, and physiological aspects need to be considered here, as elsewhere (Needham 1967; Rouget 1985).

3. For example, there are women's songs, young men's songs, drinking songs, ceremony songs, elephant song, hive songs, Okiek songs, and Maasai songs.

4. Men sing the elephant songs. Many age-set songs are also for men, but some are sung with women. Numerous Okiek age-set songs are shared with Maasai; most are sung in Maa.

5. Nonceremonial songs have significant thematic patterns in the types of call line sung by different singers in different contexts. Two types are critical in expressing differential Okiek identity as men, women, boys, and girls: those that name or describe places and those that name or describe persons (Kratz 1981b). Ceremony songs contrast with these in that their call lines are largely modal statements, directives, or descriptive lines that are neither personal nor locative.

6. The absence of men's songs for girls makes rejoicing more significant and salient as a climactic moment. All adults sing, united in joy yet maintaining gender distinctions with different songs.

7. Young and old men alike might sing during breaks in the ritual or while drinking, but their song is unscheduled, not necessary to the ritual process.

8. Women also participate in *cepketilet,* joining the responses.

9. Other songs are sung in Maa—for example, age-set songs and several women's songs for shaving ceremonies. The Okiek elephant song is also in Maa, though Maasai claim they don't understand it; singers truncate and divide words with song syllables.

10. This is true even among Kaplelach, who rarely use the Kipsigis words in speech among themselves. Examples of Kipsigis include: *musaar ce lalang'* (warm fermented porridge), *puuc* (useless), *inkuuni* (now), and *weektoi* (return); examples of Kiswahili include: *pitina* (gossip, backbiting), *safarit* (trip), *marembu* (lovely girls), and *kwaheri* (good-bye).

11. The first two also show Kipsigis words in song; Okiek usually use *roonkooriik* (porridge) and *aarteet* (sheep).

12. There are a few exceptions to the usual six-syllable call-line pattern. As discussed below, the ritual songs of dawn have three-syllable calls, often breaking six-syllable lines into two turns. Two processional songs use nine-syllable lines made of smaller three-syllable groups.

13. The groups correspond to van Gennep's (1960) divisions of rites of passage, developed by V. Turner (1969) and T. Turner (1977). I use temporal distinctions here instead of their terms (separation, liminality, and reaggregation) in order to pay attention to thematic diversity and balances in the songs. Preseclusion songs not only are about separation but also highlight the test of will and bravery. Seclusion songs are about gender roles and solidarity as well as liminal aspects of seclusion. Postseclusion songs are indeed part of reaggregation into daily life but focus thematically on the transformation that has been accomplished.

14. These categories cover most call lines, but are neither exhaustive nor completely exclusive; some lines confound categories, often in informative ways. Call line are inventoried in Kratz 1988c: appendix E.

15. Initial lines are always the most numerous, and there are always more lines that can be second expansions than third-expansion lines. The place of a call line as expansion is evident in grammatical structure when it begins with a connective, particle, or genitive marker (such as *si,* so that; *ot,* until; *ne,* that [singular], *aap,* of). Connection with a previous line can also be semantic, for example, repeating its last three-syllable phrase (the second line of example 5). In other cases, the place of a call line in relation to others is not evident, but a convention of formulaic phrasing instead.

16. Since this analysis covers a large number of songs, the corpus used to develop call-line categories was usually limited to two recordings of each song made in different ceremonies. Judging from attendance at other ceremonies and a less-detailed comparison with other recordings, the corpus does represent the common thematic patterns and progressions of the songs.

17. For instance, calls of the same type (similar thematically or pragmatically) might be used only in particular songs. Songs also differ considerably in call repertoire. An extensive array of lines are directives, challenges, or requests to initiates, for example, but many are used primarily in girls' songs; a much smaller subset are sung regularly in ritual songs.

18. *Tolooek* literally means the remains of food eaten by initiates during seclusion, but synecdochally it means initiates.

19. *Kaptiikee* refers to women as they sit leaning against the house, drinking and singing, during a ceremony (> -*tii*, to lean against).

20. The recent past is also used in dawn songs before the operation to convey its closeness; this tense can convey a sense of "just about to do X."

21. This refers to girls' ritual order in initiation.

22. Some of the lines are limited to girls' songs in one specific performance context. When girls sing farewells and distribute cigarettes, they sing directions to a helper to specify whom to call and how many cigarettes to give. They also sing about their friends' fits of anxiety:

(1)	*s'inamcin sigarook*	so give him/her cigarettes
	itese koik somoku	increase [them] to be three
(2)	*meiwiirtoi poortang'uung'*	don't throw your body about
	makenin mulayat	the whore isn't fooling you

23. The first three *kaiyantaaita*, sung daily at dawn and dusk, differ from the others and are discussed later in the chapter. Secret songs of seclusion ceremonies will be referred to comparatively, but not discussed fully because they are sensitive and guarded secrets and also, more pragmatically, because my recordings and transcriptions of them are extensive enough only to look at general patterns.

24. For example, in girls' songs, *kipeenti ot kosiim* (we'll go until they rejoice) could be completed with "until everyone rejoices," "until the passerby rejoices," "until the childless one rejoices," or "until they rejoice a month and a week" (*ot kosiim ciit tukul, ot kosiim ne sirtoi, ot kosiim cememaa, ot kosiim araaweet ak wiikiit*).

25. A few expansions are grammatically marked as continuations by initial connectives or relative particles, as in preseclusion songs. Others are also semantically related.

26. This line has several song words. Literally, it means "we are going on a slow trip, a slow trip, [when] the foot [should] not [be] stubbed."

27. Even when there is greater possible variety, only a few (about five) are sung repeatedly.

28. Women have a choice between two songs for the second dawn song. Only one parallels the first melodically. Thematic and linguistic parallelism bridges the musical contrast in the second case, creating a tension between verbal similarity and marked musical difference at the moment of dramatic tension before the girls' operations.

29. Individuals' call sequences are similar to those of earlier women's songs: after opening time lines, often calling the initiates, singers sing a series of directive and request lines. In earlier songs, individuals opened with framing occasion lines or metapragmatic ones. This pattern of women's lines in ritual songs parallels the sequential development of men's encouraging speeches discussed in chapter 6, emphasizing the parallel functions of speech and song for men and women.

30. This review did not include ritual songs of the final ceremony. Final river procession songs again mark and announce the girls' progress through initiation as they simultaneously move them through it. Their unique call lines mainly proclaim the completed transformation. The short song to open the way is a performative ritual action in a sense close to that of speech-act theory, and includes a kind of performative construction: *o yaatweec oor* (open the way for us). The way is opened by singing the song with appropriate actions, context, and actors. Unlike other ritual songs, this song is repeated a specific number of times; this definition relates it clearly to other ritual actions, also repeated four times. The song has a very limited set of unique lines. One refers to the ox-pecker that picks food from cows and wild buffalo, linking it to the key metaphor of girls' river songs (young women as heifers).

31. I looked at musical form in eight songs, the 1982–1985 "hit parade." About half the transcribed songs use four tones covering the range of a sixth, with intervalic distances of 1, 1, and 1.5 semitones. The rest add a fifth tone to the same tonal range. Response usually begins as the call ends, with no overlap. The call begins with the last word or two of the response (two to five syllables). The overlapping words are sung on a high-pitched terrace that then drops to

another terrace, sometimes with one step in the fall. In general, girls' songs have descending phrase contours, falling stepwise to each tonal terrace. They are not terraced contours in the usual sense, because the song can rise to previous tonal levels before continuing the descent. The sharp, rising tonal jumps usually mark other call segments. The end of the last call segment is usually mimetic in contour to the last response segment. Kratz 1988c:419–22 discusses phrase contour segments in call and response. Thanks to Steve Feld, who helped me formulate descriptions of general phrase shapes.

32. However, women point out that boys' operations are done in the secrecy of the forest, where women cannot see the boys' reactions and their cries can be hidden. *They,* on the other hand, are cut in full public view; there can be no doubt of girls' bravery.

33. Lines that specifically announce that appear first here, though they are more common at the end of initiation. For girls, such lines appear only when they leave seclusion.

34. Men also develop themes in *cepketilet* that are less important in girls' songs. For instance, the image of initiates' staring eyes is amplified, again a way to talk about men's self-encouragement and their difference from women.

35. Similarities in musical form within each of the initial series reinforce their cohesion as subgroups of *kaiyantaaita* for each sex. Female initiates' first songs use different tonal material than do their other songs and also differ internally, with three, four, and five tones. *Kipawes* songs are diatonic in their calls, with two additional tones in the response sections. Melodic similarities also link the initial songs in each case (Kratz 1988c:440–41). The two *kipawes* are so similar that the second sounds like a double-time version of the first.

36. This was the most common mistake people identified from tapes (for example, singing *kiteece laakwa pai* instead of the two parts *kiteece ceptolool, ceptolool laakwa pai*). When I attended a teaching session held before the girls were initiated, their singing was noticeably hesitant, often mumbled or mispronounced, and had both melodic and verbal mistakes.

37. The initial dawn/dusk songs also reproduce ritual authority; initiates follow their teacher's injunctions when they sing each day. See Kratz 1988c:442–43 for a discussion of their unique call lines.

38. A linked sonic and semantic parallelism in a small number of line pairs adds yet another thread to the poetic net that pervades the songs (Kratz 1988c:444).

39. A more complete analysis cannot be presented here, but would look at which aspects of social relations are emphasized and which passed over silently. Selective emphasis in seclusion ceremonies helps produce a certain representation of social relations. Differential emphases in songs as compared to speech or ritual acts can also portray different, contrary attitudes toward the very images they help create.

40. Similar gender patterns in ceremonial participation have been noted elsewhere (cf. Sherzer 1983:70, 143; Bloch 1986; Collier and Rosaldo 1981:305).

41. Lutz 1990 describes similar links between cultural constructions of women, emotion, and power. Briggs 1992 is a superb analysis of how such links are constructed and made effective within the Warao verbal economy.

42. Abu-Lughod (1986) discusses a similar situation among Egyptian Bedouin, with an ideology of honor expressed in public life and a contrary ideology of self and sentiment expressed in poetry. She suggests that the values expressed in poetry might extend the limits of the ideology of honor and compensate for its extremes, providing a means for articulating other experiences.

43. Thanks to Steve Feld for discussion of these issues.

Chapter 8

1. These variations and alternatives are discussed further in Kratz 1988c:464–94.

2. I thank him for generously sharing his material on initiation.

3. The beginning of the century is my start because available evidence cannot reach further back. The cutoff is arbitrary in historical terms, an artifact of memory and discourse, and in no way suggests that Okiek ceremonies before 1900 were unchanging.

4. It was these general discussions about ceremonial history that most often contradicted one another. Contradictions might arise from several sources, and are hard to sort out. For instance, different accounts might collapse and combine variations in ceremonial traditions, making it more difficult to recognize those variations retrospectively as performative alternatives. There might also be local variations in processes of change and simple misrememberings as well as a few hard-to-identify facetious responses.

5. This is also how Okiek presented ceremonial history to me. They talked about components of initiation rather than age-sets during which ceremonial change occurred. Only afterward did periods of coordinated changes in ceremonial practice become evident.

6. The most recent description available, however, is from the late 1960s (Daniels 1970). Kipsigis, too, may have instituted a separate blesser's role since then, splitting the ritual role. Peristiany (1964:216-23) describes *paayaat aap tuumto* (the term he uses is *poiyot ap tumda*) as a hereditary, learned ritual office concerned centrally with blessings, but involving participation in a wider set of ritual occasions.

7. One of the oldest men alive at the time (*il tareto*) taught a number of *eseuri* and *il ny'angusi* men. An *il terito* man, father of my 1974 assistant, said his own father (of *il tuati*) had been a *matiriyaat*. Another friend, a lively and kind woman initiated during the *il kitoip* subset, reported that the same man's grandmother (who was married by the time of *il peles* age-set) was her teacher. Within living memory, then, Okiek initiation has included *matireenik*.

8. Her own *matireenik* were Kipsigis. She was born into Kap Geemi, a patrilineage west of Nkaroni that had regular early interactions with Kipsigis.

9. Again, factors in the change are now obscure. The structural logic of auspicious numbers might reinforce regularization of the number of teachers at two, but would not cause it. Similarly, standardizing the pair strengthens structural arrangements that help re-create and secure the continuity of tradition, but that result is unintentional.

10. One *eseuri* man named dates, recalling having seen the first girls' flags about 1961, with boys' beginning to appear in 1974-75. These estimates correspond to the age-sets named.

11. The Kaplelach average was lower, the Kipchornwonek one somewhat higher. These increases were in line with Kenyan inflation between those times. In 1975, the U.S. dollar was worth about seven shillings; in 1983 it was about thirteen shillings.

12. While the *koroseek* procession and *pesenweek* are done by all Kaplelach and Kipchorn-wonek, however, the building of the *toloocik* is not, and some people predict its end. Whether or not the *toloocik* is built varies by lineage; there are differing views on the former extent of its practice (Kratz 1988c:471). Only Kipchornwonek suggested that the *toloocik* will gradually be abandoned. They linked their expectation to decreasing honey supplies and decreasing Okiek efforts at collecting honey. The *toloocik* event is completed by brewing honey wine.

13. The lineages named are Kap Kobei, Kap Geemi, Kap Mopir, Kap Mapelu, and branches of Kap Tanki. Tracing ritual networks farther west to include the Oltikambo families would make the significance of this directionality clearer.

14. No *il terito* women lived in my immediate research area; the *il ny'angusi* women that I spoke with all came from other areas.

15. Again, tracing ritual networks farther east would be informative; the only more easterly Kaplelach ceremony I attended recruited one *matiriyaat* locally and one from the Kaplelach area where I lived.

16. I attended a Kaplelach ceremony in 1975 that was reportedly one of the first with dance costume, brought by the Kipchornwonek husband-to-be.

17. Another detail of ceremonial costume was also changed. In the past, people at ceremonies smeared their heads with red ocher and fat, as Maasai still do. Okiek rarely use ocher now; they

found it incompatible with Western clothing. In ritual use, it is maintained only during shaving ceremonies.

18. Despite condensation, the full sequence of ceremonies is celebrated, though some might be combined. Shortening initiation does not seem to entail simplification. Time constraints on those preparing and holding ceremonies, however, go hand in hand with changes in initiates' own view of the process and the lessons they learn (Kratz 1988c:482).

19. Those now in school should eventually become ritual instructors. More limited or less frequent participation in initiation ceremonies, along with the reorientations of value and interest that often come with education, could help transform initiation through the incorporation of new practices or perhaps the simplification of older ones.

20. The *matatu* developed as part of the Kenyan transportation system in the 1950s. "The name itself has its origin in Kikuyu dialect, *mang'otore matatu* (30 cents), which was the standard fare" (Nairobi *Daily Nation,* 29 November 1982).

21. They might have sung current words to old tunes, but words and tune fit together somewhat differently than in contemporary songs.

22. One *il ny'angusi* woman, however, remembered there being *riret* at her ceremony. *Riret* is also men's celebration song for girls. Women's celebration song (*kimace eceek kesiim*) was also learned from Kipsigis at about the same time. Previously, men and women both rejoiced with *cepketilet.*

23. Orchardson 1961:66 and Peristiany 1964:22 both record similar chants for opening the way.

24. Compare Kipsigis *kipaes* in Orchardson 1961:132–33.

25. For instance, shifts in the significance and associations of signs are closely related to changing social and material circumstances; often formally unmarked and difficult to trace, such shifts might be especially likely in the language of events such as *ceerseet* or *pesenweek.*

26. Formal markedness refers to an opposition between related elements, one with an overt, discernable mark and one without (for instance, the *-s* mark of plurality in English, "girl" and "girls"). Semantic markedness distinguishes between related words in terms of specificity of reference, as illustrated by "dog" and "bitch." "Dog," the unmarked term, can refer to both male and female canines, while "bitch," marked as female, has a more limited and specific referential scope. Finally, distributional or functional markedness refers to relative restriction and specificity of occurrence. The marked term is used in a smaller, specifiable range of contexts; the unmarked term occurs elsewhere. Distributional marking often correlates with formal and/or semantic marking, but not always (Lyons 1977:305–11).

27. The addition of the flag, for instance, followed a structural logic in placement that crosscuts what markedness would suggest without necessarily contradicting it. The flag is another marker of ceremonial place, appropriately included in the same sequence as the *mabwaita* and *toloocik* constructions and the processions, which weave forest and home together, creating ritual space. Elaborating spatial marking with another index outside, the flag precedes *toloocik* construction inside and marks the ceremonial home on an added, vertical dimension. Placement of the event follows from the structural logic defined through ceremonial sequence, but it is also easier to climb a tree during the day, when a flag can be seen.

28. Relative to ordinary interaction, seclusion life between ceremonies is also highly marked (though publicly invisible), both by the absence of the opposite sex and by other special behavior.

29. Urban 1985 proposes a related hypothesis about expressive restriction in marked speech styles, that is, ordinarily marked pragmatic features will be the unmarked choice within functionally marked speech styles. Thus, functionally marked speech styles become more highly marked through these unusual pragmatic features and formal elaboration.

30. Okiek also note related shifts in affinal relations, such as a narrowing definition of who should be respected and assisted (Kratz 1990c:n.5).

31. For instance, Galaty 1991:4–5 describes serious conflict between old and young Maasai on some group ranches during "a highly charged period of land allocations."

32. Nominal, that is, compared to contract jobs, land sales, or total initiation costs (see table 3). Twenty shillings is less nominal from the perspective of daily household economy when people go without sugar or children are sent home from school because they can't pay the fees.

33. However, there are limits to the equality of ceremonial practice. One important limit for Okiek is the practice of circumcision as part of adult initiation; Luo (who do not circumcise) are considered very peculiar.

34. Compare Sapir's discussion of generalizing and particularizing synecdoche (Sapir 1977:14–19).

35. Volosinov (1987:100) uses the notion of enthymeme to discuss the social and communicative production of ideology; Parkin (1984:354) emphasizes enthymemic argument in political language. Our discussions of ceremonial tradition touched both these domains.

36. My characterizations of Mambai ritual tradition are much simplified. Ritual authority is itself hierarchically differentiated; it is one aspect of a complex dualistic system. Mambai ritual specialists also have jural counterparts, all integrally involved in the sociopolitical structures of Mambai life (Traube 1986:chapter 6).

Chapter 9

1. The notion of experiential and emotional engagement is comparable in some ways to what Karp (1980) calls engrossment, and the absorption Geertz (1973) notes as part of the "deep play" of Balinese cock fights. Both Karp and Geertz, however, focus on peaks of experience rather than on the processes and means through which such engrossment is achieved (or not), and the different ways people can be drawn into events in different degrees. I have stressed the ways experiential and emotional engagement is produced over time as well as the different modes of engagement and the different ways it can be experienced, invoked, and orchestrated for different participants.

2. Chet Creider emphasized to me that this highlights another contradiction in the gendered young adult roles created by initiation. Initiation limits the range of girls' legitimate sexual possibilities, which are restricted to marriage as soon as they become women. However, for boys initiation makes possible legitimate sexual liaisons with girls and later with women in marriage, expanding their horizons. Though the initiation process is largely the same, it produces inequality between men and women in this sphere, not equality (cf. Collier and Rosaldo 1981:284).

3. It remains to be seen how all this is changing as some boys and girls become educated and as other kinds of status, income, and experience become more central to Okiek life. Such changes will affect not only the hierarchy of age, but the hierarchy of gender as well, in cases when women become more educated than some men.

Glossary

ceepkuuleet: rectangular, miterlike headdress that is part of girls' dance costume during the first ceremony of initiation

-ceer: to encourage, to reassure; *ceerseet* is an event during girls' first initiation ceremony when adult men and others make speeches and give gifts intended to encourage the initiates

celimen: ritual song sung by women during processions in the first ceremony of initiation

ceemaasiit: wild creature, monster; name of the secret instrument kept hidden from initiates until the end of seclusion, pl. *ceemaasiisyek*

cepketilet: encouraging songs of boys' first initiation ceremony

ceptoloolny'aat: child who eats food left over from initiates' meals in seclusion, < *tolooek,* "the leftover food"

ceepta: girl, pl. *tiipiik*

ceepyooseet: woman, pl. *ceepyoosook*

cerukween: the middle ones in birth order or in seclusion order, lit. "those who sleep in the middle"

ciita: person, pl. *piik,* primary form *ciit*

eemeet: country; *eemeet aap kaa* means women, "those who stay at home"

enkishilit: beaded tiara with shining, hanging extension that rises from the forehead. Worn by young women the day they come out of seclusion, at their wedding, and for special occasions, < Maa

eseuri: age-set who were *murenik* between 1955 and 1970, includes *il terekeyani* and *il tiyokoni* subsets

esiny'a: auspicious, a ritually appropriate and beneficial thing or way of doing things, such as the numbers two and four, or the directions right and up

il peles: age-set who were *murenik* between 1866 and 1886, the oldest age remembered by Okiek

il tareto: age-set who were *murenik* between 1911 and 1929, includes divisions of *il meirututu* (a.k.a. *il tareto*) and *il kitoip,* the oldest age-set with members still living in 1985

il n'yangusi: age-set who were *murenik* between 1942 and 1959, includes divisions of *il kalikal* and *il kamaniki* subsets

il terito: age-set who were *murenik* between 1926 and 1948, includes divisions of *il tiyeki, il kirmere,* and *il ny'echere* subsets *imaamook:* (pl.) relatives through the mother, sing. *maama*

injorubayt: hide cape worn by men when they go to the forest to hunt or look for honey, also used as costume of ritual actors and as the external garment of initiates in seclusion

inkeeriiny'ot: single strand of blue and white beads interrupted with small groups of four red beads, worn at the hairline as a headdress by initiates coming out of seclusion before their heads have been shaved

inkipa: slime of birth, asked for in blessings as a sign of fecundity, < *in-kipa* (Maa)

-intolip: feed ritually by putting the food (usually a spoonful of honey) to the lips four times, only taking it in on the last time

intoroogenik: colored arm beads worn wrapped around the wrists and forearms by girls during their first initiation ceremony and as part of their dance costume

inturotoit: white clay smeared on daily by initiates in seclusion

i rambau: age-set who were *murenik* between 1969 and 1980, includes divisions of *i rambau* and *i rantai* subsets

kaaptiryaang'et: outside seclusion yard built for female initiates, attached to their house of seclusion

kaiyantaaita: seclusion songs sung daily by initiates

-kas: to hear, listen, understand

kasiit: work, way of doing something, < Kiswahili *kazi*

keelteet: oval-shaped wooden or metal headdress worn framing the face as part of girls' dance costume in the first initiation ceremony

keeparpar iitiik: ear-piercing ceremony celebrated for children before initiation at about the age of twelve

kelap euun: first seclusion ceremony of initiation, after which initiates can use their hands, wear different costumes, etc.

kelong'u (en aineet): final ceremony of initiation through which initiates come out of seclusion, lit. "coming up (from the river)"

-ken: to fool, to cheat; *-kenter* to cheat shamefully

keny': long ago

kepa tuumto: initiation in general, the first ceremony of initiation in particular

kereek: contagious and weakening dirt associated with birth, child-bearing women, and young children

ketuuitos suumoosyek: third ceremony of initiation, second seclusion ceremony

kipawes (kipaes): sticks beaten by male initiates in a set of seclusion songs by the same name

kipooretet: first in ritual order in a group of initiates

kipteruaan: staff carried by initiates in seclusion

kisincot: hive adze, also used in ritual acts of ceremonies

konoito: lineage forests that run along the slope of the escarpment, taking in each different ecological zone

korosyaat: sapling brought in the opening processions of ceremonies for ear piercing and initiation, pl. *koroseek*

koyuumkoo (koyuumkok): the last one of a group of initiates in ritual order

kooko: grandmother(s)

kuuka: grandfather(s)

kuumiik: honey, its primary form (often used in song) is *kuumin*

-kuuru: to call a song; the motion-toward form of *-kuur,* to call, to invite

laakweet: child, pl. *laakok*

latyet: wide neighborhood, a group of households and settlements that come to meetings to solve area problems and can be called on for help

loong'eet: shield, piece of skin beaten by men while singing cepketilet songs during boys' first initiation ceremony; small piece of wood decorated by initiates in seclusion

lukuumiik: honey water, drunk by children and also used in libations, to shave the heads of ritual actors, and in other ritual acts in ceremonies

maama: MoBr and a number of other relatives traced through the mother, pl. *imaamook*

mabwaita: ritual structure built of poles, leafy branches, and vines during ceremonies and at which many other ritual events take place, pl. *mabwaiyuek*

matatu: small vehicle used for public transport, < Kiswahili

-matir: to give ritual instruction

matiriyaat: ritual teacher who leads children through initiation, pl. *matireenik*

mau: highest ecological zone on the Mau escarpment (about 2,600 meters), open glade area after bamboo forest

mebayt: big girl ready for initiation, pl. *mebaysyek*

melyaat: big girl ready for initiation, pl. *meliik*

menceet: place of seclusion for initiates

menekobeyt: smooth hide clothing, with hair removed, worn by initiates in seclusion as inner garment

mooyta: calf, metaphorically child, pl. *mooeek,* primary form *mooi*

muny'aawa: leg bells worn on the calves by girls as part of their dance costume during the first initiation ceremony

murereet: young woman who has just come out of seclusion, young married woman, pl. *murereenik*

muran: young man, pl. *murenik*

muusareek: food and drink given to guests in ceremonies, < Kipsigis "fermented porridge," primary form (often used in song) *muusar*

muutya: slowly, carefully, sorry

muunkeenik: dance costume worn by girls during the first initiation ceremony

-mwei: to fear

-myan: to be sick, description used of initiates immediately after excision or circumcision operations, pl. *myantoos*

-nereec: to be or get worked up, upset, annoyed, anxious, determined

ng'eetik: boys [in song], < Kipsigis

ng'eetat: man, pl. *ng'eetotik*

ng'etunta: lion, metaphorically man or young man (esp. in song), pl. *ng'etuuny'ik*

-ng'aamiit: to become clever, description of effect of initiation

ntetut: beaded leather skirt worn as a cape by ritual actors and worn by young women coming out of seclusion as both cape and skirt, pl. *ntetusyek*

olartatit: long, slender staff used in ritual events, usually made of either bamboo or *olerienit* wood

olashurtit: narrow headband with blue beads and four pieces of chain hanging down the forehead worn by initiates in seclusion

oldurumetit: string of large, dark blue beads usually worn by old men and women who have many children, also put on the head of the father of initiates in the first initiation ceremony by members of certain lineages

olerienit: wild olive tree, used in ceremonies, ritual events, and blessings

ol masi: head of hair grown by initiates in seclusion, their ritual teachers, and mothers, and also the hair grown out by a woman after birth, < Maa

oormariicet: arch built onto the *mabwaita* for the final initiation ceremony, or similar arch built at a crossroads in the bush as part of the first seclusion ceremony

-pa: to go

paayaat: elder, mature man, pl. *paaiik* or *paaiisyaanik*

pakule: coinitiate, pl. *pakuleysyek*

paleito: honey basket woven of *taparariyaat* grass, used in ritual acts and events, e.g. to ritually feed, to pour liquid when shaving heads, to pour a libation

pesenta: debt, in first initiation ceremony a social debt, an argument or disagreement that ended in an adult being angry with the child being initiated, pl. *pesenweek*

-piit: to spray, to bless by spraying honey wine

piitintet: elder who blesses things in initiation

pitina: gossip, politics, cheating, backbiting, < Kiswahili *fitina*

riirik: ox-pecker birds that eat ticks and other pests from cows, buffalo, and other animals, referred to in the song for opening the way when initiates come out of seclusion

-rropil: to be sweetly fragrant, used in blessings, < Maa (Okiek synonym: *ng'omtut*)

-rur: to ripen, also used of song when it comes together well

rurupto: area down along a river valley

-saam: to ask for, to borrow, to beg, to be initiated in a home other than one's parents'

saleito: pregnant woman, woman of childbearing age, pl. *solootwik*

sasaontet: middle-range ecological zone on the Mau escarpment, forest up to about 2,400 meters.

-siim: to rejoice in song and ululation

simparaakoonik: girls

sinenteet: leafy green vine used in ritual acts and events

sirtiityet: sapling with propolis and a piece of cow or sheep skin given to initiate on coming out of seclusion and later cut by her/his father, pl. *sirtiisyek*

sisiyuet: zone of high-altitude bamboo forest, up to about 2,600 meters

soyua: low-altitude open forest, up to about 2,100 meters

suumuut: small seclusion enclosure built inside the house where initiates sleep and sit, called *tuumnet* in Maresionik, pl. *suumoosyek*

taaita: first-born, first in ritual order in a group of initiates

taarusyaat: initiate in seclusion, pl. *taarusyeek*

tanguriot: wide-bladed green forest grass used in ritual acts and events and blessings

-teec: to respect, to build

tekeriyaat: a child born after others have died, or a single son born into a house of daughters, a *tekeriyaat* can request to be initiated into the secrets of the opposite sex, pl. *tekeriisyek*

temeny'et: propolis, used in secrets of initiation and on the *sirtiityet* sapling given to initiates on coming out

-tien: to sing, dance

tienta: song, dance

timta: forest

tirap: high-altitude thick forest, up to about 2,600 meters

toloocik: tablelike structure built inside by the hearth in ear-piercing ceremonies and first initiation ceremonies on which a bag of honey wine is brewed; the posts and materials used to built it; the center pole of the house

toweet: last-born, last in ritual order in a group of initiates

-torooc: to come out to meet someone coming, as women come out from home to meet processions from the forest in ceremonies

Torrobo: Maasai name for Okiek and others who live without livestock or with few animals

-tupuc: to fall into an emotional fit, esp. of anxiety during the first ceremony of initiation

tuumto: ceremony, initiation, ritual secret, pl. *tuumwek*

-waal: to swear by something, e.g. as men do when upset during *ceerseet* speeches

wareek: young ones, pups, cubs (also used in pl. to refer to people)

-was karaaiitik: to toss the colobus skins about, said of a girl who dances well in costume the night of her initiation

weeriit: boy, pl. *weeriik*

yaatet aap ooreet: part of the last ceremony of initiation that brings initiates out of seclusion, performed at the *mabwaita* and arch

-yan: to sing the chorus, to agree

-yanta: to sing seclusion songs, only of initiates; the motion-away form of *-yan*

Bibliography

Abu-Lughod, Lila
1986 *Veiled Sentiment: Honor and Poetry in a Bedouin Society.* Berkeley: University of California Press.

Adamson, Joy
1967 *The Peoples of Kenya.* London: Collins and Harvill.

Ambler, Charles
1988 *Kenyan Communities in the Age of Imperialism: The Central Region in the Late Nineteenth Century.* New Haven: Yale University Press.

Ambrose, Stanley
1986 Kenya Highlands Hunter-Gatherers: Their Relevance for the Prehistory of the Central Rift Valley. *SUGIA* 7(2):11–43.

Appadurai, Arjun
1990 Topographies of the Self: Praise and Emotion in Hindu India. In C. Lutz and L. Abu-Lughod, eds., *Language and the Politics of Emotion.* Cambridge: Cambridge University Press.

Ardener, Edwin, ed.
1971 *Social Anthropology and Language.* London: Tavistock.

Arens, W. and Ivan Karp
1989 Introduction. In W. Arens and I. Karp, eds., *Creativity of Power: Cosmology and Action in African Societies.* Washington: Smithsonian Institution Press.

Asad, Talal
1983 Notes on Body Pain and Truth in Medieval Christian Ritual. *Economy and Society* 12(3):287–327.
1987 On Ritual and Discipline in Medieval Christian Monasticism. *Economy and Society* 16(2):159–203.

Babcock, Barbara, ed.
1978 *Reversible World.* Ithaca: Cornell University Press.

Bakhtin, M. M.
1984 *Rabelais and His World.* Trans. H. Iswolsky. Cambridge, Mass.: MIT Press.
1976 *Freudianism, a Marxist Critique.* Trans. I. R. Titunik. New York: Academic Press.

Barthes, Frederick
1969   *Ethnic Groups and Boundaries.* Boston: Little, Brown.
Bateson, Gregory
1936   *Naven.* Cambridge: Cambridge University Press.
1972   *Steps to an Ecology of Mind.* San Francisco: Chandler.
Bauman, Richard
1977   *Verbal Art as Performance.* Rowley, Mass.: Newbury House.
1986   *Story, Performance, and Event: Contextual Studies of Oral Narrative.* Cambridge: Cambridge University Press.
Bauman, Richard and Charles Briggs
1990   Poetics and Performance as Critical Perspectives on Language and Social Life. *Annual Review of Anthropology* 19:59–88.
Baxter, P.T.W. and Uri Almagor, eds.
1978   *Age, Generation, and Time: Some Features of East African Age Organizations.* London: Hurst.
Bayly, C. A.
1990   Elusive Essences. *Times Literary Supplement,* 7–13 December, 1313–14.
Beidelman, T. O.
1966   Swazi Royal Ritual. *Africa* 36(4):373–405.
1970   Some Sociological Implications of Culture. In J. C. McKinney and E. A. Tiryakian, eds., *Theoretical Sociology: Perspectives and Developments.* New York: Appleton, Century, Crofts.
1986   *Moral Imagination in Kaguru Modes of Thought.* Bloomington: Indiana University Press.
Bentley, G. Carter
1987   Ethnicity and Practice. *Comparative Studies in Society and History* 29(1):24–55.
Bernsten, John
1979   Pastoralism, Raiding, and Prophets: Maasailand in the Nineteenth Century. Ph.D. dissertation, University of Wisconsin, Madison.
Bhabha, Homi
1985   Signs Taken for Wonders: Questions of Ambivalence and Authority under a Tree Outside Delhi, May 1817. *Critical Inquiry* 12:144–65.
1986   The Other Question: Difference, Discrimination, and the Discourse of Colonialism. In F. Barker et al., eds., *Literature, Politics, and Theory.* London: Methuen.
Blackburn, Roderic H.
1970   Preliminary Report of Research among the Ogiek Tribe of Kenya. Seminar paper 89, Institute of African Studies, University of Nairobi.
1971   Honey in Okiek Personality, Culture, and Society. Ph.D. dissertation, Michigan State University.
1974   The Okiek and their History. *Azania* 9:139–57.
1976   Okiek History. In B. A. Ogot, ed., *Kenya Before 1900.* Nairobi: East Africa Publishing House.

1982   In the Land of Milk and Honey: Okiek Adaptations to their Forests and Neighbors. In E. Leacock and R. Lee, eds., *Politics and History in Band Societies*. Cambridge: Cambridge University Press.

1986   Okiek Resource Tenure and Territoriality as Mechanisms for Social Control and Allocation of Resources. *SUGIA* 7(1):61–82.

Bloch, Maurice
1986   *From Blessing to Violence*. Cambridge: Cambridge University Press.

Bloch, Maurice, ed.
1975   *Political Language and Oratory in Traditional Society*. New York: Academic Press.

Blom, Jon Petter and John Gumperz
1972   Social Meaning in Linguistic Structures: Code-switching in Norway. In John Gumperz and Dell Hymes, eds., *Directions in Sociolinguistics*. New York: Holt, Rinehart, and Winston.

Boddy, Janet
1989   *Wombs and Alien Spirits*. Madison: University of Wisconsin Press.

Boon, James
1990   *Affinities and Extremes*. Chicago: University of Chicago Press.

Borges, Jorge Luis
1972   *Doctor Brodie's Report*. London: Penguin.

Bourdieu, Pierre
1977a   *Outline of a Theory of Practice*. Cambridge: Cambridge University Press.

1977b   The Economics of Linguistic Exchanges. Trans. R. Nice. *Social Science Information* 16(6):645–68.

1982   *Ce que parler veut dire*. Paris: Fayard.

1990   *The Logic of Practice*. Trans. R. Nice. Stanford: Stanford University Press.

Boyarin, Daniel
1992   "This We Know to Be the Carnal Israel": Circumcision and the Erotic Life of God and Israel. *Critical Inquiry* 18(3):474–505.

Bravman, William
1990   Shaping an Ethnic Identity: Colonial Struggles over Social Change among the WaTaita of Kenya. Paper presented at the annual meeting of the African Studies Association, Baltimore.

Brenneis, D.
1986   Shared Territory: Audience, Indirection, and Meaning. *Text* 6(3): 339–47.

Brenneis, D. and Fred Myers
1984   *Dangerous Words: Language and Politics in the Pacific*. New York: New York University Press.

Briggs, Charles
1986   *Learning How to Ask*. Cambridge: Cambridge University Press.

1992   "Since I Am a Woman, I Will Chastise my Relatives": Gender, Reported Speech, and the (Re)Production of Social Relations in Warao Ritual Wailing. *American Ethnologist* 19(2):337–61.

Brown, R. and A. Gilman
1960   The Pronouns of Solidarity and Power. In T. Sebeok, ed., *Style in Language*. Cambridge, Mass.: M.I.T. Press.

Chang, Cynthia
  1982   Nomads Without Cattle: East African Foragers in Historical Perspective. In
         E. Leacock and R. Lee, eds., *Politics and History in Band Societies*. Cam-
         bridge: Cambridge University Press.
Clifford, James
  1988   *The Predicament of Culture*. Cambridge, Mass.: Harvard University Press.
Clifford, J. and G. Marcus, eds.
  1986   *Writing Culture*. Berkeley: University of California Press.
Collier, Jane and Michelle Rosaldo
  1981   Politics and Gender in Simple Societies. In S. Ortner and H. Whitehead, eds.,
         Sexual Meanings. Cambridge: Cambridge University Press.
Colson, Elizabeth
  1984   The Reordering of Experience: Anthropological Involvement with Time.
         Journal of Anthropological Research 40(1):1–13.
Comaroff, Jean
  1985   *Body of Power, Spirit of Resistance*. Chicago: University of Chicago Press.
Comaroff, Jean and John Comaroff
  1990   Goodly Beasts, Beastly Goods: Cattle and Commodities in a South African
         Context. *American Ethnologist* 17(2):195–216.
Cott, Nancy F.
  1977   *Bonds of Womanhood: Woman's Sphere in New England, 1780–1835*. New
         Haven: Yale University Press.
Creider, Chet
  1977   Functional Sentence Perspective in a Verb-Initial Language. In P. A. Kotey
         and H. Der-Houssikian, eds., *Language and Linguistic Problems in Africa:
         Proceedings of the Seventh Annual Conference on African Linguistics*. Co-
         lumbia: Hornbeam Press.
  1981   *An Introduction to the Nandi Language*. London, Ontario: Centre for Re-
         search and Teaching of Canadian Native Languages, University of Western
         Ontario.
  1982   *Studies in Kalenjin Nominal Tonology*. Language and Dialect Atlas of Kenya,
         supplement 3. Berlin: Sietrich Reimer Verlag.
Creider, Jane T. and Chet A. Creider
  1980   Nandi Traditional Social Organization and Culture. Manuscript.
Daniels, Robert
  1970   By Rites a Man: A Study of the Societal and Individual Foundations of Tribal
         Identity among the Kipsigis of Kenya. Ph.D. dissertation, University of
         Chicago.
Davis, Natalie Zemon
  1976   "Women's History" in Transition: The European Case. *Feminist Studies*
         3:83–103.
D'Azevedo, Warren
  1962   The Uses of the Past in Gola Discourse. *Journal of African History* 3(1):11–
         34.

di Leonardo, Micaela

1991a Women's Culture and its Discontents. In Brett Williams, ed., *The Politics of Culture*. Washington, D.C.: Smithsonian Institution Press.

1991b Habits of the Cumbered Heart: Ethnic Community and Women's Culture as American Invented Traditions. In J. O'Brien and W. Roseberry, eds., *Golden Ages, Dark Ages*. Berkeley: University of California Press.

1991c Gender, Culture, and Political Economy: Feminist Anthropology in Historical Perspective. In Micaela di Leonardo, ed., *Gender at the Crossroads of Knowledge: Feminist Anthropology in the Postmodern Era*. Berkeley: University of California Press.

1991d Contingencies of Value in Feminist Anthropology. In J. Hartman and E. Messer-Davidow, *(En)Gendering Knowledge: Feminists in Academe*. Memphis: University of Tennessee Press.

Distefano, John

1985 The Precolonial History of the Kalenjin of Kenya: A Methodological Comparison of Linguistic and Oral Traditional Evidence. Ph.D. dissertation, University of California, Los Angeles.

Donovan, Michael

1987 A Discussion of Changing Land Use Patterns in Ndaraweta Sub-location, Kericho District. Seminar paper 179, Institute of African Studies, University of Nairobi.

Droogers, Andre

1980 *The Dangerous Journey: Symbolic Aspects of Boys' Initiation among the Wagenia of Kisangani Zaire*. The Hague: Mouton.

Duranti, Alessandro

1986 The Audience as Co-author. *Text* 6(3):239–48.

Ehret, Christopher

1971 *Southern Nilotic History*. Evanston: Northwestern University Press.

1980 The Nilotic Languages of Tanzania. In E. Polome and A. Hill, eds., *Language in Tanzania*. New York: Oxford University Press for International African Institute.

Fabian, Johannes

1979 Rule and Process: Thoughts on Ethnography as Communication. *Philosophy of the Social Sciences* 9:1–26.

1982 Scratching the Surface: Observations on the Poetics of Lexical Borrowing in Shaba Swahili. *Anthropological Linguistics* 24:14–50.

1990a Presence and Representation: The Other and Anthropological Writing. *Critical Inquiry* 16(4):753–72.

1990b *Power and Performance*. Madison: University of Wisconsin Press.

Feeley-Harnik, Gillian

1984 The Political Economy of Death: Communication and Change in Malagasy Colonial History. *American Ethnologist* 11(1): 1–19.

Feld, Steven

1982 *Sound and Sentiment*. Philadelphia: University of Pennsylvania Press.

Fernandez, James
1974   The Mission of Metaphor in Expressive Culture. *Current Anthropology* 15:119–45.
1977   The Performance of Ritual Metaphors. In J. D. Sapir and J. C. Crocker, eds., *The Social Use of Metaphor*. Philadelphia: University of Pennsylvania Press.
1982   *Bwiti: An Ethnography of the Religious Imagination in Africa*. Princeton: Princeton University Press.
1986   The Argument of Images and the Experience of Returning to the Whole. In V. Turner and E. Bruner, eds., *The Anthropology of Experience*. Urbana: University of Illinois Press.
1987   Edification by Puzzlement. In I. Karp and C. Bird, eds., *Explorations in African Systems of Thought*. Bloomington: Indiana University Press.

Finnegan, Ruth
1969   How to Do Things with Words: Performative Utterances among the Limba of Sierra Leone. *Man* (n.s.)4:537–52.

Flynn, E. and P. Schweickart, eds.
1986   *Gender and Reading*. Baltimore: Johns Hopkins University Press.

Fortes, Meyer
1959   *Oedipus and Job in West African Religion*. Cambridge: Cambridge University Press.
1987   *Religion, Morality, and the Person: Essays on Tallensi Religion*. Cambridge: Cambridge University Press.

Foucault, M.
1980   *History of Sexuality*, Vol. 1. New York: Vintage.

Fox, James
1977   Roman Jakobson and the Comparative Study of Parallelism. In D. Armstrong and C. H. van Schooneveld, eds., *Roman Jakobson: Echoes of his Scholarship*. Lisse: Peter de Ridder.

Friedrich, Paul
1967   Structural Implications of Russian Pronominal Use. In W. Bright, ed., *Sociolinguistics*. The Hague: Mouton.
1979   *Language, Context, and the Imagination*. Palo Alto: Stanford University Press.

Gal, Susan
1991   Between Speech and Silence: The Problematics of Research on Language and Gender. In Micaela di Leonardo, ed., *Gender at the Crossroads of Knowledge: Feminist Anthropology in the Postmodern Era*. Berkeley: University of California Press.

Galaty, John G.
1977a   In the Pastoral Image: The Dialectic of Maasai Identity. Ph.D. dissertation, University of Chicago.
1977b   East African Hunters: "So-Calling" Some Historical Myths. Paper presented at the annual meeting of the American Anthropological Association, Houston.
1979   Pollution and Anti-praxis: The Issue of Maasai Inequality. *American Ethnologist* 6:803–16.

1980   The Maasai Group-Ranch: Politics and Development in an African Pastoral Society. In P. Salzman, ed., *When Nomads Settle: Processes of Sedentarization as Adaptation and Response.* New York: Praeger.

1981   Organizations for Pastoral Development. In J. Galaty et al., eds., *The Future of Pastoral Peoples.* Ottawa: International Development Research Centre.

1982   Being "Maasai," Being "People of Cattle": Ethnic Shifters in East Africa. *American Ethnologist* 9:1–20.

1983   Ceremony and Society: The Poetics of Maasai Ritual. *Man* (18)2:361–82.

1986   East African Hunters and Pastoralists in a Regional Perspective: An "Ethnoanthropological" Approach. *SUGIA* 7(1):105–32.

1991   "The Land Is Yours, Do with It What You Will": Individuation, Subdivision, and Commoditization of the Maasai Group Ranch. Paper presented to the annual meeting of the American Anthropological Association, Chicago.

1992   Boundary Shifters in Maasai Ethnicity. In T. Spear and R. Waller, eds., *Being Maasai: Ethnicity and Identity in East Africa.* London: James Currey.

Geertz, Clifford
1973   *The Interpretation of Cultures.* New York: Basic Books.

Genovese, Eugene
1974   *Roll, Jordan, Roll: The World the Slaves Made.* New York: Pantheon.

Giddens, Anthony
1979   *Central Problems in Social Theory: Action, Structure, and Contradiction in Social Analysis.* Berkeley: University of California Press.

1984   *The Constitution of Society: Outline of a Theory of Structuration.* Berkeley: University of California Press.

Gladsjo, Leslie Asako
1991   *Stigmata: The Transfigured Body.* Documentary film. Distributor: L. A. Gladsjo, P.O. Box 411144, San Francisco, CA 94141.

Gluckman, Max, ed.
1964   *Closed Systems and Open Minds: The Limits of Naivety in Social Anthropology.* Edinburgh: Oliver and Boyd.

Godelier, Maurice
1986   *The Making of Great Men.* Cambridge: Cambridge University Press.

Goody, Esther, ed.
1978   *Questions and Politeness.* Cambridge: Cambridge University Press.

Gossen, Gary
1974   *Chamulas in the World of the Sun.* Cambridge, Mass.: Harvard University Press.

Gumperz, John
1982   *Discourse Strategies.* Cambridge: Cambridge University Press.

Gumperz, John and Dell Hymes, eds.
1964   Toward Ethnographies of Communication. Special issue of *American Anthropologist* 66 (6, part 2).

1972   *Directions in Sociolinguistics: The Ethnography of Communication.* New York: Holt, Rinehart, and Winston.

Handelman, Don
1979   Is Naven Ludic? *Social Analysis* 1:177–91

Harding, Sandra
1986   *The Science Question in Feminism.* Ithaca: Cornell University Press.
Haraway, Donna
1989   *Primate Visions: Gender, Race, and Nature in the World of Modern Science.*
        New York: Routledge.
Hay, Margaret Jean
1988   Hoes and Clothes. Paper presented at the Conference on African Material
        Culture, Bellagio, Italy.
Heald, Suzette
1982   The Making of Men: The Relevance of Vernacular Psychology to the Inter-
        pretation of a Gisu Ritual. *Africa* 52(1):15–36.
1989   *Controlling Anger: The Sociology of Gisu Violence.* Manchester: Manchester
        University Press for the International African Institute.
Heine, Berndt
1973   Vokabulare Ostafrikanischer Restsprachen. Teil 2: Sogoo und Omotik. *Afrika
        und Ubersee* 57(1):38–49.
Heise, Lori
1989   Crimes of Gender. *World Watch* 2(2):12–21.
Herren, Urs
1987   *The People of Mukogodo Division, Laikipia District: A Historical and An-
        thropological Baseline.* Laikipia Report 9, Institute of Geography, University
        of Berne, Switzerland.
Hobsbawn, Eric and Terence Ranger, eds.
1983   *The Invention of Tradition.* Cambridge: Cambridge University Press.
Hollis, A. C.
1905   *The Masai: Their Language and Folklore.* Oxford: Clarendon Press.
Holmes, Douglas
1989   *Cultural Disenchantments: Worker Peasantries in Northeast Italy.* Princeton:
        Princeton University Press.
Holquist, Michael
1988   Stereotyping in Autobiography and History. *Poetics Today* 9(2):453–72.
Hosken, Fran
1979   *The Hosken Report.* Lexington, Mass.: Women's International Network
        News.
1981   Female Genital Mutilation and Human Rights. *Feminist Issues* 1:3.
Huntingford, G.W.B.
1929   Modern Hunters: Some Account of the Kamelilo-Kapchepkendi Dorobo
        (Okiek) of Kenya Colony. *JRAI* 59:333–76.
1942   Social Organization of the Dorobo. *African Studies* 1(3):183–200.
1951   Social Institutions of the Dorobo. *Anthropos* 46:1–46.
1954   The Political Organization of the Dorobo. *Anthropos* 49:123–48.
1955   The Economic Life of the Dorobo. *Anthropos* 50:602–34.
Hymes, Dell
1975   Breakthrough into Performance. In D. Ben-Amos and K. Goldstein, eds.,
        Folklore: Performance and Communication. The Hague: Mouton.

Irvine, Judith
1979   Formality and Informality in Communicative Events. *American Anthropologist* 81:773–90.
1989   When Talk Isn't Cheap: Language and Political Economy. *American Ethnologist* 16(2):248–67.
Jackson, Michael
1989   *Paths Toward a Clearing*. Bloomington: Indiana University Press.
Jackson, Michael and Ivan Karp
1990   Introduction. In M. Jackson and I. Karp, eds., *Personhood and Agency*. Uppsala: Acta Universitatis Upsaliensis and Washington, D.C.: Smithsonian Institution Press.
Jakobson, Roman
1960   Concluding Statement: Linguistics and Poetics. In T. Sebeok, ed., *Style in Language*. Cambridge, Mass.: M.I.T. Press.
1966   Grammatical Parallelism and its Russian Facet. *Language* 42(2):399–429.
1968   The Poetry of Grammar and the Grammar of Poetry. *Lingua* 21:597–609.
1971   *Selected Writings*. Vols. 1 and 2. The Hague: Mouton.
Jakobson, Roman and Linda Waugh
1979   *Sound Shape of Language*. Sussex: Harvester Press.
Kapferer, Bruce
1979a   Ritual Process and the Transformation of Context. *Social Analysis* 1:3–19.
1979b   Entertaining Demons: Comedy, Interaction, and Meaning in a Sinhalese Healing Ritual. *Social Analysis* 1:108–52
1979c   Emotion and Feeling in Sinhalese Healing Rites. *Social Analysis* 1:153–76.
1983   *A Celebration of Demons*. Bloomington: Indiana University Press.
Karp, Ivan
1980   Beer Drinking and Social Experience in an African Society: An Essay in Formal Sociology. In I. Karp and C. Bird, eds., *Explorations in African Systems of Thought*. Bloomington: Indiana University Press.
1986a   Anthropology. In T. Sebeok, ed., *Encyclopedic Dictionary of Semiotics*. Amsterdam: Mouton de Gruyter.
1986b   Agency and Social Theory: A Review of Three Books by Anthony Giddens. *American Ethnologist* 13(1):131–37.
1987   Laughter at Marriage: Subversion in Performance. In D. Nyamwaya and D. Parkin, eds., *Transformations of African Marriage*. London: International African Institute.
Karp, Ivan and Kent Maynard
1983   Reading the Nuer. *Current Anthropology* 24(4):481–503.
Kauffman, Linda
1986   *Discourses of Desire: Gender, Genre, and Epistolary Fictions*. Ithaca: Cornell University Press.
Kenny, M.
1981   Mirror in the Forest: The Dorobo Hunter-Gatherers as an Image of the Other. *Africa* 51(1):477–96.
Kenya Land Commission (Carter Commission)
1933   *Evidence and Memorandum*. 3 vols. London.

1934   *Report: Summary of Conclusions Reached by H.M. Government.* London.
Kipury, Naomi
1983   *Oral Literature of the Maasai.* Nairobi: Heinemann Educational Books.
Kitching, Gavin
1980   *Class and Economic Change in Kenya: The Making of an African Petite-Bourgeoisie.* New Haven: Yale University Press.
Klumpp, Donna Rey and Corinne Kratz
1992   Aesthetics, Expertise, and Ethnicity: Okiek and Maasai Perspectives on Personal Ornament. In T. Spear and R. Waller, eds., *Being Maasai: Ethnicity and Identity in East Africa.* London: James Currey.
Kratz, Corinne A.
1977   The Liquors of Forest and Garden: Drinking in Okiek Life. M.A. thesis, Wesleyan University.
1981a   Are the Okiek Really Maasai? Or Kipsigis? Or Kikuyu? *Cahiers d'Etudes Africaines* 79(XX):355–68.
1981b   Identity and Context in Okiek Song. Paper presented at the annual meeting of the American Folklore Society, San Antonio.
1986   Ethnic Interaction, Economic Diversification, and Language Use. *SUGIA* 7(2):189–226.
1987   Chords of Tradition, Lens of Analogy: Iconic Signs in Okiek Ceremonies. *Journal of Ritual Studies* 1(2):75–96.
1988a   Okiek Ornaments of Transition and Transformation. *Kenya Past and Present* 20:21–26.
1988b   The Unending Ceremony and a Warm House: Representations of a Patriarchal Ideal and the Silent Complementarity in Okiek Blessings. In J. Woodburn, T. Ingold, and D. Riches, eds., *Hunter-Gatherers—Property, Power, and Ideology.* Oxford: Berg.
1988c   Emotional Power and Significant Movement: Womanly Transformation in Okiek Initiation. Ph.D. dissertation, University of Texas at Austin.
1989   Genres of Power: A Comparative Analysis of Okek Blessings, Curses and Oaths. *Man* (n.s.)24:636–56.
1990a   Persuasive Suggestions and Reassuring Promises: Emergent Parallelism and Dialogic Encouragement in Song. *Journal of American Folklore* 103:42–66.
1990b   Sexual Solidarity and the Secrets of Sight and Sound: Shifting Gender Relations and their Ceremonial Constitution. *American Ethnologist* 17(3):31–51.
1990c   Follow the Family, Follow the Husband: Gender, Agency, Ideology, and Politics in Okiek Marriage. Paper presented at the annual meeting of the American Anthropological Association, New Orleans.
1991   Amusement and Absolution: Transforming Narratives during Confession of Social Debt. *American Anthropologist* 93(4):826–51.
1993   We've Always Done it Like This . . . Except for a Few Details: "Tradition" and "Innovation" in Okiek Ceremonies. *Comparative Studies in Society and History* 35(1):28–63.
Labov, William
1973   *Sociolinguistic Patterns.* Philadelphia: University of Pennsylvania Press.

Labov, William and J. Waletzky
   1967   Narrative Analysis: Oral Versions of Personal Experience. In J. Helm, ed.,
          Essays on the Verbal and Visual Arts. Seattle: University of Washington
          Press.
La Fontaine, Jean
   1977   The Power of Rights. *Man* 12:421–37.
   1985   *Initiation.* London: Penguin.
Leach, Edmund R.
   1954   *Political Systems of Highland Burma.* London School of Economics Mono-
          graphs on Social Anthropology, no. 44. London: Athlone.
Lienhardt, Godfrey
   1961   *Divinity and Experience: The Religion of the Dinka.* Oxford: Clarendon.
Lockwood, David
   1964   Social Integration and System Integration. In G. Zollschan and W. Hirsch,
          eds., *Explorations in Social Change.* Boston: Houghton Mifflin.
Lonsdale, John
   1977   When did the Gusii (or any other Group) Become a "Tribe"? *Kenya Histor-
          ical Review* 5(1):121–33.
   1988   Wealth, Poverty, and Civic Virtue in Kikuyu Political Thought. Seminar
          paper, History Department, University of Nairobi.
Lutz, Catherine
   1990   Engendered Emotion: Gender, Power, and the Rhetoric of Emotional Control
          in American Discourse. In C. Lutz and L. Abu-Lughod, eds., *Language and
          the Politics of Emotion.* Cambridge: Cambridge University Press.
Lutz, Catherine and Lila Abu-Lughod, eds.
   1990   *Language and the Politics of Emotion.* Cambridge: Cambridge University
          Press.
Lutz, Catherine and Geoffrey White
   1986   The Anthropology of Emotions. *Annual Review of Anthropology* 15:405–36.
Lyons, John
   1977   *Semantics.* Vol. 1. Cambridge: Cambridge University Press.
MacCormack, Carol and Marilyn Strathern, eds.
   1980   *Nature, Culture, and Gender.* Cambridge: Cambridge University Press.
Mafeje, Archie
   1971   The Ideology of Tribalism. *Journal of Modern African Studies* 9:253–61.
Malinowski, Bronislaw
   1978   *Coral Gardens and Their Magic.* New York: Dover.
Manners, Robert
   1967   The Kipsigis of Kenya. In J. Steward, ed., *Contemporary Change in Tradi-
          tional Society,* vol. 1. Urbana: University of Illinois Press
Marcus, George and Michael M. J. Fischer
   1986   *Anthropology as Cultural Critique.* Chicago: University of Chicago Press.
Mauss, Marcel
   1979   Body Techniques. In *Sociology and Psychology: Essays by Marcel Mauss,*
          trans. Ben Brewster. London: Routledge and Kegan Paul.

Mertz, Elizabeth
  1985   Beyond Symbolic Anthropology: Introducing Semiotic Mediation. In
          E. Mertz and R. Parmentier, eds., *Semiotic Mediation: Sociocultural and
          Psychological Perspectives.* New York: Academic Press.
Meyer, Leonard
  1956   *Emotion and Meaning in Music.* Chicago: University of Chicago Press.
Meyerhoff, Elizabeth
  1981   The Socioeconomic and Ritual Roles of Pokot Women. Ph.D. dissertation,
          University of Cambridge.
Mohanty, Chandra
  1988   Under Western Eyes: Feminist Scholarship and Colonial Discourses. *Femi-
          nist Review* 30:61–88.
Mohanty, Chandra, Ann Russo, and Lourdes Torres, eds.
  1991   *Third World Feminism and the Politics of Feminism.* Bloomington: Indiana
          University Press.
Mol, Fr. Frans
  1980   *Maa: A Dictionary of the Maasai Language and Folklore.* Nairobi: Market-
          ing and Publishing Ltd.
Moore, Henrietta
  1986   *Space, Text, and Gender: An Anthropological Study of the Marakwet of
          Kenya.* Cambridge: Cambridge University Press.
Moore, Sally Falk
  1987   Explaining the Present: Theoretical Dilemmas in Processual Ethnography.
          American Ethnologist 14(4):727–36.
Mouffe, Chantal
  1988   Hegemony and New Political Subjects: Toward a New Concept of
          Democracy. In C. Nelson and L. Grossberg, eds., *Marxism and the Interpreta-
          tion of Culture.* Urbana: University of Illinois Press.
Muriuki, Godfrey
  1975   *A History of the Kikuyu, 1500–1900.* Nairobi: Oxford University Press.
Murray, Jocelyn
  1974   The Kikuyu Female Circumcision Controversy, with Special Reference to the
          Church Missionary Society's "Sphere of Influence." Ph.D. dissertation, Uni-
          versity of California, Los Angeles.
  1976   The Church Missionary Society and the "Female Circumcision" Issue in
          Kenya, 1929–1932. *Journal of Religion in Africa* 8(2):92–104.
Needham, Rodney
  1967   Percussion and Transition. *Man* (n.s.)2:606–14.
Nketia, J.H.K.
  1974   *Music of Africa.* New York: W. W. Norton.
O'Brien, Jay
  1986   Toward a Reconstitution of Ethnicity: Capitalist Expansion and Cultural
          Dynamics in Sudan. *American Anthropologist* 88:898–907.
Ojwang, J. B. and A.B.C. Ocholla-Ayayo
  1989   Silvano Melea Otieno: A Genealogy. In J. B. Ojwang and J.N.K. Mugambi,
          The S. M. Otieno Case. Nairobi: Nairobi University Press.

Ole Kulet, H. R.
1972   *To Become a Man*. Nairobi: Longman.
Orchardson, Ian
1961   *The Kipsigis*. Nairobi: East Africa Literature Bureau.
Ortner, Sherry
1984   Theory in Anthropology since the Sixties. *Comparative Studies in Society and History* 26:126–66.
Parkin, David
1980   The Creativity of Abuse. *Man* 15:45–64.
1984   Political Language. *Annual Review of Anthropology* 13:345–65.
Peristiany, J. G.
1964   *Social Institutions of the Kipsigis*. London: Routledge and Kegan Paul.
Prakash, Gyan
1990   Writing Post-Orientalist Histories of the Third World: Perspectives from Indian Historiography. *Comparative Studies in Society and History* 32(2):383–408.
Prins, A.H.J.
1953   *East African Age Class Systems*. Groningen: J. B. Wolters.
Quinn, Naomi
1977   Anthropological Studies on Women's Status. *Annual Review of Anthropology* 6:181–225.
Ranger, Terence
1979   European Attitudes and African Realities: The Rise and Fall of the Matola Chiefs of South-east Tanzania. *Journal of African History* 20(1):63–82.
Reed, Adolph Jr.
1992   The Underclass as Myth and Symbol: The Poverty of Discourse about Poverty. *Radical America* 24:21–40.
Reiter, Rayna, ed.
1975   *Toward an Anthropology of Women*. New York: Monthly Review Press.
Richards, Audrey
1956   *Chisungu*. London: Faber and Faber.
Riley, Denise
1988   *Am I that Name? Feminism and the Category of 'Women' in History*. Minneapolis: University of Minnesota Press.
Rogers, Susan Carol
1975   Female Forms of Power and the Myth of Male Dominance. *American Ethnologist* 2(4):727–56.
Rosaldo, M. Z.
1980   *Knowledge and Passion: Ilongot Notions of Self and Social Life*. Cambridge: Cambridge University Press.
Rosaldo, M. Z. and L. Lamphere, eds.
1974   *Women, Culture, and Society*. Stanford: Stanford University Press.
Rosaldo, R.
1980   *Ilongot Headhunting, 1883–1974*. Stanford: Stanford University Press.

Rosenberg, Daniel

1990   Language in the Discourse of the Emotions. In C. Lutz and L. Abu-Lughod, eds., *Language and the Politics of Emotion*. Cambridge: Cambridge University Press.

Rottland, Franz

1977   Zur Gliederung der Sudnilotischen Sprachen. *Zeitschrift der Deutschen Morgenländischen Gesellschaft*. Supplement 3.2:1483–94.

1981   *Die Sudnilotischen Sprachen*. Berlin: Dietrich Reimer Verlag.

Rottland, Franz and R. Vossen

1977   Grundlagen für eine Klarung des Dorobo-Problems. In W. J. G. Mohlig, F. Rottland, and B. Heine, eds., *Zur Sprachgeschichte und Ethnohistorie in Afrika*. Berlin: Dietrich Verlagen.

Rouget, G.

1985   *Music and Trance*. Chicago: University of Chicago Press.

Rubin, Gayle

1975   The Traffic in Women. In R. Reiter, ed., *Towards an Anthropology of Women*. New York: Monthly Review Press.

Sacks, Harvey and Emanuel Schegeloff

1974   Opening Up Closings. In R. Turner, ed., *Ethnomethodology*. Baltimore: Penguin.

Sahlins, Marshall

1981   *Historical Metaphors and Mythical Realities: Structure in the Early History of Sandwich Island Kingdoms*. Ann Arbor: University of Michigan Press.

Said, Edward

1988   Foreword. In R. Guha and G. Spivak, eds., *Selected Subaltern Studies*. New York: Oxford University Press.

Sanderson, Lilian P.

1981   *Against the Mutilation of Women*. London: Ithaca.

Sapir, J. David

1977   The Anatomy of Metaphor. In *The Social Use of the Metaphor*. Ed. by J. David Sapir and J. Christopher Crocker. Philadelphia: University of Pennsylvania Press.

Sapir, J. David and J. Christopher Crocker, eds.

1977   *The Social Use of Metaphor*. Philadelphia: University of Pennsylvania Press.

Sargent, Lydia

1981   *Women and Revolution: A Discussion of the Unhappy Marriage of Marxism and Feminism*. Boston: South End Press.

Scott, James

1985   *Weapons of the Weak: Everyday Forms of Peasant Resistance*. New Haven: Yale University Press.

Scott, Joan Wallach

1988   *Gender and the Politics of History*. New York: Columbia University Press.

Scotton, Carol Meyers

1983   The Negotiation of Identities in Conversation: A Theory of Markedness and Code Choice. *International Journal of the Sociology of Language* 44:115–36.

1988   Code-switching and Types of Multilingual Communities. In P. Lowenberg, ed., *Georgetown University Roundtable on Language and Linguistics 1987*. Washington, D.C.: Georgetown University Press.

Sherzer, Joel
1983   *Kuna Ways of Speaking*. Austin: University of Texas Press.
1987a   Language, Culture, and Discourse. *American Anthropologist* 89(2):295–309.
1987b   A Diversity of Voices: Men's and Women's Speech in Ethnographic Perspective. In S. Philips, S. Steele, and C. Tanz, eds., *Language, Sex, and Gender in Comparative Perspective*. Cambridge: Cambridge University Press.

Silverstein, Michael
1976   Shifters, Linguistic Categories, and Cultural Description. In K. Basso and H. Selby, eds., *Meaning in Anthropology*. Albuquerque: University of New Mexico Press.
1977   The Limits of Awareness. Lecture paper delivered to the Harvard Anthropology Seminar.
1981   Metaforces of Power in Traditional Oratory. Lecture paper delivered to the Department of Anthropology, Yale University.
1985   Language and the Culture of Gender: At the Intersection of Structure, Usage, and Ideology. In E. Meertz and R. Parmentier, eds., *Semiotic Mediation*. New York: Academic.

Singer, M.
1972   *When A Great Tradition Modernizes*. New York: Praeger.

Southall, Aiden
1970   The Illusion of Tribe. *Journal of African and Asian Studies* 5(1, 2):28–50.

Spear, Thomas and Richard Waller, eds.
1992   *Being Maasai: Ethnicity and Identity in East Africa*. London: James Currey.

Stephens, Julie
1989   Feminist Fictions: A Critique of the Category "Non-Western Woman" in Feminist Writings on India. In R. Guha, ed., *Subaltern Studies VI*. New York: Oxford University Press.

Stewart, Frank
1977   *Fundamentals of Age Group Systems*. New York: Academic Press.

Strathern, Marilyn
1981   Culture in a Netbag: The Manufacture of a Subdiscipline in Anthropology. *Man* (n.s.)16:665–88.

Tambiah, S. J.
1968   The Magical Power of Words. *Man* (n.s.)3:175–208.
1979   A Performative Approach to Ritual. *Proceedings of the British Academy* 65:113–70.

Tannen, Deborah
1990   *You Just Don't Understand*. New York: Morrow.

Toweett, Taaiita
1979a   *A Study of Kalenjin Linguistics*. Nairobi: Kenya Literature Bureau.
1979b   *English-Swahili-Kalenjin Nouns Pocket Dictionary*. Nairobi: Kenya Literature Bureau.

Thompson, John B.
1984   *Studies in the Theory of Ideology.* Berkeley: University of California Press.
Traube, Elizabeth G.
1986   *Cosmology and Social Life.* Chicago: University of Chicago Press.
Trubetskoy, N. S.
1969   *Principles of Phonology.* Trans. C.A.M. Baltaxe. Berkeley: University of
          California Press.
Tucker, A. N. and M. Bryan
1964–   Noun Classification in Kalenjin: Nandi-Kipsigis. *African Language Studies*
65   5:192–247 and 6:117–87.
1966   *Linguistic Analyses: Non-Bantu Languages of North-Eastern Africa.* Oxford:
          Oxford University Press.
Tucker, A. N. and J. T. Ole Mpaayei
1952   *A Maasai Grammar with Vocabulary.* Publication of the African Institute,
          Leyden, No. 2. London: Longmans, Green.
Turner, Terence
1977   Transformation, Hierarchy, and Transcendence: A Reformulation of Van
          Gennep's Model of the Structure of Rites of Passage. In S. F. Moore and B.
          G. Myerhoff, eds., *Secular Ritual.* Amsterdam: Van Gorcum.
1980   The Social Skin. In J. Cherfas and R. Lewis, eds., *Not Work Alone: A Cross-
          Cultural View of Activities Superfluous to Survival.* London: Temple Smith.
Turner, Victor
1967   *The Forest of Symbols.* Ithaca: Cornell University Press.
1968   *Drums of Affliction.* Oxford: Clarendon.
1969   *The Ritual Process.* Chicago: Aldine.
Turner, Victor and Edward Bruner, eds.
1986   *The Anthropology of Experience.* Urbana: University of Illinois Press.
Urban, Greg
1985   The Semiotics of Two Speech Styles in Shokleng. In E. Mertz and R.
          Parmentier, eds., *Semiotic Mediation: Sociocultural and Psychological Per-
          spectives.* New York: Academic Press.
van Gennep, Arnold
1960   *The Rites of Passage.* London: Routledge and Kegan Paul.
Volosinov, V. N.
1987   *Freudianism: A Critical Sketch.* Bloomington: Indiana University Press.
Wagner, Roy
1981   *The Invention of Culture.* Chicago: University of Chicago Press.
Waller, Richard
1984   Interaction and Identity on the Periphery: The Trans-Mara Maasai. *Interna-
          tional Journal of African Historical Studies* 17(2):243–84.
1985   Economic and Social Relations in the Central Rift Valley: The Maa-speakers
          and their Neighbors in the Nineteenth Century. *Hadith* 8:83–151.
Waugh, Linda
1976   *Roman Jakobson's Science of Language.* Lisse: Peter de Ridder.

Weiner, Annette
1984 From Words to Objects to Magic: "Hard Words" and the Boundaries of Social Interaction. In D. Brenneis and F. Myers, eds., *Dangerous Words: Language and Politics in the Pacific*. New York: New York University Press.

West, Cornell
1990 The New Cultural Politics of Difference. *October* (summer):93–109.

White, E. Frances
1990 Africa on My Mind: Gender, Counter-discourse, and African-American Nationalism. *Journal of Women's History* 2(1):73–97.

White, Hayden
1973 *Metahistory*. Baltimore: Johns Hopkins University Press.

Wilk, Richard
1990 Consumer Goods as Dialogue About Development. *Culture and History* 7:79–100.

Wilmsen, Edwin
1989 *Land Filled with Flies: A Political Economy of the Kalahari*. Chicago: University of Chicago Press.

Wilmsen, Edwin and Rainer Vossen
1990 Labour, Language, and Power in the Construction of Ethnicity in Botswana. *Critique of Anthropology* 10(1):7–37.

Winter, J. C.
1977 Maasai Shield Patterns: A Documentary Source for Political History. In *Zur Sprachgeschichte und Ethnohistorie*. Edited by W.H.J. Mohlig, F. Rottland, and B. Heine. Berlin: Dietrich Reiner Verlagen.

Young, Kate, Carol Wolkowitz, and Roslyn McCullagh, eds.
1981 *Of Marriage and the Market: Women's Subordination in International Perspective*. London: CSE.

Zuckerkandl, Victor
1956 *Sound and Symbol: Music and the External World*. New York: Pantheon.

Index

Plates are located after page 125.